J. EDGAR HOOVER ELICITI
FROM ALMOST EVER
HERE'S HOW HE WAS REVIEWED BY SOME OF

"He was a master con man, one of the greatest con men the country has ever produced, and that takes intelligence of a certain kind, an astuteness, a shrewdness."
—Hoover aide **William Sullivan**

"You don't fire God."
—Assistant FBI Director **Charles Brennan**

"I used to hear how certain senators and congressmen would get caught in cathouses over in Virginia. When the report came in, Hoover would put it in his personal safe. If there was any problem with that senator, Hoover would say, 'Don't worry, I've got those papers right in my safe. You don't have a thing to worry about.'"
—CIA Director **Richard Helms**

"If there had been a Mr. Hoover in the first half of the First Century A.D., can you imagine what he would have put into his files about a certain trouble-maker from Nazareth, his moral attitudes, and the people he consorted with?"
—**The New York Times, 1970**

"J. Edgar Hoover, head of our thought police—a martinet, a preposterous figure, but not funny."
—Poet **Theodore Roethke**

"The man who projected himself to the public as a stern moral figure, full of integrity, was a walking myth. It was so carefully crafted that he perhaps came to believe much of it himself, but it was a myth nonetheless."
—**Anthony Summers**

"J. Edgar Hoover was one twisted sister."
  —Foreign Policy Advisor to FDR and Under Secretary of State **Sumner Welles**

"Jesus Christ! That old cocksucker!"
  —**Richard M. Nixon** upon learning of the death of J. Edgar Hoover

"America is in the grip of two homosexual lovers, and there's not a god damn thing I can do about it. He's got us by the cojones, and he'll never let go until he kicks the bucket. Tolson is his henchman, his Goebbels. He does all the dirty deeds that that faggot doesn't want to dirty his hands with. They've got enough on me to bring down my presidency."
  —**Lyndon B. Johnson** to Senator George Smathers

"J. Edgar Hoover's legend—a plausibly gay man who harassed gays, a possible descendant of an African-American who harassed civil rights leaders, a top law enforcement official who placed himself above the law, all making him out as something approaching a monster—a far cry from the young eager beaver who came to work at the Justice Department in 1917, ready to make a good impression and save the country from subversives."
  —**Kenneth D. Ackerman**

"J. Edgar Hoover was not interested in just the facts: He collected every rumor, not matter how implausible. Even completely innocent people were afraid of what was in their FBI files—and in Washington, not many people were completely innocent."
  —**Larry Flynt**, publisher of *Hustler* Magazine

"We want no Gestapo or Secret Police. The FBI is tending in that direction. They are dabbling in sex life scandals and plain blackmail when they should be catching criminals."
  —**Harry S Truman**

"President Johnson has declared that he does not intend to replace J. Edgar Hoover. However, Hoover has not disclosed whether he intends to replace Johnson."
—NBC-TV's **That Was the Week That Was,** 1964

"J. Edna is the kind of guy who has to squat to pee. I hear Clyde Tolson is in the hospital. What was it, a hysterectomy? Hoover has gone mad. He's a fucking cocksucker. Any day now, I expect him to show up at work wearing one of Jackie's Dior creations."
—Robert F. Kennedy

Kid Napoleon [J. Edgar Hoover] launched a crusade against pornography and created his Obscene File. Agents around the country sent in stag movies, photographs, books, pamphlets, freehand drawings, comic strips, and playing cards decorated with girlie pictures."
—David Eisenbach

"J. Edgar Hoover passed along gossip to the President. That practice certainly raised questions in the President's mind. What did Hoover know about him? In theoretical terms, that put Hoover in the position of a veiled blackmailer."
—Secretary of State **Dean Rusk**

"J. Edgar Hoover was like a sewer that collected dirt. I now believe he was the worst public servant in our history"
—Acting Attorney General **Laurence Silberman**

"Hoover endured too long. He ended his life embittered and isolated, his Bureau a monument to his past—and to his memories of an America that hardly existed outside its walls."
—Richard Gid Powers

J. EDGAR HOOVER
& CLYDE TOLSON

INVESTIGATING THE SEXUAL SECRETS OF AMERICA'S MOST FAMOUS MEN AND WOMEN

BLOOD MOON Productions, Ltd.

OTHER BOOKS BY DARWIN PORTER

BIOGRAPHIES
Frank Sinatra, The Boudoir Singer, All the Gossip Unfit to Print
The Kennedys, All the Gossip Unfit to Print
Humphrey Bogart, the Making of a Legend
Howard Hughes: Hell's Angel
Steve McQueen, King of Cool, Tales of a Lurid Life
Paul Newman, The Man Behind the Baby Blues
Merv Griffin, A Life in the Closet
Brando Unzipped
The Secret Life of Humphrey Bogart
Katharine the Great: Hepburn, Secrets of a Lifetime Revealed
Jacko, His Rise and Fall (The Social and Sexual History of Michael Jackson)
and, co-authored with Roy Moseley
*Damn You, Scarlett O'Hara, The Private Lives of Vivien Leigh and
Laurence Olivier*

COMING SOON:
Marilyn at Rainbow's End--Sex, Lies, and the Great Cover-up.

FILM CRITICISM
50 Years of Queer Cinema--500 of the Best GLBTQ Films Ever Made (2010)
*Blood Moon's Guide to Recent Gay & Lesbian Film-Volumes One (2006) and
Two (2007)*
Best Gay and Lesbian Films- The Glitter Awards, 2005

NON-FICTION
Hollywood Babylon-It's Back!
Hollywood Babylon Strikes Again!

NOVELS
Butterflies in Heat
Marika
Venus (a roman à clef based on the life of Anaïs Nin)
Razzle-Dazzle
Midnight in Savannah
Rhinestone Country
Blood Moon
Hollywood's Silent Closet

TRAVEL GUIDES
Many editions and many variations of *The Frommer Guides* to
Europe, the Caribbean, California, Georgia and the Carolinas,
Bermuda, and The Bahamas

J. EDGAR HOOVER
& CLYDE TOLSON

INVESTIGATING THE SEXUAL SECRETS OF AMERICA'S MOST FAMOUS MEN AND WOMEN

DARWIN PORTER

BLOOD MOON Productions, Ltd.

J. Edgar Hoover & Clyde Tolson
Investigating the Sexual Secrets
of America's Most Famous Men and Women

by Darwin Porter

Manufactured in the United States of America

ISBN 978-1-936003-25-9

Cover designs by Richard Leeds (Bigwigdesign.com)
Videography and Publicity Trailers by Piotr Kajstura
Special thanks to Photofest in New York City
The author extends special acknowledgment and thanks to
Monica Dunn for her invaluable help and support

Distributed in North America and Australia
through National Book Network (www.NBNbooks.com)
and in the UK through Turnaround (www.turnaround-uk.com)

1 2 3 4 5 6 7 8 9 10

This book is dedicated to

James Kirkwood, Jr. and Guy Hotell

Without their inspiration and spadework
it might never have happened.

Clyde Tolson and J. Edgar Hoover at the racetrack

"There's something addicting about a secret."

—J. Edgar Hoover

"I have a philosophy. You are honored by your friends, and you are distinguished by your enemies. I have been very distinguished."

—**J. Edgar Hoover**

CHAPTER ONE

In the predawn hours of January 1, 1895, as revelers were returning from their New Year's parties, a cold, bitter, and windy day had been forecast for Pipetown, a residential community in the shadow of the Capitol building in Washington, D.C.

The cobble-covered streets, shaded in summer by elms, would be too heavy with snow for horse-drawn carriages. Gas lamps at the Grant-era house at 413 Seward Square witnessed the birth of a new baby who one day would strike fear throughout the city. The innocent-looking infant was John Edgar Hoover.

His older sister, Lillian Hoover, remembered that the baby boy entered the world "kicking, screaming, and crying. He was immediately hungry." In addition to Lillian, Hoover had an older brother, Dickerson Hoover, Jr.

Hoover's mother was Annie Marie Scheitlin, who had descended from Swiss mercenaries. His father, Dickerson Naylor Hoover, traced his ancestors back to Germany and England.

Although J. Edgar became a legend in modern America, in the year of his birth, Queen Victoria still presided over a vast empire and was the Empress of India. The Dalton gang still terrorized the West, and the czar ruled in Moscow. Germany still had an emperor. In North Carolina, the Wright Brothers would not fly their airplane for another eight years. In 1909, young Hoover, or so he claimed, would be the "first person in Washington to shake Orville Wright's hand."

The United States flag needed only forty-five stars to designate its member states. As J. Edgar came into the world, there was talk of waging war against Britain over Latin American territories. Only four years before Hoover was born, white men had ended their war against the Indians at Wounded Knee.

From the beginning, J. Edgar became a "mama's boy" and would remain so until her death at the age of seventy-eight in 1938. He was forty-three years old at the time and had always lived with her.

She called him a "late bloomer," or the "runt of my litter," yet remained completely devoted to him, living her life for her son.

A young **Dickerson Hoover Sr.** *(upper photo)* and his bride **Annie** appeared resigned to marriage.

In the lower photo, Annie's face had become grim as Dickerson suffered from mental illness. Even their unhappy first born, **Dickerson Jr.,** seemed resigned.

As a boy, he was always shorter than most of his classmates, although he did grow to the height of 5'7". On documents he listed his height as "under 6 feet."

J. Edgar was devoted to his mother, but she was a strict disciplinarian. She punished wrongdoing like a military army sergeant cracking down on a young recruit. Until he was twelve years old, J. Edgar had to strip down in front of his mother to receive a bare-butt paddling. As he grew older, the shy boy tried to conceal his genitals from her.

"Mother Hoover," as she would be called by FBI agents in her future, could have posed for that portrait of Whistler's Mother.

J. Edgar grew up with the puritan ethic that characterized many of America's values at the dawn of the 20th century. Like many other boys of his day, He found inspiration in Horatio Alger stories. Actually, his favorite reading material was dime-store detective novels. For a while he wanted to be a minister, which would later earn him the appellation of "an Elmer Gantry in lawman's clothes."

As a young boy, J. Edgar never joined in the battles between the Pipetown boys and those gangs from the bordering areas of "Cowtown" and "Foggy Bottom."

He was a loner and preferred to walk the streets of Pipetown by himself, as did a neighbor, John Philip Sousa, who would grow up to become America's militaristic "March King."

J. Edgar's father lectured him on the evils of masturbation—"it's something monkeys do in a zoo."

The boy was also taught lessons by his grandmother, Margaret Scheitlin. He'd seen "colored people," as they were called, come and go. In Pipetown a colony of white gov-

As a toddler in the nation's capital *(top photo)*, **J. Edgar** revealed his ambition: To become President of the United States.

In the lower photo, he was four years old and feared that an orange seed he'd swallowed would produce a tree growing from his belly button.

ernment clerks and shop owners lived. Unusual for the South, many African Americans had moved in too, although they lived by themselves on the fringe of Pipetown.

Margaret told him that blacks "were drunkards and heathens and not to be trusted. Birds of a feather flock together, and whites should remain with their own kind."

As a youth, J. Edgar developed crushes on older boys or men. Even before his fifth birthday, he seemed mesmerized by Dr. Donald Campbell MacLeod, a minister at the First Presbyterian Church. Unlike J. Edgar's often sickly father, MacLeod was good looking, charismatic, and a superb athlete, joining schoolboys on the field in ball games. MacLeod seemed to take a joy in living. Although a minister, he was not stern or regimented. He even helped the boy overcome his stutter by instilling in him more confidence.

J. Edgar later claimed that MacLeod taught him "duty, love of country, patriotism, honor, virtue, and piety."

Under MacLeod's guidance, J. Edgar took an interest in sports, although he was far too puny and underweight for football. It was on a school playground that he earned his "prizefighter's nose" as the result of a direct hit by a fly ball.

Later J. Edgar transferred his crush from MacLeod onto Lawrence (Biff) Jones, who became a celebrated coach at West Point. For J. Edgar, it was a case of hero worship.

Classmates didn't understand why this powerhouse of an athlete, who could have any girl in the school he wanted, preferred to spend his spare time with this little boy who was about half his size.

"They were Mutt and Jeff," Fred Acker,

Young J. Edgar developed his first "crush" on **Dr. David Campbell MacLeod,** a Presbyterian minister. "My ideal of manhood," J. Edgar wrote in his diary.

a classmate, recalled about forty years later. "We were innocent back then. Today we'd suspect that Edgar was giving Biff blow-jobs. Edgar's mouth came up to Biff's fly. But I'm getting vulgar. We didn't really know what gay was back in those days."

At Central High School, J. Edgar became a skilled debater, winning his greatest honors with the argument that Cuba should be annexed to the United States. At the time of the U.S. missile crisis when John F. Kennedy was president, he proposed much the same argument, claiming that a communist country only sixty miles from the United States coastline "was an unacceptable threat to the nation's security."

He also won a debate in which he complained that women did not have the maturity and wisdom to be allowed to vote. All his life he would favor capital punishment. But in a school debate, he claimed that the death penalty should also be extended to include those accused of armed robbery and bestiality.

One day when Lillian asked her younger brother what he wanted to be when he grew up, he said, "I want to be a minister like Rev. MacLeod."

From a table in the living room, probably motivated by a wish to torment and upset him, she picked up the family bible and tossed it into the fire.

He may never have forgiven her.

His brother, Dickerson, Jr., fifteen years older than him, had already married and moved next door with his bride. His older sister, Lillian, had married in June of 1908, the ceremony performed by the Rev. MacLeod himself, whom young J. Edgar still worshipped.

The night after Lillian's wedding, J. Edgar promised his mother that he would never marry and leave her side. He would keep that promise.

"I met his sister once," Acker said, "when I came home with Edgar. That was one bitch, cold as a witch's tit."

As a widow, Lillian would eventually succumb to Parkinson's disease. J. Edgar showed up at her funeral but left in the middle of the eulogy.

The older siblings had grown up to be well adjusted, but not the head of the family, who began to deteriorate mentally as the years went by.

Dickerson Naylor Hoover, upon whom the family depended, was sent in 1913 to a psychiatric ward in Laurel, Maryland. His wife tried to suppress news of his mental illness, even from her family, but it became obvious that he had had a nervous breakdown. He was suffering from acute depression and had to undergo shock therapy. At times he had to be restrained physically by the staff after several psychotic episodes.

After months in the hospital, he returned to his government job as an engraver with the Coast and Geodetic Survey. But after some outbursts he was dismissed with no pension. Mostly he would sit silently in a corner of the family living room, brooding in a chair.

J. Edgar had loved his father dearly, but soon learned that contact or intimacy between them was impossible. "He has gone to some far and distant place," J. Edgar later recalled.

With his father out of work, J. Edgar created a job for himself outside the Eastern City Market, which supplied most of the groceries for Washington and had done so since 1873. He carried groceries for customers at the market, sometimes toting a heavy load for two miles for a ten-cent tip. He'd then run back to the market so as not to miss another customer. For that effort, he earned the nickname of "Speed." Ironically, this was the nickname his future lover, Clyde Tolson, would often call him in private.

Acker disputed some versions of how J. Edgar got the nickname of "Speed."

"He talked so God damn fast, like an FBI machine gun," Acker said. "Real staccato. That's how he got that name, not because he ran so fast. I think James Cagney in the movies imitated Edgar's fast talking."

As "J.E. Hoover," Edgar became the captain in his high school's Cadet Corps. In March of 1913—"my all-time greatest thrill"—was when he, looking stiffly formal in his uniform, led his company in its march down Pennsylvania Avenue during the four-hour inaugural parade of President Woodrow Wilson.

In 1913, Hoover was graduated as the valedictorian of his class at Central High School.

At the age of eighteen, at the Central High Regimental Ball, J. Edgar showed up at Washington D.C.'s Cairo Hotel with his mother. He looked spiffy in his blue-and-

J. Edgar's childhood home at 413 Seward Square in "Pipetown." From its front porch, a young J. Edgar with his trusty slingshot "beaned" many a passing African American on the street.

white uniform and wore a saber. Every young man had a dance book. But in the spaces reserved for female partners, the page appears blank in J. Edgar's book. He sat out the dance talking to his mother.

J. Edgar enrolled as a night student at George Washington University, only four blocks from the White House, whose future occupants he would one day terrorize.

During the day he worked as a file reviewer in the Order Division of the Library of Congress. He was paid $30 a month.

At the Library of Congress, he mastered the Dewey Decimal System. That skill he learned became the organizational model for the FBI's Central Files and General Indices in the decades to come.

He earned a Bachelor of Law degree in 1916, a master's in 1917, which gained his admission to the District of Columbia Bar. He went to work in January of 1917 as a clerk in the Department of Justice for the meager salary of $990 a year. He would remain connected in some capacity with

At the age of sixteen, **J. Edgar** *(left)* was a zealous commander of his high school cadet corps, which marched at **the inauguration of Woodrow Wilson** *(right photo)* in 1913. In spite of his military training, J. Edgar chose to avoid military service in World War I.

Throughout his life, J. Edgar detested clammy handshakes. Once, he got to shake President Wilson's hand and he later compared the experience to "a ten-cent pickled mackerel in brown paper." As president, Wilson shocked J. Edgar by recommending that all government agents should see D.W. Griffith's *The Birth of a Nation,* a film that glorified the Ku Klux Klan.

this department for the next fifty-five years.

In 1917, J. Edgar was hired by John Lord O'Brian, a former lawyer from Buffalo, New York, who took charge of the War Emergency Division of the Department of Justice. J. Edgar was assigned to the Alien Enemy Bureau and given the task of tracking down the rumor that German spies had sabotaged the food supply of America by putting ground glass in flour.

He was also charged with seeking out spies and cracking down on anarchists. He not only ordered the arrest of accused or even potential saboteurs, but he wanted German seamen, marooned in U.S. ports at the outbreak of the war, sent to alien detention camps. The young and ambitious prosecutor also led a drive to register 450,000 Germans and force them to carry a government-issued ID.

According to O'Brian, J. Edgar's boss, his young protégé "saw a spy around every corner, a saboteur in any man who walked the waterfront, and a slacker under every rock." A slacker was a man who avoided the draft. There was a certain irony in J. Edgar pursuing slackers, as he fitted the bill himself.

The man who would one day prosecute Vietnam draft dodgers "dodged the bullet" himself and didn't have to serve in the military. He later claimed that the "espionage work" he was doing on the home front prevented him from going into the army.

The claim about being essential does not ring true. The United States entered the war on April 6, 1917, but he did not join the U.S. Department of Justice until July 26, which gave him plenty of time to enlist if he had wanted to. Besides, his $990-a-year clerkship would hardly be considered essential to the war effort.

Actually he was needed at home to help pay for his father's confinement in that sanatorium in Maryland. His father suffered such acute depression that he repeatedly vomited throughout the day. What caused this sudden breakdown in his mental condition is not known. In later years, J. Edgar tried to erase his father's condition from his biography.

Young, ambitious, and determined, **J. Edgar** viewed all Germans as suspicious in World War I and became the curse of German brewery owners. "To drink the Kaiser's brew is treason," he claimed.

In his war against the slackers, J. Edgar unknowingly was aided by a young man named Clyde Anderson Tolson, whom he had yet to meet. Tol-

7

son was hired as the confidential secretary to Newton D. Baker, the Secretary of War. As such, Tolson was one of the men who organized a raid on Manhattan and Brooklyn where young men who didn't have proper identification were arrested at bayonet point on street corners and herded into a concentration camp. There was standing room only in these camps. Not enough food, water, or toilets were provided, and the young men, most of whom were innocent, were forced to live in these harsh conditions for forty-eight hours before their cases were individually heard.

One of J. Edgar's first memos carried a recommendation of what to do to an eighteen-year-old boy who had been arrested on the Texan-Mexican border. He was a supporter of the German Kaiser and called President Woodrow Wilson "a cocksucker and a thief."

J. Edgar wanted him jailed until the end of the war, although his recommendation was overruled as "too drastic."

After the United States went to war with Germany, vigilantes indiscriminately arrested aliens, especially those with a German accent, on suspicion of being spies and saboteurs. J. Edgar came to suspect that even some church leaders were secret agents of the Kaiser. Hundreds of immigrants were not only incarcerated but beaten and, in some cases, tortured. In all cases they were threatened with deportation.

By 1917, he was participating in a drive to register all German women in the United States, fearing they may be spies or saboteurs. At the department, J. Edgar would become a vociferous advocate of "The Hun Scare."

At the age of twenty-two, J. Edgar stated his lifetime goal to those who knew him. "I once thought I might become a minister. But I have now decided on my lifelong ambition. I will become a hunter of men, or maybe a lady or two if she's an anarchist."

J. Edgar worked on a memo recommending that restaurants in America should no longer list Sauerkraut on their menu, even in Milwaukee. He preferred the name "Liberty cabbage." He also wanted the music of Bach and Beethoven banned from concerts. Of course, German was no longer to be taught in public schools.

After the victory celebrations associated with the end of World War I, J.

J. Edgar's boss, U.S. Attorney General **A. Mitchell Palmer** was called "The Fighting Quaker." In 1920, he ran for president, but his notorious wartime "Red Raids" had produced a public backlash.

Edgar faced the end of his job with the War Emergency Division. He asked to join the Bureau of Immigration but was turned down. He even requested a transfer to the Bureau of Investigation (BOI). Ironically he was turned down for a job in a department he'd later rule with an iron fist for forty-eight years.

In March of 1919, Attorney General A. Mitchell Palmer selected J. Edgar to aid his campaign of "prosecuting alien agitators. I want to get rid of every god damn 'Red' in this country and make it safe for democracy," Palmer told the 24-year-old.

"Leave it to me, chief," J. Edgar said.

Accompanied with an increase in his salary to the hefty sum of $3,000 a year, J. Edgar was assigned to the new "Radical "Division" of the Department of Justice. With the Kaiser's spies no longer a threat, he turned to the "Red Menace" that he was convinced was enveloping the United States.

Palmer, J. Edgar's new boss, was a Pennsylvania-born Quaker, who raised many eyebrows during World War I when he, as Alien Property Custodian, seized millions in German assets which ended up in the coffers of his Democratic cronies.

Palmer had come down particularly hard on German brewers, finding conspiracies in virtually every tankard of beer sold. He wanted to make U.S. industry free of evil German ownership. "Every time you drink a German beer, you're putting money into the pockets of our enemy."

Palmer was Attorney General from March 5, 1919 to March 4, 1921, with J. Edgar his chief "flunky."

On a daily basis, J. Edgar worked with Assistant Attorney General Francis Garvan and became known in the bureau as "Garvan's pet hound dog, snooping his bulldog nose in everybody else's business."

Garvan was both a chemist from Connecticut and a zealot who detested foreigners, especially Germans and Russians.

As a means of understanding the mind of his enemy, J. Edgar studied the writings of Lenin, who was calling for world revolution, as well as Marx and Engels.

Methodically, he began to accumulate dossiers on the enemy, studying arrest records. He secretly obtained Communist Party member records, and he subscribed to every radical newspaper in America, scanning them for leads to direct him to enemy agents.

J. Edgar and his special assistant, George Ruch, whom he called "Blimp," asserted that the writings and speech of "left wingers" should be suppressed. Ruch, a friend from high school, would later go on to hire thugs to attack labor activists at the Pittsburgh Coal Company. In honor of "my close and intimate friend," Ruch named his son "J. Edgar."

At a private dinner, Ruch asked J. Edgar if he had any plans to get married. He told Ruch that he was "wed" to the department and had no time "to waste on a family."

Had it not been for what later evolved into an anti-Bolshevik "witch hunt," J. Edgar might never have become head of the world's largest law enforcement agency.

Long before anyone had heard of Senator Joseph McCarthy, a Red Scare prevailed under Palmer. When he directed the infamous "Palmer Red Raids," backed up by J. Edgar, he was nicknamed "The Fighting Quaker."

In late April of 1919, an anarchist, Luigi Galleani, made an attempt on the life of Palmer by sending a booby trap bomb to his home. The explosive was intercepted and defused.

About five weeks later, on June 2, 1919, shortly before midnight, two "alien saboteurs" planted a bomb in front of Palmer's house. The blast destroyed half of his home. In their attempts to escape, the terrorists were blown to bits. Some of their body parts landed across the street on the porch of Franklin D. Roosevelt, Secretary of the Navy.

Before the night ended, other explosions at government buildings went off. A note was found declaring the beginning of a class war and predicting ultimate victory for the international proletariat.

In the days ahead, nearly forty bombs were sent out, arriving at the offices of John D. Rockefeller, J.P. Morgan, a Supreme Court Justice, three cabinet members, four senators, a U.S. district judge, two governors, and two members of the House of Representatives.

Fortunately, none of the bombs reached their targets, as they were each intercepted or exploded by the police. Only one injury was reported, and that was from a servant who opened a suspicious package.

J. Edgar wanted not only to arrest radicals and anarchists, but to have them deported. Although thousands of American citizens were arrested, only 500 foreigners were kicked out of the country. "These people are planting poisonous seeds of disloyalty," J. Edgar charged. "They must be crushed out like you would a two-headed serpent about to strike you with a deadly venom."

On November 7, in raids planned by J. Edgar himself, local police, directed by the Bu-

Emma Goldman, "Queen of the Anarchists," seen here with **Berkman** in 1917 as they are being deported.

J. Edgar defined Goldman as "My biggest red game yet." She advocated politically motivated murder and violent revolution.

reau of Investigation, launched a violent sweep of Russian workers in a dozen American cities. Many suspected Bolsheviks were badly beaten during the assault. Dozens of innocent Americans, some Irish or Swedish, were arrested but later set free. Of the 650 arrested in New York City that day, only 43 were deported.

Even as a very young stalker of communists and anarchists, J. Edgar was clever enough to know he needed to capture a very high profile person if he wanted to generate favorable publicity in the press. Emma Goldman, "the Queen of the Anarchists," emerged as his most notorious target. Her character is familiar to those who saw Warren Beatty's film *Reds*.

"If I can get this Jew bitch deported back to Russia, it will make headlines for me across America," J. Edgar accurately predicted. "I might even get a promotion."

Born in the Lithuanian city of Kovno on June 27, 1869, Goldman came to the United States in 1885, settling in New York City. Throughout much of her life she was linked to Alexander Berkman, her lover and partner in anarchy. J. Edgar claimed that "beyond any doubt, these two are the most dangerous anarchists in America." His case against Berkman was stronger, and he knew that getting Goldman deported would an uphill fight. She had lived in the United States for more than three decades, and both her father and her former husband were U.S. citizens.

In 1892, Goldman and Berkman plotted to assassinate Henry Clay Frick, the multimillionaire industrialist and financier who was called "the most hated man in America." Berkman was selected to enter his office and fire bullets into his heart. The anarchists had the mistaken belief that by killing Frick, they would "strike terror into the soul of his upper class and bring their teachings of anarchism before the world."

No one represented the evils of the capitalist system more than the ruthless Frick himself. He was vilified by the public for his lack of morality in business dealings and for exploiting, even brutalizing, his underpaid workers who lived in wretched ghettos.

Chairman of Carnegie Steel, he played a major role in the formation of the giant U.S. Steel manufacturing concern, and also financed the construction of the Pennsylvania Railroad and the Reading Company. It was an exaggeration, of course, but he was said to own the city of Pittsburgh, and he had vast land holdings in the state of Pennsylvania. Some historians have named him "the single worst CEO in the history of America."

In the Homestead Strike of 1892, workers at his steel plant in Pennsylvania were locked out of the giant plant when negotiations failed. Frick hired three hundred armed guards from the Pinkerton Detective Agency to break the union's picket lines. On the morning of July 6, 1892, a gunfight broke out. A battled ensued, lasting twelve hours, during which time nine union workers and seven guards were killed.

Originally, with Goldman's approval, Berkman planned to shoot Frick and then commit suicide.

On July 23, 1892, Berkman dressed up in an expensive suit he'd bought two days before. Security in the late 19th century was not what it is today. One office seeker had only recently walked into the office of the president of the United States without any real challenge. Berkman went unchallenged past two secretaries and entered Frick's private chambers, where he sat alone at his desk. Frick did not even look up at the intruder, but muttered, "What in hell do you want?"

Berkman had arrived armed with a gun and a sharpened steel file, which he planned to stab into Frick's heart. He fired three bullets at him, but Frick jumped up and fought back. With the steel file, Berkman stabbed Frick's leg. Alarmed by the shouts, five of the plant's security guards rushed into the office to save Frick's life. They beat Berkman unconscious.

The assassination attempt was condemned by both workers and anarchists. Since Frick survived, Berkman was tried and convicted of an assassination attempt and not sentenced to the death penalty. Given a twenty-two year prison sentence, he served fourteen years. He was released on May 18, 1906.

Privately, J. Edgar endorsed the brutal putdown of union strikers ordered by the hated capitalist steel baron, **Henry Clay Frick** (photo above). J. Edgar suspected that most union strikes were communist inspired.

Berkman teamed up with Goldman again and once again launched their campaign of anarchy in America. Amazingly, in spite of often violent rallies, they were not arrested until 1917, when the U.S. entered World War I and passed a Selective Service act. Goldman and Berkman opposed conscription and widely denounced it, which led to their arrest on June 15, 1917. They were charged with conspiracy, tried, and sent to jail with a two-year prison sentence.

Goldman had many friends who were angered by her arrest. She was viewed as a free-thinking rebel and a rigorous intellectual who championed free love, birth control, freedom of speech, and even homosexuality.

When Goldman was released from the Missouri State Penitentiary on September 27, 1919, J. Edgar was waiting with another court order to re-arrest her. When Berkman was released from an Atlanta penitentiary on October 1,

1919, he, too, compliments of J. Edgar, was immediately re-arrested.

At a hearing, she was ordered deported, along with Berkman. As J. Edgar later confessed, "I threw the book at her." He even accused her of plotting the 1910 bombing of the offices of the *Los Angeles Examiner*, although he knew that she had had nothing to do with that act of terrorism. J. Edgar's most serious charge was that her speeches inspired the September 9, 1901 assassination of President William McKinley in Buffalo. He was shot by Leon Czolgosz, a Polish-American factory worker, who had once attended one of Goldman's speeches.

At 4:15AM, on the bitterly cold morning of December 21, 1919, in New York Harbor, J. Edgar and the bureau's chief, William Flynn, boarded a cutter which took them to Ellis Island. There they boarded the antiquated vessel, *The Burford* which was set to transport 249 "radicals" back to the Soviet Union.

J. Edgar personally confronted both Goldman and Berkman, who told J. Edgar, "We'll be back, you dirty bastard."

Later, on shore at Ellis Island, J. Edgar predicted that "other Soviet Arks will sail for Europe—we will not tolerate treason in this country." He was pleased to read an endorsement of his actions in *The New York Times*. The paper attacked the "blasphemous creatures who not only rejected America's hospitality and assailed her institutions but also sought by a campaign of assassination and terrorism to ruin her as a nation of free men."

Back at his office, J. Edgar predicted, "After today, I will be frontpage news throughout America until I go to meet my Maker. First thing up there, I'll probably demand that God give me his fingerprints."

***

Much to the delight of J. Edgar, another of Palmer's "Red Menace Raids" was launched on January 2, 1920. The raids took place in thirty-three American cities, and 10,000 aliens were beaten and arrested.

Most of the "deviants" seized were later released because they were *bona fide* American citizens without any record or any evidence that they had done something wrong.

J. Edgar maintained that a vast arsenal of bombs had been discovered that would have destroyed the heart of such cities as New York. Actually, all that the raiders discovered was a cache of four pistols in New York City.

Using his position, he began to investigate suspicious lawyers and other officials whom he suspected of being "disseminators of Bolshevik propaganda." The most classic case was Felix Frankfurter, a Law School professor at Harvard who would later become a justice of the U.S. Supreme

Court. In a memo dated in 1921, J. Edgar defined Frankfurter as "the most dangerous man in America."

Frankfurter had been born into a Jewish family in Vienna in 1882 during the most confident chapter of the Austro-Hungarian Empire. His family immigrated to the United States. While still a student, he attended political rallies advocating socialism and communism.

He had supported Theodore Roosevelt during his unsuccessful Bull Moose campaign in 1912. When Roosevelt lost, Frankfurter described himself as "politically homeless." The U.S. entered World War I in 1917, and Frankfurter became special assistant to Secretary of War Newton D. Baker.

Frankfurter and J. Edgar would clash many times in the future. Everything that the future Supreme Court Justice did during his rise to the bench infuriated J. Edgar. Frankfurter got involved in labor politics and came to be viewed, according to J. Edgar, as a "lawyer in favor of radical principles." Frankfurter was also a Zionist and helped found the American Civil Liberties Union.

Along the way, he stomped down on some of J. Edgar's favorite tactics as a law enforcement officer. Frankfurter attacked police entrapment and brutality and objected, in court, to prolonged detention and violations of due process. He frequently defended members of oppressed religious minorities and socialists.

After the election of Franklin D. Roosevelt, Frankfurter bonded with the new president and commissioned many bright young lawyers to promote the New Deal. They became known as "Felix's Happy Hot Dogs."

When Justice Benjamin N. Cardozo died in July of 1938, FDR appointed Frankfurter to the Supreme Court. He was confirmed without dissent, although J. Edgar worked in the background to discredit him. As a Supreme Court Justice, Frankfurter became the most outspoken advocate of judicial restraint, but in 1955, he urged desegregation of schools with "all deliberate speed."

When J. Edgar learned that his long-time enemy had died in February of 1965, he said, "Now I know there is a God in Heaven."

**

In the January, 1920 "red raids" that J. Edgar orchestrated, he later admitted there were "clear cases of brutality." What he meant to say, but didn't, was that many innocent people were arrested, beaten, and tortured.

But ironically, in the political firestorm that followed it was Palmer, not J. Edgar, who was attacked by hundreds of lawyers, labor leaders, and newspaper editors across the country.

Palmer's dreams of becoming president collapsed in the fallout from the raids, and nationwide, he was generally discredited. Violent anarchist bombs, however, continued to explode at targets, mainly along the East Coast of the U.S., for the next twelve years.

Palmer was also roundly condemned by Harlan Fiske Stone, dean of the Columbia University School of Law. Ironically, it was Stone who would later appoint J. Edgar as director of the FBI.

Even though he had directly designated many of the "red targets," J. Edgar emerged unscathed throughout the backlash against Palmer.

He continued to pursue alleged "Reds." In fact, he earned his first press mention, one editorial calling him "a slender bundle of high-charged electric wire." It would be the beginning of many a press rave or attack.

In private, J. Edgar later claimed that he virtually destroyed the Communist Party before it could overthrew the U.S. government. Before the raids, membership numbered some 80,000 party workers. After the raids, only 6,000 "diehards" continued to label themselves as communists.

One suspected communist was actor Charlie Chaplin, at that time the most famous man in the world. J. Edgar's file on Chaplin would never be closed, as he collected more and more evidence on the comedian as the years went by.

As the Roaring Twenties dawned, and flappers ruled the night and drank bootleg gin, J. Edgar still showed no interest in women. He did become enamored of Frank Baughman, a classmate from law school. They both dressed the same in summer in immaculate white linen suits. Both of them adopted the custom of wearing a pink carnation in their lapels.

Über-macho **Frank Baughman**, spiffy dresser and ladies' man. Was J. Edgar secretly enamored with him?

Patrons reported seeing them discreetly holding hands every Sunday night at the Fox Movie Theater in Washington. They often sat through a double feature before having a candlelit dinner in some tavern.

It is surprising that Baughman chose J. Edgar as a best friend. He was shy, Baughman extroverted, a spiffy dresser who enjoyed poker, crap games, and heavy drinking, all of which J. Edgar abhorred. But he was nonetheless attracted to the super masculine qualities of Baughman, in spite of his interest in young women, which he made abundantly clear to J. Edgar, who was not only having difficulty in his pursuit of love, but facing tragedy on his home

15

front.

On March 30, 1921, J. Edgar's father, Dickerson Sr., died, having wasted away from self-induced starvation. He'd once loved his father, but during his final years, he had been ashamed of him. J. Edgar did not tolerate people who suffered from mental illness, blaming it on their own weakness.

He and his mother seemed freed of a great burden and could now live alone quietly in their small house on Seward Square, where J. Edgar had been born.

After two days of mourning, J. Edgar's beloved "Mama" went out and bought four spring outfits—sunflower yellow, pumpkin orange, scarlet, and mint green—and charged them to her son.

J. Edgar was positioned to benefit from the direction of the political winds. On August 22, 1921, President Warren G. Harding's attorney general, Harry Daugherty, fired William J. Flynn, chief of the Bureau of Investigation. He was replaced with William J. Burns, a celebrated detective, who named J. Edgar as his assistant director.

Detective **William J. Burns** *(photo above)* was called "the Sherlock Holmes of America" when he was appointed as director of the Bureau of Investigation by Thomas Daugherty, the U.S. Attorney General who was implicated in many of the scandals spearheaded by president Warren G. Harding.

A notorious womanizer, Burns became J. Edgar's new boss. He was thoroughly corrupt.

Burns was not the first chief of the bureau. Stanley W. Finch had helmed it between its establishment in 1908 and 1912. Before Burns, the bureau was run by Alexander B. Bielaski (1912-1919), William E. Allen (1919; he served the shortest term), and William J. Flynn (1919-1921).

J. Edgar reported directly to William Burns, but soon realized that his new boss was mired in so much corruption that he couldn't last long in that top post that J. Edgar coveted.

Although he admired how Burns "became the idol of every schoolboy," he also viewed his boss as corrupt, and plotted to overthrow him. It was by privately investigating his chief that J. Edgar learned how to destroy a political figure.

As a close friend of Daugherty (William Harding's Attorney General) Burns almost daily was getting embroiled in the notorious Teapot Dome Scandal, which involved the secret leasing of naval oil reserve lands to private companies.

Burns gave J. Edgar some advice that he would heed until his last day in office. "When you have a political enemy, investigate him. Everybody's got a smelly skeleton hidden in the closet."

The most famous detective in America, Burns was known as the country's Sherlock Holmes and also as a notorious ladies' man. Although J. Edgar admired some of his police accomplishments, he found much about his cigar-chomping boss repulsive. But J. Edgar would nonetheless use him as a role model if the occasion suited him.

J. Edgar liked the way Burns had an instinct for publicity, which turned him into a national figure, his exploits making tabloid news. The very popular magazines of the time wrote of his "true crime stories" based on his exploits, both real and exaggerated.

A personal friend of the corrupt President Harding, Burns was allowed to simultaneously direct both the bureau as well as his Burns Detective Agency throughout his tenure with the government.

Conspiring with Attorney General Daugherty, Burns launched an investigation of Thomas J. Walsh, the congressman from Montana. The probe was in retaliation for Walsh opposing oil leases granted by Secretary of the Interior, Albert Fall, a friend of Daugherty.

When a congressional probe demanded that Burns turn over confidential documents, he refused. The Senate retaliated by investigating the Bureau of Investigation, uncovering several misdeeds, though none of them touched J. Edgar. "I was as clean as a hound's tooth," he later claimed.

The Burns-Daugherty scandal became tabloid fodder, and Burns was forced to resign in 1924.

On May 10, 1924, Hoover took over his boss's post, at first as a temporary appointment.

In 1923, when Burns had helmed the bureau, its number of employees shrank from 1,127 men to just 600 employees. Under J. Edgar, the FBI would eventually expand into a mighty empire,

Daugherty secretly wanted to run for president, and J. Edgar began collecting incriminating data on him, thinking that if he did become president, he might blackmail him into naming him

Stanley W. Finch was appointed chief examiner to head a force of special investigative agents in 1908. In time, it became the Federal Bureau of Investigation. He was called the handsomest man ever to head the agency.

In contrast, bulldog-faced J. Edgar was deemed the ugliest. His tasks included the arrest of white slavers accused of transporting women across state lines for "immoral purposes."

bureau chief permanently.

Daugherty was the Republican Party boss, a member of the "Ohio Gang" surrounding Harding. He had virtually put Harding into office, and that's why the president had named him Attorney General. During his three years in office, he became the most notorious Attorney General in U.S. history.

He was plagued with charges and indictments and was alleged to have been involved in a kickback scam involving bootleggers. Under pressure, and with more scandals enveloping him, he resigned on March 28, 1924, his presidential dream gone forever.

J. Edgar quickly closed his secret file on him and turned to probing into the private lives of other subjects, namely, a rising politician from New York named Franklin D. Roosevelt.

The new attorney general was Harlan Fiske Stone. J. Edgar's new boss liked him and determined that he should head the bureau permanently. He was joined in his support by Herbert Hoover who at the time functioned as Secretary of Commerce. Later, Hoover would become the ill-fated president who was at the switch at the time of, and who would eventually be blamed for, the Wall Street crash of 1929.

Confirmed for the position, J. Edgar would hold onto the post, tenaciously, for the next forty-eight years, in spite of presidents who wanted to fire him but did not dare to. He knew too much about their private lives.

During his tenure, he would accumulate blackmail evidence on all the Chief Executives, especially Franklin and Eleanor Roosevelt and, in later years, a particularly massive volume on John F. Kennedy.

Warren Harding, U.S. president from 1921 to 1923, died just two years into his presidency. He didn't live to see his cabinet become embroiled in the notorious Teapot Dome scandal, which centered around the illegal leasing, with bribes, of government oil reserves. In the White House, he had two mistresses and a domineering wife, **Florence Kling De Wolfe**, who he referred to as "The Duchess."

After his landslide victory, he whined to her, "I am not fit for the office and should never have been here."

No president ever uttered more truth. In the White House, he claimed, "My god, but this is a hell of a place for a man like me to be." His lifelong obsession was poker. One night he bet the priceless White House china...and lost.

CHAPTER TWO

Pasty-faced, overweight, and growing increasingly ugly as he matured and edged toward thirty, J. Edgar was facing professional success. Privately, his social life was a disaster, and he was a very lonely man, desperately wanting companionship.

He complained to his mother that women did not find him attractive. Had he brought up the subject, he could also have claimed that that was doubly true for men. Every man he'd developed a crush on turned out to be straight, leaving him feeling abandoned when the object of his affection married.

No one could be sure, but J. Edgar appeared to be a virgin. His schoolboy crushes on men more virile than himself never seemed to have developed into any man-on-man passion. At one point he told Frank Baughman that, "My mother is the only person in the world who loves me. Unlike you, I will never get married."

The announcement that on December 22, 1924, J. Edgar had been appointed as the permanent director of the Bureau of Investigation came ten days before his thirtieth birthday.

As he told his mother, "This was the best combined birthday and Christmas present I could ever hope to receive. But as much as I want the job, I want an even bigger job. I will use the appointment to win a larger prize. No later than 1940, your son will be sitting in the Oval Office of the White House."

The press paid little attention when J. Edgar was given a permanent appointment as the head of the Bureau of Investigation. The *Washington Evening Star* even ran the news on the obituary page. J. Edgar was heralded as the head of "a new school of crime detection, the old sleuth of shadows and frame-ups gone forever."

As director of the Bureau, J. Edgar decided to celebrate, as his salary had been boosted from $5,000 annually to $7,500. He and "the man in his life," Frank Baughman, took their mothers to a Broadway play.

At the Liberty Theater on Forty-Second Street, the happy quartet sat through Fred and Adele Astaire starring in *Lady, Be Good!* At the end of the show by the Gershwin brothers, J. Edgar privately whispered to Baughman, "I think Fred Astaire is a homosexual. The Bureau should investigate that."

J. Edgar was friendly backstage, congratulating the Astaires. Fred would later remember his "vise-like grip as if he were putting handcuffs on me."

Later, J. Edgar noted that after the show the "flappers and sugar daddies" in the theater audience headed to illegal speakeasies throughout New York. However, the enforcement of Prohibition was the responsibility of the Treasury Department, not the Bureau.

In his new post, J. Edgar had big plans for the Bureau, most of which were implemented. But he never achieved his dream of "Universal Fingerprinting." He wanted to have a record of the fingerprints of every man and woman in America.

In World War II, he did succeed in obtaining the fingerprints of every person in the Army, Air Force, or Navy, as well as every worker in the war industries, as he feared massive sabotage.

At the end of his life, his fingerprint division had grown to the point where it occupied a six-story structure taking up a whole city block in Washington. His Crime Laboratory became the greatest in the world, and remains so to this day.

When he took over the Bureau, he called it "a cesspool, filled with graft and corruption." Many agents were living on bribes, and some men supported themselves by extortion and blackmail. J. Edgar set about to get rid of "these thieves, bandits, and perverts," returning the Bureau to the pristine vision that Theodore Roosevelt had conceived for it back in 1908.

A journalist in 1923 wrote that, "The Bureau of Investigation is a private hole in the corner goon squad for the attorney general. Its arts are devoted to snooping, bribery, and blackmail."

J. Edgar was horrified at the morality of his agents, especially when he found them hanging out in a room known as the "Buzzard's Roost." They used the room for heavy drinking, viewing pornography they'd seized in raids, and telling dirty jokes. He fired all the patrons of the room, and even threatened to fire men caught drinking after work.

Secretly, J. Edgar set about perfecting some of his major weapons—wiretapping, opening mail, bugging, and even burglary if necessary. He wanted information and didn't seem to care how he went about getting it. Some critics have called him "The Father of the Watergate" break-in during the Richard Nixon administration.

On his first day on the job, J. Edgar ordered background checks on all the men under his command. He especially wanted to know if any of them were suspected of homosexuality or if any had ever been a member of the discredited Communist Party.

After an internal probe, many agents were fired or dismissed. J. Edgar claimed they were "hacks," actually political appointees, "incapable of doing their jobs." In the wake of that, he received at least three death threats.

This would be but the beginning of a volley of death threats he could receive over the decades. On the day he died, two letters threatening his life were delivered to FBI headquarters.

He took these mailed threats seriously, but his agents almost never found the anonymous men (or in some cases, women) who wanted him dead. Most of the letters were not from psychotic killers, but from outraged citizens expressing their extreme displeasure at the way he ran the FBI.

One agent, critical of J. Edgar after he fired him, claimed, "He walks like a woman, like mincing steps. He dresses like a dandy wearing oyster-gray spats covering patent leather shoes. He prefers snap-brimmed hats. His clothes appear tailored, not off the rack. He's rather flamboyant and smells of lavender water. Always a white shirt and striped tie. He must spend an hour folding the stiffly starched handkerchief he wears in his lapel."

"'Eleanor blue,' as it is called, is his favorite color for his matched shades of tie, handkerchief, and socks," the agent said. "He's on the chubby side. He always wears a star sapphire ring studded with diamonds. He has a dark complexion. There are rumors that he has a bit of the tarbush from his ancestors. I'm not sure about this, but he is said to change his underwear three times a day. Not only that, but he is thought to wear his panties in different colors. Since all men's underwear comes only in white, he must dye his drawers himself. If I didn't know better, I would swear that he is a homosexual, although he claims he abhors perverts and fires any agent he even suspects of being one. He once booted an agent who walks in the same mincing way he does."

A former aide claimed that J. Edgar was "short, squat, and with the smallest feet I've ever seen on a man. He walks like he talks, fast. When seen from the rear, his bottom—well, it sort of bounced."

J. Edgar did not like blacks, feeling they were "lazy bastards and un-reliable—low Red Cap sorts." When he received reports of violence against blacks in the South coming from the hooded Ku Klux Klan, J. Edgar dismissed it as "harmless intimidation—after all, someone has to keep these darkies in line."

Earlier in his career, J. Edgar had learned that President Warren Harding had been sworn into the KKK in the Green Room of the White House. The Klan's Imperial Wizard, William Joseph Simmons, conducted this secret ceremony.

J. Edgar in a memo attacked the "scourge of Kluxism," yet he was a great believer in white supremacy himself. As he later told his life-long companion, Clyde Tolson, "the face you present to the world is not necessarily the bare ass you show after midnight."

In his early days as director of the Bureau, J. Edgar "experimented" by hiring two women as special agents. But he was never pleased with their job performance. Both women lasted less than three years with the Bureau. When they resigned, he called his experiment of hiring women a dismal failure.

Actually many of his G-Men called him "a woman hater." In investigating a case, he taught them to "look for dirty, filthy, diseased women" who might lead an agent to his prey. "Behind every crook, there's probably a woman even more evil than the bastard himself. Many robberies, most robberies, occur because some stupid man is trying to get expensive things for some woman who is home goading him into crime, even if he gets shot trying to bring home the trophies for her."

In later years J. Edgar liked to drink Jack Daniels, but when he took charge, Prohibition was the law of the land, and he demanded that it be rigidly enforced. Any agent indulging in intoxicants would be immediately dismissed.

When an official stopped off to visit the Denver office of the Bureau, and the chief there offered the travel-fatigued visitor a drink, that agent was fired the next day. J. Edgar seemed to have spies in every state.

Soon he was called upon to make speeches. In his first addresses, he sounded like Bobby Kennedy in the 1960s, blaming poverty as the cause

Though J. Edgar was no great advocate of civil rights for African Americans, as head of the Bureau of Investigation, he often had to investigate the activities of the KKK when it violated Federal law.

His agents uncovered evidence that certain KKK-affiliated prison officials "sold" Negro prisoners to local farmers for free labor.

To cover up, one local plantation owner in Georgia killed a dozen Negroes to conceal the evidence. But he was eventually exposed.

The cross-burning **KKK rally** depicted above took place in Georgia in 1922.

of crime.

J. Edgar did not like his agents to engage in sex, at least the unmarried ones, which were the men he preferred to hire. When he heard that an agent had had sex with a woman in his office in Knoxville, he fired him at once. J. Edgar went so far as to break up the marriages of agents of which he didn't approve. In several cases he sent incriminating evidence to the wives, often falsely charging their husbands with adultery, causing the women to sue for divorce.

Agents actually caught in adulterous affairs—called "double yolkers" by J. Edgar—were routinely fired without recommendations to a future employer. Such a dismissal prevented them from getting hired by any other government agency.

When he really disliked an agent, but had no charge against him, he ordered him to a different office in a different part of the country, every six weeks until he broke the man's spirit and he resigned.

J. Edgar issued orders as to how an agent should dress and look, and he also vowed he'd never hire a man who extended him a clammy hand to shake. His mandate required that "no agent shall have protruding ears, bad posture, a pear-shaped head, or bushy eyebrows. Hair must be neatly trimmed, and shirts must always be white with no loud ties. Socks should always be black, and shoes must be shined until you can see your face reflected in them."

J. Edgar went from "The Red Hunter" to a protector of civil liberties, assuring a Senate committee that no American citizen should be investigated because of his or her political views. Of course, what he said and what he actually did were two different things.

The stress of the job began to wear on J. Edgar. He began to look tired and haggard and went to his doctor for a thorough examination. The physician could find nothing wrong with his patient, but recommended that he take up smoking to relax. J. Edgar followed his advice and became addicted to smoking Lucky Strike cigarettes, which was a strange choice for him since the brand at that time was considered a woman's ciga-

Tormented at times by his own sexual confusion, **J. Edgar Hoover** nonetheless preached stern moral sermons to America.

Secretly, he indulged in homosexuality, even transvestism.

One of his closest colleagues, FBI agent William Sullivan, called him "the master blackmailer." Yet on rare occasions, he was the victim of blackmail himself.

rette. Lucky Strike urged women who wanted to keep their figures trim to "reach for a Lucky instead of a sweet."

Although he was power hungry, he avoided exposing the Bureau to certain activities he knew he could not control—smuggling, violations of Prohibition, drugs, forgery, and illegal immigration.

"We would never look good taking on such things, because they're too big for us. It would be like trying to empty the Atlantic Ocean with a cup."

***

In 1928, J. Edgar's lonely days were about to end forever. Never again would he hunger for male companionship. He was introduced to the man of his dreams, Clyde Tolson, who would never leave his side "till death do us part," and who would keep alive his memory until his own demise.

Born in 1900, five years after J. Edgar, in Laredo, Missouri, Clyde Tolson was a "man's man," who would in the 1930s be called "the Gary Cooper of the FBI." He was just as ambitious as J. Edgar and was prepared not only to work to get where he wanted to go, but to use people like stepping stones if necessary.

The day the strapping, dark-haired **Clyde Tolson** walked into the office of J. Edgar Hoover, the director met the man of his dreams. The two G-men walked lockstep together for the rest of their lives.

Almost overnight, this agent-trainee occupied the second-highest post in the Bureau.

After Missouri, he attended Cedar Rapids Business College in Iowa. At eighteen he moved to Washington, D.C. where he worked as a clerk in the War Department. He had little intention of getting stuck there, so he attended night classes at George Washington University.

In the locker room of the gymnasium, he was admired by other men when he took a shower. One rather obvious man asked him, "Are all men from Missouri as big as you? If so, I'm taking the next train."

"Get away from me, you queer," Clyde shouted at him.

His big break came in 1919 when he became the confidential secretary to the Secretary of War, serving in three administrations under Newton D. Baker, John W. Weeks, and Dwight F. Davis.

At George Washington University, he earned his B.A. degree in 1925, followed by his law degree in 1927.

Clyde applied for a job in the Bureau of Investigation. He'd heard wonderful things about what J. Edgar was doing at the Bureau and wanted to be a part of it.

Regrettably, he was turned down, but he was persistent. The following year he applied once again to the Bureau. This time his photograph and application were spotted by J. Edgar, who told his assistant, "Set up a meeting with this Tolson. I think he's just the kind of man I've been looking for." That statement, of course, could be interpreted in two different ways.

J. Edgar read all the references praising Clyde, including one from the former Secretary of War, Newton D. Baker, who found him to be "a boy of fine presence who pays serious attention to his duties. He has an excellent intelligence." But the recommendation J. Edgar found the most intriguing came from John W. Martyn who was an executive assistant in the War Department. "Clyde Tolson shows no particular interest in women, but his habits have always been of the best."

When the handsome, masculine, soft-spoken Clyde Tolson, fresh from America's Corn Belt, walked into the office of J. Edgar Hoover, he was to remain by his side for nearly half a century with only minor interruptions.

J. Edgar took in the way he filled out his cream-colored linen jacket, his lime-green slacks, and looked into his piercing black eyes. Finally, he focused on his alligator shoes. He said, "Our Bureau needs more men like you."

Although J. Edgar really wanted Clyde in the office beside him, he figured, at least for appearance's sake, that his new man should get some field training. He was transferred as a special agent to the branch office in Boston. By September, J. Edgar could stand it no more and sent for Clyde to return to Washington, where he was made supervisor of the clerical staff.

Rather impulsively, J. Edgar assigned him as a special agent in charge of the office at Buffalo, New York. But before Clyde had completely unpacked, he received a call from his boss to return to Washington at once. "I need you here with me permanently," Clyde was told. "Forget your dream of becoming a lawyer in that hick town of Cedar Rapids. I'm making you assistant director."

Agents speculated that J. Edgar's decision was prompted by the recent marriage of Frank Baughman, who was no longer available for dinners, parties, and night clubbing.

Back in Washington, Clyde learned that no agent in the history of the Bureau had ever risen so high, so fast. Later, agents speculated that to get to the top it was a good idea to sleep with your boss.

J. Edgar certainly played favorites, promoting Clyde into a top position, while extinguishing the flame of yesterday, Frank Baughman. Perhaps to humiliate his former friend, J. Edgar made Baughman Clyde's assistant. But the two men bickered constantly. Clyde stayed on, but Baughman was eventually put in charge of the Bureau's firearms training program at Quantico, Virginia.

Clyde was put in charge of personnel and discipline, not frontline crime-fighting. He was given complete authority to hire and fire at his discretion and seemed to take special delight in firing men.

"He was one cold fish," said one dismissed agent. "Around the office he was called the Sphinx. No one knew what he was thinking. You'd think you were doing a good job and then, like a cobra, he would strike at you and kick you out."

"He could intimidate you by staring at you with those beady black eyes," said another agent. "He was a first-class asshole, always scheming. But when Hoover came around, his face lit up."

After one week, J. Edgar asked Clyde out for dinner. It was the beginning of thousands of dinners over the decades to come. No one knows exactly what happened that night, but Clyde became J. Edgar's constant companion, although they would have their arguments and rough spots over the years. Even so, they remained lifelong lovers "until death do us part."

After their first night together, the pair coined nicknames for each other. Clyde became "Junior." In public, Clyde referred to J. Edgar as "Mr. Boss," but in private he called him "Speed," his childhood nickname. When Clyde was being particularly affectionate, J. Edgar became "Eddie."

Around the office Clyde quickly became known as J. Edgar's *protégé,* although that wasn't the term most agents used. Behind their backs, agents referred to them as "J. Edna and Mother Tolson." Years later author Truman Capote, a fellow homosexual, had another name for them—"Johnny and Clyde."

Because J. Edgar and Clyde were seen everywhere together, it was concluded that their relationship was

As **J. Edgar**'s affair with **Clyde Tolson** deepened, so did his cover-up of his secret desires.

Historian Dr. David Eisenbach said, "Hoover's fear of being exposed fed his determination to assemble files on other people's sex secrets. But his files were daily reminders that he, too, could be exposed. He was a pathetic, angry, little man, whose anxiety about his own sexuality spurred him to become the most obsessed, most powerful, and most dangerous sexual blackmailer on earth."

intimate, which it was, of course. "They virtually lived in each other's crotches," said one dismissed agent. "One day I said something in private to another agent, and Tolson fired me the following morning. The Gestapo probably learned their techniques from them."

Ray Berry, a government worker, once remarked at a party. "I think they are sodomites." The next day the charge had reached J. Edgar's office. "A drunken degenerate," he said. He instructed Clyde to contact someone in the Department of Commerce and have Berry fired.

A male secretary for President Hoover spread the word that "Tolson is J. Edgar Hoover's boyfriend. They are both fairies."

J. Edgar shot back that "this foul-minded, malicious rat, this despicable, depraved psycho must not be allowed to work for the clean-minded U.S. government." He ordered Clyde to "dig up something on the son of a bitch. He probably molests thirteen-year-old boys."

Life somehow fell into a routine for them. Every day at noon, they lunched at the Mayflower Hotel to which they were driven by limousine. One afternoon while dining, J. Edgar recognized a man who was "the third most wanted" in America at a table nearby. He ordered Clyde to go over and arrest him, signaling two agents nearby to take the criminal away. After doing that, Clyde returned to table and resumed his meal.

The Mayflower was a particular favorite of J. Edgar. As the decades went by, J. Edgar and Clyde had spies staked out at the Mayflower. "They wanted to know every time a cockroach walked across the floor," said the manager. The most scandals at the hotel occurred in the late 1950s, when Senator John F. Kennedy rented a permanent suite there.

Very few photographs remain among the hundreds that **J. Edgar** snapped of **Clyde Tolson.** Some agent from afar managed to snap this blurred photograph of J. Edgar taking a picture of Clyde at Miami Beach during one of their many vacations.

According to Guy Hotell, J. Edgar took pride in Clyde's body and often bragged about his friend's endowment. He was known to have taken many nudes of his friend, which may no longer exist.

Upon J. Edgar's death, Clyde was said to have destroyed this enormous cache of "forbidden photographs."

Judy Garland remembered attending orgies at the hotel. And after JFK became president, his mistress, Judith Campbell Exner, was stashed here during secret sexual trysts when he couldn't bring her to the White House because Jackie was there.

In 1999, Monica Lewinsky fought her way through throngs of the press to the presidential suite at the Mayflower to recount details of her affair (including that cigar!) to congressional impeachment managers. More recently, the then-governor of New York, Eliot Spitzer, was exposed as "Client 9" as revealed in a federal prostitution sting conducted at the Mayflower.

At night J. Edgar and Clyde dined at a restaurant called Harvey's, which charged them only $2.50 for dinner. J. Edgar never paid, but got a "friend of the Bureau," to pick up the tab. Both Clyde and J. Edgar ordered the same items every night, green turtle soup followed by a thick medium-rare porterhouse steak. The meal was topped off by three big scoops of vanilla ice cream.

In the winter months an oyster-eating competition was held on Saturday night at the restaurant. J. Edgar always won. "Oysters make you virile," he claimed. He demanded that Clyde order them every time they appeared on the menu, whether his companion wanted them or not.

Wherever J. Edgar was, Clyde was also there. J. Edgar admitted that "he is my alter ego. He can even read my mind."

A senior agent at the Bureau, who would not allow the use of his name, said, "They fitted together like a hand in a glove. There was one big difference. Tolson was a lot smarter than Hoover. That boy from Missouri had a mind that was razor sharp. He could have been a big cheese all on his own had he not given up his life to slavishly follow Hoover's every whim. There was no doubt as to who was the boss in the relationship. During the day, Hoover was a little Napoleon. But, from what I heard, once they went home, once those doors were locked, it was Hoover who was the slave, waiting on his top man. When they crawled into the sack, I had no doubt that it was Tolson who was on top of the pile."

In his 1978 novel, *The Chancellor Manuscript*, a tale inspired by the duo directing the FBI, author Robert Ludlum assigned the name "Clyde" to the character based on Tolson and wrote that his "soft pampered face—struggling for masculinity—had for decades been the flower to the bristled cactus."

Not only did J. Edgar and Clyde dine together, they went to nightclubs and parties. They even took their vacations together.

One Washington hostess, Marjorie Merriweather Post, said, "We learned never to invite Hoover without including Tolson. They were an item—called the happiest married couple in Washington society."

J. Edgar and Clyde also developed a fondness for the race track. Saturday afternoons became their favorite time for the track. The director placed $2 bets but that was just for show. He had his agents place his real bets at the hundred dollar window. When they vacationed in California, they headed for the Del Mar track at La Jolla. Each December they flew to Miami, for some winter sunshine, which J. Edgar preferred far more than Clyde. There they often lived in a private villa guarded by agents of the FBI. In Florida, they became especially fond of watching and betting on greyhound racing.

Back in Washington, officially, they maintained separate residences, although Clyde seemed to visit his quarters just for a change of clothing, having spent the night with his boss.

Much of what we know about the early relationship of J. Edgar and Clyde comes from Guy Hottel, a special agent in charge of the Washington, D.C. field office. For a while, Hottel shared a bachelor apartment with Clyde. "He was never at home," Hottel later claimed. "He was out every night with Hoover. Sometimes he'd come back to the apartment at five o'clock in the morning to shave, shit, take a shower, and get dressed to meet Hoover in time for breakfast. It was obvious to me from the beginning they were having an affair. I couldn't believe that a good-looking guy like Clyde would fall for a toad like Hoover. I think he was screwing our director only for career advancement."

In spite of that early and negative assessment, Guy would later become a party in the intimate lives of J. Edgar and Clyde. In carrying out J. Edgar's every wish, he, too, learned how to advance himself within the Bureau.

Their close relationship did not always escape press scrutiny. In an article in *Time*, a reporter stated, "Hoover is seldom seen without a male companion, most frequently solemn-faced Clyde Tolson." When the story was published, that journalist found himself investigated.

Yet another journalist, Ray Tucker, hinted at J. Edgar's homosexuality in an article for *Collier's*. After its publication, Tucker was investigated by the FBI, and information about his private life was leaked to the media. Tucker was denounced as a "degenerate alcoholic." That seemed to frighten other reporters from exploring the secret life of J. Edgar more thoroughly.

As a means of presenting a different image, Clyde contacted the editor of another national magazine, *Liberty*. Its reporter agreed to write that J. Edgar had "a compact body, with the shoulders of a light heavyweight boxer. He carries no ounce of extra weight—just 170 pounds of live, virile masculinity."

For his kind words, the editor of *Liberty* was awarded with some

In the rare, out-of-focus photo above, **J. Edgar** (*right*) is seen having a gay old time with FBI agent **Guy Hotell.**

Technically, he was Clyde Tolson's roommate in an apartment that Clyde maintained for appearance's sake.

Guy was only "gay for profit," as he liked to chase after young women when not otherwise occupied by J. Edgar and Clyde, who insisted that he vacation with them.

"scoops" from Clyde, increasing circulation of his magazine.

In Kansas City on business, Clyde and J. Edgar checked into the Muehlebach Hotel, occupying connecting suites paid for by the Bureau. The next morning, a room service waiter delivered breakfast to J. Edgar's suite. It was Clyde who opened the door, rapidly covering his nude body with a *café au lait* colored terrycloth robe.

Later that day a reporter for *The Kansas City Star* dared asked J. Edgar if he were married. "His look was as mysterious as a Garbo smile," the journalist wrote.

While on vacation, J. Edgar developed an obsession for taking pictures of Clyde, although most of these photographs were apparently destroyed. He snapped candid shots of his lover in a bathing suit by a swimming pool on Miami Beach, in his shirt tails and underwear getting dressed, having a cold rum drink on a tropical terrace, or sound asleep in bed. He even took a frontal nude of him in a courtyard, which he had blown up and placed at the head of his bed. At least that is what a maid reported when she pulled back a curtain that concealed the photograph during the day.

One of the Bureau's lab technicians said that he once developed a roll of Kodak film that was a series of pictures of a large and erect male penis. J. Edgar told him it was part of an investigation he was conducting about sending pornography through the mails. "I knew better," the technician later revealed. "I would bet my life that those were pictures taken by J. Edgar of Tolson with a hard-on."

The taking of these pornographic pictures would in time become a life-long obsession of J. Edgar's. He acquired a vast collection of pornography, but he didn't want pictures of "unknowns." He preferred secret pictures taken of some of the most famous men and women in America, ranging over the years from John F. Kennedy to Elvis Presley and Marilyn Monroe.

"Kid Napoleon," as J. Edgar was called, launched a crusade against pornography, a campaign that was secretly directed by Clyde. Clyde began to accumulate a repository of so-called obscene materials, including stag movies, candid photographs snapped of couples engaged in sex when doors were kicked in, books, pamphlets, freehand drawings, and even comic strips and "dirty" playing cards.

At night, J. Edgar and Clyde brought this porno to the director's home where they viewed it for their own amusement. While ranting against it, they became life-long devotees of pornography.

Working as a team, both Clyde and J. Edgar celebrated a victory on November 6, 1928. A Republican, Herbert Clark Hoover, had just been elected president, defeating Alfred E. Smith, a Democrat and a Catholic. J. Edgar told Clyde that "I now have an entrée into the Oval Office." Rightly or wrongly, he credited the newly elected president with his appointment as head of the Bureau of Investigation.

Hoover named William D. Mitchell as attorney general. A Protestant, he was a "dry," meaning he wanted to continue Prohibition across America. He would be J. Edgar's new boss.

Although officially he spoke out against alcohol, J. Edgar had become a secret drinker. Most evenings, at Harvey's Restaurant, he would order six or even eight bourbons before dinner. Clyde concealed the drinks for him under a big linen napkin. A son of the manager later said, "From where I stood, I'd call Hoover an alcoholic."

On his first meeting with J. Edgar, the newly appointed Attorney General Mitchell told him that, "If you stay with us for another thirty years under different attorney generals, follow this advice: Wiretapping will be the key to your future success."

Four years before, in 1924, then Attorney General Harlan Fiske Stone had banned wiretapping. At the time, J. Edgar had echoed his ruling, referring to the practice as "dirty, invasive, and unethical." Subsequently, he assured Roger Baldwin of the American Civil Liberties Union that "the practice is now history."

Under Mitchell, however, he secretly ordered his agents to begin tapping phones. In the beginning, J. Edgar and Clyde confined tapping mainly to kidnapping and white-slave investigations. But as the years went by, J.

Edgar ordered tapping of everybody from Eleanor Roosevelt to Howard Hughes to Barbara Hutton.

Privately, J. Edgar told Clyde that President Hoover viewed them favorably, at least for the moment, but depending on circumstances, Hoover

could change his opinion of them tomorrow and dismiss them. "Everybody's got skeletons hidden in their closet," J. Edgar said. "Let's find out the dirt on him. That way, if he tries to fire us, we'll blackmail him. Call it job security, my good man."

Beginning that afternoon, and for all the years to come, Clyde, although a usually modest man, would later admit, "I'm the best Sherlock Holmes in America for digging up dirt. I don't care who they are or how saintly, there's something nasty that can be found out about anybody."

Future presidents would provide J. Edgar and Clyde with far more damaging evidence than any scandal that they dug up on President Hoover.

In his book, *Sex Lives of the U.S. Presidents*, Nigel Cawthorne wrote: "Sadly, Herbert Hoover's life was nowhere near as bizarre as his namesake and contemporary, J. Edgar Hoover's was. There is no evidence that Herbert Hoover pored over pornography, liked dressing up in women's clothing, gave oral sex to his deputy, or liked being masturbated by a young boy wearing rubber gloves while another leather-clad youth read passages from the

The first U.S. president from west of the Mississippi, Iowa-born **Herbert Hoover** was in office from March 1929 until 1933. He presided over the Wall Street crash and the coming of the Great Depression, which he did absolutely nothing to alleviate.

In spite of her dour, Victorian-era appearance, his wife, globe-trotting **Lou Henry Hoover**, had transported supplies to the front lines via bicycle during mainland China's Boxer Rebellion in 1900.

While First Lady, she broke the color barrier in the White House and invited a black woman, Mrs. De-Priest, wife of Illinois Republican Oscar DePriest, for tea. *Tout* Washington was shocked.

Bible."

After a tedious investigation, Clyde could turn up no extramarital affairs of the president. The only known affair he'd had before marriage was when he worked in Australia for a British company backing a gold mining operation. There, the young Herbert Hoover had fallen madly in love with a barmaid in Kalgoorlie. Apparently, they had a torrid affair. He wrote her a love poem which was later published in *Those Were the Days* by Arthur Reid in Perth in 1933.

While the starlight-spangled heavens rolled around us when we stood,
And a tide of bliss kept surging through the currents of our blood,
And I spent my soul in kisses, crushed upon your scarlet mouth,
Oh! My red-lipped, sunbrowned, sweetheart, dark-eyed daughter of
the south.

Back in California, the future U.S. president married Lou Henry, his Stanford sweetheart, with whom he had two sons. All that could be discovered was that Mr. and Mrs. Hoover ate seven-course lunches and dinners in formal attire while millions of the unemployed stood in long lines forming at soup kitchens.

Hoover did not want to encounter White House servants, and three rings of a bell announced his approach. Staff members were to duck into the nearest closet or hide behind a corner until he passed out of sight. The same policy held true for groundskeepers who had to conceal themselves behind the shrubbery until "The Great Engineer," as he was called, passed by.

When the Stock Market crashed on October 29, 1929, eight months after Hoover's ascension to the presidency, both Clyde and J. Edgar knew that Hoover would be a one-term president.

The question that plagued J. Edgar and Clyde was this: Would the newly elected "post-Crash" president, scheduled for inauguration in 1933 and almost certain to be a Democrat, want a clean sweep? Would he fire all of President Hoover's "boys", especially J. Edgar himself?

Even though Clyde and J. Edgar drank heavily, they both agreed that Prohibition had been a national disaster, turning thousands of citizens into lawbreakers and giving rise to gangs of bootleggers who made billions off illegal booze, and its spin-offs, such as protection rackets, prostitution, and pay-offs to the police.

The enforcement of Prohibition remained the responsibility of the meager corps of only 4,000 agents assigned to the Treasury Department. Gangs, especially in New York and Chicago, battled each other over liquor sales and rackets, much as drug cartels operate in the 21st century. The Treasury

Department's agents were unarmed, and they were unable to make an arrest.

With the permission and approval of Attorney General Harlan F. Stone, J. Edgar and his investigators uncovered links between police departments and bootleggers which led to arrests, indictments and convictions.

***

Sitting alone in his study at night, J. Edgar dreamed of "the big case" that would put him on every front page in America. As if to answer his prayer, his telephone rang at eleven o'clock on the night of March 1, 1932. Charles and Anne Morrow Lindbergh had reported that their twenty-month-old son, Charles Augustus Lindbergh Jr., was missing from their home at Hopewell, New Jersey.

Overnight, the story became front-page news across America and the number one subject on everybody's lips. After all, at the time, Charles A. Lindbergh was a genuine American hero in the wake of his solo flight from New York's Long Island to Le Bourget in Paris on May 20-21, 1927.

H.L. Mencken called the saga of the Lindbergh baby kidnapping "the greatest story since the resurrection." The writer was right in his assessment. The kidnapping of the Lindbergh baby became known as "The Crime on the Century."

J. Edgar was bitterly disappointed that kidnapping had not been made a federal offense. All he could do was sit around and be handed bulletins, even though he wanted to direct the case himself. Arriving the next day at headquarters, J. Edgar learned that the famed aviator and his wife had received a ransom note, calling for $50,000 in small denominations. Operating outside his authority, J. Edgar set up an unofficial "Lindbergh Baby Squad" to assist in the investigation.

This angered the agents of the Treasury Department and local law enforcement officers in New Jersey. Each agency was vying for the publicity that solving the case might generate. "If I can solve this case and find the kidnapper, I can become a household word," J. Edgar told his agents. He asked Clyde to coordinate the Bureau's investigation. "You're the only man I can really trust to get the job done."

J. Edgar ran into conflict with Col. H. Norman Schwarzkopf, who was the head of the police department for the state of New Jersey. He refused J. Edgar's offer of assistance, which caused the Bureau chief to remark, "His only experience in solving a crime was as a floor walker at Bamberger's Department Store."

The colonel's son, General Norman Schwarzkopf, was the supreme commander of Desert Storm during the Persian Gulf War.

Without an invitation, J. Edgar visited the Lindbergh estate, where Charles Lindbergh himself, in a perhaps futile attempt to recover some of his family's privacy, refused him admission. The famed aviator later referred to J. Edgar "a fussy, nosey little man."

J. Edgar demanded that his agents find the missing baby and return him unharmed to his parents. Every day he mentioned to Clyde and some of his top staff members the publicity that a resolution of the case would generate. "Everyone in America is talking about nothing else," he said. His jealous law enforcement rivals called J. Edgar and his agents "federal glory hunters."

About ten weeks after the child's abduction, on May 12, 1931, the body of the little boy was found in a shallow grave less than five miles from the Lindbergh home. J. Edgar sent a personal plea to President Hoover to put the Bureau of Investigation in charge. Hoover didn't specifically grant that request, demanding instead that all federal law enforcement agencies get involved.

In spite of accusations about pro-Nazi leanings in the late 1930s, **Charles A. Lindbergh** (photo above) was a genuine American hero after flying his Spirit of St. Louis nonstop to Paris in 1927.

The kidnapping of his baby, Charles A. Lindbergh Jr., in 1932 generated almost as much publicity. J. Edgar longed to handle the case personally, though much of it fell under the authority of New Jersey law enforcement officials.

"I do not like being in a subordinate role," J. Edgar told Clyde and his agents. "I should run the show."

But President Hoover, bowing to public pressure, finally designated J. Edgar as coordinator of federal assistance, hoping that a collaboration of various agencies could solve the case. At long last J. Edgar was assigned to lead a Federal network of law enforcement agencies, including the Secret Service. However, there was still no Federal kidnapping law, and as such, J. Edgar had only limited authority.

He seized the initiative and began to issue press releases about the hunt for the kidnapper. Soon the American public came to believe that he was personally in charge.

The public became disillusioned at the failure to bring the kidnapper to justice. But along the way there were some bright notes for J. Edgar. Such papers as *The Philadelphia Record* advocated a central agency to oversee America's battle against organized crime. Several papers thought J. Edgar would be the ideal choice to head such an agency.

Even though under attack for the tragic outcome of the Lindbergh kidnapping, he was sometimes given undue credit. Such was the case when he was praised for sending America's number one gangster, Al Capone, to prison for income tax evasion. The credit really belonged to the Internal Revenue Service.

In the somber and politically galvanized aftermath of the Lindbergh kidnapping, the jurisdiction of the Bureau of Investigation was re-defined and expanded by a law passed by Congress on June 22, 1932. Known as the Lindbergh Law, it cited kidnapping as a federal offense and gave the Bureau jurisdiction if a kidnap victim was transported across state lines. Of course, that eliminated the Lindbergh case, whose kidnapping and murder had occurred entirely within the borders of New Jersey.

"If it is the last thing I ever do, I am going to see that the man who kidnapped the Lindbergh baby will die in the electric chair," J. Edgar vowed.

To his ultimate dismay, the case would drag on in the courts for another two and a half long years.

***

Charles A. Lindbergh is pictured in the top photo with his famous wife, **Anne Morrow Lindbergh**. The picture of their kidnapped baby was plastered with a WANTED poster all over America.

Using the kidnapping as an excuse, J. Edgar lobbied to get Congress to pass the Lindbergh Law, making it a federal crime to kidnap a person within the borders of the United States.

For J. Edgar and Clyde, life was not always about work. They had to have some amusement other than sexual release with each other.

As the 1930s dawned, they started going to the movies a lot, their favorite films being the 1930 *Little Caesar* starring Edward G. Robinson or the 1931 *The Public Enemy* with James Cagney. They also attended the original prison drama, *The Big House* (1930) with Chester Morris, and *20,000 Years in Sing Sing* (1932) with Spencer Tracy and Bette Davis.

After watching their favorite gangster movies, Clyde and J. Edgar would eagerly look forward to reading the morning comics. In 1931 Chester Gould had introduced his new comic strip detective, Dick Tracy. With the enthusiasm of little boys, the men followed Dick Tracy's daily adventure before reading the news of the day.

***

Back at his office every morning, often after a night at the movies, J. Edgar was always anxious to read his morning mail.

He received correspondence from such groups as the American Legion, calling for floggings for most crimes and, in one case, a demand that a criminal arrested a second time be publicly hanged as a deterrent for anyone contemplating a life of crime. Although he didn't say so in public, J. Edgar privately believed that the death penalty should be strenuously and frequently mandated and inflicted by the courts.

During the Great Depression of the 1930s, prior to the imposition of later, more liberal policies of Franklin Roosevelt, crime was interpreted as a symptom of national decay, and calls were strident and frequent for the establishment of a powerful Federal agency to coordinate national anti-crime efforts.

The official designation of what constituted a Federal crime began to change in the 1930s, as J. Edgar's Bureau assumed increased power. When he had any time, he studied Federal laws, going over the legal codes with his experts to see if his Bureau could extend its power. He began to view his lowly Bureau as an agency that one day would assume the power of a national police force, even extending its tentacles around the globe.

The Mann Act, passed by Congress in 1910, particularly intrigued him. It made it a Federal crime for unmarried couples to travel across a state line to have sex in a hotel or even in a private residence.

J. Edgar sat back in his chair and informed Clyde and the Bureau's legal experts of his opinion. "If I read this act correctly, and I am certain that I do, this empowers us to investigate any man or woman in the United States, from the President of the United States himself to the lowliest B-picture movie star—and, of course, any person I consider a dangerous American, and, as you know, there are plenty of those who must be caught in the act."

But night after night, J. Edgar feared his dream of a powerful national police force might never be realized. Then, on November 8, 1932, he lost the support of his namesake, Herbert Hoover, when a liberal Democrat, Franklin D. Roosevelt, was swept into the Oval Office by a landslide. In the middle of a worldwide Depression, the former New York governor offered hope to the downtrodden and the unemployed, whose ranks comprised 25 percent of the work force.

Whether it was true or not, word quickly reached J. Edgar that FDR had said, "My first official duty will be to remove J. Edgar Hoover as the chief of the Bureau of Investigation."

As J. Edgar told Clyde and his chief aides, "Fortunately, ever since the Wall Street crash of 1929, I knew that Hoover would be swept out of office. We've been looking into the private lives of Mr. Roosevelt and his ugly wife, Eleanor. We have turned up scandals that could destroy his presidency even before it gets off the ground. I understand he's a reasonable man and will listen to me."

"Are you suggesting blackmail, Mr. Hoover?" one of his lawyers asked.

"That is such a dirty word!" J. Edgar said. "Our work here is vital. We must be allowed to carry on with it. If we have to use intimidation, then so be it."

Unknown to the Bureau at large, Clyde and three agents had for months conducted secret investigations into the private lives of the Roosevelts.

"They both have mistresses," Clyde told J. Edgar, revealing the contents of the various reports.

"You mean Franklin has a mistress and Eleanor has a lover on the side."

"That is true, but she also has a mistress," Clyde revealed. "The bitch is a switch hitter."

For entertainment, J. Edgar and Clyde went to gangster movies. Along with much of America, the two G-Men were thrilled as **Edward G. Robinson** *(top photo)* played Little Rico in the fast-paced Mervyn LeRoy production of *Little Caesar* (1930).

Their second-favorite movie was *The Public Enemy* (1931). This story of a Prohibition gangster's rise and fall put Cagney on the map—that and the scene where he smashes a grapefruit into **Mae Clarke**'s face.

CHAPTER THREE

Even before meeting FDR at the White House, J. Edgar had concluded that the president's marriage was not patterned in a traditional "American family values" style, but a working political relationship instead.

From 1920 on, Eleanor in private preferred the company of lesbians, allowing FDR to conduct his own private sexual trysts, or so J. Edgar concluded.

No one will ever know exactly what took place in the Oval Office between FDR and J. Edgar. The Bureau director not only kept his job that day, but by the mid-1930s had nearly all effective restraints on his surveillance powers removed.

"J. Edgar Hoover, in essence, became the head of the American Gestapo," Harry S Truman later said. "Franklin told me personally that Hoover had accumulated massive evidence on not only his private life but on Eleanor's. Hoover continued to spy on Franklin until his death in 1945 and on Eleanor until her death in 1962. They had a lot of skeletons rattling in their closets."

FDR, the suave, martini-drinking American aristocrat, was like no person J. Edgar had met before. Although confined to a wheelchair, he had a commanding presence. J. Edgar had learned that even at Harvard he was known as a ladies' man, and loved to flirt outrageously with pretty women, although he knew he should marry a relatively straight-laced one if he wanted to pursue political power.

Thanks to Clyde, J. Edgar had all his facts straight concerning details of the private life of the Roosevelts, who were on the dawn of becoming "the power couple" of the 20th Century.

In 1905, FDR married his fifth cousin, "the ugly duckling," Eleanor, whose uncle was former U.S. president Theodore Roosevelt. "It's a good thing to keep the name in the family," Theodore said. From the beginning, the marriage was anything but idyllic, although it produced four sons and one daughter, Anna. The boys included Elliott, James, John, and Franklin D. Roosevelt Jr. Franklin Jr. was the second son to carry that name, as the first-named baby had died. Even from the marriage's debut, the handsome and dashing young FDR was a notorious rake.

In 1918, Eleanor discovered a pack of love letters exchanged between her husband and her social secretary, Lucy Mercer (later Rutherfurd). She threatened her young husband with divorce unless he ended his relationship with Lucy. To save both the marriage and his political career, he promised that he would. But he lied.

From that day forth, Eleanor cut off all intimate contact with her husband, who turned elsewhere for his sexual pleasures.

In 1921, Franklin was stricken with polio, which led to the loss of his use of his legs and his confinement for the rest of his life to a wheelchair. Amazingly, that fact remained unknown to most of the American public at the time. Nevertheless as *The New York Times* put it, "In plain English, he could still sustain an erection."

With his libido intact, FDR took a second mistress, Marguerite (Missy) LeHand, the daughter of an alcoholic Irish Catholic gardener. She was described as having "lips parted in that strange secret smile composed of cunning influence, forever baffling."

When Missy came to work for FDR as a secretary, he was smitten. He began an affair with her that would last until her death in 1944 of a cerebral embolism.

For reasons of her own, Eleanor wasn't as upset over her husband's affair with Missy as she had been with Lucy. "After all, the pot can't call the kettle black," said Sir Winston Churchill, the seventh-cousin-once-

Franklin D. Roosevelt *(left photo)* was America's only President elected four times. After being crippled from polio, he told his imperious mother, Sara Delano Roosevelt, "I have not been put out of commission on all fronts, and I'm still a man where it counts."

Throughout his life, he had a number of affairs, but his two alltime favorite mistresses were **Lucy Mercy Rutherfurd** *(center photo)* and **Marguerite LeHand** *(right photo)*, whom he affectionately called "Missy." Privately, reporters referred to her as "the Second Lady of the White House" or "the Second First Lady.:"

removed of FDR.

Eleanor, meanwhile, had been having affairs of her own. In 1928, this prim and proper Victorian woman threw off the shackles of her own strict upbringing and launched two simultaneous affairs—one with a woman, another with a man.

In his official role as governor of New York, FDR assigned a handsome, virile, New York State trooper, Earl Miller, as his wife's bodyguard. A bodybuilder and notorious womanizer, Earl launched an affair with Eleanor. She was 45, Earl was 32. Her many lesbian friends were disturbed by this new liaison, and utterly horrified by the way Miller "manhandled" her in public.

Eleanor and Earl even made what was jokingly referred to years later as a "softcore porn film" entitled *The Kidnapping of the First Lady*. For

Three views of **Eleanor Roosevelt**, arguably the most famous and influential woman of the 20th Century. **Lorena Hickok** (*left photo*) gazes affectionately at her lover, Eleanor, who's wearing a fox stole and beaming at one of Hickok's satirical jokes. "Hick," as Eleanor called her, told her lesbian friends, "I like poker, bootleg bourbon, Cuban cigars, bawdy jokes...and Eleanor Roosevelt."

Eleanor (*center photo*) poses in the most elegant gown and fur she'd ever been seen in. "When my old friend, Bernard Baruch, saw me dressed like this, he proposed that I divorce Franklin and marry him," she said.

In one of her more typical dowdy dresses, **Eleanor** (*right photo*) poses with her handsome lover, New York State Trooper **Earl Miller**, who was known as a ladies' man and famed for his athletic prowess as a horseback rider, champion swimmer, and in the boudoir of the First Lady.

years, the film was believed to have been destroyed, but acclaimed historian, Joseph E. Persico, found clips from it and published them in his book *Franklin and Lucy: President Roosevelt, Mrs. Rutherfurd, and Other Remarkable Women in His Life.* In the home movie, Earl, in a tight-fitting bathing suit, plays a bearded pirate with a bandanna. He abducts Eleanor, and hauls her away with him "for immoral purposes."

After her husband had been in office for two years, Eleanor called J. Edgar and told him she was sending over copies of eight separate death threats she'd received in the mail. "I think you, as head of the FBI, should have your agents evaluate them to see if they are serious."

He agreed to do that, although privately he said, "I wish she were dead."

Before she rang off that day, he suggested seriously that she could carry a loaded pistol with her at all times. "I don't know how to shoot, Mr. Hoover," she protested.

"Then get someone to teach you."

Bravely she made an attempt to become a markswoman. When she vacationed at Chazty Lake, New York, with her State trooper lover Earl Miller, in August of 1934, he tried to teach her how to fire a gun. She never could hit her target and told Miller, "Annie Oakley, I'm not."

In this still shot *(left photo)* from a home movie, at a vacation retreat beside a lake in New York State, **Eleanor Roosevelt**, the First Lady, was "kidnapped," "manhandled," and "bound and gagged" by her lover. Earl Miller, the New York State trooper assigned to her as a bodyguard, disguised himself as a pirate wearing a bathing suit, bandanna, and false beard. He entitled their soft-core porn movie "The Lady and the Pirate." He was filmed carrying her off into the woods for immoral purposes.

(center photo) **Eleanor** posed for this kind and endearing photo, which was the alltime favorite of her female lover, the White House correspondent **Lorena Hickok** *(right photo)*, the First Lady's beloved "Hick." Lovingly inscribed, Eleanor's photo was found on the night stand beside Hickok's death bed.

Nonetheless, he urged her to carry around the pistol to protect herself. She obeyed him, and put the gun, unloaded, in the glove compartment of her car.

An equal opportunity seducer, Eleanor also took up with Lorena Hickok, a notorious, cigar-smoking lesbian, who stood five feet eight inches tall, and weighed more than 200 pounds. A journalist who was assigned to cover the Roosevelts for the Associated Press, Lorena drank a quart of bourbon a day and referred to herself as "one of the boys. I dress like a man, talk like a man, and curse better than any sailor," she said.

Eleanor fell under her spell, launching an affair that would last from 1928 to 1940, when Lorena dumped the First Lady for a female tax court judge.

By the time J. Edgar made his first visit to the White House under the Roosevelt administration, Eleanor had already moved Lorena into the bedroom opposite hers.

Returning that day to his office at the Bureau, J. Edgar found Clyde eagerly waiting for a report on the meeting in the Oval Office. "We've got that crippled whoremonger in the bag for the rest of his administration, which I predict will be a short one," J. Edgar said. "As for the lezzie, we'll keep Old Horse Face silenced as well."

Privately in the months ahead, when any of his agents asked why he never married, J. Edgar said, "One of the reasons is that God made a woman like Hoot Owl."

"Who is Hoot Owl?" an agent might ask.

"Eleanor Roosevelt, the First Lady of the land. But she's hardly what I would call a lady."

In spite of his personal attacks on Eleanor, when the First Lady arrived for a tour of Bureau headquarters, he and Clyde were most gracious in escorting her around. When he met famous people whom he had extensive documentation on, he seemed more charming to them than those he did not. Perhaps in some way, he was more comfortable around those whose private lives he had already thoroughly documented, knowing that they would be of no harm to him because of the blackmail evidence he had accumulated on their private lives.

***

On October 19, 1933, frustrated over the failure of local law enforcement officials, Roosevelt issued a presidential directive putting J. Edgar in charge of the federal aspects of the Lindbergh baby's kidnapping case. Even so, a year went by with no major breaks.

Actually, it was an alert gas station attendant who broke the case on September 15, 1934. A motorist bought five gallons of gas from a station in Upper Manhattan, using a $10 gold certificate. He wrote down the driver's license number. The bill's number turned out to be part of the ransom money, and the license was traced to Bruno Richard Hauptmann, an unemployed carpenter living in the Bronx.

After a trial defined by some as "a mockery," Hauptmann was convicted of the murder of the Lindbergh baby and was electrocuted on April 3, 1936. Privately J. Edgar admitted to his agents that he was "skeptical as to some of the evidence."

In the years to come, he took credit for the FBI's breaking of the case, but the role the Bureau played was only minor. New York law enforcement officials and agents of the Treasury Department played a much larger but unheralded role. Treasury agent Thomas H. Sisk later said, "How typical: we do the work to break the case and Hoover takes the god damn credit, as always."

To further boost J. Edgar's power, FDR in 1933 announced that the Prohibition Bureau, the Bureau of Investigation, and the Bureau of Identification would become part of a new Division of Investigation, with J. Edgar as its director. Prohibition was gradually being phased out.

J. Edgar had frequently expressed utter contempt for the Prohibition Bureau, referring to its agents as "a pack of thieves, the most corrupt branch of the American government in history. They've got a thousand agents working for them—working did I say? They are worthless trash, all of the crooks on the take. They're getting fat and bloated from illegal graft from the hooch

An unemployed carpenter, **Bruno Richard Hauptmann** became the most hated man in America when he was arrested for the kidnapping and murder of Charles A. Lindbergh Jr., the baby of the fabled aviator.

When he was informed of Hauptmann's arrest, J. Edgar, with Clyde, took the next train from Washington to New York. The director attended the police lineup where Hauptmann was identified by a (dubious) witness to the kidnapping as the perpetrator of the crime.

The other men selected for the lineup included a dozen New York detectives.

Leon Turrow, part of the investigative team that choreographed the arrest, later said, "It was no contest. The detectives were strapping six-footers who looked like college football captains. Hauptmann looked like a midget who'd roamed the halls of a Turkish bath for two sleepless days and nights."

business."

J. Edgar did not want to run the Prohibition Bureau as it was phased out. He went to his new boss, Homer S. Cummings, who had been appointed the U.S. Attorney General by FDR. He pleaded with Cummings not to integrate his Bureau "with those Prohibition boys, who are corrupt down to their little toenails." He also claimed that with the repeal of the Eighteenth Amendment, the Prohibition Bureau would recede in size and diminish in importance. Unlike some attorney generals J. Edgar would face in life, Cummings lent him a sympathetic ear. Roosevelt's executive order ended up in the dead letter office.

***

In 1934, a year that generated many headlines, J. Edgar and Clyde embarked on the greatest crime-fighting spree of their careers.

The early 1930s had been an era of gangsters centered around New York and Chicago. Dons wore spats like George Raft in the Marilyn Monroe film *Some Like It Hot*. Submachine guns sold briskly. From illegal activities, money poured into their coffers.

In contrast to the lifestyle of these gangsters, hoboes rode in boxcars from town to town, and the unemployed stood in breadlines across the nation. FDR was offering hope at last to the disenfranchised with his New Deal.

J. Edgar had a new reason to live, the subduing of gangsterism in America. He personally vowed to take on Public Enemies Number One as they fled from state to state. That fact of flight made it difficult for local authorities who could not cross state lines in pursuit of criminals. J. Edgar's boys were relentless in pursuit of their enemies, with John Dillinger topping their wanted lists, followed by Baby Face Nelson and Pretty Boy Floyd.

He instructed Clyde, "Tell our men not to let anything stand in their way. To track down these thugs, we may have to become the most ruthless branch of the government. Do you think that Hitler fanatic over in Berlin would allow gangsters to run his country?"

J. Edgar would later say, "There are those who say I flaunt the law, but the results I have achieved in apprehending the foremost criminals of our day should make me immune from such attacks—probably communist-inspired."

Congress had banned wiretapping in 1934, but J. Edgar ignored the mandate. "Why should the Bureau get rid of one of our most effective weapons in fighting crime?" he asked. "Just because some idiots on the Hill say so? What do they know? I'll fight crime in any way I god damn

One of the most infamous of the Pro-hibition-era criminals was Tennessee-born **George Kelly Barnes,** nicknamed **"Machine Gun Kelly"** because that was his favorite weapon. A psychotic, he was known for armed robbery and kidnapping, demanding ransoms whose size was awesome for that time. Caught without a weapon near Memphis, he shouted, "Don't shoot, G-Men! Don't shoot, G-Men!" The legend of the G-Man was born.

In the lower photo, he's seen, hand-cuffed,the second figure from the left, being escorted by a phalanx of gun-toting G-Men.

At age 59, in 1954, he died in Leaven-worth Federal Penitentiary, Kansas.

please without interference from these jerks."

In 1933 and 1934, J. Edgar's agents rounded up some of the most leg-endary gangsters in America, and the term "G-Men" (Government Men) be-came a household word. All of these ar-rests were high profile cases that virtually put the newly named Federal Bureau of Investigation (FBI) on the map in 1935. And although J. Edgar was basking in glory, he didn't like to share the publicity with his agents. He and he alone wanted all the acclaim.

The first legendary gangster J. Edgar's agents nabbed was George Kelly Barnes, nicknamed "Machine Gun Kelly" because his favorite weapon was a Thompson submachine gun. One of the most notorious criminals during Prohibition days, he committed his most infamous crime in July of 1933, the kid-napping of oil tycoon Charles Urschel. He and his gang were paid a $200,000 ransom, the highest ever in the history of the United States. Kelly's gang was pursued across six states, and he even sent J. Edgar letters taunting him as a "sissy."

Somehow, Machine Gun Kelly obtained the phone number of J. Edgar's mother and made threatening calls to her.

In 1928 he had teamed up with the equally corrupt Katherine Thorne, who wore a hideous red wig to cover up bald spots on her head. Machine Gun Kelly and Katherine, evocative of Bon-nie Parker and Clyde Barrow, robbed small banks.

After Urschel's kidnapping,

agents traced his hideout to a modest home in Memphis. They raided the house on September 26, 1933. Caught without a weapon, Machine Gun yelled, "Don't shoot, G-Men, don't shoot, G-Men." He not only surrendered to agents of the Bureau, but created a new term for them. For years to come, G-Men or government men became synonymous with FBI agents.

Katherine was also arrested in the raid, which led to J. Edgar adopting a bizarre theory that "the most vicious criminal, even more so than a man, is a female with red hair. If she doesn't have red hair, she will wear a red wig."

In October of 1933, Machine Gun and Katherine were convicted and sentenced to life imprisonment. And although Machine Gun died in prison in 1954, she was released in 1958 from a prison in Cincinnati.

This was the first major case solved by J. Edgar and his G-Men, and it was the first crime in which the defendants were transported by airplane. Machine Gun has entered popular culture, and has been idolized in song and film. Charles Bronson starred in the 1958 film *Machine Gun Kelly* and countless songs have immortalized the gangster, including a 1984 single "Machine Gun Kelly," released by the punk band Angelic Upstarts. Along with Pretty Boy Floyd and Baby Face Nelson, Machine Gun Kelly is one of the main characters in the comic book series "Pretty, Baby, Machine."

Three views of **Melvin Purvis** (on the left, walking with **J. Edgar** himself); on the phone *(center)*, and posing *(right photo)* as a dapper and somewhat campy dresser.

During the heady era of spats and speakeasies, pint-sized "Little Mel" became the most famous G-Man of his day, taking out John Dillinger and Pretty Boy Floyd. By the end of 1934, he was the most famous symbol of the law in America. But his triumphs sowed the seeds of his eventual downfall.

***

If Clyde had a rival for J. Edgar's affection, it was Melvin Horace Purvis Jr., the son of a tobacco farmer from South Carolina, who had joined the Bureau of Investigation in 1927. He had headed division headquarters in such cities as Birmingham and Cincinnati.

Melvin stood five feet, nine inches and weighed only 140 pounds. The newspapers began to call him "Little Mel." Although he was a crack shot, he did not look forward to gun battles. This courtly Southern gentleman with impeccable manners had been trained as a lawyer, and was addicted to the ballet, theater, and opera.

In 1932, J. Edgar appointed Melvin head of the Chicago office of the Bureau. That city became Ground Zero in the Bureau's war on crime. Chicago was the headline-making assignment of the decade.

Clyde destroyed much of J. Edgar's personal mail upon his death. But an amazing 500 letters exchanged between Melvin and J. Edgar between 1927 and 1936 have survived.

J. Edgar affectionately addressed him as "Dear Mel," with Melvin responding "Dear Jayee." J. Edgar noted how women were very attracted to the handsome Southern gentleman. In one conversation, J. Edgar jokingly told him, "You're just a short guy but you must carry a heavy gun. I suspect Little Mel actually should be named Big Mel."

"You've got that right, Chief."

As time went on, J. Edgar's letters to Melvin became more intimate. "I just saw *It Happened One Night*," he wrote. "All the gals are crazy about this new sensation, Clark Gable. The Bureau has its own Clark Gable, and he's a slender, blond-haired, brown-eyed gentleman named Melvin Purvis." Letters such as this have come to be viewed as J. Edgar's homosexual wooing of Melvin, who, so far as it is known, was heterosexual.

One Hoover historian claimed that the letters clearly reveal that J. Edgar was sexually attracted to Melvin. In letter after letter, J. Edgar pays homage to Melvin's looks. In the words of his son, Alston Purvis, "Hoover saw in my father the style and charm he lacked himself, and perceived a romantic, idealized extension of himself."

Melvin's secretary, Doris Rogers, claimed, "It is not surprising that someone would have a crush on my boss. Many of us had crushes on Mel."

Occasionally J. Edgar would send the object of his affection expensive gifts. He never paid for these. The gifts actually came from loot which agents had uncovered during raids on gangster hideouts. One morning when Melvin told J. Edgar he had a sore throat, the chief ordered an agent to deliver a Bel Air Smoke Consumer to his home to aid in his recovery.

48

There is ample evidence that J. Edgar wanted to carry this relationship much farther than Melvin was willing to go. Clyde, of course, became aware of the excessive attention J. Edgar was paying to Melvin, and he came to resent the agent. There were screaming feuds inspired by jealousy at J. Edgar's home, but never at the office, where Clyde always treated his boss with the greatest of respect.

During a twenty-month span from 1933 to 1934, J. Edgar and Melvin joined forces to round up public enemies. Today, their names are entered as one of history's greatest crime-fighting teams.

In 1934 Melvin captured more public enemies than any other agent in FBI history, a record that still stands. He led the manhunts that tracked down such outlaws as Baby Face Nelson and Pretty Boy Floyd. But the shooting death of John Dillinger was the one that garnered the most head-lines. Unfortunately Melvin didn't seem to realize at first that all these high-profile slayings, and all the subsequent publicity for him, would incur the jealous wrath of J. Edgar.

***

In the Depression-soaked 1930s, criminals robbed almost at will. For thirteen violent months, John Dillinger and his gang swept through the Middle West robbing banks such as the Central National Bank in Green-castle, Indiana, for $74,000; the Securities National Bank in Sioux Falls, South Dakota for $49,500; or the First National Bank in Mason City, Iowa, for $52,000.

These daring robberies thrilled a despondent country, who read of Dillinger's exploits. He even developed a fan base, some of the most ardent followers of his exploits viewing him as a modern-day American Robin Hood, since he stole only from banks, which were confiscating homes and farms throughout the country when owners could no longer pay their mort-gages.

J. Edgar called Dillinger "a beer-drinking plug ugly." He knew that capturing or killing Dillinger would be the greatest case in FBI history. No criminal since Jesse James had received more newsprint than Dillinger. The manhunt for the thirty-one year-old bandit was on. J. Edgar beefed up propaganda for his Bureau, claiming "the underworld has more armed men than the combined army and navy."

Even though an order of "shoot to kill" was issued, Dillinger continued to evade capture. Such was the case on March 31, 1934, when two of J. Edgar's men had him trapped in St. Paul, Minnesota. He managed to escape through a rear door, but suffered a gun wound in the leg. Trapped again, this time at a resort, Little Bohemia, in northern Wisconsin, Dillinger managed to escape once more. Baby Face Nelson, also staying at the lodge, fled in another direction.

In his eagerness, J. Edgar had summoned a press conference to announce, "There will be no escaping this time. Luck has run out on this modern-day Houdini."

Officials in Washington called for the dismissal of both J. Edgar and Melvin. J. Edgar, who had wanted to be hailed as a hero in the press, was openly ridiculed. Clyde found him in a state of permanent agitation. Capturing Dillinger had become an obsession with the director.

After Dillinger escaped in Wisconsin, J. Edgar's letters to Melvin took on a different tone. They became cold and formal. "Little Mel" had become "Dear Mr. Purvis."

Earlier in his career of crime, Dillinger had been jailed twice but had managed to escape both times. He bragged, "There is no prison that can hold John Dillinger."

With his lopsided grin and a murderous gleam in his eye, a wisecracking Indiana farmboy, **John Dillinger,** became the most notorious of the Depression era gangsters. Feeling betrayed by their government, much of poverty-stricken America made him an underdog and ultimately the alltime American anti-hero. "Great desperadoes from little urchins grow," crowed *Time* magazine.

In newsreels at movie houses across the country, Dillinger drew more applause than either FDR or the aviator, Charles A. Lindbergh.

Such a defiant remark infuriated J. Edgar. He told Melvin, "That may be true. But perhaps Dillinger will never see another prison cell, because we'll gun the dirty dog down in the street, firing bullet after bullet into him so we'll know the bastard is dead. I want your guys to get that son of a bitch at any cost. Take any risk, but try not to mow down a crowd of people while you're doing it. The public doesn't like that."

On Saturday, July 21, 1934, the Bureau's luck changed. Ana Sage, a Romanian *émigré* and the madam of a whorehouse in East Chicago, placed a call to Melvin. She told him that she was facing deportation but promised him if he'd help her, she would tell him "how you can bring down Dillinger." At first he dismissed her, as he was getting a lot of crank calls. But eventually, he believed her story.

Sage said that she and Polly Hamilton, Dillinger's prostitute girlfriend, would be visiting Chicago's Biograph Theater to see a film, *Manhattan Melodrama*, starring Clark Gable, Myrna Loy, and William Powell. Melvin immediately called J. Edgar to tell him the news. "If he escapes this time, they will call for our heads," J. Edgar warned Melvin.

"Don't worry, Chief," Melvin said. "Dillinger's luck has run out. If he draws a gun or tries to escape, we'll shoot him down."

Hamilton was a twenty-six-year-old divorcée and prostitute, and a waitress at Chicago's S&S Café on Wilson Avenue. She would be the last of Dillinger's women.

The film let out at 10:30pm. J. Edgar had issued orders not to tangle with Dillinger in the crowded auditorium.

As arranged in advance, Sage agreed to wear an orange dress, which in the neon lights of the theater looked red. Later the press would dub her "The Woman in the Red Dress." Along with the exiting crowd, Dillinger came out of the theater, with Sage and Hamilton following close behind.

Melvin took in the very recognizable figure even though his "straw boater" hat was pulled low over his eyes. He noted he wore no jacket on this hot night in which he might conceal a pistol, but had on gunmetal gray trousers and a white and stiffly starched Kenilworth shirt.

"He looked into my eyes," Melvin claimed, "but obviously didn't recognize my face, which had appeared in a lot of newspapers. If he detected something more than casual interest from me, he didn't seem aware of it."

Melvin later recalled, "I was so nervous I sounded like a girl soprano when I said, 'Stick 'em up, Johnny! We have you surrounded.'"

Dillinger ran ahead, trying to retrieve his .38 automatic pistol from the pocket of his trousers. It was too late.

Agent Charlie B. Winstead fired four bullets into Dillinger, the fourth and the fatal one, blasting through the back of his neck and fracturing his second cervical vertebra before crashing through his spinal

A waitress/prostitute, **Polly Hamilton** was John Dillinger's last girlfriend. "On the afternoon of his death, he had relations with me four times—I'll never find a man like that ever again," she reportedly said during her interviews with the Bureau.

Two agents interviewed Hamilton after she saw Dillinger shot down, but her information was sketchy and later evaluated as false. Nonetheless, she was released and promptly disappeared forever, presumably into the wilds of the Dakota Badlands.

cord and plowing into the right side of his brain, then exiting through the lower lid of his right eye.

Melvin said, "He spun like a top before toppling over dead on the sidewalk."

Running up from behind, Melvin bent over the body to hear any final words. "But he was already dead," he said.

Word spread across Chicago. Literally thousands of rubber-neckers rushed to the scene, many taking their white handkerchiefs and dipping them in Dillinger's blood as a souvenir.

His body was taken to the dank Cook County Morgue, where it was stripped naked before it was covered with a white sheet. Hundreds of rubber-neckers gathered outside wanting to get in to view the body. In a surprise decision, Melvin allowed them to come in, providing they filed by the corpse in an orderly fashion and didn't linger too long.

One daring woman ripped the sheet from Dillinger's body, exposing his nudity. She gaped at the size of his mammoth penis. In front of some 200 spectators lined up, she shouted, "Some woman has lost a good friend." In this ghoulish atmosphere, the other men and women laughed, as a policeman hastily covered the body again.

That woman's act of exposing Dillinger that night formed part of the gangster's legend. He soon was called "the most heavily endowed man in America."

For his own amusement, J. Edgar ordered Melvin to have a Bureau photographer take a nude of Dillinger as he lay on that slab in the Cook County morgue. Voyeuristically, he wanted to see if all those rumors of the gangster's massive appendage were true. When a photograph arrived in Washington, J. Edgar studied it intently. "The rumor is true . . . even more so. The man was a bull."

When Johnny Depp starred in *Public Enemies* in 2000, a gossip columnist wrote, "Only 'Donkey Dong' himself could play Dillinger—talk about typecasting."

To J. Edgar's jealous fury, Melvin, his former *protégé*, was given all the glory in the press. Newspaper reporters wrote that he was a genuine American hero having killed "the most notorious criminal in American history," although some critics felt that honor should go to the outlaw, Jesse James.

J. Edgar virtually had to ride on Melvin's coattails in trying to get press coverage for the Bureau itself and for him specifically, even though the killing came from an anonymous tip and not from any Bureau sleuthing.

Even Adolf Hitler, in the Berlin-based newspaper of the Nazi party, *Völkische Beobachter,* voiced his opinion: "The Chicago chief of police shot him like a mad dog in a public street, filling him full of holes, as a sieve, without regard to bystanders. Does a land where such things happen still deserve to be called a country where law rules? Without court procedure, without a single question, the man was shot into the Great Beyond."

From the New York islands to the Pacific Ocean, "Little Mel Purvis" reached hero status as "the G-Man who got Dillinger."

For years after, J. Edgar tried to take responsibility for Dillinger's assassination, creating a Dillinger Museum in FBI headquarters in Washington that displayed his death mask, the straw hat he was wearing, even the La Corona-Belvedere cigar he'd carried in his shirt pocket.

When a reporter for *The New Yorker* viewed Dillinger's death mask, he said that his mustache evoked that of the German Kaiser in WWI.

Two years before J. Edgar died in Washington, he virtually had a stroke when he read a copy of *The Dillinger Dossier*, published by author Jay Robert Nash in 1970. In the book, the writer claimed that Dillinger was not killed that summer night in Chicago.

The claim was that Dillinger was tipped off that he was going to be gunned down and picked a fall guy to go to the Biograph in his place. Striking flaws were cited in the autopsy evidence. The FBI never produced any counter-evidence to refute Nash's charges.

***

"If you'll gather 'round me, children, a story I will tell 'bout Pretty Boy Floyd, an Outlaw. Oklahoma knew him well."
—Folk singer **Woody Guthrie**

After Dillinger's death and the massive publicity, the next on J. Edgar's hit

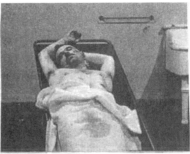

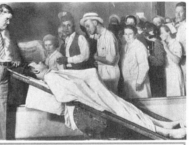

The nude body of John Dillinger was placed on public display at the Cook County Morgue after doctors performed an autopsy.

Gawkers came in to stare up close at his face, and one woman ripped the sheet off his body to expose his mammoth penis.

It was not erect, but the lower of the two photos above made history. Rigor mortis had set in and when the public saw this picture. The position of Dillinger's hands seemed to simulate an erection. The urban legend spread that he had died with a fully erect foot-long penis.

About one hundred inquiries come into the Smithsonian Institution annually, inquiring if the preserved penis of John Dillinger can be viewed.

list was Charles Arthur Floyd. The public called him "Pretty Boy Floyd," a name the bank robber hated, preferring to be known as "Choc" instead. The nickname came from a payroll master who stared into Floyd's face during a robbery, later describing him to the police as "a mere boy—a pretty boy with apple cheeks."

This American bank robber rose from a callus-fingered cotton-picking Georgia boy to a trigger-fingered desperado who terrorized much of the Middle West.

He was famously associated with Oklahoma where he grew up. A song, "The Ballad of Pretty Boy Floyd," claimed, "He took to the trees and rivers to lead a life of shame. Every crime in Oklahoma was added to his name."

His criminal record began when he was eighteen years old and was arrested for stealing $3.50 in coins from a local post office. By the time he'd turned twenty-one, he was arrested again for a payroll robbery in September of 1925 in St. Louis. For this, he served five years in prison.

Out of prison he vowed he'd

WANTED posters of **John Dillinger** were displayed in post offices and federal buildings throughout the United States. Wanting to claim the award in an America racked by the Great Depression, hundreds of people placed calls to the FBI, stating that they had seen the notorious gangster. He was spotted having dinner in New York's Chinatown; going to a movie starring Kay Francis in Hollywood, shopping for three pairs of white Hanes briefs, size 34, at a Chicago department store. All of these leads turned up nothing.

After Dillinger's death, the movie theater, **Biograph**, became a tourist attraction. There was always a hassle about patrons who wanted to sit in the same seat where Dillinger saw a Clark Gable movie.

In the lowest row of photos, a head shot of the real Dillinger (*left*) and the reel John Dillinger (*right*, as played by actor **Johnny Depp**), keep fanning the fires of the outlaw's legend.

never be jailed again, as he began a series of robberies. After several minor arrests, he was sentenced in November of 1930 to fifteen years in the Ohio State Penitentiary for a bank robbery in Sylvania, Ohio, but he escaped.

Floyd robbed banks that were foreclosing on hundreds of farms, homes, and small businesses. In addition to lots of cash, he also took mortgage records, thereby turning himself into a sort of populist salvation hero to farmers losing their lands.

The FBI under J. Edgar became involved on June 17, 1933 in the notorious gunfight known as the "Kansas City Massacre," resulting in the deaths of four law officers.

Four Bureau of Investigation agents, together with an Oklahoma police chief and two local detectives, were escorting the escaped convict, Frank ("Jelly") Nash, to Leavenworth when machine gun-wielding bandits ambushed them. They killed Nash, which may have been the intent of the raid. Special Agent Raymond J. Caffrey, along with three local police officers, were also gunned down.

In a decision that was interpreted even at the time as rather odd, in the wake of the attack on Nash, J. Edgar ordered Melvin to go on an all-out pursuit of Floyd. Many eyewitnesses vehemently denied Floyd's involvement in this crime.

J. Edgar was given ample evidence to suggest that Floyd was not involved in the massacre, but he publicly continued to maintain that he was. He was hoping to leverage the publicity value of Floyd's capture as a means of getting more funding for the FBI.

Pretty Boy Floyd, pictured above with his FBI fingerprints, wasn't really pretty, but the nickname stuck. He felt the label made him sound like a homosexual. "As a thousand women from Oklahoma to Chicago can testify, I ain't no god damn faggot."

Actually, his face was moony and flat, resembling the baseball great, a young Babe Ruth, with whom he was often mistaken. He did have a "touch of the lavender," as one reporter wrote, because he also doused himself with lilac water. "You could smell him coming around the corner," one of his gangster cronies claimed.

"Hoover wanted to enhance his own position and beef up his Bureau, and how better to do that than netting another notorious criminal, Pretty Boy Floyd himself," wrote a reporter in Kansas City.

Finally, Congress reacted by removing legal barriers that had hindered his ability to chase criminals across state lines. The passage of the Fugitive Felon Act made an escape across state lines to avoid prosecution a federal crime. J. Edgar was jubilant, claiming, "Now we have the power to go anywhere and shoot any-body. I want my G-Men to shoot any rattler in the grass."

FBI agents were authorized to carry firearms with full arrest powers. "My dream has come true," J. Edgar told Clyde and others. "We now have an empowered national police force."

Basking in his power, J. Edgar drew up a Public Enemies List, which his critics called a "Morgue List in the Making." With Dillinger dead, the elusive Pretty Boy Floyd now topped the list.

In early October of 1934, J. Edgar assured the American people that Floyd would be dead "before Santa heads down from the North Pole with his reindeer." That night he placed a call to Melvin. "Don't make a god damn liar out of me," he barked at his agent, whom he increasingly re-sented, all affection in their relationship seemingly gone.

The press continued to lionize Melvin, who began to pay more and more attention to his dress, changing his white shirt three times a day so that he would look fresh in the photos frequently taken of him.

In a *Literary Digest* poll taken in 1934, he came in eighth on a list of the ten most important people in the world. In Washington, J. Edgar did not conceal his anger when reading the poll. "Who does this midget think he is?"

At this point, Floyd began to believe the many press reports about Melvin being an agent who always got his suspect, usually shooting them down. He decided to flee from Ohio to Mexico to avoid death.

In a midnight blue Ford sedan, he set out at night with three compan-ions—his sidekick, Adam Richetti, along with two women who happened to be sisters, Rose and Juanita Baird.

The date was October 18, 1934. Floyd's plan was to drive back to the Cookson Hills in eastern Oklahoma where he grew up. There he wanted to pick up his family before heading south of the border.

On Interstate 7, deep in the valley of the Ohio River, Floyd as the driver encountered a pea-soup fog. Even so, he told his passengers that he planned to press on in spite of the dangerous curves in the road. Thirty minutes later he lost control of his car and crashed into a telephone pole.

Fearing he'd be recognized, Floyd ordered Juanita to walk into town. Miles back, they'd passed an all-night mechanic's shop. Rose was ordered to wait in the car while Floyd and Richetti took his machine gun and two blankets, heading for a wooded hill to wait it out.

An hour later, the car with the two women was towed away, and Floyd and Richetti decided to wait off Route 7 until their return. Foolishly, they were visible from the highway. Motorist Joe Fryman found it suspicious that two men would be sitting on a hill wearing a suit and tie but with no vehicle in sight. He wondered what they were doing there and how did they get there from town. It seemed too far to walk.

In town himself, he reported his suspicions to Police Chief John H. Fultz of Wellsville, Ohio. "There's something going on here," Fultz said, rounding up some law officers to take with him. Delivering a familiar line, he said, "These men sound like they are armed and dangerous."

Although Richetti was captured, Floyd fled into the dense woods. After all, he had evaded the police so many times he was known as "the Phantom of the Ozarks."

As depicted in many films, Floyd managed to elude the local sheriff. When J. Edgar found this out, he was furious, calling Melvin in Cincinnati, where he removed him from a case, ordering him to Wellsville at once to take charge.

Immediately Melvin rounded up some twenty-four of J. Edgar's agents in the area, drawing them from such diverse cities as Pittsburgh and Cleveland. All bridges in the targeted area were closed, and roadblocks were set up on all exits.

In pouring rain, armed agents with flashlights and dogs combed the dense Spencer Woods into which Floyd had vanished.

After surviving in the woods on berries for almost four days, Floyd spotted a farmhouse in the distance on October 22, 1934. He arrived at the back door, which was answered by Ellen Conkle. He told her he'd gotten lost in the forest and offered to give her a dollar if she'd fix him a dinner. Although suspicious, she agreed.

Adam Richetti, Pretty Boy Floyd's partner in crime, was also one of the primary suspects in the June 17, 1933 gunfight that infamously became known as the "Kansas City Massacre," resulting in the deaths of four law officers.

Some of the evidence against Richetti derived from a fingerprint that was said to have been recovered from a beer bottle. Both Floyd and Richetti, although admitting to other crimes, maintained that they were innocent of any involvement in that massacre, and the testimony that identified Floyd and Richetti as the killers was disputed by others, who maintained their innocence.

A recent book on the massacre attributes some of the slayings to "friendly fire" by a lawman unfamiliar with his weapon.

While eating, he noticed a Model A standing near a ramshackle corncrib. She told him it belonged to her brother, Stewart Dyke, who would soon be returning from the fields. Floyd asked her if for ten dollars Dyke would drive him to the nearest bus station.

When Dyke arrived, he too was suspicious of Floyd. Fearing that he might be dangerous, he wanted to drive him away from the women in the house. As he started his car, he noticed two cars entering his driveway, blocking his only exit. Each car contained four men, one of whom was Melvin Purvis.

Feeling entrapped, Floyd leaped from the Model A and, with his .45 automatic gripped in his hand, ran once again toward the dense woods.

The sharpshooter of the law enforcement officers, Chester Smith, fired a single bullet from his rifle, hitting Floyd in the right arm. Knocked to the ground, he rose again and started running.

Melvin shouted for him to halt, but Floyd only ran faster. Melvin ordered the G-Men to open fire. Ellen Conkle later said, "The sound was like thunder from heaven."

Nearly one hundred shots were fired, a second bullet penetrating Floyd's back, shattering a rib before entering his stomach. Yet a third bullet plowed through his body to ravage his right kidney. Blood was flowing from his severed arteries.

He fell to the ground but was still alive when Melvin came to stand over him. Both men recognized each other, Melvin from the WANTED posters of Floyd, Floyd from all the newspaper photographs of Melvin. After all they were two of the most famous men in America.

"Are you Pretty Boy Floyd?" Melvin asked.

He winced at the Pretty Boy nickname. In a raspy voice, he said, "I am Charles Arthur Floyd." Then blood gushed from his mouth.

Melvin delivered the body to the Sturgis Funeral Home in East Liverpool, Ohio. Once there, Melvin put through a call to J. Edgar in Washington, telling him that "Public Enemy Number One is dead."

Meanwhile, an autopsy was performed. The coroners took scissors and cut off small swatches of Floyd's blue suit to hand out as keepsakes.

Floyd's nude body lay on a marble slab. A coroner covered his genitals with a sheet and opened the doors of the funeral home. It was estimated that day that some 10,000 spectators filed through, one of the staff moving them along at fifty gapers per minute. It took more than three hours for all of them to view the body. One woman said, "He sure don't look like no Pretty Boy to me."

Back in Washington, J. Edgar gleefully handled calls from the press coming in from coast to coast. Somehow J. Edgar managed to get a call through to Melvin, telling him to leave Ohio to "lay low" for a few days. He also told him to silence his agents and disperse them. He did not want Melvin to talk to reporters. He'd made a mistake when he did that after the

Dillinger shooting.

He wanted to take all the credit for himself. Melvin later recalled, "I think he wanted me to become the invisible man." When reporters wanted to interview Melvin himself, J. Edgar told them that he was ill and needed rest.

In spite of J. Edgar's muzzle on Melvin, reporters still claimed he was "the slayer of Pretty Boy, gunning him down like a dog," in the words of one journalist. "MELVIN PURVIS: PANIC FOR GANGSTERS" screamed one headline.

In Salisaw, Oklahoma, Floyd's body arrived in a cheap pine-box coffin. More than 20,000 people attended his funeral, the largest ever held in the state. To most of these Depression-riddled souls, Pretty Boy Floyd was their hero because of his role in fighting the banks that threatened them daily with foreclosures.

Melvin, once again a national hero, spent a lonely October 24, 1934 in his apartment on the North Side of Chicago. Perhaps remembering the day when their relationship was close, J. Edgar sent him a telegram: HAPPY BIRTH-DAY. Melvin was thirty-one years old, and somehow felt his career as a crime fighter might be coming to an end.

In spite of J. Edgar's black-out on Melvin, headlines once again declared: MELVIN PURVIS TRIUMPHS AGAIN.

Pretty Boy Floyd became a legend after his death, depicted in books, film, and song. In *The Grapes of Wrath*, a novel by John Steinbeck, Ma Joad refers to Floyd several times, claiming he was a young man driven to a tragic fate by the Great Depression. Larry McMurty and Diana Ossana wrote a fictionalized account of his life called *Pretty Boy Floyd*. Some of the handsomest actors in Hollywood have played Floyd on the

Rose Baird *(left)* poses with her sister, **Juanita Baird** (aka Beulah Baird) for an FBI cameraman. Unlike Bonnie Parker, another famous fugitive of their era, the sisters were not accused of any active involvement in the robbing of any bank.

The long-suffering Baird sisters were the girlfriends of Richetti and Pretty Boy Floyd back in the 1930s, when they were colorfully known as "gun molls." They were in the getaway car that Floyd crashed in Ohio. While the sisters coaxed the damaged car along an Ohio highway to a mechanic, both Floyd and Richetti escaped into the forest.

The sisters never saw their gangster lovers again, and faded into the history books of 20th century crimes.

screen—John Ericson in *Pretty Boy Floyd* (1960); Robert Conrad in *Young Dillinger* (1965); Fabian in *A Bullet for Pretty Boy* (1970); Martin Sheen in *The Story of Pretty Boy Floyd* (1974), and Channing Tatum in *Public Enemies* (2009).

***

Baby Face Nelson, the runty bank robber whose *modus operandi* was to shoot anyone in his way in and out of the banks he attacked, was next on J. Edgar's list. The Bureau's director also followed the exploits of Bonnie Parker and Clyde Barrow, calling them "those mad dogs from Dallas

Ellen Conkle is pictured inside the kitchen of the modest farmhouse where Pretty Boy Floyd had his last meal. He arrived out of the woods and offered her "a fast buck" if she'd cook some supper for a hungry man. She whipped him up some pork chops, collards, mashed potatoes, and biscuits—and got her dollar.

After he was slain nearby, she charged fifty cents to stray tourists who came and wanted to see the table where the gangster ate his supper. She never washed the dishes until the tourists stopped coming. She later sold the dishes for a hundred dollars.

Born in Chicago's near West Side, the son of Belgian immigrants, Lester Joseph Gillis used a pseudonym for most of his life, George Nelson. When he became a bank robber, the public came to know him as "Baby Face" Nelson, because of his youthful appearance and small stature.

As a teenager, Nelson had moved in and out of the state reformatory. By 1928, he was running bootleg liquor to speakeasies in the Chicago suburbs where he fell in with a Capone-like mob, "The Touhy Gang," who specialized in armed robberies.

On April 21, 1930, his first bank robbery netted him $4,000. He continued a spree of bank robberies and house break-ins, often making off with $25,000 worth of gemstones from robberies of private homes.

By the winter of 1931, his luck ran out. He was arrested and sentenced to one year to life in the state penitentiary at Joliet, Illinois. By then Baby Face Nelson had become tabloid fodder. He escaped from prison in February of 1932 and once again turned to robbing banks.

After a botched robbery in 1933, Nelson decided to form his own gang. During robberies, Nelson wildly sprayed machine gun

60

The body of the recently slain **Pretty Boy Floyd** was propped up in the back of Melvin Purvis's car and taken to the **Sturgis Funeral Home** *(top photo)* in East Liverpool, Ohio.

He was stripped of his clothing and laid out on a slab, where he was fingerprinted. His blue suit was cut into small swatches, later to be sold to souvenir hunters for $5 a piece.

Sightseers were allowed to come into the funeral parlor to view the body *(center photo)*. At 8:30 that night, some 10,000 people *(bottom photo)* had gathered.

The next morning, the local newspaper defined it as, "The greatest show on earth. But in Floyd's condition, he didn't look very pretty."

bullets to make his getaway, not caring whom he killed. His wife, Helen Gillis, and young son, Ronald, often were in the back seat of his getaway car.

In the spring of 1934 Nelson had forged a quasi-partnership with Dillinger.

After a shoot-out between Nelson and Dillinger vs. FBI agents at the Little Bohemia Lodge in Wisconsin, both gangsters escaped. There were calls for J. Edgar's resignation, and a widely circulated petition demanded that Melvin be suspended.

Nelson and Dillinger, along with other gang members, robbed the Merchants National Bank in South Bend, Indiana, carrying off sacks of bills whose value amounted to $28,000. Police and bystanders died that day, but the gang escaped. This was the last robbery for Dillinger and Nelson.

J. Edgar intensified the FBI dragnet. When Dillinger was ambushed at the Biograph Theater in Chicago on July 22, 1934, Nelson knew he'd be next. By August of that year, Nelson had emerged as the sole survivor of the "Second Dillinger Gang."

In the annals of the FBI, Nelson became known for killing more of its agents in the line of duty than any other American criminal. John Dillinger and Pretty Boy Floyd became folk heroes. Not so Nelson—in fact, he was the very antithesis of popular.

No one considered him one of the "Robin Hood gangsters" of the Depression era. Nelson, "the cold-blooded killer with the hot temper" killed both law officers and any innocent bystanders nearby. Surprisingly, he was a devoted family man who often ran from the law with his wife and kids following him.

After fleeing to California, Nelson made the worst decision of his life. He returned

East with his wife, Helen and son.

The FBI had staked out Lake Como in Geneva, Wisconsin, thinking Nelson would return for the winter. He did. But once again Nelson made a daring escape heading for the town of Barrington, Wisconsin. Here on November 27, 1934, he was shot to death along with FBI agents Ed Hollis and Samuel P. Cowley.

Nelson was shot a total of seventeen times. Seven submachine gun slugs had lodged in his body and ten shotgun pellets had ripped into his leg. He told Helen, "I'm done in." She fled with him to a "safe house" in Wilmette, Illinois, where he died in bed that night.

On a tip, FBI agents tracked down Nelson's corpse, finding it in a ditch, wrapped in a blanket, in front of St. Peter's Catholic Cemetery in Skokie, Illinois. As his wife later explained to police, "I put the blanket around his body because he always hated the cold."

Learning that Helen was free, J. Edgar issued her "death order." The young widow became "the first female Public Enemy." Arrested in Chicago on Thanksgiving Day, she served a year in prison for harboring her late husband. She told police that Nelson uttered his final words at 7:35pm. "It's getting dark, Helen. I can't see anymore."

***

This mug shots from 1931 show **Baby Face Nelson** (aka Lester Gillis) who had been born on Chicago's Near West Side in 1908. For a period of his reckless life, he was a partner of John Dillinger.

"Nelson liked killing for killing's sake," claimed Melvin Purvis. "He was diabolical in appearance. He grinned when he killed. Because of his brutality, his sadistic delight in the sheer joy of killing, he stands in a class by himself."

Either directly or indirectly, Melvin Purvis had played a key role in ridding society of its Public Enemies Number One. "It's time we cut our big hero down to size," a jealous J. Edgar told Clyde and other agents. "In my opinion, the FBI has room for only one star. Anything else confuses the public."

Actually, J. Edgar feared that FDR might replace him with Melvin as Bureau director. Many newspaper editorials suggested that the President do just that.

Doris Lockerman, secretary to Melvin, claimed, "Hoover had the green eye of jealousy. His letters to Melvin, and I read every one of them, were cold and distant. At one point they became like some harsh schoolmaster disciplining an unruly pupil."

"It's true that Melvin was drinking a bit after hunting down all those mad dog criminals, but that was because of the abuse he

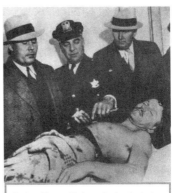

Baby Face Nelson's body is inspected by a police officer and two FBI agents. J. Edgar wanted a full report with photos that included full frontal nudes. An autopsy showed that Nelson died from seven bullet wounds inflicted by G-Men. The most damage was caused to his abdomen, through which a .45 caliber bullet had blasted.

was getting from Hoover," she said. "The most outrageous charge was that Melvin got so drunk at a party in Chicago that he pulled out his penis and urinated on the sofa of the hostess. That was a damn lie. There was another story that he went wild in a department store, pulled out his gun and shot at the chandelier."

"These unadulterated lies were so ridiculous I didn't think any sane person would believe them," she said. "Unfortunately, some very stupid people in the Bureau believed all the rumors spread about Melvin, which were told by those, especially Hoover, who wanted to destroy him because he'd done such a good job and taken the national spotlight off Hoover himself. He couldn't stand someone else getting credit for anything. Fortunately, Clyde Tolson knew how to hide in the background."

J. Edgar had a real dilemma. Melvin was too high profile as an agent, a national hero, in fact, and could not just be dismissed. There had to be another way.

J. Edgar dispatched agents to Chicago to investigate how Melvin was running the Bureau there. Without J. Edgar actually saying so, the agents knew they should file negative reports.

One somewhat petty charge made in one of the reports claimed that Chicago agents, especially those involved in long stakeouts, habitually left their dirty underwear in the men's room whenever they changed into a fresh pair of undies. More destructive was an accusation that Melvin had amateurishly dragged his feet on the resolution of 232 FBI cases and that consequently, all of them had been bogged down "with undue delay."

After reading all the criticism, including how agents and staff were "invariably late for work," J. Edgar ordered that Melvin be stripped of authority over big cases. He ended up being assigned to a job interviewing prospective men who wanted to join the local Bureau.

Finally, Melvin could take it no more. On July 10, 1935, he sent J. Edgar a telegram, resigning his post. J. Edgar immediately accepted the resignation but didn't let it go at that. He continued to pursue Melvin as if chasing down Dillinger.

Before filing Melvin's letter of resignation, J. Edgar altered it, claiming "termination with prejudice." He ordered that Melvin be put under the sort of surveillance reserved for public enemies. For the next twenty-five years, J. Edgar received detailed dossiers on the activities of his former friend. Before J. Edgar's death, these reports were destroyed.

Clyde himself was in charge of assembling the reports. J. Edgar especially liked damaging evidence, and agents curried favor with him. It is believed that G-Men inserted made up stories about Melvin when they found that was what J. Edgar wanted to read.

On a visit to New York, Melvin was said to have received a blow-job in a men's room in a theater in the Times Square area during the screening of a Humphrey Bogart movie. On another occasion, in San Francisco, he was accused of visiting a bordello where he engaged in sex with two prostitutes over a six-hour period. Whether these reports were true or not is not known, but many were thought to be fabricated. Of course, before sending them in to J. Edgar, Clyde deliberately wanted to make the reports as damaging as possible.

"Trashing my father could even advance an agent's fortunes," said Alston Purvis in his memoirs, *The Vendetta: Special Agent Melvin Purvis, John Dillinger, and Hoover's FBI in the Age of Gangsters.*

Newspapers routinely prepare obituaries of famous people long before their deaths. In November, 1935, the Associated Press sent J. Edgar their obituary of Purvis, asking the FBI to check to see if the facts were correct. At first J. Edgar ignored it until the U.S. attorney general pointedly asked him to respond.

J. Edgar claimed that he did not feel that any one individual should be singled out to be "dramatized as the man responsible for the death or capture of a notorious desperado." His reasoning, false though it was, asserted that individualized publicity would make it impossible to use an agent in future cases because his identity would henceforth be known.

He overlooked the fact that Melvin, thanks to his involvement in the Dillinger slaying, was already a household word when he went after Pretty Boy Floyd.

There was nothing that J. Edgar could do to prevent Melvin from writing the story of his own incredible rise to fame. So in 1936, after his resignation from the Bureau, Melvin "the ace G-Man," published his memoirs, entitled *American Agent*. After its publication, J. Edgar claimed that the book was filled with nothing but "lies, distortions and exaggerations." On another occasion, he contradicted himself, saying, "I never read pulp trash."

Actually what really infuriated J. Edgar was that there was no mention of him in *American Agent*, which became a bestseller.

In *The New York Times Book Review*, a critic claimed, "Melvin Purvis makes sensational statements because he is dealing with sensational facts." After publication of the memoirs, Melvin became a celebrated figure, perhaps not knowing that agents from the Bureau were clocking his every move.

A café society party was held in his honor at the 21 Club in Manhattan, which had been a former speakeasy. Here he was introduced to his favorite movie star, Joan Crawford, dining with her new husband, Franchot Tone.

An agent later reported to J. Edgar that when Tone had to fly back to Hollywood to make a film, Crawford stayed in New York an extra week. According to the report, Melvin visited her suite on three different nights and didn't leave on any of the occasions until the following morning.

Melvin needed money, and even though he found it humiliating he accepted contracts to endorse products. "Getting the drop on Public Nuisance No. 1—unsightly beard bristles," was his promo for Gillette Safety Razors. For Dodge cars, the advertisements proclaimed "Famous G-Man Corners Dodge Economy."

Melvin achieved his greatest commercial success when he signed to promote a breakfast cereal, Post Toasties. As part of the publicity campaign for the breakfast cereal, he hosted a radio show called "Junior G-Men," which became tremendously popular with America's wannabe law enforcement agents. Melvin Purvis Junior G-Man Clubs were formed in every state. At its peak, 260,000 children were enrolled. "J. Edgar fumed, fussed, and fizzled," said secretary Betty Bufffton. J. Edgar tried to prevent the club from handing out Junior G-Man badges, but a judge rejected his request.

Later, as the media ball got rolling, and with Post Toasties as its sponsor, the Melvin Purvis G-Man Board game became wildly successful, selling for $1.50. Even though he resented it, J. Edgar also became popular with young kids because he was the head of the FBI. "Without really meaning to, Melvin increased the popularity of that old toad," said an executive at Young and Rubicam, which handled the Post Toasties account.

Melvin's fame also grew in Hollywood. After the success of James Cagney's 1935 film, *G-Men*, studios clamored for more crime stories, especially those dealing with the inner workings of the somewhat mysterious FBI. Melvin seemed a natural as a source for scriptwriters hoping for "the real low-down on the FBI." That prospect aroused anxiety in J. Edgar, who feared that Melvin would use the Hollywood media as a platform to attack him personally, as well as the Bureau in general.

In Hollywood, Darryl F. Zanuck offered Melvin a position as "crime consultant" on movie production at 20th Century Fox. But after Zanuck received a phone call from J. Edgar, the offer was withdrawn. He told Zanuck that if Fox or any other movie studio needed technical advisers, the FBI would supply them for free. In job after job which Purvis was offered, including a 1938 offer to become supervisor of police affairs at the Santa Anita (California) racetrack, J. Edgar sabotaged his chances.

In Hollywood, Melvin was a celebrity at the studios. In the 1930s, gangster pictures were all the rage, particularly those made at Warner Brothers starring George Raft, Edward G. Robinson, Humphrey Bogart, and James Cagney.

Joan Crawford called Melvin Purvis "the man of the hour" and came on strong to him. Dazzled by her stardom, he gave in to her sexual desires.

However, she later switched sides, becoming an informant for the FBI and a confidential friend of Melvin's nemesis, J. Edgar Hoover.

Producer Samuel Goldwyn negotiated with Melvin to become an adviser on the 1937 movie, *Dead End*, the picture that introduced the Dead End Kids. Melvin met one of his favorite actors, Humphrey Bogart, who had the third lead in the film.

During his time in Hollywood, Bogie introduced Melvin to Jean Harlow, the reigning blonde film goddess of her day. She gave Louella Parsons a quote she couldn't print. "Mel has twice as much as Clark Gable." Although Melvin's affair with Harlow quickly fizzled out, he was deeply saddened to learn of her early death on June 7, 1937.

One morning in Washington, J. Edgar turned to his favorite column, one written by Louella Parsons which ran in the *Washington Herald*. He devoured movie gossip. But on that particular morning, he exploded like

Mount Vesuvius. The gossip maven reported that Paramount Pictures was set to film a movie called *Federal Dick*. Melvin would be played by Cary Grant, with George Raft, a real-life gangster, cast as J. Edgar himself.

Angered and filled "with absolute horror and disgust," J. Edgar called his top agent in Los Angeles, J.E.P. Dunn, and demanded an investigation. It is not known what pressure the FBI put on the studio, but *Federal Dick* never went before the cameras.

Through Clyde, J. Edgar turned down all requests from reporters wanting to interview Melvin for feature stories. Melvin was enjoying his Hollywood celebrity and was as fascinated with movie stars as they were by him.

He started dating Janice Jarrett, the most famous advertising model in America during the era that she embodied the Lucky Strike Girl. J. Edgar was so furious when he learned about the Jarrett/Purvis affair that he quit smoking Lucky Strikes.

He became obsessed with Melvin's sexual affair. Newspaper headlines thrilled readers with news of their romance: LUCKY STRIKE FOR PURVIS and MELVIN PURVIS CAPTURED BY CUPID. In March, it was announced they would marry on April 20, 1937, and invitations were mailed out to 3,000 dignitaries, including such stars as Clark Gable, Fredric March, Joan Crawford, and even Louis B. Mayer and Samuel Goldwyn. It was hailed in the press as the celebrity wedding of the year.

When Jarrett had to travel to San Francisco for a photo shoot, Melvin remained in Los Angeles, perhaps not knowing that he was being trailed by FBI agents. J. Edgar wanted to set up an entrapment for him, and ordered an FBI photographer to get a blackmail photo of Melvin in bed with a woman.

Momentarily, Melvin may have been madly in love with Jarrett, but he was not immune to other beautiful stars, some of whom were blatantly making themselves available to this American folk hero. Bogart introduced Melvin to his co-star, Joan Blondell, who was immediately attracted to him.

The upcoming weekend found them checking into a hotel together on the beach at Malibu. Shortly after midnight, two agents and a photographer, using an FBI master key, slipped into their bedroom where a picture was snapped of a naked Melvin and Joan in bed together. A copy of this picture of Joan with Jarrett's groom-to-be was anonymously mailed to the model. In the emotional aftermath, she cancelled her widely announced and publicized wedding.

In Washington, FBI agents learned of this entrapment which was never made public. When Clyde and J. Edgar were out for lunch, one agent said, "Hoover is just pissed off because Purvis is not marrying him. Our director always wanted to get into that little guy's pants."

Eventually, Melvin married Marie Rosanne Willcox, with whom he had three sons. He drifted from job to job as the years went by. For a while he set up a law practice in San Francisco. Later he bought a radio station, WOLH, in Florence, South Carolina. During World War II, he served in the U.S. Army as a colonel.

At war's end, the army dispatched him to seek out Nazis such as Martin Bormann, evocative of the way he'd gone after Dillinger. During the famous Nürnberg trials, Melvin interviewed Hitler's war criminals.

J. Edgar tried to erase the memory of Melvin from any dramatizations of the Bureau. When *The FBI Story*, as authorized by him, was filmed in 1956, no character named Melvin Purvis appeared in the movie. When Melvin applied for a Senate job, J. Edgar sent senators an official memo, with "some disturbing facts about one Mr. Melvin Purvis." J. Edgar's accusations against his former agent were never made public.

In 1959, Melvin was suffering from chronic back pain. He became addicted to morphine which eased his agony. He spent sleepless nights wandering around his home in Florence, and was deeply troubled by the past and by J. Edgar in particular. In November, he contracted a case of the Asian flu which lingered and lingered. He was in a very weakened condition. Often, very late at night, his family heard him cursing J. Edgar. "That god damn son of a bitch. He ruined my life."

On February 29, 1960, Melvin committed suicide, or so it is believed. He shot himself using a pistol given to him by his fellow agents when he resigned from the FBI in 1935. It was rumored to have been the weapon used to take down Dillinger.

It may not have been a suicide after all, and the coroner agreed. Melvin may have shot himself accidentally trying to extract a tracer bullet jammed in the pistol. If that were the case, it is ironic that he may have died from the same weapon that had been used to kill Dillinger.

Melvin was only 56 years old.

J. Edgar did not send a letter of condolence to the widow. Nor did he send an official delegation from the FBI, although many agents, some of them retired, showed up anyway.

After the bleak funeral on a rainy day, Marie Willcox Purvis sat down and sent a Western Union telegram to J. Edgar. "We are honored that you ignored Melvin's death. Your jealousy hurt him very much but until the end I think he loved you."

CHAPTER FOUR

"Two deadly snakes—a rattler and a cobra—were crawling around some garbage one night and came across each other. Instead of striking each other with their deadly venom, they bonded to spew their poison upon the world." Or so said Eleanor Roosevelt's lesbian girlfriend, Lorena ("Hick") Hickok, a correspondent for Associated Press.

When Walter Winchell and J. Edgar met in the 1920s, the influential newspaper columnist and the director of the Bureau of Investigation must have sized each other up. J. Edgar could supply Winchell with secrets for his column, and in return, the newspaperman could build up J. Edgar's reputation as a powerful law enforcement figure.

J. Edgar was willing to overlook the fact that Winchell was "a New York Jew," and these two men became best friends, known as "the odd couple."

Winchell was no great devotee of homosexuals, calling them "lavender lads," but he tolerated J. Edgar's obsession with Clyde Tolson, who was always included on any nighttime outing. The columnist asked no questions about the nature of their relationship and was given none.

Born in New York, Winchell had always wanted to be a journalist and finally made it in the summer of 1929, when he joined the *New York Daily Mirror*, working himself up to become a syndicated columnist. His work would, in time, appear in some 2,000 newspapers worldwide and be read by some 50 million people who virtually had to learn a new language of "Winchellisms." Examples included use of the word "handcuffed" for marriage, and "pashing it" for falling in love.

Instead of J. Edgar and Clyde, Winchell in the 1920s preferred to hang out with gangsters, especially Owney Madden, the No. 1 gang leader in New York during the Prohibition era. When he felt his life in danger because "I knew too much," Winchell fled to Los Angeles.

After several months, he returned to his native New York "a changed man" in his words. Almost overnight, or so it seemed, he'd become a cheerleader for Uncle Sam, law and order, mom, and apple pie.

The most faithful patrons of the Stork Club, columnist **Walter Winchell** *(top photo)* appears in the bottom photo *(left)* with **J. Edgar**. Clyde Tolson was seated on J. Edgar's left, but was conveniently left out of the photograph.

Even though J. Edgar professed to be Winchell's "great and good friend," he secretly spied on him, ordering the compilation of an FBI dossier that eventually grew to 3,908 pages.

He later told Clyde and other FBI agents, "Walter Winchell is the most crooked journalist in America."

J. Edgar had gotten to know him when he reported on the Lindbergh kidnapping case. His stories received national exposure. Their friendship grew.

Clyde and J. Edgar were invited to join Winchell in his nightly rounds of the Stork Club in Manhattan, whenever they were up from Washington. This was America's most famous night spot and the last dying gasp of the lost world of café society.

Born in the Roaring Twenties, "the Stork" was run by Sherman Billingsley, an ex-bootlegger from Oklahoma. As he moved into the 1930s, he created a glittering, glamorous world labeled by one reporter as "a haven for guns, diamonds, champagne, and caviar where starlets, high-class whores, and lavender boys with talented butts chased perverted millionaires with dubious reputations." In the midst of the Depression, it was not unknown for the headwaiter to be given a $20,000 tip.

Winchell was the scribe-in-residence, mingling with movie stars, aristocrats, generals, political bosses, and stage actresses. Patrons included Tallulah Bankhead, Ernest Hemingway, Cole Porter, Milton Berle, Bob Hope, Robert Benchley, Bing Crosby, Humphrey Bogart, Charlie Chaplin, Louise Brooks, Gary Cooper, Joan Crawford, Bette Davis, Jack ("Legs") Diamond, Dwight D. Eisenhower, F. Scott Fitzgerald, Clark Gable, Cary Grant (with Randolph Scott), and Myrna Loy. Gangster Dutch Schultz was seen drinking one night with the aviator hero Charles A. Lindbergh. Another aviator, Howard Hughes, showed up one night with two "dates"—Errol Flynn and Tyrone Power.

In the words of Winchell, the Stork Club was "the New Yorkiest spot in New York." He always held court at the choice table, No. 50. Whenever they were in town, Clyde and

J. Edgar were usually seated beside him.

On those nights, Billingsley instructed Yetta Golove, a robust Russian Jewish immigrant in charge of tables, "Hold those seats for J. Edgar and Mrs. Hoover."

"I didn't know he was married," Golove said.

"Don't be an idiot," he said. "I mean Clyde Tolson."

Winchell's lawyer, Ernest Cuneo, claimed that Table 50 in the Stork Club's Cub Room was the virtual center of gravity in Manhattan. "To Walter's table came the most important men in the world—newspaper and book publishers, bankers, Hollywood magnates, celebrities of all kinds, an international Who's Who." He added under his breath, "Even J. Edgar Hoover and his boy friend."

Cuneo reflected nostalgically on an age gone by, recalling "beautiful women, beautifully clothed—terrific form, terrific grace, and terrific style. It was like the *Belle Époque* in France, like a Dufy painting of Longchamps on Grand Prix Day."

J. Edgar liked the Stork Club so much he invited Clyde there on a date to celebrate New Year's Eve in 1936. Of course, Billingsley wanted to work a beautiful girl into the photo. He asked the fashion model, Luisa Stuart, to pose for a gag photo, wielding a toy gun. The picture was widely published in newspapers, suggesting that Stuart, not Clyde, might have been J. Edgar's "date" that night.

"I was not his date," she later recalled. "It was all staged for the benefit of a photographer. As the evening wore on, I caught J. Edgar holding hands with Clyde."

More than any other person in America, Winchell sold the heroic image of the G-Man to the public, with J. Edgar configured as the nation's valiant crime fighter. To return the favor, J. Edgar provided Winchell with some of the biggest scoops of his career. The FBI director always denied that. "I never play favors with the press," he lied.

***

With John Dillinger, Baby Face Nelson, and Pretty Boy Floyd wiped out, there remained Alvin Karpis, the last "Public Enemy Number One" at large.

Born to Lithuanian immigrants in Montreal, Karpis was nicknamed "Creepy" because of his sinister smile. He grew up with gamblers, bootleggers, and pimps, and turned to a life of crime that included bank robberies and kidnapping. He became particularly sought after when he hooked up with the notorious Barker gang.

J. Edgar wanted his G-Men to make another high-profile arrest, hoping to get the bureau's annual operating budget increased. He'd also applied for an increase in salary from $9,000 to $10,000 a year. At a budget hearing, J. Edgar was called before a congressional committee.

In April, 1936, at a U.S. Senate hearing, Kenneth D. McKellar of Tennessee lambasted J. Edgar for his performance at the FBI. "You're called America's greatest lawman, but you personally have never arrested anyone. Is that true?"

Turning red in the face, J. Edgar could barely suppress his anger. He felt he'd been publicly humiliated by the senator, but was forced to admit that his words were true.

"So, you're telling me that you and your so-called Babe Ruth physique have sat on your butt in some office during your entire career as head of the Bureau?" Enraged, J. Edgar only nodded.

Congressman Marion Zioncheck made the hearing even worse by accusing J. Edgar of being "a dictator, a master of fiction, a product of self-generated public relations to create a macho image completely divorced from reality. You're supposed to hunt down the nation's most dangerous criminals, but I read in a feature story you take only mincing steps. Maybe your little feet are too dainty to catch these gangsters."

U. S. PENITENTIARY
ALCATRAZ
325

J. Edgar could hardly speak. Finally, he said, "My record of rounding up Public Enemies Number One is well known."

Outside the building, an infuriated J. Edgar told Clyde that he was going to launch an immediate investigation of both McKellar and Zioncheck. "How dare those cocksuckers blacken my masculine image. We'll get the dirt on them even if we have to create the mud to sling."

Alvin ("Creepy") Karpis is seen in handcuffs preceded by **J. Edgar** *(lower left figure in upper photo)* at the time of his capture in New Orleans. The lower photo replicates Carpis' mug shot at Alcatraz.

Today, his claim to fame might be as the prison inmate who taught a fellow prisoner, the psycho Charles Manson, how to play the guitar.

After suffering through public ridicule at the hearing, rumors of his homosexuality spread through official Washington. A furious J. Edgar vowed to the press, "I will capture Creepy Karpis single-handedly."

During Karpis' incarceration at the Kansas State Penitentiary in Lansing, Kansas, he'd met Fred Barker, a notorious member of "The Bloody Barkers."

Fred invited him to join their gang after both of them were released from prison in 1931. Karpis headed to Oklahoma where he hooked up with "the most dangerous mad-dog criminals of the Depression era." The Barkers never hesitated to kill anyone who stood in their way, including innocent bystanders, as they robbed banks or hijacked mail deliveries.

At some point, Karpis convinced the Barkers that they could earn more money through kidnapping than in robbing banks. Their first kidnapping was a millionaire Minnesota brewer, William Hamm, which netted them $100,000.

When Karpis and the Barkers abducted a Minnesota banker, Edward Bremer, Jr., the ransom was $200,000, a vast fortune in those days. Bremer, as it turned out, was a friend of FDR, who threw the weight of the White House behind rounding up the Barker gang.

In Oklahoma, Karpis met the notorious "Ma" Barker who had given birth to four boys, Herman, Arthur, Lloyd, and Fred, each of whom had evolved from juvenile delinquents into dangerous criminals. Ma's real name was most unusual—"Arizona Donnie" Clark.

As legend had it, Ma Barker was the

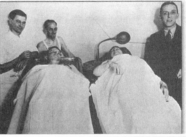

J. Edgar defined **"Ma" Barker** *(top photo)* as "a she-wolf, a veritable beast of prey." But movies and books have grossly exaggerated her role as the leader of her notorious killer sons. She wasn't the criminal mastermind that she was said to be. According to one of her associates, "Ma Barker couldn't even plan breakfast." On some occasions, while her boys were out killing and looting, she'd go to the butcher shop to buy them sirloins for grilling that night.

After she and her son, **Fred Barker,** were mowed down at their hideout on Lake Weir in Florida, J. Edgar ordered that their bodies be put on public display *(bottom photo)*.

Fred, her most faithful son, had always told her, "We'll die together, Ma."

brains behind the robberies. But Karpis soon discovered that this rather ignorant woman "couldn't even plan breakfast." He took over the plotting of their future bank robberies. The story that Ma Barker was the mastermind of the Karpis-Barker gang was pure fiction. Karpis charged that J. Edgar had created that myth to justify the killing of an old lady when agents gunned down "Ma" on January 16, 1935. After an intense, hour-long gun battle, both Ma and her son, Fred, were killed within the premises of a modest house in Ocklawaha, Florida. J. Edgar falsely reported that the FBI had found a tommy gun in Ma's dying hands, and ordered that their bodies be put on public display.

The J. Edgar myth, not the truth, has entered popular culture. In the 1966 *Batman* series, one of the villains is Ma Barker, played by Shelley Winters. Her story was also adapted in the low-budget film *Bloody Mama* (1970), and "Ma Barker and Her Boy" was an episode of *The Untouchables* with Eliot Ness leading the assault on the Barker hideout, which was a total fabrication. The opera, *Ma Barker*, by John Eaton in 1955, is still presented at concerts.

With the gang narrowing down, another rumor was spread that Karpis had threatened to kill J. Edgar in revenge for the shooting of Ma Barker. But, as it turned out, J. Edgar himself was the source of this wild rumor.

Late one night, when J. Edgar was in bed with Clyde, he received the phone call he'd wanted for a very long time. His FBI agents had traced Karpis, who was wanted on charges of kidnapping and murder, to an apartment house in a residential section of New Orleans.

Unusual for the time, J. Edgar chartered a 14-seater airplane. With Clyde at his side, he flew to Louisiana with a dozen other FBI men. "We're going to take Karpis this time, dead or alive," he said.

In New Orleans, J. Edgar, Clyde, and other FBI agents surrounded the apartment building where Karpis was hiding with another gang member, Fred Hunter. The FBI had to wait only one hour before Karpis and Hunter emerged from the building heading for their car. Both men got into the vehicle before agents surrounded them.

Karpis and Hunter were arrested on May 1, 1936. The arrest was routine and fairly uneventful, although it became fodder for a legend in the making.

Clyde later claimed "We ripped the joint apart with machine gun fire." However, not one bullet was fired. J. Edgar wrote a letter praising Clyde's assistance in nabbing Karpis, although Clyde had been posted as a look-out.

Only when J. Edgar was assured that the prisoners were being held at gunpoint did he emerge from around the corner. When J. Edgar found it safe to approach the car, he informed Karpis that he was under arrest. He ordered his agents to handcuff Karpis and Hunter, but discovered they had not brought the handcuffs with them. The two criminals were tied up with neckties worn by the agents.

In the official FBI version, J. Edgar and agent E. J. Connelley, the head of the special squad division, approached the car. J. Edgar, or so he claimed, lunged at Karpis through an open window and grabbed him by the collar, as Connelley moved in on Hunter who was, according to the official version, seated on the driver's side.

In J. Edgar's words, "The man upon who was bestowed the title of Public Enemy Number One folded up like the yellow rat he is. He was stammering, stuttering, shaking as if he had palsy."

J. Edgar received massive publicity in the wake of the arrest of Karpis. His favorite headline was HOOVER ORDERS STICK 'EM UP! His version of that night was pure fantasy, as he claimed he personally approached the car, putting Karpis and Hunter under arrest at gunpoint before Karpis could reach for his rifle in the backseat.

Karpis later claimed that it was not J. Edgar but agent Clarence Hurt who ran up to the side of his car and put a .351 automatic rifle to his temple. Hurt was one of the special agents who'd shot Dillinger.

After he was subdued, Karpis claimed he heard Hurt yell, "It's all clear, Chief. I saw two well-dressed men emerging from behind the apartment building wearing suits and blue shirts. One was slight and blond, the other was heavy-set with dark complexion. I recognized him at once. It was J. Edgar Hoover." Unknown to Karpis at the time, the other well-dressed man was Clyde Tolson.

In his memoirs, Karpis claimed, "The story of Hoover the hero is false. He didn't lead the attack on me. He hid until I was safely covered by many guns. He waited until he was told the coast was clear. Then he came out to reap the glory. That May day in 1936, I made Hoover's reputation as a fearless lawman. It's a reputation he doesn't deserve. I made the son-of-a-bitch."

J. Edgar's story about the rifle in the back seat was discounted. "I drove a 1936 Plymouth coupe," Karpis said. "There was no fucking back seat."

With the arrest of Karpis, the era of "Depression" criminals was coming to an end. Only Harry Brunette, another bank robber and outlaw, remained at large. He, too, was declared a Public Enemy by the FBI.

One by one, these high-profile criminals were taken down to become the stuff of legend. Wiped out were such gangsters as Jack ("Legs") Diamond whom J. Edgar, knowingly or otherwise, had sat next to at the Stork Club. Vincent ("Maddog") Coll bit the dust, as did Dutch Schultz. As for Al Capone, he was in Alcatraz slowly going insane from syphilis.

Karpis, too, ended up at Alcatraz in 1962. As the notorious prison was being shut down, he was transferred to McNeil Island Penitentiary in Washington State. There, he met a young Charles Manson and taught him how to play the guitar.

In his autobiography Karpis noted that "Little Charlie" was lazy and shiftless, the son of a prostitute who "is meek and mild for a convict." He told Karpis that he was a musician and would one day be "bigger than The Beatles."

Released from prison, Karpis fled to Spain where he died on August 26, 1979. Since sleeping pills were found by his body, it was ruled a suicide, although no autopsy was performed.

J. Edgar was one year from death himself when Karpis published his memoirs in 1971 "exposing what a coward" the FBI director was around guns.

It was the last book the FBI chief ever read. "I should have ordered him shot on sight that night in New Orleans, so he'd never live to write this pack of lies," J. Edgar said.

***

After all the publicity surrounding the arrest of Alvin Karpis, J. Edgar and Clyde were ready for another "showcase" arrest. The American bank robber and Depression-era outlaw, Harry Brunette, became their next target. After all, he'd been defined as Public Enemy Number One, the subject of WANTED posters displayed in post offices around the country.

A twenty-five year old former librarian, Harry Brunette, along with his partner in crime, Merle Vandenbush, had robbed a series of banks in the New York City area. Their biggest crime during 1936 involved the kidnapping of William A. Turnbull, a New Jersey state trooper.

The police in New York, cooperating with law enforcement officials in New Jersey, traced Brunette to an apartment on West 102nd Street in Manhattan, a residence they put under surveillance.

Out of professional courtesy, the NYPD contacted the Bureau and notified them of their stakeout, claiming that on the afternoon of December 14, 1936, they planned to raid the apartment and capture Brunette dead or alive.

Working behind the scenes, J. Edgar decided that he wanted to bring some glory to Clyde, his second in command at the Bureau, and allow him to personally arrest Brunette.

"Let's jump the gun," J. Edgar told Clyde and his agents, fully intending the double meaning. Then he concocted a plan to raid the Brunette apartment fourteen hours ahead of the schedule meticulously established by the NYPD. The city's detectives were shocked at the noisy and highly visible arrival, unannounced, of a phalanx of agents from the Bureau.

Armed with a machine gun, Clyde shot the lock off the door to Brunette's apartment. Awakened from sleep, Brunette shot back. Two agents in back of Clyde lobbed tear gas shells into the apartment, setting it ablaze.

Brunette's wife surrendered immediately but he fled down the hall and into a storage closet where Clyde and two agents discovered him. From the closet, he fired at them until he ran out of ammunition.

The New York City Fire Department, with alarms sounding, arrived on the scene. An overzealous G-Man held them back. As a reporter from *Newsweek* described the incident, amid the hubbub, a flustered G-Man poked a submachine gun at a husky fireman. "Dammit, can't you read?" growled the fireman, pointing at his helmet. "If you don't take the gun out of my stomach, I'll bash your head in."

The fire was subdued and Brunette surrendered. This time J. Edgar saved the glory for Clyde, who was photographed leading Brunette to a squad car.

His partner, Vandenbush, arrived on the scene and saw Brunette's apartment under siege. When he was captured two months later, the fugitive claimed, "I stood close enough to Hoover to tap the fart on his shoulder."

After capturing **Harry Brunette** *(right)*, **Clyde Tolson** *(left)* became known, sometimes sarcastically, around FBI headquarters as "Killer Tolson."

Armed with a Thompson machine gun, Tolson and FBI agents shot their way into the apartment of the librarian-turned-bank robber.

J. Edgar milked this arrest for all the publicity he could get. A letter he wrote his lover was made public: "You were subjected during the course of this raid to great physical danger, and you measured up to the high standard expected of all men of the Federal Bureau of Investigation. Your courage and fearlessness upon this occasion are to be highly commended."

A much-publicized triumph for Clyde, during an episode that both betrayed and enraged the NYPD, the Brunette capture represented the only incidence during his long career at the FBI where he was personally and directly associated with the use of a weapon.

77

The G-Men captured the first headlines, but Police Commissioner Lewis J. Valentine shot back in the days that followed, accusing J. Edgar of "trying to steal the glory."

He issued an FBI press release, claiming that who captured Brunette wasn't the issue. "The issue is that we have this crook in Federal custody."

Much to J. Edgar's amusement, Clyde became known as "Killer Tolson."

***

One day while lunching at the Mayflower, Clyde clutched his lower stomach, complaining of a sharp, jabbing pain. J. Edgar went into a panic and ordered a nearby agent to rush him to the hospital in the Bureau's limousine, as "I don't trust ambulances."

On the way there, J. Edgar, in the rear of the limousine, offered what comfort he could, holding Clyde's hand and assuring him it was going to be all right. Clyde began to sweat profusely, and J. Edgar mopped his brow.

At the hospital, doctors informed J. Edgar that Clyde had a ruptured appendix which would require immediate surgery. Assuming the role of Clyde's legal spouse, J. Edgar gave his permission, Clyde was hauled into the operating room for a successful surgery.

When he regained consciousness, J. Edgar was at his side in his private room, holding his hand. "It's going to be okay."

For an entire week, Clyde remained in the hospital recuperating, with J. Edgar sitting by his bed. Except for routine office work, the Bureau of Investigation came to a grinding halt. All major decisions were delayed until the Chief returned to duty.

Clyde recovered rapidly and was released from the hospital. J. Edgar decided they needed a four-day post-operative vacation in New York. To his staff, he announced that they were going on a tour of the Bureau's offices in Manhattan.

In New York, they were graciously welcomed at the St. Moritz Hotel on Central Park South and given the presidential suite with a large double bed. The manager assured them the suite was complimentary. There would be no charges, even for food and drink.

Every night during their stay in New York, they were invited to the Stork Club as special guests of the columnist Walter Winchell.

Privately one night, perhaps after both J. Edgar and Winchell had had too much to drink, the columnist told his friend, "A lot of people are talking in this town. I think it's time you meet and are seen with some very glamorous women. You need some arm candy, and these stars I know are always hot for publicity. I think a deal can be worked out to give you two confirmed bachelors some much-needed exposure with the distaff side."

Winchell kept his word. To Table 50 he invited some of the headline-making, beautiful women of his day. They were often seated or photographed next to J. Edgar with Clyde sitting at the far end of the table out of camera range. No one seemed particularly interested in him, even though he was a handsome, masculine man. Perhaps the word was already out that Clyde was J. Edgar's personal property—"so hands off."

Winchell introduced Clyde and J. Edgar to the reigning model of her day, the beautiful Anita Colby, daughter of the cartoonist Bud Counihan, a legendary figure among New York artists. Making fifty dollars an hour, she was the highest paid model in New York, her lovely face and svelte figure plastered on billboards and in newspaper advertisements across the country. She was especially popular hawking cigarettes. At the time she met J. Edgar, she was planning a move to Hollywood, because "I want to be a movie star."

"You have the looks for it," J. Edgar told her.

She remembered that Clyde didn't say much to her, but "he couldn't take his eyes off me. I definitely had the feeling he was sexually attracted to me, although Sherman Billingsley had told me I was to flirt with Hoover."

Instead of building himself up as America's No. 1 G-Man, J. Edgar bragged on Clyde. J. Edgar claimed that it was Clyde, not Melvin Purvis, who had gunned down Dillinger. "I asked Clyde to tell me all about it," Anita said. "He went into a long, elaborate story about how he'd killed Dillinger, but decided to let Purvis take the credit. Later on I found out that was a complete lie. Clyde, or so I was told, wasn't even in

Called "The Face," **Anita Colby** became the most sought-after female model in America. For publicity purposes, she hung out with J. Edgar and Clyde at the Stork Club in Manhattan. She always maintained that she felt Clyde would have lived the life of a straight man had he not gone to work for J. Edgar.

"He probably would have married some woman and settled down. But what's a guy going to do when the most powerful law enforcement officer in America orders you to strip off your clothes and come to bed?"

the same town the night Dillinger was shot."

"Winchell had told me that my two new buddies were homosexuals," she said. "That they had no interest in women whatsoever. I think that was true of Hoover. He could laugh and talk around women, but I'm sure that was as far as it went. As for Clyde, I was not so sure. Throughout our night together, I felt he was definitely interested in me. When Hoover excused himself to go to the gents' room to powder his nose, Clyde put the moves on me. He asked if he could come by my apartment the following evening, his last night in town, and perhaps take me out for dinner and dancing. I was intrigued by this silent, Gary Cooper type. I agreed and invited him for drinks at 6:30."

"He arrived exactly on the dot," she said. "Not at 6:31 or 6:29 but at 6:30pm. I was still putting on my makeup. I found him very shy around women. At one point I asked him if he were dating anyone in Washington. He said his work occupied all his time day and night. What he really meant to say, but didn't, was that Hoover occupied all his time morning, noon, and night."

"At one point he began to loosen up a bit and talk to me, but then suddenly there was an urgent ringing of my doorbell. I opened it and was shocked to see Hoover there. Without being invited, he barged into the apartment. Clyde seemed very upset to encounter his boss."

"Hoover took over the evening," she claimed. "He said he had a limousine waiting downstairs to take us to dinner at 21. In other words, he was just inserting himself into the evening."

"I decided to make it a three-way date," she said. "It was good for my image to be seen with two of the most powerful men in America. Actually we had a great evening. When I loosened up the boys with a drink or two, I found them amusing. They certainly had the dirt on every name that was mentioned. They even told stories on their friend Winchell. They said one night in a bordello in Los Angeles, he visited a house run by a madam. The girl Winchell selected for the night rejected him because his dick was too short."

"I thought whores had to take on all customers," she said to them.

"Not always," J. Edgar said. "We've made a study of this. In a cheap cathouse, anything goes. But some of the more high-class call gals are picky about who they'll screw. From what I hear, the whores in the bordellos always want Errol Flynn to come back again and again, but one night with W.C. Fields is one night too many. I'm sure Mae West will agree."

"Did you know Miss West likes big black dick, preferably attached to a boxer?" Clyde interjected.

"No, I didn't," she said. "But I do now. I'll spread the news."

"That night at my door, Clyde gave me a kiss on one cheek, J. Edgar on the other, and that was as far as our relationship went. I gave them my phone number in Hollywood, and each of them said he'd call."

Anita was billed throughout the country as "The Face." "It made me wonder about the rest of my body."

In spite of the awkward beginning of their relationship, Anita became friends with both G-Men. "They were really voyeurs," she said. "I was dating both Clark Gable and Jimmy Stewart. They wanted to know details, all the details, even anatomical ones, about both of these stars. I told them that Jimmy was the real stud in bed and that Clark, to my disappointment, was rather underendowed. They seemed to find that fascinating."

"They were particularly intrigued when I told them that one night, in Palm Springs, Clark took me to a cocktail party. There were nothing but homosexuals there. I was surprised. Clark seemed too macho for that!"

"It could be all pretense," J. Edgar said, "although we have a long list of women he's bedded at MGM. Clyde and I will look into this. He had some homosexual liaisons in his past, especially when he was a young, struggling actor. We know for a fact that he spent entire nights at the homes of William Haines, Ramon Novarro, and George Cukor. Howard Hughes took him away for a weekend in San Francisco where they shared a suite with a double bed."

"I became their Louella Parsons in Hollywood," Anita said. "Sometimes I called them two or three times a week with little tidbits of gossip. I was invited to a party at the home of Barbara Hutton when she was married to Cary Grant. Clark Gable took me. At some point in the evening, Barbara told me that Clark had once asked her to marry him. 'I should have accepted his proposal,' she said. 'I love Cary dearly, but he's a homosexual.'"

"We know that," J. Edgar said. "He and Randolph Scott were more than roommates. Once Grant was arrested in the men's room of a department store in downtown Los Angeles. Money exchanged hands. It was hushed up. He also had to pay off a mother who threatened to sue him for picking up her teenage boy and propositioning him."

On another night, Anita said that she'd been taken by actor Bruce Cabot to a party at the home of Errol Flynn. "There were about thirty people there. The most amazing thing happened. Errol went around greeting and talking to his guests, but he had unzipped his trousers and was displaying his penis. Later he masturbated himself until he was erect. Then he played a little tune on his piano, using his penis, not his fingers."

J. Edgar told Anita that, "We're getting a lot of disturbing reports on Flynn, and we'll definitely have to add your tidbit to his dossier."

Before he put down the phone, Clyde wanted to know if Errol was circumcised. She told him he wasn't.

"What about Clark?" J. Edgar asked.

"Definitely not, but in his case he should have been," she said. "His foreskin extends far too long."

"When I decided that Hollywood wasn't for me—or, more accurately—I wasn't for Hollywood, I returned to New York to resume my modeling career. Through Winchell I encountered Clyde and Hoover on a few occasions—at the Stork, Morocco, or the Colony. They were quite the night clubbers in those days. But by then I knew what the situation was. Clyde was Hoover's boy. Once they invited me and my companion to tour the FBI headquarters in Washington, and we did."

She was referring to Frank Ryan, a wealthy young Washingtonian who was showering her with jewelry.

In the late 1950s, when Anita was invited as the house guest of Princess Grace of Monaco, J. Edgar and Clyde contacted her after she flew back to New York.

"They wanted to know all the details," she said. "I viewed myself at that point as an FBI informant. I told them that Grace already had taken upon herself a handsome young beach boy from Nice and that Prince Rainier often flew to Paris to shack up with his mistress who was installed in a luxurious apartment there."

By the time Anita married Palen Flagler in 1970, she more or less lost touch with Clyde and J. Edgar, who were getting old. J. Edgar would soon die.

"I really miss those two boys," she told her long-time friend and former model of the early 40s, author Stanley Mills Haggart.

"Stanley had been a leg man for Hedda Hopper years ago, and he was interested in all the gossip I'd told Hoover," she said, "especially the really wicked stuff. Of course, Hedda couldn't print the stuff that I came up with. Stanley also told me that many of the items he discovered couldn't be printed either. Times were different then."

"I've spent most of my life looking and talking like a lady, but with Clyde and Hoover I could talk dirty without being judged a whore. How many women can pull off that trick?"

***

J. Edgar was delighted to meet a New Orleans-born singer at the Stork Club. She was in her twenties and called herself Dorothy Lamour, a name inspired by that of her stepfather, Clarence Lambour. Heading to Chicago after she won the Miss New Orleans beauty contest, she ended up working as an elevator operator at Marshall Field's. Finally, she got a gig singing with bandleader Herbie Kay on his radio show, "The Yeast Foamers." She married him while still a teenager but they were incompatible.

Fleeing to New York she worked briefly as a prostitute for Polly Adler, who was the reigning madam of the city, although frequently raided by the police.

Billingsley introduced Dorothy to J. Edgar. The Stork Club owner had a crush on her, and he'd hired her as a singer, later finding her "without talent." He'd warned Dorothy, "It's just for show. Hoover and Tolson are as queer as a three-dollar bill, but it'll get you some publicity if you become Hoover's arm candy."

Sherman Billingsley ran the Stork Club, the most famous night spot in Manhattan, where he frequently entertained J. Edgar and his lover, Clyde Tolson.

The press erroneously promoted a *faux* romance between J. Edgar and screen siren **Dorothy Lamour** *(above)*. But instead of the FBI director, she was having an affair with a former bootlegger, **Sherman Billingsley,** who ran the celebrity-haunted Stork Club in Manhattan.

When Dorothy migrated to Hollywood, J. Edgar and Clyde often stayed at the home she shared with her new husband. "On several occasions, Eddie like to dress up wearing one of my famous sarongs. He didn't look all that great impersonating me, but what the hell, the guy worked hard and deserved some fun in life."

Founded as a Jazz Age speakeasy, the club achieved its greatest fame in the 1940s, attracting movie stars such as Clark Gable and Joan Crawford, New York City mayors, gangsters such as Dutch Schultz, and royalty which included the Duke and Duchess of Windsor. As the years went on, John F. Kennedy wooed Jacqueline Bouvier here, and Prince Rainier showed up with the blonde film goddess, Grace Kelly.

"Sherman ruled the club with a velvet fist," said Dorothy Lamour, who was his lover when Ethel Merman wasn't around.

Veteran newsman Ralph de Toledano covered the FBI as one of his beats for *Newsweek*. He admitted that J. Edgar knew the "reigning sirens of the period, including Dorothy. But he was never serious in his attentions."

He told newsmen, "I was in love once when I was young." He never named the object of his affection. Nor did he indicate the sex of the person he was referring to. It could have been one of his schoolboy crushes on a man.

Rumors spread quickly through the New York grapevine, reaching Washington. The word was out, J. Edgar had fallen for the glamorous Stork Club singer, Dorothy Lamour. "It took a Louisiana Southern beauty, a real sweet magnolia, to melt the ultimate icy cold G-Man," wrote one columnist, getting the facts all wrong. J. Edgar, of course, had fallen for the third party at the table, Clyde Tolson himself, who looked on and appeared somewhat irritated at times at the charade they had to play in public.

What started out as a mere publicity stunt developed into a friendship that would last a lifetime, as J. Edgar saw Dorothy through the ups and downs of movie stardom. She knew she could always turn to him for advice "and to rescue me whenever I fell into a manhole."

In her own memoirs, *My Side of the Road*, Dorothy called J. Edgar "a friend of the family," which is a far more accurate description than those who have ridiculously suggested some grand romance between the two of them.

Eventually, in 1936, Dorothy gravitated to Hollywood where she became a star playing Ulah, a sort of female Tarzan in *The Jungle Princess*. She wore a sarong, which became an outfit famously associated with her, especially when she burst into international fame with Bob Hope and Bing Crosby in a series of box office champions, the Road pictures, beginning with *Road to Singapore* in 1940.

For his fifty-eighth birthday celebration, Franklin D. Roosevelt invited both Dorothy and J. Edgar Hoover to the White House for a gala celebration. Dorothy appeared on the arm of the handsome matinee idol, Tyrone Power, with whom she'd starred in *Johnny Apollo* (1940). When she had a moment alone with J. Edgar, she whispered to him, "We're having a torrid affair."

He asked her to call him the following day because he had quite a dossier on Power that he felt she should know about.

For his date that night, J. Edgar invited Lela Rogers, the mother of Ginger. FDR went against Washington protocol. Most hosts always invited J. Edgar and Clyde as a couple, but FDR thought it would be better for him to have a woman accompany him to the White House celebration.

A furious Clyde was left at home. Throughout the rest of his life, he always said, "I hate Roosevelt's guts."

When Dorothy called J. Edgar the following morning, she was stunned at his revelations about the sexual life of Tyrone. She was unaware that he was bisexual and was virtually the kept boy of aviator Howard Hughes. She also learned that he was engaged in ongoing affairs with the other two reigning matinee idols of the day, Errol Flynn and Robert Taylor.

While seeing Dorothy, Tyrone was also slipping around in and out of the bedrooms of Betty Grable, his co-star in *A Yank in the RAF* (1941) and Rita Hayworth, his co-star in *Blood and Sand* (1941).

J. Edgar saved the final, shocking revelation for last. "He indulges in coprophagia."

"What in hell is that?" she asked.

"Feces eating."

There was a long pause. "I want to vomit."

"Clyde interviewed an eighteen-year-old boy who was hired for the occasion. A gathering of these shit-eaters took place at the apartment of Monty Woolley. Our file on that lusty old perv would stretch from the Capitol building to Annapolis."

Shocked and horrified, Dorothy dropped Tyrone at once and refused to come to the phone when he called her. He never knew why.

In lieu of a father, Dorothy turned to J. Edgar with her problems. Once when she complained that a producer didn't have the money to finance a play in which she wanted to star, he came to her rescue. Through Clyde, he arranged for a Texas oil millionaire, who owed J. Edgar a big favor or two, to put up the money. Regrettably, the play flopped.

The biggest rescue of Dorothy came, however, when *Confidential* magazine in the 1950s was going to publish an exposé of Dorothy, revealing that during a bleak period in her life she'd been a prostitute for the New York madam, Polly Adler. No one knows what exactly took place, but Clyde paid a visit to the offices of *Confidential*. The story about Dorothy was never published.

Ovid Demaris wrote an biography of J. Edgar, based on the memories of those who remembered him, in 1975 shortly after his death. Called *The Director*, it contained an interview with William Ross Howard III, Dorothy's second husband, whom she'd married in 1943. The couple had two sons.

Howard claimed that J. Edgar and Clyde stayed with them during their annual visits to La Jolla in California. "He was an expert at barbecue and made a wicked drink called a G-Man," Howard said.

J. Edgar and Clyde slept in a double bed in their guest room.

One evening, without an invitation, gossip maven Louella Parsons arrived unannounced on the Howard doorstep. Dorothy let her in, but was afraid she might put something in her column about the intimate relationship of J. Edgar and Clyde. But Parsons admired J. Edgar and the FBI and kept his secrets.

Don Smith, the former manager of the Del Mar racetrack when Bing Crosby operated it, would also be visited by Clyde and J. Edgar after they'd spent time with Dorothy and her husband. "Clyde did everything for J. Edgar," Smith said. "They were as close as any two men could be."

Allegedly, he said, "that stuff about J. Edgar and Dorothy being lovers is pure bullshit."

When Dorothy and Howard lived on the outskirts of Baltimore, she would often drive into Washington to dine with J. Edgar and Clyde at Harvey's. "In some ways they were my closest friends. They visited me on at least two occasions when I was doing a Road picture with Bob Hope. Whenever we traveled abroad, such as to London, they always had agents who paved the way for us and handled any problem that arose on the road."

"The sweetest gesture," she recalled, "was when our boy, Tommy Howard, was born. Edgar sent an agent and had his toe prints put on a gold coin. As Tommy grew older, he started calling him Uncle Edgar."

Dorothy recalled one of the last times she saw Clyde and J. Edgar was when they showed up for her nightclub act in the 1960s at El Rancho Vegas in Las Vegas. "Clyde had lost a lot of weight and looked haggard." She found out later that he'd suffered two massive strokes. "I fear he didn't have much longer to live, and I didn't know what J. Edgar would do without him. They were so close I feared J. Edgar might commit suicide."

J. Edgar, in private moments, wished to deflect his homosexuality by

J. Edgar broke up the blossoming affair between **Tyrone Power** and **Dorothy Lamour**, with whom she'd starred in *Johnny Apollo* (1940). She was unaware at the time that he was bisexual, having affairs with both Howard Hughes and Robert Taylor.

But what really ended Dorothy's affair with him was when J. Edgar revealed a sexual perversion that the "Queen of the Sarongs" found "disgusting."

J. Edgar had also learned that Errol Flynn broke up with Power "because he wanted me to do things to him I considered vile."

painting a picture of Dorothy as "the gal who got away. After my romance with her, no other woman would do." Of course, that was pure hype with no basis in reality.

Dorothy's name surfaced after J. Edgar's death when the Senate launched an investigation into FBI corruption. It was later revealed that J. Edgar frequently used FBI money to entertain Dorothy and Howard. One investigator recalled that J. Edgar and his agents spent a lot of FBI cash creating an artificial moon, an electric globe way up in a tree, as a prop for a lavish party for Dorothy. She had made a movie called *Moon Over Burma* (1940), and she'd also introduced the song "The Moon of Manakoora," which became her standard.

***

J. Edgar and Clyde usually detested vulgar women, especially the outspoken Tallulah Bankhead, a Stork regular. She was always making veiled references to their homosexuality. "The bitch is one to talk," Clyde said. "She's had more pussy than Porfirio Rubirosa, not to mention everyone in pants."

One night, fueled by too much alcohol, Tallulah stopped by their Table 50 at the Stork Club when Winchell was interviewing someone at the bar. "Good evening, Mr. Hoover," she said. "I understand that to join the FBI, a G-Man has to have at least nine inches." He ignored her. She looked over at Clyde. "And how is Mrs. Hoover tonight?"

As **J. Edgar Hoover** aged, his face grew stern and rigid. It was often compared to that of a bulldog. But regardless of how he looked, Clyde Tolson was always there for him, always at his side, morning, noon, and night.

A closeted homosexual and a transvestite, J. Edgar intimidated presidents who were afraid to fire him because of the damaging secrets he possessed. He ruled the FBI for nearly fifty years and struck fear in everyone from public officials to private citizens.

But in a complete reversal of their usual tastes in women, J. Edgar and Clyde virtually adopted Ethel Merman as "our all-time gal pal." With her powerful and strident voice, she seemed the epitome of vulgarity and was known for her dirty jokes. The first time she heard what eventually became her standard, "Everything's Coming Up Roses," she quipped, "Everything's coming up Rose's what?"

She even sent out tasteless Christmas cards. On one was a picture of Santa Claus, proclaiming "Have I got a big surprise for you." When the recipient opened the card, a large penis popped up.

For reasons known only to themselves, Clyde and J. Edgar viewed Ethel as their favorite entertainer, both on and off the stage.

When Sherman Billingsley first escorted J. Edgar and Clyde into the Cub Room, he said he created this annex to the rest of his club by cutting through the wall into a neighboring building. He converted it into the most exclusive part of the Stork Club because he wanted a place for his flame, Ethel Merman, to drink and relax after delivering a performance on Broadway.

"When Sherman told me that Clyde and J. Edgar considered me their favorite star, I had to meet them, and he arranged a dinner for us at the Stork Club," Ethel said. "It was one of those things where we bonded for a lifetime. They became my best friends. What a swell pair of guys, and they were so much in love. Under those draped linen tables at the Stork Club they held hands. I found that very romantic."

J. Edgar and Clyde had met Ethel when she'd opened on Broadway with Bob Hope in the musical *Red, Hot, & Blue!* by Cole Porter. In the show she'd introduced a song, "It's De-Lovely," which became one of her standards.

At a late-night champagne dinner, the two G-Men were enchanted by this brassy New Yorker who had been born in Astoria, Queens as "Agnes Zimmermann."

Amazingly, she brought these two closeted homosexuals out of hiding and immediately accepted their relationship. Of course, she'd been prepped by Billingsley himself before meeting the two FBI lovers. As the night wore on, she bonded with Clyde and J. Edgar, paying equal attention to both members of the pair.

To Clyde, she jokingly whispered, "Every time you top John, do you borrow my song, 'I Got Rhythm?'" When he laughed, she said, "I've made the Sphinx laugh!"

"Of course, you might also want to borrow another one of my songs, 'Blow, Gabriel, Blow,'" she said. "You can change it, of course, to 'Blow, John, Blow.'"

She was the only person who ever called J. Edgar "John." She later said, "John wasn't the talkative type. Clyde was the one with the quips. And John was careful never to lend the FBI's name to any commercial endorsements, especially anything a little risqué. But one way or another he came through for *Red, Hot, and Blue!*, telling the *New York Post*'s Michael Mok, "It's a bright entertainment, put over with lots of style, and there's quite a lot of truth in the cracks."

J. Edgar told her he approved of her love affair with Billingsley. "A perfect mating. The Queen of Broadway meets the King of the Night."

"Sherman treats me like a queen," she said. "I bet he does the same for you."

In normal circumstances, J. Edgar would never tolerate such kidding, but he found it amusing coming from the belting mouth of Ethel. "I adore you guys," she said after their first meeting. "From this night on, consider me your den mother."

Their first night had gone so well J. Edgar and Clyde came to see her show again, escorting her to the club after the performance.

At the door to the Stork Club, she greeted "Albino," the long-time doorman. She flipped up her skirt, exposing bare flesh, as she wore no bloomers. "That's in lieu of a tip." Albino later told Clyde, "I'd rather have a dollar tip. Looking at that overworked pussy of hers doesn't help me feed a wife and kids."

J. Edgar agreed that Ethel was treated like royalty. Billingsley even kept a waiter by her side just to light her cigarettes, and he gave her expensive presents including bottles of *Sortilège*, a chic perfume whose distributorship he had acquired. For no reason at all, he sent her cases of the best French champagne.

Ethel's biographer, Brian Kellow, wrote of her immense sexual attraction to Billingsley, whom she found extremely masculine. She told J. Edgar and Clyde, "At first he frightened me but I learned to melt those ice blue eyes of his. He is uncompromising about running the Stork Club the way you run the FBI, monitoring everything yourself. When I met him, I knew I'd found my soulmate, the way you did when you met this adorable Clyde here. I know Clyde looks stiff and formal on the outside. But, as they say, still waters run deep."

On another visit to New York, Clyde and J. Edgar double-dated with Ethel and Billingsley and were seen dining at the Italian Pavilion of the 1939-40 World's Fair. In the arcade shooting gallery, both J. Edgar and Clyde showed her what crack shots they were. "You guys hit those fake rabbits and ducks so well I can understand why Dillinger didn't have a chance against you two." Of course, J. Edgar and Clyde had not been at the scene of the slaughter of Dillinger, but they didn't really want anyone to think differently.

One night at the Stork Club, J. Edgar had a double date—he with Clyde and Ethel with the bisexual actress, Bea Lillie. She amused them with her quick wit. She preferred lager, a lot of it, as Ethel downed champagne. That night Ethel revealed to J. Edgar that she, too, had a dark secret to equal his

It was an unconventional friendship, but the Broadway stage star, **Ethel Merman,** who could belt out a song like no other, became [her words] "John and Clyde's gun moll."

She told the G-Men about her affairs, both with men and women, and they shared details about the intimate aspects of their lives with her.

She often purchased gowns and lingerie for J. Edgar when he wanted to dress in drag. J. Edgar warned her that "Judy Garland's a bit young for you...you might get into trouble." Garland was only a teenager at the time Merman seduced her.

The first time J. Edgar and Clyde visited Ethel at her home in California, she took them to her bedroom, where she opened her closet door. "Those two urns contain mom and dad. I like to open the closet and see those I love the most."

closeted homosexuality. "I'm a lesbian on alternate Sundays. Bea and I are having an affair."

As Ethel remembered Bea, "She looked as if she had just come out of a bandbox—always with that little Juliet cap she wore. She had lovely skin and wore only light powder and a little rouge. In her own peculiar way, I thought she was stunning. And funny!"

J. Edgar trusted Ethel enough to reveal to her one of his darkest secrets. He was a cross-dresser but only in the privacy of his home—never at a private party. She took this revelation in stride. In the words of Ethel's biographer, Geoffrey Mark, "She even helped him go shopping for ladies' apparel at the finest stores." Of course, the sales clerks understood that the star was buying apparel for herself—certainly not for the director of the FBI.

Clyde and J. Edgar had to miss Ethel's opening of *Stars in Your Eyes* (1939) because of pressing FBI business in Washington. But a telegram arrived on opening night. SINCERE GOOD WISHES TO YOU AND YOUR NEW SHOW. WE'RE SORRY WE CAN'T BE IN THE FRONT ROW TO HISS—TO KISS YOU. She told her co-star that Clyde must have written that telegram. "John doesn't have that much humor."

In 1978, years after both the deaths of J. Edgar and Clyde, Anita Bryant, the orange juice queen of Florida, launched her homophobic campaign against gay men, labeling them child molesters.

Beginning in Dade County, her campaign spread across the nation. A reporter cornered Ethel for her reaction. "Miss Merman, what do you think about what Bryant is doing?"

"Some of my best friends were or are homosexuals," Ethel said. "Take J. Edgar Hoover, for instance. He virtually created the FBI. Many homosexuals are the most creative and dynamic people in America. I'm all for these guys. To each his own."

***

Except for very brief mention here and there, Guy Hotell is almost a non-presence in biographies of J. Edgar Hoover. Guy has virtually disappeared from the FBI roll call. Yet for twenty-five years, he was the second most important man in J. Edgar's life, ranking just behind Clyde Tolson himself.

J. Edgar had met the football player at George Washington University, but their friendship didn't begin until decades later. Guy was a very masculine, rambunctious playboy. As J. Edgar remembered it, he was recognized as the stud of the university, and many of the female students chased after him. "In those days, Guy could have his pick of almost any gal he wanted," J. Edgar said.

Clyde did not want it known that he was actually living with his boss, so J. Edgar rented him a two-bedroom apartment at the Westchester Apartments on Cathedral Avenue in Washington, DC. Clyde suggested that to cut down on his rent, he should rent out the extra bedroom.

"We have to rent it to someone we trust," J. Edgar told him. "I know just the right man. Guy Hotell."

At the time, Guy worked as a young executive for AETNA, an insurance company. Within two years, the insurance people wanted to transfer him to the Rocky Mountain states, but he didn't want to go. Subsequently, J. Edgar hired him as a special agent at the FBI.

Right after Guy moved in, he was soon seen dining almost every night with J. Edgar and Clyde at Harvey's, their favorite hangout.

"I was Clyde's roommate in name only," Guy later claimed. "The apartment was only for appearance's sake, as he spent his nights with Eddie, coming home for a change of clothing."

One agent had to deliver an urgent document on a Sunday to J. Edgar's modest home. He found the director in his back yard, dressed in slacks and a jazzy sports shirt. He was digging in the dirt around his beloved tea roses. Clyde was frying pork chops on the stove, and Guy was raking the grass, removing debris from a recent rainstorm. "The scene was very domestic, very cozy, a happy trio tending to their home," the agent claimed.

In later years, J. Edgar would try to erase any connection he had with

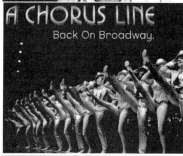

A CHORUS LINE
Back On Broadway.

"I did not kill President Kennedy," **Clay Shaw** *(top photo)* told his biographer, **James Kirkwood** *(middle photo)*, an author who won the Pulitzer Prize for his Broadway musical *A Chorus Line*.

Shaw had been charged with conspiring to murder the President, but was later exonerated. Shaw flew to Key West for extensive interviews with Kirkwood. With him was Guy Hotell, who had been Clyde Tolson's roommate in Washington, DC, and one of the few persons who ever witnessed firsthand the intimate dynamic between "Eddie and Clyde."

Guy, and the file he kept on his special agent mysteriously disappeared after Guy left the bureau.

J. Edgar eventually turned on Guy because he was one of those "loose-lipped type of guys who sink ships." When he drank excessively, which he did frequently in later years, Guy dined out on stories about his years with J. Edgar and Clyde.

At one point in the 1980s, he agreed to "tell all" to the author James Kirkwood Jr., who won the Pulitzer Prize for his Broadway musical, *A Chorus Line*.

"Jimmy," as he was called by his friends, was the lover of another novelist, James Leo Herlihy author of *Midnight Cowboy,* the book that inspired the Oscar-winning movie (in 1969) with the same name. Jimmy was also a personal friend of Clay Shaw, a homosexual New Orleans businessman tried by district attorney Jim Garrison in New Orleans on trumped-up conspiracy charges associated with the assassination of President John F. Kennedy in Dallas in November of 1963. Shaw was later acquitted.

As an author and investigative reporter, Jimmy thought the story of Shaw's ordeal would make a lively yarn, and he signed to write the first-ever biography on Shaw, whom he invited down to his residence in Key West. Shaw showed up with Guy Hotell, who had been his lover in younger days.

During a yachting excursion to an offshore and uninhabited island in the Florida Keys, arranged by local businessman Bill Johnson, Jimmy spent hours talking with Guy, who told him "fantastic stories" about his life with J. Edgar and Clyde, each of whom were long dead, of course. Jimmy became so intrigued that he began to negotiate with Guy to do a second biography after he finished his memoirs of Shaw, which was eventually published under the title of *American Grotesque.*

A first-rate *raconteur*, Jimmy was the son of two famous actors, James Kirkwood Sr. (the lover of Mary Pickford) and Lila Lee (who had starred with Rudolph Valentino). Jimmy entertained guests at parties in Los Angeles, New York, and Key West with tales of J. Edgar, Guy, and Clyde. At one point, he planned to call his second biography *The Gay Adventures of J. Edgar Hoover and Clyde Tolson.*

Regrettably, Jimmy died of spinal cancer in 1989, and Guy died a few months later. But much of what is known about Guy's FBI days came from what Jimmy Kirkwood learned from Guy about this strange trio and the complexities of their relationship.

Had J. Edgar not found Guy so compelling, he would have dismissed him as a pervert and fired him from the bureau. Guy was a true bisexual, often proclaiming "all cats are gray at night."

In his book, *Hoover's F.B.I.*, former agent William W. Turner claimed that J. Edgar was the ultimate hypocrite, preaching family values during the day but leading a secret homosexual life at night. "As director, he bashed homosexuals with a vengeance," Turner said. "They were barred from Bureau employment at any level. The few who slipped through the screening process simply disappeared when discovered."

After two months of working for "**Clyde and Eddie**" *(left and middle figures, above),* FBI agent **Guy Hotell** *(right figure, above)* came to realize that his duties, which continued over the course of several years, involved "arranging private things for these guys who lived deep in the closet."

"Pimp is too nasty a word," Guy revealed, "but these boys couldn't very well arrange sexual liaisons themselves. They were too famous. I spent several nights with them when I was younger and still had a full head of hair."

"They also wanted me to go with them on nearly all their vacations. We had fun in those days. But unlike Clyde and Eddie, I was also a lady killer."

It wasn't just homosexuals that J. Edgar would fire. Turner claimed he was known for his arbitrary harshness. Once when the director rode up on the elevator with one of the Bureau's teenage clerks, he noticed his face was covered with unsightly pimples. That afternoon the nineteen-year-old received his pink slip.

Married four times, Guy was known as a "wife beater." He always maintained that, "I am basically straight, but tempted by boy ass every other week." He also complained that he felt his roommate, Clyde, was basically straight as well, but was "detoured" into homosexuality by J. Edgar.

Guy maintained that Clyde formed attachments to two different women in 1939—one Edna Daulyton, a waitress in a café near the Justice Department, and another, Louise Edwards, who worked as a secretary in the Bureau's Washington headquarters.

In anger, Clyde broke off with Daulyton because she accused him of being "a fairy at Hoover's beck and call." When J. Edgar found out about Clyde's relationship with Edwards, he had her transferred to the Bureau's office in Kansas City.

FBI agents found Guy the friendliest of the trio, with the most engaging personality. "Tolson wore a perpetual frown like he was worried about something all the time," said one agent. G-Men claimed that J. Edgar had the face of a bulldog complete with that spatulate nose.

In the words of one G-Man in the Washington Bureau, "Hoover had a crooked smile but almost never smiled. When he fixed those brown eyes on you, I'm sure he looked like those monsters who dropped the gas pellets in the Nazi concentration camps. When he talked, it was with the syncopation of an FBI submachine gun."

"I liked women more than I liked men," Guy revealed to Jimmy. "But I engaged in a three-way with Clyde and Eddie whenever they wanted me to. I was a top man. So was Clyde. J. Edgar liked to be a sandwich between us."

"They also liked me to arrange certain gay parties for them, since each of them would never dare do it on their own," Guy said. "I was, in essence, their pimp. In fact, I seemed to have been hired for that job alone as I didn't do much work for the Bureau."

"I went with them on their vacations to Florida, California, and the Caribbean," Guy said. "These were disguised as inspection tours, but they spent more time at the nightclubs and race tracks than inspecting any local bureaus."

"I also attended fabulous parties with them," Guy said. "Eddie had many wealthy admirers who entertained him, along with Clyde and me. At banquets and parties those tire people and those car moguls made us feel like we were Louis XIV at the Court of Versailles." He no doubt was referring to executives of Firestone and Ford.

Guy recalled two trips with J. Edgar and Clyde when they were booked into the Flamingo Hotel in Miami. "We had a private terrace where we could sunbathe in the nude. Eddie wasn't all that endowed, and he liked to see Clyde and me walk around in the nude because both of us were low danglers. It was on one such afternoon there on that terrace that the notorious photograph was taken."

He was referring to an underground photograph that was alleged to have been taken of J. Edgar performing fellatio on Clyde. Although shot at a distance, no doubt from a tree, J. Edgar's face was clearly visible, Clyde's face less so, according to Guy who saw the photograph when it arrived at J. Edgar's private address in Washington.

It was rumored that the long distance photographer was hired by the Jewish gangster Meyer Lansky, who maintained his headquarters in Miami. Lansky once bragged to Frank Sinatra in Havana that he possessed such an incriminating photograph. "It's blackmail, sweetheart," Lansky told the singer. "That picture will keep Hoover a very good boy and out of my business."

"That's what I would call a Mexican standoff," Frank later told his friends.

On another occasion, at a gathering of the nation's arch criminals in Havana at the Hotel Nacional in 1947, Lansky exhibited the fellatio photograph. He announced to the assembled group of gangsters, "The director of the Federal Bureau of Investigation has been fixed. Of course, all of us should still be discreet when we have to kill someone like Bugsy Siegel."

On another trip to Florida, Clyde, Guy, and J. Edgar checked into Miami's Gulfstream Hotel. The following day Clyde joined some agents who wanted to head early in the morning to the Florida Keys on a fishing trip. J. Edgar remained behind with Guy.

Later in the day Guy was contacted about a case in Miami where the Bureau had apprehended a seventeen-year-old boy, Ricky Mazzini. He had stolen a car in Atlanta, robbed a service station, and had driven all the way to Miami where he was arrested by local police. Since the boy had crossed state lines while committing these crimes, it was viewed as a matter for the FBI.

Guy was sent to interview the boy. He told his would-be biographer, Jimmy Kirkwood, "The kid was a knock-out, a real sexy looker even at his age. I arranged to have Ricky released in my custody. I took him over to our suite at the Gulfstream. Eddie was at a private cabana on the beach at the time. While he was away, the kid and I had a hot time. He must have been broken in when he was eight years old."

"When Eddie returned, I could tell he was hot for Ricky, too," Guy claimed. "He asked me if he could spend a couple of hours in the bedroom with Ricky. The boy was only too willing. They spent a good part of the afternoon in that bedroom. I could just imagine what went on. Before five o'clock Eddie told me to give the boy a hundred dollar bill, drive him to the Greyhound bus station in Miami, and buy him a ticket back to Atlanta where he lived with his grandmother. The Bureau's case against him was dropped. When Clyde returned from the Keys, we had supper together and nothing was ever said about how Eddie and I spent the afternoon."

On yet another vacation to Miami Beach, J. Edgar booked a suite for himself, Clyde, and Guy at the Gulfstream Hotel, a return visit. "Since I knew Eddie cheated on Clyde behind his back, I figured Clyde should have some fun on the side. I was still convinced he was basically straight. Boy, did I make a mistake. I arranged a double date with two models, who were really prostitutes. We were going to make it a foursome for the evening."

"The Jew was the brains of the outfit." Or so said Lucky Luciano about the gangster **Meyer Lansky,** pictured above.

"He was one smart guy and had blackmail evidence on Hoover. He more or less told the FBI to back off so we could go about our business. I never liked him, but Lansky was useful. You can stay in the mob as long as we find you useful. After that, it's the kiss of death."

As late as 1950, J. Edgar maintained to the Senate Special Committee to investigate Organized Crime in Interstate Commerce that "there is no such thing as a national crime syndicate."

"The next day, when Eddie found out, he threw a hissy fit," Guy said. "He locked himself in the bathroom and started screaming and banging on the walls. At one point he threatened to cut his wrists with a razor. I couldn't believe this was happening, and the plans for our four-way were nipped in the bud. Clyde helped me break down the door. No, this time, 'Killer Tolson' didn't use a machine gun. I even slapped Eddie's face to try to bring him to his senses."

Because of Guy's "loose lips," the story made its way back to the FBI Bureau in Washington. Former agent William W. Turner referred to it in his book *Hoover's F.B.I.*

"After Eddie warned me never to do that again, I left the Gulfstream and had to take care of the two whores by myself, which was an easy task for a man like me," Guy said. "I once took on five *putas* in one night. When I got back to the suite that night, Eddie and Clyde were sleeping peacefully in each other's arms. Very romantic, I would say, though Eddie sure wasn't much of a looker, although some dog fanciers actually see a certain beauty in a bulldog's face."

As Guy later related to Jimmy Kirkwood, "The most compromising vacation Clyde, Eddie, and I took together was to Havana, Nassau, and San Juan. The trip would have far-reaching political and espionage implications."

***

Guy and J. Edgar loved to go on vacations under the pretense of executing the business of the FBI. Since the arms of the Bureau stretched virtually everywhere, he could devise and disguise a business trip whenever it suited his need for a holiday.

One morning, he woke up with a mission. He decided that what he, as well as Clyde and Guy, needed was a luxurious eight-night vacation which would incorporate visits to Miami, Havana, San Juan, and Nassau. From his office, he ordered Special Agent Robert Page Burrus to make all the arrangements.

In a memo dated February 11, 1936, Burris wrote "The Boss," claiming that his luggage would not be inspected at any port of call and that his presence in these exotic locales would not be made available to the press.

Winging their way to Florida, the trio checked in once again for an overnight stay at the Flamingo Hotel in Miami, before flying on to decadent Havana. In Cuba their luggage was transferred to the deluxe Sevilla-Biltmore Hotel on the Prado.

In this heady world of tropical nights, J. Edgar discovered "the Paris of the Americas," and he joined forces with Clyde and Guy to sample the forbidden pleasures of the city. But he warned his agents they had to be very discreet. "I've got a lot of enemies, and they'd love to entrap me in something."

In nighttime Havana, high rollers could mambo their way through the casinos, and later attend sex shows or patronize bordellos. In these well-decorated whorehouses, there was a steady supply of beautiful young girls or handsome young men, depending on a client's preference.

Guy later recalled to author James Kirkwood, "Eddie wore a silly mustache, a pair of dark glasses, and a hat pulled down as we made the rounds, but no one seemed to recognize him. At that time in his life, his bulldog face was not much known to the Cuban people. Clark Gable and Franklin D.

97

Roosevelt they knew."

"Boy prostitution was rampant, and I slipped away with Clyde and Eddie to sample the treats at what we were told was the best male bordello in Havana. It was known as 'Cocktail.' We expected the rooms to be painted cherry red, and so they were. I'd arranged for Eddie and Clyde to inspect the boys in a private salon because they didn't want to be observed by the other male clients, most of whom were visiting Americans. The madam was actually a male. She paraded some twenty young men in front of us. All of them were shirtless and had on very revealing, tight white pants. Before the night was over, we'd booked four of them, maybe five. Clyde and J. Edgar shared a bedroom, and I had a room all to myself. Both of my studs had golden skin and were willing to do everything. Right before we left, I slipped the madam a five-hundred dollar tip, which was a lot of money in those days."

"You've trained your boy whores well," I told the madam.

"And what fun it was," the madam shot back.

On the following evening, Guy directed J. Edgar and Clyde to a sexual exhibition at a club called Smörgåsbord. Both men claimed they'd never viewed one before. "Inside, in a small arena, some twenty performers, both male and female, staged a show for us on a revolving stage. Every known sexual act was performed on that platform—men with men, men with women, women with women. All that was missing was a donkey. Most of the brown-skinned girls looked like teenagers. The men were slightly older, probably in their early twenties. There were two beautiful blond boys who were rather effeminate and looked Scandinavian. They got raped by two big burly Mandingos. J. Edgar was practically salivating. And this was the same guy who had walked out of the Cotton Club in Harlem when he saw a blonde-haired woman dancing with a black man. He was hard to figure out. Apparently, what was not acceptable to him in New York was titillating, when the gender combinations were changed, in Havana."

"In one of those amazing coincidences that happens in a Charles Dickens novel, J. Edgar ran into Sumner Welles, emerging from one of the bedrooms. We found out later he'd been entertained by two strapping black boys. J. Edgar knew Sumner, but the two men did not acknowledge each other early that morning."

A long-time diplomat in the Foreign Service, Welles was one of FDR's favorites. Fluent in Spanish, he had served since 1933 as Assistant Secretary of State for Latin American Affairs. That same year, FDR sent him to Cuba as a special envoy, since the island nation was in the throes of a revolution.

At the time of their awkward encounter, J. Edgar did not know that

Sumner was a homosexual. Before leaving Havana, J. Edgar found out all he could about Sumner's private life. He told Guy and Clyde, "He knows too much about me. I've got to find out even more about him. He could destroy me."

Weeks after their encounter, William Bullitt, the U.S. Ambassador to France and a longtime antagonist of Welles, called J. Edgar. Bullitt had just learned that Sumner had been kicked out of Cuba. Apparently, he'd moved two young black boys into his private apartments, and a scandal had ensued, apparently from an enraged father.

Having had "a hot time in the old town of Havana," as J. Edgar put it, the three men flew to San Juan, Puerto Rico. Burrus had arranged for them to stay free in the penthouse suite at the luxurious Condado-Vanderbilt Hotel along the beachfront. More adventures lay in store for them.

***

After the tropical nights of Havana, San Juan seemed a bit dull. But on J. Edgar's second night there, his interest was piqued. "Hawk Eyes never misses anything," he bragged to Guy and Clyde, explaining what he meant when they were seated in a booth in the hotel restaurant.

At a far and distant booth he had spotted Porfirio Rubirosa dining with Joan Crawford in what was obviously an off-the-record weekend. They seemed oblivious to the rest of the world. Joan was a friendly acquaintance of his, although he did not plan to intrude on her privacy, because he did not want to be seen chatting with "Rubi," who already was being billed as "The Playboy of the Western World." He'd been married to the whorish Flor de Oro Trujillo, daughter of Rafael Trujillo, the notorious dictator of the Dominican Republic.

J. Edgar's real interest in Rubi would not become a full-scale obsession until 1947 when he married the tobacco

In an attempted disguise, J. Edgar sampled some of the wild nightlife of Havana. Clyde and Guy Hotell accompanied J. Edgar on his nighttime rounds. His favorite was **The Superman Show** at the Shanghai.

The star of the show, El Toro, came on stage boasting a fourteen-inch, very thick and erect penis. He was a tall, slender Cuban of African descent who wore a scarlet cape—and nothing else. Three beautiful women lay nude on cots before him. One by one he penetrated each of them.

heiress, Doris Duke. But on that night in San Juan he ordered Clyde to begin a file on "that woman magnet." Eventually, Rubi's FBI file would stretch to 1,100 pages.

Rubi was wanted for questioning by the New York police about a murder, and he had been avoiding the mainland of the United States. J. Edgar was familiar with the case.

Dr. Angel Morales, a Dominican statesman, was the chief rival of General Trujillo, and had fled his native island fearing that Trujillo would have him killed. In New York he lived in a modest rooming house as an exile, sharing quarters with Sergio Bencosme (aka Doctor Pascasio Toribio Bencosme Garcia), the son of a general who had opposed Trujillo.

The last person J. Edgar expected to see in one of Havana's male bordellos was **Sumner Welles** *(photo above),* one of the top advisers to (and a personal friend of) Franklin D. Roosevelt.

As Guy Hotell later recalled, "Both Sumner and Eddie by accident outed themselves to each other as being gay, but the two powerhouses did not acknowledge each other. Although homosexual in nature, their sexual tastes differed when it came to color. Eddie dug white boys and Sumner was turned on by those black dicks. It was this love of forbidden fruit that led to Sumner's downfall. Otherwise, he would have become U.S. Secretary of State during the war."

J. Edgar learned about the case from the chief of the New York City Police Department. He had never been on friendly terms with "New York's finest," viewing the NYPD as a potential rival of the FBI. But he was told that in April of 1935, Rubi had arrived in New York harbor aboard the *S.S. Camao* carrying $7,000 in each (the equivalent of $100,000 today).

He stayed at the Dominican Consulate, where he met with his cousin, Luis de la Fuente Rubirosa (nicknamed Chichi), and one other potential assassin. The police assumed that Rubi turned the money over to these men with orders to gun down Morales.

While Morales was out of his room one evening, meeting with fellow Dominican dissents, Bencosme was alone in the apartment. An assailant broke down the front door, ran up the steps and barged into the bedroom where he fired two shots into Bencosme's chest. As he did, he yelled, "Die Morales."

He then escaped, although the landlady, Carmen Higgs, would later identify the assassin as Chichi when shown a file of possible suspects at the police station. It appeared that Chichi had meant to assassinate Morales, but had shot Bencosme instead.

Rubi's cousin fled the country but was indicted in absentia for murder on February 18, 1936. The police also wanted to summon Rubi for questioning, but he was out of their reach. Since Puerto Rico was a U.S. possession, J. Edgar had the power to arrest Rubi and bring him in for questioning. But he chose not to.

He explained to Guy and Clyde that Joan Crawford was a friend of his, and he didn't want to unduly involve her in a potential scandal. Consequently, Rubi got a reprieve from the FBI that night.

Over dinner, Guy noted that J. Edgar seemed far more concerned with Rubi's legendary endowment than he did about any murder in New York. Through the grapevine, J. Edgar, along with half the rest of the world, had heard that Rubi's penis looked like "a fat baby's arm dangling from his trousers."

J. Edgar told Guy and Clyde that, "Somehow we've got to get a nude of him for our private album. Since he's known to seduce hundreds of women, and an occasional young man, I'm sure that can be arranged."

"Leave it to me, Boss," Clyde said.

Although J. Edgar spent a great deal of his life investigating the sex lives of movie stars, he always protected Joan from scandal. "When it came to law enforcement," Guy said, "Eddie played favorites."

J. Edgar's friendship with Joan went back to the early 1930s when he had visited the studios of Metro-Goldwyn-Mayer, and she had been his tour guide, introducing him to stars such as Clark Gable (her lover), Norma Shearer, Lionel Barrymore, and even Greta Garbo. Since that day, Joan and J. Edgar had bonded.

She must have had the same hawk eye J. Edgar possessed, as she had seen him in the dining room last night.

The next afternoon she called him on the house phone and asked him if she could come up to his suite for a drink. He told her he'd be delighted to see her again. "Incidentally, I'll be alone," she said, indicating she knew that it would be insensitive to bring Rubi up with her.

In respect for her privacy, J. Edgar also ushered Clyde and Guy out of the suite, suggesting they lounge by the pool for a while.

Guy found out later what J. Edgar's arrangement with Joan was. Since their meeting at MGM, Joan had kept him supplied with insider gossip about "who was fucking who in Hollywood," as she so graphically put it. J. Edgar was hungry for gossip, and she confided the secrets to him, some of which he found scandalous, such as Norma Shearer sleeping with Mickey Rooney, who was just a kid at the time.

Of course, Joan had her motivations for befriending J. Edgar. One day she had called him for a favor. She admitted that she had a police record in Detroit, where she was once arrested for prostitution.

Dancing in the chorus line, she, along with the other girls, accepted invitations for dinner with the Stage Door Johnnies who waited outside. This was in the 1920s when she was billed as Lucille Le Sueur.

One night after dinner she had returned to a hotel room with one of her johns. As he was seducing her on the bed, the house detective, along with an armed policeman, broke into the room and arrested her, letting the john go free.

At the city jail, she was booked and fingerprinted, having to spend the night with eight other prostitutes in a cell. Early the next morning, the backstage manager arrived to bail her out. She explained to J. Edgar that she was afraid that her police record would surface one day. He told her he'd handle the matter. He contacted the police in Detroit who sent him Joan's file. Presumably, J. Edgar destroyed it.

In a confessional mood, Joan also claimed that she and Brooklyn-born Ruby Stevens had briefly been prostitutes at a house run by Polly Adler, New York's most notorious madam.

Ruby later became Joan's best friend, a lesbian relationship existing between them when she went to Hollywood and became Barbara Stanwyck in the 1930s. Their liaison would continue until their mutual deaths. On her nightstand on the day Joan died rested a picture of Stanwyck.

J. Edgar never told Joan, nor did she ever admit it, but he'd also acquired a collection of the stag films she'd made in the 1920s to be shown to men at smokers. The so-called "blue movies" had been filmed in Astoria, Queens, New York.

Guy and Clyde had viewed J. Edgar's collection of Joan's films, which had begun as stills designed for display in machines in penny arcades. Porno loops she made included *What the Butler Saw*, *The Plumber*, *Velvet Lips*, *Coming Home*, *She Shows Him How*, and *The Casting Couch*. These were heterosexual films. In *Bosom Buddies*, she had a lesbian romp with another chorus girl.

Without alerting Joan, J. Edgar had his agents conduct an investigation of these porno movies and their distribution. That led to the arrest of two postal inspectors. Why they were arrested or the outcome of their cases is not known.

After Joan became a star, a copy of *The Casting Couch* was sent to Louis B. Mayer at MGM. Apparently, $50,000 was demanded by a blackmailer. When Joan's contract was cancelled in 1943 by Mayer, he wanted her out the studio gates. But she had to settle $50,000 on MGM, ostensibly to buy out her contract. But since Mayer didn't want to hold onto her,

J. Edgar concluded that $50,000 was to pay MGM back for putting up the money demanded by that long-ago blackmailer.

For the next thirty years, Joan would stay in touch with J. Edgar, usually by mail or over the phone—not in person. She told her best friend, gay actor William Haines, "Edgar and I have a barter arrangement. I feed him information, and he takes care of some potentially embarrassing problems for me."

"That sounds like a fair exchange to me," the impish Haines said. "Now, tell me the dirt: Does Mr. Hoover take it up the ass?"

"I'll set up a date with you two, dear heart, and you'll find out for yourself and can tell me."

"I know a bottom when I see one," he said.

***

Landing at the airport in Nassau, The Bahamas, J. Edgar, Clyde, and Guy checked into the second best suite at the Fort Montague Hotel, which The Chief had been told was the most exclusive hotel on New Providence island. He was disappointed that the best suite had not been reserved for him. "We have a very special guest in that suite who does not want his identity known," the manager told him. J. Edgar was furious that the manager would not give him the name. In America, he would have insisted on it.

En route from the airport, he had surveyed the ramshackle buildings and had told Clyde and Guy, "We should have spent all our nights in Havana instead of coming to this backwater."

Bored with his suite, J. Edgar sunned himself on the terrace. He'd placed a call to the FBI to see what VIP was staying at the Fort Montague. Clyde didn't like the sun as much and preferred to lounge in the nude in bed, reading a 10-cent paperback novel called *Gangbusters*. Later he told J. Edgar, "I could have written better shit than that. The writer got everything wrong."

Guy had left the suite "in pursuit of some poontang pussy," as he would later tell his would-be biographer, Jimmy Kirkwood.

At two o'clock, a call came in to J. Edgar from FBI headquarters. "The guest in the presidential suite is Axel Wenner-Gren," a name very familiar to J. Edgar. After talking to his office, he called the hotel's manager, who had left for the afternoon. Instead, he spoke to Ronnie Symonette, the assistant manager.

"I would like to speak to Wenner-Gren," he said. "I'm sure he will talk to J. Edgar Hoover of the Federal Bureau of Investigation."

"One bigshot always talks to another bigshot," Symonette said. He

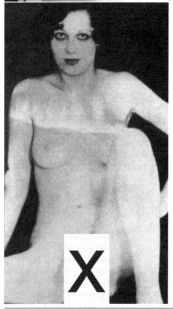

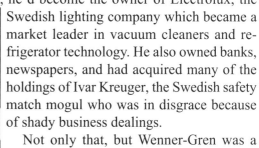

called Wenner-Gren's suite, and the industrialist agreed to talk to J. Edgar. It is not known what these two giants had to say to each other, but Wenner-Gren invited J. Edgar "and his boys" to dinner that night in the hotel dining room.

Since Wenner-Gren was possibly the richest man in the world, his biography was tabloid fodder. He'd made his fortune adapting the industrial vacuum cleaner for domestic use in households. By the early 1930s, he'd become the owner of Electrolux, the Swedish lighting company which became a market leader in vacuum cleaners and refrigerator technology. He also owned banks, newspapers, and had acquired many of the holdings of Ivar Kreuger, the Swedish safety match mogul who was in disgrace because of shady business dealings.

Not only that, but Wenner-Gren was a weapons manufacturer helping with the rearmament of Hitler's Nazi soldiers. He was also said to be a close friend of Hermann Göring, whose first wife, like Wenner-Gren himself, was a Swede.

Over dinner that night, Guy, Clyde, and J. Edgar found Wenner-Gren to be charming, sophisticated, and erudite, still retaining some of the visages of a once-handsome and young face. As Charles Higham, Errol Flynn's biographer, wrote: "Tall, magnificently built, Wenner-Gren looked like a Viking, but had the soul of a rattlesnake."

He told FBI agents that he was considering building a luxurious estate for himself on the adjoining Hog Island (later renamed Paradise Island). "In spite of its name, it's idyllic. You and your boys must come down for a holiday when I've completed it," he said to J. Edgar.

"We'll be there," J. Edgar prom-

Although they compiled a private file on her sexual escapades, J. Edgar and Clyde maintained a friendship with **Joan Crawford**. She admitted to them that she'd once worked for Polly Adler, the New York madam, as a prostitute when she was down and out. She also admitted that during the same period, she had been a player in porno films (See Miss Crawford, above, in a still from one of her lesser-known movies.)

Clyde acquired copies of these films, and enjoyed watching them, especially one entitled *The Casting Couch*. MGM frantically tried to buy every available copy, although versions of it still exist today.

ised.

Wenner-Gren tantalized them by telling them he was expecting a very exciting guest who had just arrived at the airport. "He'll be a surprise. You gentlemen will know at once who he is."

Fifteen minutes later a waiter told Wenner-Gren that his guest had arrived and would be down in twenty minutes to join them for dinner.

All four men were having key lime pie for dessert when Errol Flynn came into the dining room. At that point in his career, a lot of the guests had not seen any of his movies yet, but J. Edgar and Clyde had been captivated by him when he'd starred in *Captain Blood*. J. Edgar had called the film "a banquet of homoeroticism from the first reel to the final reel." He'd also proclaimed that the new film star from Tasmania was "the most devastatingly handsome man I've ever laid eyes on."

Errol apologized that his plane had been late, and after shaking hands and flashing his brilliant smile, he sat down and immediately ordered a drink. In the flesh, Errol seemed even more alluring than he was on the screen, if that were possible. He told his fellow diners that he'd just completed a movie called *The Perfect Specimen*.

"Sounds like typecasting to me," J. Edgar said, as if flirting with him.

"Coming from the top G-Man in the country, I'll take that as a real compliment," Errol said.

Under Errol's gaze, J. Edgar seemed to be experiencing a meltdown, if Guy was to be believed when he related the incident years later.

After dinner and drinks—lots of drinks—J. Edgar noted that Errol was occupying the same presidential suite as Wenner-Gren.

Back in their own suite, J. Edgar speculated that the industrialist might be a homosexual. "Why else would he be shacked up with Flynn?"

An even more troubling question for J. Edgar was why Errol was in Nassau socializing with a rumored munitions tycoon supplying arms to Hitler?

Before retiring that night, J. Edgar told Clyde and Guy that he wanted the FBI to start files on both men.

The night was not over for J. Edgar, who later said he could not sleep. Jimmy Kirkwood didn't know if he should trust Guy's next revelation, suspecting it might be a cheap shot to sell his biography. But Guy claimed in all sincerity that J. Edgar that night wandered down by the pool area where the honor bar remained open until morning.

He later told Clyde and Guy that he saw a nude young man swimming at three o'clock in the morning. Seeing J. Edgar, the man emerged from the pool completely nude.

"Got a towel, sport?" a dripping Errol asked J. Edgar. When the Chief found a towel, Errol asked him, "Would you dry me off, sport?"

Later, J. Edgar admitted to Guy and Clyde that he was only too willing to perform this service. Errol produced an erection as he was being rubbed down. "Care to help me with this thing, sport?"

The next morning over breakfast, J. Edgar told Guy and Clyde that, "I showed him what a sword-swallower I am. I've had a lot of practice on you guys."

The allegation could be true or apocryphal. But Guy later swore that J. Edgar claimed that he'd performed fellatio on Errol by the pool.

If he did that, he did not develop a schoolgirl crush on Errol. When he returned to Washington, he ordered an ongoing investigation of both Errol and Wenner-Gren. The Chief began an almost two-decades-long obsession with Errol, his FBI file growing every month until it became voluminous.

In Nassau, The Bahamas, **Axel Wenner-Gren** *(photo above)* entertained Guy Hotell, J. Edgar, and Clyde, introducing them to the dashing new film star, Errol Flynn.

A Swede, Wenner-Gren was the richest man in the world, his personal fortune estimated at a billion dollars. At least some of that money came from the sale to Hitler of munitions and other strategic materials.

During the war, Wenner-Gren arranged with Hermann Göring for a neutral Sweden to allow passage across its borders of German munitions to war-torn Norway.

At dinner, he told the vacationing trio from the FBI, "I'm so rich, I'm above international law."

J. Edgar's suspicions about Errol and his Nazi connections were confirmed when the FBI received a report from Clyde that the film star had flown to Spain in 1937 with the Austrian-born Dr. Hermann Erben, who was rumored to be an espionage agent with strong links to Nazi Berlin.

Erben and Errol had been friends since meeting in 1933. Born in Vienna, Erben traveled the world, most often as a ship's doctor, and he was a suspected spy for the Nazis. Once he'd worked in Berlin for the film industry, at which time he'd doctored a young Greta Garbo and a young Marlene Dietrich.

A friendship between Erben and Errol was forged on April 14, in Salamaua, a town on the north shore of Papua New Guinea, when they sailed for a plantation on nearby Garowe Island. They became so close on the voyage that Errol was invited to move into Erben's cabin.

Writing in his 1959 autobiography, Errol said that "thanks to Erben and his lusty practical outlook on men and mice, sex, morals, and morons, I was seldom ever trapped again in this world between Skylla [he'd meant to write Scylla] and good clean living and the wicked Charybdis of a good solid hard-on."

On Garowe Island, Erben, an avid photographer, took shirtless pictures of Errol wearing a pair of white shorts. Later, Errol stripped off the shorts and posed nude for his friend. Years later these nudes fell into the hands of J. Edgar, who gave them an honored place in his album of celebrity frontals.

After a visit to Garowe island, the tall, handsome, and well-hung future film star, according to FBI reports, visited Hong Kong and Saigon with Erben. In Vietnam at a bordello, he con-tracted what he called "the pearl of great price" (actually gonorrhea).

In discussing his reports with J. Edgar and other agents, Clyde said, "Our friend is playing a very dangerous game with these Nazis. There's a war coming on. I think the FBI should stay on this guy's ass for the duration."

***

After a long battle with cancer, Annie Hoover died in 1938. She had been so long attached to her son that even after her death, she remained a hovering presence. Clyde told Ethel Merman, "I never could completely relax with Eddie when she was around. I felt he would never belong to me until she passed on."

J. Edgar had been at her side in the bedroom where she'd died. It was the same room where she'd given birth to him in 1895.

At the time of Annie's death, J. Edgar was forty-three years old, and he'd lived with her all his life. Often, however, he was out of town with Clyde at his side, but he would call her two or three times a day. Clyde once told Dorothy Lamour, "Annie's apron

While filming *Captain Blood* in 1935, **Errol Flynn** *(photo above)* was fre-quently visited by his boyhood friend from Sydney, Freddie McEvoy, a Nazi spy and legendary playboy sought out by wealthy women for his sexual prowess. Errol made frequent trips to Mexico City with Freddie, where they were entertained by Mexican fascists and Nazi spies. Errol and McEvoy often shared a suite at the Beverly Hills Hotel, where they made love to every-body from movie star Joan Bennett to tobacco heiress Doris Duke.

On several occasions, the American-born Nazi beauty Tara Marsh, who had lived in Berlin, was their guest. She later told Countess Dorothy di Frasso, "The difference between making love to Freddie and Errol as opposed to Hitler and Goebbels is the difference between washing dishes in a soup kitchen and experiencing seven fan-tastic orgasms, the greatest in your en-tire life, within a period of twenty-four hours."

strings extended all the way from Washington to La Jolla."

J. Edgar would never completely free himself from her overwhelming presence. Her memory, in his own words, "hung like a cloud over me." He often would say, "Annie would not approve of this," as if she were still around to judge whatever he was doing.

Bosom buddies in Nazi espionage and sin, Austria-born **Dr. Hermann Erben** *(left)* and **Errol Flynn** *(right)* shared a cabin when they sailed aboard the *Queen Mary* ocean liner in 1937.

After Errol filmed *Captain Blood,* Erben joined him in Hollywood. The doctor had bragged to Errol and his other Fascist friends that he'd planned the assassination of the Austrian Chancellor, Engelbert Dollfuss. That event occurred on July 25, 1934, when a member of the Nazi S.A., Oskar Planetta, fired a bullet into Dollfus' throat. Several members of the Gestapo, including Erben, watched the anti-Nazi Dollfuss suffer an agonizing and protracted death.

In the assassination's aftermath, Vienna police ransacked Erben's villa, finding drugs, munitions, forged passports, and obscene photographs, including those taken of Errol Flynn having sex with both women and teenage Austrian boys.

Dorothy Lamour once visited Annie when invited by Clyde and J. Edgar for a dinner at the director's home. "I visited with her alone in her bedroom, and she looked into my eyes," Dorothy said. "She told me that she didn't have much time left on this earth, and that she knew I would make a good wife for her Edgar. I just went along with it, playing the game. She told me her own marriage had been a sham, and her husband was a weakling. She claimed her entire life had been a disappointment except for the achievements of her son. To my astonishment, she admitted 'I'm living my life through him.'"

Once he'd buried Annie, J. Edgar no longer wanted to live in her house with all its memories. He purchased a one-story brick house at 4936 Thirtieth Place in the Rock Creek section of Washington, DC, where he would live until his death in 1972. Clyde continued to maintain a separate residence for appearance's sake. He urged J. Edgar to add a second floor.

Although a male-on-male love affair was taking place right in front of her eyes, Annie was always in denial about her son's homosexuality. She claimed that Clyde and her son were working late at night on official FBI business even if they were going to a night club or vacationing together.

When she heard that a neighbor's son, who was constantly bullied because of his effeminate manner, had committed suicide, she told J. Edgar, "It's better that way. If I had a son who was homosexual, I think I would kill him, then kill myself."

***

"When are you two lovebirds going to get married?" That was Franklin D. Roosevelt talking at the White House on the occasion of his fifty-eighth birthday celebration.

The President had long ago learned that J. Edgar was a homosexual, so he was addressing the FBI director tongue in cheek. At the gala, J. Edgar was escorting Lela Rogers to the birthday bash. She was the powerful stage mother who had propelled her dancing daughter, Ginger Rogers, into international stardom, especially in those RKO musicals with Fred Astaire.

Although Lela was forty-seven, only four years older than J. Edgar, she was an experienced, even adventurous woman of the world—or "one tough broad," as her friend Walter Winchell characterized her. On the dawn of World War I, she'd been one of the first ten female recruits into the previously all-male bastion of the U.S. Marine Corps, handling publicity issues. She soon became editor of *Leatherneck*, the magazine of the Corps.

Winchell also noted that she was "to the right of Attila the Hun in her political views and would become a founding member of the Motion Picture Alliance for the Preservation of American Ideals. J. Edgar admired her Right Wing political position, although not totally agreeing with her that the United States should bring back the guillotine of the French Revolution to handle its enemies on the far Left.

Lela and J. Edgar were frequently seen together, causing speculation that they might get married one day. Actually, he never had any intention of marrying her. Without any legal recognition, he was already "wed" to Clyde Tolson. J. Edgar admired and respected Lela, finding her a gutsy woman. He began seeing her very soon after the death of his mother, Annie Hoover. Friends of J. Edgar speculated that he was drawn to this strong-willed woman because he needed a mother substitute in his life.

Lela had been introduced to J. Edgar at Manhattan's Stork Club by their mutual friend, the model, Anita Colby. What reporters didn't write about was the fact that Clyde accompanied J. Edgar on all his "dates" with Lela. Harry Viner, a close friend and businessman, as a gesture of good will, always picked up the tabs for Clyde and J. Edgar at Harvey's Restaurant in Washington.

"Sometimes when she was in town, Lela would dine with the boys," Viner said. "I'd pay for her dinner, too. J. Edgar never took Lela back to her hotel. He gave her a little peck on the cheek and had one of his FBI agents drive her back to where she was staying. He and Clyde always remained be-

109

FBI agents referred to J. Edgar's mother, Annie, as **"Mother Hoover."** To her critics, she was known as "The Mother from Hell." She was smothering in her love for J. Edgar, overly possessive, domineering, and unnaturally attached to her son. She insisted he live with her and never leave home, and he gave in to her wishes. "I want to be alive on the day Eddie is named President of the United States," she told friends.

When author Philip Wylie was writing his attack on "Momism," *Generation of Vipers,* he told an interviewer that one of the women he was attacking for "motherly evil" was Annie Hoover.

A vicious homophobe, she always said that if she found out her son was a homosexual, she would shoot him and then commit suicide.

After a long bout with cancer, she died with her loyal son at her bedside. Clyde Tolson told Guy Hotell that, "It wasn't the cancer eating away at her body that killed her, but the cancer eating away at her soul."

hind to enjoy a brandy before disappearing into the night together. As I said, I know because I picked up the bill."

The press constantly asked Lela if she planned to marry J. Edgar. She had a pat answer: "That's up to him." The director's usual response was, "Lela Rogers is a fine and decent woman."

A first-rate raconteur, Lela amused J. Edgar with insider gossip about Hollywood and tales from her own life. She claimed that her mother, Saphrona Ball, a grocery store clerk, had to give birth to her on Christmas Day in 1891 in the family barn where, at the same time, she had to fend off a hungry bear.

One magazine reported that J. Edgar "is known as a man's man. Lela Rogers fits into that category. She acts more like a bull-headed father to her daughter, Ginger Rogers; has a shrewd head for business, iron nerves like an FBI sharpshooter, colossal self-assurance, indestructible intestinal fortitude, and a belief that all enemies of America should be wiped off the face of the earth. If she ever married J. Edgar—highly unlikely—she would definitely wear the pants in the family."

Over the years there have been published accounts of J. Edgar slipping off with Lela for illicit sexual trysts, but these appear to be inventions to give him credentials as a straight man. Ginger was extremely close to Lela and called her mother at least twice a day. She would have been aware if Lela had ever run off to such places as Florida with J. Edgar.

"The claims about my mother and Edgar are ridiculous," Ginger said after his death. "Lela was perfectly aware of Edgar's relationship with Clyde Tolson, and it posed no threat to her. From 1938 until 1955 they were close friends until they had some falling out over some silly little disagreement. My mother found Edgar a convenient friend to have. Edgar used both my mother and Dorothy Lamour to throw off the bloodhounds who claimed he was a homosexual. Was he a homosexual? Lela told me he definitely was. I don't know. I never hid under the bed of Edgar and Clyde. But back in Missouri where I was born, we had this saying: If it waddles like a duck, quacks like a duck, and looks like a duck, then it must be a duck."

Another friend of J. Edgar's, Cobina Wright, a society hostess and Hollywood gossip columnist, also became aware of the Hoover/Tolson affair. But she never wrote about it. Once, when queried, she said, "There are some things, such as my age, that must never appear in print." She was born in Oregon back in 1887.

Whenever Lela's beloved "Ginja" encountered any trouble in Hollywood or New York, Lela turned to J. Edgar for advice and help.

Ginger had married actor Lew Ayres on November 14, 1934. But by 1939 she was having other affairs, including one with Howard Hughes, and no longer slept with her husband, although she was still married to him. As Ginger later candidly confessed, "After a few years of marriage, I really wanted to experience the joys of being a single gal again."

In those books, such as *Did She or Didn't She?* by Mart Martin, Desi Arnaz always tops the list of her lovers, probably because his name begins with an "A."

Born in Cuba, he had fled to Miami following the 1933 revolution led by Fulgencio Batista. Ginger had been attracted to him in 1939 when he appeared on Broadway in the musical *Too Many Girls*. She'd gone backstage to congratulate him. In his pre-Lucille Ball

A girl's best friend is her mother," or so said **Ginger Rogers** *(right)* in a cuddly pose with her "tough-as-nails" stage mother, **Lela Rogers** *(left)*. Lela for years was a close friend of J. Edgar's, and he was delighted as rumors spread that they were going to get married. Some gossip columns even maintained that J. Edgar was slipping off to such places as Palm Beach for illicit sexual trysts with Lela.

After J. Edgar died, Ginger claimed that such reports were ridiculous. She believed that J. Edgar used her mother as a "beard" to cover up his love affair with Clyde Tolson.

days, he found the blonde beauty extremely attractive. An off-the-record affair ensued, since she was still a wedded wife.

Three months later she'd gone to Lela and told her, "I'm pregnant. The father is Desi Arnaz."

When Ayres saw that Ginger was pregnant, he reacted angrily since he knew he wasn't the father. He told her that he was going to divorce her and name Desi as co-respondent.

J. Edgar was never as close to **Ginger Rogers**, pictured above, as he was to her mother, Lela. But J. Edgar, much later in Ginger's career, gave her a sexual education, or so claimed Guy Hotell.

"Like many people in those days, Ginger wasn't really familiar with the concept of bisexuality. One day when Ginger and Lela visited J. Edgar and Clyde at the FBI, I was ordered to bring out a file on the bisexual activities of many of Ginger's former lovers. The FBI had documented homosexual affairs that her previous lovers had indulged in. The list included Desi Arnaz, Fred Astaire, Cary Grant, Howard Hughes, George Montgomery, David Niven, Jimmy Stewart, and Rudy Vallee. Ginger looked shocked."

"Surely not David and Jimmy," she said to J. Edgar. He rose from his chair and said, "Yes, Niven with Errol Flynn and Stewart with Henry Fonda."

Ginger was horrified knowing that such a scandal would sabotage her career in the moralistic 1930s. Flying to Washington with Ayres' threat, Lela pleaded with J. Edgar to "bail out my poor Ginja who has made a terrible mistake."

He assured her that he would look into the situation. She interpreted that to mean that he would provide the solution as he did to most troubles his friends encountered.

Lela's close friend, Anita Colby, was made aware of the Ginger Rogers/Desi Arnaz affair, and also of J. Edgar's involvement in it. She waited until both J. Edgar and Clyde had died before she gave some tantalizing details about the scandal, although it had been fodder for gossip in Hollywood for years.

J. Edgar and Clyde had heard many rumors about the handsome young actor, Lew Ayres, who had shot to fame in *All Quiet on the Western Front* where he played a young German soldier disillusioned by the realities of war. The anti-war sentiments expressed in this 1930 film, directed by Lewis Milestone, had such a profound effect on Ayres that he became a conscientious objector during WWII.

To silence Ayres and to blackmail him, FBI agents in Hollywood were ordered to investigate his private life, as he was rumored to be a bisexual. At this time, Ayres was enjoying wide popularity in America through his appearance in Dr. Kildare movies.

Almost immediately, the FBI learned that Ayres had engaged in a homosexual love affair with a very closeted gay, Spencer Tracy. When J. Edgar learned that, he called off the investigation.

"That's all we need," he said. "We don't need more evidence of other affairs. The thing with Tracy is dynamite enough. That Tracy! He's so masculine on the screen." He ordered Clyde to arrange a private meeting with Ayres. "Show him our evidence about his affair with Tracy. That will silence Dr. Kildare for good. He won't make any trouble for Ginger."

Just in case Desi Arnaz considered making trouble for Ginger and didn't cooperate by "keeping silent forever," J. Edgar ordered that he be investigated as well.

It was relatively easy following Desi's sexual escapades, as the Cuban entertainer usually left what Clyde called "a road map to what he was up to." After only three weeks, FBI agents concluded that TV's future Ricky Ricardo "would stuff his Cuban sausage into any hole he could find," as one agent so bluntly put it.

Since arriving on Broadway, Desi had quickly established himself as the intimate friend of every chorus girl. When he was cast in *Too Many Girls*, he claimed that "the title of this play suits me perfectly."

He freely admitted to some of his

The Hollywood gossip columnist **Cobina Wright** made the cover of *Life* magazine's February 17, 1941 issue. Throughout her career, she kept J. Edgar and Clyde informed of "all the stuff I couldn't print."

Cobina was aware of many scandals about J. Edgar, not all of them sexual. She learned that three of J. Edgar's books, including *Masters of Deceit*, had actually been written by FBI personnel at taxpayers' expense, even though he pocketed the royalties.

In 1950, when a respected attorney, Max Lowenthal, published a book, *The Federal Bureau of Investigation*, which contained criticisms of J. Edgar, Cobina noted the dozens of attacks Lowenthal suffered from pro-Hooverites.

About the only dirt J. Edgar's supporters found on Lowenthal was that he attended Harvard Law School "like many other Parlor Pinks, fellow-travelers, Communists, and convicted perjurers."

escapades such as the night he encountered Polly Adler, New York's most notorious madam. At Club 21, she headed for his table, clutching the early morning editions, each containing a rave review of *Too Many Girls*.

"Cuban!" she said in her baritone voice, "you are the biggest fucking hit in town." She grabbed him and kissed him.

That wasn't all. To celebrate, she had arranged for him to spend the night in her apartment, which was really a bordello. For his pleasure were one redhead, one blonde, and one brunette.

By the time Desi made curtain call at eight-thirty the following night, he said, "I was pooped out, petered out, and drained dry."

Of an even more embarrassing nature than patronizing prostitutes, it was discovered that Desi was also allowing the Broadway lyricist Lorenz Hart to fellate him. He was one of the co-authors of *Too Many Girls*. As Clyde and J. Edgar, along with three FBI agents agreed, Desi was not above "climbing the lavender ladder" to success on Broadway, as so many young men had done before him.

The second husband of **Ginger Rogers** *(left)* was **Lew Ayres** *(center),* with whom she'd co-starred in the 1933 film *Don't Bet on Love.* He is embracing **Lela Rogers** *(right)* his mother-in-law. Here they seem friendly enough, but both Ayres and Lela detested each other. The composer, George Gershwin, one of Ginger's many lovers, said, "She has a little love for a lot of people, but not a lot of love for anybody."

That included her handsome husband. As she told her mother, "I did not always make myself sexually available to Lew. I don't think a wife should be treated like cattle, always available for her husband to fuck her like some bull with a cow. I don't mean for a minute that Lew was a bull. He was not. With some of his male friends, he played the role of a cow, or so Hoover informed me one afternoon."

Clyde ordered agents to have Desi picked up after one of his performances on Broadway and brought to the Bureau's headquarters in Manhattan. There he was fingerprinted, stripped, searched, and photographed in the nude. There was some vague talk that his immigration papers had not been in order when he entered Florida.

Desi would later tell another one of his fellators, gay actor Cesar Romero, that "I was so dumb. I thought taking that nude photograph of me was the way police matters in America were handled. Years later I found out that Hoover and his buddy liked to collect nudes of celebrities, both men and women. Someone who saw the collection told me that I am number two in the album, following a nude picture of John Dillinger taken in the morgue. At least I'm sure I looked a bit livelier."

An agent lent Desi an FBI car, and he was told to drive Ginger to Montreal where the Bureau, under Clyde's direction, had arranged for her to have an abortion.

Desi was warned never to speak of the matter again.

If Desi thought that that was the last of J. Edgar in his life, he was mistaken.

***

Throughout the 1930s, and lasting until the eve of World War II, J. Edgar, assisted by his loyal Clyde, continued to pursue high-profile, headline-grabbing criminals in dramatic arrests or shootouts. In all cases, J. Edgar's role in these arrests was either exaggerated or else completely fictionalized.

Beating his drum at La Conga in Miami, **Desi Arnaz** attracted the attention of Lorez Hart, the popular Broadway composer. He was immediately attracted to the young Cuban. In New York, he had him cast in his first Broadway musical, *Too Many Girls*.

After an audition, Hart invited Arnaz to dinner, followed by an invitation to come to his apartment. A football uniform lay on his sofa. "You're supposed to play an eighteen-year-old football player, the best in Latin Amerca," Hart said. "Would you strip down and try on the uniform so I can see if you'll look right in the part?"

As Arnaz later confided to Cesar Romero, "I stripped down, but I never got a chance to try on that uniform."

One such case, avidly followed by millions, was the arrest of Louis (nicknamed "Lepke") Buchalter—a Jewish-American mobster who was the chief honcho of a hit squad notoriously known as "Murder, Inc."

At the time, J. Edgar, who wanted Lepke on Federal charges, was locked in a major battle with New York's attorney general, racket-busting Thomas Dewey. The race was on as to which law-enforcement officer would nab Lepke and the subsequent headlines.

Lepke is a name that will live in the saga of the FBI's arch criminals. At the age of twenty-two in 1919, he had already served two maximum security prison terms at Sing-Sing. After his second release, he went about taking control of the garment industry unions on the Lower East Side of Manhattan. He terrorized factory owners with paralyzing strikes and demands for weekly "alimony" payments.

In the early 1930s Lepke joined forces with Charles (Lucky) Luciano,

Benjamin (Bugsy) Siegel, and Meyer Lansky to form Murder, Inc., a deadly organization that specialized in fulfilling mob murder contracts. In that role, Lepke worked hand in glove with Albert ("the Mad Hatter," or "the Executioner") Anastasia in committing murders coast to coast. Their most famous murder was that of mob boss Dutch Schultz.

A $50,000 reward was offered for the capture of Lepke, who was living secretly in a modest room next door to police headquarters in Brooklyn.

In August of 1939, while at the Stork Club, Walter Winchell received an unexpected call. The gruff-talking man on the other end claimed he was a friend of Lepke, who was willing to surrender but only to J. Edgar. Whereas Dewey had threatened to seek the death penalty for Lepke if New York authorities captured him, on charges of murder and extortion. The FBI wanted him only for narcotics trafficking.

In an urgent call, Winchell reached J. Edgar in Iowa where he was attending the funeral of Clyde's father. He and Clyde immediately flew to New York to await the surrender of Lepke. "Here's our chance to upstage that shithead Dewey," J. Edgar told his agents.

During Winchell's famous Sunday night radio broadcast, J. Edgar and Clyde were sitting beside him in the studio. The broadcast that night shocked the nation. "Attention Public Enemy Number One, Louis (Lepke) Buchalter, I am authorized by John Edgar Hoover of the FBI to guarantee your safe delivery if you surrender to them."

Fifteen minutes after going off the air, another call came in for Winchell. It was from Lepke himself. "That was fine, Walter. I'll soon be seeing you and Hoover. I'll keep in touch."

Clyde and J. Edgar waited for three days in New York before another call came in. A gang member asked Winchell, "Lepke wants to know how many years he'll get if he turns himself over to the Feds."

The columnist didn't know and rushed over to the Waldorf-Astoria where he found J. Edgar and Clyde relaxing in their underwear.

"Dewey will send him to the chair for a good sizzle," J. Edgar told Winchell. "But for Federal charges, he's likely to get fourteen years."

Testing J. Edgar's limited patience, negotiations dragged on for three weeks in New York. Flashing anger, J. Edgar turned on Winchell, accusing him of being "New York's champ bullshitter." He charged that Winchell was just trying to increase readership of his column and more listeners to his radio show.

A bitterly wounded Winchell denied these charges before J. Edgar issued a threat. "If Lepke doesn't turn himself in, in forty-eight hours, I'll order him shot on sight."

Stung by J. Edgar's allegations, Winchell broadcast an appeal for Lepke to turn himself in at once. Finally, the call Winchell had been waiting for came in. It was from Lepke, who told him that "between ten-ten and ten-twenty on the night of August 24, 1939, I'll be waiting at the corner of Fifth Avenue and 28th Street."

J. Edgar later claimed that he stood on the lonely corner waiting to arrest Lepke. That was not true, as Clyde had ordered nearly two dozen FBI agents to stake out the area. In a separate vehicle, Winchell had picked up Lepke five blocks away and had driven him to J. Edgar's limousine where he waited, armed, in the back seat.

After two agents thoroughly searched Lepke, he was allowed into the rear of the limousine with Winchell. J. Edgar sat far in the corner of his seat, his face partially hidden behind a pair of dark sunglasses.

After Winchell introduced Lepke, he said, "Glad to meet you, Chief." He extended his hand but J. Edgar didn't shake it, but told him, "You did a smart thing turning yourself in like this."

En route to police headquarters, Lepke soon realized he'd been betrayed. During his final phone call to Winchell, he had been told that J. Edgar thought he'd get no more than ten years, of which he would probably serve only five if he got off for good behavior.

But in the back of the limo, J. Edgar stated his original judgment. "You're staring at least fourteen years in the face."

"You dirty double-crosser," Lepke charged. Taking his gun, J. Edgar whacked the murderer across the face, bloodying his nose. Actually, that was a deliberate action. He wanted it to appear that Lepke had put up a fight at the time of his arrest, and that J. Edgar had subdued him.

Still infuriated at the nearly month-long "horsing around" that J. Edgar felt Winchell had subjected him to, he decided to betray his friend, who wanted an exclusive on the story, which he well deserved. While Winchell was being questioned by the police, J. Edgar went into an adjoining office and called the Associated Press. Glorifying his own role, he gave reporters the complete story in time for them to make morning editions across the country.

Dewey wanted to interview Lepke about a number of murders, but J. Edgar refused to release him from Federal custody.

"I'm going to run for President of the United States," Dewey told him. "My first official duty will be to fire you."

"Perhaps," J. Edgar said, "unless I decide to seek the presidency for myself in 1940."

Tried on Federal charges, Lepke was sentenced to fourteen years at Leavenworth. He would not remain there. An authority higher than Dewey or J. Edgar intervened. Republican newspapers, including *The Chicago Tribune*, claimed that the FBI and FDR had made a deal with Lepke to keep him from revealing the Roosevelt's administration's link with Murder, Inc. Enraged, FDR ordered "that the son-of-a-bitch be turned over to Dewey."

Consequently, under the jurisdiction of the New York State judicial system, Lepke was tried and convicted for murder and sentenced to death in the electric chair at Sing-Sing, in Ossining, New York, on March 4, 1944.

His last words were, "I hope the God damn Nazis and Japs take over this fucking country, put a guillotine in front of the White House and hang that fucking Roosevelt, Hoover, and Dewey after publicly castrating each of the bastards."

In 1975, Tony Curtis revived the fame of the gangster when he starred in the movie *Lepke*. Curtis was intrigued with the fact that the only mobster ever sent to the electric chair was Jewish. The savage realism of the electric chair climax was horrifying to film-goers.

"I fell in love with Lepke when I played him in my movie," said Tony Curtis. He was referring to **Louis ("Lepke") Buchalter** *(above)*, the mobster who ran "Murder, Inc.," killing people designated with the kiss of death by the mob.

In 1975, Curtis starred in a "my comeback film," *Lepke,* playing the Brooklyn mob leader. "Even though Lepke had a compulsive viciousness, you come to love the character you're playing, even a killer," Curtis claimed.

Lepke was betrayed by J. Edgar Hoover, who misled him, signaling that he was going to get off with only five years served in a Federal prison. Instead, in 1944, at the age of forty-seven, Lepke was hauled kicking and screaming to the electric chair.

***

Was J. Edgar a closeted child molester?

If he ever had an obsession with a female, it was little Miss Shirley Temple herself. At the age of five, she'd become acclaimed as the most famous child on the planet. In her movies of the 1930s, she perked up the spirits of an America caught in the grip of a lingering Depression. Guarded like royalty, she made more money than the President of the United States.

J. Edgar took Clyde to see every one of the films of this chubby-cheeked moppet who delivered goody-goody lines on the screen, trying to wring forth every tear. Clyde preferred gangster movies, but sat patiently with J. Edgar through such froth as *The Little Colonel* (1935) and *Wee Willie Winkie* (1937).

J. Edgar personally requested that Shirley's studio send him a series of shorts called "Baby Burlesks," which Shirley made at the dawn of her career, spoofing notable movie stars of the time. Today these skits are a favorite of pedophiles. Viewed in a more enlightened era, the shorts are really soft-core child porn.

As one of the most celebrated personages in the world, Shirley was sought out not only by other movie stars but by politicians, each and every one of them wanting to have their pictures taken with Shirley because of her publicity value.

In 1935, she'd received an invitation to the White House from Franklin and Eleanor Roosevelt. Her mother, Gertrude Temple, told her daughter, "You are a Republican, Roosevelt a Democrat, but since he's the President we can't turn him down."

She recalled her meeting with FDR, who was disappointed that she didn't smile, as she was celebrated for her smile. "I'm sorry, Mr. President, but I've lost a front tooth, and I'm ashamed."

That day he invited her to his weekend country estate at Hyde Park. Once there, she saw Eleanor bending over an outdoor grill checking the burgers. Shirley had taken her slingshot to Hyde Park hoping to down a bird or two. Eleanor made such a tempting target, Shirley couldn't resist. She picked up a pebble and fired at the First Lady, scoring a bull's eye on her butt. Shirley concealed her weapon, and neither Eleanor nor the Secret Service knew who did it.

J. Edgar became involved in Shirley's life when she faced two daunting challenges—the first in 1936, another in 1938. Since she enjoyed world-wide fame as a moneymaker for Fox, she was often threatened with kidnapping. On a few occasions, psychos sent in death threats. Some of these threats were discarded by the Fox mail department, but occasionally one would emerge as a genuine threat to her safety.

A threat was received at Fox at the time Shirley and her parents, Gertrude and George, were driving up the northwest coast to Vancouver Island in Canada for their summer vacation. Fox sent them an urgent cable. According to the letter, if $25,000 were not dropped from an airplane on May 15, 1936 near Grant, Nebraska, Shirley would be assassinated.

Since interstate blackmail was a federal crime, George contacted the FBI. Shirley got to speak to J. Edgar for the first time. "I knew if anybody in America could save my life, it was J. Edgar Hoover himself," she later said.

He agreed to handle the case personally, assigning Clyde as the chief investigator for the FBI. By July 13, the G-Men found their man, a sixteen-year-old Nebraska farmhand who appeared in a cornfield at the time a small airplane dropped the money. Actually, the bag of "cash" was stuffed only with newspapers. When arrested, the teenager claimed he got the idea of threatening Shirley from having watched a movie about a ransom plot.

On hearing of the naïve boy's arrest, J. Edgar said, "Rodents like that should be exterminated."

Weeks later, yet another death threat arrived at Fox, this one also demanding "$25,000 or Shirley's life." This newer threat was mailed from Atlanta. Once again, J. Edgar assigned his trusted Clyde to the case.

Shirley's faith in the FBI and its G-Men was justified on September 15, 1936, when agents seized a boy who was also sixteen years old like the previous farm boy from Nebraska. This time he confessed he was inspired to threaten Shirley after watching a gangster film starring George Raft.

"I wanted the money to entertain my gal in style," he told FBI agents. On October 6, a Federal judge sentenced him to a reformatory school near Washington DC until he was twenty-one years old.

In gratitude, Shirley called J. Edgar to thank him personally "for saving my life" and to invite him to visit her when he came to California.

"My little sweetheart," J. Edgar told her, "that's an invitation I will accept."

As J. Edgar would learn, Shirley's troubles weren't over.

A blaring headline on August 22, 1938 shocked the young girl's millions of fans—IS SHIRLEY TEMPLE A COMMUNIST?

Representative Martin Dies, a right wing congressman from Texas, not the brightest bulb on the hill, was gathering testimony from workers in the movie colony about actors and directors accused of spreading communist propaganda.

In testimony before a congressional hearing, James B. Matthews, a former Communist Party official, had accused six actors of spreading communist propaganda. The actors, each a devout patriot, were Clark Gable, Robert Taylor, and James Cagney. The actresses included arch rivals Miriam Hopkins and Bette Davis. Shirley's name on the list came as a shock. She called J. Edgar asking him to investigate. "I'm not a communist," she told him. "I hate communists."

Both Hopkins and Davis were charged because they were members of the League of Women Shoppers, an alleged communist front organization. Actually, it was anything but. It had been formed as a group boycotting Japanese silk stockings in favor of cotton ones from American fields.

As J. Edgar and Clyde discovered, Shirley's link to a communist organization did not exist. Her signature had been among those included in an anniversary cable to the offices of *Ce Soir*, a daily newspaper published in France. Paula Walling, Shirley's former tutor in French and a Hollywood correspondent for *Ce Soir*, had included Shirley's name in the cable. Actually the newspaper was owned by a consortium of loyal French bankers, each a patriot.

J. Edgar personally cleared Shirley of any communist affiliation. However, Dies inserted in the *Congressional Record* a damning statement: "Shirley Temple unwittingly has served the purposes of the Communist Party. The testimony given before our committee has never been denied by the screen star herself." Privately Dies, to his supporters, accused J. Edgar of covering up the communist links of "this little lollipop-sucking Red jailbait gooey glob working to overthrow the American government."

Three years later, the *Los Angeles Times*, in a satirical article, wrote: "Shirley Temple was only ten years old when she was accused of spreading Communist propaganda. Since then she has become quite respectable."

On a vacation to California, J. Edgar, along with Clyde and seven other agents, wearing cream-colored snap-brim hats, went to visit Shirley. He had a gift for her, a Minox camera used by his G-Men to take clandestine photographs. She told him she would have preferred a tommy gun.

He jokingly asked her to sit on his lap so he could take her fingerprints.

She later recalled, "As laps go, his thighs were just fleshy enough, his knees held calmly together, and there was no bouncing or wiggling. One arm circled me protectively and mine curled around his neck as I rested my cheek against his. For me the whole FBI was romantically encapsulated in his strong, quiet presence."

"Are you married?" she asked.

"No, I've been living all my life with my mother until her recent death," he told her.

"Then I'll kiss you." A photographer was on hand to take a picture of her lips pressed tightly against Hoover's, the only known time he ever kissed a female on the lips. It was a kiss seen around the world, as newspapers in countries as varied as Russia and Brazil ran the photograph.

It was also the beginning of an unlikely "odd couple" friendship that would last a lifetime.

***

Early one morning as J. Edgar was rising from the bed where he'd spent the night with Clyde, a call came in from the White House. It was a secretary who informed him that President Franklin D. Roosevelt wanted to speak to him.

Pictured above, **Shirley Temple** is being escorted around FBI headquarters in Washington by **J. Edgar**, who even gave her an autograph. She rewarded him with a kiss, but only after he assured her that he was not married. "I will never get married," he informed her, "until you turn twenty-one years old."

"Oh, Mr. Hoover," she cooed.

Shirley never did marry J. Edgar, of course, but she did check with him when her second husband, Charles Black, proposed marriage. "Only after learning he was clean did I finally marry Charles. I should have had Mr. Hoover investigate my first husband, John Agar."

In 1948, Shirley had co-starred with Agar in *Fort Apache,* directed by John Ford and featuring such big names as John Wayne and Henry Fonda. J. Edgar and Clyde later learned that Fonda had walked into Ford's office one afternoon without knocking and found the director "with his tongue down Agar's throat."

Fearing trouble, J. Edgar nervously held the receiver.

"Hoover," came the familiar voice of FDR. He wasted no time in idle chit-chat. "A little birdie told me that you plan to seek my job in the 1940 elections, although I don't know which party you're affiliated with— no doubt, Republican. I've got some real bad news for you. Last night I met with Eleanor, a rare occasion for us, and we decided to put up a brave front of our marriage and stay in the White House for another term. Not only that, but I plan to run again in 1944, 1948, 1952, and 1956. When my last term is finished in 1960, I'll turn the field over to you. Perhaps even throw my support to you if some gangster hasn't shot you by then."

"Mr. President, you will have my complete support in all your campaigns, and I'd like to be your loyal chief through all the years."

"My God, my good man," FDR said. "Do I have any other choice? You know too much about Eleanor and me."

Later that day, J. Edgar told Clyde and some agents, "That was the most disappointing call of my life. I have always harbored a secret desire to run for president. I know I'm a popular hero in America. I'm even featured in G-Man comics. Yet it's an ill wind that doesn't blow somebody some good. At least with FDR still in the Oval Office, I'll be able to keep my job."

CHAPTER FIVE

The months leading up to World War II and the war itself provided the excuse J. Edgar needed to pry into the secrets of virtually anybody, to open closet doors previously locked tight, and to expand FBI files on everybody from Frank Sinatra to Albert Einstein.

The award-winning historian, Dr. David Eisenbach, wrote, "J. Edgar Hoover was a snoop even as a little boy growing up in Washington. At eleven years old, he meticulously recorded the daily activities of his neighbors and published a one-cent newsletter filled with gossip. He was not interested in just the facts, he collected every rumor, no matter how implausible."

"As a grown man in charge of the Bureau of Investigation, he continued to collect both facts and gossip on famous Americans," Eisenbach wrote. "Even innocent people were afraid of what their FBI files contained, and in Washington very few people were completely innocent. Not even FDR, the man who battled Adolf Hitler, could stop Hoover from spying on his wife." Dr. Eisenbach might have added—from spying on his wife or even on the President himself.

No friend of J. Edgar's, Robert H. Jackson became the United States Attorney General in 1940, resigning to become Associate Justice of the Supreme Court in 1941. This "county seat lawyer" would later become the Chief U.S. Prosecutor at the Nürnberg war trials.

At times, the Supreme Court weighed in on the topic of wiretapping. In a decision on March 15, 1940, Attorney General Jackson issued an order forbidding the FBI from indulging in wiretapping.

To the public, J. Edgar praised the decision: "I don't wish to head an agency of potential blackmailers." Privately, and perhaps with the tacit permission of FDR, he continued to use wiretapping as a device to ensnare criminals and Nazis, or else to spy on any American who crossed his path.

Finally he got the ban overturned because he persuaded FDR that wiretapping was necessary to root out Nazi spies and saboteurs within the U.S. government. At one point he asserted that his G-Men had overheard Nazis plotting to blow up the British ocean liner, the *Queen Mary*.

Later, Jackson told his staff, "I hate this man Hoover. I should have fired him. I'm supposed to be over him, but he has far more power than I do. He's got so much blackmail on Roosevelt that the President more or less has to give in to him."

Right before Jackson's death, he addressed the danger of having a national police force, "especially one controlled by a despot who follows the old Nazi handbook of going after perceived enemies."

On the eve of World War II, J. Edgar and Clyde turned their attentions to investigating Nazi infiltration into the United States. "They saw a spy around every corner," said Jackson. "Hoover was very suspicious of German Americans, especially the Bund, and he feared that if war came they would quickly be turned into enemy agents hell bent on sabotage."

Clyde had agents infiltrate the Bund [a highly organized pro-Nazi group of German sympathizers], and they succeeded in planting three spies in their midst. They provided detailed reports on the group's activities. However, the FBI director rejected a report from newspaper columnist Heywood Hale Broun, a member of the legendary Algonquin Round table, who claimed that there were already pro-Nazi storm troopers in America.

J. Edgar and Clyde were particularly concerned that communists would successfully persuade American labor unions to block production of munitions in an attempt to sabotage FDR's announced intention of turning the United States into an "arsenal of democracy."

In a decisive move, J. Edgar expanded the reach of both the FBI and his own personal power, fomenting alliances with Britain's MI-5 and Scotland Yard, and even with France's *Deuxième Bureau*. He also worked with the Office of Naval Intelligence.

Months before the United States entered the war, J. Edgar and his FBI launched a war against subversion, espionage, and sabotage. FDR instructed him he didn't need to waste the Bureau's power and money on Italians residing in the U.S. "They're nothing but opera singers anyway."

FDR did not like J. Edgar personally, and Eleanor "detested" him, but nonetheless, J. Edgar rose in power during the Roosevelt administration. FDR told his aides, "The nation needs a police chief in time of war. We not only have enemies abroad but at home. The land is filled with saboteurs."

Hugh S. Johnson, who had headed FDR's National Recovery Administration during the 1930s, defined the attacks on J. Edgar as "obscene." He also criticized "sucker columnists and sucker politicians who support sabotage against the United States."

Westbrook Pegler, an influential columnist for *The Washington Post*, who won the Pulitzer Prize for journalism in 1940, accused FBI agents of bugging rooms and taking clandestine pictures of Washington politicians, "even if they are man and wife." J. Edgar shot back that Pegler had "mental halitosis."

Ironically, J. Edgar seemed to have run out of domestic gangsters and "public enemies" to subdue. But as war seemed to inevitably descend over Europe, other enemies loomed on the horizon to justify his increased budget demands. He perceived ample opportunities to resurrect the menace of communism and there was, of course, Hitler and his Nazi sympathizers working subversively within America.

At a secret gathering for top FBI agents within J. Edgar's private home, the director warned that war in Europe could break out at any time. He also expressed his firm belief that "Roosevelt and Britain in time will see that the United States rushes in. There's no way that Britain can triumph over Hitler's armies without us sending troops to the rescue like we did in 1917."

At the meeting, he outlined a string of espionage proposals that would be secretly conducted by the FBI. "Saboteurs and enemy aliens will be overrunning this country. They are, in fact, already here. Our job is to catch the dirty bastards. Let the spying begin. My trusted man here, Mr. Tolson, will oversee the day-to-day operations."

***

Before he launched an all-out espionage war, J. Edgar decided he and Clyde needed a vacation in Florida. Guy Hotell was invited, too, mainly to handle the urgent calls flooding in from FBI headquarters in Washington. Many were of the crank nature, one woman in the Hamptons on Long Island having spotted Hitler shopping for frankfurters and Sauerkraut in the local market.

One call that came in for J. Edgar was from the wealthy Axel Wenner-Gren inviting him to Hog Island in The Bahamas where he was hosting the widely disgraced Duke of Windsor, the newly appointed governor of The Bahamas, along with his notorious Duchess.

After the death of King George V on January 20, 1936, the Duke had ascended the throne as King Edward VIII. At the time, he was having an affair with the still-married Wallis Warfield Simpson. When she was free to remarry, the King told Prime Minister Stanley Baldwin that he wanted to wed this recently divorced woman. Baldwin had informed him that as Supreme Governor of the Church of England, he could not marry a divorced woman. If he insisted and married the American divorcée, he would be forced to abdicate the throne.

That is exactly what the Duke did on December 11, 1936 when he addressed what was left of the British Empire. As he put it, "I have found it impossible to carry the heavy burden of responsibility and to discharge my duties as King as I would wish to do without the help and support of the woman I love."

Ever since his abdication, Clyde and J. Edgar had been compiling a dossier on the Duke and Duchess, including mounting evidence that both of them were bisexuals, and that each of them had suppressed a respective string of scandal, which may be one of the reasons they had opted to marry in the first place. But a more serious charge had surfaced: that each of them was a Nazi sympathizer.

They were viewed as security leaks. In FBI files designated as "International Espionage Behind Edward's Abdication," there appeared a memo. "Certain would-be State secrets were passed on to Edward, and when it was found that Joachim von Ribbentrop actually received the same information, immediately Stanley Baldwin was forced to accept that the leakage had been located. It was Edward himself. Even though King, he was actually spying on England."

By the time J. Edgar, Clyde, and Guy Hotell flew to Nassau, the director had read the most pertinent revelations in his file on the newly appointed governor of The Bahamas. J. Edgar was particularly interested in reports of the Duke's homosexual trysts. The most notorious revelations had occurred in the 1920s when the then Prince of Wales had gone on a tour of the British Empire with his celebrated cousin, Louis Mountbatten, during which they were said to have conducted a homosexual love affair.

In another report, the Prince was accused of commanding the dashingly handsome Lord Chaud Hamilton of the Grenadier Guards to strip naked in front of him and then sodomize him. It seemed that the Duke often liked to strip down himself except for a diaper. On several occasions, he was accused of commanding Admiral Sir Lionel Halsey to push him through the halls of his residence in a perambulator.

The deposed king of England, now the **Duke of Windsor**, is seen on his wedding day, June 3, 1937, with his bride, **the Duchess**, at the Château de Condé, in the Picardy region of northeastern France.

As early as May, 1937, the Duke demanded that his future wife be addressed as "Her Royal Highness." No one obeyed that command.

But these were considered minor perversions when stacked against a far more serious accusation that bordered on treason. Against the wishes of the British government, the Duke and Duchess of Windsor visited Nazi Germany in the wake of his abdication. In October of 1937 the royal couple was received by Adolf Hitler at his vacation retreat at Obersalzberg.

The Duke gave *der Führer* the Nazi salute. The FBI file claimed that the Duke endorsed Nazism, viewing it as a bulwark against the communist menace from the east. If he had stayed on the throne, he planned to pursue an alliance with Nazi Germany against the Soviet Union. Hitler himself is reported to have said, "The abdication of Edward VIII is a severe loss for us."

In Lisbon, after his abdication, the Duke had in an interview suggested that Britain could not win a war with Germany. Upon learning of this, Britain's new prime minister, Winston Churchill, decided such a defeatist attitude could not be tolerated from a former king. He was ordered (some say "banished") to the "backwater" of The Bahamas where he was named governor. "In that post he could do the least damage to the British war effort," Churchill said.

Arriving in Nassau, the Duke referred to The Bahamas as "a third-rate British colony." Within a week, the Duke and Duchess were seen aboard Axel Wenner-Gren's yacht, reaffirming J. Edgar's conviction that all three parties were entrenching their links to *Luftwaffecommander* Hermann Göring.

Joachim von Ribbentrop was Hitler's special adviser in foreign affairs and ambassador without portfolio.

During his affair with the Duchess, he sent her seventeen red roses every day. In return, she gave him sex and state secrets.

Before leaving Europe, the Duke, according to the FBI files, had received a personal letter from Hitler, promising that if the Duke would publicly support the establishment of a fascist Britain, the Führer would return him to the throne and make his Duchess the ruling queen. Both would have imperial power, as Hitler planned to dissolve Parliament and establish a Nazi Council to govern the U.K.

Many of these reports reached Roosevelt, who ordered the FBI to begin "covert surveillance of the Duke and Duchess." J. Edgar carried out these orders, even assigning eight agents to spy on the Windsors when they visited Palm Beach in April of 1941.

Before flying to Nassau, Clyde gave J. Edgar a secret communiqué from Lord Caldecote in London. In it, he claimed that British intelligence had learned that the Duchess had been the mistress of von Rippentrop when he had functioned as Germany's ambassador to Britain. She was said to have leaked highly confidential information to the diplomat, who then systematically forwarded it to Berlin.

At a dinner party on Hog Island, J. Edgar, Clyde, and Guy were astonished at how vain the Duke was and how self-involved and imperial the Duchess was. "I don't usually dine with the police," she said, insulting J. Edgar.

The Duke spent most of the dinner conversation talking about how he kept his waist so thin. He even stood up and modeled to the dinner table how fit and trim he was.

When a conch salad was served, he nibbled at the lettuce leaf encasing it. Even though Wenner-Gren had ordered his Bahamian chef to roast a suckling pig, the Duke insisted on a small cut of boiled grouper, no sauce, which he followed by eating an apple for dessert.

J. Edgar maneuvered the venue so that he could have some time to talk alone with the Duke, hoping to learn something of his plans. The Duke wasn't very revelatory. When J. Edgar mentioned Hitler, the Duke startled him by saying, "I don't think he's such a bad chap."

As part of his after-dinner entertainment, Wenner-Gren had hired a junkanoo band. It seemed that the Windsors liked to dance. The Duke preferred to dance the night away, doing the fox trot with Guy. Clyde invited the Duchess to be his partner while J. Edgar and Wenner-Gren looked on, each of them slightly bemused.

Later in the evening Guy showed the Duke the way to the bathroom, where the two men remained an inordinate amount of time. Guy later told J. Edgar and Clyde, "The Duke's a homosexual all right, and has the world's smallest dick. He is the active partner in fellatio and the passive partner in sodomy, because he doesn't have much to work with."

J. Edgar told Wenner-Gren, "Your new governor and his First Lady appear to be quite a horny couple." J. Edgar couldn't help noticing that when the Duchess was dancing with Clyde, she pressed her body into his.

"My dear fellow, you don't know the half of it," Wenner-Gren said. "In his new home, the Duke often wears only a diaper, or so a servant told me. He dirties that diaper and gets a wicked spanking from the Duchess."

"I'm sure England has had more perverted kings than the Duke," J. Edgar said.

Before J.Edgar's departure from Nassau, he arranged to have two agents stationed on the island of New Providence to feed him information about the exiled Duke and Duchess's every movement. In utter secrecy, Clyde also contacted that gossipy manservant at the Windsor's residence. For a hundred dollars a week, the Bahamian agreed to file a weekly report on everything going on in the royal household.

Back in Washington, J. Edgar sent FDR a confidential memo. "We have the Windsors under constant surveillance now that they're living in our part of the world. If the Duke tries to make a deal with the Nazis to use Bahamian ports as a base to launch an attack on Florida, we will be the first to know."

For years to come, the Duke and Duchess would remain on J. Edgar's radar screen even when they were no longer security threats. Guy later recalled, "Eddie found that their lifestyle made titillating reading late at night."

***

Flying back into Miami from Nassau, J. Edgar and Clyde found themselves involved in a round-up of "white slavers" in Florida. His G-Men had discovered a ring of men exploiting young boys and girls, forcing them into the sex trade. Many of the male and female prostitutes were from Cuba or the Dominican Republic. Young girls seeking a better life in the United States fell victim to pimps. There were incidents of gang rapes.

Even more shocking to G-Men was the discovery that some homeless young boys had been illegally brought into Florida to be auctioned off nude to pedophiles.

The FBI's handling of this white slave trade won J. Edgar praise from Walter Winchell in his column. Since their days at the Stork Club, J. Edgar's friendship with the journalist had chilled, but Winchell was still supplied with tips from Clyde in exchange for a favorable press.

Back in Washington, J. Edgar seemed reconciled to the fact that the Roosevelts might become permanent "squatters" within the White House. "I think the only way Roosevelt will leave that Oval Office is when the Grim Reaper knocks on his door."

He ordered Clyde to step up the FBI's investigation of Franklin and Eleanor, and especially those men in power around them. J. Edgar singled out Sumner Welles in particular. His influence on FDR seemed to be growing monthly, and the politician knew too much about J. Edgar after that embarrassing encounter at the male bordello in Havana.

The FBI director constantly referred to Welles as a "connoisseur of black meat." To Clyde and Guy, J. Edgar predicted, "We'll get enough on this guy to bring him down. As for FDR and his ugly squaw, they are the most scandalous couple ever to occupy the White House, including that whore Dolly Madison."

Since she outlived her husband by about seventeen years, Eleanor's FBI file came to occupy two overstuffed filing cabinets. Of that original file, only a meager 450 pages survive. After the death of the First Lady in

1962, J. Edgar ordered that most of her files be destroyed.

At private parties attended by fellow bigots, J. Edgar had learned to do an almost perfect imitation of Eleanor's high-pitched and rather prim voice. Playing only to a select group, including Clyde, he called his fifteen-minute presentation, "An Evening With the Nigger Lover in the White House." In his attempts at hilarity, J. Edgar, as Eleanor, would expound on the "divine pleasures of cunnilingus," a subject with which he utterly lacked familiarity.

He was always willing to read the most unflattering editorials about the First Lady, and Clyde collected caricatures of her in newsprint. One day Clyde opened a package from W.C. Fields, the comedian appearing in movies with Mae West. At first viewing, they appeared to be merely ugly pictures of the First Lady. But when turned upside down, they looked like anatomical close-ups of some hideous vagina.

J. Edgar sent Fields a letter thanking him for "this most wonderful gift—it made my day."

He encountered Eleanor at functions more frequently than he wanted to, and was once deeply offended while having lunch with Clyde at the Mayflower Hotel. Eleanor attempted to enter the dining room with two black women as her guests. The manager of the restaurant stepped up to her. "Mrs. Roosevelt, we will be honored to accommodate you. In fact, you might like to join Mr. J. Edgar Hoover at table. But I'm afraid we'll have to accommodate your colored guests in the kitchen."

The First Lady said, "If my friends aren't good enough to dine here, I'll invite them to lunch with me at the White House." As J. Edgar watched scornfully, she turned her back on the manager and headed back to her car, followed by the two black women.

As America moved toward war with Japan and Germany, J. Edgar had spies everywhere. He even heard how Eleanor referred to him, at one point calling him "a Fascist bastard," and on another occasion labeling him an "arrogant would-be Himmler."

Two years before her death, J. Edgar was still calling her "the most dangerous woman in America."

Clyde, with the help of three agents, conducted an extensive probe of Malvina ("Tommy") Thompson and Edith Helm, two of Eleanor's chief aides. He even sent agents to their hometowns, digging for dirt on the women. Eventually, news of that reached Eleanor. When she heard of this, she fired off a letter to J. Edgar accusing him of "using Gestapo methods to discredit loyal American citizens."

He didn't like Eleanor before she wrote that letter. But after he received it, the First Lady had made a dangerous enemy for life. He wrote her a letter of apology and said he would call off the investigation of Thompson and Helm. But he didn't agree to stop probing into her life.

During the war, "Eleanor Clubs" were launched, and J. Edgar observed them closely. These clubs were composed mainly of black domestic workers. He assumed they were planning subversive activities, although their main purpose seemed to be to eliminate segregation.

The clubs were named for Eleanor because of her opposition to segregation. In standing up for African Americans, she received numerous death threats, beginning in 1943 in the middle of the war. These threats were turned over to the FBI.

J. Edgar told Clyde "to file the fucking things. If the KKK gets rid of that old bitch, what a bright world it will be. Imagine a world without Hitler, Stalin, and Eleanor Roosevelt."

His "snoop squad" discovered that Eleanor maintained a secret apartment in New York's Greenwich Village "where she meets with communists and lesbians."

"That's why she refuses Secret Service protection," J. Edgar said. "To conceal her own dirty secrets."

The FBI learned that since 1921 Eleanor had maintained very intimate relationships with Elizabeth Read, an attorney, and Esther Lape, a publicist. Eleanor later recorded in her journal, "No form of love is to be despised."

As First Lady, she became even more intimate with another lesbian couple, Marion Dickerman, a liberal firecracker for the New York State Democratic Committee, and her lover, Nancy Cook, a carpenter and potter. Both were ardent feminists. FDR referred to them as "Eleanor's squaws." Alice Roosevelt Longworth, the outspoken and socially prominent daughter of Theodore Roosevelt, referred to them as female impersonators. Cook and Dickerman nicknamed Eleanor "Muddie."

At one point, so the FBI learned, FDR agreed to construct Val-Kil, a residence in an isolated position on his Hyde Park estate which he called "a shack for my wife's shemales." When at Hyde Park, Eleanor slept with the two women in a single bedroom.

In a remote section of Hyde Park, FDR's family estate north of New York City, **Val-Kil Cottage** was built as a retreat for Eleanor Roosevelt. She lived here with an entourage that FDR referred to as her "squaws." Members included political activist Marion Dickerman and Nancy Cook, a carpenter and potter.

FDR derided Val-Kil as "my wife's honeymoon cottage." He tolerated her lesbian liaisons because it freed him to pursue his own affairs.

When the President learned of that, he renamed Val-Kil "Honeymoon Cottage." All the furniture, silverware, and linen were inscribed with the women's combined initials of EMN.

In a letter that still survives, Eleanor wrote to Marion and Nancy: "I feel I'd like to go off with you and forget the rest of the world exists."

As First Lady, **Eleanor Roosevelt** *(left)* spent many cozy evenings at the White House with **Marion Dickerman** *(right)*, one of her closest friends and a woman who adored her, calling her "Muddie."

"Muddie" and Marion often talked of their plans to live together, after Muddie's involvement in the White House, with Marion's lover, Nancy Cook.

At Val-Kil Cottage, Marion became increasingly annoyed by the visits of Eleanor's lover, New York State trooper Earl Miller, and her relatives and grandchildren.

In a jealous mode, Marion eventually wrote Eleanor, "Nancy and I feel increasingly abandoned and rejected by your other interests."

J. Edgar and Clyde discovered that, in spite of her "matronly aunt" appearance, she had a fairly active sex life, and not just with state trooper Earl Miller or Lorena Hickok, the lesbian reporter whose beat was the White House.

Whether it was true or not, Clyde revealed to J. Edgar that during the previous four years, she had had sex with her black chauffeur, her own private doctor, David Gurewitsch, a colonel in the U.S. Army, and two rugged officials of the National Maritime Union, both of whom had served in the Navy. They were Joseph Curran, president of the National Maritime Union, and Frederick ("Blackie") Myers, his vice president.

In one bugging, the FBI had listened in to the two union men talking to each other. "Goddamn it, Blackie," one of them said, "My dick has made enough sacrifices to the ugly old bitch. Now is your time to service that flabby cunt!" To make matters even more provocative, Clyde discovered that one of the union men Eleanor had slept with was a member of the Communist Party.

Clyde and J. Edgar focused not on these passing liaisons Eleanor had indulged in, but on her infatuation with a studious young man, Joseph Lash, whom she'd met at a 1939 session of the House Un-American Activities Committee. The young man had just turned thirty but looked much younger.

"Bat Breath [J. Edgar's name for Leona Hickok] is a 100 percent lesbian, but it seems Eleanor likes a young dick every now and then," J. Edgar told Clyde and his agents.

An outspoken student radical—"a Com-

132

munist through and through," in J. Edgar's words—Lash remained under FBI surveillance for the duration of the war. The CIC (Counterintelligence Corps) also had Lash under surveillance. During the war, the CIC was known as the "FBI of the Army."

Clyde learned through his agent that Lash had visited "communist cells" on trips to Spain during its civil war and during a journey to Moscow, where he was a guest at the Kremlin.

Eleanor seemed mesmerized by Lash and adopted him as her *protégé*, inviting him to dine with her at the White House. She also contributed $1,000 toward his education.

Clyde's dossier on Lash grew and grew every passing month. In an illegal move evocative of Richard Nixon's Watergate break-in in the years to come, Clyde directed two agents to break into the headquarters of the American Youth Congress, of which Lash was an officer. The agents discovered intimate letters between Eleanor and Lash, which they photographed.

In the FBI's "bureauspeak," planting a bug or breaking into someone's home or office became known as "surreptitious entry" or a "black bag job." As Clyde said, "We stole only secrets—nothing of material value."

While Eleanor was romantically involved with Lash, she was still carrying on her lesbian affair with Hickok. One night at a Washington party, J. Edgar and Clyde encountered Eleanor's spiteful cousin, Alice Roosevelt Longworth.

J. Edgar quizzed her about Eleanor's relationship with Hickok. "Eleanor Roosevelt is a card-carrying lesbian," the outspoken Alice claimed. "When I was growing up, I didn't know what that meant.

One of **Eleanor Roosevelt's** "squaws," (as FDR described her), **Nancy Cook** *(left figure, above)* is characteristically pictured with a hammer in her hand, as she worked as a carpenter and furniture maker. Here, at Val-Kil cottage, she nails up a poster promoting FDR's National Recovery Administration (NRA).

In 1933, shortly after Eleanor and FDR moved in, the First Lady invited Nancy to the White House. Together, they redecorated, hanging pictures and eventually defining Lincoln's bedroom suite as Eleanor's sleeping quarters within the White House.

With Nancy's help, Eleanor moved her own pictures into the Lincoln Suite, with Nancy hammering nails into the walls to hang Roosevelt family photographs. Eleanor complained to Nancy that Lincoln's bed was too large for her, so the two women, aided by two White House staff members, placed a bed for the First Lady into a small adjoining dressing room.

Lorena Hickok, Eleanor's other lesbian lover, referred to Nancy and Marion as "self-absorbed snobs."

It seemed physically impossible, but now I know more about it. They're sleeping together in the White House and having sex."

Alice wasn't engaged in reckless gossip. Eleanor's steamy love letters to Hickock were published in a 1998 book *Empty Without You*. In one of the letters Hickok wrote: "I wish I could lie down beside you tonight and take you in my arms. I ache to hold you close. Most clearly, I remember your eyes, with a kind of teasing smile in them, and the feeling of that soft spot just northeast of the corner of your mouth against my lips."

After its reviewer read the book, *The New York Times* concluded that J. Edgar had been right—"it was a homosexual affair." *The Los Angeles Times* found that a same-sex involvement was "incontrovertible." The *Washington Post* labeled the Hickok/Roosevelt liaison "a lesbian love affair," as did *Newsweek*.

After the United States entered the war in December of 1941, the patriotic Lash signed up for enlistment in the Navy. Although he was physically in excellent shape, he was turned down, which he later reported to Eleanor. She immediately wrote Attorney General Francis Biddle demanding to know why Lash was rejected.

He sent the letter to J. Edgar, who personally wrote Eleanor that the FBI had not conducted any investigation of Lash, nor had it filed any unfavorable reports about him to the Navy.

Actually, J. Edgar himself had called the Secretary of the Navy, claiming that Lash was a security risk. Even so, the U.S. Army drafted him, and he was inducted. For his farewell party in New York, Eleanor hired a band and paid for the bottles of imported French champagne.

Unrelenting in tailing Lash, FBI agents learned that in the spring of 1943, he had been assigned to Army headquarters in Illinois. On March 5, Eleanor checked into Room 332 of the Urbana-Lincoln Hotel in Urbana, and Lash occupied No. 330. The two bedrooms had connecting French doors. Knowing their arrival details in advance, FBI agents had bugged the room. Later they reported that Eleanor and Lash stayed in their adjoining rooms for thirty-six hours, taking out only forty-five minutes during the evening for a quick dinner in the hotel dining room.

When Clyde and J. Edgar heard the recording at the FBI headquarters in Washington, both men determined that the First Lady and Lash were definitely engaged in sexual intercourse.

On the train back to Washington, Eleanor wrote one of her "Joe dearest" letters. In it, she said, "Separation between people who love each other makes the reunion always like a new discovery. Thanks for such a happy time. All my love, E.R."

In another brief note, Eleanor indicated she was aware that Lash would be occupying the same bedroom with Trude Pratt, a married woman. Instead of being jealous, she seemed to give the illicit union her blessing. She even placed a call to their hotel room to wish them well.

In a letter to Trude, Lash wrote that Eleanor had taken him shopping in Chicago, buying him garish underwear, "one pair with a tiger on the crotch."

After listening to details about Eleanor and Trude's respective sexual encounters with Lash, the young man's superior, Lt. P.F. Boyer, a colonel, contacted Army officers, claiming that Eleanor, Trude, and Lash were involved in a "gigantic conspiracy," although offering no evidence. He asked that FBI agents break into the bedroom where Trude, who had journeyed by train from Washington to Urbana, was

Student activists **Agnes Reynolds** *(left)* and **Joseph P. Lash,** as member of the American Student Union, were summoned before the House Un-American Activities Committee in 1939 to testify about his communist past.

That same year, he'd met Eleanor Roosevelt on a train, and he became her life-long friend and lover. Later, he would gain his greatest fame as her biographer.

staying with Lash and arrest him "for having intercourse with the much-married Mrs. Pratt." Boyer's superior ignored the request, although J. Edgar thought it would be a valid action to take. Following her divorce, Trude would eventually marry Lash.

On another occasion, J. Edgar and Clyde learned that Eleanor was meeting Lash at the Blackstone Hotel in Chicago. Once again, agents bugged their bedrooms. When J. Edgar and his agents heard the recording, he said, "Horse Face must really have been enjoying herself."

In the same recording, Eleanor admitted that, "I'm not in love with Franklin but I render him a labor of love by helping him carry out his hopes and dreams. I ask only that I be treated as an equal partner." She also shared similar feelings in a letter to Hickok. She wrote, "I'm a stranger to Franklin, and I don't want to be anything else. I realize he is a great man."

On the train back to Washington, Eleanor wrote lovingly to Lash relating how much she loved stroking him as he slept. Back at the White House, Eleanor continued to write Lash. In one letter, she said, "I feel so excited about the thought of hearing your voice. What will I do when I actually see you?" He wrote back, "You know exactly what will happen when I see you again."

In many of her letters, she claimed, "I need you so very much." In one letter, she said, "I want to hold you in my arms during these troubled times." She slept with his picture encased in a gold locket under her pillow.

George Burton was J. Edgar's chief liaison with the U.S. Army. He informed the FBI director that the recordings and letters between Lash and Eleanor had been turned over to FDR. After reviewing the material, FDR summoned general officers of Army Intelligence to the White House. He also summoned Eleanor to the Oval Office and confronted her with the evidence right in front of Army Intelligence.

According to Burton, Eleanor fought back, accusing her husband of adultery "many, many times." "It was a terrible argument between these two powerhouses," Burton said.

The next morning, FDR called officials of the Army Air Corps and directed them to have Lash shipped to a dangerous combat post in the South Pacific. "Perhaps a Jap bullet has Lash's name on it," the President said. He also ordered that Army agents directly involved in that intelligence gathering on Lash and Eleanor "also be sent to the South Pacific to confront the Japs."

Eleanor flew to San Francisco to tell Lash good-bye. As he sailed to the Pacific, she wrote to him, "The hard part of loving is that one has to learn so often to let go of those we love."

Even as late as 1960, while Eleanor was still alive, J. Edgar told an agent that she almost caused the FBI to fail in its mission to contain the menace of communism. "I think in her heart she wanted America to go Red."

In spite of the blackmail evidence J. Edgar had compiled on Eleanor, she continued to complain about "the Gestapo tactics of the FBI" throughout the war.

In a private meeting with FDR in the Oval Office, J. Edgar voiced his own complaints about the First Lady and her "left wing activities."

The President sighed. "Edgar, don't get too worked up. Feel some pity for me. I have to live with her. She's going through a change of life, and we'll just have to put up with it."

***

When FDR appointed Joseph P. Kennedy, the founding father of the political clan, ambassador to Great Britain in 1938, the President suggested he might be discreet to break off his affair with Gloria Swanson, who had been the leading vamp of the silent screen.

The brash Irishman told FDR, "but only if you set a good example and break off your affair with Missy."

He was referring to FDR's second most favored mistress, Marguerite LeHand. Perhaps unknown to FDR at the time, Ambassador Kennedy and Missy had previously been lovers. In Boston, Kennedy had introduced Missy to his oldest son, Joseph P. Kennedy Jr., and they'd enjoyed a two-week affair. She later wrote Shirley Bassingworth, a long-time friend, "Joe Jr. is far more masculine and a far better lover than dear ol' dad. He's also the handsomest devil of the Kennedy clan."

As Michael John Sullivan wrote in *Presidential Passions*, "Missy shared almost every aspect of the President's daily life. She swam with him, she dined with him, she shared his hobbies with him, and, most importantly of all, she had fun with him and made him laugh, something Eleanor was never able to do."

"She is the unofficial First Lady of the land," J. Edgar told Clyde and his agents. "If the American public only knew. Even on official motor trips, FDR sits with Missy, not Eleanor."

J. Edgar and Clyde had stationed a spy (name unknown) in the White House, who gave them daily bulletins on the comings and goings of Franklin and Eleanor. The two men were informed that Missy was the "Second Lady" of the White House, and that FDR had ordered the staff to treat her "in the same manner in which they would treat Mrs. Roosevelt."

During **Franklin D. Roosevelt**'s term in the White House, he had both a "Second Lady," **Marguerite (Missy) LeHand** *(center)*, and an official First Lady, **Eleanor** *(right)*.

"Missy" was the President's true love, and she performed all the "wifely" duties in the White House, even dispersing the allowances for the Roosevelt children.

She also had an active sex life with FDR. Even though disabled from polio and permanently confined to a wheelchair, he could still maintain an erection.

Although Eleanor had abandoned the bed of her husband in 1918 when she discovered his love letters to Lucy Mercer, she seemed to accept Missy as one of the family. In fact, with Missy in charge during her long and frequent absences, she felt no guilt about any abandonment of her husband.

Missy had long ago assumed the duties of a second wife to FDR, giving his sons and daughters their allowances, paying the personal bills for FDR, and even supervising Eleanor's travel budget, which was often exorbitant to tight-fisted Missy.

Around April of 1941, J. Edgar received a call from a doctor to learn news that hadn't even been passed on to FDR. The President's mistress had been diagnosed with a brain tumor. Two days later she suffered a stroke which left her incapacitated.

When FDR went to see her, he found her irrational. She demanded that he move into the hospital suite with her. He told her he couldn't and returned to the White House.

That night she set herself on fire. Eventually he had to send her back to her own family in Massachusetts. Under the watchful eye of her family she was cared for but never had any more contact with FDR. At the age of forty-six, she was hit by a cerebral embolism and died suddenly in the summer of 1944.

After FDR's death in 1945 in Warm Springs, Georgia, when his will was read, his family was shocked to learn that he'd left half of everything he owned to Missy, even though she'd died months before.

Marguerite LeHand *(above)*, whom FDR affectionately called "Missy," was the second greatest love of his life, after Lucy Mercer Rutherfurd.

When Eleanor Roosevelt was away somewhere else, Missy lived with the President in the White House, aboard a Florida houseboat, and in Warm Springs, Georgia, helping him recover from polio.

Franklin D. Roosevelt Jr. said that she was "as close to being a wife as my father ever had. For most of Dad's term of office, it was Missy who was actually the First Lady of the land, and the American public had not a clue."

Although Eleanor had gotten along with Missy, she could not abide Franklin's first mistress, Lucy Mercer, who had been his lover during World War I. In 1920, Lucy Mercer had married Winthrop Rutherfurd, an aging North Carolina socialite. After that, she was known as "Mrs. Rutherfurd."

Eleanor had assumed that her agreement with FDR from 1918 was still in effect. The President could see Missy at any time of the day or night, but he was forbidden to visit Lucy again. Even so, over the years, FDR continued to see her on infrequent occasions, sometimes at the South Carolina estate of Bernard Baruch.

Winthrop suffered a severe stroke in 1941, leaving him so incapacitated he didn't know if Lucy were in the house or not. With Missy dead, FDR began to slip Lucy in and out of the White House when Eleanor was away, perhaps visiting a coal mine in West Virginia or addressing the congregation of a black church in Georgia.

When Eleanor was in Washington, FDR sometimes ordered his Secret Service caravan to take him into the wilds of Virginia where he would have pre-arranged a meeting with Lucy. Standing by the road, she would get into the back of FDR's limousine, and the caravan would drive off.

A glass partition was curtained off to afford the pair some privacy from the chauffeur. Franklin D. Roosevelt Jr. later claimed that his father had continued to have sex with Lucy until the presidential election of 1944, when his health began to decline very seriously. Photographs taken of him at the time show him looking very haggard.

FDR Jr. recalled that once he'd walked into his father's library and caught Lucy massaging the President's crippled legs.

On a yacht trip on the Potomac in 1959, the young Roosevelt told John and Jacqueline Kennedy that, "I think the true love of dad's life was Mrs. Lucy Rutherfurd. Through World War II, she was his mistress."

"When Jack becomes president of the United States," Jackie said, "and he slips a mistress into the White House . . . well, let me put it this way. I'm an expert manicurist. Can you imagine Jack a soprano?"

***

J. Edgar spent a great deal of his time during the war years digging up dirt on the Roosevelts, but on many an embarrassing occasion he was confronted with his own misdeeds of yesterday. As revealed in Anthony Summers biography, *Official and Confidential: The Secret Life of J. Edgar Hoover*, Jimmy G.C. Corcoran emerged from J. Edgar's past. He had been one of his chief aides at the Bureau of Investigation back in the 1920s.

He had learned much about J. Edgar while working so intimately with him. Their paths had never crossed since he left the Bureau to become a highly paid lobbyist in Washington. After the United States entered WWII, it became illegal for lobbyists to solicit money from businessmen hoping to get congressional approval to set up munitions factories.

Using his powerful connections, Jimmy ignored the ban and sought help from some congressmen to open such a wartime factory. For his services, he was to be paid somewhere around $80,000.

Not being familiar with J. Edgar's link to Jimmy, Clyde carried out a sting operation. Along with two agents, he was going to burst into a hotel room at the Mayflower Hotel and catch Jimmy in the act of accepting the bribe.

The operation was carried out successfully and Jimmy was arrested. But before he could be hauled off to jail, he privately informed Clyde about blackmail evidence he had on J. Edgar.

In New Orleans around 1927, J. Edgar had been arrested in a men's room while fellating a teenage fisherman, son of a local shrimp boat owner.

There was a record of that arrest. Jimmy told Clyde he would go to the newspapers if the FBI carted him off to prison.

At the time, J. Edgar was dining at Harvey's. Leaving Jimmy in the custody of two agents, Clyde hurried to the restaurant, informing J. Edgar of Jimmy and his allegations.

"I thought that record was destroyed long ago," he told Clyde. "See to it that it is. Also let Jimmy go and get his $80,000. I'm sure he earned it. Give him my regards. Case closed."

Jimmy continued as a lobbyist until his death in a mysterious plane crash in 1956 off the coast of Spanish Wells in The Bahamas. There were rumors that the privately owned craft had been tampered with by an unknown mechanic before takeoff. In spite of suspicions, no investigation was ever launched. Jimmy's FBI file was destroyed upon his death. Throughout the war there were "other brush fires to put out," in J. Edgar words. "No man is better than Clyde," he said, "in squelching a story."

***

If J. Edgar had been alive in 1993 when Anthony Summers published this **controversial book** *(above)*, he would surely have had the author arrested.

Summers was the first investigative reporter to establish that the FBI director was a closet homosexual and a transvestite.

Other than Clyde, J. Edgar's most loyal agent in the FBI was Louis ("Nick the Greek") Nichols, a corn-fed football hunk from the Middle West who had a powerful, almost intimidating presence except when he was around "The Boss."

Nichols joined the bureau in 1934 around the time of the John Dillinger slaying and would remain there until 1957. His rise within the Bureau was so rapid that most his fellow agents assumed that J. Edgar had taken on another lover, although that does not appear to be the case.

By 1937, Nichols had become head of the Research Division but, in essence, he was the publicity director for the Bureau and the de facto second-in-command after Clyde. His main job seemed to involve the promotion of the "glory and accomplishments" of J. Edgar and to squelch all stories associated with the director's homosexuality.

Often Nichols was tipped off before a story was published, as he seemingly had spies everywhere. Such was the case in the early 1950s when reporter Jack Nelson investigated and wrote a feature for *The Los Angeles Times*, citing mounting evidence that J. Edgar was a homosexual.

Nichols was immediately dispatched to Los Angeles, where he met with the publisher of the newspaper, during which time he presented evidence that Nelson was a serious alcoholic and engaged in "degenerate sex" with underage girls. The article was dropped, but the publisher did not give in to Nichols' demand that Nelson be fired.

By some means not known, Nichols also prevented *American Mercury* from running an article in which J. Edgar was accused of perversion. Nichols met privately with Lawrence Spivak, the publisher. No notes remain of that meeting, so whatever intimidation Nichols used on Spivak remains a mystery. The feature story was dropped on the grounds that it had not been adequately investigated, although its contents seemed accurate, at least when judged by hindsight. It is believed that Nichols turned up damaging evidence about Spivak's private life.

Under J. Edgar's direction, Nichols drew up a list of publications with whom the FBI would cooperate and those whom it would not. On his hate list were *The New York Times* and *Time* magazine. J. Edgar despised *The Washington Post*, but liked *The Washington Star*.

Nichols even sent gifts to reporters on the *Star*, paid for by FBI funds. He liked stories about how J. Edgar rooted out "commie rats" in the U.S. government, and he attacked reporters critical of the FBI, calling them "journalist prostitutes who should be dealt with like a two-dollar Saturday night whore."

When *The Washington Post* wrote an unflattering story on J. Edgar, Nichols told him, "Had I known, I would have gone over there and hurled myself into the press machines to prevent its publication."

Nichols seemed determined to respond to J. Edgar's every whim. A workaholic, he was devoted to his job. To curry favor on the side, he gave J. Edgar expensive gifts that he could ill afford since he had to support a family.

He even named his son "J. Edgar," which caused Nichols to be ridiculed behind his back. The private joke in the Bureau was that if the child had been born a girl, "Nichols would have named it Clyde."

He wrote sycophantic letters to his boss, including one in 1935 when he claimed that "listening to your utterances is one of the greatest experiences of my life."

Not all allegations about J. Edgar's homosexuality came from the press. There were other leaks, as in a case in Kentucky, when T.C. Purdue, a carpenter, claimed that once in Miami J. Edgar had had sex with a seventeen-year-old boy, who was in FBI custody at the time. Purdue, who had once hired the boy as an apprentice carpenter in Georgia, went public about this brief liaison. Nichols was ready to have Purdue arrested for his statements until Guy privately admitted the story was true and that he was responsible for having set up the sexual tryst.

Learning that, Nichols switched to a cover-up mode. One doesn't know what he privately thought, but he spent at least his public life denying stories of the homosexuality of his boss, J. Edgar. To be confronted with this "disconnect" between the private and "official" versions of the story most have caused him much anxiety.

Nonetheless, Nichols ordered M.W. McFarlin, the chief of the FBI field office in Louisville, to track down Purdue and force him to sign an affidavit "confessing" that he had lied.

In his report to J. Edgar, McFarlin wrote: "You may be assured, Mr. Hoover, that so long as there is a Federal Bureau of Investigation, those associated with you will exert every means in their power to protect you from lying attacks and throw the lies down the throats of those who utter them." He called Purdue "a vile and dastardly bastard."

In Washington, when Nichols read that, he told Guy, "My God, this McFarlin can be as much of a sycophant as I am. I'd better watch out: he's after my job."

In 1936, having put in an extra forty hours week after week, Nichols collapsed from nervous exhaustion and was sent to the hospital in an FBI limousine. The next day, accompanied by Clyde, J. Edgar visited him in his private room. So exhausted he couldn't even get up to go to the bathroom, Nichols was being given a sponge bath by a male nurse.

After the nurse left, Nichols did not bother to cover his nudity with a sheet, perhaps deliberately putting on an exhibition for his boss.

J. Edgar told Nichols to rest here as long as he needed. When he and Clyde left the hospital after an hour, they headed for an FBI limousine. Guy was waiting in the back seat for them.

He heard J. Edgar and Clyde talking about Nichols. "Did you see the dick on our football hero?" J. Edgar asked. "There's meat for the poor there. Too bad he's straight."

***

When FDR ran for an unprecedented third presidential term in 1940, it was a tense time in the world. Britain and Germany were at war in the wake of the Nazi invasion of Poland in September of 1939. It seemed inevitable that America would be drawn into that conflict, but millions of Americans emphatically opposed the involvement of the United States.

Roosevelt ran on a ticket that insisted that he'd keep the country out of foreign wars. During a private meeting, J. Edgar asked, "What if we're attacked?" FDR shot back, "then that is no foreign war."

At the Democratic Convention of 1940, Henry A. Wallace was named as the vice presidential candidate to run on the ticket with FDR, seeking to win an unprecedented third term in office. From the cornfields of Iowa, the controversial Wallace had risen to become the President's Secretary of Agriculture during FDR's first two terms. He'd gained recognition when he'd devised the first "corn-hog ratio charts," indicating the probable course of the markets.

Many voters feared that FDR would not make it through a third term and focused more than the usual attention on Wallace. J. Edgar and Clyde ordered some of their agents to begin an investigation of him. Increasingly, they were hearing rumors that he was a card-carrying communist. Republicans started a smear campaign that he was actually an agent of the Kremlin.

The FBI uncovered what they viewed as an "unnatural relationship" between Wallace and Nicholas Roerich, a Russian *émigré*, painter, and theosophist. "God knows what the Red bastard has implanted in the brain of our upcoming vice president," J. Edgar told his agents.

During the 1930s, Wallace had written rather adoring letters to Roerich, calling him "Dear Guru" and signing them with a "G," meaning Galahad. To the Christian fundamentalists of that era, the intimate letters suggested that Wallace was a Buddhist, one of the people of "Northern Shambhalla," the Buddhist term for the Kingdom of Heaven. When confronted by these letters from his political enemies, Wallace called J. Edgar and asked him what to do. The answer was blunt: "Deny you ever wrote them."

When the GOP officials called him a liar and announced that they were going to release

Henry Wallace was Franklin D. Roosevelt's vice president throughout most of World War II, although he was dropped from the Democratic ticket in 1944 in favor of Harry S Truman. Before becoming Veep, Wallace had been FDR's Secretary of Agriculture. He is seen in his garden, above.

John Franklin Carter, writing in *The New Dealers* (1934), said, "Wallace is as earthy as the black loam of the corn belt, as gaunt and grim as a pioneer."

J. Edgar had a different opinion: "Wallace is a communist bastard working behind the scenes to overthrow the American government. I know for a fact that Wallace and Eleanor are planning to run for the office of President and Vice President in the 1948 elections. They plan to make the United States a colony of the Soviet Union."

them to the press, J. Edgar and Clyde summoned them to FBI headquarters.

Three members of the Republican National Committee were presented with Clyde's evidence that their candidate, Wendell Willkie, was engaged in an extramarital affair with Irita Van Doren, an editor in Manhattan. J. Edgar even presented photographic proof. Before the afternoon ended, he told Clyde, "We've got them at a Mexican stand-off."

The letters were not released, and news of the Willkie/Van Doren adultery was suppressed. FDR was guilty of having a mistress himself and was disturbed at Democrats publicizing his opponent's affair. "In my case," he told J. Edgar, "wouldn't it be like the kettle calling the pot black?"

J. Edgar and Clyde would keep their radar on Wallace not only throughout the war but until his death in 1965. More scandal was on the way.

Wendell Willkie *(above),* a Republican who opposed "the government waste and inefficiencies of the New Deal," ran against Franklin Roosevelt, who, in 1940, was seeking an unprecedented third term as President of the United States.

Both men had mistresses, so each could not expose the other's adultery for fear of retaliation. Even so, the anti-Roosevelt campaign of 1940 was venomous, the most vicious since Abraham Lincoln ran for president before the Civil War.

Much of the abuse centered on Eleanor herself. In secret, J. Edgar was only too willing to supply Willkie with damaging information about the First Lady.

***

Technically, since America was a neutral country, any agents working for British intelligence were spies and could be arrested as such. J. Edgar and Clyde set out to have their West Coast agents supply them with data on "the nefarious activities of both British and German spies in the film industry."

Clyde drew up a list of stars whom he felt deserved surveillance. Much of the data that J. Edgar's G-Men collected on these movie stars would be discredited in later years, but in the tense, paranoid, and suspicious months of 1940 and 1941, virtually anyone was suspect.

He divided film stars into three categories—those who were unabashedly pro-American; others who were working strictly for British interests, and the most dangerous of all, pro-Nazis, especially those plotting with Mexican Fascists with the promise that Hitler would cede them California and the Southwest when the Nazis won the war.

Caught up in the whirlwind of espionage and possible sabotage, J. Edgar and Clyde entered one of the busiest and most confused periods of their lives—i.e., the period between Britain's declaration of war against Germany in September of 1939 and America's entry into the war in December of 1941 after the Japanese attack on Pearl Harbor.

Even so, their fascination with Hollywood continued unabated. Both G-Men realized the power of film as propaganda. They were also aware that Hollywood was divided between pro-German and pro-British warring clans, each of which was frantically busy inserting propaganda into movies under production.

"Hollywood, as you know, is controlled by the Jews," J. Edgar told his agents. "You know those bastards will be trying to lure America into the war."

In their first reports, G-Men reported a disturbing discovery, claiming that some stars who outwardly presented a strong pro-American stance were secretly meeting and socializing with the pro-Hitler colony. Errol Flynn, whom J. Edgar and Clyde had met in The Bahamas, was singled out as a particularly dangerous individual.

Hedy Lamarr, the sultry MGM star, also attracted the attention of the FBI. Clyde and J. Edgar had first become aware of Hedy Kiesler (her original name) when they saw her first film, *Ecstasy*, in which she'd appeared nude. J. Edgar felt the film should have been labeled as pornographic and not allowed to be shown in the United States.

In the late summer of 1937, Hedy escaped from Austria and the bed of her ruthless and sadistic husband. Fritz Mandl, the wealthy munitions king who supplied arms to Hitler's Nazi soldiers. An FBI informant in Vienna claimed that unknown to the Führer, Mandl was masquerading as an Aryan, concealing his Jewish heritage. So was Hedy, who was actually the daughter of a Jewish banker in Vienna.

In the most startling part of the report, J. Edgar and Clyde read that Mandl, to win favor with the Fascist dictators, had actually "pimped" his beautiful wife to both Benito Mussolini and Hitler himself.

In the early autumn of 1937, Hedy arrived in the United States, heading for Los Angeles where she'd been granted a contract by Louis B. Mayer of MGM. She told immigration officials that she "detested" Hitler, although they found a gold cigarette case with a diamond-studded Swastika embedded in its center. She admitted that it was a gift from Hitler, and she was only bringing it into the United States to hock in case she ran out of cash. J. Edgar and Clyde were suspicious of her claims, fearing she might be a "plant" taking her orders directly from Berlin.

When interviewed by the FBI, Hedy claimed that Hitler was "posturing" and Mussolini "pompous," but provided no other details.

On the West Coast, the FBI continued to monitor her nocturnal adventures, discovering that she was a bisexual. One report claimed she was "oversexed," and noted that she was carrying on affairs with Charles Boyer, her co-star in *Algiers* (1938) and Clark Gable, her co-star in *Boom Town* (1940). Hedy was also involved with another one of her *Boom Town* co-stars, Claudette Colbert, with whom she was engaged in a lesbian affair. She also had flings with Charlie Chaplin, Marlene Dietrich, and Joan Crawford. "That's one busy Kraut," J. Edgar told his agents.

During all these months of investigation, agents did not discover one piece of hard evidence that she was reporting sensitive information to the Nazis. On the eve of the Japanese attack on Pearl Harbor, Hedy redeemed herself. She came up with an idea for a radio-directed torpedo guidance system that was later adapted to modern warfare and remains today an essential part of cellphone technology. Of course, Hedy may have stolen the

idea from endless hours sitting with Mandl and his cronies as they discussed Hitler's plan for wireless communication. She gave her patent idea to the U.S. government for use in the war effort. The device later proved invaluable to the U.S. Navy in its submarine warfare with Germany. Hedy later claimed, "I helped the Americans win World War II by my device."

During the war, the Treasury Department called J. Edgar to inform him that Hedy had volunteered to sell war bonds. "Is she pro-American or a secret Kraut?"

"She's clean," J. Edgar said, "but watch her on tours. She'll fuck anything that moves."

Closing the file on Hedy, J. Edgar told Clyde and his agents, "We've wasted time on Hitler's mistress. We must turn to a far more dangerous and diabolical Kraut. I think she's a double agent."

He was referring, of course, to Marlene Dietrich.

So far as it is known, the glamorous and sultry Austrian beauty, **Hedy Lamarr** may have been one of only two woman in history who went to bed with both Adolf Hitler and John F. Kennedy.

A nude scene she filmed in *Ecstasy,* released in 1933, propelled her into international stardom. After she fled across Europe to Hollywood, Louis B. Mayer was stunned by her beauty.

In time, it was learned that she was far more than merely Delilah to Victor Mature's Samson. She fulfilled an unexpected role as the inventor of a technological breakthrough that has become a vital part of everything from military weapons to cellphones.

***

Alfred Duff Cooper, Minister of Information for the British government, found it vital to set up a spy network in the United States during that 27-month period between Britain's declaration of war and the American entrance into the conflict in the wake of the Japanese attack on Pearl Harbor.

He singled out producer Alexander Korda to be the front man for British espionage in America, instructing him to set up offices in Washington, Los Angeles, and New York. These offices, or so it was hoped, would ostensibly be conducting film industry business but would, in essence, be a camouflage for British agents working in the still neutral United States. "A movie studio would be an ideal cover to mask intelligence operations," Winston Churchill told Korda, who was to become the chief British spy in the United States.

From the very beginning, J. Edgar and Clyde had been aware of these operations. Clyde had even planted informants in each of Korda's offices. J. Edgar in time accumulated enough information on this illegal operation that he could have had Korda arrested, but FDR refused to give him permission. "One day very soon, or so I fear, we'll be fighting side by side with our British friends."

Clyde at FBI headquarters received a report that Korda told British intelligence he was "prepared to take all risks, even the possibility of assassination." J. Edgar was particularly disturbed with one of Korda's

Hedy Lamarr's first husband was **Fritz Mandl** *(above)*, with whom she was trapped in a loveless marriage.

An Austrian munitions czar, he was ambitious and ruthless, a friend of Mussolini who sold armaments to Hitler, yet concealed his own Jewish heritage. He didn't see anything wrong in pimping his beautiful young wife to Fascist dictators if it served his advancement as an "honorary Aryan."

Hedy later recalled, "At first I felt like Cinderella, trapped in furs, designer gowns, and jewels, but I was soon locked away, where I had to wait behind seven locked doors for him. He was a sadist. The servants could hear my screams."

reports to London which the FBI had intercepted. Korda asserted that "even Hoover doesn't know the full extent of German foreign agents operating in the U.S."

Clyde presented J. Edgar with another message that Duff Cooper had sent to Korda. "At all costs," Duff Cooper instructed him, "avoid the scrutiny of the FBI and the U.S. Senate." After reading that, J. Edgar told Clyde and some top agents, "We know every move these limeys make."

Lord Lothian, the British ambassador to Washington, called for British movie stars and directors working in Hollywood to remain there to counter anti-British propaganda put out by German interests in the film industry.

The ambassador instructed UK citizens to endorse an aggressive and ongoing roster of charity events, both as a means of raising money for the British war effort and as a means, once again, to offset Nazi propaganda. It was not just the Germans who worked against British interests. First- and second-generation Irish Americans had long held a loathing of Great Britain, and some had even publicly claimed that they'd like to see Hitler win the war.

Before departing for America, Korda spent countless hours being briefed by the SOE, and the men of MI-6, the British Intelligence Service. Established in 1940, the "Special Operations Executive" (SOE) was known as "Churchill's Secret Army." The prime minister called SOE "The Ministry of Ungentlemanly Warfare."

At its peak, the SOE employed some 13,000 recruits, conducting more than a million worldwide secret operations. Actually, they weren't that secret from the FBI. Almost from the day it was established, J. Edgar had his "moles" entrenched within both MI-6 and the SOE reporting on British espionage. As far as it is known, not one of these double agents was ever exposed.

Recruited as a British agent in 1933, Korda became the most important British spy working in the United States. The information the producer collected during the period when England virtually stood alone against Nazi Germany was later viewed as "vital" to British intelligence.

J. Edgar and Clyde were particularly intrigued at the number of homosexuals SOE recruited, even though they were not allowed to join the armed services. Bad conduct records or even criminal files in the armed forces were not a strike against a potential SOE employee.

The hiring of homosexuals actually planted an idea in J. Edgar's head, which he secretly submitted to Clyde and Guy. Guy later claimed that "Eddie came to realize that a homosexual might be useful in some cases, even that of sleeping with the enemy to gain information, a sort of male Mata Hari type for the Second World War."

J. Edgar's official policy remained firm—"no homosexuals in the FBI"—but behind the scenes, Clyde began to privately recruit them, especially closeted homosexuals who had the protective net of a marriage, even children, to conceal their true sexual preferences.

The policy paid off right from the beginning. One of his well-built, attractive homosexual agents managed to get a leading official at the Russian Embassy to fall in love with him. Over pillow talk, the gay G-Man learned many secrets, including that Josef Stalin feared that Hitler would betray him and launch an invasion of the Soviet Union. This information, of course, proved absolutely true.

A homosexual G-Man, through his sexual involvement with a member of the Argentine Embassy, eventually met a valuable contact in the form of an ambitious young man named Juan Peron. A strongly built young boxer and champion fencer of the army, Peron had ambitions to become president of Argentina.

As a military attaché, he had traveled to Europe in 1938 and had been impressed with the rise of the Fascists in Italy and their counterpart, Hitler's Nazis, in Germany. J. Edgar and Clyde learned that he was a secret member of a military group that was plotting the violent collapse of the civilian government of Argentina.

Peron had secretly communicated with Josef Goebbels in Berlin, promising him that when and if his *junta* seized power, he would allow the Nazis to use Buenos Aires as their official headquarters in South America. "Our city can become the Berlin of South America," the future Argentine dictator promised the Nazis.

When J. Edgar and Clyde learned that at least a dozen major officials in Washington's Mexican Embassy were homosexuals, and that they had a preference for blond-haired men, Clyde ordered that six of his men with dark hair dye their hair blond to seduce these Mexicans. Valuable information was learned, especially about Mexico's contacts with Berlin, and even which American movie stars, during their holidays south of the border, were getting involved with Fascists.

Consequently, several Hollywood stars, especially Errol Flynn and Tyrone Power, came under heavy scrutiny.

After only two months of hiring homosexuals as agents, J. Edgar pronounced his new hiring practice a success. He would continue secretly to employ homosexuals throughout his final decades in office. "After all," he asked Clyde and Guy, "how many straight men will volunteer to take it up the ass for their country?"

***

Korda set about compiling a list of movie industry stars or players suspected of having Nazi links. Within a day, the list reached Clyde's office. J. Edgar read it that night.

Wallace Beery topped the list, followed by Victor McLaglen, Errol Flynn, Gary Cooper, and Walt Disney. J. Edgar also suspected producer Winfield Sheehan, former head of 20th Century Fox, of having Nazi sympathies. He interpreted his relationship with George Gyssling as "highly suspicious." Gyssling was the German Consul General for the Los Angeles area, and his headquarters was the center of Nazi activities on the West Coast.

After an intensive investigation that, obviously, was separate from anything Korda supplied, J. Edgar and Clyde concluded that two famous British stars, Vivien Leigh and Laurence Olivier, were undeclared and unofficial British spies working within the California film colony. As such, he could have them arrested as unregistered foreign agents, even though Britain was a secret ally, at least with the Roosevelt administration.

Unknown to the Oliviers, J. Edgar's G-Men had them trailed, learning that they had volunteered their services to British intelligence when England had declared war on Germany after its attack on Poland.

Risking imprisonment and even assassination by the Nazis, Olivier became an agent for the SOE in 1940, working out of Los Angeles. Vivien would join later. Korda was later quoted as saying, "If Nazi agents knew the full extent of the activities of Vivien and Larry, I'm sure they would have gone after them. Josef Goebbels would have seen to that."

"I was a regular Mata Hari," Vivien told director George Cukor after the war.

The FBI also launched an investigation of Barbara Hutton, the Woolworth heiress. Her code name was "Red Rose." Because she was about to marry the British star, Cary Grant, he too came under suspicion, even though financially they were doing more for the British war effort than any other couple in Hollywood.

Grant worked with

One of their era's "fun couples," the Argentine dictator, **Juan Peron**, and his powerful wife, **Eva Peron**, a former prostitute, ruled their country with an iron fist.

Suspecting from the beginning that they were secret Nazis, J. Edgar had them under surveillance during the duration of their power over their volatile country. J. Edgar learned that Juan Peron hoped to transform Buenos Aires into the Nazi capital of South America, in the mistaken belief that the Fascists would triumph over the Allies.

As for Evita, J. Edgar concluded that, "She wants to look like Lana Turner and fuck Tyrone Power and Errol Flynn."

William Stephenson, who was head of British Security, and no friend of J. Edgar, although he had the ear of both FDR and Churchill.

After private dinners with Hutton and Grant, Vivien and her husband, Olivier, concluded that Hutton and Grant were under suspicion only because of their friendship with the notorious Countess Dorothy di Frasso, who had been the lover of Gary Cooper. The FBI had accumulated a thick file on her, noting that she was a *confidante* of Benito Mussolini and had even entertained Field Marshal Hermann Göring at her villa near Rome.

Hutton herself continued to entertain Nazi sympathizers, even though there was no evidence the FBI found to label her a spy. One agent reported that she was "incredibly naïve about world politics." Many of the FBI reports on the heiress were based on false information. Even though she planned to marry Grant in 1942, she was said to be enamored of a certain "German baron with pro-Hitler leanings," according to her dossier.

The accusation was false and a reference to the dashing Baron von Gramm, a national tennis hero in Germany. Although he was accused in the West of being a Nazi, it was later discovered that he had expressed anti-Hitler views and had been arrested and imprisoned in March of 1938 for having a homosexual relationship with another male member of the German Davis Cup Team.

Vivien and Olivier soon appeared on the guest list of the Countess di Frasso. The FBI obtained a copy of their report to Korda, in which Olivier claimed that di Frasso was definitely on the side of Mussolini and hoped that he would emerge triumphant from the ashes of WWII. At a dinner party, she said she "detested" Churchill, and asserted that Britain was fighting the war only to hold onto its empire.

The Countess invited Vivien and Olivier for a vacation at her hacienda in Mexico City where Hutton and Grant would later visit as part of their honeymoon. But the invitation was declined because Korda had warned Vivien and Larry that

Unthinkable but true: Heathcliff (**Laurence Olivier**) and Scarlett O'Hara (**Vivien Leigh**) operated as British spies.

Risking assassination by the Nazis, or at the very least imprisonment as foreign agents operating on American soil, Olivier became an agent of the "Special Operations Executive (SOE)" in 1940, and Vivien joined Korda's espionage coterie shortly thereafter.

"I was a regular Mata Hari," she asserted at war's end.

"the Nazis are on to you two. There's a plot to kill both of you."

On the eve of America's declaration of war against the Axis, Mexico City was like Lisbon in Europe, a haven for international spy rings, smugglers, and black market operators. On instructions from "The Boss," Clyde posted several agents there.

Some insiders in Hollywood thought the Countess di Frasso had ended her romance with Gary Cooper, but G-Men in Mexico reported that over a period of six months he'd made three visits to her villa. J. Edgar suspected that Cooper was supplying information to the countess, which she would then turn over to Nazi agents in Mexico City.

"Put that Montana Mule under surveillance," J. Edgar ordered Clyde.

The reference to the "mule" derived from Cooper's legendary endowment. J. Edgar had obtained a nude picture of him snapped while he was shaving in his dressing room. He placed it alongside his nude of Errol Flynn.

"Cash and Cary," as **Cary Grant** and Woolworth heiress **Barbara Hutton** were called on their wedding day, July 8, 1942.

Despite that label, Grant did not hustle money from his wife, the second-richest woman in the world after tobacco heiress Doris Duke.

Alexander Korda later admitted that Grant was a true British patriot and that Hutton contributed greatly to the British War Relief.

J. Edgar, however, sniped that "they numbered many Nazi sympathizers among their degenerate friends."

***

Cooper had long been under FBI scrutiny, ever since both Clyde and J. Edgar had become fascinated by his conquests of both men and women. As the gay director, George Cukor said, "Cooper found out pretty quick that he could do two things well—ride a horse and fuck."

Clyde had chronicled a string of affairs Cooper had had in Hollywood, including a long-term relationship with the tobacco heir Anderson Lawler. His list of conquests was impressive: the photographer Cecil Beaton, Tallulah Bankhead, Claudette Colbert, Marlene Dietrich, Clara Bow, and director Edmund Goulding, who was said to have "worshipped" him twice a day. The list went on and on—Randolph Scott, Carole Lombard, Merle Oberon, Lupe Velez, Mae West, and Cary Grant himself.

In Washington, J. Edgar learned that Cooper was a close friend of Wendell Willkie, and that the actor had shared women with the candidate trying to unseat

152

FDR. No one ever accused Cooper of being a liberal. He'd voted twice for Calvin Coolidge and for Herbert Hoover.

In their investigation of Cooper, FBI agents learned he was a founding member of the "Hollywood Hussars." Funded by press baron William Randolph Hearst, it was a reactionary group with Fascist sympathies. Actors Victor McLaghlen and Ward Bond were also charter members. Before the war, this right wing club paraded around at social events in fancy uniforms and practiced military drills. Louis B. Mayer referred to them as "Nazi Jew haters."

Clyde booked a spy to attend their secret meetings. The conclusion of the agent was that these men, including Cooper, ran the para-military organization not for international espionage. The members wanted to "protect" the United States from the New Deal and the "red menace." The report submitted to Clyde concluded, "They are not a stalking horse for Nazism. They are just corn-fed American Fascists who would probably welcome a dictator instead of a U.S. president."

Of all the Hussars, Cooper was singled out for special attention as he became the most suspicious, especially when it was learned that he dined weekly with the German Consulate General in Los Angeles.

What really put Clyde on his trail was when Cooper visited Nazi Germany in 1938 when it was not politically correct to do so. Later, when

The press called them "The Cowboy and the Countess," referring to **Countess Dorothy di Frasso** (born Dorothy Taylor in Watertown, New York, in 1888) and **Gary Cooper**.

The frequently widowed Dorothy was struck by "love at first sight" when she first met Coop in Italy. As described by Cooper's biographer, Jane Ellen Wayne, "His clothes were rumpled and hung like a burlap sack. There in the opulence of her palace stood a timid, half-smiling, pathetically thin Adonis. Dorothy promptly fell in love and set out to turn him into her well-dressed and debonair escort. She footed the bill, and he had his pick of sports cars and limousines, which were often seen parked in front of exclusive jewelry stores while the Countess chose the proper gold cuff links, watches, and tie tacks."

After her first sexual union with Coop, she confided to heiress Barbara Hutton, "I didn't known American men came in that size."

153

America went to war against Germany, Cooper was extensively questioned by Clyde himself in Los Angeles. The actor claimed that the trip had actually been ordered by FDR.

Cooper's father-in-law, Paul Shields, stepfather to Cooper's wife at the time (Veronica Balfe), was a liberal and an economic adviser to FDR. The President sent him to Berlin that year to investigate the German war machine and its financing. He was actually a spy for the Americans.

Cooper, J. Edgar learned, was sent along as "bait," because Josef Goebbels was his movie fan and had seen all his films. In fact, Goebbels rhapsodized so frequently about Cooper that many in the Berlin film colony suspected that he had a crush on the American actor.

In the wake of the Japanese attack on Pearl Harbor in December of 1941, Cooper assured the FBI that he was a patriotic American and had abandoned the isolationist view he had endorsed when he confronted the build-up of the Nazi war machine in Berlin in 1938.

Although he eventually dropped out of the Hussars, Cooper and McLaghlen continued their friendship. Both actors were known to make anti-Semitic remarks.

But whereas the FBI dossier asserted that Cooper had turned against the Nazis, they went on to claim that Cooper did not appear to be pro-British either. Korda concluded, "Gary Cooper will not help our cause, but he won't harm us either, although he holds such right wing views he might be called an American Fascist."

J. Edgar and Clyde no longer viewed Cooper as a security threat, but they continued to monitor the actor's love life. Clyde finally concluded, "If it moves, Coop will fuck it."

***

In 1940, in a surprise coincidence, J. Edgar and Vivien Leigh, enjoying popularity across the country in the 1939 box office bonanza *Gone With the Wind*, almost simultaneously focused their attentions on Walt Disney.

As a secret British agent, Vivien had been asked by Korda to investigate Disney to determine if he were pro-Nazi. In contrast, J. Edgar wanted to enlist Disney's help in uncovering communists working in the film industry.

Korda had selected Vivien because he'd received reports that Disney was a great admirer of both Mussolini and Hitler, and that he'd attended meetings of Nazi sympathizers in Los Angeles in the late 1930s.

Further suspicion arose when Disney extended an invitation to Leni Riefenstahl to tour his studio during her visit to California. Reported to be the mistress of Hitler, she had directed the most effective propaganda film in cinematic history, *Triumph of the Will* (*Triumph des Willens*). Released in 1935, it chronicled the 1934 Nazi Party Congress in Nürnberg, glorifying Hitler and the Third Reich.

After her visit, Riefenstahl pronounced Disney "the greatest personage in American film." The pair had hugged and kissed outside of camera range.

Vivien was selected as Korda's spy because the creator of Mickey Mouse had sent her a fan letter praising her performance as Scarlett O'Hara. She called Disney, and he invited her to dinner. She later typed up a report for Korda, a copy of which J. Edgar's "mole" sent to him in Washington.

In it Vivien reported that she could not determine if Disney were pro-Nazi or not. "But he will do nothing for the British cause, however. His position is 'let 'em fight their own wars over in Europe.' I do not think he is secretly funding any pro-German groups. Frankly, his main concern is losing the lucrative German market for Disney films if Hitler goes to war against the West." She added a postscript: "Larry and I have heard rumors that he is a homosexual."

The news of Disney's presumed homosexuality was no thunderbolt to Clyde and J. Edgar, who had long ago figured out Disney's sexual preference. Even so, the two FBI men wanted him to become an FBI informant, keeping them abreast of the infiltration of "reds in the film industry."

In a confidential letter to Disney, J. Edgar had written: "I believe that communists have infiltrated every branch of the film industry, and that it is filled with political subversives who are a threat to the security of the United States, as we inevitably head for war. We need your help in identifying these subversives."

It took a lot of persuasion, but Disney finally agreed to come aboard as an FBI informant, a position he would hold for twenty-five years, although there would be some rough points and some misunderstandings between J. Edgar and Disney. At one point J. Edgar gave Disney a title—"Special Agent in Charge."

On November 10, 1940, Disney clarified his position with the FBI, agreeing to help the Bureau root out communists in the film industry. Over a period of two days, Disney was spotted in Washington. It has since been assumed that he spent most of that time meeting with J. Edgar and Clyde.

Fully aware that he was a closeted homosexual, Guy Hotell arranged a sexual tryst between Disney and a young FBI man who was most willing "to meet my hero" at the Mayflower Hotel. Clyde had the room bugged because he wanted to secure blackmail evidence on Disney if he ever tried to cause the FBI any trouble at some future date.

Having Disney as its special agent presented some problems for the Bureau. Disney had attended "America First" rallies with Charles A. Lindbergh, and he'd previously been accused of being both pro-Nazi and anti-Semitic. One reporter charged he was sending "secret signals" to the Germans through his Mickey Mouse comic strip, claiming that in the final panel of one of the rodent's cartoons appeared a fast-flashing swastika.

In the aftermath of Disney's official designation, J. Edgar was bombarded with letters attacking Disney. He ordered Clyde to file such protests in a drawer marked CASE CLOSED.

Later J. Edgar persuaded Disney to go on a good will tour of South America. Disney was told that by presenting himself as a patriotic American, it would help erase his pro-Nazi image.

The trip went smoothly except for one flaw. J. Edgar sent Disney an urgent telegram, suggesting that he not refer to the people of Brazil as "natives."

At the end of the tour, J. Edgar told Clyde and Guy, "We've got Mickey Mouse in our pocket. He'll cooperate with us from now on. If not, thanks to Guy here, we can blackmail him. In the future, let's use more of our homosexual agents to blackmail politicians to do our bidding. I think most of them are faggots anyway, especially the Democrats."

Adolf Hitler and his rumored mistress, **Leni Riefenstahl**, the genius filmmaker, met in August of 1934 in Nürnberg to discuss the final logistics for her historic *Triumph of the Will,* a film glorifying Hitler and the emerging Nazi empire.

During its actual filming, her cameras were everywhere in the city, even perched high atop fire ladders. She had a cast of thousands at her disposal.

Propaganda minister Josef Goebbels suspected that Riefenstahl might be Jewish. He harbored the same unvoiced suspicions about Hitler himself.

***

Arguably, Tyrone Power was the leading matinee idol of Hollywood in 1940, directly competing with Errol Flynn and Robert Taylor, who were his on-again, off-again lovers. Power was also having an affair with the billionaire aviator and mogul Howard Hughes.

As his biographer Hector Arce wrote in *The Secret Life of Tyrone Power*, "Sex with other men wasn't something Ty could either take or leave alone. He risked losing everything should it become public knowledge, and yet he continued having

156

such affairs. He'd not only had to hide this fact of his sex life from the masses, but also from the sedate Hollywood crowd he'd taken up with. A great percentage of the conservative Beverly Hills establishment were Jews, who'd been taught that sex with another man was the ultimate taboo."

Many of Power's male lovers, such as Cesar Romero or Nöel Coward, felt that their seducer was basically homosexual but had affairs with women to keep up his masculine screen image. He actually married three times, his first wedding to the French actress Annabella, with whom he'd co-starred in the 1938 *Suez*.

Power's longtime "trick," Smitty Hanson, summed it up this way: "Ty was basically gay but liked a girl like Lana Turner from time to time, occasionally marrying one."

Since Power started at 20th Century Fox earning only a hundred dollars a week, he never had much money. Howard Hughes, however, paid most of his bills, buying him, among other things, a new wardrobe and a new car.

Although J. Edgar was voyeuristically intrigued by Power's sexual escapades, what brought him under FBI surveillance in the early 1940s were the people he associated with, especially the Fascist-leaning Countess Dorothy di Frasso coterie. According to FBI files, Power made frequent trips to Mexico City for reasons unknown.

Finally, Clyde, through his agents in Mexico, discovered the reason for the star's frequent trips South of the Border. Power was sexually involved with Maximino Ávila Camacho, the brother of the president of Mexico, Manuel Ávila Camacho. Maximino was a notorious womanizer, known for his carousing, especially with underage *putas*. He was also a four-star general in Mexico's revolutionary forces and was the political boss of his home state of Puebla.

By late 1940 the FBI concluded that Maximino, unlike his brother, the president, was actually conspiring with the Nazis to tilt Mexico into the orbit of the Axis. That way the Nazis could use Mexican ports for an eventual attack on the California coast. The

Walt Disney and **Mickey Mouse** welcomed Leni Riefenstahl to Hollywood. Their rendezvous evolved into a mutual admiration society, one artist lavishly admiring the talents of the other.

As Steven Bach, biographer of Riefenstahl, wrote: "Disney expressed a desire to see *Olympia* in his own screen room, but backed off in the end, citing fears of a boycott of his films by left-wing union projectionists should the screening become public knowledge."

Olympia was the director's glorification of the Aryan team's performance at the 1936 Olympic Games in Berlin.

157

Bureau also discovered that Maximino was a key player in a group known as the National Synarchists, an organization created in 1937 by the Nazis, working in conjunction with the Japanese and the Spanish Falange. Power was frequently seen socializing with Maximino's closest political allies from Axis powers.

Yet the FBI could turn up no hardcore evidence that Power was doing anything to aid the Fascists. In December 1, 1940, he'd hosted a house party in Hollywood for Manuel Ávila Camacho, who had been elected president of Mexico. But that wasn't incriminating. Franklin D. Roosevelt had done the same thing.

In Hollywood, Power was frequently seen in the company of Laurence Olivier, and Bureau agents concluded the two handsome actors were having an affair. "Tyrone Power is nothing but a boy whore," one FBI report concluded. "Like Gary Cooper, he will fuck anybody, man or woman."

Having failed to provide any espionage evidence against Power, J. Edgar and Clyde studied the file that Olivier had submitted to his secret boss, Alexander Korda. Although sleeping with Power, Olivier was spying on his lover at the same time.

In Olivier's report to British intelligence, which J. Edgar's "mole" copied for him, it was written that "Tyrone Power is no security risk, it seems. But he has a poor choice of friends and constantly fraternizes with Fascist sympathizers in the orbit of the notorious Dorothy di Frasso. It appears that he has developed some sort of male crush on the flashy Maximino, who has been known on occasion to have sex with very beautiful four-

(left photo) **Tyrone Power**, playing the title role in *Jesse James* (1939), one of his most macho impersonations. Like Robert Taylor, he worked hard to combat rumors that he was a "pretty boy homosexual."

He indulged in a torrid romance with **Laurence Olivier** *(right photo)*. When it ended, they became lifelong friends. During their affair, Olivier was spying on Power, reporting his activities to master spy Alexander Korda. It was eventually determined that Power was not working for Fascists based in Los Angeles, but merely consorting with them. Later, Power's heroism during World War II helped remove him from J. Edgar's list of Nazi sympathizers.

The FBI was fully aware of Olivier's role as a British spy operating illegally within the then-neutral U.S. before its entry into the war in 1941. But insofar as Olivier was concerned, they consistently maintained a policy of "hands off."

teen-year-old boys, although he seems intent on seducing every young girl in the province of his native Puebla. Power may be politically naïve, or else he is playing on both teams because he also agreed to aid Olivier and others in charity events for British War Relief. A very confused picture here, but typical of homosexuals who find it impossible to make up their minds."

On May 22, 1942, the Nazi attempt to forge an alliance with Mexico came to an abrupt end for reasons never fully explained. Maximino's brother, Manuel, declared war on Germany in the wake of a Nazi submarine attack on two Mexican ships carrying oil supplies in the Gulf of Mexico near the port of New Orleans.

Maximino's Fascist friends hastily retreated from Mexico City. With the outbreak of war, Power joined the Marine Corps as a pilot, seeing action in the South Pacific.

"We'll take him off the list of suspected enemy agents," J. Edgar told Clyde and Louis Nichols. "However, we'll still monitor his private life to learn what important people he is seducing, especially Howard Hughes. This information might be extremely valuable to us in the future."

***

Ever since aviator Charles A. Lindbergh had refused to admit J. Edgar into his home during the investigation of the kidnapping of the Lindbergh baby, the FBI director had harbored a grudge against this American hero. Clyde was personally in charge of Lindbergh's FBI dossier, which had grown year by year. Long before Germany declared war on the United States, J. Edgar and Clyde suspected him of pro-Nazi sympathies.

Between 1936 and 1938, Lindbergh began a series of flights to Nazi Germany. With his wife, Anne Morrow Lindbergh, at his side, on July 28, 1936, he accepted the German Medal of Honor. It was presented on behalf of Adolf Hitler.

Lindbergh would make several more trips to Nazi Germany to report on that country's aviation industry. At the invitation of Hermann Göring, he became the first American allowed to examine the Luftwaffe's newest bomber, the Junkers Ju 88. He also conducted a thorough inspection of the Messerschmitt Bf109, Germany's frontline fighter aircraft. In a surprise move, Göring granted him permission to fly the Bf109.

Unknown to Göring and Lindbergh, J. Edgar and Clyde had planted a "mole" within Göring's entourage. The spy reported on Lindbergh's activities night and day, including details of his private life.

Lindbergh had nothing but praise for the Nazis, calling the Luftwaffe

Franklin D. Roosevelt *(left seated figure, above)* wanted to maintain a good neighbor policy with the president of Mexico, **Manuel Ávila Camacho** *(right)*. They met in Monterrey, Mexico, where FDR was entertained with a lavish Mexican banquet and fiesta.

J. Edgar kept the U.S. president informed of the activities of Manuel's brother, Maximino, and how he was being wooed by political allies of the Axis powers, who wanted to use Mexican ports as part of a possible attack on the United States. That dream faded for the Nazis when Mexico declared war on Germany in 1942.

"the greatest air force on earth." He also claimed that "Hitler is a great man who has done much for the German race." In another interview, he said that in Germany "I have discovered a sense of decency and values far ahead of our own." He also shocked reporters by delivering an anti-Semitic attack, accusing the American Jew of "being the chief agitator urging America into a European war."

After that interview, Lindbergh's FBI report accused the aviator of being a "traitor and a Nazi." Privately, J. Edgar told Clyde and his agents, "If Hitler had asked Lindbergh to lick the dingleberries off his asshole, I'm sure the *Spirit of St. Louis* would have obliged."

J. Edgar also monitored Lindbergh's trips in America, and in California discovered that he was indulging in sexual trysts with Sonja Henie, the Norwegian ice-skating champion that Hollywood had been trying to turn into a movie star.

Perky, blonde, blue-eyed, and a Nordic beauty of sorts, she fitted Lindbergh's female ideal of the superiority of the white race, as also espoused by Hitler. She'd won the World Figure Skating Championship at the age of eleven, and had followed with Gold Medals at the 1928, 1932, and 1936 Olympics. She'd dazzled the Nazi hierarchy in Berlin. In a skating exhibition, she'd shouted HEIL HITLER! in front of the *Führer*. She'd also perfected the Nazi salute.

J. Edgar and Clyde received a report that in 1938, Lindbergh dined with Göring at the American Embassy in Berlin, where he was introduced to the greatest engineers of the burgeoning Nazi aviation field. Here he was presented with another award by Göring, the Commander Cross of the German Eagle.

After *Kristallnacht*, Lindbergh critics demanded that he return the award. But he refused, claiming, "If I were to return the German medal, given in times of peace, it would be an unnecessary insult. Even if war comes, I can see no gain in indulging in a spitting contest with Germany."

J. Edgar and Clyde discovered another damaging piece of evidence. Ambassador Joseph P. Kennedy, the unpopular U.S. Ambassador in London, persuaded Lindbergh to write a secret memo to the British prime minister. In it, the aviator warned Britain that even though Hitler had violated the Munich Agreement—"peace in our time"—it would be suicidal to go to war with Hitler.

"France is unprepared for any war, and Britain relies too much on naval power. Its ground forces and its air arsenal are hopelessly out of date. Germany would win in any war between the two coun-

Hermann Göring *(far right)* presents "my favorite American," **Charles A. Lindbergh** with a medal on behalf of Adolf Hitler. **Anne Morrow Lindbergh** *(far left)* stands by her husband, looking on. The ceremony occurred on July 28, 1936.

The U.S. military asked Lindbergh to travel to Germany several times between 1936 and 1938 as a means of getting information about the *Luftwaffe*. Amazingly, Göring didn't seem to view Lindbergh as a spy, but fed him vital data about the new Nazi bomber, the Junkers Ju 88, and allowed him first-hand views of German aviation facilities. Göring later said, "We viewed him as being on our side, opposing the communist menace to the east."

tries." He also warned that France was so unprepared it might be overrun by Nazi storm troopers in a matter of weeks, and he advocated a war between Germany and Russia. "The Soviet Union and the growing spread of communism are the true menaces in the world today, not Nazi Germany."

Late in 1940, one year before America's entrance into WWII, Lindbergh became the chief spokesman for the America First Committee, urging the country to avoid all involvements in what appeared to be an imminent European War. Heard by millions, his speeches attracted overflow crowds in New York's Madison Square Garden and Chicago's Soldier Field. In one of his strongest speeches, Lindbergh claimed that if America attacked Nazi Germany, it might "lay Europe open to rape, loot, and barbarism of Soviet Russia's force, causing possibly the fatal wounding of western civilization."

In a speech he delivered in January, 1941, Lindbergh attacked FDR's Lend-Lease Bill on which Winston Churchill so eagerly depended. He proposed instead that the United States negotiate a neutrality pact with Germany, evocative of the German/Soviet nonaggression pact that the Soviet Union had previously signed.

FDR fought back, calling Lindbergh a "defeatist and appeaser," comparing him to Clement L. Vallandigham, Democrat of Ohio, the leader of

Adolf Hitler considered Charles A. Lindbergh, the fabled aviator, and the Norwegian ice-skating champion **Sonja Henie** *(both photos above)* the Aryan ideal—"the perfect man and the perfect woman." Those who knew Henie intimately, and that included Tyrone Power, claimed that she was possessed by an insatiable passion for money, diamonds, furs, and men.

She liked heroic men, the Nazi ideal, and found lovers in a very young John F. Kennedy and Charles Lindbergh himself.

She once told the aviator, "We could make beautiful babies together, superior babies."

Lindbergh never admitted to an affair with Henie, but JFK confessed to his best friend, actor Robert Stack, "Sonja is a great fuck, sexily adaptable to any position requested. Because of all that ice skating, she's developed vaginal muscles from hell."

the "Copperhead" movement that had opposed Abraham Lincoln's declaration of war on the Confederate States.

Lindbergh resigned his commission in the U.S. Army Corps three days later, following FDR's speech on April 25, 1941. "Having been accused by my commander and chief of being a traitor, I have no honorable alternative."

As Lindbergh's attacks upon FDR and his advocacy of U.S. involvement against the Nazis grew more strident, FDR called J. Edgar. "If I should die tomorrow, I want you to know this," Roosevelt said. "I am absolutely convinced that Charles A. Lindbergh is a card-carrying Nazi."

Having passed almost unnoticed by the Bureau, Clyde discovered a Lindbergh essay in *Reader's Digest* in 1939 that elucidated his beliefs in the superiority of the white race. The aviator praised "our inheritance of European blood," as opposed to black blood or Asian blood. He opposed the "dilution" of that blood by foreign races. Many Americans at the time echoed Lindbergh's anti-communism and his belief in "Nordicism" and eugenics.

Even if it meant a political alliance between the United States and Nazi Germany, Lindbergh believed in the preservation of those of European descent. He feared that "My people might be drowned in the pressing sea of yellow, black, and brown."

Right up until the attack on Pearl Harbor in December of 1941, Lindbergh continued to oppose the war, denouncing the British, the American Jews, and the Roosevelt administration, whom he claimed were "agitating for war." He cited Jewish influence over American media, including motion pictures, the press, the radio, and even the government in Washington.

After the Japanese attack on Pearl Harbor, Lindbergh sought to be re-commissioned in the U.S. Army Corps. FDR ordered Henry L. Stimson, Secretary of War, to decline the aviator's request.

Even so, Lindbergh spent six months in the Pacific in 1944 taking part as a civilian in bomber raids on Japanese positions. In all, he flew 50 combat missions and was officially praised by Gen. Douglas MacArthur. All the U.S. Marine, Army, and Air Force pilots who served with Lindbergh had only praise for his innovations in aircraft defense and for his courage in the face of the enemy. They also defended his patriotism.

Regardless of the political spectrum that endorsed or condemned Lindbergh, it was widely acknowledged that the aviator and his wife, Anne, never really recovered from the kidnapping and murder of their infant son, Charles A. Lindbergh Jr. Anne did go on to give birth to five other children—Jon, Land Morrow, Anne Spencer, Scott, and Reeve. To the public they appeared to be one of the most famous and distinguished families of America. Lindbergh was a national hero, and memories of his political platforms prior to the outbreak of World War II faded from the public mind.

At the end of the war, Lindbergh returned to Germany for a tour of Nazi concentration camps. He later said, "I was disgusted. I was angry."

His fascination with Germany and the Germans continued, however. As J. Edgar and Clyde learned, but never exposed to the public, the aviator had three German mistresses and three different families, and visited each of them five to seven times a year from 1957 until he died in 1974.

As the German author, Rudolf Schroeck, revealed in his shocking 2005 book, *The Double Life of Charles A. Lindbergh*, he had seven children in Germany.

Two of his mistresses were sisters, Brigitte and Marietta Hesshaimer. They lived in Geretsried, a small Bavarian town 35 kilometers south of Munich. With Brigitte, he fathered three children, Duyrk (1958), Astrid (1960), and David (1967). The children did not know the true identity of Lindbergh. When he came to visit them, he used the alias of "Careau Kent."

He was also sleeping with Brigitte's sister, Marietta, with whom he bore two sons—Vago in 1960 and Christoph in 1966. None of these children knew their father was an international aviation hero until Astrid read a feature story in a German magazine about Lindbergh's exploits.

An East Prussian aristocrat, known only as "Valeska," had introduced the Hesshaimer sisters to Lindbergh. She was his private secretary in Europe. With him, she had a son in 1959 and a daughter in 1961. At one time, all three mistresses lived together in the same apartment in Rome until Brigitte admitted she was pregnant, eventually giving birth to Lindbergh's first European child.

J. Edgar learned that on Lindbergh's death bed in August of 1974, he wrote all three of his mistresses, pleading for "utmost secrecy" in not revealing that he had "supplemented" his U.S.-based family with an additional three families in Germany.

In 2008, Reeve, the youngest daughter of the American branch of the Lindbergh family, wrote a book *Forward from Here,* in which she included her discovery in 2003 of the truth about her hero father's three secret European families.

In reading over Lindbergh's file, J. Edgar scribbled a note: "He called himself a Lutheran but with all those wives, he should have been a Mormon."

Clyde discovered a final tantalizing detail to amuse J. Edgar. "I talked to this airman who had become friends with our aviator friend in the Pacific in 1944. He told me that one night Lindbergh confessed to him that he masturbated three times while flying the *Spirit of St. Louis* to Paris."

***

At the beginning of World War II, the United States had been officially neutral, even though the sympathies of the Roosevelt administration leaned, of course, toward Britain. In a private call to J. Edgar, FDR had asked him to cooperate with British intelligence.

This led to the secret meeting of the FBI director with William Stephenson, a Canadian-born industrialist who became known as the famous British spy "Intrepid," as depicted in the 1979 bestseller *A Man Called Intrepid.*

Reporting directly to Churchill himself, Stephenson was Britain's chief of intelligence in the Western Hemisphere, with particularly far-reaching authority in Canada and the United States, during World War II.

Before he became the master of cloak-and-dagger espionage, Stephenson had been one of Britain's top fighter pilots in WWI. His approval among his commanders reached its peak during his stint as a member of the Royal Flying Corps, when he shot down 26 German planes. Eventually captured and imprisoned in an internment camp by the Nazis, he came across an ingenious can opener that had been patented in Germany. At war's end, he adapted this can opener and obtained patents worldwide for it. In time, this lowly can opener made him a multi-millionaire. He branched off into radio, phonographs, automobiles, airplanes, real estate, and steel. He was also a clever inventor, creating the first device for sending photographs by radio. He even won the European lightweight boxing championship.

Years before his internment, in Germany on business in the months before the outbreak of World War II, Stephenson sent Churchill undercover information on Nazi steel, arms, and munitions production. He sent these secrets directly to Churchill himself, who had not become Prime Minister at the time.

In April of 1940, both FDR and Churchill told Stephenson to meet privately with J. Edgar to coordinate activities, such as the training of potential American spies in Canada.

Stephenson did not want to be seen entering FBI headquarters in Washington, so J. Edgar agreed to meet with him at his home on Thirtieth Place. Stephenson was informed in advance that Clyde Tolson would be present.

Long freed of his mother's control, J. Edgar could decorate his home as he desired. Stephenson later claimed he was stunned when he came in, finding both the house and garden filled with nude pictures, nude statues, and nude figurines, all male. "When I had to take a leak, I found the walls of the bathroom decorated with reproductions of Roman friezes of men sodomizing each other. I was taken aback. I had heard that J. Edgar and Clyde were the most closeted homosexuals in Washington. Yet anybody who came into their home would recognize the place as the abode of a homosexual couple."

At the bottom of his report to Churchill, Stephenson also added that "J. Edgar is a formidable halfback, but I suspect Clyde Tolson is the real coach in this bizarre relationship."

At first J. Edgar was rather leery of Stephenson. As FBI agent William Sullivan later claimed, "Hoover didn't like the British, didn't care for the French, hated the Dutch, and couldn't stand Australians."

The meeting between J. Edgar and Stephenson revealed startling information. J. Edgar was told that England had captured an Enigma machine, the key to decoding Nazi military communications. "With this machine, we can win the war," Churchill had said. "But it is a deadly secret."

Stephenson decided that FDR would be the only non-British authority figure who would be informed of the existence of Enigma and its capture by the British. Even though the United States was still neutral, the summary of German intelligence would be sent to the President.

Churchill had decided that J. Edgar was the man to receive these secret messages, which he would then convey to the White House. Before the night had ended, J. Edgar had agreed to become the liaison between the coded Enigma messages from London and the White House. At the conclusion of the evening, J. Edgar said, "The FBI has just married British intelligence."

It is estimated that in one year alone, J. Edgar at the FBI received some 100,000 secret messages as decoded from the Nazi High Command.

The debate still rages: Was **William Stephenson** *(above)* the inspiration for Ian Fleming's James Bond character, or was it Dusko Popov, another master spy?

Fleming once wrote, "James Bond is a highly romanticized version of a true spy. The real thing is William Stephenson."

Standing only five feet, five inches, Stephenson was head of British Intelligence in the Western Hemisphere during World War II. He is best known by his code name, "Intrepid."

in 1976, a writer (William Stevenson) published a biography of the master spy, *A Man Called Intrepid,* which brought international attention to the spy's role during World War II.

In 1979, the spy was portrayed by David Niven in a film (also called *A Man Called Intrepid*), based on the bestseller. Because of the similarities in the names of the book's author and its protagonist, (Stevenson vs. Stephenson), consumers thought the book was an autobiography, which it was not.

Stephenson said, "That allowed us to round up Nazi spies in America, and we let J. Edgar take the credit. At no point did we want it revealed that we were providing the information that led to these arrests."

At Rockefeller Plaza in New York, Stephenson set up headquarters of the British Security Coordination (BSC). This organization intercepted all suspicious mail between the United States, South America, and Europe. Diplomatic pouches were illegally sent here to be opened. "We became the letter-opening center of the world," Stephenson later said. "We could break almost any code. We shared the fruits of our labor with Hoover." Stephenson, however, found J. Edgar completely uncooperative and of virtually no help in reciprocating with data that was deemed vital to British Intelligence.

Up until July of 1941, J. Edgar believed that he and Clyde were the kingpins of American intelligence and counterespionage. "Then Stephenson betrayed me," in J. Edgar's words.

Stephenson threw his weight behind William J. Donovan in the process of getting him appointed as head of the Office of the Coordinator of Information (COI), which later was renamed Office of Strategic Services (OSS). Donovan was put in charge of an integrated strategic intelligence service, which made him J. Edgar's boss. Stephenson continued to deliver secret messages to J. Edgar, but the Bureau chief reacted vengefully by refusing any further cooperation with Stephenson because of his involvement with Donovan's appointment.

J. Edgar openly criticized the president's appointment of Donovan, calling it "FDR's folly," and never forgave Stephenson for supporting Donovan.

When Churchill was informed of J. Edgar's lack of cooperation, the Prime Minister said, "Our least favorite homosexual in America is living up to his reputation—a true Anglophobe."

J. Edgar spent most of the war years involved in espionage against the Japanese and the Nazis, but "my worst enemy" (his words) was William J. Donovan, nicknamed "Wild Bill." In time, Donovan, not J. Edgar, would be known as the "Father of Central Intelligence." His OSS was the forerunner of today's CIA.

"Wild Bill" earned his name when he led a cavalry troop of the New York State Militia in the 1916 Pancho Villa campaign along the Mexican and U.S. border. FDR admired him greatly, even though he was a Republican and had run unsuccessfully in 1932 in a bid for FDR's former office as governor of New York.

In the summer of 1941, the President assigned to Donovan the almost impossible task of coordinating the intelligence divisions of the Army, Navy, State Department, and the FBI. These warring factions were not pulling together, and not presenting a solid front against their Fascist enemies. J. Edgar didn't want to share his organization's intelligence with the other branches.

From the beginning, Donovan found roadblocks along the way, as J. Edgar insisted on retaining the autonomy of the FBI in South America, and the OSS was blocked from the Philippines by the opposition of General Douglas MacArthur, the commander of the Southwest Pacific Theater.

The FBI director was especially concerned with what he feared was "the increasingly dangerous theater of South America." He also seriously doubted Mexico's loyalty, and uncovered a secret Nazi memo written to the Mexican president. Hitler agreed to return the lands Mexico had lost to the United States if that country would allow Germany to use its ports for an eventual attack on the north.

J. Edgar was convinced that Hitler was plotting to first subdue South America and then use it as a launching pad for an invasion of the United States, with enemy troops landing first in Mexico. In reaction, the Bureau's agents poured into Brazil, Chile, Colombia, and especially Argentina.

British agents always received a dubious reception from J. Edgar at the FBI. Commander Ian Fleming, who later created the James Bond stories, recalled one of his visits to the office of J. Edgar. "He was a chunky, enigmatic man with slow eyes and a trap of a mouth who received us graciously, listening with close attention to our exposé of certain security problems. His assistant, Tolson, stood up during the entire time, taking in our every move with his judgmental black eyes. Hoover made it perfectly clear he had no

167

interest in aiding British intelligence in the United States. His negative response was soft as a cat's paw. With a firm, dry handclasp, we were shown the way out."

When Churchill himself read Fleming's wartime report on J. Edgar's reception, he told his aides, "That old sod Hoover thinks like a cop. He doesn't know how to make use of the intelligence supplied by the British."

"Had Hoover not shown such hostility toward us, maybe Pearl Harbor could have been prevented," Stephenson later recalled. "Does that god damn pansy think he's still fighting the Red Coats on Bunker Hill? Does he not know Britain is an ally of the United States?"

J. Edgar conceived of the Special Intelligence Service (SIS) that kept Axis spies from winning countries in South America to their side. To hold onto his South American turf, J. Edgar bombarded FDR with reports of his success in such Fascist-leaning countries as Argentina. Somehow the FBI obtained copies of secret letters that Juan Peron in Buenos Aires was sending to Hitler in Berlin.

The FBI had begun operating in Central and South America in the summer of 1940. From then on, they systematically rounded up Axis agents, arrested saboteurs, disrupted the smuggling of strategic war materials, and confiscated funds the Nazis planned to use to finance their infiltration of South America.

Before war's end, J. Edgar's G-Men would shut down three dozen clandestine radio stations broadcasting Spanish and Portuguese-language Nazi propaganda within South America. J. Edgar ordered that Nazis agents be captured as far away as Chile or Brazil and held in prisons in the U.S. Canal Zone. A roundup of Nazi agents in just one city, Rio de Janeiro, resulted in some five hundred arrests.

In time, J. Edgar was so proud of his achievements South of the Border that he hoped to head all divisions of U.S. intelligence at war's end, although the rise of the CIA would burst that dream balloon.

Throughout the war J. Edgar consistently sabotaged Donovan. When OSS men were breaking into the Spanish Embassy in Washington, two FBI cars arrived outside with dome lights flashing and sirens sounding an alarm. Donovan's men were arrested and Spanish officials, sympathetic to the Nazis, alerted.

Since Donovan viewed this OSS attempt at intelligence gathering vital to the Allied war effort, he called FDR and accused J. Edgar of "committing treason." The President agreed and was furious at the FBI director. "The only way I'll get rid of the fart is if you guys break into FBI headquarters and steal the files on Eleanor and me."

Donovan guaranteed that J. Edgar would be his enemy for life when he ordered his agents to conduct a very private investigation to determine if J. Edgar and Clyde were homosexual lovers. He suspected strongly that they were, and Stephenson firmly believed that the two men were lovers in the wake of his visit to their home with all those male nudes and erotic drawings.

When Guy Hotell became inebriated, and that was almost nightly, he was "loose-lipped," in the words of J. Edgar. But Guy knew far too much to be fired.

One night, Donovan employed a very attractive, well-built blond OSS agent of Scandinavian ancestry. His assignment was to pump all the information he could out of Guy and learn what he knew about the intimate details of the sex lives of J. Edgar and Clyde. Donovan even got the agent to agree to allow Guy to seduce him if he provided the right kind of information.

The OSS dressed the agent like an *homme fatale* and sent him to the tavern in Georgetown that was frequented by Guy. Guy did not show up on the first or second nights but came into the bar on the third night. The agent found that Guy was only too willing to sit drinking with him in a private booth.

The agent admitted that he'd recently divorced his wife and was horny now that his sex life had been cut off. "I think I know how that can be remedied," Guy told him. He also bragged about his close relationships with J. Edgar and Clyde, hinting at great degrees of intimacy between them when they went on vacations together.

William ("Wild Bill") Donovan, an Irish/American doughboy during World War I, is best known as the wartime head of the Office of Strategic Services (OSS), which technically made him J. Edgar's boss, a designation which led to the FBI director's massive resentment.

Dead by 1959, Donovan today is known as "the Father of Central Intelligence."

Harry S Truman also disliked Donovan, and although Donovan laid the framework for what became the modern-day CIA, he never actually ran it. In its early days, it was denounced as "An American Gestapo" by its critics.

At the Nürnberg trials, Donovan had the satisfaction of seeing some of the Nazi leaders responsible for the torture and murder of his OSS agents brought to justice. President Eisenhower referred to him as "The Last Hero."

Somehow, Clyde learned about this possible entrapment, and immediately sent an FBI squad car to the bar, where Guy was escorted out of the tavern and placed under FBI custody until he sobered up. He later admitted, "I faced the worst scolding of my life from Eddie. He used every word he could think of to denounce me, but he had no choice but to keep me on the force. I knew where all the bodies were buried."

Even though Guy did not provide as much private data on the two FBI lovers that Donovan wanted, he had enough to file a report that was sent directly to the Oval Office. In his report, Donovan pointed out that both J. Edgar and Clyde, as homosexuals, were in danger of being blackmailed and compromising the work of the FBI.

The President chose not to take any immediate action in the wake of Donovan's allegations. Actually, Donovan's charges were well known to FDR. In fact, from various sources he'd long ago been alerted to those "she-males" who ran the FBI.

***

Dusko Popov, the playboy son of a rich Serbian family, became the most famous double agent of World War II. His cryptonym was "Tricycle," a nickname he earned for his sexual preference of sleeping with two women at the same time. Actually, he preferred that these two women be identical twins, and he spent a life of sexual frustration because he could not often arrange such a tryst.

When he died in 1981, he claimed that he had achieved his sexual fantasy with some two dozen twins, but that he would have preferred "so many more."

Author Ian Fleming ripped off the life of Tricycle, who was one of the inspirations for the creation of his James Bond character.

Fluent in German, Popov was approached in 1940 by Nazi agents of the Abwehr, Hitler's high command espionage service. He did so well in their intensive training program that he was asked to become a master Nazi spy. He'd survived torture better than any agent the Abwehr had recruited before. Part of his endurance training had been an intensive assault of his testicles, which according to reports, were quite large and made an easy target for Abwehr interrogators, who had been recruited from a bar in Berlin catering to sadists.

Unknown to the Abwehr, Popov detested Hitler and his Nazis. Flown to London, he immediately contacted MI-6, telling him he was sent to England to spy on the British war effort. Without the torture, the British also subjected him to an intensive interrogation and came to believe he was telling the truth and was not a "plant."

MI-6 agents fed Popov "useful but relatively harmless" military secrets to funnel back to Abwehr headquarters in Germany. In some cases, these secrets led to the loss of British lives, but the agents of MI-6 felt the sacrifice was worth the price to establish the validity of Popov and not let the Nazis know he was a double agent.

Abwehr was so impressed with the military data Popov collected in Britain that in the summer of 1941 he was dispatched to New York on a secret mission which the Germans viewed as vital to their espionage work in the Western Hemisphere.

Before leaving London, MI-6 was apprised of Popov's mission. The Nazis had arranged to provide him with an initial $50,000 in American currency which would be waiting for him in New York. He was told that his contact in America could supply him with an almost unlimited budget on an as-need basis, because they wanted him to set up Nazi spy cells that stretched from New York to California and on to Hawaii.

Prior to his departure for his clandestine assignment in the U.S., Popov was given an "intelligence questionnaire," with instructions to fill in the blanks within a reasonable time of his arrival. Popov passed it on to British intelligence, where it was studied by J.C. Masterman, chief of the British XX Committee, the XX standing for "Double Cross." Masterson ascertained that one third of the questions concerned logistics associated with Pearl Harbor. Where was the mine depot on the Isle of Kushhua? How far had the dredging at the entrance to Pearl Harbor proceeded? What was the depth of the water in the main harbor? How many airplanes stood at Hickam, Wheeler, Luke, and Kaneche airports?

German spies in the United States were sending reports about the extension of American airfields and troop movements throughout the U.S. The routes ammunition ships used as they headed for England were deemed of vital importance. The most sensitive queries demanded information about the U.S. atomic energy program. As early as 1940, Germans suspected that the Americans were trying to develop an atomic bomb. There were many questions about enriched uranium.

A spy had reported that Hitler had told Göring's chief aides that, "If we can build an arsenal of atomic bombs, we will dominate the planet. With three bombs, we could destroy London, Washington, and New York."

When Popov arrived in New York, he later told London that the FBI was picking up perceived Nazi sympathizers "like whores off the Reeperbahn," a reference to the bordello district of Hamburg.

Popov had two major goals to achieve in America. First, he wanted to meet with J. Edgar at FBI headquarters in Washington. To clear his pathway to J. Edgar, he was given letters of introduction by British intelligence, who stated that he was a double agent of the highest importance.

Before heading to Washington to meet with J. Edgar, Popov decided to spend some of those lavish dollars bestowed on him by the Germans. He checked into a suite at the Waldorf-Astoria in Manhattan.

During a secret mission to France, he'd met a beautiful French film actress, Simone Simon, who had been a singer, model, and fashion designer. She'd made her screen debut in Paris in 1931 and became so successful that she was brought to Hollywood by Darryl F. Zanuck in 1935. The cigar-smoking producer immediately seduced her after warning her that his penis was so large "I might split you in two."

In Hollywood, she'd faced one career disaster after another. Cast in *A Message for Garcia* (1936), she was replaced by Rita Hayworth. In 1936, she was cast as the female lead in *Under Two Flags* but was discharged for being too temperamental. She later claimed that she'd taken the advice of Marlene Dietrich, who had told her, "To be a star, you must make yourself behave like one every day on the set. You have to be imperial. You can't walk out of your dressing room like Minnie Mouse."

Although a nymphomaniac, seducing one male after another, Simone also had a lesbian streak and was involved in a torrid affair with Marlene at the time.

Simon did make *Seventh Heaven* in 1937 with Janet Gaynor, at which time she had affairs with both of its stars—not only with Gaynor but with James Stewart, who always said, "I polluted myself" after having sex. Cast in *Danger—Love at Work* (1937), she later lost the part to Ann Sothern because the director found her French accent too thick.

Abandoning Hollywood, embittered, she returned to France but came back to New York at the outbreak of the war, heading for Hollywood. When Popov learned she was in Manhattan, he resumed his affair with the actress.

Unknown to both Simone and Popov, Clyde had assigned FBI agents to watch their every move. Both lovers already had a dossier at the FBI.

During her years in Hollywood, Simone had become one of Clyde's "persons to watch." She'd scandalously been known as "The Lady with the Golden Key," and was said to have given any man she desired a gold-painted key to her boudoir, including Robert Taylor, Errol Flynn, George Gershwin, Johnny Weissmuller, Tyrone Power, and Charlie Chaplin. She had also involved herself in a number of lesbian affairs.

Knowing that Popov liked three-ways, and reading that Marlene was in New York, Simone called her and invited her to spend a night at the Waldorf with Popov and her. Apparently, she told Marlene that Popov was romantically devilish and "has the largest pair of testicles of any man in

Europe and a penis that doesn't seem to end." She made that claim to several women with whom she arranged threesomes with Popov.

At the time of Simone's wartime hookup with Popov, the actress had just achieved her greatest success in English language cinema with the release of *The Devil and Daniel Webster* (1941). She had also signed to star in two films that would become cult classics in the horror genre—*Cat People* (1942) and *The Curse of the Cat People* (1944).

When Clyde informed J. Edgar that Marlene Dietrich was sleeping with Simone and Popov, the director said, "My suspicion is confirmed. I think that Dietrich, though pretending to be anti-Nazi, is using Popov as her secret agent to supply data directly to the Abwehr. We must increase our surveillance of this blonde Kraut whore, who, no doubt, like Hedy Lamarr, has been fucked by Hitler's paltry three and a half inches."

Before leaving New York, it had been understood that Popov would meet with Percy Foxworth, who worked in the FBI's Manhattan office. J. Edgar wanted Foxworth to review the double agent's data before he met with him.

Caught up in FBI red tape, Popov learned that his information had also been forwarded to Earl Connelley, assistant FBI director in New York. The officer found Popov's reports "too detailed, far too precise and well organized. It sounds like a trap to me. The British may be taken in, but I think he's a loyal member of the Abwehr. He's fucking us, getting information from us. But I'll send his reports along to see what Hoover thinks."

At the Waldorf, Popov received an invitation to visit the FBI in Washington. In an assessment he shared with MI-6, he felt his data was of major importance to J. Edgar, because it suggested that an attack on Pearl Harbor might be imminent.

Popov had also been sent data from the Nazis which confirmed that Japanese naval officials had visited Taranto, Italy, at that country's southern tip. The Japanese had wanted to learn how British torpedo planes, launched from an aircraft carrier, had nearly obliterated the Italian fleet.

Reaching Washington with his vital data, Popov was told that J. Edgar along with his associate director, Clyde Tolson, had gone on a business trip to Miami. Guy Hotell had accompanied them.

Guy later recalled to his would-be biographer, James Kirkwood, "While the Japs were warming up their airplane engines to fly to Hawaii, Eddie, Clyde, and I were chasing after young dick in Florida."

Since J. Edgar was in Florida and would be there for at least two weeks, Popov, ever the playboy, found two Chinese teenage twins. Offering them $2,000 each, he drove them to Florida for a bacchanalian holiday, checking into a suite at the Roney Plaza on Miami Beach.

Codenamed "Tricycle" because he liked to sleep with two women at the same time, **Dusko Popov** was the most extraordinary spy of World War II.

Recruited by Nazi Intelligence (*Abwehr*) in 1940, the 27-year-old became a turncoat, working secretly for the British. He fed the Germans a constant stream of military "intelligence" after it had been vetted by MI-6.

Sent to the United States to establish a Nazi spy network, he met with J. Edgar Hoover late in 1941, warning him of an imminent attack on Pearl Harbor. The FBI director failed to heed his warnings and spent a great part of the rest of his life trying to cover up a fatal mistake that virtually wiped out the U.S. Pacific Fleet.

Weeks later, he learned that J. Edgar had considered having him arrested for violation of the Mann Act for taking a woman across state lines for the purpose of seduction. He also learned that Clyde had ordered agents to bug his suite at the Waldorf, and J. Edgar had personally listened to a tape of him having sex with Marlene and Simone.

J. Edgar suspected the French actress of being a Nazi agent. "She is known in homosexual circles in Paris where she has many friends including the pervert Jean Cocteau," Clyde claimed. "From what I'm told these boys are willing to be deflowered nightly by Nazi soldiers in Paris. It's called sleeping with the enemy."

Popov very accurately assumed that the information he was providing was important enough to alter the course of World War II and was vital information for the United States. He had told MI-6, "Instead of going through pansy boy Hoover, I should be dealing directly with Franklin Roosevelt, warning him of an imminent attack on Pearl Harbor."

Finally, after endless delays, Popov was ushered into the office of a suntanned J. Edgar. Clyde stood ten feet away, looking out the window. Neither man shook his hand. Popov later recalled that the face of J. Edgar looked "like a sledgehammer in search of an anvil."

"Sit down, Popov," J. Edgar virtually shouted at him. The spy would later recall, "I was greeted with the enthusiasm of a fresh dog turd which had had the audacity of placing itself beneath Hoover's polished patent leather shoes."

Instead of listening and digesting his information, J. Edgar astonished Popov by attacking him as a bogus spy. "Ever since you've arrived on our shores, you've fucked movie stars, drank too much champagne, ate too much at the Waldorf, taken teenage girls across the state line to engage in sexual intercourse, and patronized low-grade prostitutes. In Miami you were caught running nude around the pool area chasing after a married woman."

"My high life was paid for by the Germans," he claimed. "They're giving me an endless supply of the Yankee dollar."

"In America, and especially from our agents, we believe in good clean living. We are a much more moral country than you people over in London. I think you're just playing the British against the Nazis. Probably feeding misinformation to both sides."

He pounded his fists on the desk. "You've done nothing but behave like a degenerate. Who do you think you are? Porfirio Rubirosa?"

"I have valuable information about a possible Japanese attack on Pearl Harbor."

"I get all sorts of crank information like that every day," J. Edgar said. "Do you think I need you to teach me how to do my job? If Japan plans to attack Pearl Harbor, I will be the first to know about it. General Douglas MacArthur and I have spies in the Japanese High Command."

"Roosevelt must be alerted," Popov protested. "Your Pacific fleet is a sitting duck for a surprise attack. Abwehr believes that what they call their 'yellow allies' will attack sometime between your Thanksgiving and the Christmas holiday of this year, maybe sooner."

"If such a move is planned, I assure you I'll be the first to know. I do want to know

A relatively forgotten actress today, **Simone Simon** was a French film star who began her movie career in 1931. She is remembered by American audiences, if at all, for the cult classic *Cat People* (1942) and *The Curse of the Cat People* (1944).

She was brought to the attention of the FBI because of her affair with Dusko Popov, code name "Tricycle."

The agent submitted a request to J. Edgar for the rental of a summer cottage and for the payment of a $2,000 "bonus," payable directly to Simone.

In the aftermath of this request, the FBI tapped Simone's phone calls. As Guy Hotell reported, "Those two hot tamales invented phone sex.'

something from you. Did Marlene Dietrich quiz you about any information about an attack on Pearl Harbor?"

"She did not," Popov said defensively. "She's loyal to the Allies. All that stuff about Hitler and her is pure crap."

"Or so you say," J. Edgar said.

Realizing how hopeless the meeting was, Popov rose to his feet extending his hand. J. Edgar ignored it and remained seated. Clyde had never left his position at the window and had not said a word during the all-too-brief interview.

After the meeting, Popov sent a coded message to MI-6 in London. "Meeting with Hoover a disaster. Churchill should address FDR directly with this."

After Popov left FBI headquarters, J. Edgar called Donovan and demanded that the double agent be deported from the United States. "I am not prepared to turn over our dossier on him at this minute, but we have proof he's lying to the British and feeding them false information. He's not a double agent working for Britain and Germany. He's a Nazi spy through and through—no doubt about it."

***

It was a peaceful early afternoon in New York on Sunday, December 7, 1941. J. Edgar and Clyde were having lunch in their complimentary suite in Manhattan's Waldorf-Astoria. The time was 1:25. J. Edgar had just finished a sirloin steak and was savoring his cherries jubilee when the telephone sounded. It had an urgent ring.

A frantic call had come in from SAC Robert Shivers in Honolulu. He was connected to the switchboard in FBI headquarters in Washington, where the operator was able to link him to J. Edgar and Clyde at the Waldorf.

Clyde picked up the receiver to hear Shivers' hysterical voice. The sound of exploding bombs could be heard in the background.

Across the static-filled wire came the news. "The Japs are bombing Pearl Harbor. Hundreds of our men are dying. The Pacific fleet has been wiped out."

Clyde turned to J. Edgar who was looking up from his luscious dessert, noting the panic on Clyde's face, which was usually devoid of emotion.

He handed the receiver to J. Edgar. "Boss, you're not going to like this call."

Nervously coming onto the line, J. Edgar listened for an entire minute before turning to Clyde. "We're at war with the Japs."

CHAPTER SIX

In their suite at Manhattan's Waldorf-Astoria, J. Edgar hastily packed his possessions. Already packed, Clyde was on the phone, chartering a plane at La Guardia airport to fly them at once to FBI headquarters in Washington. All of their employees in the District of Columbia had heard the news and were waiting for the pair to arrive.

By midnight J. Edgar was still waiting for an authorization from FDR to begin arresting "enemy agents." Finally, it arrived, and he gave the orders through Clyde. "We'll get them even if we have to drag the bastards naked from their beds. By tomorrow these spies won't be sleeping on soft beds but on cold concrete floors with a gun pointed at their heads."

At FBI headquarters, J. Edgar and Clyde worked throughout the night, ordering the compilation of a list of all aliens, especially Japanese ones. The director feared massive sabotage. As soon as approval was granted, he directed law enforcement officials to take into custody all Japanese. In less than 72 hours, 3,846 aliens were arrested. Before 1945, J. Edgar would have as many as 16,000 enemy agents in custody. Clyde sent out a memo to all airlines not to fly Japanese passengers.

As the war proceeded, the number of prisoners reached beyond the 400,000 mark. Every month some seventy of these aliens escaped, and the FBI's job was to round them up. Not only that, but the Bureau was assigned the task of rounding up draft dodgers. In a sweep in one night in New York, 150 potential soldiers were arrested.

FBI laboratories also worked overtime to discover faulty military material supplied by war contractors, including defective hand grenades with insufficient charges.

Early on the morning of December 10, 1941, J. Edgar and Clyde were rushing into FBI headquarters. Mary MacNaulty, a housewife from Baltimore, stood on the sidewalk wearing a heavy black overcoat. "You killed 2,400 men," she shouted at J. Edgar. "My son was killed because of you."

She reached into her coat and pulled out a pistol, aiming it at J. Edgar, The highly trained Clyde quickly subdued her, knocking her to the pavement. Two FBI security guards apprehended the woman and took her into FBI custody. But later in the day. J. Edgar ordered his agents to release her because he didn't want the publicity.

The pistol that had almost been the weapon to assassinate him was brought to his office where he kept it. Clyde checked and found that it had been legally registered in the name of her dead son.

Usually J. Edgar did not drink on the job. But on this particular day he had several hefty shots from a bottle of Old Grand Dad that rested nearby in his liquor cabinet.

A call came in later that day from Francis Biddle, a Harvard-educated lawyer and judge who had been appointed Attorney General. Technically, he was J. Edgar's boss, although the FBI director often went over his head, reporting directly to FDR himself. Biddle informed him that he had no objection to that. Without saying so, Biddle more or less green-lighted "any tool necessary to discover America's enemies working within the country."

J. Edgar accepted that as authorization to do anything he wanted, legal or otherwise. "We're at war," Biddle told him. "Desperate times call for desperate measures."

Biddle informed J. Edgar that FDR wanted him to be in charge of wartime press censorship. It was a position J. Edgar didn't want. He managed to maneuver his way out of that job, the position eventually going to Byron Price, executive news editor of Associated Press.

"The FBI doesn't have time to get into the censorship business," J. Edgar informed Biddle. "We need to devote all of our energy to counterespionage."

With Price, Biddle worked to suppress "vermin publications."

In the week that followed the attack on Pearl Harbor, J. Edgar had a major conflict with Clyde, who usually gave in to nearly all decisions made by "The Boss." Clyde was a reserve naval commander, and, as a super patriot, he wanted to go on active duty "to serve my country in its hour of need. If Hitler wins this war, we'll be herded into a concentration camp or the gas chamber."

J. Edgar adamantly refused his request, and appealed directly to Henry Stimson, the Secretary of War. The next day Stimson sent Clyde a personal letter, asking him to resign his commission. He was told he would contribute more to the defense effort by remaining at his post at the FBI.

"There is no way in hell I'm ever going to let Clyde Tolson leave me," J. Edgar told Frank Knox, the Secretary of the Navy.

Knox later recalled, "I was stunned by such a statement. It convinced me that Hoover was in love with our boy Tolson. That was fine with me because we didn't allow homosexuals in the Navy anyway."

Even in wartime, Knox was not the only one wondering about the private lives of J. Edgar and Clyde. Over the years J. Edgar had been asked many times why he never married. Before the war, a Washington woman's page editor ran an article on the confirmed bachelor, entitled "J. Edgar Hoover Wants an Old-Fashioned Girl."

In the feature he said, "Every time I find a girl I'd like to marry, she is already married to someone else. I will meet a girl and think, 'Now there's a girl for me.' And what happens? She is either the hostess or the wife of someone else. Someone always beats me to the girl. If I ever marry and the girl fails me, ceases to love me, and our marriage is dissolved, it would ruin me. I couldn't take it and I would not be responsible for my actions."

But except for a rare voice raised here and there about his sexual preference, most of the FBI director's critics focused on why Pearl Harbor had to happen and who was to blame for America's all-time biggest naval disaster.

In the days, weeks, years, and decades that followed Pearl Harbor, J. Edgar came in for severe attacks when politicians looked for scapegoats. On the very night of Sunday, December 7, 1941's surprise aerial bombardment, Senator Tom Connally of Texas arrived enraged at the White House. As head of the Senate Foreign Relations Committee, he was called to an urgent meeting with FDR and other officials.

At the meeting Connally pointedly asked, "Why did the Japs catch us with our pants down so they could stick a firecracker up our ass? Didn't Hoover have some warning from his so-called far-flung spy network?"

John O'Donnell, writing for the McCormick chain of newspapers, claimed that, "The nation's super Dick Tracy, FBI Director J. Edgar Hoover, is directly under the gun. The blame for Pearl Harbor rests in his lap."

In his book, *J. Edgar Hoover, The Man in His Time*, Ralph de Toledano wrote: "The question arises, where was the FBI in those critical days in December of 1941? Why did they not alert the President, the Army, and the Navy of the impending attack on Pearl Harbor? Was its counter-intelligence force asleep or incompetent?"

An enraged Admiral Edwin Layton, the fleet intelligence officer at Pearl Harbor, charged that "Hoover's ego got in the way. He wouldn't share intelligence with other agencies. He dropped the ball completely just when America was depending on him. He seemed more interested in who Dusko Popov was fucking than he did in the upcoming Japanese surprise air attack. That fumble of his put us on the road to hell. Hoover literally sacrificed the lives of all those poor boys."

Master spy Popov, who had tried to alert J. Edgar and the United States about an imminent attack on Pearl Harbor, called J. Edgar "A god damn fool. If Hoover had cooperated, and I had been allowed to set up spy cells across America for Abwehr, the shithead would have known everything going on in German espionage in America."

"Hoover knew he'd made a mistake and attempted to cover up his guilty tracks," Popov also claimed. "I hope the history books will catch up with him. He didn't even share my information with Donovan."

The Boston Post [EXTRA]

JAPS DECLARE WAR ON U.S.
ATTACK HAWAII--KILL 350
BIG NAVAL BATTLE RAGING

Waves of Bombers Swoop Down on U. S. Pearl Harbor Base--Battleships West Virginia and Oklahoma and Several Destroyers Reported Hit--U. S. Fleet Steams to Sea--Heavy Gunfire Indicates Ocean Fight Under Way--Jap Airplane Carrier Believed First Victim--Six Planes and Four Subs Also Destroyed--Other Attacks on Honolulu and Guam--Japs Occupy U. S.-Owned Wake Island
PRESIDENT TO

Both J. Edgar Hoover and Clyde Tolson received warnings that a Japanese attack on Pearl Harbor was imminent, but they chose to ignore them.

Many historians and military experts blamed J. Edgar for the tragedy that wiped out most of the U.S. Pacific fleet, including the *USS Arizona* (whose wreckage is depicted above), going down.

An hour before the actual attack, a mysterious call came in from "somewhere in the islands," stating that a large fleet of planes with the rising sun on their bodies was heading toward Honolulu. At FBI headquarters, a memo was typed up and placed on J. Edgar's desk, where he discovered it Monday morning.

The attack had occurred on the previous day, Sunday.

William J. Donovan, assigned the task of coordinating all American intelligence, also attacked J. Edgar. "Hoover should have digested the data and brought it to my immediate attention. I would have gone to Roosevelt within the hour. Thousands of American lives could have been saved, not to mention the U.S. Pacific fleet. Damn him!"

Speaking privately for British intelligence, William Stephenson said, "Hoover failed to pick up what Popov was trying to tell him about Pearl Harbor. The consequences were disastrous for the United States. Roosevelt should have fired him on the Monday that followed the Japanese attack."

In 1941, the CIA, of course, had not come into existence, but even its future director, William Casey, was still blaming Hoover for Pearl Harbor. "The director showed a total incompetence for sophisticated wartime intelligence. The way he handled Popov showed that he should have been reassigned the job of a cop on the beat. Pearl Harbor was but a tip-off about Hoover's future legendary secretiveness and oversimplified way of thinking."

Over the decades, many historians have come down hard on J. Edgar, especially Leslie Rout and John Bratzel in their *American Historical Review*. They blamed J. Edgar for failing to share information with the White House and Army and Naval intelligence agencies. Their claim was that J. Edgar "showed both a poverty of judgment on his part and the crippling consequences of rivalry among those government agencies charged with gathering and evaluating information essential to the United States at a critical time in its history."

J. Edgar tried to distance himself "from Pearl Harbor blame," claiming at one point to Assistant Attorney General Joseph Keenan that Roosevelt "suppressed vital Pearl Harbor intelligence." On another occasion he suggested that Winston Churchill withheld last-minute intelligence warnings that an attack on Pearl Harbor was imminent.

"That was the fucker's way of luring us into a war," J. Edgar charged.

Many Americans at the time were not familiar with J. Edgar's role in Pearl Harbor and lavished praise on him for his wartime surveillance activities on the home front. But his overzealous tendency to find a possible spy around every corner also made enemies for him on the left. Senator George Norris of Nebraska accused him "of overstepping and overreaching" his authority, claiming "J. Edgar Hoover is the greatest publicity hound on the North American continent."

VOTE FOR VITO!

The New Republic wrote that J. Edgar's "chief support comes from those who go to gangster movies and purchase detective magazines for a dime." J. Edgar's major enemy in Congress, Vito Marcantonio, ridiculed the director as "the Stork Club detective." In all seriousness, on the floor of the House of Representatives, he called for the "decapitation" of J. Edgar Hoover.

J. Edgar's worst enemy in Congress was the dapper, flamboyant, **Vito Marcantonio** *(two photos above)*, who represented New York City's East Harlem. He'd graduated from New York University's Law School and evolved into the populist champion of the working-class poor in his district, where he built up a loyal following.

His denunciations on the floor of the House of Representatives against J. Edgar Hoover were the most violent ever delivered in Congress. He virtually wanted to bring back the guillotine to cut off J. Edgar's head for the failure of his intelligence regarding Pearl Harbor.

Through the years, the FBI file on Marcantonio grew to 1,000 pages before the congressman's death in 1954. When J. Edgar learned of the passing of his enemy, he said, "The biggest Communist in America is burning in hell tonight."

When Marcantonio was finally defeated in 1950, Italians were enraged. They blamed the newly arriving Puerto Ricans for the defeat of "our beloved Vito."

As a cop in East Harlem admitted, "All the Italians were jumping every Spic they saw."

The only attacks that J.

Edgar relished were those that accused him of being a womanizer. *Time* magazine claimed that "his dread is that someone, someday, somewhere, will plant a naked woman in his path to try to frame him."

Winchell in his column wrote, "The only girl he really adores and sends gifts to is a famous movie star who makes more in a fortnight than he does in a year . . . Shirley Temple."

***

J. Edgar and Clyde became key players in the great sex scandal of the Roosevelt administration. Sumner Welles, FDR's Undersecretary of State, had already learned that J. Edgar and Clyde were homosexual lovers. Both these FBI men knew that Welles liked to perform oral sex on black men, whom he would pursue indiscreetly when intoxicated. His love of fellatio had already gotten him kicked out of Cuba.

America's two top G-Men were not the only ones who wanted Welles eliminated from government. His official boss, Secretary of State Cordell Hull, despised him. The ailing Secretary loathed the thought that Welles was set to replace him. Hull's health was failing, and he feared he might have to step down.

Over the years, FDR had heard many scandalous stories about Welles. Through it all they had remained friends.

FDR felt that Welles could hide his homosexuality behind the cloak of marriage to Mathilde Scott Townsend, a noted international beauty whose portrait had been painted by John Singer Sargent. Mr. and Mrs. Welles lived in a 49-room mansion outside of Washington on a 245-acre estate. FDR often used their home, Oxon Hill Manor, for weekend escapes with one of his mistresses.

The Welles family and the Roosevelts were very close. A twelve-year-old Welles was a page at FDR's wedding to Eleanor in March of 1905 and had even carried her bridal gown. At Groton, Welles had roomed with Eleanor's brother, and she'd always been his major champion in the Roosevelt administration.

J. Edgar told Clyde, Louis Nichols, and Guy Hotell that he wanted to bug the hotel rooms Welles occupied. "If we could secretly film him performing fellatio on a Negro, that would do it. Nothing could be more incriminating than that, except filming him getting fucked by some black buck. I detest people who have sex outside their race. We need stronger laws against that."

The first chance to entrap Welles having illicit sex had manifested itself back in September of 1940. Senator William Bankhead, the Speaker of

182

the House, had died. He was the father of actress Tallulah Bankhead, who detested J. Edgar. Several government dignitaries, including Welles himself and Secretary of the Interior Harold Ickes, traveled by train to Jasper, Alabama, to attend the funeral.

J. Edgar sent Clyde and Guy to accompany the party. While Welles was at the funeral, supporting a grieving Tallulah, Clyde bugged his compartment on the train.

En route back to Washington, Clyde and Guy paid two good-looking black Pullman porters to make themselves sexually available to Welles. "He'll take the bait," Guy accurately predicted.

Clyde paid each of the porters one hundred dollars, which was more money than either of them had ever seen before.

When the porters visited Welles' compartment, they found him drunk and willing to sexually take on both of them simultaneously. It was all caught on the secret recording, which Clyde and Guy almost gleefully transported back to J. Edgar for his listening pleasure.

Through other congressmen attending the Bankhead funeral, and not through the FBI, William Bullitt became aware of Welles' seductions of the black men on that funeral train. Bullitt had a motive. He'd been FDR's ambassador to France but left Paris in the wake of the Nazi invasion. He wanted to become the new Secretary of State when Hull stepped down. To achieve that goal, he had to eliminate Welles, his major competitor.

A self-promoting political opportunist, Bullitt was called "the Iago of Iagos" by columnist Marquis Childs. Roosevelt had a personal reason to dislike Bullitt. Privately he referred to FDR as "that cripple in the White House," and he had even seduced the President's mistress, Marguerite LeHand ("Missy"). He bragged

As one of Franklin D. Roosevelt's chief aides, a "peacemonger" like **Sumner Welles** had maintained close ties to the Roosevelt family since his childhood. Some experts defined him as "the number three man in FDR's administration," with special expertise in U.S. relations with Latin America. As such, he was honored on the cover of the August 11, 1941 edition of *Time* magazine.

But by 1956, Welles had fallen into disgrace, and as such, appeared in a scandalous cover story of *Confidential* magazine. His habit of performing fellatio on studly African-American and African-Hispanic men became common knowledge during the Eisenhower era.

183

to Hull and others, "At least she knew what it was like to have a real man, not someone in a wheelchair."

Bullitt met with J. Edgar and pleaded with him to turn over the FBI report on Welles, but J. Edgar refused the request. He wanted to collect far more incriminating evidence before he had his own meeting with the President. Rebuffed, Bullitt decided to go to FDR himself and present his case against Welles.

FDR didn't want to hear it. "I never want to hear what a man does when he's drunk," he told Bullitt. However, he appointed a "bodyguard" for Welles the next day. But after their second night together, J. Edgar learned that Welles was getting drunk with his bodyguard and seducing him as well.

When Eleanor learned of the charges against Welles, she intervened with her husband, claiming that he would surely commit suicide if he lost his post.

Bullitt then wrote FDR a confidential letter, asking "What if America's brave fighting men learned that the Number Two man in our State Department was a criminal and a sex deviate?"

Pressure mounted on FDR, as Bullitt was threatening to go to some Republican members of Congress to launch an investigation.

Louis Nichols and Clyde came up with another damaging report that occurred on a train ride Welles took to Cleveland. A very rich man, Welles had spread the word that any black man on the train who wanted to make a hundred dollars could knock on the door to his compartment. "All he asked was for me to take it out so he could suck it," one of the porters had claimed. "A lot of my brothers went for that kind of money since that was all they had to do to earn it."

When Hull heard these reports, he too wanted an audience with the President. But first the Secretary of State called J. Edgar asking for him to turn over his file on Welles. Seeing no advantage in helping Hull, J. Edgar refused. He personally wanted to break the case on him.

J. Edgar, Guy, and Nichols continued to accumulate more evidence. Around Christmastime of 1942, Welles almost froze to death, having stumbled and fallen into an icy stream on his estate. He was so drunk, he passed out. He was pursuing a very reluctant black workman on his property.

Another report reached J. Edgar's desk. On a visit to Paris in 1939 before the Nazi invasion, Welles had been seen in a bar right off the Champs-Elysées. This incident later became so gossiped about in Washington that it appeared as a passage in *Answered Prayers*, the novel that the gay author, Truman Capote, was working on (or pretending to be working on) at the time of his death.

The passage reads:

It was after midnight in Paris in the bar of Boeuf-sur-Le Toit, when he was sitting at a pink-clothed table with three men, two of them expensive tarts, Corsican pirates in British flannel, and the third none other than Sumner Welles— fans of CONFIDENTIAL will remember the patrician Mr. Welles, former Undersecretary of State, great and good friend of the Brotherhood of Sleeping Car Porters. It made rather a tableau, one especially vivant, when His Excellency, pickled as brandied peaches, began nibbling those Corsican ears.

Secretary of State **Cordell Hull** *(left)* takes a walk with his undersecretary, **Sumner Welles** *(right)*, who wanted to replace him. Hull was in ailing health and could hardly withstand the awful tension of being Secretary of State during a World War. But as Hull knew all too well, thanks to reports from J. Edgar Hoover, Welles was a notorious homosexual, specializing in sex with black men. His career within the Roosevelt administration was doomed.

J. Edgar finally descended on the Oval Office with a very detailed and damaging report on "how dangerously and indiscreet Welles had behaved." With a 1944 re-election campaign coming up, FDR finally capitulated, especially when Hull was told that a congressional investigation was about to be launched. It was August of 1943 when FDR painfully called Welles and asked him to resign, suggesting he cite the ill health of his wife.

Back at his office, J. Edgar told Clyde and Guy, "That old biddy, Horse Face herself, can't protect her boy anymore." He was referring, of course, to Eleanor Roosevelt.

Author Ted Morgan in his book *FDR: A Biography* maintained the resignation of Welles had a devastating effect on Pan American solidarity and the Good Neighbor Policy. Not only that, but Welles was the most sympathetic person in the Roosevelt administration to the plight of Jews fleeing the terror of Hitler's Germany. Some historians credit Welles with the design for the future United Nations.

Welles had appeared on the cover of *Time* magazine in 1941, and had been profiled in *The New York Times* that same year. The paper called him, "Tall and erect, never without his cane. He has enough dignity to be a Viceroy of India and enough influence in this critical era to make his ideas, principles, and dreams count."

185

Welles died a broken man in September of 1961, but lived long enough to see his homosexual secret life exposed in *Confidential* in 1956. The tabloid scandal magazine published a story about the train incidents with the black Pullman porters.

Sir Winston Churchill once said, "I learned one thing from Sumner Welles. He made the phrase 'no comment' famous."

In the case of Sumner Welles, J. Edgar and Clyde perfected their technique of rounding up incriminating evidence on presumed homosexuals. They would carry on such secret missions for the rest of their lives, involving allegations against such men as Adlai Stevenson and Martin Luther King, Jr.

***

By the spring of 1942, there were many letters reaching J. Edgar's office, asking why Errol Flynn had been deferred by his draft board. Many of his friends and or male lovers were already in uniform, including Clark Gable, David Niven, Tyrone Power, and Robert Taylor.

An outcry was heard on June 19, 1942 when Igor Cassini published a blurb in the *Washington Times Herald*:

> *"Errol Flynn was deferred by his H'wood draft board because of a heart condition. Funny that this should happen to the hero of the greatest screen battles, to the tennis champion of the movie colony, to an ex-boxer, and to the greatest athlete of all Hollywood. Flynn's friends, however, say that he's burned up about criticism and that he wants to get into the army at all costs. We'll see. Errol looks healthier to us than many men they take every day. If it's his heart that is weak, Flynn should have been buried a long time ago."*

A draft dodger himself in WWI, J. Edgar ordered an immediate investigation. To his special agent in Los Angeles, Richard Hood, the director wrote: "You should furnish the Bureau with the complete facts concerning Flynn's deferment within seven days. This inquiry should be conducted in a very discreet manner so that the fact it is being made will not be publicized."

To Guy and Clyde, J. Edgar said, "He looked pretty healthy to me when he emerged from that pool in Nassau."

Hood's report was complete, claiming that in spite of his outward physical appearance, Errol was "a very sick man," suffering from infectious tuberculosis, a condition worsened by his "excessive" lifestyle, including chain smoking." In New Guinea, he'd contracted malaria and still suffered from recurring bouts of this disease.

That was not all: It was determined that he had a dangerous heart murmur, and he also suffered from sinusitis, a serious inflammation of a sinus within his skull.

His examining physician, Joseph Szukalski, allegedly said, "The only thing about Mr. Errol Flynn that seems in working order is his penis." Errol was said to have produced an erection when his testicles were being juggled by a physician.

In 1937, under instructions from J. Edgar, Clyde had begun an FBI file on Errol Flynn whom they had met with Axel Wenner-Gren in The Bahamas. The trip the movie star had taken to Spain in 1937 was cause for alarm, since Flynn's traveling companion was Dr. Hermann Erben, who had strong and sinister links to the Nazi Party.

J. Edgar feared Erben might be a possible espionage agent, and that Flynn was dangerously linked to him. Errol was questioned by an FBI agent, Richard Hood, at Warner Brothers in September of 1940 but he claimed that Erben was merely a longtime friend and denied that his associate had any Nazi ties.

Biographer Charles Higham claimed that Erben was a soldier of fortune and an adventurer of the seven seas. "His anti-Semitism and love of Hitler were the overpowering impulses in his life." In his youth, he bore a marked resemblance to the Führer himself.

In 1933, in a letter to Erben, Flynn had written: "A slimy Jew is trying to cheat me. I do wish we could bring Hitler over here to teach these Isaacs a thing or two. The bastards have absolutely no business probity or honour whatsoever."

In Errol's memoirs, *My Wicked, Wicked Ways*, he changed Erben's name to "Dr. Gerrit H. Koets," because at the time he didn't know if his long-ago friend were still alive and might sue for libel.

In the book he described Erben as he looked upon their first meeting in 1933: "He wore a broad, Dutch grin, showing enormous teeth parted. His ears were monsters that stood out at about the angle of an enraged elephant about to charge. His face was covered with blond hair. His bare legs and thighs showed the same hirsuteness, so that he looked like an amiable orangutan in a mink coat."

In 1933, Erben, a specialist in tropical diseases, became a U.S. citizen by falsifying his application. The FBI had recommended the suspension of Erben's U.S. citizenship because he had been arrested for "nefarious activities" in Spain. Errol had driven him from a point within the U.S. to the Mexican border as a means of escaping arrest. Even so, after Mexico, he arrived in Shanghai in 1936, where he was arrested and imprisoned by the

U.S. Army, which suspected him of being a double agent. His U.S. citizenship was rescinded and he was forbidden to return to the United States.

In a surprise move, Errol then intervened with Eleanor Roosevelt to help Erben. She'd met Errol in Miami in the spring of 1940 when both of them were raising money for the March of Dimes. Errol was also a friend of her son, Franklin D. Roosevelt Jr., who used to go fox hunting with him in the wilds of Virginia.

Errol appealed to her concern for the underdog, and claimed that Erben was only appearing to be a Nazi under a threat from Berlin of killing all the members of the family he'd left behind in Germany if he didn't cooperate. Eleanor believed Errol and intervened in the case. Back in Washington she called J. Edgar and demanded that surveillance of Erben and Errol be suspended, and that Erben retain his U.S. citizenship.

J. Edgar also learned that Errol had written a five-page letter to William J. Donovan at the Office of Strategic Services, requesting an assignment as an informal and unofficial ambassador of good will to Ireland. He was, of course, immediately turned down. J. Edgar suspected he wanted to use that post to gather Allied secrets to turn over to his Nazi friend Erben.

In the midst of all his other troubles, Errol was indicted in Los Angeles on three counts of rape. The district attorney's office filed a complaint on November 20, 1942, outlining the charges.

Although the case was not within the jurisdiction of J. Edgar and Clyde, they voyeuristically followed the trial, adding details about its progress to Errol's FBI file.

Trouble began with Betty Hansen, a fifteen-year-old girl from Nebraska, claiming that Errol raped her. The second and third counts alleged that he also seduced Peggy Satterlee aboard his yacht, the *Sirocco*, on August 3, 1941. She was rather late in filing her complaint.

As events in the trial unfolded, it was discovered that she had worked as a dancer and showgirl at the Florence Gardens Burlesque House in Los Angeles, and she'd been an extra on Errol's film, *They Died With Their Boots On*. Unlike Betty, whose case qualified as statutory rape of a minor, Peggy was twenty-one years old at the time of her grievance.

One of Errol's most venomous attackers was Peggy's father, William C. Satterlee, who accused Errol of "degrading American womanhood." Clyde later learned that her father had previously been charged and convicted of molesting two underage girls himself.

During his trial on charges of rape, Errol had "to lay low," as he put it. To supply him with young boys and young girls in the interim, he turned to his stuntman friend, Buster Wiles, who subsequently pimped for the star. When either a gay boy or a straight girl was asked if they'd like to go to bed with Errol, nearly all of them volunteered.

As J. Edgar learned, Errol during his trial became intrigued with a beautiful young girl, Nora Eddington, who ran the tobacconist's kiosk at the Los Angeles County Courthouse. He demanded that Wiles find out if she were a virgin, although how the stuntman was expected to do that was never explained.

Errol finally concluded that she was a virgin, and may—just may—have been of legal age, which was eighteen. Hood, functioning as J. Edgar's ears and eyes in Los Angeles, filed a report stating that Nora had "just turned sixteen." This was not accurate. She was nineteen.

Right in the middle of his trial, Errol was alleged to have raped Nora, at least according to an interview she gave Flynn's biographer, Charles Higham, in 1978. She charged that, "I was terrified. Suddenly, he was thrusting into me. It was like a knife. I felt I was being killed. I screamed and screamed."

The act may have been brutal, but as Nora confessed in her own autobiography *Errol and Me*, she agreed to go on a trip to Mexico with him. Unknown to the pair, J. Edgar's agents had them spied on throughout the entire trip.

Amazingly in the middle of World War II, J. Edgar spent time and money trying to entrap Errol for being in violation of the Mann Act, which prohibited a man from taking a woman across a state line for the purposes of seduction.

The rape trial and other rumors were seriously damaging Flynn's popularity in the public eye as a screen swashbuckler. Even though he seemed to be winning World War II single-handedly on the screen, his clout at the box office had begun to wane. It seemed to his fans that he was inclined to do almost anything for his sexual gratification.

After the investigation, the FBI filed a memorandum on Errol regarding his "moral turpitude and publicity lies."

"Errol Flynn, movie actor, was held for trial on

Dr. Hermann F. Erben, a close friend of Errol Flynn, was a dedicated member of the Nazi Party. In 1935, he embarked on a zoological expedition to study monkeys, with implications for their role in inoculations against leprosy.

Years later, in a description of his friend, Errol claimed that Erben revealed to him "in a humorous, bawdy, Rabelaisian, tough, rough way the difference between a man with no soul and a man with one, even though neither of us knew what a soul was."

Erben was less charitable when describing Flynn to his Nazi associates: "Flynn is weak, easily bamboozled. His trust and friendship can be ruthlessly exploited."

two charges of rape, after hearings in Hollywood. One of the accusers said she was 15 when Flynn raped her on his yacht; the California law protects children by making the age of consent 18.

Behind the news: In 1937 Errol Flynn came to Madrid, saying he was bringing a large sum of money and the good will of the movie colony to the Loyalists in their fight against Hitler, Mussolini, and Franco, the Axis. This was a falsehood.

One night Flynn disappeared. Next morning he left for Valencia. The same day the entire American press front-paged a thrilling story of how Flynn was wounded in the frontline trenches of Madrid.

This story was a lie. Madrid censor, Constancia de la Mera, stated officially that Flynn had filed an innocent-looking telegram to Paris, that this telegram was the tipoff to release the news, and that the hoax was one of the most foul and callous actions ever admitted by a Hollywood actor to gain publicity at the expense of the fight against world fascism. Associated Press, United Press and other news agencies phoned their man in Valencia who confirmed fact Flynn was there without a scratch."

Errol Flynn *(right)* met his second wife, **Nora Eddington** *(left)*, a teenager, when she sold him a glass of cold cider in the courthouse where he was being tried on rape charges.

Not having learned any lessons, he soon proceeded to rape Nora. As she confessed in her memoir, "I was impaled on the end of a sword. The pain was unbearable. 'Oh, no, no!' I shrieked."

After the act, she lay there "sobbing and sobbing on a mess of bloodied sheets."

The FBI trailed Errol during his romance and eventual marriage to Nora.

On February 6, 1943 the jury returned a verdict of not guilty on all three counts of rape. Leslie Still, the presiding Superior Court judge, claimed, "I have enjoyed this case." Looking over at the jury, he added, "and I think you have, too."

In November of 1942, back when Errol was still facing an indictment on rape charges, he became involved in an extortion case, which did involve the FBI. Richard Hood, the special FBI agent in Los Angeles, sent J. Edgar and Clyde the threatening letter. The writer of the letter threatened the life of Errol if he did not deliver ten-thousand dollars in cash to an address in San Bernardino. The money was to be delivered to "Jack Gelstrom" at a malt shop at 383 East Street.

J. Edgar ordered his agents to place the malt shop under surveillance. The extortionist turned out to be Billy Seamster, age 13. He was photographed and fingerprinted, but the District Attorney's office in Los Angeles decided not to prosecute Seamster because of his age.

On February 23, 1943, Errol received another extortion letter which claimed, "If you know what is good for you, you will pay attention to them girls you raped. I know you did it. You can't fool me so you better fork over some dough." Errol was told to answer the threat in the *Boston Daily Record* near Walter Winchell's column. The extortionist had demanded $15,000.

J. Edgar ordered his agents in Boston to place an ad as instructed. It read simply, "Received your letter, Mr. Flynn."

Eventually the letter was traced to a man called Robert Street, who claimed he hated Errol. He was never prosecuted by the FBI. J. Edgar had bigger game to pursue, and that was Errol himself.

FBI agents in Mexico had failed to nail Errol on any white slavery charges concerning Nora Eddington.

In 1943, Errol would marry Nora, although he was never faithful to her. On that trip to Mexico with her he spent as much time with a very good-looking beach boy, Apollonio Díaz, as he did with Nora. Several times he left Nora back in their hotel room while he went sailing with the boy he'd affectionately nicknamed "Apollo."

From Los Angeles, Errol had flown to Mexico with the notorious Freddie McEvoy, his "second best friend" after Dr. Erben. Hoping to throw the FBI off his trail, Errol had booked Nora on a separate flight.

Errol's friendship with McEvoy dated from their boyhood days growing up in Australia. In Mexico, McEvoy vied with Porfirio Rubirosa for the title of "Playboy of the Western World," both studs known for their legendary endowments.

As J. Edgar learned, McEvoy and Rubi were not competitors, but instead, actively pimped for each other. In fact, McEvoy in later life charged Rubi a fee of $100,000 for him to arrange an introduction to Barbara Hutton, the Woolworth heiress whom Rubi eventually married. Before Rubi, Hutton had indiscreetly proclaimed to her friends that superstud McEvoy was the only man in the world who'd ever given her an orgasm.

Weighing 175 pounds, McEvoy bragged about his thick twelve-inch penis, referring to it as "one of the wonders of the world." As dozens of wealthy women in both Europe and North America could testify, he did not exaggerate. He became history's highest paid gigolo.

He'd also seduced such Hollywood stars as Mae West, Joan Crawford, tobacco heiress Doris Duke, Hedy Lamarr, Merle Oberon, Marlene Dietrich, and Judy Garland.

FBI agents in Mexico diverted their surveillance of Errol to concentrate on McEvoy, after a tipster revealed to J. Edgar that he was a Nazi collaborator.

An expert spy and master of intrigue and espionage, McEvoy had become involved with the Nazis in 1936 when he visited Berlin as captain of the British bobsled team.

On his second night in the Nazi capital, he was seen dining with Josef Goebbels himself. Somewhere along the way, he was recruited as a spy for the Nazis. Since he moved in exalted circles around the world, McEvoy was able to supply the Nazis with valuable information.

Errol had made Mexico his weekend retreat, attending bullfights in Mexico City, going spear fishing in Acapulco, visiting the spa and "sin palaces" in Cuernavaca. Among the *gringo* celebrities, he was the best known of the Hollywood crowd, a familiar face to bordello owners, who rented out a bevy of handsome boys or beautiful girls. Errol preferred them underage.

As a sideline, McEvoy recruited about two dozen of the handsomest and most virile men in the world, with origins ranging from Senegal to Norway. He established stud services for rich women in various countries, pocketing fifty percent of the earnings of his male prostitutes. As such, he was said to have been the most successful pimp of the 20th century.

During some of his visits to Mexico, Errol was the guest of the American heiress, Beatrice Cartwright, who was confined to a wheelchair. McEvoy had agreed to marry this disabled woman for her money, with the stipulation that he could have other women on certain nights of the week.

He confided to Errol that, "Beatrice is the most sexually demanding partner I've ever had—night and day, the bitch can't get enough deep dicking. And I'm a sexual athlete. I've got a foot of dick, as you well know, and even that is not enough to satisfy her."

Other evenings with the McEvoys were spent at the Mexico City mansion of the American-born Countess Dorothy di Frasso, who was a vivacious friend of everybody from Mussolini to gangster Bugsy Siegel. J. Edgar ordered that she remain under constant surveillance.

At one party at her home, McEvoy proclaimed, "I avoided the draft. There's no way the British will get me to fight the Nazis."

During the war, McEvoy shared a secret and very dangerous plan with Errol. The Nazis wanted his aid in setting up U-boat refueling bases off the Pacific coasts of Mexico and Central America.

Learning of this plot, an FBI agent went over J. Edgar's head and reported this startling information to U.S. Naval Intelligence. When the F.B.I. director learned of this insubordination, he immediately fired the agent in Mexico City.

In Mexico City, McEvoy arranged for Errol to have a brief fling with the reigning *femme fatale*, Tara Marsh. J. Edgar's agents unraveled the details. Marsh, a Nazi agent assigned to Mexico, claimed she'd been to bed with both Josef Goebbels and Hitler in Berlin. To Errol, she denied reports that the Führer was impotent but did confirm that he'd lost one testicle which was shot off during World War I.

McEvoy had also introduced Errol to the pleasures of Cuernavaca where he flew for secret visits. He stayed at the mansion of Harry Carstairs, a British homosexual and Nazi spy. With some accuracy, this heir to a bakery fortune billed himself as "the handsomest man in Cuernavaca."

Installed in his mansion, Errol enjoyed all twelve of Carstairs' "special employees," a series of beautiful young boys from all over the world, from Germany to Brazil. The nude boys arranged themselves on chaises longues around Carstairs' pool, and Errol made his choices.

Carstairs also took Errol to a club where he could watch women have sex with horses and large dogs.

After one of his wild weekends in Cuernavaca, Errol flew back to Warner Brothers to finish *Santa Fe Trail*. He was accompanied by his pimp, Johnny Meyer, who had, among other assignations, arranged a sexual liaison between him

In October of 1950, **Errol Flynn** *(left)* and the notorious playboy and gigolo, **Freddie McEvoy** *(right)* are all dressed up for Errol's third and final marriage, this time to the beautiful actress Patrice Wymore.

McEvoy and Flynn went way back, and shared many dark secrets. None was as notorious as an event that occurred at the Helen Mar Hotel on Miami Beach early in 1950. McEvoy had arranged for a half-brother and his half-sister, both immigrants from Cuba, to spend the weekend at their hotel suite.

They had arrived in Miami with their mother, who shortly thereafter died. They were supporting themselves through prostitution, renting themselves out, usually as a team, as bisexuals. The girl was only fourteen, her half-brother, sixteen. The story has never been completely revealed, but McEvoy and Errol wanted to conduct some pseudo-scientific experiments to determine "if certain acts were better with a girl or a boy."

On the Monday that followed a weekend of debauchery, the girl was found dead in bed. A lot of money passed hands in the form of a bribe, but the investigating officers from the Miami Beach Police eventually declared that the girl had died of a heart attack. Errol paid for her funeral.

and the billionaire aviator Howard Hughes.

As part of the Good Neighbor Policy arranged by the U.S. government and Errol's P.R. staff, which included Meyer, Errol had been persuaded to embark on a trip that incorporated stopovers in twenty-one Latin American countries. It was understood that Meyer would accompany him on this trip. Major stopovers included Buenos Aires where Errol had an affair with the beautiful, elegant Evita Peron, a former prostitute. During his stopover in Rio de Janeiro, Meyer arranged for Errol to seduce some of that city's most beautiful boys and girls.

Dr. Erben had warned Errol to denounce Nazism at the same time that he was gathering secret information for them.

Charles Higham, in his controversial biography, *Errol Flynn, The Untold Story*, interviewed Meyer years later. The former pimp confirmed that Errol had met Gestapo agents in South America, especially in Buenos Aires, "at the highest level in the Nazi hierarchy."

As a visiting American film star, Errol was the guest of American ambassadors and was allowed to tour secret U.S. Army and Naval installations. He was even invited aboard American warships in the area. According to Meyer, Errol accumulated a great deal of secrets to turn over to Erben.

Back in the States, Erben once again confronted immigration authorities. J. Edgar had convinced them that Erben was a dangerous Nazi agent. Without the protective umbrella previously provided by Eleanor Roosevelt, he was deported from America for the final time.

To throw the FBI and other detractors off his trail, Errol gave interviews upon his return to California. The most famous of these was published in *Photoplay* magazine.

> *"I did not go down there on a binge. They—Germany and Italy—are getting ready to fight the United States, not just the British Empire, and they want to fight us in our own back yard, South America. I know, I was there and saw the preparations, the 'tourists,' the Fifth Columnists, the huge radio programs, the saboteurs. I fought them every way I could. That's why I went! They gave me quite a write-up. According to Virgie [Virginio Gayda, editor of GIORNAL D'ITALIA and an ardent supporter of Mussolini] I'm the tops, the deadliest, dirtiest, conniving son of a macaw that the unspeakably cunning British Propaganda Minister has ever sent out!"*

J. Edgar and Clyde read that article with complete skepticism. "He's not fooling us," J. Edgar told his agents. "We're on to him. But he's a tricky one. I hear he's even working for British intelligence, a true double agent."

In spite of wasting what was a vast fortune of government money, J. Edgar and Clyde never nailed any concrete evidence on Errol that confirmed his role as a Nazi spy. A British patriot and fellow actor, David Niven, who once shared living quarters with Errol, denied that he was an actual spy for the Nazis.

"This pro-German crowd simply entertained Errol with the best sex he'd ever had," Niven said. "If the party was good enough, Errol didn't give a damn whether the party was thrown by a friend of Roosevelt or Churchill or even Mussolini and Hitler. He once told me, 'There isn't that much difference between a Nazi pussy and an Allied pussy, especially when the lights are out.'"

Shortly after Flynn's death in 1959, J. Edgar and Clyde had answered what they viewed as two very important questions about the former swashbuckler.

At the tender age of twelve years, he'd lost his virginity to the family maid. They also discovered the secret of Errol's sexual prowess: Before intercourse, he smeared a film of cocaine on the tip of his penis.

***

J. Edgar and Clyde never trusted Marlene Dietrich, whom they suspected of being a double agent during World War II, secretly spying for the Nazis while entertaining American troops in the trenches of Western Europe.

The FBI file on her dated from May 17, 1924, years before she starred in *The Blue Angel,* a film that catapulted her into international stardom in 1930.

In the *Kaiser Wilhelm Gedächtniskirche* in Berlin, she and Rudolph Sieber ("Rudi") were wed. During her early years in Berlin, while married, as always, to Rudi, Marlene entered into a number of affairs with both women and men, most notably Greta Garbo during the Swede's years in Berlin.

J. Edgar learned that at the time of her marriage, Dietrich occupied the same apartment building as Leni Riefenstahl, the German film star who later became Adolf Hitler's favorite filmmaker for works that included her masterpiece, *Triumph of the Will*. Marlene was seen coming and going from the Riefenstahl apartment at 54 Kaiserallee in Berlin.

Through introductions by Riefenstahl, Marlene was seen at various parties which were attended by the hierarchy of the fast-rising Nazi party. Among others, she was introduced to Josef Goebbels and Hermann Göring.

Even before she left Berlin for Hollywood, Goebbels approached her, telling her she should stay in Germany where she could become "Queen of UFA," the German film studio. She was said to have spat in his face, but that could have been a later invention of her biographers.

On hearing these stories about how Marlene turned her back on Hitler and the Nazis, J. Edgar was suspicious. "It could be just an act to throw us off her trail," he told Clyde and his agents. "A clever espionage trick on the part of the Nazis."

As reports came in from the Hollywood of the 1930s, J. Edgar came to view Marlene as "an international slut. She'll sleep with anybody, man or woman, from Gary Cooper to Tallulah Bankhead."

Although her own sexual record was one of the most tarnished in Hollywood, Joan Crawford took delight in feeding J. Edgar and Clyde the latest scandals revolving around Marlene. Crawford was confident that if she ever got involved in a major scandal that threatened her own career, J. Edgar and Clyde would rescue her.

While making *Knight Without Armour* (1937) in London, Marlene was approached by the German actress, Mady Soyka, who delivered a message from Goebbels. He'd orchestrated vicious attacks on Marlene within the German press, accusing her of being a traitor for her allegiance to the United States. However, Soyka claimed that he'd call off his attack dogs if she'd agree to return to Berlin and make just one film in one month. He offered her fifty thousand British pounds if she'd agree. According to reports reaching J. Edgar, Marlene rejected Goebbels' offer once again.

In spite of this latest evidence, J. Edgar remained stubborn in his belief that "the Kraut is a committed Nazi. All these offers and rejections are staged just for our benefit to conceal what the lesbian bitch is really up to."

Back in Hollywood during that winter of 1937, Hitler was said to have presented Marlene with an elaborate piece of jewelry at Christmas, which was delivered by an official of the German Embassy in Los Angeles. The gift included a letter from Goebbels, urging her to sign with UFA and return to Berlin.

Even though at the time she had been labeled "box office poison" in the United States, Marlene turned down the offer one final time. This latest rejection was widely publicized and endeared Marlene to her still-loyal fans. But it didn't impress J. Edgar. "She's an actress. It's just a ruse to throw us off her trail."

Just weeks before the Japanese attack on Pearl Harbor, J. Edgar and Clyde supplied secret information to the House Un-American Activities Committee, whose members were in Hollywood looking for violations of the U.S. Neutrality Act. They were trying to ferret out Fascists secretly working for the Nazi cause.

J. Edgar privately informed committee members that the name of Marlene Dietrich should be added to the list. As evidence, he cited that she'd made the German actor Rudolf Forster the godfather of her daughter, Maria Sieber. J. Edgar had learned that in a moment of artistic pique, he'd walked out on rehearsals for a production on Broadway, sending Otto Preminger a note which read, "I'm going home to rejoin Adolf."

"Even if it's only guilt by association, Frau Dietrich knows just too many Nazis," J. Edgar told the investigating committee.

In 1942, at the beginning of America's entry into World War II, Marlene asked the Office of Strategic Services if she could entertain U.S. troops in Europe. Behind her back, J. Edgar and Clyde filed a report with the OSS that accused her of being a security risk, defining her as a suspected spy for the Third Reich. OSS officials ignored the report and granted her permission to entertain the troops. She was also allowed to sing American songs with German lyrics on shortwave broadcasts to Nazi soldiers.

J. Edgar suspected even those songs, claiming that she was sending coded messages behind German lines. He was told by one of his German-speaking agents that the lyrics to "Taking a Chance on Love," for example, assumed a completely

Although it originated as a German-language song, American soldiers, including members of the 63rd Infantry Division in 1945 (*lower photo*) wanted **Marlene Dietrich** *(in both photos, above)* to sing *Lili Marlene*.

(Before she adopted it as her "theme," the original German-language spelling of the song had been *Lili Marleen.*)

Dietrich starred in frequent radio broadcasts on the Armed Forces network. At one point, she shouted (in German) into the microphone: "Boys! Don't sacrifice yourselves! The war is a shit! Hitler is an idiot!"

In Army hospitals and on the front lines, the entertainment of American troops became her passion. A legend was being born.

As one soldier recalled, "Marlene had no modesty. While we were showering, she would come right in with us, carrying her soap and towel, and shower with us. Every guy got a hard-on."

different meaning in German.

Lt. Colonel Robert Armstrong was assigned the role of Marlene's military escort in Italy and France, as those countries were respectively invaded by the Allies. He later reported that in Europe, Marlene was threatened by messages from Goebbels, who warned her that both her sister and her mother were citizens of the Third Reich. "I, of course, do not want any harm to come to them. But if you continue to entertain enemy troops of your Fatherland, I cannot guarantee their safety."

As her biographer Charles Higham wrote: "Sometimes she would perform on rough wooden platforms set up out on the fields, with only the headlights of Jeeps to light her, or in rain under umbrellas or feeble little canvas canopies. She never had more than one suitcase for her makeup and her stage costumes. She wore GI uniforms: an Eisenhower jacket, regulation trousers, boots, and often a helmet or overseas cap. She liked being a soldier. One of the boys."

J. Edgar was not impressed when he learned of this. "A very clever woman, this German *Frau*. She could have taught Mata Hari."

Marlene insisted on going to the dangerous front lines to entertain the troops. In addition to numerous soldiers, which she allowed to seduce her, she also had affairs with two of the leading generals of WWII, George Patton and James Gavin.

Patton, whose men called him "Blood and Guts," was a great admirer of Marlene's. "They began an intense affair," claimed Frank McCarthy, who later produced the film *Patton*. "He often summoned Dietrich to his headquarters late at night, ostensibly to inquire about her tour. He assigned her the password of 'Legs.'"

Over pillow talk, she told him of her fears that she'd be captured by the Nazis. "I'm not afraid of dying, but they will shave off my hair and have horses drag me through the streets of Berlin."

He gave her a pearl-handled revolver just like his own. "If that ever happens, shoot yourself. After all, you said you're not afraid to die. Neither am I."

J. Edgar and Clyde were horrified to learn that Marlene was sleeping with Patton. "What military secrets will he pass on to the Kraut?" J. Edgar asked.

Patton's rival was the handsome, dashing General Gavin, one of the youngest commanders in the U.S. Army. He, too, had launched an affair with Marlene and had made her song, "Lili Marlene," the anthem of the 82nd Airborne Infantry Division of the United States Army, a unit specializing in parachute landing operations. Over pillow talk at the Ritz Hotel in Paris, he shared secrets with her, including his knowledge of Operation

198

Eclipse, in which Allied planes would storm Berlin with paratroopers. Plans for this operation were later abandoned.

Marlene even went to the Ardennes in Eastern France where she suffered frostbite. To her horror, she found herself entrapped with Allied troops during the Battle of the Bulge, the last great German offensive in the West. The Nazi general, Sepp Dietrich (no relation), almost captured her.

In a real-life development which resembled a theme from one of her films, her "gallant cavalier," General Gavin, flew to her rescue, aiming one of his "Flying Fortresses" into the war-torn area and landing virtually at her feet. Bundling her into a Jeep, he broke through enemy lines and drove on with her to Paris, with a few stopovers for lovemaking along the way.

At war's end, in spite of his expensive and time-consuming investigations and probes, and in spite of his many spies reporting on Marlene's activities, J. Edgar was terribly disappointed to hear she was staying at the Ritz Hotel in a liberated Paris with Gavin. He chastised Clyde and his agents, "We didn't dig deep enough. If we'd had better informants, we could have caught her red-handed. Let's keep after her. Find out what that whoring Kraut is up to after the war. We'll have her trailed when she returns to Berlin for that reunion with her Nazi mother."

Frau Dietrich liked American generals fighting World War II in Europe, especially old "Blood and Guts," **George Patton** *(left)* or the young, movie star handsome **James Gavin** *(right)*, whom she found more passionate and even more impressively endowed.

As she recalled, "I advanced with General Patton and the Third Army toward my homeland of Germany. I remember it well—I washed my undies in snow melted in my helmet and survived in sleeping bags in ruins. With the GIs, I dined on K-rations. There were rats and even more crabs."

"My darling James Gavin should have been my leading man in the movies. What a dashing paratrooper. As a man, he would have been Hitler's ideal. I fell in love with him in a Russian bar in Paris listening to gypsy music."

General Gavin was portrayed by Robert Ryan in *The Longest Day,* and by Ryan O'Neal in *A Bridge Too Far.* He accepted John F. Kennedy's offer of becoming U.S. Ambassador to France in 1961, but, at the age of 70, in 1976, he turned down Jimmy Carter's offer to become director of the CIA.

***

In early 1942, some of the darkest days for the United States in World War II, neighbors near the Brooklyn Naval Yard became suspicious of uniformed sailors arriving at all hours of the day and night at a private townhouse. Well-dressed men in three-piece suits, often looking like Wall Street bankers, came and went like a steady flood.

Wondering what was going on, Sally Bethune put through a call to the FBI. She managed to get as far up in the chain as Louis Nichols, who told her he would investigate.

When Nichols reported to Clyde and J. Edgar, he found out they were already familiar with what was operating as a male bordello by a "madam," Gustave Beekman, who over a course of fourteen months had hired as many as fifty sailors, each agreeing to become a male prostitute, for a fee of fifty dollars per client. Of course, Beekman insisted on sampling the sailors in bed himself to make sure they were well built and well endowed and could sexually satisfy a client.

Weeks before the scandal broke, Guy Hotell had gladly volunteered to become a spy for the FBI within the brothel.

Originally, J. Edgar had sent Guy to the whorehouse to gather incriminating information on Sumner Welles and other highly placed government officials, who were rumored to be steady patrons of Beekman and his hot-to-trot sailors.

At that point, U.S. Naval Intelligence seemed unaware of even the existence of the bordello. Guy was only too eager to sample the sailors, especially since the FBI picked up the tab. He also had become aware that the brothel had been infiltrated by at least three Nazi spies, who gave each of the sailors a hundred dollar bill and plied them with liquor. Perhaps unknowingly, the Navy men provided these German spies with far more information than they meant to, especially classified data about the Brooklyn Naval Yard.

Long before the FBI wanted it known, this "house of degradation" was exposed in an article in the May 7, 1942 edition of *The New York Post*. The modesty of the press in those days dared not refer to it as a male bordello, since most Americans had never heard of such a thing, assuming that all brothels were by definition staffed exclusively with female prostitutes. The story was considered "unfit to print by most papers," including *The New York Times*. When the story finally made its way into the pages of *The New York Times*, that paper referred to the bordello as a "resort."

J. Edgar's friend, the columnist Walter Winchell, was more explicit, referring to it as "Brooklyn's spy nest, also known as the swastika swishery."

Many of the sailors who hired themselves out were rounded up. As Guy had reported to J. Edgar, Saturday, when Beekman auctioned off the young men on a small stage, was the bordello's most popular night. A curtain was pulled back, and each Navy man presented himself with an erection. Bidding was the highest on those nights, and some of the sailors were sold five or six times before the dawn.

When questioned by Naval Intelligence, the sailors usually denied that they were selling their bodies. Most of them said they had never participated in any homosexual acts. One sailor claimed he sold himself to raise money for dates with Brooklyn women. Another Navy man from Missouri claimed he thought the building was a branch of the U.S.O. One man maintained he only accepted clients who were Catholic priests because his parents had raised him to obey "Holy Fathers."

Three foreign agents were arrested, and somehow they just disappeared from the radar screen. Perhaps the U.S. government executed them.

What turned the bordello into a major national news event was the charge that Senator David I. Walsh, the 69-year-old chairman of the Naval Affairs Committee, was one of the more frequent patrons, at one time calling for a total of five young men to visit his room in a single evening. According to testimony, he was also seen talking to the Nazi agents already arrested.

Walsh was one of the most famous men in Massachusetts, having been its 46th governor (1914-1916). He later was elected to the U.S. Senate (1919-1947). He was the leading isolationist in the U.S. Senate, opposing Roosevelt's Lend Lease to Britain up until the attack on Pearl Harbor. As the first Irish Catholic senator from Massachusetts, he paved the way for John F. Kennedy in later years.

At the 1940 Democratic National convention, Walsh supported James Farley for president rather than FDR. His stand against Britain and against FDR assured him a host of enemies who wanted to see him destroyed.

Under intense questioning from Naval Intelligence, Beekman admitted that "Senator X" was indeed Walsh. The Massachusetts senator charged that he had been framed, and denounced the press, claiming that the charges were a "diabolical lie" and that his political enemies were trying to destroy him.

J. Edgar was asked for a full report. He was aware that Walsh knew that one of his top agents, Guy himself, was also a patron of the bordello. At no point did J. Edgar want it known that the FBI had planted a spy in the bordello to entrap politicians.

Known to J. Edgar and Clyde, but not reported in the press, were some famous non-political clients who also patronized "Beekman's Boys." Chief among them was Virgil Thomson, the celebrated composer whose work was described by critic Peggy Glanville-Hicks as "an Olympian blend of

David L. Walsh, the former governor of Massachusetts and later its senator, was trapped at the center of one of the most politically compromising sex scandals of the 1940s. It was so embarrassing that newspapers, even after they learned the facts, judged it as too hot to print.

Walsh, chairman at the time of the Senate's Naval Affairs committee, was one of the busiest patrons at a house of male prostitution that flourished during World War II near the Brooklyn Naval Yard. Every Saturday night, it "auctioned" young, well-endowed sailors to wealthy male patrons for a standard fee of $50, plus liquor and gratuities.

J. Edgar was well aware of what was going on within the bordello, which was patronized by Nazi spies eager to extract military secrets from its associates.

On May 20, 1942, the FBI issued a false report to Senator Alben W. Barkley, the Senate Majority Leader, denying that Walsh had ever been a patron of the male whorehouse.

The establishment's "madam," however, Gustave Beekman, was sent "up the river" for a long prison sentence.

humanity and detachment." Although he was rounded up that fateful night near the Brooklyn Naval Yard, he was later released. Under interrogation, Beekman revealed that some of his movie star clients included Tyrone Power and Cary Grant. According to testimony, the socially prominent stage, film, and radio personality, Monty Woolley, whenever he was in New York, spent every night at the bordello, and another composer, Cole Porter, frequented the house as well.

No report was made of Clyde's private meeting with Beekman after he'd been jailed. However, he must have threatened him in some diabolical way because after their heated confab, Beekman issued a statement. "I was mistaken. I must have confused Senator Walsh with another man, known to me as 'Doc' and residing in Connecticut."

Beekman claimed that the client thought to be Walsh was a different visitor altogether. "Although portly like the Senator and roughly the same age, he resembled him no more than I look like Haile Selassie."

Beekman was sentenced to twenty years for sodomy, and remained in prison until 1963.

When FDR was confronted with the information about his political enemy Walsh, he told J. Edgar that he had long known that the Senator was a homosexual but never wanted to use the charge against him. FDR also told Alben W. Barkley, the Senate's majority leader, that Walsh was indeed a homosexual. But for the "sake of the party," the President suggested that Barkley, who later became Harry S Truman's vice president, denounce the charges as false.

Before the Senate, Barkley refused to insert the investigative report on Walsh into the Congressional Record "because it contains disgusting and unprintable things. The details are too loathsome to mention on the Senate floor or in any group of ladies and gentlemen." For all official purposes, Walsh was cleared. The FBI found no evidence he passed on any information to Nazi spies, even though he had patronized the sailor prostitutes, in spite of his denials.

Through Clyde, J. Edgar pretended to conduct an investigation, later issuing a report that the newspapers had been wrong. He even attacked *The New York Post* for its "irresponsibility." His report cleared Walsh, even though dozens of witnesses knew he was guilty. J. Edgar officially stated that Walsh had an "unsullied reputation." The grateful New Englander wrote J. Edgar a thank you letter and continued in his post as senator.

Except for those in New York City, the rest of the American newspapers avoided the story, fearing libel or "not wanting to print dirt."

After Barkley's speech, Bennett Clark, senator from Missouri, demanded an investigation of "the old hussy who runs the *Post*." He was referring to 38-year-old Dorothy Schiff Backer.

To complicate matters, Schiff was said to have had an affair with FDR after ascertaining from his doctor that he was capable of having an erection.

In retaliation, the publisher demanded that J. Edgar file a complete report on the case and that it be made public. It never was.

The New York Post finally concluded, "The known facts made only one thing indisputable: Either a serious scandal was being hushed up or a really diabolical libel had been perpetrated."

In 1946, in Massachusetts, Walsh was defeated in his bid for re-election by Henry Cabot Lodge Jr., a Republican and an enemy of the Kennedy clan. Walsh remained a bachelor until his death on June 11, 1947. If he'd been re-elected, death would have claimed him before he served out his term.

In the future, another more famous senator from Massachusetts would be intensely investigated by J. Edgar and Clyde.

***

One foggy early morning on June 13, 1942, four Nazi saboteurs emerged from a German U-boat, *Innsbruck*, at the shore near Amagansett, Long Island. They were in the vanguard of a massive operation planned for the arrival of Nazi submarines on the East Coast of the U.S. Each of the saboteurs had been ordered to instigate a "Reign of Terror" through bomb-ings and sabotage, creating panic on the American homefront.

From the shore, John C. Cullen, a twenty-year-old Coast Guard seaman second class, was trying to see through the dense pea-soup fog that night. He spotted the glistening of a submarine. Although unarmed, he bravely approached the party of four men as they stood on the beach.

Their leader, George Dasch, spoke perfect English and lied to Cullen, telling him that they were fishermen whose boat had run aground. Almost immediately, Cullen suspected they were Nazi spies, but didn't want to alarm them, fearing he'd be killed. He suggested they return with him to a nearby Coast Guard station and wait until dawn broke.

One of the men, Heinrich Heinck, accidentally said something in German but was quickly silenced by Dasch. Actually, he'd told Dasch to kill Cullen.

Ignoring the request, Dasch offered Cullen $260 in American twenty-dollar bills, "If you'll forget you ever saw us."

Pretending to go along with that, Cullen appeared eager to accept the bribe. "I've never seen any of you before. I know nothing." Cullen quickly left his lookout post, fearing he'd be shot in the back, but Dasch let him go free. Cullen immediately hurried to the Coast Guard station, where his superiors did not believe his story.

"We don't want to make fools of ourselves," one of the Coast Guard officers said. "They'll give us hell."

When daylight came, Cullen, along with two officers of the Coast Guard, went to the landing site, where they found evidence that something had been recently buried.

After digging, the guardsmen found a hidden cache of blasting caps, incendiary devices, fuses, timers, and explosives, along with some Nazi uniforms, even German cigarettes and French brandy.

By six that morning the four saboteurs had taken the Amagansett train heading for New York City. They agreed to split into pairs. Dasch, thirty-nine years old, chose Ernst Peter Burger, thirty-five years old. Both of them had lived for a while in the United States. The other two German agents, Heinck and Robert Quirin, went their separate way.

In Manhattan, Dasch and Burger checked into the Hotel Martinique at Broadway and Thirty Second Street, where they enjoyed a sumptuous lunch, having arrived with $84,000 their Nazi bosses at Abwehr had given them.

Back in their hotel room, Dasch told Burger that he had no intention of carrying through with the sabotage and that he planned to call the FBI and turn himself in. He urged Burger to do the same. But his partner had another plan. He wanted to take the horde of cash and disappear into the American heartland. When he heard that, Dasch took control of the money.

Dasch later claimed that if Burger had not gone along with his plan, he was going to shove him out the window, where he'd plunge eight floors to his death.

Within the hour, Dasch called the New York branch office of the FBI and revealed the entire German plan and details associated with the arrival of the saboteurs. He was ready to turn himself in, along with Burger. "I just got off the phone with Marie Antoinette," the FBI agent said before slamming down the receiver. He later explained himself by saying, "You wouldn't believe how many crank calls I get."

Leaving Burger behind, Dasch flew to Washington and checked into the Mayflower Hotel. With a briefcase stuffed with cash, he headed for the FBI headquarters where he requested a private meeting with J. Edgar himself. He was turned down, but shown into the office of D.M. Ladd ("Mickey"). Ladd didn't believe his story and called Duane L. Traynor into his office. Head of the Sabotage Division of the FBI, Traynor was far more receptive.

The FBI had been notified by the Coast Guard at noon on June 13 about the arrival of the saboteurs. Precious hours had been wasted. But Cullen had told Traynor that the Nazi leader had a white streak in his hair. Traynor noticed that same white streak in Dasch's hair.

Right in front of Ladd, Dasch opened his briefcase which at that point contained $80,000 in cash, the rest of the money left at his hotel. In a dramatic gesture, Dasch tossed the bills across Ladd's desk. Suddenly, Dasch was believed.

When the call about Dasch came in to J. Edgar's office, he was studying a report from one of his secret agents in Berlin. It revealed that tap-dancing Eleanor Powell was Adolf Hitler's favorite movie star. The agent wrote, "Old *Schickelgruber* never misses one of Powell's films and orders the Gestapo to smuggle her movies in through neutral Zurich. *Broadway Melody of 1940* is the favorite of *der Führer*."

On learning the secret data provided by Dasch, J. Edgar rushed over to the office of his boss, Attorney General Francis Biddle. Both men agreed there should be a news blackout until all the Nazi saboteurs were in custody.

Biddle later recalled, "Hoover was practically foaming at the mouth. He was just imagining what a hero he was going to be to every red-blooded American boy reading G-Man comics."

For eight brutal days, Dasch underwent a terrible ordeal of interrogation. First, J. Edgar's G-Men wanted to find out who he was.

Born in Speyer, Germany, Dasch had entered the United States illegally in 1923 as a stowaway aboard a German ship. He later enlisted as a private in the U.S. Army Air Force. Receiving an honorable discharge, he worked as a waiter in New York City, where, in 1930, he had married an American citizen, Rose Marie Guille. He became a naturalized citizen in 1933. Disheartened when his marriage failed, he returned to the Fatherland in 1941 when Germany was at war with Britain.

For the first few months, he was impressed with the rising Nazi power, and he trained in a school for espionage on an estate outside Berlin. But before he was assigned the sabotage work on the American East Coast, he had already soured on Hitler and the Nazis. He planned to use the submarine leaving from western France as a vehicle for his permanent return to the United States.

During his long drilling by the FBI, Dasch revealed the targets of sabotage for his group. They included the Aluminum Corporation of America, the Ohio River Locks, and the hydroelectric plant at Niagara Falls. He'd also been ordered to bomb Jewish-owned department stores and places of business, as well as synagogues.

He provided a valuable insight into Abwehr's school for sabotage in Berlin, and gave the FBI German secret codes.

He startled agents by revealing that Germany had developed a submarine

A Nazi espionage agent, **George Dasch**, was the centerpiece of what J. Edgar defined as "the most sensational espionage case of World War II to occur on American shores."

He finally got to tell his side of the story in 1959, when he wrote a memoir, *Eight Spies Against America,* with an accurate report—not J. Edgar's version—of what really happened, but no one was listening. The book did not sell well, and it was virtually ignored by the press. Yet the episode that inspired it led to some of the most intriguing chain of events on the U.S. homefront during World War II.

The young German, with three others, piloted a Nazi submarine to the shores of Long Island, one of a string of such incursions planned as instruments to incite terror. The Nazi's plan involved the sabotage of strategic targets that would sow chaos across America—first on the East Coast, then later in California.

Although J. Edgar suppressed the true story, lying about it even to the U.S. president, Dasch had voluntarily turned himself in to the FBI, its agents not at first believing him.

He should have been hailed as a U.S. hero, but after his betrayal by J. Edgar, he drew a long prison sentence instead. All but one of his comrades were executed.

that could go six-hundred feet deeper than competing American vessels, which put them out of reach of U.S. depth charges. This information was vital, as the "Wolf Packs," as the German subs were called, had been taking a staggering toll on Allied shipping across the Atlantic.

Dasch also revealed that the Nazis planned to send a U-boat filled with saboteurs to some point along the East Coast every six weeks, not only to destroy facilities but as a means of creating havoc throughout America. One plan involved the bombing of Grand Central Station in Manhattan during rush hour.

He also informed them that a second submarine had previously landed at Ponte Vedra Beach near Jacksonville, Florida. J. Edgar ordered his agents into action, and these four potential saboteurs were eventually tracked down and arrested in New York and Chicago. They were Edward J. Kerling, Werner Thiel, Hermann Neubauer, and Herbert Haupt.

Dasch also told the FBI where they could arrest Burger, and he led them to the other two saboteurs who'd landed with him on Long Island. Consequently, the FBI rounded up Quirin and Heinck.

J. Edgar was eager to release the news to the papers. First, he informed FDR, but deliberately did not mention that Dasch had voluntarily turned himself in, an act which had led to all the arrests. J. Edgar suggested that his agents had discovered the plot when they found butts of German cigarettes in ashtrays on that Long Island train to Manhattan.

The next morning, headlines blared—FBI CAPTURES 8 GERMAN AGENTS LANDED IN SUBS. Details were lacking as to how the Bureau did that, but J. Edgar's prestige rose to the top of the popularity polls.

The suggestion remained that the FBI had infiltrated not only the Gestapo but also the German High Command. One reporter on Long Island falsely claimed that J. Edgar himself was on the beach watching as the Nazi submarine moved in toward the Long Island shore.

U.S. Army Intelligence and the Secretary of War, Henry Stimson, were each furious with J. Edgar for prematurely breaking the story. They'd received reports from American spies in Germany that more U-boats with saboteurs would be arriving on the East Coast within six weeks, and the Army wanted to be ready to intercept them.

"Hoover wanted those headlines," Stimson charged. "Whatever he thinks will bring him glory. He always exaggerates or even lies about his role in everything he does or doesn't do."

In front of a military tribunal composed only of generals, Biddle presented the case for the prosecution with information handed to him by J. Edgar, who sat at his side. There was no defense.

Before the trial, J. Edgar met privately with Dasch, telling him the up-

THE FACES OF TERRORISM
circa 1942

| Dasch | Burger | Haupt | Heinck |

| Kerling | Quirin | Theil | Neubauer |

Former FBI agent William W. Turner, wrote in his book, *Hoover's FBI,* "George Dasch is probably an authentic American war hero, responsible for saving many lives. But fate made him a threat to the FBI's public image."

J. Edgar wanted to take all the credit for rounding up these Nazi terrorists, which meant he had to suppress the fact that Dasch never had any intention of blowing up any facilities in America, preferring to reveal many of the Nazi plans and to defect to the U.S. instead.

J. Edgar promised Dasch that he'd be released after a face-saving mock trial, but reneged on the deal, and was instrumental in getting Dasch sentenced to thirty years in prison. His collaborator, Burger, was given a life sentence, and the other Nazi saboteurs were executed.

When he was finally freed, Dasch was deported back to Germany, where he was viewed as a traitor.

coming legal proceedings would be a sham. He promised him that he'd be tried and convicted, but that he would be set free six days later and awarded a secret presidential pardon. J. Edgar didn't want Nazi agents to know he'd exposed their plot of terror against the United States.

As Dasch later confessed in his memoirs, he was stunned when he heard the sentencing and Biddle told him there would be no pardon. Dasch received a sentence of thirty years in prison, and Burger drew a life sentence. On August 8, 1942, the other six Nazis were executed in the electric chair in a Washington, DC prison.

It was not until 1959 that Dasch told his side of the story when he wrote *Eight Spies Against America*. His memoir sold very few copies and was ignored by the press.

After his trial, Dasch came face to face with J. Edgar and pleaded with him. He shouted, "Mr. Hoover, aren't you really ashamed of yourself?"

In his memoir, he wrote: "An FBI agent walking nearby struck me on the face, sending me sprawling on to the floor. One of the Army guards helped me to my feet. Through the tears brought on by the hot sting of the agent's hand, I saw the chief disappear down the hall, seemingly surrounded by an impregnable wall of justice and strength."

In response to Dasch's charges, J. Edgar later maintained that he defected only at the last moment "when he got cold feet" and feared he'd be arrested and put to death. That, of course, was not true.

Actually, it was later revealed that Dasch found Hitler "a disgustingly funny little man with a horrible mustache." Trapped in Germany when that country declared war on the United States, he was forced into the espionage act because he spoke excellent English and knew the East Coast of the United States. He'd been ordered to kill any witnesses to their landing, but allowed the young Coast Guardsmen who sighted him that fateful early morning to go free.

In 1948, when Harry Truman learned the full details of the case, he pardoned both Dasch and Burger but ordered them deported at once to the American Zone of a then-occupied Germany, where they were viewed as traitors. Alone and dejected, and living in poverty, Dasch died in Germany in 1991, a forgotten figure but still a key player in World War II.

Former FBI agent William W. Turner claimed, "He is most probably an American war hero, responsible for saving many lives. But fate had made him a threat to the FBI's public image."

After the executions, Louis Nichols, J. Edgar's faithful sycophant, began a campaign to have the FBI director granted a Congressional Medal of Honor. That didn't happen, to J. Edgar's disappointment, as he was set to celebrate his twenty-fifth anniversary with the Department of Justice.

In the wake of the arrests and executions, the Nazis felt that the American coastline was far better guarded than reports had it. On November 29, 1944, two more Nazi spies landed by U-boat at Point Hancock, Maine, but they were quickly spotted and arrested, paying the ultimate penalty.

Despite the efforts of J. Edgar and Clyde, they failed to suppress the story of Dasch's role in rounding up the elite saboteurs. At war's end, during the autumn of 1945, reporter John Terrell, writing for *Newsweek*, asked to read the file on the saboteurs. In a private meeting with Tom Clark, whom Truman had appointed Attorney General, the Justice Department's data was made available to him. Hearing of its imminent publication, J. Edgar called Clark, pleading with him to suppress the article. It was too late. The article was on the press.

Working frantically with Nichols throughout the night, the FBI issued a press release, putting out their own version, revealing what future President Richard Nixon would call "a limited hangout."

In Nichols's press release, he downplayed Dasch's role and omitted the revelation that the FBI wasted valuable time by not believing his testimony at first.

J. Edgar claimed the case was "the most sensational espionage case of World War II" to occur on the homefront.

In later years, J. Edgar said, "Clyde Tolson and I, working around the clock, prevented a Nazi campaign of massive sabotage where secret agents would arrive in U-boats, and, working arm in arm with homefront secret spies, would virtually cripple the homefront. If we hadn't stopped this, the infrastructure of the United States would have been seriously harmed. We might not have won the war until 1950."

***

Japanese espionage represented only a fraction of what German spying was. But J. Edgar ordered his agents and its wartime censors to ferret out spies working for the empire of Japan.

One of the most notorious arrests involved Velvalee Dickinson, known in the press as the "Doll Woman." She used her shop, which sold and repaired antique dolls, to send coded information on U.S. Naval forces to Japanese contacts in Buenos Aires via stenographic messages.

A California woman, she married Lee T. Dickinson, and socially, in San Francisco before the attack on Pearl Harbor, they attended gatherings in which Japanese Navy members and other high-ranking Nippon government officials were present. She was often seen coming and going from the Japanese Consulate in that city.

In 1937, she moved to New York City and opened the Dickinson Doll Shop, on Madison Avenue, catering to affluent collectors throughout America.

In February of 1942, a letter allegedly sent from a woman in Portland, Oregon, talked of a "wonderful doll hospital" and noted that "three Old English dolls" were being repaired. There were also references to "fish nets" and "balloons." Cryptographers determined that the "dolls" referred to three warships, and that the "doll hospital" was actually a West Coast-based shipyard where repairs were being made. Balloons and fishing nets were references to coastal defenses along the West Coast of the United States.

More letters were intercepted after being sent to Buenos Aires from fake addresses in the United States. A reference to one doll, "Mr. Shaw," was actually data associated with the USS *Shaw*, which had been damaged in Pearl Harbor.

The FBI determined that these letters were being sent by Dickinson. It was discovered that before the war, she had been a friend of Ichiro Yokoyama, the Japanese Naval attaché in Washington.

Agents arrested Dickinson in January of 1944 where they discovered in her safe thousands of dollars which were traced to Japan. Tried and convicted, she was sentenced in August of 1944 to ten years in prison. However, she was released in the spring of 1951 and faded into the dustbin of history.

She was rumored to have died around 1980 long after she became a footnote in WWII history as the notorious "Doll Woman."

J. Edgar ordered most of his agents to focus on Nazi espionage within the U.S. during World War II. But the FBI was also sensitive to Japanese spying, which was much less pronounced.

One of the major spies caught was California-born **Velvalee Dickenson** *(left and center photos, above)* who operated a shop for antique dolls *(one of which is depicted on right, above)* on Madison Avenue in New York City.

She sent coded messages to the Japanese through a contact in Buenos Aires. If she claimed she was working on a doll known as "Mr. Shaw," she was actually saying that the USS Shaw, which had been severely damaged at Pearl Harbor, was being made seaworthy once again.

***

On the surface at least, the personal relationship between J. Edgar and Clyde seemed to travel down a smooth road. But there were a lot of potholes along that rocky highway. Like all couples, the two G-Men had their jealous temper fits, and, on rare occasions, engaged in violent confrontations.

One of their most notorious incidents occurred in the waning months of World War II, when they flew to Los Angeles for a two-week vacation. They were house guests of their dear friend, Dorothy Lamour, and her husband, William Ross Howard III.

After a weekend the four of them spent together, Dorothy and her husband had to fly to San Francisco, leaving their house to J. Edgar and Clyde, whom Dorothy privately referred to as "The Hoovers."

Clyde later told Guy Hotell an amazing story that happened while they vacationed at the Howard household. Clyde discovered a side to J. Edgar's makeup that he'd never experienced before after returning from a trip into town for supplies.

He claimed to Guy that when he returned from shopping, he entered the darkened living room. "A woman was sitting on the sofa smoking a cigarette. At first I thought Dorothy had come back early from San Francisco. When I switched on the light, I was shocked. It was Eddie in full drag. He'd assembled a tropical motif wardrobe from Dorothy's closet. In drag, Eddie wasn't exactly *The Jungle Princess,* but he was A-OK in my book."

"Weren't you disgusted?" Guy asked.

"Not at all," Clyde said. "I realized our relationship had entered another dimension. As you well know, I'm only thirty-three and one-third percent homosexual. As a woman, Eddie brought out the beast in me. I'd always had this fantasy of ripping off a woman's clothes and raping hell out of her. Now I had my chance, and I took full advantage."

Some biographers dismiss stories of J. Edgar being a cross-dresser, claiming that these tales are but a myth, an urban legend. Yet sources as diverse as Ethel Merman, who often purchased garments for him, and gay attorney Roy Cohn, Joseph McCarthy's chief aide, have told friends that these revelations are indeed true. Of course, they made these comments not for publication, and only after J. Edgar was safely in his grave.

Guy may have been the first person to spread the story of J. Edgar's cross-dressing. In his preliminary talks with his would-be biographer, James Kirkwood, Guy revealed explicit details and numerous private parties where J. Edgar appeared in drag. Kirkwood believed him, "they were just too astonishing not to be true."

In the words of author Thomas Doherty, "For American popular culture, the image of a *zaftig* FBI director as a Christine Jorgensen wanna-be was too delicious not to savor."

The favorite pastime of J. Edgar and Clyde was attending horse races at Del Mar Racetrack, twenty miles north of San Diego, where they were guests of Bing Crosby. The singer had been one of the founding fathers of the Del Mar Thoroughbred Club in 1936 and remained its primary stockholder. Bing was easy to spot, always wearing a loud Hawaiian shirt and a jaunty yachting cap.

In a very odd instance of collusion among couples, J. Edgar and Clyde appeared there on several occasions with Lucille Ball and Desi Arnaz, who were divorcing each other and then not divorcing each other.

Clyde was jealous of Desi and didn't want these encounters, but J. Edgar insisted. J. Edgar had known Desi since his abortion scandal with Ginger Rogers, and always seemed both mesmerized and amused by the entertainer whenever they encountered each other.

Unaware that J. Edgar coveted her husband and had compiled an investigative file on both Desi and herself, Lucille seemed flattered to be seen in the company of such a powerful national figure as J. Edgar. "He likes me better than he does that Ethel Merman," Lucille bragged to friends. Of course, at this point in her career, the red-haired actress could hardly know all the trouble that the FBI director would make for her in the future.

When Desi had to visit the men's room, J. Edgar volunteered to go with him so he could use the key he'd been given to an executive washroom reserved for VIPs. "Bing Crosby never wanted guys like Clark Gable having to take a piss at a public urinal," J. Edgar jokingly told Desi.

It can be assumed that it was Clyde, not Lucille, who cast a suspicious eye at J. Edgar toddling off to the men's room with Desi. He long knew that his boss and lover

Guy Hotell claimed that actress **Dorothy Lamour** and **J. Edgar Hoover** were certainly friends, but he also knew that each trusted the other not to betray their deepest secrets. J. Edgar had long ago learned that Dorothy, in her early days, had for a brief time been one of Polly Adler's hookers, a detail that was not revealed in Adler's autobiography, *A House is Not a Home*.

Dorothy fully realized that J. Edgar was involved in a homosexual relationship and that he was a secret cross-dresser. "Chances were good," Guy said, "that neither of them would be writing memoirs spilling the beans on each other."

During World War II, only a sarong separated Lamour from the erotic dreams of many GIs fighting hand-to-hand with the Japanese on South Pacific beaches. Dorothy was known as "The Queen of all Robinson Crusoes."

had harbored a "crush" on Desi, whose picture remained a favorite frontal nude in his private album.

What happened next has been claimed by only one witness, the Hungarian-born film producer, Joe Pasternak. Apparently, J. Edgar stationed an FBI agent at the door to the executive washroom with instructions not to let anyone enter until "we've finished with our business."

After a preliminary check, J. Edgar and Desi may have thought they were alone in the washroom, whose private booths were outfitted with floor-to-ceiling doors and walls. Unknown to them, Pasternak was in a toilet booth at the far end of the washroom.

Pasternak would later "dine out" on what he claimed took place that hot afternoon. "I couldn't see them but I could hear them," he told such friends as Marlene Dietrich and James Stewart. "From the sounds of it, Hoover was giving Arnaz a blow-job, and the Cuban was egging him on, in Spanish no less. I heard the men up until they washed up and headed out the door."

"Eddie was always jealous of **Lucille Ball** because she had that Cuban fireball, **Desi Arnaz**, and he didn't," or so claimed Guy Hotell.

Two of America's most improbable couples, J. Edgar with Clyde and Lucy with Desi, often "double dated." They were seen together in Los Angeles night clubs, at the race track, at the beach, and in restaurants together whenever Clyde and J. Edgar made vacation trips to California.

By 1950, the FBI had already accumulated a fairly large dossier on Lucille, tracing how she'd worked her way up from a starving hooker/model in New York to B-film stardom in Hollywood.

More revelations about her past were about to explode.

Pasternak spread the story like a raging fire across Hollywood. "It was just too good to keep to myself.

In the years ahead, Pasternak saw J. Edgar several times at Del Mar. The producer claimed, "Hoover was a homosexual. Every year, he used to come down to the Del Mar racetrack with a different boy. He was caught in the bathroom by a newspaperman. They made sure he didn't speak. Nobody dared say anything because Hoover was too powerful."

These allegations appeared in the most revelatory book about J. Edgar ever published, Anthony's Summers' *Official and Confidential: The Secret Life of J. Edgar Hoover.*

In that later quote, Pasternak is referring a period in the late 1950s and 60s when Clyde and J. Edgar, perhaps tiring of too steady a diet of each other, began to patronize hustlers, especially in Florida and California. But at the time of the Arnaz episode, Clyde was still intensely jealous of J. Edgar and wanted to protect his turf.

During the weekend of the Arnaz/Pasternak incident, J. Edgar and Clyde had been given a free suite at a deluxe hotel in Laguna Beach. The night manager, Bernard Gaal, later reported that when J. Edgar and Clyde returned from the Del Mar track that evening, "the fight of the century was heard. I was called to their floor by complaints coming to the front desk. The word 'Arnaz' was shouted into the hallway."

No one knows exactly what happened inside the suite. But dishes were broken and furniture overturned. At one point, J. Hoover must have tossed something at Clyde. It struck him in the left eye and caused serious damage to his lip.

"When I buzzed the door and was let in," Gaal said, "Hoover had disappeared into the bedroom. But Tolson came to the door. He was a bloody mess. He claimed he'd had an accident and needed to be taken to the nearest hospital. I agreed to drive him there."

"At the hospital, the doctor treated his eye and put a patch over it," Gaal said. "His lip required stitches. After he was released, he asked me to drive him to the airport in Los Angeles. He didn't return to the hotel for his luggage. Hoover was left alone in our complimentary suite."

J. Edgar remained on the West Coast for another two weeks, conducting business out of the San Diego office. Back in Washington, Clyde called FBI headquarters and told his staff that he had a serious case of "Jap flu" and would be out for almost two weeks while he recovered.

Ethel Merman always claimed that the Hungarian-born film producer, **Joe Pasternak**, did more than anyone to fan rumors about J. Edgar's homosexuality in the wake of an incident in a men's toilet at the Del Mar race track.

When FBI agents in Los Angeles reported that Pasternak was spreading "these vicious lies," J. Edgar ordered an immediate investigation into Pasternak's past.

He wanted to know if Pasternak had previously dabbled in Nazism. FBI agents learned that he'd produced German-language musicals in Weimar Berlin, and that Pasternak hadn't emigrated out of Germany until 1936, three years after Hitler rose to power.

Pasternak's first major Hollywood victory derived from his transformation of a 14-year-old Canadian singer, Deanna Durbin, into an international star.

No one knows the details, but obviously those battling warriors made up with each other over the phone. When the director returned to Bureau headquarters, flying into National Airport in Washington, Guy Hotell was the chauffeur and Clyde the eager passenger wanting to have a reunion with

J. Edgar.

"They both had their make-up session in the back seat of the limo, or should I call it make-out session," Guy said. "Fortunately, the windows were so darkened you couldn't see in. In the rear-view mirror I watched so much kissing and ass-grabbing it was like a soldier returning to his wife after three years in the Pacific. I cooked steaks for them that night at their home. They were upstairs in the bedroom for three hours. The next day I had lunch with them at the Mayflower. They were like two love-birds."

***

J. Edgar conceived many plots for the FBI to execute to protect the home front in World War II. But the most bizarre episode he ever planned called for its execution on German soil. In this wild fantasy, never carried out, he was obviously in search of "the ultimate headline."

"I think in his megalomania, he completely failed to see his limitations and was hoping for a glory that would make him legendary—and not just for running the FBI," Guy claimed.

During the investigations by FBI agents of the American Nazi beauty, Tara Marsh, in Mexico City, they had learned many intriguing details. Engaged at the time in a brief but torrid romance with Errol Flynn, she had spoken openly about her affair with Adolf Hitler when she attended parties thrown by Mussolini's friend, the Countess Dorothy di Frasso.

According to an eyewitness, she'd claimed that Hitler had stashed the equivalent of one hundred million dollars in gold bars in the cellars of his alpine retreat at Berchtesgaden in southern Germany near the Austrian border. The rather indiscreet Marsh had also revealed that Nazi aviation engineers were designing an airplane capable of flying *der Führer* to Buenos Aires without refueling in case Germany lost the war.

Of course, that major claim revealed that Hitler at least was considering the possibility that Germany might emerge from World War II as a vanquished nation. At least that was something the propaganda minister, Josef Goebbels, never admitted.

Guy claimed that during the closing months of the war, J. Edgar began to conceive a fantastic role for himself. Apparently that long-distance airplane was never developed. Informants within the Nazi regime were reporting to the Allies that Hitler in the closing weeks of World War II planned to leave Berlin on April 20, 1945, and return to Obersalzberg, above Berchtesgaden, to defend Nazi Germany until the death of its last soldier.

"I will make our last stand for the Third Reich in the legendary mountain fastness of Barbarossa," *der Führer* announced.

J. Edgar learned that Hitler's household staff had already arrived in Berchtesgaden to prepare for his return to his mountain villa, the Berghof. The director knew that the U.S. Third Army was in nearby Linz, Austria, and he was told that from there, the Allies would move north into Berchtesgaden.

Night after night J. Edgar became obsessed with the idea that he, Clyde, and his trusted agent, Louis B. Nichols, would fly to the headquarters of the Third Army, and that with them, they would advance toward Berchtesgaden. When Hitler's final security guards were subdued, J. Edgar, according to his fantastic plan, would proceed directly into the chamber of the Nazi dictator. Armed with machine guns, J. Edgar, Clyde, and Nichols would move in to arrest Hitler. Of course, if he resisted, J. Edgar himself would mow him down with an FBI machine gun.

After either arresting or assassinating Hitler, and after all the photographs were taken, J. Edgar would make one final grand play. Along with Clyde and Nichols, he wanted to descend into the cellars of the Berghof and rescue millions of dollars in gold bars, which would then be flown back to the United States to help alleviate the vast war debt America had incurred during this epic battle.

J. Edgar diverted some of his top agents to help him draft an elaborate plan to carry out this scheme. When it was ready, he made an appointment to meet privately with Secretary of State Edward Stettinius Jr., who had replaced Cordell Hull, who had to resign because of ill health. J. Edgar had worked very little with this prematurely white-haired, rather handsome man, and had not a clue as to how he would respond to his scheme. Stettinius had been described as a meticulous, no-nonsense bureaucrat with an almost obsessive attention to detail.

In front of Stettinius, J. Edgar was only five minutes into his presentation of "the coup of the century" when Stettinius rose in anger from his desk. "Who in hell do you think you are? Dwight David Eisenhower? A lot of plots have been presented to me, but this is the most ridiculous. Are you out of your mind?"

"But it could work," J. Edgar protested.

"You are terribly misinformed," Stettinius said. "Hitler has waited too long. There's no way he can fly out of Berlin at this point. The Russians are already bombarding the Chancellery. He's trapped in his bunker with Goebbels and others. There's little doubt he'll be taken alive by the Soviets and shipped in a cage to Josef Stalin. We think he'll commit suicide instead. Now get out of my office. Europe is falling apart, and I've got important business to attend to. No time to listen to some dumb fantasy

Der Berghof
Hitler ganz Privat

In a reflective mood, **Adolf Hitler** *(top photo)* contemplates his next diabolical scheme: Perhaps his plan to bring Winston Churchill to Berlin after the Nazi victory and parade him in chains through the streets, but only after the *Führer* himself had castrated the wartime British leader.

As a site for the contemplation of his next moves, the Nazi dictator enjoyed an idyllic setting that would during the years to come serve as a backdrop for the Julie Andrews movie, *The Sound of Music.*

Hitler vacationed with his mistress, Eva Braun, at the **Berghof** *(lower photo)* in the Bavarian Alps near the Austrian border. He lived in an imposing villa like a villain from a future James Bond film.

During the 1930s, the neighboring village of Obersalzberg became a place of pilgrimage for Nazi fanatics; hysterical women took away stones on which Hitler's feet had trodden.

that sounds as if it were concocted by a twelve-year old G-Man wannabe. You've got to find a new mission, Hoover. The Nazis are defeated. Why don't you go on a commie hunt?"

Enraged and fuming with anger, J. Edgar arrived back at FBI headquarters. Clyde found him in such a state that he decided to drive him home for the day. Before J. Edgar departed, he instructed Nichols to destroy all the plans for their Berchtesgaden coup. "There must not be one trace of it left."

On the way out the door, Guy joined J. Edgar and Clyde. "Behind the anger he showed on his face was a determination I'd never seen before. He told us, 'The Nazis are defeated. Hitler will be dead soon. We must turn our attention to the communists infiltrating our government. I suspect Stettinius himself takes his marching orders directly from the Kremlin.'"

***

Stettinius didn't need to give J. Edgar advice about ferreting out communists in the government. Before the presidential elections of 1944, he'd already launched such a campaign. His main target was Henry A. Wallace, FDR's Vice President, whom J. Edgar suspected "was as red as his nosebleed."

Secretly delivered to J. Edgar was a highly classified report from Roosevelt's doctors. The report noted that the President's heart might not survive a grueling fourth run for the White House in 1944. The doctors had advised FDR to retire from office at the end of his third term.

In a private confab with Clyde, Louis Nichols, and Guy Hotell, J. Edgar informed them that FDR's selection of a vice president was vital. "The man elected as veep will become President of the United States, perhaps just months after the election—that is, if Roosevelt makes it through the campaign at all."

Fearing that a Wallace presidency would mean a complete communist takeover of the U.S government, Clyde launched a major campaign within the FBI, directing his agents to dig up whatever they could about the Vice President's left-leaning politics.

On May 8, 1942 Wallace had delivered his most famous but most controversial speech in New York. Called the "Century of the Common Man," it was delivered to the leftist Free World Association. In the speech, the Vice President laid out his vision for a New World Order, following the defeat of the Fascist powers.

Unknown to Wallace, Clyde had set up an extensive monitoring system that tapped into the phone wires of the Vice President. He heard and reported, word for word, what Wallace said to the Joint Anti-Fascist Refugee Committee. The FBI considered the organization "a commie front group." Clyde also listened as Wallace talked to the president of the leftist Los Angeles Union, which Clyde claimed was "completely red."

In 1943, an FBI agent was in the audience as Wallace appeared before a public rally consisting mostly of African-Americans who had suffered police brutality during recent race riots. "We cannot fight to crush Nazi brutality abroad while engaging in such harsh tactics at home against our own citizens," Wallace said. "For some reason, white supremacists always want to join the police force."

Also in 1943, Wallace made the first of two controversial visits to Latin America. He spoke out in defense of underpaid workers laboring under dangerous conditions. Without authority, he even claimed that the United States would pay half the costs of improving working conditions throughout Latin America. This obviously brought him into a violent confrontation with the U.S. Department of Commerce.

Two FBI agents trailed Wallace wherever he went in Latin America expressing alarm in their reports that he had come under the influence of Bolivian Communists. In a secret memo, J. Edgar expressed his grave concerns to Attorney General Francis B. Biddle.

In one of his memos to Biddle, J. Edgar complained, "Wallace and Eleanor Roosevelt are locked into a conspiracy. I do not for a minute believe she is as naïve as she pretends to be. Both of them are known to so-

219

cialize or even endorse some of the most dangerous communists in the country, both party members and pro-Soviet groups."

Clyde presented J. Edgar with a detailed report on a private phone conversation between Eleanor and Wallace, in which he asked her if she might consider running with him for the Presidency of the United States in 1948. "You would obviously attract more voters than I would, so you should head the ticket with me being the vice presidential candidate like I was to Franklin." The transcript of the conversation, perhaps for technical reasons, was not complete. The First Lady's response to that radical suggestion was not recorded.

On May 23, 1944, Wallace left on yet another controversial trip, departing via Alaska to the barren wilderness of the "Wild East" of Russia, including Siberia, where communist authorities steered him away from the slave camps. On Soviet soil, he praised the Bolshevik Revolution as the greatest since the American Revolution.

After this trip, J. Edgar sent a notation to Biddle. "There can be no doubt: Henry A. Wallace is engaged in a communist conspiracy. He has secret pro-Soviet ties both in Russia and in America. His actions might not be approved of by FDR, but Eleanor is very influenced by his far left positions."

FDR was also receiving these reports and was seriously alarmed by them. Historians may disagree, but what may have influenced FDR to drop Wallace from the 1944 ticket was a report from his closest advisers that he would lose three-million votes if he kept Wallace on the ticket.

Finally, a decision came through. Wallace would be dropped from the ticket, and FDR would run with Harry S Truman, a relatively obscure senator from Missouri, as his vice president. As history records, Wallace was replaced on the Democratic ticket just 82 days be-

It was not a happy ride when **Franklin D. Roosevelt** *(left)* brought Vice President-elect **Harry S Truman** *(center)* and Vice President **Henry A. Wallace** *(right)* together for a ride back to the White House from Washington's Union Station in 1944.

As Wallace told friends, "I was still in a state of shock that Roosevelt had replaced me as his vice president in favor of the shit-kicker from Missouri, a machine-backed politician. He offered me the job of Secretary of Commerce. Truman had already told his cronies that he was going to become the next President of the United States. We both knew that Roosevelt had death written all over his face. Even his handshake felt like that of a cadaver."

fore the elections of 1944, and consequently, thanks to the death of FDR in 1945, missed becoming the 33rd president of the United States.

To placate Wallace, FDR named him Secretary of Commerce, but he was fired by Truman in September of 1946 because he objected to the President's anti-Soviet policies.

* * *

Enraged by many of FDR's foreign and domestic policies, the Republicans nominated J. Edgar's nemesis, Thomas Dewey, the former governor of New York, to run against Roosevelt in the 1944 election. "If he gets in, somebody other than me will be running the FBI," J. Edgar confided to Clyde.

But Dewey didn't win. In spite of his ill health, the ailing FDR retained the presidency and was swept into office with Truman, his last-minute choice, as his vice president. "The Missouri mule" [J. Edgar's pejorative reference to Truman] might just as well make his inaugural speech," he said, "as he'll soon become President."

Three terms as U.S. President would age younger, healthier men. Not only was FDR in poor health throughout three previous terms of his presidency, but he had led the nation through the stress of both the Great Depression and World War II. As regards his final meeting with FDR, J. Edgar told Clyde and his aides, "I don't think he has much longer before he departs this earth."

"That feisty little Harry S Truman is just waiting in the wings to take over," J. Edgar told Clyde and Guy. "Just the other day, I heard he told some senators that, 'There is no love lost between Hoover and me.'"

Even though World War II had entered its final crucial months, J. Edgar and Clyde diverted more FBI agents to begin an intense investigation of Truman.

The director already knew that Truman had entered politics as a *protégé* of Tom Pendergast, the flamboyantly corrupt political boss whose influence had sent Truman to the Senate from the State of Missouri. J. Edgar and Clyde determined that Pendergast had cultivated ties to the Mafia. "We can use that against him," J. Edgar claimed.

Thomas Joseph Pendergast, called "Boss Tom," controlled Kansas City and its environs (including Jackson County), Missouri, and played a key role in maneuvering his hand-chosen political cronies into office during the Depression, enriching himself as part of the process. He was the most corrupt politician in the state. On election days, there were shootouts and beatings. A citizen of Kansas City faced fraud and intimidation if he voted

221

for a Republican. Turnout for Pendergast candidates was an unbelievable ninety-eight percent of voters. His machine allowed alcohol and gambling during Prohibition, as his men bribed police officers.

In 1934, Pendergast handpicked Truman as his candidate for the 1934 U.S. Senate seat, and Truman won. But after years of boss rule, in the late 1930s, the U.S. Treasury Secretary, Henry Morgenthau, went after both Pendergast and his collaborator, Mafia boss Charles Corolla as part of a crackdown on corruption and organized crime. Federal funds were pulled from the grasp of "Boss Tom," and in 1939, he was convicted of income tax evasion. J. Edgar and Clyde were in Kansas City at the time.

Corruption, bootlegging, voter fraud, election violence, and intimidation— good, old-fashioned ward politics— gave **Thomas Joseph Pendergast**, known as "Boss Tom," enormous political power in Kansas City. He is pictured in the inset photo, and also as the left-hand figure in the bigger photo during a dialogue with his arch enemy, **Lloyd C. Stark**, who set out to destroy him.

Pendergast changed the course of world history when he selected haberdasher Harry S Truman to run for political office as his hand-picked candidate. After Pendergast was convicted of income tax evasion, Stark sought to unseat Truman in the 1940 U.S. Senate election, a bitter campaign that made both men lifelong enemies after Truman was re-elected. Truman, of course, would go on to greater things, like ushering in the Atomic Age.

Lloyd C. Start, who'd won the Missouri governor's seat in 1936, eventually turned against "Boss Tom" and ran against Truman for the Senate seat in 1940. U.S. Attorney Maurice Milligan, who had prosecuted Pendergast, also ran. Truman won as the other two candidates split the anti-Pendergast vote.

When "Boss Tom" died on January 26, 1945, Truman was the only elected official who attended his funeral. Brushing aside criticism, HST said, "He was always my friend, and I have always been his."

J. Edgar and Clyde realized that Truman's link to this unsavory character could be a weapon to use against him if he opted to run for President in 1948.

But even though they tried, FBI agents could come up with no sex scandals involving Truman. "I think he has sex with Bess, and only with her, with all his clothes on—that is, if he has sex with her at all, which I doubt," one frustrated agent reported. "I bet Harry and Bess have never even seen each other naked."

"The most damaging personal thing we've come up with so far is that he leaves skid marks on his underwear," Clyde claimed. "He's afraid someone will steal a dirty pair and auction it off as a joke. That's why he washes his drawers every morning in the sink of his bathroom. He's also known for taking dinosaur dumps."

The FBI was informed that Roosevelt had left the White House on March 3, 1945, heading for Warm Springs, Georgia, for rest and recuperation. A spy among FDR's Secret Service informed J. Edgar that the President's longtime mistress, Lucy Mercer Rutherfurd, was staying with him at the Little White House.

In Washington, as the cherry trees were about to burst into bloom, J. Edgar became increasingly convinced that FDR's death was imminent.

He began to speculate about the degree of influence Eleanor Roosevelt might have on the new President Truman. One FBI agent trailed her at every appearance. On the afternoon of April 12, 1945, the agent had listened to Eleanor speak at the Seagrave Club in Washington. She had just finished her speech when he noted an agent of the Secret Service approach the platform and whisper something into the First Lady's ear. Excusing herself, she left the auditorium at once and got into a limousine, which sped her to the White House. She was last seen by another FBI agent "rushing into the White House with a sense of panic on her face."

"Keep us informed," Clyde told his underling.

Another FBI informant in the Senate called Clyde, who put him through to J. Edgar on his direct line. It was 5pm, and Truman had just finished presiding over the Senate. He retreated to the unmarked Room H-128 with Sam Rayburn, Speaker of the House. This high-ceilinged room was a kind of after-hours hideaway where Democratic Senators gathered to drink and discuss politics.

Truman, it was reported, was enjoying a hefty glass of bourbon when an agent from the White House told him to go there at once to meet Eleanor.

Within minutes, a slightly tipsy Truman was spotted dashing along the otherwise deserted passage beneath the Capitol building. He had no Secret Service protection. In a great rush, he was seen going into the Pennsylvania Avenue entrance of the White House. Over the phone, an FBI agent told J. Edgar, "Either the war is over or Roosevelt is dead."

With no more immediate news, Clyde and J. Edgar decided to take the elevator down and head for Harvey's, their favorite restaurant, for an early dinner. Clyde left strict instructions with Edward Tamm, J. Edgar's top aide during World War II, that they were to be informed of the latest news. J. Edgar didn't like not knowing what was going on.

As they got off the elevator on the ground floor, a security guard told them that Tamm wanted them to return at once upstairs.

They came back into J. Edgar's office to approach a highly agitated Tamm. The FBI had hookups with three news services, the International News Service, the Associated Press, and United Press. A five-alarm bell was going off from INS, indicating a bulletin about to be sent. Such bulletins ranked up there with news of "The Second Coming."

The time was 5:45pm, as J. Edgar and Clyde stood over the machine. Both men read the abbreviated words as soon as they appeared—FLASH WASHN—FDR DEAD.

Newspapers going to bed on the East Coast held their press runs, and radio stations were told to stand by for late-breaking news of major importance. Thousands, even millions of Americans, stopped their activities and gathered around their radios. Three minutes later, at 5:48pm, both AP and UP flashed their own bulletins—FDR DEAD.

Clyde stood with Tamm and J. Edgar in stunned silence as Guy Hotell and Louis Nichols approached.

It was Clyde who broke the deadly silence. "My God, that little haberdasher from Missouri is our new boss. What will happen to the FBI?"

A grimace crossed J. Edgar's face as he looked at Clyde. "More to the point, what in the fuck is gonna happen to us?"

In the 1950s, **J. Edgar Hoover** (seen above on vacation in Miami Beach) was Clyde Tolson's favorite subject for photographic studies.

CHAPTER SEVEN

After Harry S Truman was sworn in as President of the United States, J. Edgar called Clyde, Louis Nichols, and Guy Hotell into his office. "Harry Truman hates us and will want to cut off our balls. In Guy's case, that will take one big knife." No one said anything, but J. Edgar laughed at his own remark. "A little gallows humor, fellows."

"We've got to dig deep to get the dirt on this pig farmer from Missouri," J. Edgar said. "I think Truman will try to slice us down to size. I hear he wants to create an intelligence agency spanning the globe. I want that agency to be under the FBI. I see a few battles along the way, but ultimately we'll win this war with Truman."

The FBI spy stationed at the White House reported that a funeral cortège with a black-draped caisson drawn by six white horses had just pulled up under the portico of the White House. To his dismay, J. Edgar learned that the funeral service was to be held in the East Room. The widowed Eleanor Roosevelt had not invited him to the services, much less extended an invitation to Clyde. "We're going to the funeral," J. Edgar told Clyde.

"But I'm not wearing a black suit today," Clyde protested.

"Any fool can see that," J. Edgar said. "We're going anyway. Call our limousine."

"Without an invitation, we can't get in," Clyde protested.

"Who do you think you're talking to?" J. Edgar asked. "Name the security guard at the door to the White House who will not allow entrance to J. Edgar Hoover, director of the Federal Bureau of Investigation?" He slammed his fist down on his desk. "I think not."

On the way to the White House, J. Edgar checked his vest pocket three times. In it he had slipped an envelope with a dossier on the last day of FDR's life. He wanted the now deposed First Lady to be aware that her husband had spent the final hours of his life with not only one, but with two mistresses, Lucy Mercer Rutherfurd, whom Eleanor despised, and a second mistress, Margaret Suckley, whom FDR called "Daisy." For some reason, Eleanor tolerated Daisy but despised Lucy.

Daisy was nine years Franklin's junior and his eighth cousin. She was also a seventh cousin to Eleanor and had come into FDR's life after polio

To this day, no one has adequately explained why **FDR** (*top photo, right*) picked "The Man from Independence" (*top photo, left*) as his vice presidential running mate in the 1944 campaign for the White House.

In the lower photo, **Harry S Truman** is sworn in as President of the United States, as his wife, **Bess** (center) and his singer-daughter **Margaret** (right) look on.

On his first day in office, Truman told his aides, "One of my first official acts of duty will be to snip off one of J. Edgar Hoover's balls."

The Missouri politician was known for his plain speaking. William Sullivan of the FBI claimed, "Hoover's hatred of Harry Truman knew no bounds."

struck. Daisy had helped implement the romance between Franklin and Lucy. After Lucy was banished by Eleanor, Daisy had filled in as the future president's lover.

During his final hours, or so it was reported to J. Edgar, Lucy and Daisy had hovered around FDR as his last portrait was painted by Madame Elizabeth Shoumatoff.

J. Edgar was right. Ultimately, he and Clyde were allowed into the East Room although backed up against the wall and not given any front row preference. With Clyde, J. Edgar stood in the long receiving line to offer Eleanor his condolences. Coming face to face with the widow, he shook her hand and offered his sympathy, and he also slipped her the envelope he'd carried over to the White House from the FBI. Looking startled for a moment, she accepted the envelope and immediately passed it to her social secretary.

Reportedly, she later told her intimate friend, Joseph P. Lash, "It was a final act of cruelty and vengeance on the part of Hoover. I already knew the Rutherfurd woman and Daisy were in Warm Springs. I learned about it an hour after I arrived there."

Back in their limousine, J. Edgar and Clyde sat with Guy, who had not entered the White House. J. Edgar told Guy that he'd given "the final report" to Eleanor. "It looks like old Horse Face is out of the picture. Enter 'the Missouri Cow.'" He was referring, of course, to Bess Truman, who at that moment was arranging her personal possessions and limited wardrobe in the bedroom hastily vacated by Eleanor.

On her arrival in New York at Grand Central, a reporter had rushed up to Eleanor for an interview. She put up her hand. "The story's over."

That would have been the case with most First Ladies after their departure from the White House. Not so with Eleanor. As J. Edgar was to find out, there were many more chapters to be written in her life.

World events were passing so rapidly that J. Edgar and Clyde could hardly keep abreast of developments. U.S. troops liberated the Nazi concentration camp at Buchenwald where countless Jews, homosexuals, and Gypsies had been murdered. In Berlin, Hitler was in his bunker when he heard news of the death of FDR. It was a cause for celebration.

But Hitler himself would commit suicide on April 30, 1945, shortly after marrying his longtime mistress, Eva Braun. A Viking style funeral was hastily held in which the Führer's body was burned. The Third Reich would survive for another week.

J. Edgar and Clyde followed these events with avid interest, not knowing exactly what the new world would mean for their roles at the FBI.

They were particularly concerned to read of Germany's unconditional surrender on May 7, 1945, which effectively ended the operations of the Office of Strategic Services. The war was still raging against Japan in the east, but the OSS had never really operated there very much because of the objections of the commander in charge, General Douglas MacArthur.

With Clyde by his side, J. Edgar began to scheme to assemble all American intelligence operations under his control. That meant commandeering the former duties of the OSS, which had previously been run by his nemesis, William Donovan.

When J. Edgar received some of the first reports that Soviet troops had overrun Berlin, he told his agents, "Communists, not the Fascists, will become the new enemy of the United States. Instead of Hitler, we'll have to confront the even more cunning Josef Stalin. No one has rounded up more communists in the United States than I have. Now with the war coming to an end, watch me go. Of course, first, we'll have to do some brown-nosing with this Truman creature."

***

Wanting to carry favor with Truman, J. Edgar sent him a memo, putting himself "at your personal disposal, Mr. President."

Truman angrily shot back, "Tell Hoover if I need any help from the FBI, I'll go through proper channels and first ask the Attorney General who can then convey my wishes to Hoover."

When he heard this, J. Edgar was insulted and went into a rage. But he had to swallow his pride and figure out some way to put Truman in his debt. But then J. Edgar received even worse news when he was shown a copy of a memo Truman had dictated.

"We want no Gestapo or secret police. The FBI is tending in that direction. They are dabbling in sex life scandals and plain blackmailing when they should be catching criminals. They also have a habit of sneering at local law enforcement officers. This must stop! Cooperation is what we must have."

During his first weeks in office, Truman learned many government secrets, including an overview of massive wiretappings by the FBI. "What in the fuck is this?" the outspoken President said. "Tell Hoover to cut this crap. We don't have time for this kind of shit!"

Aware of his power, J. Edgar ignored the presidential ban and continued to acquire data illegally.

Truman never really wanted J. Edgar to come into the White House, especially the Oval Office. "Body odor offends me," he told his aides. "If I had to meet him, make sure he's at least ten feet away and there's no down wind. On the other hand we've got to watch him. Long ago I learned not to kick a pile of cow shit on a hot August day."

Although it could have been embarrassing to Truman's administration, the FBI continued with its wiretapping.

J. Edgar baited the President with tantalizing tidbits of information about what his Republican opponents were planning to do to discredit him. Sometimes FBI memos alerted Truman to potentially threatening maneuvers unfolding even within his own administration.

Confident of the degree of power he wielded, J. Edgar even snooped on his own boss, Attorney General Francis Biddle, especially when wiretapping revealed he was linked to the notorious lawyer and lobbyist known as "Tommy the Cork," the centerpiece of an FBI file nearly a foot thick.

"Tommy the Cork" was actually Harvard-educated Thomas Corcoran, an Irish Catholic lawyer who had become one of the most influential officials in Washington during Franklin Roosevelt's first two terms in office.

Elliott Roosevelt once claimed, "Apart from my father, Tom was the single most influential man in the country." He was a key factor in drafting FDR's New Deal legislation. Long before Lyndon Baines Johnson came onto the scene, Corcoran was called "the ultimate arm twister" in Congress. Senator Walter George of Georgia went so far as to claim, "He had the power of saying who shall be a senator and who shall not be a senator."

An isolationist, Corcoran in time became "too politically dangerous (FDR's words) to keep around." He was instrumental in getting Joseph P. Kennedy appointed ambassador to England, and both men opposed America's entry into the war. As FDR's aide, Harry Hopkins, told him, "Tom, you're too Catholic to trust the Russians and too Irish to trust the English."

Corcoran's days as Roosevelt's trusted adviser were numbered when the *Saturday Evening Post,* in June of 1939, accused the President's son, James Roosevelt, of being a war profiteer. James was one of Corcoran's best friends, and as a result, Corcoran got dragged into the scandal.

"It involves my son and my closest adviser." FDR told J. Edgar. "I want you to see what damage the scandal might cause."

Two weeks later, J. Edgar called FDR to report, "James and Tommy the Cork are as guilty as hell. There are many instances where Corcoran has been accused of corrupt behavior. I'm sure it was Corcoran who talked poor James into acting improperly."

Then Norman M. Littell, a high-ranking official in the Department of Justice, approached Anna Roosevelt, FDR's daughter. He warned her to intercede with her father and fire Corcoran. "Ability and brilliance of mind are not enough."

In October of 1940, FDR had to call Corcoran and tell him the bad news. "I've got to ask you to resign."

Once FDR forced him out of his administration, Corcoran became the most influential lobbyist in Washington, making a fortune in the arms trade and "wheeling and dealing (J. Edgar's words) with so many companies I don't know how he keeps them straight."

Ever since the 1930s, Clyde and J. Edgar had accumulated an extensive file on Corcoran, much of it derived from phone taps. Conversations recorded included intimate talks with justices of the Supreme Court, Federal judges, congressmen, senators, and even members of FDR's cabinet, including Attorney General Francis Biddle. From Hollywood, private talks with Louis B. Mayer and Darryl F. Zanuck were subject to eavesdropping.

To J. Edgar, the evidence indicated that Biddle, his boss, and Corcoran had "a corrupt relationship." In a memo to Truman, J. Edgar charged, "Corcoran has something on your Attorney General."

When Biddle heard that J. Edgar was trying to get him fired, he met privately with Truman and presented evidence that the FBI director was involved in a homosexual relationship with his associate director, Clyde Tolson.

"I flipped through the file," Truman years later would tell his biographer Merle Miller. "I didn't want to see it. I told Biddle I didn't give a damn about Hoover's personal life. That wasn't my business. It was what he did *while* he was at work that was my business."

During the war, a case had been brought against Sterling Pharmaceutical Company, of which Corcoran was the chief lobbyist, alleging that

Sterling had been trading with an enemy antagonist, with strong implications that the company had Nazi links. Somehow Corcoran managed to have Biddle drop the case and erase all charges. This action infuriated J. Edgar, who claimed that Biddle's decision represented "the lowest point in the history of the Department of Justice since the Harding administration."

In Congress, there were calls for an investigation both of Biddle and his links to his lawyer/lobbyist friend Corcoran. The tension poured over into Truman's office, where the president proclaimed, "The buck stops here."

On July 1, 1945 the President fired Biddle and replaced him with Tom Clark, a former lobbyist for Texas oilmen before joining the Justice Department. Ironically Biddle had only recently tried to fire Clark, who was now taking over his job.

Truman later admitted that assigning Clark the position of Attorney General "was the worst mistake of my life. It isn't so much that Clark is bad. It's just that he's such a dumb son of a bitch."

Supreme Court Justice Felix Frankfurter detested Clark, calling his "morality somewhat rancid." Even so, and even after he'd been accused of accepting a large bribe in a war profiteering case, Clark nevertheless became an Associate Justice of the Supreme Court, serving from 1949 to 1967.

J. Edgar was delighted when Clark became the Attorney General. "The fucker will more or less rubber stamp anything I want to do," J. Edgar proclaimed to Clyde, Guy, and Louis Nichols. With some exceptions, that turned out to be true.

"I didn't bother to read Hoover's secret memos," Clark later said. "If he wiretapped people, I figured he knew what he was doing. I handed his memos over to my assistant. He wrote several times about queers in the State Department. So what? Queers can show up everywhere, even as captains of football teams. In America it's possible for a queer to become director of the FBI. Hey, don't quote me on that."

J. Edgar was not only concerned with men who held great power in Washington. Both he and Clyde had an uncanny knack for figuring out who would hold power in the future.

As Guy Hotell claimed, "Eddie and Clyde wanted to start collecting incriminating data on young men who were on their way to the top. Often they figured out the politicians who would one day become President— take Richard Nixon, for example, or John F. Kennedy. Yes, they even spotted Lyndon Johnson as a rising force to be reckoned with."

***

A young couple had moved across the street from J. Edgar on Thirtieth Place NW. He was a congressman from Texas, Lyndon B. Johnson, along with his wife, known as "Lady Bird." J. Edgar told Clyde, "I hear he's a big crook who married her for her money, and that he has the morals of an alleycat. Guess what? Several secretaries he's fucked on Capitol Hill spread the word he's hung like a horse. Not only that, but his favorite dish is grilled Texas rattlesnake. Sounds like he's a man to watch."

***

After the collapse of the Third Reich, J. Edgar in Clyde's presence often dined out on how he tricked the Nazis into thinking the Allied invasion of Europe would be launched in Norway. Fueled by bourbon, he exaggerated his role one night when he invited Ethel Merman to dine with Clyde and him at Harvey's. "I recommended to Roosevelt that we erect false bases in Iceland that could be seen by German reconnaissance planes. That way, the Nazis were tricked into thinking we were establishing a base in Iceland for the eventual invasion of Norway." Nazi troops were rushed to Norway in anticipation of the landing that never was. Without me, the Normandy invasion would not have been successful."

Instead of war strategy, Merman told him what a lousy lay actor Cesar Romero was, "Gay as a goose," she said before the term had come into vogue.

On another front, J. Edgar's attention turned to "keeping the lid on the Manhattan Project" at Los Alamos. He was one of the few U.S. citizens who knew that America was close to developing an atomic bomb. The original plan, he claimed, was to bomb the port of Hamburg and ask for German's unconditional surrender. If that failed, a second bomb would be dropped on Frankfurt in an effort to bring Nazi Germany to its knees.

After the German surrender, the attention focused on Japan. J. Edgar wanted the first bomb to fall on Tokyo, but Truman vetoed the plan. "If we bomb Tokyo, there won't be any officials left to surrender. We might end up having some low-rent Jap admiral surrender."

Julius Robert Oppenheimer, an American theoretical physicist, is often called the "Father of the Atomic Bomb," based on his role in the Manhattan Project in WWII that developed the first atomic weapons. The scientist had come under surveillance by J. Edgar and Clyde since before the war when he displayed "pro-communist sympathies" while a professor at Berkeley. He was also known to associate with known communists.

As his involvement with the government became known, J. Edgar increased surveillance, bugging his office and tapping his phone. Letters sent to him were secretly opened before delivery.

J. Edgar was horrified when Oppenheimer was allowed to join the Manhattan Project in 1942, even after he admitted on his security questionnaire that he had been "a member of just about every communist front organization on the West Coast." J. Edgar had sent to the President a warning that while at Berkeley the scientist "had been the ring leader of a communist cell group." Even though he was working on the Manhattan Project, Oppenheimer was added to the FBI's "Custodial Detention Index," and slated for arrest in case of a national emergency.

Throughout the war, he was repeatedly investigated by both the FBI and the Manhattan Project's Internal Security team. When FBI agents spotted Oppenheimer talking to suspected Soviet agents trying to steal nuclear secrets, J. Edgar immediately notified Brigadier General Leslie R. Groves, Jr., director of the Manhattan Project. Groves was given a detailed report of Oppenheimer's communist associations with times and places of meetings. Groves called J. Edgar, claiming that the scientist was "absolutely essential to the project and had to be retained. We have to take the risk to end the war and save millions of lives of American soldiers perhaps by killing a few hundred Japanese civilians. At least the fuckers will surrender—or else NO TOKYO!!!"

Oppenheimer handled the work on fast neutron calculations and was given the role of "Coordinator of Rapid Rupture," a reference to the propagation of a fast neutron chain reaction in an atomic bomb.

When J. Edgar learned that Groves had named Oppenheimer as director of the project's Secret Weapons Laboratory, he notified him, "Oppenheimer is a card-carrying communist with direct links to the Kremlin. You have been warned. You are, in fact, giving Josef Stalin the secrets of how to make an atomic bomb." The Brigadier General chose not to answer.

J. Edgar became even more horrified when he learned that the Manhattan Project had grown from a few hundred people in 1943 to 6,000 employees weeks before the history's first nuclear attack. J. Edgar told Clyde and other agents, "Stalin will get our atomic secrets. There is no way in hell that 6,000 people will keep a secret, especially Oppenheimer, who is as red as Santa Claus' drawers."

Spies within the Manhattan Project kept J. Edgar and Clyde appraised of every development, especially the launch of a project code-named "Trinity."

The project paid off on July 16, 1945 when the first nuclear explosion ushered the world into the Atomic Age near Alamogordo, 230 miles south of Los Alamos. Oppenheimer later quoted a Hindu verse: "If the radiance of a thousand suns were to burst at once into the sky, that would be like the splendor of the mighty one."

For six months prior to the dropping of atomic bombs onto the mainland of Japan, the U.S. Air Force intensely fire-bombed nearly 70 cities in Japan. The Japanese ignored an ultimatum issued at Potsdam in Germany.

J. Edgar secretly learned that Truman was prepared to authorize dropping at least two atomic bombs on Japan. The first one blasted Hiroshima into eternity on August 6, 1945.

"Little Boy," as it was called, killed perhaps 160,000 people. On August 9, "Fat Man," the second bomb, dropped on Nagasaki, turning it into a mushroom cloud, killing some 80,000 people. Six days later, the stubborn Japanese finally surrendered to Allied powers.

Awarded the Presidential Medal for Merit in 1946, Oppenheimer became a national spokesman for science and a household name, appearing on the covers of both *Life* and *Time*.

J. Edgar continued to have Oppenheimer trailed, feeding information about him to his enemies. On June 7, 1949, Oppenheimer was forced to testify before the House Un-American Activities Committee, where he admitted to "associations" with the Communist Party in the 1930s. In the 1950s, Oppenheimer found himself in conflict with Edward Teller, who was working on his own project—the development of the hydrogen bomb. Whereas Op-

A cigarette-smoking "addict" (four packages a day), **Julius Robert Oppenheimer** was called "the Father of the Atomic Bomb." He knew all the secrets of the bomb and worked at Los Alamos in its development.

J. Edgar thought he was a communist. Oppenheimer topped the FBI list of possible subversives, which also included Oppenheimer's friend, Albert Einstein; U.S. Supreme court Justice William O. Douglas, and novelists John Steinbeck and Ernest Hemingway.

Many of Oppenheimer's lovers and associates were communists. The scientist never said that he had actually joined the party, but admitted that he was a "fellow traveler." J. Edgar's FBI could never pin homosexuality on him, but they did investigate his sexual life, discovering him to be "an adulterer who liked to be tortured a bit during sexual encounters."

Agents also investigated his mistress, Jean Tatlock, the daughter of a Berkeley literature professor who wrote for *The Western Worker*, a communist newspaper. Oppenheimer broke up with Tatlock in 1939 and took up with Katherine (Kitty) Puening Harrison, a radical Berkeley student and Communist Party member.. His affair with her began while she was still married to Richard Harrison, a medical researcher.

Oppenheimer impregnated Kitty on his ranch in New Mexico, and she finally divorced Harrison. She married Oppenheimer on November 1, 1940, and gave birth to his first child, Peter. During his marriage, Oppenheimer continued an adulterous affair with Jean Tatlock.

FISSION FIGURE — This picture of Rita Hayworth, film actress, has been painted on the atomic bomb, christened Gilda, to be dropped today.

(AP) Wirephoto

Rita Hayworth starred in *Gilda* (1946), her most famous movie role, in which she was cast opposite her lover, Glenn Ford. Rita had never been sexier, especially when she sang "Put the Blame on Mame." Her appearance made *Gilda* the favorite movie shown to GIs that year. To these military men, Rita incarnated American female sexuality. "Rita was the real reason we fought World War II," said one of the GIs who stencilled her image on the airplane that dropped a nuclear test bomb that exploded the Bikini Island atoll in the Marshall Islands in the Western Pacific.

Although the GIs meant it as a tribute to the love goddess, Rita was horrified. Her husband, Orson Welles, claimed, "Rita flew into the rage of her life. I've never seen her this angry before."

"I am shocked," she told Welles. "As you know, I would never hurt another human being. Why I would be linked with an atomic bomb that took thousands of innocent lives is beyond me." She wanted to fly to Washington for a press conference to defend herself. "These GIs have mixed me up with the Bitch of Buchenwald who made lampshades out of human skins," she said.

Welles talked her out of it. The head of Columbia Pictures, Harry Cohn, also talked her out of the trip, claiming that it would appear unpatriotic. "You make that trip, bitch, and J. Edgar Hoover will have you invesigated as a communist." Later, Rita blamed Cohn for the "Gilda Bomb," claiming that it was "one of his sick publicity stunts."

penheimer pushed for smaller "tactical" nuclear weapons, Teller was interested in harnessing the ultimate big blast.

J. Edgar believed that his years of spying on Oppenheimer had finally paid off on December 21, 1953, when President Dwight D. Eisenhower revoked his security clearance.

A chain smoker, Oppenheimer was diagnosed with throat cancer in late 1965 and lived until February 15, 1967 when he fell into a coma and died at the age of 62 in Princeton, New Jersey.

Clyde sent an FBI agent to the funeral to write down the names of the powerful political, military, and scientific leaders, as well as the artists who attended. They included the novelist John O'Hara and dancer/choreographer George Balanchine, the director of the New York City Ballet. "Probably red as blood," J. Edgar told Clyde who reported back to him.

Although Oppenheimer was extensively investigated by the FBI, J. Edgar and Clyde would spend far more of their time spying on Albert Einstein.

***

As revealed to his closest allies, J. Edgar was an anti-Semite, as was his friend Clyde. One of J. Edgar's many criticisms of Albert Einstein was that "he is just too much of a Jew."

J. Edgar and Clyde had compiled and maintained a bulky file on Einstein since the 1930s. After the war, they increased their surveillance of him when he began to have secret meetings with Oppenheimer. "Just what are they plotting?" J. Edgar asked Clyde and Guy. "I'm sure both of them are in direct contact with the Kremlin, probably sending love letters to Josef Stalin." An all-out investigation of the scientist would not really begin until 1950 when J. Edgar began to view Einstein as Public Enemy No. 1, like John Dillinger in the 1930s.

Years before that, J. Edgar shared some of his suspicions with Tom Clark. The Attorney General reminded J. Edgar that it was Einstein who had warned Roosevelt that Hitler had ordered scientists to develop an atomic bomb that would destroy both Washington and New York, in both cases with just one bomb for each. J. Edgar did not respond to that praise for Einstein.

Back at his office, J. Edgar ordered Clyde to intensify the FBI surveillance of Einstein. "From what I hear, he's on his way to becoming the antiwar critic of capitalism. He's an ugly little Jew, and you know what I think of Jews."

J. Edgar allowed some of his agents to

Ever since **Albert Einstein** arrived in the United States in 1933, he was viewed by J. Edgar as a dangerous pacifist, socialist, and advocate of left-wing causes. Einstein's political views provided the excuse J. Edgar needed to remove him from the Manhattan Project, code name for the development of history's first atomic bomb.

But J. Edgar was even more intrigued with another legend: Had the emerging starlet, Marilyn Monroe, bedded Einstein as she had claimed to her girl friends, Shelley Winters and Jeanne Carmen? "I admire his brains," she told one of her lovers, Peter Lawford.

One FBI agent reported to J. Edgar that "Monroe and Einstein definitely did not have an affair—she just made it up." But another agent offered a more detailed report, claiming that he had extensively interviewed two servants, each of whom maintained that Marilyn had slipped away from her apartment in New York City and driven to a restored farmhouse on the outskirts of Easthampton, Long Island, where she spent the weekend.

As relayed by Jeanne Carmen, Marilyn said, "After my weekend with 'Alberto,' I now admire more than his brain. He might not look like much, but he's a dynamo in bed."

Whether Marilyn told the truth or not may never be known. Perhaps she made it up. But then again.....

235

tell new recruits that there is nothing terribly wrong about the American Nazi Party because "it is against the Jews trying to take over America, including the media, especially the film industry."

In the late 1930s, J. Edgar and Clyde vacationed at a hotel on Miami Beach that advertised its policy of NO DOGS, NO JEWS. On their vacations to California, J. Edgar and Clyde lodged at the Hotel del Charro in La Jolla. It was owned by a friend of J. Edgar's, Clint Murchison, a Texas oilman who had a policy of housing only Gentiles.

J. Edgar was alarmed that the Manhattan Project had employed too many Jewish scientists. Guy claimed, "If Eddie found out someone was a Jew, he immediately felt they might be a security risk."

With a certain anger, J. Edgar always brushed off criticism that he had been "asleep at the wheel" in the weeks leading up to the Japanese attack on Pearl Harbor. After the war was over, he claimed that his own role in winning the epic conflict did not receive the commendation it deserved. "I blame the Jews for that," he told Louis Nichols and Clyde. "They are keeping me from many deserved honors because they are secret communists who want to diminish me."

***

Both J. Edgar and Clyde continued to see their celebrity women friends, particularly Dorothy Lamour and Ethel Merman, who they entertained with tales of their daring WWII exploits capturing Nazi spies and saboteurs on the homefront. He became especially animated when relating his involvement with Nazi spies William George Sebold and Walter Koehler.

Born in Germany in 1899, Sebold became one of the most famous German spies in WWII, a double agent for the FBI. This former dishwasher and bartender was the key player in outing the Duquesne Spy Ring, which remains the largest espionage case in U.S. history ending in convictions.

Sebold became a naturalized U.S. citizen in 1936, but returned to Germany in February of 1939, months before the outbreak of the war. In the city of Mülheim on a visit with his mother, he was approached by an Abwehr agent and asked to return to the United States and spy on America. From Major Nickolaus Ritter of Abwehr, Sebold received final instructions, including the use of codes and microphotographs. He was assigned the code name of "Harry Sawyer."

Before leaving for New York, Sebold took a daring risk and visited the U.S. consulate in Cologne. Perhaps he was in disguise, because visitors entering the U.S. consulate, which was before America's entry in the war, were often photographed and spied upon by the Gestapo. At the consulate, Sebold told the American staff that he'd been recruited as a spy by Abwehr but wanted to cooperate with the FBI.

He claimed to Dale W. Maher, the official in charge, that the Gestapo had threatened him when they discovered that he'd been jailed for a robbery in his hometown, but that he hadn't reported that detail in his application for immigration to America. He was also told by Abwehr that if he didn't cooperate, he'd be sent to a concentration camp.

Before leaving for New York, Sebold took an intensive seven-week course in Hamburg, with thorough training in radio telegraphy, Morse code, and short-wave transmitters. In New York, J. Edgar met privately with Sebold but didn't really trust him. Finally, he agreed to accept him as a double agent, but privately he warned Clyde that Sebold would have to be watched at all times. "His chief advantage, I think will be in leading us to other Nazi spies." J. Edgar was strongly urged to work with Sebold, and he very reluctantly agreed.

Sebold had been supplied with enough money to rent his own office. However, J. Edgar called millionaire Vincent Astor, who owned an office building on 42nd Street in Manhattan. When J. Edgar explained his need for such an office, Astor volunteered to let Seebold use it rent free. That way, J. Edgar could have it equipped for an FBI spy operation before Seebold moved in.

J. Edgar personally inspected the office and ordered Clyde to have it bugged and a one-way mirror installed so that all visitors could be secretly filmed while talking to Sebold. Even though moving ahead with details associated with Sebold, J. Edgar remained deeply suspicious that he was a plant still loyal to his Nazi bosses back in Hamburg. "I don't want him to make a fool of us," J. Edgar told Clyde and Guy.

Installed in his new quarters, it took Sebold two months before he could start transmitting messages from Nazi agents stationed in America to the officers at Abwehr. Clyde had personally traveled to Long Island with FBI technicians, where a building was purchased and then equipped to broadcast shortwave radio messages to Hamburg. For a period of sixteen months, this secret station remained in operation, providing the main link between the Nazi spies in the United States and the Nazi intelligence operation in Hamburg. For security reasons, J. Edgar never told Sebold the location of the radio transmitter.

Working secretly through Sebold, J. Edgar and Clyde identified dozens of Nazi spies not only in the United States but in Mexico and in such countries as Argentina and Brazil.

On orders from Abwehr, Sebold contacted the major German spy operating in America, Fritz Joubert Duquesne, code-named DUNN. He had been spying in New York for Germany since WWI and had never been caught.

After two months of getting settled and contacting Nazi spies working within the U.S., Sebold began transmitting messages to Hamburg. Officials at Abwehr were impressed with his reports and found them authentic enough to relay to the military.

In sixteen months, some 300 messages were sent to Hamburg, and the radio station became the chief communications link between Abwehr and its network of Nazi spies.

One of the biggest secrets Nazi spies were ordered to discover was how far the United States had gone in developing its atomic bomb project.

All this espionage came crashing down on June 29, 1941 when J. Edgar announced "the greatest spy round-up in American history," carefully planned by Clyde and executed with lightning speed.

The FBI rounded up thirty-three top Nazi agents, all fingered by Sebold. Collectively, the agents of the "Duquesne Spy Ring" were sentenced to serve a total of three hundred years in prison.

The only advantage Abwehr saw in the round-up was that Sebold himself had not been arrested. But their last hope disappeared when Sebold himself showed up at the trial of the Nazi spies. After that, he just disappeared from the radar screen, perhaps under the wing of the government witness protection program.

Guy once asked over dinner at Harvey's what happened to Sebold. "We had to get rid of him because he knew too much about the operation of the FBI," J. Edgar said, supplying no further details.

The exploits of Sebold formed the basis of a 1945 spy film, *The House on 92nd Street*, starring Lloyd Nolan and Signe Hasso. J. Edgar introduced the film, and FBI agents played themselves in the semi-documentary style movie produced by Louis De Rochemont.

J. Edgar later proclaimed that the ring's round-up of spies delivered "the death blow to Abwehr's espionage efforts in the United States." Perhaps that was an overstatement, but it was more or less true.

***

In 1946 in *American* magazine, J. Edgar published an article called "The Spy Who Double Crossed Hitler." It dealt with the strange case of Walter Koehler, who was hardly the romantic James Bond type of spy. As J. Edgar described Koehler, he was "a swarthy, short, heavy-set man with thick-lensed glasses who walked with a stoop—hardly the spy type."

A jeweler by trade, Koehler was a Dutchman and a staunch Roman Catholic who had worked as a spy for the Kaiser during World War I.

He came to the attention of Abwehr because of his knowledge of scientific matters. How a man who sold diamond rings to engaged couples became familiar with science is not known. Abwehr agents recruited him to go to America and learn about government proficiency in the field of nuclear research.

Koehler was flown to Lisbon, a city crowded with refugees from Hitler trying to get a visa for entrance into the United States. Interviewed by the vice consul there, Koehler immediately confessed that he'd been hired by Abwehr to go to the States to spy for the Nazis. He turned over evidence. In J. Edgar's article, he claimed, "They dealt with every detail of building and operating a shortwave radio, frequency tables, ciphers, hours of transmission, and a copy of the Dutch-language prayer book, on which his code was based. Koehler pleaded that he had never intended to work for the Nazis and that he had gone through with it just to get out of Europe. He insisted he loved the United States and would willingly serve it as a counterspy."

In his coat he carried some $20,000 in gold coins, travelers checks, cash, and jewelry.

The vice consul notified the State Department, which called J. Edgar. Clyde brought his boss an extensive file on Koehler, outlining his espionage activities in WWI. J. Edgar was greatly puzzled. He told Clyde, "I don't think a zebra can change its stripes so easily. I think he's planning to double-cross us. That confession in Lisbon was but a ruse. Let's send for him but try to outsmart him. In his attempt to double-cross us, perhaps we can figure out a way to double-cross Abwehr. Let's play a dangerous game."

When Koehler landed in New York, Clyde ordered FBI agents in Manhattan to put him under strict surveillance. In his luggage, G-Men found a spy's equipment not reported to the vice consul in Lisbon—a miniature Leica camera, chemicals for making inks not visible without special equipment, and equipment for microphotography. One agent reported to Clyde that Koehler's wife had visited a minor Nazi spy known to the FBI. He turned over $8,000 in cash to her.

From February 7, 1943 until the German surrender in May of 1945, Koehler sent coded messages to Abwehr in Hamburg through the FBI transmitter on Long Island.

In his article, J. Edgar wrote: "We gave the Nazis industrial and military information on a week-to-week basis. Most of the information we gave them was true, because we wanted to give Koehler a high degree of credibility. It was a touchy situation because we did not want to give away anything of real importance and also because we could not let it appear that Koehler knew too much. After all, he was a single agent working alone in the United States. If he had been too knowing, the Germans would have suspected us. Really, what we wanted out of the Koehler operation was to prevent the Nazis from sending others to pry into our nuclear activities. But we also wanted to learn how Nazi agents on the American continent were being paid."

The FBI director also used Koehler to feed Abwehr the false information that the allied invasion of Europe would begin in Norway through U.S. bases in Iceland.

J. Edgar's claims about Koehler in a magazine article have been disputed by later revelations by historians investigating Nazi espionage in 1971. A charge appeared that a Nazi spy operating out of Rochester, New York, frequently journeyed to Manhattan to pick up military secrets from Koehler. Although he was under surveillance, he was not guarded twenty-four hours a day.

A year before J. Edgar's death, charges were made that Koehler was THE SPY WHO FOOLED J. EDGAR HOOVER, as one article claimed. As the story unfolded, the FBI director became almost consumed with rage.

When the U.S. Army invaded Hamburg, secrets from Abwehr headquarters were retrieved. It was too much information to consume at once and did not receive high priority because the war had already ended. But as the years went by, it was discovered that secrets were sent from Koehler to Hamburg through a communications link to Abwehr from Rochester. The spy there was never found, and presumably faded into the great American heartland after the Nazis surrendered.

Born in Weinheim, Germany, in September of 1897, Koehler lived a long, mysterious life. The last decades of his life remain a mystery, and he went to his grave in January of 1989. The secrets of his role as a spy, possibly a double agent, in WWII were buried with him.

***

After celebrating his fifty-first birthday in January of 1946, J. Edgar asked Clyde to fly with him to New York for a brief vacation. At the Club of Champions in Manhattan, J. Edgar kneeled down to kiss the sapphire ring of the notorious Francis Joseph, Cardinal Spellman, Archbishop of New York. Before flying to New York, Clyde had presented J. Edgar a long file on Spellman's sometimes outrageous homosexual lifestyle, which was well known even by the Pope himself. Around the Vatican, the American archbishop was mockingly called "Nellie Spellman."

That night at the club, the audience was filled with many right wing zealots, including Spellman himself. J. Edgar launched an attack on the "new enemy," communists, who were actually his old enemy. With the Nazis defeated, he began his campaign against "the Red Menace." Arguably, more so than any other individual, including the infamous Senator Joseph McCarthy, J. Edgar was the key figure in launching the anti-communist hysteria that would rage across America in the post-war years, destroying lives and careers.

Before Spellman and the club members, J. Edgar gave a fiery speech. "Come what may, when thirty million Catholics assert themselves, the nation must pause and listen. There are only 100,000 Communists here but they are organized, articulate, and motivated by a fanatical frenzy. We must search them out and neuter them. Perhaps make *castrati* out of them." The audience laughed and applauded wildly.

Spellman was one of the leading American prelates of the Roman Catholic Church and the sixth archbishop of New York, reigning (and that's the right word) from 1939 to 1967, having served before in the archdiocese of Boston. When J. Edgar met him, he had already been designated as a cardinal. At the time, he was convincing Pope Pius XII of the need to internationalize the Vatican's investments. "They are too centered in Italy," Spellman claimed. He had such success at going global with Vatican lire that he became known as "Cardinal Moneybags."

Truman Capote in later years referred to Spellman and J. Edgar as "Mary and Franny. Spellman was the major child abuser in the Roman Catholic Church," the author claimed.

The flamboyantly gay **Francis Spellman** used to scream "more lace, more lace" at his tailor when being fitted for one of his gowns. As Guy Hotell claimed, "Spellman could appear in drag during his official duties in all that Vatican finery, but his pal, Eddie, could dress up only in private. They were two birds of a feather—or should I say 'boas'?"

No other archbishop of New York, before or since, was as controversial as "Nellie Spellman," as he was called by his enemies in the Vatican.

At the 1958 papal conclave that elected Pope John XXIII, Spellman said, "He's no Pope! He should be selling bananas!"

Even though John F. Kennedy was a Catholic, Spellman supported a Quaker, Richard Nixon, for President during the elections of 1960. "Jack Kennedy is a whoremonger with a homosexual concubine on the side," Spellman told J. Edgar Hoover. The archbishop was referring to JFK's best friend, Lem Billings, who was a homosexual.

"With Hoover, he often swapped young males, many of them underage, for the purposes of sex. Spellman's name of Franny made its way through New York's gay community. When not being an archbishop, he could in private be the campiest queen in New York. On the other hand, 'Mary' was a bit more macho and subdued, even at the gayest of parties."

Capote was known to exaggerate, but there may have been some truth to his claims, which have been substantiated by other sources.

Tracy Coombes, who later became a waiter in a Hollywood eatery, was born in New York. He went to *Confidential* in 1955 and tried to sell an article to the magazine's editors about his experiences with Spellman and J. Edgar. The hustler wanted five thousand dollars. Although the editors were enthralled with his revelations, they were considered too hot for them to expose. "Hoover would surely shut down our magazine," said one of the editors.

"I was a good-looking kid when I was fourteen, and had a good build and an impressive package," Coombes claimed. "I'd heard that Spellman paid big money for young boys, and I made myself available to his secretary who arranged things for the Cardinal. I was ushered into his chambers, and I was there for about an hour. He gave me a blow-job and really felt me up. He gave me a hundred dollars, probably from the collection plate. At the time, my going rate was ten dollars. He asked to see me again, and I was always willing. For one hundred dollars, I would have had to turn ten tricks."

Coombes told the editors that one day Spellman arranged for him to be driven to Washington in an FBI car. "I was taken to the home of J. Edgar Hoover. I once thought I wanted to be a G-Man myself. I was really shocked to find that the director of the FBI liked to make it with young kids. Later I heard about this Tolson guy who was Hoover's lover. But on the afternoon I visited, Tolson was not in the house. Hoover took me into his library. He asked me to strip down and get a hard-on. He took several pictures of me before giving me a blow-job. Since I was sent down all the way from New York and had to be driven back, he gave me two hundred dollars. I'd never made money like that before. I was so grateful I even let Hoover kiss me when the FBI driver arrived outside to take me back. I was goddamn grateful for the money. Nowadays as a waiter, I can make two hundred dollars in just one night in tips."

Somehow the boy-swapping between J. Edgar and Spellman became known to Richard Cardinal Cushing of Boston. A heavy drinker, he preferred young nuns to young boys.

Lem Billings, John F. Kennedy's best friend and a homosexual, once said, "Jack knew about Spellman and Hoover. He knew about the boy exchanges, the dressing in drag, the works. Cushing was a great friend of both Bobby and Jack, and he gave the brothers a full report. Of course, that dreaded Hoover kept a full report on both Bobby and Jack. He had all the shit on them, and they had all the shit on him. Revelations would have ended all three careers. Jack could never fire Hoover, and Hoover could never afford to expose the Kennedys. Everybody knew too much about everybody else. Call it a Mexican standoff."

In spite of decades-old cover-ups, word did leak out, of course, about both J. Edgar and the Kennedys. One of Spellman's biographers, John Cooney, interviewed several people close to the cardinal, who made claims that he was gay. "I talked to many priests," Cooney claimed. "These men worked for the cardinal and were incensed, dismayed, and angered by his conduct, which was often outrageous in private."

Journalist Michelangelo Signorile called Spellman "one of the most notorious, powerful and sexually voracious homosexuals in the American Catholic Church's history." The author claimed that pressure was brought to bear on Cooney's publisher, Times Books, and charges of Spellman's sexuality were reduced to one paragraph of accusations. One of Cooney's interviews was with the famous historian C.A. Tripp, who made many revelations about Spellman.

Signorile also cited a story that in the 1940s, Spellman had an affair with a male member of the chorus in the Broadway revue *One Touch of Venus*.

Although he had no intention of ever exposing Spellman—he couldn't afford to and had no motivation to do so—J. Edgar still gathered an extensive file on the cardinal, which he and Clyde read for voyeuristic pleasure.

As Guy Hotell later recalled, "When Eddie met Francis, it was the beginning of a beautiful friendship, just like Bogie and Claude Rains in the closing scene in *Casablanca*. They were birds of a feather. With his Vatican apparel, Francis was in a sort of drag most of the day. But with Eddie in private, he could bring out the boas, the feathers, the hosiery. Both men loved total drag, especially spiked high heels. I attended their parties in New York and Palm Beach. My greatest regret is that I never snapped a picture of both of them sitting down to dine in total drag. Surely it would have sold for a million bucks."

***

The meeting of the young Congressman from Texas, Lyndon B. Johnson, and J. Edgar became the stuff of Washington legend and lore. After moving in, Johnson learned from the neighbors that J. Edgar, who, with

Clyde, occupied the house across the street, was called "Weird Mary" by the other residents on the block.

On several occasions when he came home from his congressional office, LBJ had noticed a person "wearing either a dress or an old woman's style housecoat while watering his flowers and trimming his rose bushes, his face masked by a beekeeper's hat and face net." The future President was astonished to learn that "Weird Mary" was actually J. Edgar himself.

One afternoon, tanked up on bourbon after drinking with House Speaker Sam Rayburn, LBJ dared cross the street to present "Weird Mary" with an invitation. Striding into J. Edgar's yard, LBJ confronted J. Edgar, who at first seemed to want to flee.

"Hi, Edgar, I'm Lyndon Johnson," he said. "I meant to come over before and get acquainted."

"Hello," J. Edgar answered in a low voice.

"Lady Bird and I want you to come over for dinner tonight," he said. "She's found a place in Washington that makes real Texas barbecue. The chef's from San Antonio."

History does not record what went through J. Edgar's mind at that point. Obviously he realized that LBJ was accepting of him, even in a housecoat, and wanted to form some sort of bond.

"You like barbecue don't you?" LBJ asked.

"Clyde and I love it," he said.

"Well, why don't you and your boy get your asses across the street at seven tonight? We'll have a few Jack Daniels to get acquainted. I hear that's what you drink at Harvey's. It's about time we became asshole buddies because I think you can help me and I can help you in this town."

Details about J. Edgar's introduction and the dinner shared with Clyde at the home of LBJ and Lady Bird were related in graphic detail to Guy Hotell the following day.

Actually, LBJ, according to reports, did not approve of homosexuality, but he was clever enough to keep his prejudices under control when dealing with people in Washington who had a sexual preference other than his own. Before moving to Washington, Lady Bird had warned him, "Lyndon, you're going to have to adjust to the fact that up in D.C., people sleep together in different combinations from what you are used to—not just men with women, but men with men, or even women with women."

"I wouldn't mind watching some of that lesbian action, but cocksucking or taking it up the ass never appealed to me," he said.

"If you're going to be President one day, you've got to learn to leave your Texas prejudice behind and tolerate sexual behavior that your mama didn't teach you."

"You've got a point there, Miss Lady Bird," he told her.

Standing in the garden of his front yard, his face hardly visible, J. Edgar looked across at Johnson's rented home. "Clyde and I will be there right on the dot."

As he was leaving the yard, LBJ turned back to J. Edgar, "Oh, you guys can wear whatever you want. It's very informal. I often eat dinner in my underwear."

"No one knows what J. Edgar told Clyde when he got home that night. But promptly at seven that night, they showed up on LBJ's front porch. They were dressed in dark suits and ties. Access to the house was blocked only by a screen door, the main wooden door having been left hospitably open. Clyde rang the doorbell.

From down the hall, LBJ called to them. "Come on in," he shouted. "I'll be out in a minute."

J. Edgar and Clyde stood awkwardly in the hallway. In a few minutes, LBJ emerged dripping wet from the shower. With his penis swinging, he strode up the hallway to shake J. Edgar's hand and introduce himself to Clyde.

Far from concealing his prodigious endowment, he flaunted it. He took his penis in his left hand and shook it. "I've gotta take Ol' Jumbo here and give him a workout tonight. After the barbecue, tell Lady Bird we have some business at FBI headquarters tonight. I'll leave with you boys but skip out. I wonder who the lucky gal will be tonight who gets me to fuck her with this."

In his entire life, J. Edgar had never met a politician this open and blatant. Apparently, what LBJ was trying to do was to signal them right from the beginning that there was no need for secrets among them. It was an effective ploy.

When Lady Bird arrived thirty minutes later, the men were already enjoying their second bourbon. As she came in the door, the smell of the barbecue she carried permeated the air.

Johnson rose and gave her a wet kiss before introducing her to J. Edgar and Clyde.

Regrettably, no one recorded what was said among this soon-to-be famous quartet. That night, a liaison was formed that would grow more intense as LBJ's political power grew in Washington.

Of course, his tolerance of homosexuals went just so far. The next day at his office, he told Ted Sudling, a young aide he'd brought up from Austin, "Guess what? Last night I fed barbecue to the two most famous cocksuckers in Washington." He grabbed at his crotch. "I bet the faggots wanted me to feed them Ol' Jumbo here, but, as you know, I'm strictly a man for the

En famille in Austin, Texas, in 1948, **Lady Bird** *(left)* and **Lyndon B. Johnson** *(right)* look like one happy family in a posed portrait with their daughters. Actually, the road for Lady Bird was a rocky one, as she had to tolerate Lyndon's adulterous affairs, especially after their move to Washington. "Women were attracted to Lyndon like flies to honey," Lady Bird said in her Southern drawl.

In the 1940s, Lyndon and Lady Bird also socialized with another "couple," J. Edgar and Clyde, during the months when they lived across the street from them. When Lyndon wanted to take Lady Bird out on the town for the night, he often asked Clyde and J. Edgar to babysit for his girls. Both of these G-Men gladly volunteered.

"Babysitting with my little gals is as close as Clyde and J. Edgar will ever get to know what it's like to bring up children. After all, they can't have kids. Neither one has the right plumbing, even though J. Edgar wears a dress on occasion."

ladies."

In another part of town, J. Edgar ordered Clyde to begin a much closer FBI monitoring of the activities of LBJ. "This tall Texan is going places, and we must find out what he's up to. This town has rarely seen a wheeler dealer like him, and he certainly isn't the modest type."

Actually it was J. Edgar himself who gathered firsthand evidence of a scandal involving LBJ and one of his mistresses. He was enjoying his usual lunch at the Mayflower Hotel when he saw LBJ enter the dining room with Alice Glass, whom he introduced to Clyde and J. Edgar before going on to their own table.

J. Edgar was well aware of who Alice was. She was the live-in lover of Charles E. Marsh, the newspaper magnate, who had walked out on his wife and children to live with Alice. Politicians, including Franklin D. Roosevelt himself, had visited the couple at their 18th-century manor house, Longlea, in Northern Virginia, a short drive from the heart of Washington. Marsh also entertained some of the best-known journalists in Washington, including columnist Drew Pearson.

Ostensibly, Alice and LBJ, who were spending a lot of time together, were trying to rescue Jews from Nazi Germany. J. Edgar had suspected they were having an affair, which was dangerous on LBJ's part, because Marsh was his principal political backer. His newspapers also promoted Johnson. Not only that, but J. Edgar had been told that Marsh was contributing thousands of dollars a year for LBJ's personal fund, since he could not live well on his $10,000 annual salary as a congressman.

FBI agents had learned that in 1939, Johnson had been sold a tract of very valuable land, using $5,000, a "knock-down price," to purchase land worth nearly half a million. He used Lady Bird's money to close the deal. "Today I have secured our financial future," Johnson reportedly told his staff in Texas.

At the end of their meals, Alice and LBJ walked back to J. Edgar's table. Alice invited both men to join her lover, Marsh, and herself at Longlea for the weekend, and the two G-Men accepted. "Lyndon here and Lady Bird will be there." Almost provocatively, she said, "You guys don't mind doubling up and sharing a bedroom?"

"That will be fine," J. Edgar said.

Alice gave a knowing look at LBJ and headed toward the elevator.

With a wink, LBJ told J. Edgar and Clyde, "Don't spread it around, but Alice keeps a room upstairs. Back in Texas we believe in 'love in the afternoon.'"

When the congressman left to join Alice upstairs, J. Edgar told Clyde, "We know his secrets, and he obviously knows ours. We should get along fine. He'll not make trouble for us, and we won't make trouble for him."

For years to come, J. Edgar and Clyde would keep abreast of Alice Glass, who eventually married Charles Marsh. Her long-enduring affair with then-President Johnson lasted until 1967. She so strongly objected to his conduct of the Vietnam War that she finally told him goodbye after thirty years of seductions.

***

Lyndon Johnson wasn't the only future President that J. Edgar began courting in the early stages of a national political career.

As a young law student, Richard M. Nixon had attended a recruitment lecture in Los Angeles organized by one of J. Edgar's FBI aides. So inspired was young Nixon by the speech that he flew to Washington and applied for a position with the Bureau. He had graduated from the Duke University School of Law in 1937.

His record looked impressive, and he went so far as to have a brief interview with Clyde. Nixon was so reserved, formal, and polite with Clyde that he rejected his application. "Not aggressive enough to be an FBI man," Clyde wrote.

An entire decade would pass before J. Edgar met Nixon at a 1947 hearing before the House Un-American Activities Committee. Truman didn't trust J. Edgar, but Nixon at that stage in his career viewed him as a tireless warrior against the rising menace of communism. *Newsweek* had featured J. Edgar on its cover against a background of Stars and Stripes. Behind the scenes, J. Edgar was feverishly working to consolidate his power and take control of all foreign intelligence for the U.S. in the post-war years.

J. Edgar was delighted at *Newsweek*'s honor of him but embarrassed when the American Mothers' Committee of 1947 named him "Father of the Year." At the time these mothers were unaware of J. Edgar's private life and just assumed that he was married with children. In those days homosexuality was not mentioned in polite circles. When the committee learned that J. Edgar was not married, one of the secretaries, Elizabeth Harris, wrote J. Edgar a note of apology withdrawing the award. "Oh, dear, oh dear, we are so terribly embarrassed and must withdraw the award. Please forgive us. Our committee is certain that you'll meet the right woman and have a family of your own. When that happens, I am sure that you will be truly recognized as Father of the Year. With your pristine record in government, I feel confident that you will not only make the ideal husband and the perfect father to your sons. We just know they'll be boys and future FBI men themselves."

The Father of the Year mishap once again sparked rumors of J. Edgar's homosexuality. His guilt drove him to become a patient of Dr. Marshall Ruffin, a prominent psychiatrist in Washington. But sessions with Dr. Ruffin were not successful, because J. Edgar feared that revelations about his private life would somehow be exposed. He broke off the sessions, and he was right. Some of the secrets he confided to the psychiatrist later were made public by Ruffin's wife after her husband died.

During J. Edgar's appearance before the House Un-American Activities Committee, he was asked a number of questions by Nixon about communism. J. Edgar viewed each of these friendly queries as aiding him in his battle against communism. Unlike Clyde, J. Edgar was impressed with Nixon.

During recess, an aide to J. Edgar whispered that Nixon had used dirty tricks against Jerry Voorhis to take away his congressional seat in California. "I know all about it," J. Edgar said. "Clyde let me read his file before coming over here this morning. There's nothing wrong with using dirty tricks if the goal is to defeat communism. I think Nixon will be a man we can work with in the months ahead."

That morning when J. Edgar had read Nixon's file, he found it rather skimpy. Before J. Edgar's death, the dossier would grow into volumes. Unlike Lyndon Johnson, Nixon appeared to have been a virgin until his wedding night.

In Whittier, California, he'd dated Ola Florence Welch, the daughter of the local police chief. It was hardly a passionate romance, though it lasted for six years. She'd voted for Nixon's rival when he ran for student body president.

He and Ola were cast as Dido and Aeneas in a local production of *The Aeneid*. In the play, he was supposed to embrace Ola and declare his love for her before throwing himself on a funeral pyre. His lack of passion and simpering kiss caused the student audience in the theater to utter catcalls and boos.

Ola remembered going to her first dance with Nixon. "We sat in chairs looking at the other dancers. Nixon didn't dance."

When he finished college, Nixon was hired by the law firm of Wingert and Bewley in Whittier. But he asked to be taken off divorce cases. "I can't tolerate hearing women talk about the sexual incompatibility of their husbands. I turn fifteen colors of the rainbow."

In January of 1938, Nixon, who fancied himself becoming a movie star one day, was cast in *The Dark Tower*, a production of the Whittier Community Players. Thelma (Pat) Ryan, a twenty-six-year-old teacher, was cast in the role of Daphne. The playwright called for "a tall, dark, sullen beauty of twenty."

As Nixon later recalled, "That night a beautiful and vivacious young woman with Titian hair appeared whom I had never seen before. I found I could not take my eyes off her. For me it was a case of love at first sight."

She let him drive her home. But at her doorstep, he asked if he could date her. She rejected him, claiming "I'm very busy."

"You shouldn't say that," he told her. "Someday I'm going to marry you."

Years later she recalled, "I thought he was nuts."

Over the next few months she kept turning him down. Most biographers have missed the reason why. Dreaming of

The top photo shows **Richard Nixon**, snapped in 1937 when he was a senior-year law student at Duke University. Before his death in 1972, J. Edgar had accumulated a massive file on him.

The FBI director had also ordered the compilation of a file on **Patricia Nixon** *(lower photo)*, but except for a few "indiscretions" prior to her marriage, she seemed to be "clean as a hound's tooth." She spent most of his high-profile years within her private suite at the White House, hitting the bottle, perhaps as a means of forgetting the many woes her husband had caused her.

By the time they married, both Nixon and his wife had abandoned their dreams of becoming movie stars. "All fairly attractive young men and women who grew up in California in the 1930s wanted to be movie stars," Patricia once confided to a group of Republican women she was addressing in Washington in 1969.

becoming an actress, as did many attractive young women in Hollywood in the 1930s, Pat was cast as an extra in the film *Small Town Girl* (1936), co-starring Janet Gaynor and matinee handsome Robert Taylor.

Gossip columnists at the time speculated that Gaynor and Taylor were having a torrid romance, not knowing that Gaynor had a preference for her own sex and that Taylor was involved in a torrid affair with the aviator Howard Hughes.

But Taylor also seduced women, and he began to date Pat and even managed to take her virginity. As she later admitted, "I developed such a powerful crush on Bob—call it love if you wish."

But his attentions shifted, and he saw her less frequently, as he'd also launched an affair with Errol Flynn. She had dreams of his asking her to marry him, but soon realized it would never happen.

Almost in desperation she let Nixon date her. But he often wasn't free. Working in the law firm during the day, he labored in a plant at night. He'd secured some investors to launch a frozen orange juice business and was trying to get the packaging right. Pat warned him that no American consumer would ever purchase frozen orange juice.

One night the frozen orange juice bags exploded in a refrigerated rail boxcar, and all of Nixon's savings were wiped out. "For a while if we went to the movies, I had to pay," Pat remembered.

Finally, Pat agreed to marry Nixon in a small ceremony on June 21, 1940. Two years later they moved to Washington, where he landed a job in a government wartime agency that rationed tires to motorists.

In Washington, Nixon decided he didn't want to be a movie star or a lawyer, but a congressman. In 1945, back in California, he persuaded some powerful Republicans to back him for Congress, taking on the popular Jerry Voorhis who was a Democrat. Handsome and well educated, Voorhis had served five terms in the House of Representatives, backing Roosevelt's New Deal.

Nixon ran a dirty campaign against Voorhis, accusing him of being a communist backed by left wing groups who owed their allegiance to the Kremlin.

When Voorhis had served on the House Un-American Activities Committee, *Time* magazine asserted that he could be "counted on to temper rightist blasts for leftish lambs." He was tabbed as "Kid Atlas" in the press because he seemed to carry the weight of the world on his shoulders.

A Republican smear committee delved into Voorhis' past. No communist links were discovered, but there were charges of homosexuality. Some of these stemmed from 1923 and 1924, in Germany, when Voorhis was said to have engaged in sex with a number of German youths when he was a representative for the YMCA. In 1928, he founded and became headmaster of the Voorhis School for Boys in San Dimas, California, a post he retained until he was elected to Congress. The smear campaign located three young men who'd attended the school. Each of them claimed that he was coerced into a homosexual relationship with Voorhis.

The Republican campaign headquarters considered this too hot an issue to make known to the public. Instead they launched a whispering campaign. Voters in the district picked up their phones to hear, "Did you know that Jerry Voorhis, running for Congress, is both a homosexual and a communist?" Nixon trounced Voorhis on Election Day and was sent to Washington.

At FBI headquarters, J. Edgar told Lou Nichols, Clyde, and Guy, "Richard Nixon is just the man to help us in the Red-baiting campaign I plan to launch. He'll go far. I predict he'll become a Senator from his state, maybe even Governor of California one day."

"Why not President of the United States?" Guy asked.

"Never that!" J. Edgar said. "He's no glad-hander. No personality. In a race against our friend Lyndon, the Texan would cut off Nixon's balls. I prefer the kid's politics, though, a hell of a lot more than I do that tall Texan's."

When Nixon met privately with J. Edgar two weeks later, Nixon confessed, "I knew Jerry Voorhis wasn't a commie. The man has high ideals and is strongly motivated to do good, the do-gooder type. But I had to win. That's what a lot of people in politics don't understand. The important thing is to win."

"You're preaching to the choir, Dick," J. Edgar said.

***

J. Edgar continued to view William (Wild Bill) Donovan as his chief rival for power even at war's end. During the war, Donovan as the director of the OSS had controlled some 12,000 agents, even several dozen in Nazi Berlin, and had scored victory after victory in counter-propaganda and disinformation activities, igniting J. Edgar's jealousy. OSS agents had also indulged in sabotage and demolition.

Seeing the war coming to an end in a few months, Donovan had met with Roosevelt in November of 1944 and presented his blueprint for a peacetime intelligence agency for the United States—something distinctly separate from the existing structure of the FBI. Other countries had such agencies, and FDR was convinced of the need for such an intelligence-gathering agency. Of course, Donovan proposed himself as a candidate to

A hard-as-nails lawyer, Murray Chotiner, ran Nixon's 1946 congressional campaign against a popular Californian representing Los Angeles county, **Jerry Voorhis,** depicted above. The ruthless Chotiner had a motto: "Hit 'em, hit 'em, and hit 'em again for good measure."

He told the aspirant Richard Nixon, "What are the two most disgusting things you can be in America?—a communist and a homosexual. Actually, the worst thing of all time is to be a homosexual communist. We'll string Voorhis up by his balls on both charges."

Publicly, Nixon denounced Voorhis as a communist; privately, he launched a whispering campaign that Voorhis had a fondness for teenaged boys. Voorhis went down in a humiliating defeat and left politics forever. Nixon went on to greater and more notorious things.

Nixon was just as rough on his wife, Pat, who bore their first child, Tricia, at the start of the campaign. When she walked in while he was meeting with his aides, he shouted at her, "Would you get the fuck out of here...and stay out! I'm busy."

After the election, Voorhis told a reporter, "I'm rid of Nixon now and all his lies. His wife will have to live with him forever, or at least until she wises up and divorces the tyrant."

head such a giant spy network.

FDR claimed that Donovan "is a man who has one-hundred ideas a day, ninety-five of which are awful." [During the war, Donovan had endorsed a proposal to saturate Japan's cities with tiny delayed-action incendiary bombs attached to millions of bats, who would supposedly nest in the mostly wood-built city of Osaka. He also supported the use of chemical weapons against enemy targets.] "However," FDR continued, "how many men come up with five good ideas in a lifetime?"

As a means of accumulating feedback, Roosevelt sent copies of Donovan's plan for the establishment of a separate intelligence agency to various government agencies, including both Army and Naval intelligence, to officials at the State Department, and to J. Edgar at the FBI.

Plotting with Clyde, J. Edgar leaked the report to Walter Trohan, the Washington correspondent for the *Chicago Tribune.* Publication brought an avalanche of attacks from the nation's press, *The New York Daily News* charging that it was "another New Deal move right along the Hitler line."

The outcry became so loud that in a private meeting with Donovan, FDR informed him that he would not be allowed to set up such a new agency. Donovan accused J. Edgar of "deliberate sabotage. He wants to keep all the power for himself."

Roosevelt's untimely death put the plan for an alternative intelligence agency temporarily in mothballs, but it was revived when Truman became President. He was opposed to launching a "world-wide Gestapo-like agency," but he recognized the need for a U.S. agency that specialized in foreign intelligence. He told Brigadier General Harry Vaughan, his chief military aide, that, "No man, especially one J. Edgar Hoover, should control such an agency and also the FBI. Hoover is already too big for his britches."

Truman rarely allowed J. Edgar to come into the Oval Office, but agreed to meet with him there about the new agency. In a tense session, J. Edgar made his pitch that the agency become a subdivision within the FBI and under his control. The President flatly rejected the proposal.

When J. Edgar persisted, Truman snapped at him, "You're out of bounds. Don't forget one thing: I am the President of the United States. I decide. Case closed."

Humiliated, J. Edgar rushed out of the White House and into a waiting FBI limousine. Back at FBI headquarters, he called a confab with Clyde and some of his top agents. "We must do everything in our power to see that the Missouri jackass is not re-elected in 1948."

In 1946, Truman moved ahead to launch the Central Intelligence Agency (CIA), appointing neither J. Edgar nor Donovan as its director, but anointing Rear Admiral Sidney W. Souers, who served only five months before being replaced by Lt. General Hoyt S. Vandenberg.

A former executive of the Piggly Wiggly grocery chain, Souers had been an admiral in the Naval Reserve and had almost no background in intelligence. He found the new agency filled with jealousy, conflict, and strife, and urged that its functions be turned over to the FBI, which J. Edgar certainly wanted.

His replacement, Vandenberg, was just biding his time during his administration of the CIA, waiting for an appointment as U.S. Air Force Chief of Staff, which is the position he really wanted. He was eventually forced by presidential edict to take over the South American intelligence operations which had been run by J. Edgar up until then. When Vandenberg requested that J. Edgar turn over the FBI's complete dossiers on South America, the director ordered that all U.S. intelligence, including vital contacts, be burned. Vandenberg recalled, "We got a lot of empty safes and a pair of yellow rubber gloves—that was it!"

Privately, and without the President's approval, J. Edgar continued surveillance in Mexico, duplicating the efforts of the new CIA.

In 1947, Congress passed a bill creating the National Security Council. The CIA was placed under that board's direction. By then, the CIA was being popularly compared to the KGB in the Soviet Union.

With foreign intelligence removed from the scope of his authority, J. Edgar set out on another massive attack plan on the homefront. "If the stubborn jackass from Missouri won't let me fight communists abroad, I'll do so on the homefront, beginning with Soviet spies in the government. We'll knock them off one by one or else use a machine gun in case we run into a nest of these treasonous bastards. We'll go after the commie sons of bitches not only in Washington but in Hollywood."

***

Early on the morning of February 26, 1947, Clyde ordered two agents to begin a file on Frank Sinatra. It was learned that he was flying to Miami and on to Havana. Agents in both Florida and Cuba were told to monitor his trip and to report on the people he met. During the presidency of John F. Kennedy, the Sinatra file would balloon.

But on this cold morning, it began as a skimpy document. Many stories about Sinatra's mob connections had already been published in newspapers in New York and Los Angeles. The singer was linked to such gangsters as Willie Moretti, who was said to have launched Sinatra's career as a Big Band singer in New Jersey.

J. Edgar's spies in Cuba had tipped him off that high-ranking Mafia figures were meeting at the Hotel Nacional in Havana, where Sinatra was slated to entertain them.

One report asserted that Sinatra was scheduled to meet with Lucky Luciano, who, after his forced deportation from the United States, had moved to Cuba, hoping to run his crime syndicate ninety miles from the Florida coast.

Ever since he was a young man, J. Edgar had witnessed the burgeoning growth of the American Mafia, especially when he was director of the Bureau of Investigation in the 1920s when Prohibition was the (frequently violated) law of the land. He was told at the time that some 250,000 speakeasies were operating in the United States, a problem for the Treasury Department—not for him.

During the Roaring Twenties and into the Depression era, J. Edgar had sat silently by as bootleggers in such cities as Chicago and New York had become multi-millionaires. With all that money, many gangsters had developed side businesses such as prostitution, labor racketeering, and loan-sharking.

The role of J. Edgar and the Mafia was controversial and long criticized and debated. At one point he claimed that organized crime did not exist in the United States.

In 1993, an investigative TV documentary on PBS alleged that, "J. Edgar Hoover corrupted the very mission of the FBI. It was while he was director that the Mafia was allowed to grow rich and powerful." The rumor still persists that the mob, especially Meyer Lansky, had incriminating photographs of J. Edgar performing fellatio on Clyde on the terrace of their

254

hotel suite on Miami Beach.

While J. Edgar was denying that organized crime existed, he was regularly hob-knobbing in the 1930s with such mob figures as Frank Costello. It was reported that J. Edgar viewed some members of organized crime as his "ideological kinsmen." At the Stork Club in Manhattan, he was seen on three different occasions having drinks with Costello. He reportedly told the gangster, "Just stay out of my bailiwick, and I'll stay out of yours."

An inveterate gambler at the horse races, J. Edgar was very tolerant of gambling in America. He had good reason not to get anything on Costello. At the races he'd receive tips on the horses from columnist Walter Winchell, who picked them up from Frank Erickson, the nation's leading bookmaker. The tips came from Costello himself and were "sure things"—meaning horse races that had been fixed. The FBI director made more money at the tracks than he did working for the FBI.

J. Edgar was spotted once in the coffee shop of the Waldorf-Astoria having a light lunch with Costello. Reportedly, the gangster—supposedly in a flash of sardonic humor—told him, "I've got to be careful of my associates. They'll accuse me of consorting with questionable characters."

> In the 1940s and 50s, *La Voz* (**Frank Sinatra**, nicknamed "The Voice") decided that "Havana, not Chicago, is my kind of town."
>
> "Cuban teenagers today still speak of Sinatra," claimed Bill Lezzi, writer for *The Philadelphia Inquirer.* "They listen as their grandparents and parents play his LPs and talk about his music. Cuban TV occasionally airs his life story. Sinatra is seen by more *Habañeros* now than when he used to visit."

In August of 1937, under heavy pressure from the government, the FBI swept through three states, arresting gangsters in the prostitution racket. One mobster jailed was one of Luciano's key men. "The Boss of Bosses" had been sent to prison the year before by Manhattan Attorney General Thomas Dewey. Luciano was convicted on ninety counts of extortion and "for the direction of harlotry." But even from his cell he retained his position as the father of organized crime in America, issuing orders to Lansky, Costello, and Joe Adonis, among others.

Right after this crackdown, for no apparent reason, J. Edgar's interest in the Mafia waned. It was at this time that rumors spread that the Mafia had blackmail evidence on him.

During World War II, the FBI often worked with the Mob, members of which protected vital waterfronts such as those in New York and New Jersey from Nazi saboteurs.

At the end of the war, Luciano was released from prison and deported to his native Italy. From Naples, he ran the International Crime Syndicate, directing shipments of millions of dollars worth of heroin into the United States.

Both Clyde and J. Edgar knew that Luciano had only one reason for flying to Cuba, and that was to establish a base closer to the United States.

Through his so-called "girlfriend" and informant, Lela Rogers, J. Edgar learned that Luciano had given her daughter, Ginger Rogers, "a whole lot of money" to appear at the Copa Room at the Hotel Nacional in Havana. "Lucky told Ginger that she sure could wiggle her ass but can't sing a god damn note," Lela told J. Edgar and Clyde.

In 1947, J. Edgar and his agents were aware of the upcoming mobsters' convention in Havana, but weren't certain of Sinatra's role in it. Was he being brought in just to sing Italian songs to the gangsters?

An FBI agent was secretly observing Sinatra when he disembarked in Miami from a plane that had flown from Idlewild Airport in New York. Sinatra was seen being ushered into a black limousine, in which he was driven to the home of the Fischetti Brothers. All three of them—Charles, Rocco, and Joe—had just attended the funeral of their friend, Al Capone, in Chicago.

During Sinatra's stay at the Fischetti villa, a number of beautiful women, presumably hookers, were seen coming and going at all hours of the night.

Before flying to Cuba, Sinatra was driven to Hallandale, north of Miami Beach, where he sang a medley of ten of his favorite songs at the Colonial Inn. This was a swanky gambling casino owned by Joe Adonis and Meyer Lansky.

The following day Sinatra and the Fischetti brothers were seen boarding a plane from Miami to Havana where two FBI agents were waiting to pick up their trail. Each of the men carried an attaché case. The FBI learned that the quartet carried a total of sixteen million dollars in U.S. currency. Sinatra's attaché case contained two million of that stash from Luciano's illegal operations within the United States.

In Havana, at the Hotel Nacional, two bodyguards escorted Sinatra and the Fischetti brothers to Luciano's penthouse suite. The Fischettis later left, but Sinatra moved into the suite with Luciano. Two days later, he and Luciano traveled by Cadillac to the gangster's seaside villa in suburban Miramar where more beautiful girls had been shipped in.

The FBI reported that Albert (The Executioner) Anastasia and Joey (Bananas) Bonanno were among the gangsters checking into the Nacional. After some private meetings, the mob, on the first night of their "convention," congregated within the dining room of the hotel, where Sinatra sang some of their favorite numbers, Costello requesting "Stella by Starlight."

It was later learned that Sinatra was being offered hugely profitable business deals in Havana, including interest in a projected resort and casino which was slated to become the most luxurious in the Caribbean. That deal eventually fell through.

Much to Sinatra's regret, he was spotted by American newspapermen, and his link to the mob was widely reported back in the United States. It was the beginning of a bad reputation he'd never live down.

Clyde and J. Edgar were besieged with calls demanding to know what they were going to do about Sinatra and how they were going to handle Luciano's return. Clyde deflected such calls, claiming that President Truman had restricted their authority to the domestic front, not Cuba.

As time went by, J. Edgar and Clyde would learn more and more about Sinatra, but their early conclusion was that he was a notorious womanizer and "the least faithful husband who ever existed."

Clyde said, "Apparently, he's signing up to be a money runner for the Mafia."

J. Edgar's hands-off policy toward the Mafia drew a continuing barrage of criticism from the press, not only during the time he ran the FBI, but for years after his death.

"Hoover paid so little attention to organized crime that we can accuse him of dereliction of duty," wrote historian Albert Fried. He said that J. Edgar thought that organized crime "constituted no immediate danger to the established order and that gang members were in fact pillars of the status quo."

Privately J. Edgar said that the mob "has a vested interest in the health of the free enterprise system and represents America's triumph over communism."

A future director of the CIA, Richard Helms, said, "I always thought that the reason J. Edgar did not take on the Mafia had nothing to do with blackmail but had everything to do with the fact that he was concerned that his beloved FBI would be tarnished with all the money that was sloshing around the Mafia, that they might buy off some of his agents, bribe them, or corrupt them. He wanted a squeaky-clean outfit."

"Why take the risk of going after the Mafia," J. Edgar asked William C. Sullivan, the number three man at the FBI. "The Mafia is too powerful, too much to tackle."

One footnote reported at that 1947 mobster convention at the Hotel Nacional was the arrival of Clyde himself. He had been assigned a complimentary suite immediately adjacent to Lucky Luciano.

Frank Sinatra consistently lied about his associations with gangster **Lucky Luciano** *(above)*. The singer told Hedda Hopper, "Even if I'd caught his name when introduced, I probably wouldn't have associated it with the underworld character."

Later, Hedda claimed (but not in her column) "That was pure bullshit."

In Havana and later in Italy, Sinatra and Luciano shared hotel suites and a lot more with each other, including visits to a Havana whorehouse that advertised, "There is no human desire we can't satisfy."

"Sex for Sale" might have been the motto of pre-Castro Havana, and Lucky claimed "Sinatra enjoyed every hour he spent there. I saw to that."

Although it might appear that he was in Havana to investigate Sinatra and the mob, he was not. He had been suffering from bronchitis, and he arrived in Havana a sick man. J. Edgar sent him to Cuba to recuperate. He could not go himself because he had to testify at a hearing in Washington.

Several times, Clyde spotted Sinatra coming and going from Luciano's suite, but at the time the singer did not know who Clyde was.

At the U.S. consulate office in Havana, a legate had been instructed to wine and dine Clyde—"and provide him with anything he wants." The official knew what that meant. All the VIPs arriving from the United States wanted to be fixed up with beautiful hookers, and the young man making arrangements for Clyde assumed he wanted the same.

The first night in town, he wined and dined Clyde at the Nacional. The young man, whose name has never been revealed, was having an affair with a buxom Swedish blonde-haired actress who had run afoul of U.S. Immigration. She needed help from J. Edgar's office to clear her entry into the United States because she was known to have slept with high-ranking Nazi officers during the war.

The legate figured he could solve two problems at once—a beautiful woman for Clyde to seduce and a visa for this Swedish bombshell with the questionable past.

When Clyde flew back to Washington, he told Guy Hotell and J. Edgar what happened after he'd dined with the consulate official. "I went back to my suite and pulled off my clothes and draped them on the sofa. I wanted to soak in a hot tub. I went first into a small adjoining kitchenette where I drank a large glass of fresh orange juice."

"Then I walked buck-assed naked into my bedroom heading for the bath. There I saw this blonde thing lying on top of my bedcovers fingering her bush. I rushed to wrap a robe around myself and called downstairs. The sexpot got kicked out of my suite. I was furious that he'd pull a cheap stunt like that."

Within the hour, J. Edgar was on the phone to the U.S. consulate in Havana. "Fire that god damn pimp who tried to set up Tolson with that Nazi Swede in some sort of entrapment. You probably had hidden cameras. As for the whore, tell the bitch she'll never get a visa to enter the United States. I'll see to that." He slammed down the phone and turned to Clyde, "At least Havana cured your bronchitis."

***

Even though stripped of his international surveillance powers by the CIA, J. Edgar continued to fancy himself as the true head of America's international police network. He still had an informant in Paris who sent disturbing news that Doris Duke, the American tobacco heiress and the richest woman in the world, planned to marry playboy Porfirio Rubirosa at the Dominican Legation in Paris on September 1, 1947.

It was more than a society wedding, where an heiress was purchasing a heavily endowed stud for sex, and he was marrying her for her vast riches. J. Edgar viewed this odd couple's mating as a threat to the security of the United States.

In Rome, the Department of State had been so concerned about Duke marrying Rubi that they momentarily revoked her passport, making it impossible for her to travel. Through her vast retinue of attorneys, she managed to get her passport returned. She immediately booked the entire First Class compartment on an Air France plane to Paris where she joined Rubi, who was having a torrid affair with Zsa Zsa Gabor.

The State Department feared that Duke's vast fortune might fall into the dangerous hands of Rubi and his sponsor in international crime, Rafael Trujillo, the brutal dictator of the Dominican Republic. Rubi had wanted to marry Duke on his home island in the Caribbean. J. Edgar feared this would be a dangerous step. He was informed that the D.R. followed the Napoleonic code, which granted the husband authority over communal property. Duke rejected the idea of getting married in the D.R., but agreed to marry him at the Dominican Legation in Paris, which international law interpreted as being on Dominican soil without actually being on island.

Both the FBI and the State Department viewed Rubi and Trujillo "as shady characters, really international gangsters." J. Edgar stashed an informant at the wedding ceremony. His ultimate fear was that Rubi somehow would take over Duke's estate, which might give Trujillo and him control over Duke Power and the electrical grid of the southern United States.

Carmel Snow, the editor of *Harper's Bazaar*, prevailed upon Duke to call her lawyers and draw up a pre-nuptial agreement. Duke gave in and did just that.

Two attorneys with briefcases arrived at the Dominican Legation with papers minutes before the ceremony. They confronted Rubi and demanded he sign the pre-nuptial.

At first he balked, but he was told that if he did not sign, the marriage would not take place. At that point in his life, he had only fifty U.S. dollars in his striped pants. Infuriated, he signed the pre-nuptial.

As J. Edgar's informant later claimed, "Rubirosa looked like one of those fierce Miura bulls about to charge a red cape. I've never seen a man look so mad. To show his contempt, he smoked a cigarette throughout the wedding ceremony."

For three hours before the wedding, he'd been drinking heavily. At the end of the ceremony, he fainted. "Big Boy passed out in my arms," Duke later told Snow.

In one of the few happy moments of their short, traumatic marriage, **Porfirio Rubirosa** dines with his wife, **Doris Duke**, the richest woman in the world.

As Rubi's biographer claimed, "Women heard about it, wondered about it, whispered about it, had to see it, hold it, have it— and who was he to deny them? Doris Duke bought it, but didn't get to enjoy it as much as she'd wished."

The writer was obviously referring to the mammoth endowment of the "Last Playboy of the Western World." Rubi once told a reporter, "I am a man devoted to the pursuit of pleasure."

Rubi got his revenge on his honeymoon with Duke at Cap d'Antibes along the French Riviera. J. Edgar, through Clyde, ordered that the honeymoon bungalow of Rubi and Duke be bugged. No state secrets were discovered on the wiretapping, but J. Edgar and Clyde did learn that Rubi withheld sex from Duke for forcing him to sign that pre-nuptial.

J. Edgar also learned that Rubi excused himself on the morning of the second day of their honeymoon, claiming he was going out to purchase a package of cigarettes. He was gone for three days and nights.

It was later learned that he'd encountered a former lover, known as "Manouche," who invited him for a drink. She later spoke about their fling to Alice Leone Moats, author of *The Million Dollar Studs*. According to Manouche, "Rubi's sex organ was long and pointed and it hurt. It was nothing for *ce cher* Rubi to take on two or three women a night. Late at night when he was good and drunk, he didn't give a damn what kind of legs were opening."

Sometimes it was a young man opening up for Rubi, as well as a string of beautiful women.

After the wedding, Trujillo appointed Rubi as the Dominican Republic's Ambassador to Argentina. The U.S. government refused to issue Duke a diplomatic visa. But she went as a private citizen, flying to join her husband in Buenos Aires in a converted B-25 bomber she'd purchased for him.

On the day after her arrival, bribed servants reported to her that Rubi had been having an affair with Evita Peron, the wife of the Argentinian dictator, Juan Peron. The FBI also learned that Rubi was associating with former Nazis who had fled from Berlin shortly before or after it collapsed during the spring of 1945.

"Rubi was a real whore," claimed the author and columnist Doris Lilly, the lover of Ronald Reagan. She also claimed that Duke had tried to commit suicide over Rubi by cutting her wrists, but was discovered by a servant and rushed to the hospital in time to save her life.

Even though J. Edgar had been officially stripped of his intelligence gathering authority in South America, his job going to the CIA, he nevertheless kept his informants and occasionally sent agents South of the Border.

He openly bragged to Louis Nichols and Guy Hotell that, "I saved Latin America from going communist." His boast was that he had prevented Duke from purchasing a fleet of cargo ships in the Caribbean that, had the deal gone through, would have been controlled by Rubi. He thought he could make millions transporting arms from one Latin American republic to another republic ripe for a communist takeover, including Cuba.

J. Edgar never explained how he did that, although Clyde obviously knew. "Instead of a communist Cuba, the United States, were it not for me, might have faced twenty Latin American countries controlled by the Kremlin."

The director also claimed that he foiled a plot to have Duke assassinated and her estate taken over by Rubi. Again, he didn't reveal just how he accomplished that.

There were many unanswered questions within the dossier the FBI collected on Duke over the years. Long before J. Edgar died, most of her file was destroyed. Unknown to J. Edgar and Clyde in the early 1940s was that Duke entertained many Nazi notables, especially Hermann Göring. "Surely Duke wasn't a Nazi spy like Errol Flynn?" J. Edgar asked.

Her file showed that in 1944 and 1945 she contributed greatly to the welfare of merchant seamen and spent weeks at a time bestowing food, cigarettes, and liquor on them. "She was a traveling USO," in the words of one reporter.

"I'm happier now than I've ever been in my life being with a lot of swell, interesting guys," she told the press. "I guess I've discovered it's fun to work."

FBI agents learned that she took "dozens upon dozens" of these young men to bed. She later told Jimmy Donahue, the dissipated and chronically scandalous cousin of the Woolworth heiress Barbara Hutton, "of all the men I've seduced, I've never found one with the dimensions of Rubi. I know you've had him too. Did you ever find anyone bigger?"

"Once in Morocco I encountered this mulatto boxer from the Sudan," Donahue said. "But he was half an inch shorter than Rubi."

***

Leaving her daughter, Ginger Rogers, back in Hollywood, Lela Rogers flew into Washington, configuring herself as "arm candy" for J. Edgar at a party honoring newly elected members to Congress.

In the 1946 elections, Republicans had swept into control of both houses. Among the newly elected politicians on hand to greet J. Edgar that night were John F. Kennedy, Democrat from Massachusetts, Richard M. Nixon, Republican from California, and Senator Joseph R. McCarthy, Republican from Wisconsin. Each of these rising young politicians would be closely linked to J. Edgar in the future.

As Louis Nichols later said, "We already had files on Nixon, McCarthy, and Kennedy. They were on what J. Edgar called his watch list. Our file on Kennedy was 250 pages before he took office . . . and growing. Most of it dealt with his womanizing. McCarthy was a closet homosexual, and Nixon was squeaky clean sexually but had shady business dealings with big businessmen back in California, guys like the tycoon Gordon Howard."

In the post-war years, J. Edgar and Clyde had two main concerns during their investigations of the private lives of prominent Americans: What were they doing sexually, and were they or had they ever been a member of the Communist Party?

FBI agents fanned out to gather evidence where they could find it, planting bugs, wiretapping phones, and even committing "bag jobs," or robberies at the offices of such magazines as *Amerasia*, whose leftist views were interpreted as propaganda for the Chinese communists. Although arrests were made and the *Amerasia* editors put on trial, none of them was convicted.

262

Because of the FBI's mishandling of the investigation, Attorney General Tom Clark was publicly forced to back away from his accusations of communism. Embarrassed, he attacked J. Edgar, putting the blame entirely on the FBI.

J. Edgar never handled criticism well, and his heretofore friendly relationship with Clark soured after that.

Pressure mounted on J. Edgar to "name names" of all those Soviet agents he claimed were working within the U.S. government. The director knew he had to produce some actual spies sooner than later.

Luck had been on his side during World War II, when a saboteur (George Dasch) had walked into the offices of the FBI, revealing Nazi plans for a massive campaign of wartime sabotage within the United States. Luck shined on J. Edgar once again when an otherwise unknown woman named Elizabeth Bentley walked into the FBI headquarters in New Haven, Connecticut, and revealed to agents there that she was a Soviet spy. She was a most unlikely spy, the daughter of a straight-laced family of Episcopalian New Englanders.

In New Haven, she revealed only a fraction of what she knew about Russian spying in the United States.

Soviet spy **Elizabeth Bentley**. Although newspapers described her (without actually running her photograph) as a shapely and beautiful blonde, she wasn't that at all. J. Edgar thought she looked like some dumpy American housewife.

After Clyde investigated Bentley's sexual past, he concluded, "She'd fuck a tree if she could."

The agent didn't really seem to believe her, perhaps thinking she was an incoherent crank who had wandered accidentally in from the street. After interviewing her, he reported to the FBI in Washington that she was "very vague, appeared drunk, and did not provide any convincing evidence. I recommended that she go home and sober up."

A month later, she met with her KGB "handler," Anatoly Gorsky. Exceedingly drunk, she became angry at him and called him a "gangster." She also threatened to go to the FBI and reveal all she knew about Soviet espionage in the United States. Apparently, he was not aware that she'd already been interviewed by the FBI. The next morning when she sobered up, she realized that she was in imminent danger for having made such a threat. Indeed, it was later revealed that the Kremlin had become alarmed at her condition and had ordered Gorsky "to get rid of her."

In desperation, she drove to Washington and was interviewed by Guy Hotell at FBI headquarters. Before him, she claimed that she'd been an American spy for the Soviet Union from 1938 to 1945. She also told Guy that she thought her life was in danger.

Her story could have inspired a Cold War novel. It began when she won a fellowship to the University of Florence (Italy), where she had joined a local anti-Fascist group. There she fell in love with Mario Casella, a faculty member.

He convinced her that upon her return to America she should join a communist front group, the American League Against War and Fascism. She did just that, and in March of 1935, she became a card-carrying member of the Communist Party of the United States (CPUSA).

Bentley was employed by an organization in New York City known as the Italian Library of Information. She soon discovered that it was a propaganda bureau for Italian fascists. She reported this to CPUSA headquarters, volunteering her services to spy on Mussolini's fascists. Her contact became Jacob Golos, a Russian émigré and naturalized U.S. citizen who was the key Soviet intelligence agent in America. She did not know that at the time nor did she know that he was plotting the assassination of Leon Trotsky in Mexico, a murder which took place in 1940.

Bentley and Golos became lovers, and he assigned her the code name of *Umnitsa* or "Miss Wise." As a communist spy, she came into contact with everyone from dedicated Stalinists to "romantic idealists." When Golos suffered a fatal heart attack late in 1943, the Russians assigned Bentley to take his place.

In her new position, the Soviets had cause to worry about Bentley's stability. An alcoholic, she suffered bouts of depression and was also promiscuous, known to be "loose-lipped" with her male conquests, often U.S. servicemen.

As her paranoia deepened, she took on a new lover (unnamed), whom she suspected of working either for the Soviets or the FBI. She finally decided that he was a spy for the Kremlin after he tried to force her to emigrate to the Soviet Union, where she feared she would be put to death. Afraid for her life, she had descended, in August of 1945, onto the FBI office in New Haven.

Guy found her story convincing, and he turned her over to Clyde, who after hearing only five minutes of her testimony summoned J. Edgar. "This could be big," Clyde told his boss and lover.

To J. Edgar, she turned over a list of 150 American citizens, including 37 federal workers, whom she claimed were spies for the Kremlin.

After an extensive interview, J. Edgar had Guy drive Bentley to an undisclosed location for her own safety. J. Edgar immediately notified William Stephenson, head of British security in the Western Hemisphere. Stephenson alerted his intelligence contact in London, the soon-to-be infamous Kim Philby, who was a double agent, spying for the Soviets.

It was obvious she'd been outed because the Soviets made no further contacts with her, although she remained a potential target for assassination.

Philby eventually came under suspicion, but British intelligence did not investigate him at that time, considering him "an old school Brit, loyal as Churchill."

The Soviet agents who had been identified as such by Bentley were rounded up. In every case they either evoked the Fifth Amendment or maintained their innocence. J. Edgar had evidence that they were lying but he couldn't officially corroborate Bentley's testimony without exposing one of the U.S. government's most guarded secrets. If he had, it would have compromised an explosive piece of evidence that J. Edgar felt was too vital even to share with Harry Truman, the sitting U.S. President.

It was the "Venona Project," the core of which involved a machine that could decrypt cables between Soviet agents working in America and the Kremlin. These cabled messages, decrypted through Venona, had revealed that Bentley was telling the truth.

Tom Clark, the Attorney General and (nominally) J. Edgar's boss, agreed that the success (or the very existence) of the Venona Project should never be revealed at various trials. "There's no way we want the Soviets to know we've cracked their code," he told J. Edgar.

But for reasons of her own, in April of 1948 Bentley went public with her revelations during an interview with reporters from *The New York World-Telegram*. Without running her picture—an odd editorial decision—she was identified as "a beautiful young blonde," which she wasn't. Actually at this point in her life she'd begun to look rather dumpy. *The New York Journal American* called her a "shapely blonde and a blue-eyed New Yorker who lured secrets from her Soviet lover in the boudoir." A.J. Liebling of the *New Yorker* ridiculed her, labeling her a "Nutmeg Mata Hari."

This catchy, albeit somewhat enigmatic, phrase was picked up by other newspapers, even though no one knew exactly what Liebling meant, except to suggest that Bentley was a spicy, aromatic seed about to fall off a Soviet tree into a spice grinder.

After these press revelations, she was, of course, summoned to testify before the House Un-American Activities Committee. After the official airing of Bentley's revelations, Thomas Dewey and other Republicans attacked Truman, accusing him of covering up communist espionage within his administration.

As the weeks went by, J. Edgar and Clyde grew increasingly concerned about Bentley's credibility as a witness. In a memo, J. Edgar wrote, "She's bordering on some mental pitfall." Her drinking had increased, and she was involved in three automobile accidents while driving drunk. Surprisingly, her driving license was not suspended. One night she picked up a male hitchhiker and drove him to a secluded motel. He turned out to be psychotic and beat her so severely she almost died.

Skeptics doubted some of her revelations, especially when she claimed she had had advance knowledge of the Doolittle air raid over Japan in the middle of World War II. She also maintained that she had transmitted the exact time and place of the D-Day landings on the beaches of Normandy to the Soviet Union.

Many historians were skeptical of the claims made in her 1951 autobiography. It wasn't until the 1990s, when Venona transcripts along with some Soviet intelligence archives were made public, that many of Bentley's charges were verified.

But in spite of his many doubts about Bentley, J. Edgar stood by her testimony, perhaps to glorify his own achievements in exposing Soviet agents working within the United States.

"The testimony of Elizabeth Bentley had a major impact on making eunuchs out of many Soviet spies in America," he said.

What he didn't say was that her revelations ruined many lives, both the innocent and the guilty.

Bentley's notorious life came to an end on December 3, 1963. At the age of fifty-five, she was felled by abdominal cancer at Grace-New Haven Hospital in Connecticut. *Time* magazine gave her death only a two-sentence mention in its "Milestones" section, yet she paved the way for the emergence of Red-baiting Joseph McCarthy, and she was the fuse that lit the anti-communist explosion set off in America in the late 1940s and early 1950s.

***

One of the most shocking outings of a Soviet agent was the exposure of Harry Dexter White, an American economist who in the 1930s had been one of the chief architects of Franklin Roosevelt's New Deal. He had been a former Assistant Secretary of the U.S. Treasury.

White had participated in the 1944 Bretton Woods Conference that ultimately led to the creation of the International Monetary Fund and the World Bank. By 1946, he was calling for improved relations between the

U.S. and the Soviet Union. Truman nominated him for the post of director of the International Monetary Fund in spite of a damaging twenty-eight-page memo sent by J. Edgar to the President, accusing White of being a communist.

J. Edgar viewed Truman's rejection of his memo as a direct slap in his face. At the time, Truman was being besieged with accusations against hundreds of suspected communists, and he thought J. Edgar's charges lacked credibility.

"I'm deluged with mail accusing everybody of being a communist," Truman told Lyndon B. Johnson. "You won't believe the bullshit that comes over this desk, especially from our boy Hoover. One minute some crank claims that Eleanor Roosevelt is the mistress of Josef Stalin. The next letter claims that Clark Gable is on the payroll of the Kremlin. A letter arrived the other day charging that Ambassador Kennedy [Joseph P. Kennedy] was working with American capitalists to re-launch a new Nazi Party to bring Hitler back to power."

"But Hitler, so they say, committed suicide," Johnson said.

"Not according to my informants," Truman said with a smirk. "The next thing I hear about you, Lyndon, is that you're working to have Texas secede from the Union and become Soviet-occupied territory."

"That wouldn't be such a bad idea, Harry, if Stalin made me President of Texas," Johnson said jokingly.

Before HUAC, Elizabeth Bentley had testified that White had given the U.S. Treasury's engraving plates for the printing of the "occupation currency" then used within the American zone of occupied Germany to the Soviet Union, which had then used them to print counterfeit currency. Russian soldiers had then exchanged this counterfeit money, according to Bentley, for consumer goods and hard currency. This had created a black market and caused serious inflation in the occupied and war-torn country. It was estimated that this counterfeiting cost the United States a quarter of a billion dollars.

Summoned before HUAC on August 13, 1948, White denied he was a communist or had ever been one.

In 1950 White was positively identified as a Soviet spy by J. Edgar's FBI. Venona decrypts revealed he was operating under the code name of "Jurist."

J. Edgar claimed that White "should have been sent to the electric chair and branded a traitor."

But three days after testifying before HUAC, White died of a heart attack on his New Hampshire farm. He was fifty-five years old. An overdose of digitalis was reported as the cause of his death.

267

Bentley also exposed Laurence Duggan, who had functioned as director of the U.S. State Department's operations in South America during World War II. In New York, Clyde and Guy Hotell, on orders from J. Edgar, questioned Duggan extensively about accusations that he was engaged in espionage for the Soviet Union.

It was claimed that Duggan had been recruited as a Soviet spy in the mid-1930s by the leftist journalist Hede Massing. Duggan was charged with supplying the Soviets with intelligence, including copies of confidential cables, some of them sent by William Bullitt, U.S. Ambassador to the Soviet Union.

Indeed, although Duggan had transmitted information to the Soviets, he had resigned from his position at the State Department in 1944, telling his Soviet contacts that, "The only thing which kept me at this hateful job where I did not get out of my tuxedo for two weeks, every night attending a reception, was the idea of being useful for the communist cause."

To the FBI, however, Duggan denied all charges. But later evidence gathered as a result of the Venona Project, which decrypted Soviet intelligence cables, revealed that Duggan was indeed a spy operating under the code name of "Frank." His last message sent to the KGB in Moscow was dated November 12, 1944.

Ten days after Clyde and Guy questioned Duggan, he fell to his death from the sixteenth floor of the office of the Institute of International Education in midtown Manhattan. The New York Police Department concluded that he "either accidentally fell or jumped."

Clyde Tolson had a different conclusion. "I have little doubt that his KGB agent pushed him. Duggan knew too much about Soviet spying in America to be allowed to testify before a committee."

Another casualty of Bentley's testimony was William Remington, a mid-level government economist who was employed in various Federal government positions until "the blonde spy" presented her accusations.

He'd acquired a security clearance in 1941 when he worked for the Office of Price Administration, even though he admitted having been active in communist-allied political groups. In March of 1942, he began to pass secret information on to Bentley, including data on U.S. airplane production.

When Bentley outed Remington in 1945, FBI agents trailed him but learned little, as a result of how, by that time, he had become disillusioned with communism and had broken off his relationships with what he called "my radical friends of yesterday." When questioned by the FBI, he denied all accusations that he had ever had any communist affiliations.

To shift suspicion from himself, Remington became an anti-communist informer for the FBI, labeling as communists "Negro nationalists," extreme liberals, his estranged wife, Ann Remington, and his hated mother-in-law, Elizabeth Moos, both avowed communists.

In spite of that, another loyalty investigation of him was opened in 1948. In hearings in June of that year, he was called "a boob who was duped by commie agents," according to the *Washington Post*. At loyalty review hearings he stated, "I divorced my wife, Ann, because she's a communist."

On NBC Radio's *Meet the Press*, Bentley referred to Remington as a communist. He sued for libel and settled out of court with NBC for $10,000. But then his divorced wife turned against him, claiming he was a communist spy.

Tried and convicted for perjury, he was sentenced to five years in prison. The *Washington Daily News* claimed that "in Russia he would have been shot without a trial."

The verdict was appealed and a new trial was conducted. It concluded that Remington was guilty of two counts of perjury for lying about his communist links. This time he was sentenced to three years in prison.

Jailed at Lewisburg Federal Penitentiary in Pennsylvania, Remington met George McCoy, a violent man with an I.Q. of 61. He taunted Remington about his communism. On the morning of November 22, 1954, McCoy and another inmate, Lewis Cagle Jr., a 17-year-old juvenile delinquent, murdered Remington with a brick encased in a sock.

J. Edgar called the warden and told him to claim that the motive was robbery. He did not want to be connected to Remington's death because of the zealous investigation of the FBI. McCoy, however, denied J. Edgar's claim and testified that he and Cagle had killed Remington because he was a communist.

Gary May, Remington's biographer, later claimed that his conviction for perjury seemed justified. "Yet Remington was no pro-Soviet automaton, no slave to Party or ideology, and not even the FBI, at least privately, was willing to classify him as a Russian spy."

Remington has entered the history books as one of the few murders attributable to McCarthyism.

When J. Edgar was asked about the murder, he told a reporter, "No comment," and walked rapidly away as if to distance himself from this notorious case.

***

In the 1948 presidential election, J. Edgar faced one of his worst dilemmas. He detested Harry S Truman, and he loathed his Republican challenger, Thomas E. Dewey, with whom he'd conflicted when Dewey was the

Manhattan District Attorney.

When faced with such a daunting challenge, J. Edgar decided to throw his weight behind Dewey but only after "he'd come around" [J. Edgar's words].

"Dewey will be a tough nut to crack," J. Edgar told his aides. "I'm convinced Truman will fire me if elected. But Dewey has threatened to do the same thing."

In 1944, after his unsuccessful run against FDR for President, Dewey had told his aides, "The proper place for Hoover is a jail cell in the darkest prison."

J. Edgar was ready to cut a deal with Dewey, meeting privately with him in a Manhattan hotel suite, probably the Waldorf-Astoria. There, J. Edgar, Clyde, and Louis Nichols made what was called "The Devil's Pact" with Dewey.

J. Edgar promised to give Dewey any dirt he'd dug up on the Truman administration and promised to inaugurate an all-out war, charging that Truman was soft on communism and that his administration was riddled with Soviet spies seeking to overthrow the U.S. government. In essence, with Dewey's approval, J. Edgar was launching the anti-communist hysteria that swept over the United States in the post-war years and that ultimately led to the rise of Senator Joseph McCarthy.

"In exchange for making you president," as J. Edgar put it to Dewey, "I want to be named your Attorney General, with Clyde here as my Assistant Attorney General. I want you to name Lou here as director of the FBI."

To the surprise of his aides, Dewey gave his solemn promise that if elected President he would make those appointments. The candidate must have realized, though, that with Nichols in charge of the FBI, J. Edgar would still be running the Bureau as his boss in his new position as Attorney General.

Guy Hotell claimed that J. Edgar had long ago realized he would never become President of the United States. But his ultimate ambition, after being appointed as Dewey's Attorney General, involved being designated as Chief Justice of the U.S. Supreme Court when that post became vacated.

Armed with promises from Dewey, the Republican candidate, J. Edgar began supplying him with damaging evidence. First, Harold Stassen, Dewey's chief opponent for the Republican nomination, had to be eliminated. "I've got enough stuff on Stassen to make him toast," J. Edgar later bragged.

Stassen had been governor of Minnesota from 1939 to 1943. The year 1948 marked the first of eight times he would run for President of the United States, his last attempt in 1992.

Stassen had shown surprising strength in the primaries, and polls showed that he could beat Truman if nominated as the Republican candidate. But J. Edgar insisted that he was "a dangerous liberal" and that he had received campaign money from "a rich Baptist preacher," who was never named. [In 1963 Stassen did join Martin Luther King Jr. in his march on Washington.] The FBI also charged that Stassen had used a portion of the campaign money he collected in his run for governor of Minnesota in 1940 and 1942 for private expenses.

To his credit, after confronting this information, Dewey opted to retreat to higher moral grounds. Ultimately, Dewey concluded that Stassen was ultimately a good and decent man, and that J. Edgar's accusations should best be left unvoiced.

Stassen's aspiration for higher office was summed up by Hunter S. Thompson in *Last Train from Camelot*. That author said, "Others are not so lucky and are doomed, like Harold Stassen, to wallow for the rest of their lives in the backwaters of local politics, cheap crooks, and relentless humiliating failures."

Even without J. Edgar's mud-slinging, Stassen still lost the Republican nomination to Dewey, who privately claimed that "Stassen was far too liberal to be a Republican. He really should come out as a Democrat."

For a while at least, Dewey's chance at becoming president looked good. Truman's popularity was sinking, and a lot of votes that would have gone to Truman were divided in a three-way split between Henry A. Wallace, running on the Progressive Party ticket, and segregationist Strom Thurmond, who sought the presidency on the Dixiecrat ticket of the Deep South.

The FBI continued throughout the campaign to fuel the Dewey people with "toxic data" about his rivals. But as his campaign progressed, Dewey himself made a fatal decision in his quest for the presidency. He delegated the publicizing of "Hoover's dirt" to his Republican attack dogs and spoke in platitudes in a misguided attempt to appear like a statesman rising above gutter campaign tactics.

The Louisville Courier Journal summed up Dewey's run for President:

"No presidential candidate in the future will be so inept that four of his major speeches can be boiled down to these historic sentences: Agriculture is important. Our rivers are full of fish. You cannot have freedom without liberty. Our future lies ahead."

Although he had promised otherwise, and although his GOP backers urged him to, Dewey refused to indulge in J. Edgar's "Red baiting." J.

Edgar wanted to outlaw the Communist Party in America, but in response, Dewey said, "You can't shoot an idea with a gun. Unlike Hoover, I don't go around looking under beds."

***

Henry Wallace was the campaign's most liberal candidate, running on the Progressive Party ticket beside his vice-presidential candidate, Idaho's Democratic Senator Glen H. Taylor, Wallace called for an end to segregation, full voting rights for blacks, universal government health insurance, an end to the nascent Cold War, and friendly relations with the Soviet Union. He was a candidate far ahead of his time, and he campaigned with African American office seekers.

In the South he refused to appear before segregated audiences or stay in restricted hotels in such states as Georgia and South Carolina. He was often greeted with raw eggs and rotten tomatoes hurled at him, "with his Negro secretary beside him," wrote a newspaper in Columbia.

J. Edgar couldn't be absolutely sure that Truman would be defeated, so he decided to hedge his bets. To be on the safe side, he also supplied damaging information to Truman's campaign manager on Wallace, FDR's former Vice President. He secretly spread the word that Wallace was a homosexual, a technique he perfected in the 1948 election and would use more forcefully in the 1952 and 1956 campaigns against Democratic candidate Adlai Stevenson.

Like all good rumors, there was a nugget of truth in this accusation, and it does appear that Wallace might have engaged in two, possibly three, rather harmless affairs in the 1930s with young men when he was Secretary of Agriculture.

One man from Wallace's native Idaho, James Whiting, was willing to sign an FBI affidavit that he and Wallace had engaged in homosexual trysts during the 1930s when he traveled with Wallace on a very controversial tour where farmers were ordered to slaughter pigs and destroy cotton fields in rural America to drive the price of these commodities back up to improve the financial plight of America's farmers.

What made the homosexual rumors stick to Wallace was a controversial group of his supporters who called themselves "Bachelors for Wallace."

This was the first time a group of gay or bisexual men had ever organized as a group, much less supported a candidate for political office.

Privately Wallace had a number of campaign meetings, rather secretly, with Harry Hay, who in 1950 would go on to found the Mattachine Society, giving rise to the modern gay and lesbian movement of today.

Wallace welcomed Hay and his bachelors in both California and New York. "We didn't find any in Alabama," he recalled. But he told them it would not be possible to come out for homosexual rights at this time. "But your day will come. Maybe not in the 1950s but surely by the 1960s. If I'm still around, I will be your chief advocate."

Although he could not come out publicly and endorse homosexual rights, Wallace promised that if elected President he would end the dismissal of homosexuals from government service and that he would stop the FBI harassment of homosexuals, both men and women. For Hay, that was reason enough to support Wallace.

In his campaign for gay rights, Hay was thrilled to read the controversial Kinsey Report, published to widespread interest and furious refutations. The first volume, *Sexual Behavior in the Human Male*, released in 1948, was the most talked about book of the year, making the claim that thirty-seven percent of adult men in the United States had experienced man-on-man sex.

REVOLT OF THE HOMOSEXUAL

Two years after he supported Henry Wallace for President in the 1948 race for the White House, activist **Harry Hay** *(two photos above)* founded The Mattachine Society, giving rise to today's gay rights movement.

Called before HUAC, Hay sat through the testimony of Stephen Wereb, an FBI agent that J. Edgar had assigned to infiltrate "Hay's Boys."

In 1940, Wereb, using the name "Steven Webber," had spied on Hay, eventually reporting him as a "Marxist-Leninist who advocated the overthrow of the American voting system." The agent also cited ninety other Southern Californians as communists.

When called to the stand, Hay was "dangerously loquacious." After hours of pompous courtroom buffoonery, the proceedings were disrupted. A table was accidentally overturned, and the court reporter's transcripts uncoiled into a jumble on the floor. Spectators directed mocking laughter at the inept HUAC staff. Hay was dismissed.

Frank Tavenner, chief counsel of HUAC, became so flustered that Hay later described him as "looking like the *commandante* from *Don Giovanni* rising out of the floor."

One night at a rally, Wallace whispered to Hay, "I am among those thirty-seven percent."

Hay wanted the Progressive Party to include a plank in its platform supporting the right to "privacy"—a code name for protection of homosexuals. It seemed too much of a hot button. Even some of Wallace's so-called Progressives labeled the Bachelors "Fruits for Wallace" or "Queers for Wallace."

Hay later wrote of the enormous stonewall he faced. "I knew the government was going to look for a new enemy, a new scapegoat. It was predictable. But Blacks were beginning to organize, and the horror of the Holocaust was too recent to put the Jews in that position. The natural scapegoat would be us, the queers. They were the one group of disenfranchised people who did not even know they were a group because they had never organized before. They—*we*—have to get started. It was high time."

***

On election night, J. Edgar went to bed confident of a Dewey triumph. *The Chicago Tribune* had already flashed the night's headline—DEWEY DEFEATS TRUMAN.

The next morning, Clyde was the first to wake up to make coffee. He turned on the radio to hear the news. In panic, he rushed to the stairs and called up to his bedtime companion. "That fucking asshole from Missouri is still the President."

After breakfast that morning at the Mayflower Hotel, J. Edgar stormed into his office. He was looking for a scapegoat, and he settled, somewhat arbitrarily, on the ever so-loyal Louis Nichols. "You pushed me out on a limb, and it got sawed off," he charged. "I wouldn't be in this mess if it weren't for you. Four more years of Harry Truman. I don't think I can take it. I'm going to resign."

He didn't resign, of course, and was in Washington to hear Truman take the oath of office.

J. Edgar was so depressed on Inauguration Day, January 20, 1949 that he claimed "only Shirley Temple could cheer me up." Consequently, he invited her to Washington to join him on his office balcony to watch the parade, as Truman passed along Pennsylvania Avenue.

J. Edgar later told his aides, he was a bit disappointed "to see Shirley all grown up." She was twenty-one years old at the time. "But I guess she couldn't be a little girl forever."

As a goodbye present, she claimed he "flashed his best Santa Claus smile as he gave me a present, a tear-gas gun disguised as a fountain pen. It's one of my most prized possessions."

CHAPTER EIGHT

J. Edgar Hoover, with a lot of right-wing help, launched the most sweeping and penetrating witch hunts in American history. He saw Red everywhere, a river of corruption whose tentacles, he claimed, incorporated the highest offices in Washington to movie studios and film stars in Hollywood. The hunt was on to ferret out communists in all walks of life, but mostly in politics and the film colony. In the "Red Scare" that J. Edgar spearheaded in the aftermath of World War II, lives, friendships, reputations, and careers would be destroyed.

Now that America's "official" enemies, Japan and Germany, had been defeated, he turned the full force of the FBI into an assault on what he called "the enemies within." At least in the beginning, he had the support of the majority of the American public. Of course, there were dissenting voices, such as those expressed by historian Bernard DeVoto in October of 1949:

> *"I say it has gone too far. We are dividing into the hunted and the hunters. There is loose in the United States today the same evil that once split Salem Village between the bewitched and the accused and stole men's reason quite away. We are informers to the secret police. Honest men are spying on their neighbors for patriotism's sake."*

New Jersey-born J. Parnell Thomas, a former stockbroker, was elected seven times to Congress before being sent to prison. He was known for his controversial statement, calling James Forrestal, U.S. Secretary of Defense, "the most dangerous man in America. If he's not removed from office, he'll cause World War III."

A staunch opponent of Roosevelt's New Deal, Thomas was an avowed anti-communist. He claimed that the Federal Theatre Project presented nothing but "sheer communism propaganda," and he seemed to have a special aversion to Hollywood. When Thomas became chairman of the House Un-American Activities Committee, J. Edgar supported him totally. The

FBI fed Thomas a constant stream of accusations as to who was a communist and who might make a friendly witness before HUAC.

Drew Pearson in his column, *Washington Merry-Go-Round,* wrote, "Those watching Lou Nichols, [the FBI Agent in charge of public relations, reporting directly to J. Edgar] note that he goes in and out of the office of Congressman J. Parnell Thomas like an animated shuttlecock."

J. Edgar never seemed quite certain what a communist actually was. At one time he suggested that it was a "diabolic figure" or else a "sinister person." He also claimed that a communist was someone "strangely out of step with American values." In the wave of his own self-generated hysteria, he found the pervasive influence of communism virtually everywhere, even in the theme song for two films and a radio show about the FBI. Called "Love for Three Oranges," the song was written by Sergei Prokofiev, the Soviet composer. "Who knows what communist messages are embedded in that song?" J. Edgar asked.

When **J. Parnell Thomas** *(above)* took over as head of HUAC, he informed J. Edgar, "Now you have a grand opportunity to say anything you want to."

Privately, J. Edgar told Thomas that "President Truman is the embodiment of evil by defending those I've accused of being disloyal to America." In the midst of the hearings, J. Edgar learned that the congressman was operating a kickback racket, but he did nothing about it.

After a "fact-finding" trip to Hollywood in May of 1947, Thomas returned to Washington to launch the investigations of HUAC, with America tuned in. At first only friendly witnesses were called. Many of the spectators turned on not to hear who was a communist, but to view movie heartthrobs such as Gary Cooper and Robert Taylor.

Begun on October 20, 1947, the hearings were held in the overcrowded Caucus Room of the Old House Office building in Washington.

Some friendly witnesses in their testimony cited nineteen people working in the film industry, accusing them of holding left-wing views, with the suggestion that each of them was a card-carrying member of the Communist Party.

Taylor's appearance was so spectacular that police had to erect barricades to hold back the surging crowds. Before the committee, Taylor referred to communists in Hollywood as "the rotten apples in the barrel. If I had my way, they would all be sent back to Russia." He also claimed that, "I was forced to work in the film *Song of Russia* glorifying that country." He testified he turned down many scripts because "they are pinko influ-

Deadly charm projected from two of Hollywood's biggest heartthrobs, **Robert Taylor** *(top photo)* and **Gary Cooper** *(below)*. Fans at the Senate hearing mobbed them, far more interested in seeing them, ripping their clothes, and getting an autograph than they were in any "friendly witness" testimony they had to deliver about communists infiltrating the film industry.

enced. I will not work with a Hollywood communist even if it means the end of my career."

At the end of his testimony, pandemonium broke out and several people were injured. Clothes were ripped and one woman dangerously injured when she fell in the stampede.

A young congressman, Richard Nixon, congratulated Taylor, praising his "patriotism and fearlessness in testifying." It is not known at this point if Nixon knew that Taylor was the star who had taken his wife Patricia's virginity.

J. Edgar maintained a file on Taylor, learning that he was having an affair with a very young Elizabeth Taylor. It was also revealed that he was bisexual and had had affairs with Howard Hughes, Errol Flynn, and Tyrone Power. He was married at the time to Barbara Stanwyck in a "lavender marriage" to conceal his homosexual lifestyle. Stanwyck was also bisexual.

Other stars such as Robert Montgomery and George Murphy also arrived to testify, but the greatest mob scene occurred on the day Gary Cooper showed up. He was mobbed by nearly a thousand women, some of whom tried to rip off pieces of his clothing.

Before HUAC, Cooper claimed, "I'm no danged Red, never have been a Red, don't like Reds, and will never be a Red." He freely admitted he didn't know Karl Marx from Groucho Marx. "I could never take any of this pinko mouthing seriously," he claimed.

Cooper had long been under the scrutiny of J. Edgar and Clyde for his political beliefs. For their voyeuristic pleasure, they also kept an extensive file on his sexual affairs, learning that like Robert Taylor he was also bisexual, having had affairs with Clara Bow, Tallulah Bankhead, director Edmund Goulding, Cary Grant, William Haines, Rod La Rocque, Barbara Stanwyck, Lupe Velez, Mae West, Marlene Dietrich, and a long-enduring relationship with the wealthy tobacco heir Anderson Lawler.

Cooper's morning session was followed that afternoon by the appearance of Walt Disney.

Disney attacked the League of Women Voters as a "commie front group," although he meant the League of Women Shoppers, which included members such as Bette Davis. Women Shoppers was a nonpolitical consumers' group. In an astonishing statement, Disney also claimed that communists in his studio in the 1930s had tried to use the cartoon figure of Mickey Mouse to spread propaganda.

Just one of the careers he destroyed that day was that of animator David Hilberman, who had studied for six months in 1922 at the Leningrad Art Institute. There was absolutely no evidence he was a communist. After that, Hilberman never found work in Hollywood. In just one minute of testimony from Disney, his life's career and livelihood had been destroyed.

Before HUAC, Sam Wood, one of the directors of *Gone With the Wind*, claimed, "If you pull down the pants of a communist you will find a hammer and sickle tattooed on their ass."

After the hearings, the films of Cooper, Taylor, Montgomery, and the aging right-wing Adolphe Menjou were banned from Iron Curtain countries, even those of Ginger Rogers because her mother, Lela Rogers, had testified before HUAC.

Before Parnell and others, Lela had been introduced as one of the outstanding experts on communism in the United States. She attacked films such as Cary Grant's *None But the Lonely Heart* (1940), which had been directed by playwright Clifford Odets, whom Lela considered a communist. She charged that this moody Odets drama of a Cockney drifter was filled with communist propaganda.

Although it had nothing to do with communism, J. Edgar slipped Thomas secret data that Grant and Odets were lovers.

***

Ronald Reagan had been an informant for the FBI (file no. 100-382196) since 1943. Early in the communist witch hunt of the 1940s, he agreed to provide secret information about his fellow actors, directors, and writers. He did not want to name names in public hearings like some actors did, preferring instead to warn J. Edgar and Clyde about artists in Hollywood that he felt were so left wing in their politics that they should be investigated.

James Cagney claimed Reagan was a "rat" on his fellow actors. "Hoover wanted more than reports on left wing politics. He wanted to know who had a drug problem, who contracted venereal disease, who had homosexual relationships in secret, and what stars, other than Errol Flynn, were fucking teenage gals? Reagan reported to Hoover that Audie Mur-

Ronald Reagan *(above)* was a friendly witness before HUAC, but he took a far more moderate position than his boss, Jack Warner. Before committee members, Warner attacked communists in the film industry, calling them "ideological termites" and "subversive germs that breed in dark corners."

Reagan called Humphrey Bogart's Committee for the First Amendment "for suckers only." Commentator Quentin Reynolds claimed that "Reagan stole the show from the better known stars," a reference to Robert Taylor and Gary Cooper.

phy, the most decorated hero of World War II, was plugging me in the bedroom cottage on the property I'd rented to him."

From Hollywood, Reagan flew to Washington two days before his appearance at HUAC. He met privately with J. Edgar, Clyde, and Louis Nichols at the FBI director's private home. He did not want to blow his cover as an informant by appearing at FBI headquarters.

Before Reagan's dinner ended that night at J. Edgar's home, he had launched the FBI on a road of discovery that would destroy the career of one of Hollywood's biggest and most popular stars, John Garfield. He finished off a minor star, Larry Parks, and threw suspicion on Ida Lupino, Fredric March, Edward G. Robinson, and Paul Muni.

He named a number of actors— only one woman—whom he suggested should be placed on the FBI's "watch list," because of their extreme left-wing views that bordered on communism, even if they were not actual card-carrying members.

Although Reagan was painting many artists red, he complained to J. Edgar, "There are some of my associates, I'm sure, who believe that I am as red as Moscow."

To popping flashbulbs, Reagan's appearance before HUAC hardly prompted the heartthrob hysteria that sexpots Robert Taylor and Gary Cooper did. By 1947, Reagan's screen career was in serious decline.

Before flying to Washington on October 7, 1947, he'd received a phone call from his wife, Jane Wyman, who had been shooting a film with Lew Ayres called *Johnny Belinda* (released in 1948). It would win her an Oscar. She told Reagan that she'd fallen in love with her handsome co-star.

Ironically Ayres had been the husband of Ginger Rogers and the former son-in-law of J. Edgar's much-admired Lela Rogers.

Having already promised to combat the movie industry's "domination by communists, radicals, and crackpots," Reagan had volunteered to appear before HUAC. In March he'd been elected president of the Screen Actors Guild, replacing the right wing Robert Montgomery.

Reagan looked rather studious in a white gabardine suit complete with thick glasses. As president of SAG, he claimed he had always opposed communist propaganda. "I do not believe that the communists have ever at any time been able to use the motion picture screen as a sounding board for their ideology." He contradicted testimony by Robert Taylor in that regard.

Startling the committee, he took a position directly opposite to that of MGM mogul Louis B. Mayer. Reagan defended the rights of communists to exist so long as they remained a legitimate political party and not an agent of a foreign power. That contradicted his previous statements.

Before the committee, Reagan seemed to be undergoing a major political change, drifting uncomfortably from an FDR New Deal liberal into a conservative Republican. On some weeks he would take one position, appealing to his liberal friends, and at another time he would be turning them in as suspected communists.

Earlier, he'd told J. Edgar that "I am firmly convinced that the Congress should declare the Communist Party illegal."

Back in Hollywood, Reagan desperately tried to save his marriage. He even told Hedda Hopper that he was aware of his wife's affair with Lew Ayres. "Right now, Jane needs very much to have a fling, and I intend to let her have it."

He finally persuaded Wyman to return home, where she occupied the guest bedroom. She even accompanied him to a party, where he spent the evening ignoring her and making political speeches.

Finally, in front of everybody, she shouted at him, "You bore me. You're a god damn windbag. Our marriage is over. You're as good in bed as you were in *Night Unto Night*." She stormed out the door never to return.

She was referring to a 1947 film in which Reagan starred with the Swedish actress Viveca Lindfors. It was a somber, unconvincing movie about a dying scientist and a mentally disturbed widow. When Jack Warner saw it, he was so horrified at how awful it was, he delayed its release for two years.

After Wyman walked out on him, Reagan had dinner with his mentor, George Murphy, who would later go on to become a senator from California. "I owe you a great deal in helping me wipe away my white-clouded liberal daze," Reagan told him. "My liberalism is becoming a liability."

Months later, Murphy would give Reagan some marital advice. He was having an affair with both Doris Day as well as starlet Nancy Davis, with a side trip to Miami Beach with a Hollywood hopeful who had changed her name to Marilyn Monroe.

"Marry Doris Day and drop the other two bimbos," Murphy advised Reagan.

Later, when fearing he'd made Nancy pregnant, Reagan proposed marriage to her. The next morning he called Murphy. "It's Nancy. There's something in the oven."

"My friend," Murphy said, "you'll live to regret that marriage. Besides, I hear she's in love with both Frank Sinatra and Clark Gable, not you."

***

Aided by investigations by FBI agents, J. Edgar and Clyde worked in the background to create what became known as the "Hollywood Blacklist." This career-destroying finger pointing was a list of actors, directors, screenwriters, producers, and other entertainment professionals who were denied employment in their fields because of their political beliefs or left wing associations. Sometimes an exposé of a communist past was real; in many instances, the artists were innocent or were banned because they refused to assist in investigations of their fellow workers. Even starlet Nancy Davis, who later married Ronald Reagan, came under suspicion because of the mail she received. As it turned out, Nancy had been confused with another actress with the same name.

Records are sketchy, but Reagan was known to have outed at least five actors as communists, as well as Ida Lupino. After his return to Hollywood, he continued to add names to the *Red Channels* list.

His first victim was the American stage and film actor, Fredric March, who had won two Oscars, the first for Best Actor in the 1932 *Dr. Jekyll and Mr. Hyde* and the second in 1946 for *The Best Years of Our Lives*. When he learned Reagan had outed him, he said,

"All my life I've supported the Democratic Party, not the Communist Party. But my support for the Republican side during the Spanish Civil War caused great controversy and made me suspect because the Soviet Union had funded the anti-Franco side. They even sent communist volunteers. Because I was opposed to Fascists, I was called a communist. I know that the FBI also spied on me when I lived next door to Arthur Miller in Connecticut."

March was an inveterate womanizer, and the FBI explored his private life. One report to J. Edgar and Clyde claimed that "March is the most lecherous fanny grabber in films."

Shelley Winters said, "March was able to perform an emotional scene with tears in his eyes while feeling my ass at the same time."

The star got a taste of his own medicine during the making of *The Sign of the Cross* (1932). Charles Laughton, the gay British actor, kept chasing him across the sound stages, trying to look up March's toga to get a glimpse of his genitals.

A young Katharine Hepburn also got her revenge on March when they co-starred in *Mary of Scotland* (1936). She had heard from Carole Lombard how he ran his hand up women's dresses. In her sixteenth century costume, Kate retrieved a banana and taped it over her vagina. When she felt March's hand go up her dress, she let it travel until it reached a phallic-like object. He withdrew his hand at once and quickly left her dressing room. J. Edgar and Clyde found that story terribly amusing.

Reagan reported to J. Edgar and Clyde that he and his best friend, fellow actor William Holden, once attended a SAG meeting at the home of Ida Lupino, who called herself "the Poor Man's Bette Davis."

Her home was crawling with communists," Reagan claimed. "Not only John Garfield, but Sterling Hayden and Howard Da Silva. Da Silva gets up in the morning only if the Kremlin says he can," Reagan said.

The future American president also reported that he had received anonymous threats of physical violence, particularly when the Guild went on strike. "Some commies didn't like the way I was handling the strike, and I was told that they were going to 'fix my face'—and that I'd never work in pictures again."

When he reported this to the police, the chief ordered him to be "fitted with a shoulder holster and a loaded .32 Smith and Wesson. "It was the first thing I strapped on every morning and the last thing I took off at night."

Third on Reagan's hit list was Edward G. Robinson, born in Bucharest, Romania, in 1893. He and his Jewish family emigrated to the United States when he was nine years old.

Although he despised movies, a bad economy drove him from the stage to the Hollywood film studios in the 1930s where he gained fame playing the gangster Caesar Enrico (Rico) Bandello in *Little Caesar*. This was one of the favorite movies of J. Edgar and Clyde.

When Reagan outed Robinson, J. Edgar didn't want to pursue a full FBI investigation of him. As Guy Hotell later said, "They gave Rico a pass."

Charges of being a communist sympathizer arose when Robinson sent author Dalton Trumbo a check for $2,500 while he was in prison, jailed for contempt of Congress. His family was having financial difficulties. "That brought the vultures down around my neck," Robinson said. "Apparently, Reagan heard about that and labeled me a pinko. I even appeared in an all-star film with Reagan called *It's a Great Feeling*, so I must have said something to him. At the time I thought he was a liberal Democrat."

In his autobiography, *All My Yesterdays*, Robinson said it all—"Imagine, Ronnie Reagan!" Robinson was first outed by the Catholic Information Society of New York in an article called "Red Star Over Hollywood" by Oliver Carlson:

> *"Names like Edward G. Robinson—to take a notorious example of an actor who has sponsored literally dozens of Red undertakings and organizations—gain for Red enterprises an audience a hundred thousand times greater than any avowed communist can muster."*

In the beginning, **Ida Lupino** *(above)* and Ronald Reagan were friends, and she often dined with Jane Wyman and him in their apartment at 1326 Londonderry in Beverly Hills. Both were liberal Democrats and had supported FDR.

Later, Lupino was horrified to see the political transformation of Ronald Reagan into a conservative Republican during his bid for election as governor of California.

Robinson immediately contacted J. Edgar, "I was hoping I would receive a letter from him clearing me or at least telling me of what other dire crimes I had been accused of by unknown witnesses." He received a mimeographed reply from J. Edgar's office.

Robinson appeared three times before HUAC, his first testimony given on December 21, 1950. He denied he was a communist, and he claimed he had never been a party member.

"What the hell good was all that?" he later claimed. "What they wanted me to say was that I was a dope, a sucker, a fool, an idiot, that I'd been double-crossed and that everything I believed in was negated by the clubs to which I belonged—that I was a tool, an unsuspecting agent of the communist conspiracy. I didn't say it because I didn't believe it."

But desperate for movie work, he finally broke down and said what was expected of him at his third HUAC appearance on April 30, 1952.

Francis Walter, chairman of the committee, said, "We never had any evidence presented to indicate you were anything more than a very choice sucker."

Back in Hollywood, there was no more work for Robinson. "Nobody would dare hire a sucker."

According to his FBI file, Robinson's fellow star, Paul Muni, was far more of a suspect than he was. "He has Jew, Jew, Jew written all over his face," J. Edgar told his aides, "and you know by now how far you can trust a Jew."

The Austro-Hungarian born American stage and film actor was the son of a Polish-Jewish family in what is now the Ukraine. The Muni family emigrated to the United States in 1902. Launching his career on the Yiddish stage, he became so clever with makeup he was dubbed "the new Lon Chaney." Edward G. Robinson was a distant cousin.

J. Edgar had liked Robinson's performance in *Little Caesar*, but had only ugly remarks to make about Muni in his 1932 roles in *Scarface* and *I Am a Fugitive from a Chain Gang*. Warner Brothers called him "the screen's greatest actor." In 1935 he starred in *The Story of Louis Pasteur* which brought him an Oscar.

There was one piece of evidence about Muni that J. Edgar could not decipher. For such a "dedicated communist," in J. Edgar's estimation, Muni flew into hysterical rage whenever one of his fellow actors showed up wearing anything red. His almost psychotic aversion to the color was never explained. Playwright Arthur Miller felt it had "something to do with an event that happened in his childhood."

In 1946 Muni appeared on Broadway in *A Flag is Born*, written by Ben Hecht, whom the FBI labeled "Red."

Everyone connected with *A Flag Is Born* was viewed by the FBI as subversive, not only its star, Muni, but the director, Luther Adler.

"The only goy in the cast" was Marlon Brando, who came to the attention of the FBI for the first time. Over the years, his file would mushroom in association with both his bisexual escapades and his civil rights clashes. The play was a strident propaganda piece revealing Hecht's zealous commitment to Zionism. Obviously he hated the British.

A Flag Is Born marked Marlon's first experience with a political commitment that in time would lead to his fight for the rights of the American Indian. At the time American Jews were divided over how a Jewish homeland should be established in Palestine. Marlon backed the more militant wing, the Irgun, a group lead by Menachem Begin that advocated violence and was vehemently anti-British. Most American Zionists, however, leaned more to the Haganah movement advocating a less violent approach, as proclaimed by the more moderate David Ben-Gurion.

After the play had run its course, Marlon traveled across the United States, raising money for the Irgun. "I was a hot-headed terrorist back then, advocating violence," he recalled later in life. "As I matured, I came to understand all sides, even the Arab point of view. I was a bit over the top when I proclaimed in speeches that British troops blocking Jewish immigration to Palestine were committing far greater atrocities than the Nazis. Blame it on my youth!"

Hecht lost his sense of fairness and balance when he zealously took out a newspaper advertisement in the *New York Herald Tribune*. In that ad, he proclaimed that every time a British soldier dies, "I have a little holiday in my heart."

This uncompromising support of Irgun terrorists would eventually cost Hecht his movie career. It certainly led to a boycott of all his work in Britain. Even such leading Jewish figures as Robinson dropped his support after Hecht's blatant advertisements.

But Marlon remained loyal to Hecht, and basically agreed with the screenwriter. In his memoirs, Hecht claimed that *A Flag Is Born* raised one million dollars for the Irgun "Freedom Fighters." Actually, it raised $400,000. That money went to purchase a large ocean liner, named the *S. S. Ben Hecht*, which ferried nine hundred refugees to Palestine in March, 1947. The British Navy captured the ship and sent six hundred of its passengers to detention camps in Cyprus. The rest of the passengers escaped to Palestine where they joined the ranks of the militant Irgun. Later the *S. S. Ben Hecht* became the flagship of the Israeli Navy.

Although Marlon was appearing in a political role, his presence as a sexual animal on stage did not go unnoticed. "Scads of young Jewish girls flocked every night not to listen to the message of our play but to see Marlon perform," Luther Adler said. Marlon wore a black turtleneck sweater that showed off his powerful physique and a pair of black trousers tied with a rope belt. One male writer proclaimed that he was "breathtakingly handsome, a figure of charismatic, mythic beauty."

"I think during the run of the play, Marlon must have fucked half the Jewish gals in New York," Adler said. "They flocked backstage to meet him, and he took his pick every night."

In the words of his first wife, Anna Kashfi, "Marlon seduced an ardent harem of voluptuaries. He told me, 'I wanted a house filled with women. One for every occasion—a picnic in the woods, a day at the beach. One to screw in bed. One to screw standing up.'"

***

When Larry Parks, the American stage and movie actor, was outed as a communist by Reagan, he was at the peak of his film career. Like Reagan, he had been born in Illinois.

He was an unremarkable stock player of the 1940s before achieving

The bad, bad, very bad **Marlon Brando** *(above)*. The young actor appeared with Paul Muni in a pro-Israel play called *A Flag is Born*. It was written by the anti-British playwright, Ben Hecht, whom the *London Daily Express* called "a Nazi at heart."

Hecht took out an ad in the *New York Herald Tribune* congratulating Jewish terrorists and praising them for slaying British soldiers. Brando enthusiastically backed him, earning him his first entry in J. Edgar's files.

film success in *The Jolson Story* (1946), earning him a Best Actor Academy Award nomination. It was followed by another huge box office hit, *Jolson Sings Again* (1949).

Just as he was really rising in the Hollywood firmament came rumblings that the FBI was investigating him for his communist background.

J. Edgar and Clyde discovered that he had indeed been a member of a Communist Party cell. Summoned before HUAC, he faced the threat of being blacklisted if he didn't testify. "Don't present me with the choice of either being in contempt of this committee or going to jail or forcing me to really crawl through the mud to be an informer. For what purpose? I don't think that is a choice at all. I don't think this is American. I don't think this is American justice!"

When J. Edgar heard these remarks, he told his aides, "We'll fix Parks. Snip off his balls if he has any."

Parks eventually gave in to the pressure of HUAC, testifying in tears and outing former communists. Sadly, he was blacklisted anyway. His testimony made former friends turn against him. "He was a god damn rat," said left-wing actress Gale Sondergaard, who faced her own blacklist problems.

Columbia Pictures dropped Parks. A film he'd made at MGM was shelved for three years. His career virtually over, he established a successful construction business which supported him and his wife, actress Betty Garrett, who later became known as Archie Bunker's Irene Lorenzo on TV's *All in the Family* and as landlady Edna Babish on *Laverne and Shirley*.

Parks once said, "I'll hate Ronald Reagan until the day I die." Death from a heart attack came at age 60 in 1975. By then he'd been long out of sight.

Garrett reportedly once said, "Larry would have been the world's most surprised man if he'd lived another five years to see Reagan elected president. He viewed him as a hopeless lightweight in the brain department."

286

***

The biggest name actor Reagan brought to his knees was his fellow star at Warner Brothers, John Garfield. Born to Russian Jewish immigrants, this New York actor was a key player in Manhattan's avant-garde Group Theater before moving to Hollywood in 1937.

After the war, he starred in some of his biggest hits including *The Postman Always Rings Twice* (1946) with Lana Turner, with whom he'd had an affair.

As his FBI file revealed, after hitting Los Angeles, he quickly began to seduce some of its leading stars, such as Joan Crawford, Hedy Lamarr, Ann Sheridan, Shelley Winters, and Ida Lupino. "He loves being John Garfield because of all the pussy and the perks," claimed musician Artie Shaw.

Occasionally he seduced a young male, including author Truman Capote, and somehow he even managed to take the French singer Edith Piaf to bed, plus dozens of showgirls, script girls, starlets, and female students at the American Laboratory Theatre.

The tough New Yorker virtually invented the term "bad boy. He had a penchant for picking up girls two at a time," claimed Lana Turner. "He also had a reputation as a demon lover. He died young and in bed with a woman. How fitting!"

The gossip columnist Sheilah Graham summed up Garfield's technique. "He made love like a sexy puppy, huffing and puffing in quick gasps. Before intercourse, he preferred women to go on an around-the-world trip on his body."

Garfield's wife, Roberta Seidman, whom he'd married in 1935, was a communist but he never was, or at least there is no evidence that he was. Nonetheless, he was called before HUAC during the Red Scare. He voiced his support for the Committee for the First Amendment, which opposed government investigations of people's political beliefs.

Before the committee, he claimed he didn't know any communists in the film industry. In later years, he hoped to redeem himself in front of the blacklisters who had ruined his career. He wrote an article, "I Was a Sucker for the Left Hook," claiming that he'd been duped by communist ideology. The title was a reference to his movies about boxing.

However, his initial appearance before HUAC had placed him on the *Red Channels* list. The stress of that may have caused his early death at the age of 39 from a heart attack.

Today he is acknowledged as the predecessor of such Method actors as Marlon Brando, James Dean, and Montgomery Clift.

***

To gather data about witnesses scheduled for upcoming appearances before HUAC, the FBI tapped phones, opened private mail, and put suspicious persons under surveillance. As a result, the FBI often learned more about their sex lives than they did about their politics.

Upon viewing the accumulating evidence, J. Edgar said to Guy Hotell, "Instead of asking a suspect, 'Are you a communist or have you ever been a communist,' the line should be changed to 'Are you a sexual pervert or have you ever been a sexual pervert?' According to my educated guess, I'd say that seventy-five percent of the people in Hollywood have engaged in sexual perversion, even guys like Gary Cooper and John Wayne. Cooper, I can believe. He'd fuck anything with a hole in it. But John Wayne! Of course, in Wayne's case, he had to give in to the twisted desires of that pervert, John Ford, to get launched in the movies. Even he-man Clark Gable got his start climbing the lavender ladder."

"But, Eddie, it's been a tradition for two hundred years in the theater that actors have to drop their trousers to get a part," Guy said. "Actually, it began with William Shakespeare. He created the original casting couch."

"Are you suggesting that Shakespeare himself was queer?" J. Edgar asked.

"My dear, have you read his homoerotic love sonnets?" Guy asked.

***

On November 25, 1947, the first systematic Hollywood Blacklist was issued

On April 23, 1951, **John Garfield** *(above)* was called to testify before HUAC about his alleged communist affiliations. At the hearing, he insisted, "I have never been a member of the Communist Party. I am no Red. I am no pink, I am no fellow traveler." He denounced the Communist Party as "subversive, a dictatorship, and against democracy."

Despite his performance, he was blacklisted in Hollywood. The Committee members just did not believe his testimony. J. Edgar was called and asked to investigate Garfield.

Victor Riesel, a columnist for the *New York Daily Mirror*, spoke to Garfield right before he died on May 21, 1952 of a heart attack. The journalist claimed that Garfield planned to recant his testimony and that he would hold nothing back. "He'd tell the whole truth about his being a communist."

Garfield's funeral in Manhattan attracted some 10,000 fans to Riverside Memorial Chapel on 76th Street. A squealing mob of bobby soxers and ardent older female fans evolved into a riot.

John Garfield came like a meteor, and like a meteor, he departed.

288

when ten writers and directors were cited for contempt of Congress for refusing to give testimony before HUAC. These artists were collectively and notoriously labeled through the decades that followed as the "Hollywood Ten."

As the months went by, more names would be added to the list. On June 22, 1950, the FBI-inspired *Red Channels* list was published, naming 151 entertainment industry figures, accusing each of them of being "Red Fascist."

Hollywood changed almost overnight. In what is known as the Waldorf Statement, because it was issued at the Waldorf-Astoria Hotel in New York, Eric Johnston, president of the Motion Picture Association of America (MPAA), declared that every member of the "Hollywood Ten" would be fired or suspended without pay and not reemployed.

Each of the "Hollywood Ten" was found guilty of contempt of Congress, and each was sentenced to between six and twelve months in prison.

During the 1947 investigations, witnesses had claimed protection under the First Amendment. By the 1951-52 investigations, they invoked the Fifth Amendment against self-incrimination. But "taking the Fifth" before HUAC meant an automatic blacklisting. Incidentally, at no point had membership in the Communist Party been illegal.

Since there weren't any big-time movie stars on the list of the "Hollywood Ten," their names were not household words in America.

A novelist, journalist, and screenwriter, Alvah Bessie was imprisoned for ten months for contempt of Congress and blacklisted by studio bosses. In 1938 he'd fought as a volunteer soldier in the communist Abraham Lincoln Brigade during the Spanish Civil War. His experiences, recaptured in a book, *Men in Battle*, won the praise of Ernest Hemingway, a novelist who was also on J. Edgar's list of suspected communists.

Bessie was nominated for an Oscar for Best Original Story for *Objective Burma!* (1945), starring Errol Flynn, whose FBI file by that time challenged the size of the *Gone With the Wind* manuscript. Far from being filled with communist propaganda, *Objective Burma!* was a super-patriotic WWII action film about a company of U.S. paratroopers invading Burma to wipe out a key Japanese post.

His career destroyed by HUAC, Bessie ended up running the lights and sound at the hungry i nightclub in San Francisco. In 1965, he published *Inquisition in Eden*, attacking his tormentors.

J. Edgar later claimed, "The book is filled with libelous lies coming from this commie pinko. In his initial sentencing, he should have gotten at least ten years. Some patriot in prison should have beaten the shit out of him."

***

Bespectacled, Philadelphia-born Herbert Biberman was the husband of the famous actress, Gale Sondergaard, who won the first Oscar for Best Supporting Actress for her film debut in *Anthony Adverse* (1936), in which she appeared opposite Claude Rains. The movie also starred Fredric March and Olivia de Havilland.

Today Biberman is best known for his direction of the 1954 film *Salt of the Earth* about a zinc miners' strike in New Mexico, which is listed for preservation by the National Film Registry.

Biberman's pre-Blacklist career included writing such films as *Meet Nero Wolfe* (1936), *When Tomorrow Comes* (1939), and *The Master Race* (1944). Biberman's wife, Sondergaard, paid a terrible price for standing by her man. It cost her almost a quarter of a century of work in films.

Sondergaard lives in Hollywood trivia as the original Wicked Witch cast in *The Wizard of Oz* (1939). Because she didn't want to appear in disfiguring makeup, she withdrew from the role, which immortalized character actress Margaret Hamilton instead.

Sondergaard, as J. Edgar learned, also had lesbian tendencies and had a brief fling with her bisexual co-star Barbara Stanwyck in *East Side, West Side*, which also co-starred Ava Gardner and Nancy Davis (Reagan).

When Dorothy Lamour, beloved friend of J. Edgar and Clyde, filmed one of the Crosby and Hope pictures, *Road to Rio* (1947), she claimed that Sondergaard made unwelcome lesbian advances toward her.

In gay history, long before the advent of Elizabeth Taylor, Biberman and Sondergaard were the first celebrities to endorse gay rights before that became a political goal. They lent their support to Harry Hay's emerging Mattachine Society, an activist group composed of homosexual men.

After his fall from grace and imprisonment, Biberman worked for several years selling small plots of land in the Hollywood Hills.

***

Lester Cole, a New York-born screenwriter "remained a hardcore communist until his death in 1985," according to historian Ronald Radosh. Before he was blacklisted in 1947, Cole wrote more than forty screenplays. In 1934 he joined the Communist Party.

Hauled before HUAC, he refused to answer questions and was convicted of contempt. Fined $1,000, he served ten months in the Federal Correctional Institution in Danbury, Connecticut.

Returning to Hollywood, he wrote a few screenplays, especially the highly successful *Born Free* (1966), but submitted the scripts under the name of Gerald L.C. Copley.

Unable to find a writing job most of the time, Cole worked for five years in New York as a waiter or a short-order cook. In one job he moved slabs of marble around a Brooklyn warehouse.

***

One of the most famous directors of Hollywood, Canadian-born Edward Dmytryk, was known for directing films such as *Back to Bataan* (1945), starring super patriot John Wayne, whom J. Edgar always maintained "took it up the ass" when he was known as Marion Morrison in the 1920s.

At the time he got sucked into the Red Menace vortex, Dmytryk had directed *Crossfire* (1947), starring three actors named Robert—Mitchum, Ryan, and Young. This *film noir* involved a victim of anti-Semitism and was handled with taste and intelligence. The novel on which it was based cast the victim as a homosexual, but that was viewed as too hot to handle for post-war American audiences. Dmytryk made the victim a Jew instead.

Summoned to appear before HUAC in 1947, he refused to testify and was sent to prison. After a few months, he felt he was going insane while "caged like a wild animal." On April 25, 1951, he asked to appear a second time before HUAC. This time, "the canary sang" [his words].

He admitted to a brief membership in the Communist Party in 1945 and named twenty-six former members of left-wing groups. He ratted on Adrian Scott, Albert Maltz, and John Howard Lawson, fellow members of the Hollywood Ten. He testified that all of them had pressured him to include communist propaganda in his films.

Regrettably, his testimony damaged pending court cases where these men were trying to exonerate themselves. In a revealing 1996 book, *Odd Man Out: A Memoir of the Hollywood Ten*, he recounted his horrible ordeal.

Unlike the others, his directorial career wasn't wrecked. He would go on to helm one of Humphrey Bogart's greatest films, *The Caine Mutiny* (1954). He would also direct Elizabeth Taylor, Bette Davis, Marlon Brando, Montgomery Clift, Sean Connery, Clark Gable, Spencer Tracy, Richard Burton, Richard Widmark, Henry Fonda, and Barbara Stanwyck typecast as a lesbian in *Walk on the Wild Side* (1962).

***

The famous humorist and journalist, Ring Lardner, was the father of

291

Ringgold ("Ring") Lardner Jr., who followed in his father's footsteps, scripting such films as *Woman of the Year*, a 1942 movie starring Katharine Hepburn and Spencer Tracy. He also worked on the classic film *Laura* (1944) starring Gene Tierney.

In 1947 at the time he was scripting *Forever Amber* (1947), he was the highest paid scriptwriter in Hollywood, making $2,000 a week at 20th Century Fox.

In 1936 he'd joined the Communist Party, and his left-wing politics often upset the studio. Summoned on October 30, 1947 before HUAC, he refused to answer questions. Tried and convicted for contempt of Congress, he served a year in Danbury Prison and was dismissed from Fox.

After that, he wrote under pseudonyms, but in 1965, Norman Jewison gave him screen credit for 1965's *The Cincinnati Kid*, starring Steve McQueen.

Shortly before Lardner's death in 2000, he was visited by the Hungarian writer Miklos Vamos. Lardner told him that one of the movies he wrote under a pseudonym won an Oscar. But he refused to name the picture, claiming it would be unfair to the writer who allowed him to use his name. At the time of his death, he was the last surviving member of the "Hollywood Ten."

Ring Lardner Jr. often wrote under the name of Oliver Skene.

***

One of the oldest members of the "Hollywood Ten," John Howard Lawson was also the "reddest." He was the chief officer of the Hollywood branch of the Communist Party, answering directly to the major cell in New York City. He was the first president of the Writers Guild of America, which eventually changed its name to Screen Writers Guild.

He was born in New York City; his family name was Levy, but his father changed it to Lawson "so that my son would obtain reservations at expensive resort hotels." He was referring to the policy of certain restricted hotels which would not accept Jewish clients.

Lawson was one of the most controversial Hollywood authors and screenwriters. Like the rest of the "Hollywood Ten," he was tried and convicted for not answering questions about his communist past.

Some critics claimed that based on his writings, Lawson was out of step with the proletarian. In 1934, the magazine, *The New Masses*, attacked him as "A Bourgeois Hamlet of Our Time." Perhaps in reaction to those critiques, he joined the Communist Party in 1934 to educate himself about the plight of the working man. Heading south, he studied bloody labor conflicts in Alabama and Georgia and wrote articles for *The Daily Worker*, which led to his arrest on several occasions.

More than any of the "Hollywood Ten," his scripts were laden with political themes and innuendos. They included Henry Fonda's 1938 *Blockade* about the Spanish Civil War. For that drama, he received a nomination for an Oscar. His 1945 *Counter-Attack* was a tribute to the USA/Soviet alliance during WWII. He also wrote less obviously politicized films such as *Algiers* in 1938 with Charles Boyer and Hedy Lamarr, and two Humphrey Bogart movies in 1943, *Action in the North Atlantic* and *Sahara*.

Summoned before HUAC on October 29, 1947, he refused to answer questions. Tried and convicted with the others, he was sentenced for a year in Ashland (Kentucky) Federal Prison.

After he was released, he moved to Mexico where he wrote Marxist dramas and remained a dedicated communist until his death in 1977, claiming that Hollywood falsifies the life of the American worker. His writings infuriated J. Edgar, who somehow may have prevented the publication of his autobiography.

Lawson became one of the first male advocates of feminism, claiming that Hollywood degrades the image of women "treating glamour and sex appeal as the sum total of a woman's personality."

One statement Lawson wrote particularly enraged J. Edgar. He said that in the movies "when a woman succeeds in the world of competition, Hollywood holds that her success is achieved by trickery, deceit, and the amoral use of sex appeal."

J. Edgar told his aides, "Lawson is completely wrong on that account. When it comes to women, Hollywood gets it completely right."

***

Brooklyn-born Albert Maltz wrote the first of his eighteen screenplays for Hollywood in 1932. One of his most famous dramas was the 1942 *This Gun for Hire*, the movie that propelled those WWII "shorties," Veronica Lake and Alan Ladd, into stardom. For his 1945 script, *Pride of the Marines*, starring John Garfield, Maltz was nominated for an Oscar in the category of Writing Adapted Screenplay.

After serving time in prison for contempt of Congress, he had to go uncredited for such highly successful films as the 1950 *Broken Arrow*, starring James Stewart, or the 1953 *The Robe*, starring Richard Burton. Maltz was uncredited because of the blacklist.

In March of 1960, Frank Sinatra wanted to end the blacklisting of some of the most talented artists in Hollywood. He called Maltz "the best goddamn writer around," and hired him to do the screenplay for a film based on the soldier, Eddie Slovik, executed during the closing months of WWII. Slovik was a soldier charged with desertion, and he was shot by a firing squad, the only soldier executed by the U.S. Army since the Civil War.

Sinatra's hiring of the blacklisted writer sent shock waves through the Kennedy campaign, creating an enormous backlash because of the singer's close personal friendship with John F. Kennedy, who was running for president that year against red-baiting Richard Nixon, who could have used this as a club against his Democratic rival.

"If Sinatra loves his country, he won't do this," wrote columnist Hedda Hopper, a fervent right winger. Finally, Ambassador Joseph P. Kennedy called Sinatra. "That pro-Communist shit is more than our campaign can take. Jack being Catholic is enough to derail us. Now this. Make up your mind. It's either Maltz or the road."

After that threat, and to the delight of J. Edgar, Sinatra caved in and removed Maltz from the project, although he paid him $75,000, the full amount he would have received for doing the script. "Chalk up another victory for the lynch-law mentality," charged *Publishers Weekly*.

***

Samuel Ornitz, another of the "Hollywood Ten" sent to prison, was the son of a prosperous dry goods merchant in New York. At the age of twelve, he was a dedicated socialist, standing on the street corner giving speeches to the poor on the Lower East Side. He rejected the prosperous life of a Jewish merchant and became a social worker in the New York prison system.

After moving to Hollywood in 1929 at the advent of the Talkies, he wrote twenty-nine screenplays, including *Three Faces West* (1940), starring John Wayne, who engaged in political debates with him all during the shoot. At the time, Ornitz was the most outspoken political figure in Hollywood, praising the glories of the Soviet Union.

At the end of his life, when he learned what a brutal dictator Josef Stalin was and how many millions he had killed, Ornitz claimed he felt betrayed by communism and totally misled. "Stalin was worse than Hitler himself," he said. He died on March 10, 1957, of cancer at the Motion Picture Country Home in Los Angeles.

***

An American screenwriter and producer, Adrian Scott, rose from the bogs of New Jersey to become one of the "Young Turks" working at RKO in the 1940s. He was the quintessential Popular Front Communist, committed to anti-fascism, anti-racism, and progressive unionism. To him, making films was the most effective expression of political activism.

In 1944 he had a runaway *film noir* success, *Murder, My Sweet*, which gave singer Dick Powell a new image as the hard-boiled detective Philip Marlowe. Suddenly, Scott became one of the hottest producers in town, hailed as "The New Thalberg," or "The New Boy Wonder."

Scott also helmed *Cornered* (1945), a high-tension drama in which he cast Dick Powell once again. The film's female lead was played by Anne Shirley, who married him a year later. She had previously been married to heartthrob John Payne. One of J. Edgar's favorite candid nude shots was of Payne snapped in his dressing room as he showered after shooting a boxing scene in a movie.

One of Scott's most visible and controversial films was *Crossfire* (1947), directed by Edward Dmytryk, another member of the "Hollywood Ten."

Scott's appearance before HUAC was on October 29, 1947, when he refused to discuss his personal politics or name names. On November 25, the president of RKO, N.P. Rathvon, fired him, criticizing his general conduct and claiming he had placed himself in "disrepute."

Like the other members of the "Hollywood Ten," Scott, too, was sent to prison for contempt of Congress.

Upon his release he announced to his wife, Shirley, that he was going to Europe to try to find work. She wrote him a "Dear John" letter, claiming she preferred to remain in Hollywood to divorce him.

"I was a threat to the security of the United States," he said. "My screenplay, *Mr. Lincoln's Whiskers*, was dropped. From 1947 to 1952 my earning capacity was almost nil—some years, zero. How to eat? How to live?"

***

Arguably the best writer jailed for contempt of Congress among the "Hollywood Ten" was Dalton Trumbo. After jail time, he won two Oscars while blacklisted—one originally given to a "front" writer, another awarded to Robert Rich, Trumbo's pseudonym.

Emerging from the arid plains of Colorado, Trumbo in the 1940s was one of Hollywood's highest paid writers, turning out such hits as *Thirty Seconds Over Tokyo* (1944) with Van Johnson and Spencer Tracy, or *Our Vines Have Tender Grapes* (1945), starring Edward G. Robinson.

For *Kitty Foyle* (1940), he was nominated for an Academy Award for Writing Adapted Screenplay. Ginger Rogers walked away with an Oscar as Best Actress for her take as a working girl heroine in *Kitty Foyle.*

In 1939 Trumbo published his anti-war novel, *Johnny Got His Gun*, which won the National Book Award. It told the story of a Canadian soldier who had lost all his limbs during World War I. But for motives known only to himself, Trumbo suspended publication of the popular novel during World War II, perhaps not wanting to incite fear in young men being drafted into military service. Even so, he received highly controversial mail from both sides of the political spectrum throughout the course of World War II, some writers calling for "an immediate negotiated peace" with Nazi Germany, others "denouncing the Jews for getting us into this horror." Trumbo systematically turned the mail over to the FBI.

J. Edgar sent two agents to his home. Later Trumbo said, "I regretted my decision. I soon realized that their interest lay not in the letters but in me."

What J. Edgar and Clyde discovered was that Trumbo had been a member of the Communist Party from 1943 to 1948 and had once written for *The Daily Worker.*

After being convicted for contempt of Congress, Trumbo spent eleven months in the Federal Penitentiary in Ashland, Kentucky.

Fleeing to Mexico after being released from prison, Trumbo continued to turn out scripts, nearly three dozen, all under pseudonyms. Many became quite famous, including the 1950 *Gun Crazy,* starring Peggy Cummins, a film often noted as a precursor to *Bonnie and Clyde.*

Writing under the name of Robert Rich, Trumbo won an Oscar for Best Original Story for *The Brave One* in 1956. The Oscar went unclaimed until 1975 when Trumbo came forward to admit authorship.

Supported by director Otto Preminger, Trumbo wrote the screenplay for his 1960 film *Exodus,* adapted from the bestseller by Leon Uris. After that, Kirk Douglas hired Trumbo to write the screenplay for *Spartacus* (1960). These widely acknowledged triumphs were viewed as the beginning of the end for the blacklist.

In 1971 Trumbo adapted his own novel, *Johnny Got His Gun*, for the screen and also directed it. One of his last films, *Executive Action* (1973) starring Burt Lancaster, was based on various conspiracy theories about the assassination of President Kennedy.

In 1993 Trumbo won his posthumous Oscar for *Roman Holiday,* which starred Audrey Hepburn and Gregory Peck in 1953. The Oscar had previously been given to Ian McLellan Hunter, who had served as a "front" for Trumbo.

Trumbo died of a heart attack at the age of 70 in 1976, donating his body to science.

***

Another blacklisted writer, Guy Endore, wrote an article in *The Nation* on December 20, 1952, describing what it felt like being blacklisted.

"You are lost. You have no country, no civil rights, no means of livelihood. And you have heard so much about guilt by association that you hesitate to go to see anyone. When you meet an acquaintance you wait to be recognized, not wishing to spread the infection. You feel that like the lepers of the Middle Ages you ought to tinkle a bell and cry out the old warning, 'Unclean!' 'Unclean!'"

One of the best but also the most infamous screenwriters in Hollywood was Colorado-born **Dalton Trumbo,** depicted in his prison mug shot above.

He was a member of the Communist Party from 1943 to 1948. At the outbreak of World War II, in September of 1939, he argued, like many other intellectuals and liberals at the time, that the United States should not get involved in the war on the side of Britain.

Adrian Scott later claimed, "J. Edgar Hoover played real dirty with the 'Hollywood Ten.' It was later learned that he went not only after us, but after our attorneys such as Bartley Crum."

In violation of the 1934 Communications Act, and Supreme Court rulings, J. Edgar and Clyde listened in, through wiretaps, as the "Hollywood Ten" lawyers talked to their clients. The Justice Department was given advance notice of all of their legal defenses. In presenting his evidence, J. Edgar said it came "from highly confidential sources," not mentioning illegal wiretapping. Attorney General Tom Clark did not challenge him on that.

An outstanding lawyer, Bartley Crum was a confidante of press baron William Randolph Hearst and of the liberal Republican, Wendell Willkie, who ran unsuccessfully against FDR for President in 1940. Crum had advised President Harry S Truman to allow unrestricted Jewish immigration to Palestine and to permit the creation of a Jewish state.

Crum agreed to defend some writers who were subpoenaed to appear before HUAC. For doing that, J. Edgar ordered that his phone be tapped, his mail opened, and that he be shadowed by an FBI agent. Eventually Crum was labeled a subversive and lost most of his clients.

He drifted into alcoholism and on December 9, 1959 swallowed an entire bottle of Seconal, washing down the pills with whiskey.

His daughter, Patricia Bosworth, became a notable biographer, writing books on such "left wing" iconic figures as Montgomery Clift, Marlon Brando, and Jane Fonda.

***

The aging actor, Adolphe Menjou, who was to the right of Josef Goebbels, declared, "I am a witch hunter if the witches are communists. I am a Red-baiter. I would like to see them all go back to Russia."

In extreme contrast to his statement, some of the leading figures of Hollywood, a group of Hollywood liberals, appalled at the Red scare destroying careers, decided to fly to Washington to protest the "un-American" activities of the House Un-American Activities Committee. Jack Warner opposed the idea, since he had many of these stars, including Humphrey Bogart, under contract. "Bogie's making a mistake!" the studio chief shouted at his staff.

"Like Don Quixote," Bogie said, "we're just fighting a lot of windmills, but I'm going anyway. Betty is too." He was, of course, referring to his wife, Lauren Bacall.

In addition to the Bogarts, the roster of protesters included Gene Kelly, June Havoc (sister of stripper Gypsy Rose Lee), Danny Kaye, Evelyn Keyes, Marsha Hunt, Geraldine Brooks, Richard Conte, Jane Wyatt, and Ira Gershwin. The spokesmen for the group were director John Huston and screenwriter Philip Dunne (*How Green Was My Valley*).

Huston said, "Bogie is our big ace, a media magnet."

Howard Hughes, who in his capacity as director of RKO would himself be named on the blacklist in the 1950s, offered one of his airplanes to fly the group from the West Coast to Washington. The galaxy of stars left California on October 26, 1947.

In a statement, Bogie said, "Is democracy so feeble that it can be subverted merely by a look or a line? The beliefs of men and women who write for the screen are nobody's business but their own. Congress is not empowered to dictate what Americans shall think."

Paul Henreid, who had co-starred with Bogie in *Casablanca*, didn't really want to go. "It was stupid. I didn't want to have anything to do with it." His wife, Liesel Henreid, coerced him. Later Henreid himself would become a victim of the blacklist.

Huston told Bacall, "Tell Bogie to keep his trap shut. I'll do the talking for us."

It evolved into a tabloid feeding frenzy when the Hollywood delegation appeared at the Old House Office building, posing for pictures with the

Capitol dome in the background.

The day of testimony, John Garfield arrived from New York with another delegation. Months later, his own career would be destroyed.

The appearance of the Hollywood delegation was a disaster that day, as seasoned politicians embarrassed them. *Life* magazine gave them its own review, calling them "Lost Liberals." Dalton Trumbo, later one of the "Hollywood Ten," called the HUAC proceedings "the beginning of American concentration camps."

J. Parnell Thomas, the head of HUAC, "pulled every dirty trick in the books," according to Huston. "He and J. Edgar Hoover, with a little help from Tricky Dickie." As far as it is known, Huston was the first person to refer to a young congressman, Richard Nixon, with that label.

The Hollywood celebrities presented a petition to the Speaker of the House, but he was too busy to receive them. Their petition claimed, "The procedures adopted by the House Committee on Un-American Activities violates the civil liberties of American citizens." The delegation later tried to see their California representative in Congress, Nixon, but learned he had fled town.

Throughout their trip to Washington and during their trip back West with stopovers, J. Edgar and Clyde had ordered FBI agents to monitor "their every move." Clyde was in charge of the file which he headed: COMMUNIST INFILTRATION OF THE MOVIE INDUSTRY.

Columnist Ed Sullivan noted that the plane carrying the stars was called *Star of the Red Sea.*

In spite of the chilly reception the delegation received in Washington, Bogie issued a statement calling the hearings "a failure, a travesty of justice, an abuse of the defenseless, and a subversion of the courts."

In a call to columnist Ed Sullivan, his drinking buddy in New York in the 1920s, Bogie claimed, "I'm about as much a Communist as J. Edgar Hoover."

During his stay in Washington, Bogie placed a call to J. Edgar himself at FBI headquarters, but the director refused to come on the line. However, Clyde in an adjoining office took the call. To Clyde, Bogie denied that he had been involved at any time in any communist activities.

"I admired your performance in *Casablanca,*" Clyde told him. "You were on the right side back then." Then he put down the phone.

On the way back across the vast American continent, Bogie began to have second thoughts about his appearance in Washington, especially when news reached him that members of the "Hollywood Ten" were or had been communists.

Evelyn Keyes, John Huston's wife and "Scarlett O'Hara's Younger Sister," felt the stars had failed on that trip to Washington. "If it's a choice of who is the bigger star, Hollywood or the U.S. government, it's no contest. People who hold the power always win."

By the time Howard Hughes' TWA plane set down in Los Angeles, gloom had settled over the stars. Screenwriter Abraham Polonsky called it "evocative of a flu epidemic." Bogie seemed in a rage, shouting at Danny Kaye, "You fuckers sold me out!"

Former friend and now right-wing columnist, Ed Sullivan, called Bogie. "The public is beginning to think you're Red. Get that through your skull, Bogie."

Bogart began to drink even more heavily than usual and feared he'd jeopardized his future career in pictures. Jack Warner continued to issue dire warnings. Bogart responded, "Jack, if I made an ass out of myself in Washington, you in your testimony not only showed them your ass but parted cheeks and flashed your rosebud."

"You've been accused of being a commie before," Warner shouted before slamming down the phone.

He was referring to the testimony of John L. Leech, who had been the executive secretary of the Communist Party in Los Angeles from 1931 to 1937. The party had expelled him when it was discovered that Leech was a paid police informer.

Before a grand jury in 1940, Leech testified that the following stars were red: Humphrey Bogart, James Cagney, Fredric March, Melvyn Douglas, and Franchot Tone during his marriage to J. Edgar's friend, Joan Crawford.

Furious and filled with rage, Bogie, while shooting *High Sierra*, issued an angry denial. He denounced the charges as "absurd and one-hundred percent untrue because I've never been a member of any party or contributed one cent."

Looking haggard and beaten down, Bogie went into the offices of Warner Brothers in New York in the dying days of autumn in 1947. No record exists of what transpired. But on the following morning, December 1, 1947, Jack Warner in Los Angeles received a telegram from his New York office. It was short and blunt—BOGIE TO RECANT.

J. Edgar had already secretly been sent a copy of a telegram that Warner had flashed to Bogie in New York: "Do you ever want to work in this town again? Do you want to be tried for treason? Look at yourself. You're fifty and balding. *Casablanca* was a long time ago. You've got a wife that the papers are calling a defender of traitors."

During a change of trains in Chicago, Bogie, along with Bacall, held a hastily called news conference, where he said:

> *"I went to Washington because I thought fellow Americans were being deprived of their Constitutional rights, and for that reason alone. That the trip was ill-advised, even foolish, I am very ready to admit. At the time it seemed the right thing to do.*
>
> *I have absolutely no use for Communism nor for anyone who serves that philosophy. I am an American. And very likely, like a good many of you, sometimes a foolish and impetuous American."*

What was not known to the press at the time was that Clyde had called Bogie at his New York hotel before his appointment at the Manhattan office of Warner Brothers. In his most threatening voice, he told Bogie that if he did not recant the statements he'd made during his trip to Washington, an embarrassing aspect of his private life would be exposed.

"Our agents have learned that you have been conducting an affair with Verita Peterson, your hairdresser. We know you've been carrying on with her ever since you met her on the set of *Casablanca*. Even after marrying Ba-

ALL ABOARD
A JOURNEY INTO DISASTER

In October of 1947, the Committee for the First Amendment, composed of Hollywood stars, flew to Washington to protest the "un-American" activities of the House Un-American Activities Committee. Among the stars aboard were **Geraldine Brooks, Paul Henreid, June Havoc, Marsha Hunt, Lauren Bacall, Richard Conte,** and **Evelyn Keyes.** Howard Hughes, who owned TWA, provided the airplane.

Their trip was ill-conceived, and much damage was caused when Bogie later recanted his testimony.

"I had to be a turncoat," he later confessed. "I was not a personal friend of any of the Hollywood Ten, and I had worked fifteen years to reach the top in Hollywood. It seemed senseless to throw all that away. At least my trip got my picture on the frontpage of the *Daily Worker.*"

call, you're still involved with Peterson. You often go sailing with her on weekends. The press hails your idyllic marriage to Bacall, but it is hardly that. Bacall is young enough to be your daughter, and yet you desert her to pursue this other woman. You really don't want us to leak all the details to Walter Winchell, now do you?"

This time Bogie slammed down the phone on Clyde, but he'd listened to every word of the threat and knew that J. Edgar was serious.

That night over dinner at Harvey's, Clyde entertained Guy and J. Edgar, relating how he'd talked tough to the screen's tough guy.

The next day, Clyde typed up the notes of his phone conversation with Bogie and placed them in his file, which in time would grow to two inches thick. He filed his notes next to a favorable review of Bogie's appearance in Washington, which appeared in Moscow's *Daily Worker*.

Back in Chicago before boarding the train to Los Angeles, Bogie made a parting statement to the press. "We went in green to Washington and they beat our brains out!"

In spite of his recanting, the press was largely hostile to Bogie, with such headlines as TOUGH GUY WAVES FLAG. A columnist in Indiana wrote, "All right, Bogie, you can get up off your knees now."

However, *The Washington Post* sort of defended Bogie, claiming, "We are rather sorry for Mr. Bogart. He had nothing at all to be ashamed of until he began to be ashamed."

His liberal acquaintances in Hollywood were horrified, especially Paul Henreid, who'd detested Bogie ever since their mutual appearance in *Casablanca*. "Bogart has no character, nothing," Henreid told the press. "He's a shit." One reporter commented that "Victor Laszlo has gotten his revenge on Rick for taking Ilsa's heart in *Casablanca*."

Actor Luther Adler, who would become blacklisted himself, voiced his extreme disappointment at Bogie's "betrayal." He later said, "And then Gene Kelly reneged and Danny Kaye reneged, and Frank Sinatra reneged, and those of us who didn't stood out like carbuncles."

Marsha Hunt called Bogie's recanting a "body blow," and Evelyn Keyes accused him of "a cowardly sell-out."

In spite of his capitulation, Bogie received bags of hate mail pouring into Warner Brothers. He was called "a pansy," "a cheap sissy," and a "so-called tough guy with no balls."

After Bogie did what J. Edgar wanted him to, J. Edgar wrote J. Parnell Thomas at HUAC, asserting that Bogie had been cleared by the FBI and could continue to work in pictures. "I think the tough guy has learned his lesson now, and will no longer make trouble for us. In the future, he'll chase after villains on the screen and not look for them in Washington."

After Bogie's appearance in Washington with the other left-wing stars, the blacklist, fueled by J. Edgar and Clyde, grew larger and larger, destroying careers and lives. In the aftermath of Thomas' HUAC hearings, a rumor in Hollywood spread that J. Edgar and the FBI would take over the actual casting of future roles throughout the film industry.

Lillian Ross, while researching an article for *The New Yorker*, visited Errol Flynn on the set of *The Adventures of Don Juan* at Warner Brothers. He was attired in royal blue tights for his performance as a 16th Century swashbuckler.

"As a casting director, I have no doubt that J. Hoover will insist on the casting couch," Errol said. "I'm sure I'll have to pull off these blue tights. Of course, in his case, he already knows what the package is like."

Of course, Ross couldn't print those comments.

***

Left wing Katharine Hepburn had starred in *Undercurrent* with right-wing Robert Taylor. During the shoot, they often clashed bitterly over politics. The picture was a flop. More personally damaging than a string of bad pictures were harmful rumors about her affair with Spencer Tracy, who was not only a married man but, like J. Edgar himself, a closeted homosexual. There were whispers about her lesbianism and criticism of her left-wing politics. She was so controversial she came under the radar of Clyde and J. Edgar at the FBI. "She's as pink as her underwear," or so the FBI director proclaimed.

Some of the stars she'd worked with, not just Taylor but Adolphe Menjou, spread the word that she was definitely a communist and should be hauled before HUAC in Washington. Menjou claimed that every member of her outspoken New England family was a Stalinist.

Her boss at MGM, Louis B. Mayer, had already testified before HUAC as a friendly witness, and he was "increasingly horrified" at comments that she was sympathetic to communism, if not a party member. Hepburn stridently deplored the witch hunt going on in Hollywood, not realizing that she was being sucked into the whirlpool herself.

It all began with a call from Edward G. Robinson, who told her he was sick and could not deliver an important speech about censorship in films. Without knowing all the details, she agreed to appear in his place.

During the war years, Kate had escaped political fallout for her so-called left-wing politics, mainly because of her friendship with the Roosevelts and contributions to the war effort that included patriotic radio broadcasts and her appearance in the morale-boosting *Stage Door Can-*

teen.

Perhaps angered that Harry S Truman had invited Spencer Tracy to the White House and not her, Kate refused to back the sitting President during his 1948 run for re-election against Governor Thomas Dewey of New York. Whereas Tracy remained with Truman, Kate announced that she was backing the Progressive ticket and endorsed the left-winger, Henry Wallace, instead.

Wallace's attack of Truman's "get tough" policy toward the Soviet Union eventually cost him his position as Secretary of Commerce within the Truman administration. Wallace himself was under investigation from the increasingly powerful HUAC, in which a rising young politician from California, Nixon, was emerging into prominence. Nixon publicly referred to Wallace as "a Communist dupe."

In May of 1947, Edward G. Robinson called Kate, explaining that he was ill and asking her to deliver an anti-censorship rally at the Los Angeles Gilmore auditorium. "Sure, I'll go on in your place," she told the actor. "If you weren't ill, I'm sure you'd be speaking out for the right principles. I have always opposed people who try to censor motion pictures."

She even persuaded a rather unpoliticized Judy Garland to address the audience as well. J. Edgar had learned that Kate was having an affair with the bisexual Judy at the time.

Kate later regretted her decision, claiming that her first big mistake was in her choice of clothing. "At first I was going to wear white," she later recalled. "But then I thought I'd look like the Dove of Peace. So I decided to wear a red Valentino dress. Red, of all colors. Believe me, it wasn't deliberate. I just wasn't thinking. When my enemies, including Miss Hedda Hopper, whose politics were to the right of Attila the Hun, heard of my choice of colors the next day, it was as if I had endorsed Josef Stalin for president instead of Wallace. Even though my ancestors had sailed over on the *Mayflower* and I'd never joined any group in my life, I suddenly became part of the communist conspiracy to overthrow the American government. Actually, I'd written Eleanor Roosevelt, urging her to run for President against Truman, but she ever so gently turned me down."

Kate had seen how powerful J. Parnell Thomas's HUAC committee was. Thomas, the chairman and chief investigator, had been responsible in part for destroying the careers of such friends as screenwriter Donald Ogden Stewart. Stewart, in fact, had been blacklisted because of the anti-Fascist—and allegedly pro-socialist—statements he'd made when writing the screenplay for the Tracy/Hepburn film, *Keeper of the Flame.*

Witnesses at the auditorium that night reported that Kate's voice grew shrill as she warmed up to her attack. She launched into an assault on "super patriots who call themselves the Motion Picture Alliance for the Preservation of American Ideals."

"For myself," she shouted, "I want no part of their ideals or those of Mr. Thomas."

In her impassioned speech before twenty thousand people, Kate personally attacked Thomas for engaging in a "smear campaign against the motion picture industry. The artist since the beginning of time has always expressed the aspirations and dreams of the people. Silence the artist and you have silenced the most articulate voice the people have."

Even little Judy Garland got up on the podium, although no one expected her at a political rally. She, too, attacked HUAC as the "Un-American Committee," and urged the audience to write their congressmen, protesting "Mr. Thomas's kicking the living daylights out of the Bill of Rights."

Anti-Hepburn forces rallied, enraged, the next day. Louis B. Mayer called Kate in to explain why she'd made such an incendiary speech. She told him, "In my heart, I had to stand up for my beliefs like my mother, Kit, has done all her life. I wanted Kit to be proud of me."

Since Kate had already been cast in *Song of Love*, and since he had legally contracted her for the role, Mayer went ahead with the production despite the negative implications of Kate's designation as a "pinko." But although he didn't inform her immediately, the studio chief, in the months ahead was "unable to find any worthy scripts" for her.

More to the right in his politics than Kate, Tracy did not attend the rally, nor did he join Kate in any of her political protests. When asked what he thought about actors going into politics, he said, "Remember who shot Lincoln?"

Wearing a red dress, **Katharine Hepburn** *(above)* gave a speech at the Gilmore Auditorium that angered most of right-wing Hollywood, bringing a denunciation from Ronald Reagan, head of the Screen Actors Guild.

In the wake of that speech, "Lady in Red" stories were published across the nation. In his column, newspaperman Jimmie Fidler said director Leo McCarey "was right to can her from his upcoming film *Good Sam*. Her hot political speeches may queer her at the box office."

In his column, Drew Pearson predicted that Kate would be called before HUAC to be grilled about her communist affiliations. Of course, she wasn't a communist, but you wouldn't know that from reading the newspapers.

After the speech, in spite of Mayer's protests, Kate joined in with hundreds of other actors, writers, directors, and non-studio producers—including David O. Selznick, John Ford, Bogart, and George Stevens—to launch the Committee for the First Amendment, hoping to combat the unfavorable portrait of the film industry rising out of the bad publicity of the HUAC hearings.

Tracy's name surfaced a few times at the HUAC hearings, but references to him did not harm his career. The movie-going public just didn't believe that Tracy was part of any communist conspiracy to overthrow the American government.

Kate stood by and watched the careers of such actors as John Garfield and Larry Parks destroyed. Amazingly, in spite of all her left-wing activities, she was never called before the committee, although almost daily she rehearsed what she'd say if she did receive such a subpoena.

Her name was mentioned several times, and always unfavorably, at the hearings. She sat by her radio in Los Angeles and heard directors Sam Wood and Leo McCarey testify that they knew "for a fact" that she had helped raise nearly ninety thousand dollars for "a very special political party, and we're not talking the Boy Scouts of America." The directors did not name the party.

Traveling between New York and Washington, Kate's very young friend, actress Patricia Peardon, called her with an alarming report. Perhaps over "pillow talk" with Nelson Rockefeller, Peardon had learned that J. Edgar Hoover of the FBI had amassed a dossier on both Tracy and Kate that "would stretch around a city block and then some." J. Edgar, according to Peardon, was making noises that he was about to destroy the careers of both Tracy and Kate herself.

For reasons known only to himself, J. Edgar had long been fascinated by the private lives of Katharine Hepburn and Spencer Tracy, Tracy even more than Kate.

A closeted and cross-dressing homosexual himself, J. Edgar was particularly intrigued by Tracy's gay life and the actor's patronage of male hustlers. He ordered his agents to dig up all the material they could find on both Kate and Tracy. Eventually, he accumulated massive documentation on Kate's lesbian affairs, especially with Laura Harding, the American Express heiress.

After Kate's speech attacking HUAC, J. Edgar became more determined than ever to expose both Kate and Tracy not only for what he alleged was their communist leanings, but for their private lives as well.

As he told his associates, "Just wait and see what happens when America learns that its self-styled most ideal couple are really a faggot and a dyke."

Meeting with Nixon, he unveiled how he was going to help the HUAC committee members. At the end of their conversation, J. Edgar dropped a "bombshell" about Hepburn and Tracy.

Although he thought that he'd be applauded by Nixon for his efforts, the young congressman was horrified about the Hepburn/Tracy file J. Edgar revealed to him, but for reasons that the FBI chief had not anticipated.

"For the very precise reason that Tracy and Hepburn are America's most ideal couple is why you have to burn this file," Nixon warned J. Edgar. "It will kick back on all of us and all the work we're doing to clean out the Commies. Hepburn and Tracy are too much of an entrenched institution by now. Besides, all these revelations about homosexual stuff would be too much. There are homosexuals working everywhere."

Perhaps Nixon was sending a subtle signal to J. Edgar when he delivered his final zinger. "There are even homosexuals working for the FBI!"

The conclusion of the dialogue between Nixon and J. Edgar isn't known. However, J. Edgar must have gotten the message, because he destroyed most of the Hepburn/Tracy file, leaving only some minor and relatively unimportant details, such as press clippings about Kate's speech in Los Angeles.

As Nixon later told his cronies, "I personally saved the career of Tracy and Hepburn. They may never know that, but they should always be in my debt. I kept that fag from blowing the whistle on America's favorite box-office love birds."

Nixon even quoted himself, "Drag Tracy and Hepburn through the mud and you'll trigger a backlash."

Years later, when Joseph Mankiewicz heard about the Nixon/Hoover meeting, he weighed in with his own assessment. "If the American public had learned that Father Flanagan was cheating on his sainted wife, Louise, with a Bryn Mawr lesbian, it would have triggered a nation-wide scandal. It would even have undermined the film industry. Besides, it would definitely have killed Spence's image to learn that he had beaten up whores in bordellos and rented male hustlers. His having an extramarital affair with Hepburn would have been the least shocking revelation. Could you see Tracy being convincing as Elizabeth Taylor's dad in *Father of the Bride* if the public knew that he was a closeted cocksucker in his private life?"

When Harry Truman learned of the FBI file on Hepburn and Tracy, he more or less agreed with Nixon, perhaps the only time these two political enemies ever agreed on anything. "Let it lay," Truman advised J. Edgar. "Don't touch that with a ten-foot pole. You say you're going after communists—that's enough. Don't start seeking out homosexuals, much less lesbians, or else we'll go back to burning people at the stake in America, like they did in Salem."

Throughout his life, Nixon remained image-conscious. In 1956 when he was running for vice president on a ticket with Eisenhower, his media

Even though **Spencer Tracy** was married to another woman, news of his association with **Katharine Hepburn** was widely accepted as a passionate affair throughout Hollywood.

Their closest friend, director George Cukor, knew differently. According to him, they had more of a platonic relationship. Tracy was a closeted homosexual, with occasional affairs with women, and Hepburn was a closeted lesbian with occasional affairs with men.

Ironically, Richard Nixon became their "guardian angel" because of his having persuaded J. Edgar not to expose "this all-American couple."

adviser was Edward A. Rogers, who arranged for him to appear on a televised question-and-answer session at Cornell University. Facing a barrage of some of the toughest questions of his career, Nixon appeared in total control as he answered his attackers.

Yet afterwards, when Nixon boarded the campaign plane with Rogers, he yelled at him. "You son of a bitch! You put me on with those fucking, asshole, liberal sons of bitches. You tried to destroy me in front of thirty million people!" Completely losing control, Nixon physically attacked Rogers, pounding his face until two newspapermen restrained the vice president.

That same year, 1956, Nixon wrote a joint letter to Kate and Tracy, seeking their support for his election campaign with Eisenhower. "I think you owe me a favor," he said. "It is important that we carry California and if you can get some of your many friends and admirers to support us, it might help in what could shape up to be a close race."

It is presumed that at this point, Nixon knew that both Kate and Tracy had become fully aware of his efforts to have J. Edgar destroy their FBI files. He sent the message in the form of a typewritten personal letter, and arranged for it to be hand-delivered to Kate at her home.

Kate, as she told director George Cukor, was startled. "I don't think I had ever received a letter addressed to 'Miss Katharine Hepburn and Mr. Spencer Tracy' before. Did you notice he put my name first? Smart man." That very afternoon she wrote back to Nixon. Tracy chose not to respond.

"I heard what you did to help maintain my privacy, and I guess in my way I'll always be grateful for that. However, I must also be true to my convictions, and I believe that my parents would disown me if I offered my support in any way to a Republican vice-presidential candidate. Mr. Tracy shares my convictions."

She signed her note to the White House as: THE LADY IN RED.

In March of 1945, as WWII was coming to its long, dreadful end that would see the arrival of the Atomic Age in August, much of the attention of America was focused on the newly formed United Nations meeting in San Francisco. The temporary Secretary General of the UN was Alger Hiss, who would soon become a household word in the country, but for the wrong reasons.

Handsome, articulate, and debonair, Hiss was an American lawyer, government official, author, and lecturer, the son of an old Maryland family. His father had committed suicide when the boy was two years old. He grew up in "shabby gentility" but managed to receive a law degree from Harvard, where he had been a *protégé* of Felix Frankfurter, the future U.S. Supreme Court Justice. In 1933, Hiss became an attorney for FDR's New Deal.

He served various positions in the Department of Justice and Department of State. President Roosevelt respected him so highly that he invited him to attend the Yalta Conference in February of 1944, where he negotiated with Josef Stalin and Winston Churchill.

There had been rumblings, mostly from J. Edgar at the FBI, that Hiss was a communist. When President Truman heard of these, he told Treasury Secretary Henry Morgenthau Jr. that the reports were "either history, hypothesis, or deduction."

Truman also told his chief military liaison, General Harry Vaughan, "Hoover reminds me of a movie I once saw with Bess. I don't remember the name. In it, Marjorie Main was spreading vicious rumors across the back fence to her neighbors. Hoover is that nasty old maid gossip. What if I acted on all the gossip spread about him? In his case, and I know this for a fact, the gossip is true. Let's face it: He's as queer as a three-dollar bill."

J. Edgar resented the establishment of the United Nations, and was alarmed that Hiss was playing such a large role in its formation. "It will give every commie country in the world the ability to send spies to America with diplomatic immunity," he told his aides.

Clyde was ordered to round up some of the FBI's best agents and have them work behind the scenes to gather incriminating evidence against Hiss. Wiretapping was not enough. Clyde even put the Hiss household maid on the FBI payroll as a domestic spy. When J. Edgar's chief agent in London reported that Hiss had dined with Eleanor Roosevelt and Adlai Stevenson, J. Edgar proclaimed, "Now I know the fucker is a communist."

J. Edgar's own appearances before HUAC were rare but momentous occasions. A bystander, Walter Goodman, remembered one visit. "Hoover

Of all the hundreds of people accused of Soviet espionage, **Alger Hiss** *(above)*, an American lawyer and government official, became the most celebrated case.

When Hiss became the temporary secretary-general of the then-new United Nations, J. Edgar ordered Clyde to "have our agents work overtime. This is going big."

Eventually, he wasn't convicted of espionage, but of perjury, and sentenced to prison in January of 1950, ordered to serve two concurrent five-year sentences. He ended up serving three and a half years.

appeared before HUAC like an archbishop—no, the Pope—paying a call on a group of poor priests. He patronized them as they fussed over him. He was King of the Hill."

On August 3, 1948, the rather nerdy Whittaker Chambers was called as a friendly witness to testify before HUAC. The writer and editor was a favorite of Henry Luce, publisher of *Time* and *Life* magazines.

Pudgy and with a double chin, the Philadelphia-born writer had grown up in Brooklyn. There had been mental illness in his family, including his grandmother. After one year in college, his brother had committed suicide, which Chambers cited as one of the many reasons he had been drawn to the Communist Party when he was still a young man.

In 1931, Chambers married an artist, Esther Shemitz. When she became pregnant, certain key party members demanded that he and his wife abort their child, because having to tend to a baby might interfere with their work. He was told that his responsibility involved carrying out the party's work—not tying himself down to a family. Both Chambers and Esther decided to disobey these harsh instructions, and they went ahead and gave birth to their child. Later, Chambers would claim that the abortion demand marked the beginning of his disillusionment with the Communist party.

J. Edgar and Clyde vetted Chambers before he appeared on the HUAC stand. Chambers told them that he had spied for the Soviets throughout most of the 1930s, but that he had abandoned the party in 1937 when he lost faith in the movement in the wake of Josef Stalin's Great Purge of 1936.

He warned these G-Men that in an attempt to discredit him, the opposing side might bring up the numerous homosexual liaisons he'd enjoyed in the 1930s with young men. "Be prepared," he warned J. Edgar. "They'll bring it up for sure, and all of it is very true. I had numerous encounters in Washington and in New York, great cruising grounds for a man of my tastes." As it would turn out, Chambers had given the FBI only a limited report.

On August 3, 1948, he testified before HUAC, naming people who were part of a Communist underground in the 1930s. The most prominent man he cited was Alger Hiss, a name known to thousands upon thousands of Americans.

Hiss, of course, was summoned before the committee. Initially, he asserted that he did not know Chambers. However, under intensive questioning, and after seeing him up close and in person, Hiss admitted that he had known him in the 1930s under the name of "George Crosley." He claimed that he hardly knew "the deadbeat but I gave him my 1929 Ford when I found out he had no transportation. It was worth twenty-five dollars."

Up until then, Chambers had not presented much evidence that Hiss was a communist. J. Parnell Thomas wanted to establish a stronger link. Hiss testified that he gave the car away when he purchased a new one in June of 1935.

But then the FBI learned that Hiss didn't purchase a new car until three months later. This connection was deemed so important that W. Marvin Smith was called to testify. A member of the Justice Department, he had notarized the transfer of title.

But before he could testify, he fell from a five-story stairwell at the Justice Department, plunging to his death. A woman clerk claimed she heard two men shouting at each other in the hallway before the sound of a blood-curdling scream went out. There was speculation that somebody had pushed Smith to his death. Additional speculations surmised that it might have been a suicide. There seemed no other way that he could have fallen over the stairwell's protective banister.

Without any hard core evidence, most HUAC members seemed to take Hiss at his word. But he had two sworn enemies out to get him, namely J. Edgar and a young committee member from California, Richard Nixon.

J. Edgar ordered Clyde to devote all his time to an entrapment of Hiss. At Harvey's Restaurant they were seen dining with Karl Earl Mundt, a member of the Senate from South Dakota from 1948 to 1973. Mundt was a key participant in the Hiss/Chambers hearings, and also became a key figure in creating the Hollywood Blacklist.

In time, he would join with Nixon in helping pass a bill to require communists in the U.S. to register with the government and to prevent them from holding public office. Clyde passed along what information they'd gathered on Hiss. As it unraveled, it became obvious that the situation was far more complicated that either Hiss or Chambers had revealed so far.

Years later, in 1960, Mundt reflected on the heyday of the witch hunt.

Pudgy **Whittaker Chambers**, with a record of homosexuality, became the man liberal America loved to hate. A former Communist Party member, he was the key witness in the espionage trial of Alger Hiss. Chambers had had a sexual affair with both Hiss and with Hiss's stepson.

Richard Nixon detested Chambers, but knew that he'd be an effective witness in bringing about the downfall of the once influential Hiss.

Events swirling around the Hiss/Chambers case became Act One in what evolved into the "Red Hunt" orchestrated by Senator Joseph McCarthy.

"Without this case, the McCarthy thing might have been a stillborn," Nixon claimed to his aides. "Sometimes these queers [a reference to both Chambers and Hiss] can be useful."

Although a champion of the Far Right, he nonetheless denounced J. Edgar "as the most dangerous man in the United States. He has misused his office and done things to congressmen and senators that should never have happened. He has accumulated blackmail on everybody." J. Edgar repeatedly denied the existence of such dossiers, but he lied.

Nixon seized upon the Hiss/Chambers case as the cannon to launch himself like a fireball into national prominence. Under intensive grilling by the ambitious Nixon, Chambers admitted that he and Hiss had been lovers, and he'd preserved dozens of souvenirs from the relationship, including a crushed cigarette butt, a pair of trousers worn by Hiss, and fabric from a battered old love seat on which they had kissed. He also revealed that Hiss had supplied him with a rent-free apartment.

After Hiss became tired of Chambers, Chambers claimed that he had become sexually involved with the stepson of Hiss, Timothy Hiss, who had taken the name of his stepfather.

Lending credence to Chambers' claim was a review of documents that revealed that Timothy had been discharged from the Navy in 1945 on a charge of homosexuality.

Eventually, Nixon decided that the homosexual relationships were "just too much to spring on the public—those lying queers!" He felt that the best option would involve an entrapment of Hiss in perjury. He had already denounced Hiss to the press, criticizing his "condescending demeanor before the committee, which I found insulting in the extreme."

President Truman denounced the Hiss-Chambers conflict as a "Red Herring, a desperate move on the part of the Republicans to regain power after being confined to the wilderness for sixteen long years." Bowing to pressure, however, especially from the FBI, he did initiate a program of loyalty reviews for Federal employees in 1947.

Truman's loyalty oath affected some 2.1 million Federal employees. It was officially decided that no government worker could belong to any group considered "totalitarian, Fascist, Communist, or subversive."

Both Nixon and J. Edgar pressured Chambers to come up with some other strong evidence to implicate Hiss in treasonous wrongdoings, since they did not want to introduce the subject of homosexuality into the hearings.

Whereas Chambers was protected from libel litigation for whatever he said during the HUAC hearings, that protection did not apply to other venues. When he repeated his charges on radio, Hiss filed a $75,000 libel suit against him on October 8, 1948.

Under increasing pressure, Chambers produced four notes in Hiss's handwriting, sixty-five copies of typewritten State Department documents, and five strips of microfilm, some of which contained photographs of State Department documents. This evidence became infamously known as "The Pumpkin Papers," because Chambers had hidden the documents in a hollowed-out pumpkin in his garden. This data was turned over by Chambers to HUAC as proof that Hiss was engaged in espionage for the Soviet Union.

On an ocean cruise with Patricia Nixon, Nixon landed in Florida in front of waiting reporters. He announced he was returning at once to Washington to pursue the case against Hiss. "Now we have conclusive proof of the greatest conspiracy in the nation's history."

Both J. Edgar and Nixon knew that Hiss could not be tried for espionage, because the statute of limitations had long ago expired. Instead, Nixon pressed for an indictment for two counts of perjury, the main charge being that Hiss had denied giving any documents to Chambers. The second perjury charge was associated with Hiss's testimony that he hadn't seen his former friend after mid-1936.

During the first trial of Hiss, character witnesses in his defense included Supreme Court Justice Felix Frankfurter and Adlai Stevenson.

Hiss was tried in June of 1949 for perjury, but the case ended with the jury deadlocked eight to four for conviction. The key piece of evidence had involved an old Woodstock typewriter owned by Hiss. Its typeface matched the documents submitted by Chambers. Experts who had compared the documents from Hiss's machine and the Chambers papers had defined them as a perfect match.

Hiss's lawyers had brought in experts who testified that since 1944 typewriters could be doctored. A U.S. army technician testified that during World War II, military intelligence could reproduce faultlessly the imprint of any typewriter on earth.

Nixon was so furious that four members of the Hiss jury had voted for acquittal that he threatened to haul them before HUAC to be grilled for any possible communist connection.

The first trial had lasted from May 31, 1949 to July 7, and had resulted in a deadlocked jury. A second trial, under a new judge, lasted from November 17, 1949 to January 21, 1950, resulting in a conviction and a sentence of five years, of which Hiss could serve three and a half.

The implications of the Hiss trial reverberated through American lives. It thrust Nixon into the spotlight, helping him move, after the elections of 1950, from the House of Representatives to the U.S. Senate, and then on to greater glory and later infamy. As a catalyst to later developments, the Hiss case is still being debated today.

Based on Justice Department documents released in 1976, the Hiss defense team tried to get a Federal judge to reopen the cased based on prosecutorial misconduct, segments of which included the introduction of typewritten documents that could have been forged.

They presented evidence that J. Edgar knew that there was an inconsistency in the serial number of the Woodstock typewriter presented in court as evidence and the one that Hiss actually owned. On orders from J. Edgar, the FBI deliberately withheld this vital piece of evidence which might have exonerated Hiss.

But in 1982, the Federal court denied the petition for a retrial, and in 1983, the U.S. Supreme Court declined to hear an appeal.

Testimony showed that J. Edgar and Clyde had visited a secret OSS installation in Canada where typewriter fabrication and other acts of espionage were under wartime development.

John Dean, former attorney for Nixon, claimed in a 1976 memoir that the President's chief counsel, Charles Colson, told him that Nixon had admitted that the typewriter had been fabricated in an FBI laboratory. "We built one in the Hiss case," Nixon allegedly said.

"Had Nixon asked the FBI to manufacture evidence to prove the case against Hiss," claimed former FBI Assistant Director William C. Sullivan, "I'm sure Hoover would have been only too glad to oblige."

When confronted, Nixon denied that he ever made such a claim about the typewriter, contradicting his former attorney... but then, Nixon was not always known for telling the truth.

In 1952, Chambers wrote a best-selling book *Witness*, which Ronald Reagan credited as the inspiration behind his conversion from a New Deal Democrat to a conservative Republican. Chambers died of a heart attack in July of 1961 on his 300-acre farm in Westminster, Maryland.

Eventually, the committee chairman of HUAC, J. Parnell Thomas, ran into his own legal problems. Columnist Drew Pearson exposed corruption in Thomas' office in a newspaper article published on August 4, 1948. Thomas' personal secretary, Helen Campbell, sent documents to Pearson, claiming that since 1940 she had placed Myra Midkiff on his payroll as a clerk, earning $1,500 a month. Midkiff did no work but kicked back all her salary to Thomas to supplement his meager income and avoid taxes.

Before a Grand Jury, Thomas refused to answer questions, just like many a communist sympathizer had done when hauled before HUAC. He pleaded the Fifth Amendment against self-incrimination. Tried and convicted of fraud, he was given an eight-month prison term.

When Thomas was sent to the Federal prison in Danville, Connecticut, his sentence included an ironic touch. Fellow inmates included both Lester Cole and Ring Lardner, Jr., two members of the "Hollywood Ten," whom he had sent to jail during his ill-fated tenure as head of HUAC.

Very generously, President Truman pardoned Thomas on Christmas Eve in 1952. In the President's words, "I'm letting the man who tried to destroy my presidency out of jail."

After his release from prison, Thomas admitted that the HUAC hearings had been inspired by Hugh Scott, the Republican National Committee's chairman, "He told me to set up all that spy stuff to keep the heat on Truman and the Democrats."

Truman had left office by 1953 when J. Edgar made a rare appearance before the U.S. Senate. His frustration, even his anger, over Truman was still so strong at this point that in front of the law-making body he called the former President a liar.

After retiring from office, Truman later remembered, "All that witch hunting, all those ruined lives. The Constitution had never been in such danger. Could you imagine Nixon as President one day, with Hoover as his Vice President? It would be Hitler and Goebbels all over again." Tanked up on bourbon, he said that one night at Sheriff John Spottswood's home in Key West, Florida in 1959.

The case of Alger Hiss became the most controversial, the most de-

With his chipmunk cheeks, this is one of the grimmest pictures ever taken of **Richard M. Nixon**, a congressman from California who was moving up the ladder of government, based to a large degree on the notorious Alger Hiss/ Whittaker Chambers case.

Eager for the publicity, Nixon spearheaded the investigation of Hiss, garnering one headline after another.

"I want to be known as the mighty warrior against commies. A politician can make his reputation chasing commies in the State Department."

Nixon configured the Hiss Case as the first crisis in his best-selling 1962 book *Six Crises*, which was his eulogy to himself.

bated, and the most celebrated case of communist espionage during the Cold War. Hiss died in 1996, taking his personal secrets to the grave. Today, pro-Hiss and anti-Hiss historians continue to debate his guilt or innocence.

As late as 2007, researchers probing Soviet archives made claims ranging from "We found no mention of Hiss" to "His name appears countless times—he was a spy all right. Guilty as hell!"

***

Two weeks after the conviction of Alger Hiss, an ambitious young junior senator from Wisconsin sat in an airport lounge in the nation's capital. Waiting for his plane, he'd just ordered his fourth glass of Jack Daniels on the rocks.

All his fellow Republican senators were fanning out across the nation to make speeches on Lincoln's Birthday, February 9, 1950. Instead of New York, Los Angeles, or Chicago, Joseph McCarthy had been assigned to what he called "the backwaters of America," beginning in Wheeling, West Virginia. This former dirt farm boy, contemptuously said to his aide, "The town is probably inhabited by redneck aborigines." He was to address the Republican Women's Club—or, in his words, "a lot of blue-haired old farts who probably were last fucked before World War II."

An alcoholic, McCarthy was drunk when his limousine pulled up at the McClure Hotel in Wheeling. But, as he so often bragged, "Keep the bourbon coming, 'cause Joe is a guy who can hold his liquor."

As he walked into the crowded room, he was reasonably steady on his feet, and, except for a few slurred words, he seemed physically under control. He might have been assigned a backwater, but he'd vowed that by the end of his speech, he would garner more headlines than all the senior senators on Lincoln's Birthday.

Waiting to be introduced, McCarthy had whispered to his aide, "The House Un-American Activities Committee think they can make headlines with their witch hunt. You ain't seen nothing yet. Watch me go! I'm gonna round up commies like Hitler's boys rounded up the Jews."

A man of his word, bellicose and shameless, the senator faced a field of right-wing women who thought even President Truman was a communist taking orders from Stalin.

That afternoon, he stroked the fiery furnace of the "Red Menace," and subsequently, its flames would engulf much of American life and culture until they consumed even the senator himself.

CHAPTER NINE

No actual audio recording exists of that drunken speech that Senator Joseph McCarthy gave to the Republican Women's Club in Wheeling, West Virginia, on February 9, 1950, in honor of Lincoln's birthday. But it became a speech of legend.

As recorded in handwriting by a local reporter on note paper, McCarthy electrified the women by claiming, "The State Department is infested with communists. I have here in my hand a list of 205 names that were made known to the Secretary of State as being members of the Communist Party and who nevertheless are still working and shaping policy in the State Department."

He also claimed that Dean Acheson, the Secretary of State, was "a pompous diplomat in striped pants, with a phony British accent."

The speech was delivered at a crucial moment in the Cold War. China had fallen to the Communists, Alger Hiss had been convicted of perjury, Eastern Europe had come under the domination of Josef Stalin, and the Soviet Union knew how to manufacture an atomic bomb.

A German-born scientist and naturalized British citizen, Klaus Fuchs, was convicted in 1950 of supplying information about the Manhattan Project to the Soviet Union. From late 1947 to May 1949, he gave a Soviet agent the principal theoretical outline for creating a hydrogen bomb.

Press interest in McCarthy's speech would explode like another atomic bomb, but it was at first slow to build. Eighteen newspapers carried a report of his speech after the Associated Press filed the story on February 10. By February 11, ten other newspapers carried the senator's accusations. The *Nashville Tennessean* accepted McCarthy's word at face value, with a headline—STATE DEPARTMENT HAS 205 COMMIES.

His next stops were Salt Lake City, Denver, and Reno. By the time McCarthy's plane set down in Reno that Saturday, the State Department was demanding that he produce the list of these "so-called commies." The senator faced a major embarrassment. He had no such list.

He claimed to the press he had been misquoted as to the number. "I've got a sockful of shit," he told reporters, "and I know how to sling it. There

A false smile hides a soul of evil and malice on the face of **Senator Joseph McCarthy** of Wisconsin. With a lot of help from J. Edgar Hoover, McCarthy created the "Red Scare" of the 1950s, eventually transforming himself into the most hated senator in the history of the Republic.

Bellicose and shameless, he was an extraordinary witch hunter, whipping up hysteria across the land and ruining lives.

are 57 card-carrying communists in the State Department." The number had shrunk since Wheeling. At every stop in West Virginia, he was besieged by reporters.

He'd succeeded in capturing the nation's attention. In Washington, President Truman privately denounced McCarthy as a "drunk and a liar," and in public he claimed his statements were not true. "McCarthy is not even fit to have a hand in the operation of the United States government."

Immediately after he landed in Washington, McCarthy placed an urgent call to J. Edgar, who had befriended him since 1946, viewing him "as a soldier in the field against the Red Menace."

Soon McCarthy was dining with J. Edgar and Clyde at Harvey's. Over a blood-red steak and several glasses of bourbon, he told the G-Men, "I don't have such a list. I just made up the whole thing to get a headline or two."

The next day J. Edgar, Clyde, and Lou Nichols became a virtual public relations firm for McCarthy, even writing some of his speeches and changing his accusations to "communist sympathizers" or "loyalty risks," since these charges would be easier to prove than "card-carrying communists." J. Edgar also suggested to McCarthy that he hire Donald Surine, a former FBI agent, as a private investigator "to dig up the dirt on the commies."

McCarthy also received help from Richard Nixon, who secretly gave him classified files from the House Un-American Activities Committee.

Another well-wisher was Ronald Reagan.

During the McCarthy hearings, many actors such as John Wayne wanted to ingratiate themselves with J. Edgar, knowing how powerful he was and aware that he could destroy carefully constructed careers.

Before the Republican Convention of 1952, Ronald Reagan sent J. Edgar a confidential memo. "Whatever you do, you should do all you can to prevent the emergence of Thomas Dewey if he dares seek the nomination, having failed in 1944 and 1948. On his swing through California during one of his campaigns, he said there were not enough jails in America to hold all the people he planned to convict. 'The first person I will put in jail is John Edgar Hoover himself.' I thought you should know what an enemy he is. I want you to know that in any future conflict like that, I am definitely inclined to side with America's esteemed FBI director."

Back in Washington, a new type of political war cloud loomed on the home front as America prepared to go to war again, this time in Korea to prevent a communist takeover.

The Tydings subcommittee opened its hearings on McCarthy's charges on March 8, 1950 in the Senate Caucus Room.

Senator Millard Tydings wanted McCarthy to name names to back up his accusations, but McCarthy floundered. Actually, Surine had hardly begun his investigations into the Red Menace.

Under pressure, McCarthy introduced the names of nine men and women whom he claimed were communist sympathizers. One person cited was Dorothy Kenyon, a sixty-two-year-old New York lawyer who told the press, "Senator McCarthy is a liar." An embarrassment for McCarthy followed when it was revealed that Kenyon had never been a member of the State Department.

Although headlines in the Hearst papers screamed NEW YORK LAWYER LINKED TO REDS, *The New York Times* noted that "Joe got off to a thin start." As it turned out, Kenyon was a friend of Eleanor Roosevelt. In her column, *My Day*, she wrote: "If all of the honorable senator's 'subversives' are as subversive as Miss Kenyon, I think the State Department is entirely safe and the nation will continue on an even keel."

It also turned out that Kenyon had been a delegate to the United Nations Commission on the Status of Women from 1947 to 1949 and had clashed bitterly with representatives from the Soviet Union, denouncing them.

At the end of the hearing, the first of McCarthy's attempts to expose a communist, the *Washington Post* noted: "In truth, Case no. 1, turned out to be not only an outraged and innocent American, but also a woman of spirit."

At midpoint, Chairman Tydings told the press that McCarthy had not provided his committee with the "name of a single State Department employee accused of being a communist."

The next day McCarthy fired back that he was going to reveal "the name of the man, connected with the State Department whom I consider the top Russian espionage agent in this country."

In an emergency call that night to J. Edgar's home, McCarthy sounded desperate. "I don't know why, but that statement about my naming this big communist just popped out of my head. You've got to help me. I'm going to have to face Tydings, and I've got to come up with someone."

"Clyde's here with me," J. Edgar said. "We'll come up with someone, maybe not a household name. But before the dawn breaks, we'll have that name for you."

Although his support from the right wing in American politics mushroomed overnight, many newspapers shot back at McCarthy. The *Washington Post* accused him of "sewer politics—rarely has a man in public life crawled and squirmed so abjectly."

McCarthyism began to seep into all corners of American culture.

A jittery Hollywood studio cancelled a movie based on Longfellow's *Hiawatha* out of fear it would be viewed as "communist peace propaganda." Citizens demanded that librarians remove books from the shelves, including *Adventures of Robin Hood*, because of "its subversive message." The Cincinnati Reds temporarily changed the name of their team to "Redlegs." In New York, even washroom attendants had to submit to loyalty tests.

Shortly after she won the Oscar for *Born Yesterday*, **Judy Holliday** was profiled in *Hollywood Life* by right-wing columnist Jimmy Tarantino:

"Judy Holliday only acts dumb. She's a smart cookie. The commies got her a long time ago. She was a singer with the National Council of Arts and Sciences and Professions, a commie front group. In 1948, she was a guest speaker during a rally at New York's Hotel Astor for the STOP CENSORSHIP COMMITTEE, a communist front. She was sponsor for the World Federation of Democratic Youth, a known communist front. In 1948, she wired greetings of good luck to the Moscow Art Theatre. She is a supporter of the Civil Rights Congress, a Red outfit. She performed at a dance sponsored by the *Commie Daily Worker*. She always knew what she was doing."

***

While they worked with McCarthy to dig up communists in the government, especially the State Department, J. Edgar and Clyde also focused on weeding out communists in the film industry.

Far more intriguing than hunting down public enemies such as John Dillinger in the 1930s, J. Edgar and Clyde especially liked to investigate the private lives of movie stars if they found evidence of homosexuality, regardless of how infrequent the occurrence.

Judy Holliday, the brilliant blonde-haired comedienne of the 1940s and 50s, came into their focus, as they'd receive several calls from "informers," claiming that she was a member of the Communist Party.

The daughter of Russian-Jewish immigrants, she grew up in a world of Yiddish culture. Although known for her dumb blonde roles, such as that of Billie Dawn in the Oscar-winning performance in *Born Yesterday* (1950), she had an IQ score of 172, placing her above the 99.999[th] percentile.

The FBI launched an investigation of her in 1950, but after three months found no direct evidence of her communist links. They were willing to give her a pass, as they'd learned far more about her sex life than her politics.

Like so many actresses they probed, they found that Judy, in addition to her affairs with several men, also had lesbian liaisons. It appeared that she'd lost her virginity to Yetta Cohn, a prominent policewoman in New York who reportedly did have links to the Communist Party. Agents also discovered that Judy had her first heterosexual experience with the British actor John Buckmaster, whom she alleged had raped her.

She'd also had high-profile affairs with journalist Heywood Hale Broun, Sydney Chaplin (son of Charlie), jazz musician Gerry Mulligan, and even Peter Lawford when he wasn't sleeping with one of his boys.

J. Edgar and Clyde were well aware of Katharine Hepburn's lesbian adventures, so they were not surprised that Judy shared her bed at Hepburn's Turtle Bay residence in Manhattan on many a night. Judy was appearing in Garson Kanin's film *Adam's Rib*, directed by George Cukor and starring Kate's companion, Spencer Tracy, who was well aware of Kate's fascination with Judy.

So many "stool pigeons" cited Judy as a communist that in 1952 she was called upon to testify before the Senate Internal Security Subcommittee to "explain" why her name was linked to so many communist front groups.

Garson Kanin, who wrote *Born Yesterday*, was also being labeled a communist. Along with Kanin, Judy began to appear on the *Red Channels* list. The Catholic War Veterans had picketed *Born Yesterday* when it played on Broadway, and placards had denounced Judy as a Red. She suddenly faded from radio and television, because pressure groups warned sponsors not to use her.

Even her Oscar win did not help her case. NBC pulled the plug on a proposed variety show that could have made her wealthy. Liggett and Meyers also cancelled her appearance on the Bob Hope Show, not wanting their product, Chesterfield cigarettes, to be linked to a woman who had donated a hundred dollars to the Peace Crusade.

At Columbia, studio boss Harry Cohn withdrew his bid to purchase

Gentlemen Prefer Blondes for Judy, the career-making role eventually going to Marilyn Monroe, another not-so-dumb blonde.

Privately, two senators called Judy and told her that if she would appear at the Senate hearings and name just four communists, the pressure on her would end. She told Katharine Hepburn that she would view such testimony as a "betrayal of former friends."

On July 12, 1950 before her appearance, she sent Lou Nichols at the FBI a sworn statement, denouncing communism and denying that she had been a member of the party. She pleaded with him to present the document to J. Edgar himself. There was no response from the director.

In spite of her intelligence, Judy's attorney told her to play the role of the dumb blonde at the hearings, and she followed that advice, giving her best Billie Dawn impersonation. Before the committee, she'd claimed she'd been taken advantage of by communist front groups using her name without her permission.

She was cleared of any wrongdoing, but her career was seriously damaged. "Survival is not enough," she told Cukor. "My public image has been tainted. People will forever think I'm a Red. After that grilling on the Hill, I've entered purgatory."

She continued to find work where she could, appearing in a 1960 film, *Bells Are Ringing. The New York Times* noted that "the squeaky voice, the embarrassed giggle, the brassy naïveté, the dimples, the teeter-totter walk remain unimpaired."

Disillusioned and saddened by life, Judy died of breast cancer on June 7, 1965.

Gloria Swanson had sent her a sympathy card of sorts. "I hope you get well, but I can never forgive you for taking that Oscar from me." The former silent screen vamp still harbored bitter feelings toward Judy for losing the Academy Award to her for Swanson's own role as Norma Desmond in *Sunset Blvd.*

***

One of J. Edgar's favorite frontal nudes was of the handsome, strapping actor, Sterling Hayden, once billed as "The Beautiful Blond Viking God."

He ran away to the sea at the age of seventeen and became a ship's boy. He was stalked day and night from the men aboard. "I had to beat off my admirers," he later claimed.

At six feet, five inches, he was one of the tallest actors in Hollywood, and was famous among the women for his endowment. An adventurer and man of action, he made grand voyages around the world, skippering a square rigger from Massachusetts to Tahiti in 1938. He was only twenty-two years old.

Drifting to Hollywood, he'd become a movie star, marrying his co-star, British-born Madeleine Carroll, one of the most elegantly beautiful leading ladies of the 1930s. The marriage lasted four years and wasn't helped when he joined the Marines in World War II.

During that war, J. Edgar was very distressed to learn that under the military pseudonym of "John Hamilton," Hayden had worked for William J. Donovan as an OSS agent. J. Edgar never got over his jealousy of "Wild Bill." J. Edgar and Clyde kept a dossier on Hayden, learning that along with Yugoslav partisans, he'd parachuted into fascist Croatia. He also was a hero of air crew rescue teams behind enemy lines in the Naples area.

J. Edgar admired actor **Sterling Hayden's** physique, not his left-wing politics. Unconventional and always controversial, he led a life of adventure on both land and sea.

His most famous screen performances included *The Asphalt Jungle,* during which he seduced Marilyn Monroe off screen in 1950, *Dr. Strangelove* in 1964, and *The Godfather* in 1972.

Dorothy Lamour, the close friend of J. Edgar and Clyde, made *Manhandled* with Hayden in 1949. "When he strips down, he truly lives up to his reputation as a Viking God. God himself did not make all men equal."

After the war, when he returned to Hollywood, Hayden became known for seducing his leading ladies, including Anne Baxter in *Blaze of Noon*; J. Edgar's friend Dorothy Lamour in *Manhandled*; Marilyn Monroe in *The Asphalt Jungle*, and Jane Wyman, the former Mrs. Ronald Reagan, in *So Big*. He was going to play Quint in *Jaws* but couldn't come back into the United States because he'd be arrested for tax evasion.

After Lex Barker left the Tarzan role, it was offered to Hayden, but he found it undignified to play a character who swings on a vine from tree to tree.

In 1945, he'd been so impressed with the bravery of his communist partisans that he briefly joined the Communist Party. J. Edgar discovered that membership and in 1951 presented it to the House Un-American Activities Committee who called upon Hayden to testify.

Under pressure to keep his career and livelihood, Hayden was coerced into naming names in the film industry with links to the party. In a move so uncharacteristic of him, he cited Bea Winters, a stenographer for Horizon Pictures; Abraham Polonsky, author of the film noir classic *Body and Soul* (1947), as well as Robert Lees (*Abbot and*

Costello Meet Frankenstein; 1948). He also named other industry workers but later said, "It was the stupidest, most ignorant thing I ever did in my life."

Winters was fired the next day, and Polonsky would have to wait two decades before he got another screen credit. Lees never wrote another screenplay.

Ronald Reagan, president of the AFL Screen Actors Guild, said, "The guild congratulates Sterling Hayden on his honesty and frankness in his testimony which confirms the fact that the guild, with the full support of 98% of the Hollywood actors, defeated the Communist Party's attempts to use the guild for their causes."

Later on, Hayden, contemptuous of his HUAC testimony, called it a "one-shot stoolie show." In his autobiography, he wrote, "I was a real daddy longlegs of a worm when it came to crawling. Not often does a man find himself eulogized for having behaved in a manner that he himself despises."

After his testimony and upon his return to the screen, Hayden became the first actor subpoenaed by HUAC to land a major acting assignment after admitting to having been a member of the Communist Party, if only for seven months.

A heavy drinker all his life, Hayden suffered a complete nervous breakdown in 1972. For a while, he gave up liquor, turning to marijuana and hashish—"grass and hash," as he called it.

In the 1970s he wore a gray beard. "I never want to be taken for a male starlet again like I was in the 1940s. Never again will I be a pinup boy for J. Edgar Hoover." Somehow over the years, he must have learned that the FBI director was in possession of that frontal nude of him.

In Sausalito in 1986, Hayden died of prostate cancer after a long battle with the disease.

Writer Howard Skiles said, "He was always somehow larger than life, a pillar of strength and energy, a force of nature. That he could also act was sort of like putting a few stray diamonds on top of a solid gold Cadillac."

***

Woolworth heir and a cousin of Barbara Hutton, Jimmy Donahue was the archetypal post-war playboy known for his wit, charm, and gay personality. He made a career of mischief—his critics said evil. In 1949, at the age of thirty-five, he befriended the Duke and Duchess of Windsor, and became the lover of both of them. Around the world at all the glamorous watering holes, they were an inseparable trio. The royal couple became obsessed "with our darling Jimmy."

When news of this *ménage à trois* became public, the *New York Observer* wrote, "It's like finding out that the epic love affair of Abelard and Heloise was really just a quickie in a Left Bank nightclub's men's room."

In spite of Jimmy's notorious reputation, he still tried to be a good Catholic. In 1949, he'd met Cardinal Francis Spellman, the Archbishop of New York, who was very grateful for Jimmy's generous bequests to the New York Foundling Hospital. Through Spellman's sponsorship, Jimmy became its chairman.

""She married a King, but screwed a queen," as it was often said of the Duchess of Windsor, referring to her marriage to Edward VIII, which cost him his crown and to her affair with the homosexual **Jimmy Donahue,** the Woolworth heir.

He had a penchant for drag, as did his close friends J. Edgar and Cardinal Spellman.

He was born to be bad, and with his wealth and social position as the cousin of one of the world's richest women, Barbara Huttom, Jimmy pursued a life devoted to decadence and debauchery.

It didn't take Cardinal Spellman and Jimmy very long to figure out that they had more in common than their devotion to the Catholic Church. They both had a taste for well-endowed young male hustlers. With all those five-and-dime dollars from Woolworth's, Jimmy could purchase the very best.

As Jimmy's biographer, Christopher Wilson, stated: "Jimmy became intimately involved with Francis Spellman, the Archbishop of New York, a notorious homosexual. St. Patrick's Cathedral was a great cruising ground, particularly late Mass on a Sunday, and the Cardinal was rumored to have deflowered many young men."

Wilson also noted, Jimmy often went with the Cardinal "to get some new dresses," as Jimmy put it. Like J. Edgar, both men indulged in their penchant for drag. One tailor recalled the Cardinal calling out, "More lace! More lace!"

The author also claimed that after Jimmy broke up with the Windsors, Cardinal Spellman arranged for him to fly to Rome to meet the Holy Father. When Woolworth Donahue, Jimmy's brother, heard of this, he snidely remarked: "Now that he hasn't got the Windsors any more, I suppose he's gone to Rome to fuck the Pope."

J. Edgar and Clyde frequently visited New York and were often the guests of Cardinal Spellman. One Saturday night in 1950 he invited them to meet "this divine creature, Jimmy Donahue." The reputation of the playboy was already well known to the G-Men, who had a file on Jimmy and his many exploits.

At the appointed time, J. Edgar, Clyde, and Cardinal Spellman arrived at the apartment of Jessie Donahue, Jimmy's mother, at 834 Fifth Avenue. His mother was in Palm Beach at the time. A butler ushered them into a large living room filled with about twenty young and handsome men (average age of twenty-two) in provocative dress, each evoking an archetype—cowboy, truck driver, sailor, marine, boxer, or "nights in leather."

The arriving trio were directed to an elegant sofa where Jimmy had arranged himself. As he offered his hand to J. Edgar, the FBI director, perhaps with envy, took in his scarlet velvet haute couture ball gown. He had on a pair of "Joan Crawford fuck me" high heels.

When J. Edgar shook Jimmy's hand, he said, "If I had known, I would have dressed more formally," no doubt a reference to their mutual love of cross dressing.

"You *must*, dear heart," Jimmy said, "the next time."

Details are missing on that night, since Guy Hotell wasn't invited, but he heard about the party two days later. Apparently, three of the young men were professional strippers. According to Guy, Clyde confessed that he and J. Edgar around midnight disappeared with one of the well-muscled "Greek Gods" into one of Jimmy's bedrooms for a three-way. In those days, J. Edgar and Clyde liked to seduce a young man in the same bed.

After that night, Jimmy became "one of the delights" of J. Edgar and Clyde, according to Guy. "They shouted his praise. He could arrange things. J. Edgar and Clyde shared something in common with the Duke and Duchess of Windsor. Each member of this sponging quartet adored it when Jimmy picked up the tab, as he invariably did."

J. Edgar and Clyde learned something that Cardinal Spellman already knew. In the days when homosexuality was illegal, Jimmy gave the best of gay parties, where money was no object. "When it comes to men, I find that any guy can be had for a price. The only difference between a butch straight man and a gay one is a five-hundred dollar bill."

Often J. Edgar and Clyde were entertained in Jericho, Long Island, within the palatial mansion which had originally been built by Alfred Vanderbilt, and which Jimmy had purchased. According to gay underground legend, the parties "were wild, wild, and then some" in the seclusion of that mansion, and where Jimmy was known to have spiked many of his guest's cocktails with mysterious substances which included, among oth-

ers, Benzedrine.

It was inevitable that Jimmy would eventually be introduced by J. Edgar to his dear friend Ethel Merman. "We clicked from the first night I met him," Merman recalled. "He was my kind of guy. Like my favorite FBI man, Jimmy was partial to gowns."

"Jimmy was the Elsa Maxwell of the gay set," according to Merman. When his mother, Jessie, was away, he threw fabulous parties at her home, Cielito Lindo, in Palm Beach. That massive pile was a monument to social ambition.

Sometimes as many as thirty-five waiters would be hired for the night, with the provision they would wear only a G-string and make themselves available later that night to whatever male guests requested their services.

Guy related to his would-be biographer, James Kirkwood, the greatest scandal that ever took place at Cielito Lindo. Apparently, a drunken and drugged Jimmy had taken one of the handsome young waiters to his bedroom for amusement. As part of his perverted fun, he told the man that he'd give him a thousand-dollar bill if he'd let him shave off his pubic hair. The hapless victim agreed. Perhaps not deliberately but in his drugged condition, Jimmy accidentally cut off the young man's penis with a long, sharp razor. His screams echoed throughout the mansion.

Guy was fuzzy on what happened next. "Eddie was in Washington but he intervened somehow and got the whole thing hushed up. There was a big outlay of cash. I don't know how much. Just how much would you pay a man for cutting off his dick?"

As Guy claimed, "Jimmy Donahue became Ethel Merman's Stage Door Johnny, though she never lost her

When it came to male friends, **Ethel Merman**, the Queen of Broadway, had unusual taste in men. The ones she hung out with included J. Edgar, Clyde Tolson, and Jimmy Donahue, who backed her Broadway revival of *Annie Get Your Gun* shortly before his untimely death. "Life is outrageous," Merman said, "so why can't Jimmy be outrageous if he wants to?"

When Jimmy came backstage on opening night to take Merman to the Stork Club, he also invited her handsome, 6'5", curly-haired and blue-eyed leading man, Bruce Yarnell.

Merman went home alone that night. Jimmy invited Yarnell to his apartment, where, except for appearnces on stage, he remained for two and a half weeks.

Yarnell always claimed that he worked undercover for the FBI, but he never told his friends exactly what he was spying on. Merman once asked J. Edgar if Yarnell had ever worked for his Bureau. "He smiled enigmatically and told me he'd rather not discuss it."

affection for Clyde and Eddie. They knew that with her they could indulge and drop all that macho pretense."

Guy also recalled that one night Jimmy hosted a grand party for Merman at El Morocco in Manhattan. "The place was dripping with queens, and J. Edgar and Clyde sat drinking in the midst of it all. The only negative was when J. Edgar refused a drag queen's request to dance with him. I filled in for Eddie and later was awarded with a blow job in the men's room."

On a few occasions, Merman entertained what she called "the boys" at her apartment in Manhattan. She later said that Cardinal Spellman, J. Edgar, Clyde, and Jimmy would arrive in business suits. "While Clyde and I sat in my living room, the boys would disappear into my bedroom where I had laid out some gowns on my bed. It took them about an hour before they made their appearance in my living room dressed in all their finery. We always had such a gay old time back then. To entertain them, I played my recording of *Annie Get Your Gun*. Sometimes Jimmy would play the piano and accompany me as I sang 'There's No Business Like Show Business' to the boys. They applauded like there were fifty people in the room. It felt great."

In her autobiography, Merman claimed that she was invited to only the more respectable parties at Jericho, where women in elegant gowns appeared. "Even so, the talk at table in Jimmy's magnificent dining room got pretty racy. J. Edgar revealed sexual secrets of movie stars we'd never heard before, and I thought I'd heard them all. Did you know, for example, that James Stewart and Henry Fonda were lovers in the early 1930s? At Jericho, Jimmy was said to have hired partially deaf waiters so they couldn't eavesdrop and call the tabloids the next morning."

Jimmy and Merman remained friends for life. She'd once been hailed as the Queen of Broadway, but in her later years, engagements dwindled, as did her audience. Her friend, Dorothy Streslin, recalled that Jimmy would take her to a club in Manhattan on 53rd Street called The Lido. One night he invited J. Edgar and Clyde to hear her sing. As the manager said, "We had only about eight clients that night, but the applause of Donahue and those FBI boys made up for it."

To show his devotion to Merman, on September 21, 1966 Jimmy attended opening night of her revival of *Annie Get Your Gun* at the Broadway Theater. He'd backed the production with his own money.

J. Edgar and Clyde flew in for the occasion and attended a black-tie dinner and dance at Goldie's Restaurant on 42nd Street. In gratitude, Merman presented Jimmy with a pair of gold cufflinks. Jimmy died that year and was buried with those cufflinks.

When J. Edgar heard of his passing, he told Clyde, "I fear all the fun has gone out of our life. Jimmy knew how to have fun, and he knew that better than anyone."

***

In Miami, in May of 1945, J. Edgar had appeared before the International Association of Chiefs of Police and delivered an address. "In the war, foreign powers tried to steal not only the secrets of the atomic bomb but other vital military secrets. With the FBI's counter-espionage program, we encircled the spies and rendered them harmless."

J. Edgar viewed the trial of **Julius and Ethel Rosenberg** as the most sensational spy case of the Cold War. They were tried, convicted, and sentenced for passing atom bomb secrets to the Kremlin.

In sentencing the Rosenbergs, Judge Irving R. Kaufman claimed that "this country is engaged in a life-and-death struggle with a completely different system." Although the Rosenbergs had their defenders—and still do— many of the nation's press referred to their crime as "worse than murder." Even the Communist aggression in North Korea was blamed on the Rosenbergs.

Some observers believe that the data Julius passed to the Soviets was not information associated with the eventual creation of the atomic bomb in the Soviet Union.

At the time he made that speech, Soviet agents were stealing the concept for the development of an atomic bomb and passing this top secret data on to the Kremlin.

In a total breakdown of security, the Los Alamos project in New Mexico had hired an Army sergeant named David Greenglass to work as a machinist on elements of the interior of the first atomic bomb.

He passed the secrets he had gleaned from his work to his sister, Ethel Greenglass Rosenberg, a one-time member of the Communist Party. She in turn gave them to her communist husband, Julius Rosenberg. Through a courier, a chemist in Philadelphia named Harry Gold, these secrets made their way to Moscow. Within months, Russia was working on its own atomic bomb.

On August 29, 1949 the Soviets exploded their first nuclear test of "Joe I," named after Josef Stalin.

A German-born theoretical physicist, Karl Fuchs, was arrested in 1950 and tried for spying on the Manhattan Project for the Soviets. His statements to British and FBI intelligence, later at his trial, were used to further implicate Gold, who later became a key

329

witness in the subsequent trials of David Greenglass and Julius and Ethel Rosenberg.

Gold's arrest on May 23, 1950 led to a link with Sergeant David Greenglass.

Under intensive pressure from the FBI, David and his wife, Ruth Greenhouse, presented evidence to implicate both Ethel and Julius. She was the sister-in-law of Ruth and David was her brother, of course. It was a very damaging case the FBI had of family members testifying against each other.

Both Ruth and David testified against Ethel, claiming that she had typed up U.S. nuclear secrets in the Rosenberg apartment in New York in September of 1945. David also testified that he had turned over to Julius a sketch of the cross-section of an implosion type atomic bomb that was actually the "Fat Man" dropped on Nagasaki, Japan in 1945.

The Greenglasses presented their allegations to a Grand Jury in August of 1950, their testimony leading to the eventual arrests of both Julius and Ethel. When their trial began on March 6, 1961, it captured the attention of a nation caught up in Cold War hysteria and the McCarthy witch hunts.

As author Ronald Kessler wrote, "Her round face and tiny mouth and his mustache and protruding ears became burned into the American consciousness."

Morton Sobell was also arrested as part of the Soviet spy network and tried with the Rosenbergs.

Gold's testimony was crucial to the trial, and J. Edgar ordered his agents to spend four hundred hours going over and over his allegations. "I want him letter perfect when he goes on that stand," J. Edgar instructed his agents.

As former FBI man, William W. Turner, claimed, "The much-trumpeted FBI 'feat' in tracking down the spies was actually a case of closing the barn door after the horse was gone."

Both Ethel and Julius took the Fifth Amendment during their trial, saying that they refused to answer questions based on the fact that their answers might tend to incriminate them. On April 5 they were sentenced to death by Judge Irving Kaufman, their conviction helping both J. Edgar and McCarthy in their anti-communist campaign.

The Rosenbergs became the only two American civilians executed for espionage during the Cold War. Kaufman attacked them from the bench, claiming that their treachery might cost millions of innocent lives in the future.

Born to Jewish parents in New York, Ethel Greenglass and Julius

Rosenberg, later man and wife, became the most high-profile communist agents during the McCarthy era.

Many Americans believed the Rosenbergs were innocent and launched an unsuccessful grassroots campaign to prevent their going to the electric chair. Charges of anti-semitism were raised. An international uproar rose, Pablo Picasso calling it "a crime against humanity," Jean-Paul Sartre labeling it as a "legal lynching that smears with blood a whole nation." Pope Pius XII appealed to President Eisenhower to spare the couple, but Ike rejected the request coming from the Vatican. The Rosenbergs went to their deaths at New York's Sing Sing Prison on June 19, 1953.

Julius died after the first series of electrocutions, but Ethel did not. Doctors determined her heart was still beating. Three more courses of electrocution were ultimately applied before eyewitnesses reported smoke rising from her head.

To J. Edgar's credit, he had opposed the death sentence of Ethel, but agreed that Julius should face the chair. Clyde was of the opinion that both husband and wife "should feel the juice."

Sobell, the co-defendant, received a sentence of thirty years in prison, but served slightly less than eighteen years.

The debate over their guilt or innocence continues. However, in 1995, once secret information decoded from Soviet cables, code-named VENONA, supported testimony that Julius was a spy but cast doubt on the extent of Ethel's involvement.

On the 50th anniversary of the Rosenberg executions, June 19, 2003, *The New York Times* in an editorial claimed, "The Rosenberg case still haunts American history, reminding us of the injustice that can be done when a nation gets caught up in hysteria."

***

During World War II, J. Edgar had ordered his agents to tap the telephone lines of aviator and movie mogul Howard Hughes. He had never trusted Hughes, especially when his aviation company began conducting business with the U.S. government. He became particularly alarmed when Hughes, at least briefly, considered making a bid to run for President of the United States. A report reached J. Edgar that, if elected, Hughes' first act of duty would be to fire the FBI director.

During the war years, J. Edgar could always spare two agents to spy on Hughes wherever he went. If he were dining at the swank Chasen's in Los Angeles, often with a beautiful starlet such as Faith Domergue, you could virtually count on a black sedan parked in shadows some one hundred yards away. From listening to secret tapes garnered from bugging, Guy Hotell said, "I am convinced that Howard Hughes is the greatest oral artist in the boudoir in the history of Hollywood."

In the summer of 1944, J. Edgar's agents trailed Elliott Roosevelt to Hollywood, where Hughes Aircraft lavishly entertained the President's son. Almost desperately eager, Hughes wanted Elliott to recommend his company to build war-time planes for the government.

In spite of massive opposition, denunciations, and protest, Elliott won the battle when he obtained the permission of Jesse Jones, Secretary of Commerce, to greenlight the project. Hughes was awarded a $43 million contract to deliver nine prototypes and ninety-seven production models of the D-2 in less than ten months.

Hughes began to doubt his own D-2, telling his aide Johnny Meyer, "It sucks." On the night of November 11, 1943, a hanger housing the craft caught on fire, and the very flammable D-2 was destroyed. With his order for one-hundred planes still intact, Hughes reworked the design for the D-2, emerging with the superior D-5, which the Air Force designated as the XF-11. J. Edgar's agents reported almost daily to him on the disarray at Hughes Aircraft.

On Sunday morning, July 7, 1946, J. Edgar received a call that Hughes' reconnaissance plane, the bullet-nosed XF-11, had crashed on its test flight, plowing into homes in Beverly Hills. The aviator, or so J. Edgar was informed, had piloted the plane, and he was still alive. "Let me know if the bastard lives or dies, preferably dies," J. Edgar instructed his agents.

Hughes survived and came out of his coma to receive a blow-job, as he was recuperating in his hospital bed, from Ava Gardner.

Production lagged, and it appeared that Hughes Aircraft could not make its quota. The point became academic when Japan surrendered, and WWII came to an end. The Allies won without benefit of Hughes' XF-11s, which were never delivered.

He turned his attention to the need for reconnaissance planes to fly over Soviet Territory. "We need to see what the fucking communists are up to."

When Hughes announced he wanted to construct a flying ship the size of the Queen Mary, even his top aide, Noah Dietrich, denounced the idea as a "colossal boondoggle that will never fly." The aircraft's original name was *Hercules*, although the public dubbed it the *Spruce Goose*. The aircraft's "skin" and its structural parts were composed of thin sheets of spruce plywood.

In the Greater Los Angeles area, J. Edgar ordered that three of his agents keep him apprised of the progress, or the lack thereof, of the *Spruce Goose*. The director called the aircraft, "Hughes' Folly."

In time, *Hercules* would weigh 200 tons, making it three times heavier than "anything that had ever flown through the air, including a flotilla of flying dinosaurs."

Hughes claimed that it would be capable of transporting 400,000 pounds of cargo as well as 700 fighting men and their equipment. Its hull would be taller than a three-story building.

J. Edgar learned that on November 16, 1942, Hughes had been sent a government check for $18 million to construct three different prototypes of *Hercules*, each for delivery within ten months.

Of course, such a contract could never be fulfilled under those terms, and J. Edgar knew it. He called the War Department and urged that the Hughes contract be cancelled.

In July 28, 1947, Hughes had been summoned to Washington to testify about what had gone wrong with his wartime government contracts. Millions had been granted to him, but not one single aircraft had emerged.

The man out to get Hughes was a bombastic Republican senator from Maine, Ralph Owen Brewster, a Harvard-educated lawyer and a one-time governor of Maine. In his second term in the U.S. Senate, he had been named chairman of the Special Senate Committee on National Defense.

Senator **Owen Brewster** *(left)* and aviator mogul **Howard Hughes** *(right)* attracted the attention of the nation when they battled over Hughes' misuse of millions of dollars worth of wartime government contracts.

At one point during the hearings, Brewster threatened to demand testimony from some of the biggest movie stars in Hollywood, telling reporters "to get your note pads ready and get plenty of film for your cameras."

He threatened to summon "at least fifty Hollywood stars," including Rita Hayworth, Faith Domergue, Jane Russell, Lana Turner, Ava Gardner, Jane Greer, Jean Peters, Susan Hayward, Katharine Hepburn, Ginger Rogers, Fay Wray, and Bette Davis. Privately, to embarrass Hughes, he sent word that he might also include two of his male lovers, Cary Grant and Errol Flynn.

At the Senate hearings, Hughes turned the tables on Brewster and virtually put him on trial as "being in the pocket of Juan Trippe," head of Pan American, Hughes' bitter enemy at TWA. *Newsweek* called the Senate hearings with Hughes "the biggest circus act that has pitched its tent in Washington in years."

With millions of Americans listening on radio, Hughes attacked his inquisitors, especially Senator Brewster, charging him with accepting bribes from Pan Am. He called him, "One of the greatest trick-shot artists in Washington."

He vigorously defended the *Spruce Goose*, admitting that his only mistake had been in supervising "each portion of it in too much detail." With millions of Americans listening, Hughes declared he'd leave the country if his beloved *Hercules* didn't fly.

Facing reporters outside, he told them, "The *Hercules* will fly by the end of the year, and the XF-11 reconnaissance plane is the finest ever built. I did not waste the government's money."

The probe into his aircraft company had been a fiasco for the Republicans. Hughes flew back to Culver City, emerging relatively intact from what he called "a vicious smear campaign." Privately he told his aides that many of the attacks on him had originated with J. Edgar Hoover.

After the Senate hearings, HUGHES FOR PRESIDENT clubs were organized around the country.

On November 2, 1947, with much of the world looking on, the notorious *Spruce Goose*, with Hughes sitting in the pilot's seat, actually became airborne, taking off from Long Beach, California.

Denounced as a "flying lumberyard" by Senator Brewster, the *Spruce Goose* flew smoothly for one mile, reaching a maximum speed of ninety miles per hour at an altitude of only seventy feet. The historic multi-million dollar plane, the most expensive in the history of the world, stayed airborne for one minute.

"Millions of taxpayer dollars spent on a worthless piece of shit," J. Edgar concluded back in Washington.

***

Hughes, a dedicated capitalist, kept his eye trained on Washington and followed the hearings conducted by the House Un-American Activities Committee, ferreting out communists in the film industry. HUAC summoned Paul Jarrico, one of his studio writers to testify. Hughes fired him immediately, even though he had not finished the screenplay for the *Las Vegas Story* set to star Jane Russell and Victor Mature, both of whom Hughes had sexually pursued.

As one journalist wrote, "No one was more swept up by this fear of creeping communism than Howard Hughes." He even shut down RKO until he had each employee sign a loyalty oath. Those who refused to do so were dismissed.

Although it had nothing to do with national security, J. Edgar assigned agents at the end of the war to trail Hughes on his sexual trysts with Tyrone

Power and Lana Turner. When not with Hughes, these celebrated beauties were having an affair with each other.

When Turner and Hughes flew to New York to stay at the Sherry-Netherland, the FBI had their rooms bugged. By the summer of 1946, J. Edgar seemed so fascinated by the private life of Hughes that he had as many as twenty-four FBI agents assigned to follow his trail in Los Angeles, New York, and Washington.

The FBI even discovered that Turner and Hughes had sex when he piloted his Sikosky as it flew 12,000 feet above the earth on autopilot. Since they were alone in the plane, the question was raised as to how the FBI made that discovery. It was later learned that Turner bragged about it to her friends, including Peter Lawford and Ava Gardner.

The romance ended when Turner called him to report that she had syphilis, which she alleged she'd caught from the Turkish/Czech actor, Turhan Bey.

To J. Edgar and Clyde, even more intriguing than Hughes' accomplishments—or lack of successes—in aviation was his list of conquests, male and female. The gender didn't matter. He asked only that his conquest be beautiful.

J. Edgar's friend, Joan Crawford, said, "Howard would fuck a tree. I turned him down."

Very few other stars did. James Bacon, the Hollywood columnist, called him "the greatest swordsman."

In his heyday, Hughes boasted of "deflowering two hundred virgins in Hollywood." Jimmy the Greek, the celebrated gambler, said, "He must have got all of them."

Hughes seductions included Jean Harlow, Bette Davis, Yvonne de Carlo, Marlene Dietrich, Ava Gardner, Paulette Goddard, Kathryn Grayson, Susan Hayward, Rita Hayworth, Katharine Hepburn, Veronica Lake, Hedy Lamarr, Carole Lombard, Ginger Rogers, Shelley Winters, Norma Shearer, Fay Wray, and Marilyn Monroe, who, as a struggling young actress, agreed to star in one of his "home movies."

Hughes never mentioned the male idols of the screen he seduced, but in addition to Cary Grant, he bedded Gary Cooper, Clark Gable, Robert Taylor, Errol Flynn, Tyrone Power, Randolph Scott, and for years pursued Jack Buetel, whom he retained under exclusive contract since starring him in the controversial *The Outlaw* (1943).

Hughes didn't always make a conquest. Among the men and women who got away were Elizabeth Taylor and a young John F. Kennedy.

Amazingly, in an act unprecedented for J. Edgar, at the end of the war, he sent Hughes a matching pair of blue leather file boxes which bore the lettering—FEDERAL BUREAU OF INVESTIGATION, DUPLICATED FILES. The director said he was sending Hughes this package "because of my high regard for you."

The hoard revealed an extraordinary FBI bugging project that operated from 1943 to 1946, in which the mogul's love nests in the Hollywood Hills and his suites in Las Vegas and Manhattan were tapped. Coming from those rooms came the clear voices of Ava Gardner, Errol Flynn, Yvonne De Carlo, Lana Turner, Cary Grant, and Jack Buetel.

From that moment on, Hughes developed a lifelong hostility toward J. Edgar. Often hiring former FBI agents, Hughes himself had a network of spies, accumulating data on both his business rivals and his lovers, either male or female.

For a long time, J. Edgar had pried into Hughes' private life, and had even illegally secured medical records. He told his aides, "Hughes is a homosexual and his brain is half eaten up with syphilis, which he may have acquired in 1930 from that whorish actress, Billie Dove."

From 1966 and lasting for two years, Hughes set out to build "My Kingdom on Earth," a vast gambling empire. He became the biggest personal investor in Las Vegas, going on a buying spree that included the Desert Inn, where he took up residence on the ninth floor.

Nevada governor Paul Laxalt had exempted Hughes from making personal appearances before the Gaming Control Board. But rumors resurfaced that Hughes was dead and an impostor was in his suite. Forced to respond, Laxalt personally called J. Edgar and asked him to investigate to determine if Hughes were alive or dead.

After FBI agents sent to Vegas investigated for ten days, J. Edgar was forced to admit defeat. He called Laxalt telling him that "we cannot guarantee that Mr. Howard Hughes is dead or alive, or that he is actually the man inhabiting the ninth floor of the Desert Inn."

There was a fear that a cabal of persons was secretly conducting vast Hughes operations, siphoning off the money. His wife, former screen actress Jean Peters, came to Las Vegas, but was not granted entry into his suite.

After the initial report, J. Edgar ordered his agents to keep investigating Hughes. In a second secret analysis, much later, it was determined that after the mogul's involvement in a plane crash in 1946, he had become a drug addict. In an FBI memo, 64-1996-6, it stated that "Mr. Hughes takes at least six codeine tablets a day. He is in constant pain, especially in his thigh bones and pelvis. He contracted syphilis in the 1930s, and it was never adequately treated. The still lingering effects cause him agonizing pain. He also has an obsessive-compulsive disorder that practically paralyzes his brain at times, leading to dysfunctional decisions. He is extremely erratic in behavior, often injecting himself, the needles sometimes breaking off in his body and not removed. He often goes as much as forty-eight hours without sleep watching B-pictures from the early 1940s."

As J. Edgar neared the end of his life in 1970, he was called upon to investigate the mental condition of Hughes, who was also entering the twilight of his life.

Since Hughes Aircraft had become the third largest supplier of weapon delivery systems to the Air Force, the Pentagon asked J. Edgar to check up on the mental stability of Hughes himself. Reports reaching the Pentagon ranged from the charge that Hughes was drugged 24 hours a day, definitely suicidal, or even that he was dead. Journalists have since called the probe "unique in the history of domestic espionage."

"A tough assignment," J. Edgar told his aides. "We've got to determine the mental condition of the fattest cat in the States."

In ten weeks, FBI agents in Washington, New York, and Las Vegas interviewed dozens of people who were known to have had some sort of contact with Hughes, even waiters in Nevada. J. Edgar himself wrote the FBI's conclusion, having his letter hand delivered to the Pentagon. As he stated in Report no. 62-1476-4, "Mr. Howard Hughes has become paranoid, vengeful, and an emotionally disturbed man, whose mind has deteriorated to the point that he is capable of both suicide and murder."

When Hughes heard that the Air Force might move against him, he outwitted all of them by donating Hughes Aircraft to the Howard Hughes Medical Institute. Not wanting to move against a charity, the Pentagon capitulated, and President Eisenhower announced to the press, "Howard Hughes has created a high water mark for American philanthropy."

Actually Hughes' brain might not have been as damaged as J. Edgar's reports indicated. His great gift turned out to be an incredible tax dodge. For every $1 million the institute gave to medical research, it had to give $2.5 million back to Hughes himself.

When the FBI investigated Hughes' two other major corporations, the movie studio, RKO, and the aviator's beloved TWA, J. Edgar received a report that both companies were "each in total chaos being run by a man who some have determined is certifiably insane."

In 1971, President Richard Nixon sent J. Edgar the government's final request for the FBI to investigate Hughes' stability. In a personal "for-your-eyes-only" memo, J. Edgar concluded after a month-long investigation by his agents, "Mr. Howard Hughes is considered by many to be an unscrupulous individual who possesses a highly unstable nature, is ruthless and capable of almost anything."

The continuing investigation into Howard Hughes was ongoing at the time of J. Edgar's death in 1972. Hughes died in 1976, but the FBI still followed a directive J. Edgar had left in the Hughes file.

"Have agents fly to whatever city Hughes dies in and get his fingerprints to see if they match those we possess at the Bureau. It is very important that we determine that it is actually Howard Hughes who died—not some impostor."

***

Whenever actress Lindsay Lohan goes into a court today, it attracts massive tabloid coverage. Back in 1949 and the early 1950s, Judith Coplon received the same treatment from the press but for different reasons. A twenty-seven-year-old *cum laude* graduate of Barnard College, and employed in the Internal Security Division of the Department of Justice, she outwardly appeared as the model postwar "government girl." She was, in fact, a spy for the Soviet Union, having been recruited by the KGB back in 1944. In her sensitive position, she had access to counter-intelligence secret data.

J. Edgar and Clyde learned about her espionage as a result of a VENONA message received in 1948, sent to her under her Soviet code name of SIMA. The code-cracking VENONA was still a top-level secret, and could not be revealed in a trial. If it had, the Soviets would learn that their code to their foreign agents had been cracked.

Under J. Edgar's confidential orders, sensitive but fake U.S. secrets were fed to Coplon, who in return relayed them to the Soviet Union.

With mounting evidence against her, she was tried in 1949 for espionage and a year later for conspiracy, both trials resulting in a conviction.

In the Coplon case, the judge had ordered that the FBI turn over the original documents in her file, including recordings and disks. Defying the judge, J. Edgar ordered the originals destroyed. President Truman later said, "During the Coplon trials, I came as close I ever did to firing Hoover."

Clyde had planned a glorious celebration to honor J. Edgar's silver (i.e., 25th) anniversary as director. But he told his fellow agents, "That commie bitch comes along to ruin everything for us and to turn Eddie sour."

Both of the convictions against Coplon were overturned in 1950 and 1951, a judge concluding that she was guilty of both charges, but J. Edgar's FBI agents had lied under oath about illegally bugging her phone. Her privileged conversations between her attorney and herself were also bugged. A new trial, though possible, was never pursued.

Coplon remained in America, marrying her attorney, Albert Socolov, with whom she lived until her death in 2011.

Writing in *The New York Times*, Gertrude Samuels raised some questions: "Why do some people become traitors? What turns some native-born Americans, as well as naturalized citizens, into Benedict Arnolds and Quislings? What motivates them to betray their country and themselves?"

Historian Bernard DeVoto at Harvard denounced J. Edgar and his FBI dossiers on Coplon, labeling them "the irresponsible chatter of retarded children."

J. Edgar wasn't going to take that, and he ordered that Clyde and his agents launch a massive investigation to weed out communist professors not only at Yale and Harvard but at some fifty campuses around the country. In the wake of this, discreet firings followed, with many academic careers destroyed.

One professor, Howard Higman, earned a 6,000-page file, which was made available to him in 1991 under the Freedom of Information Act. Not only faculty members and deans were accused of "being soft on communists," but university or college presidents were also targeted.

Once a household word during the early stages of the Cold War, the notorious **Judith Coplon** died on February 26, 2011, in a Manhattan hospital at the age of 89.

During her youth, she had been convicted in two separate trials of spying for the Soviet Union. Judges eventually overturned her convictions because of illegal wiretaps and a lack of warrants, although proclaiming her guilt nevertheless.

During their investigation of her, FBI agents vied for a chance to put her under surveillance. They soon learned that she entertained a frequently changing array of well-built male friends and, as they performed their studly duties, she didn't close the curtains or turn off the lights. As Guy Hotell later said, "It was a live porno show going on every night."

J. Edgar not only investigated communists, but continued to probe into the sexual lives of both politicians and entertainers. He sent Truman a confidential memo, claiming that one of his administrative assistants, David Niles, and Charlie Ross, his press secretary, were engaged in indiscreet and random affairs with women.

At a cabinet meeting, Truman denounced this latest report. "Being a victim of Cupid," the President said, "is not being a victim of Moscow propaganda. Having a known homosexual as the director of the country's internal security force, and making him a target for any hostile Soviet intelligence service, is far more dangerous than a little womanizing on the side."

***

As a guest on the live broadcast of a radio talk show, Lester Cole, one of the "Hollywood Ten," awkwardly encountered an ex-communist, the writer Budd Schulberg, who had testified as a friendly witness before HUAC. "Aren't you the canary who sang before the *Un-American* Committee?" Cole asked. "Aren't you just that canary? Or, are you another bird, a pigeon—the stool kind? Just sing canary, sing, you bastard!"

The radio station manager cut off Cole's mike.

For many years, J. Edgar and Clyde had maintained a file on Schulberg, a novelist, sportswriter, screenwriter, and TV producer. In 1941 he had written a highly successful novel, *What Makes Sammy Run?*, followed by another hit novel, *The Harder They Fall*.

What caught the attention of J. Edgar and Clyde was when Schulberg served in the Navy during WWII and was assigned to the Office of Strategic Services (OSS). He worked with John Ford's documentary unit, and, following VE Day, was one of the first U.S. military men to liberate Nazi-run concentration camps. "What I saw in those camps caused me

In a characteristic pose (behind a camera), the glamorous **Leni Riefenstahl** became one of the three most famous German women associated with WWII—Marlene Dietrich opposing the Nazis and Riefenstahl exploiting their "power and glory" with her propaganda movies. The third most celebrated woman, known mainly after the war, was Eva Braun, Hitler's longtime mistress who became his wife in their dying pre-suicide days in a Berlin bunker in 1945.

Author **Budd Schulberg** *(lower photo)* interrogated Riefenstahl in more ways than one during both a grilling and a "drilling" in Austria. Schulberg died in 2009 at the age of 95, the lone survivor of the OSS Field Branch that located and analyzed Nazi films, in attempts to identify men who were later charged with crimes against humanity. At the time of his death, he was working on a book entitled *The Celluloid Noose* about the Nürnberg trials.

340

to have a nightmare every night for the rest of my life," he later recalled.

At the end of the war, he was charged with gathering evidence against Nazi war criminals, which would lead to many of their deaths. His biggest assignment was to track down Hitler's favorite filmmaker, Leni Riefenstahl, at her chalet in Kitzbühel, Austria. She was needed to identify the Nazi war criminals who had appeared in some of her Nazi-sponsored film footage, which had been confiscated by Allied troops.

After the war, her reputation was trashed internationally, and she was denounced as "Hitler's girl friend," who had glorified the Nazi Party through her films such as *Olympia* and *Triumph of the Will*.

While Schulberg grilled her, he learned that she had made use of slave labor in the form of concentration camp gypsies destined for Auschwitz.

When Schulberg returned to Hollywood, he himself was grilled by FBI agents in Los Angeles. Apparently at the time, the Bureau did not know that the author had been a member of the Communist Party. That would be revealed later.

The FBI wanted to know what Schulberg had learned when he'd interrogated Riefenstahl. He described his visit to her home, Seebichl Haus. "She made a spectacular calculated entrance, wearing yellow corduroy slacks with a golden brown leather jacket. I thought she was like so many actresses of her age I had met before, fading beauties who tried to compensate in make-up and grooming what they lacked in physical appeal."

Later in the *Saturday Evening Post*, Schulberg had written about the "Nazi Pin-Up Girl." To the author, Riefenstahl denied all charges of collaboration with the Nazis, claiming, "I was the victim of Goebbels. He made me do what I did. Otherwise, he threatened to send me to a concentration camp. I hardly knew Hitler. The talk of our having an affair is a libelous lie."

To the FBI agent, Schulberg told an amazing story, whether true or not. When a report was filed, J. Edgar believed it was true.

In his confession, Schulberg admitted that he became infuriated at Riefenstahl because she was so evasive in denying her role in glorifying the Nazi Party and her intimate association with Hitler. "Call it the Jew in me, but I became so enraged I attacked her. I held a knife at her throat and warned her if she resisted me, I'd disfigure her. When I shot off in her, I said, 'That's what it feels to get fucked by a fat Jewish dick.'"

Afterward, he searched her home, taking away three suitcases of material. Several included pictures of a young Marlene Dietrich. In one, both women were bare breasted. He forced her to admit she'd had a lesbian affair with Marlene in the 1920s. That information only solidified J. Edgar's long-held opinion that Dietrich was a secret Nazi.

Schulberg later bragged to Elia Kazan on the set of *On the Waterfront* that, "I think Riefenstahl liked getting fucked by me. After all, what fun could she have had with the tiny dick of the Führer? Do you think he made her lick his one ball?"

In 1951, Schulberg became caught up in the communist witch hunt. Screenwriter Richard Collins, testifying before HUAC, outed him as a former party member. When called to testify, Schulberg, trying to save his career, became a friendly witness, naming other Communist Party members.

Unlike most writers summoned before the committee, Schulberg's career was rescued. In 1954, he won an Oscar for his screenplay of *On the Waterfront* and another for his 1957 *A Face in the Crowd*.

Other "stool pigeons" would follow Schulberg, including film director Elia Kazan, playwright Clifford Odets, and actor Lee J. Cobb.

Born in Istanbul to Greek parents, Kazan was one of the most honored and influential directors on Broadway or in Hollywood, and he introduced a new generation of unknown Method actors to movie audiences, including Marlon Brando and James Dean in such films as *A Streetcar Named Desire* (1951), *On the Waterfront* (1954), and *East of Eden* (1955). During his career, he received two Oscars as Best Director.

He was investigated by the FBI, who turned up evidence of his support of "dangerous left-wing causes." He was called before the House Un-American Activities Committee in 1952, and became a friendly witness, naming names. This move shocked Hollywood and cost him the friendship of his liberal friends such as playwright Arthur Miller.

After an investigation, J. Edgar and Clyde determined that Kazan had been a member of the American Communist Party in New York between the years 1934 and 1936.

At first Kazan refused HUAC's request to provide names of other communists who had worked with him in the Theatre Group during the 1930s. Among the many names cited by him for their communist affiliations were Paula Miller, who later married acting guru Lee Strasberg.

Kazan, according to J. Edgar's dossier, became disillusioned with the party, and he turned against communism, especially after the Hitler-Stalin pact. Consequently, its members turned against him. As Kazan told Arthur Miller, "I hate the communists and have for many years, and I don't feel right about giving up my career to defend them. I will give up my film career if it is in the interest of defending something I believe in, but not this."

Arthur Miller dropped Kazan as a friend, but he received support from another playwright, Tennessee Williams, with whom he had collaborated on numerous plays and films. An outsider himself because of his homosexuality and controversial theatrical statements, Williams "became my most loyal and understanding friend through all those black months when I was being denounced as a rat," Kazan said.

Because of his affiliation with Kazan and "other undesirables," the playwright was also investigated by J. Edgar and Clyde. They accumulated a rich dossier on his homosexual lifestyle, even exploring the rumor that he'd given John F. Kennedy a blow job in Palm Beach after having been introduced to the President by author Gore Vidal.

Kazan also found a sympathetic soul in actor Lee J. Cobb, whom he cast in *On the Waterfront*, for which Cobb was Academy Award nominated in his supporting role.

Born to a Russian-Jewish family in the Bronx, Cobb was outed by J. Edgar, Clyde, and other FBI agents for his support of political organizations suspected of being communist fronts. For two years, he refused to testify before HUAC, but he was summoned in even more forceful terms in 1953. He relented and gave testimony, naming twenty people who were former members of the Communist Party.

As he tried to explain himself, he said, "The blacklist is just the opening gambit—being deprived of work. HUAC wore me down. I had no money, no work. I had a wife and children to support. Why should I subject them to this? I decided keeping my mouth shut wasn't worth the price, wasn't worth dying for. If testifying would keep me out of the penitentiary, I'd do it. I had to be employable again."

His career resumed with the controversial *On the Waterfront*, where he worked with Kazan and Budd Schulberg, two other HUAC "friendly witnesses," although they weren't all that friendly. *On the Waterfront* itself can be interpreted as an allegory and apologia for testifying.

Frank Sinatra wanted to play the lead role, that of an ex-boxer, Terry Malloy, who is persuaded by a priest to inform on corrupt unions. At first Brando vowed never to work with Kazan again because of his outing of former communists. But eventually, Brando was persuaded to take the role. The star claimed that Kazan, Schulberg, and Cobb "squealed like pigs on castration day."

***

The one film that J. Edgar and Clyde wanted to see in 1952 was *High*

Noon, starring an aging Gary Cooper and a young Grace Kelly. Rumor had spread that the film, "disguised" as a Western, was actually an attack on McCarthyism. Through a connection in Hollywood with director Fred Zinnemann, Clyde was able to get a copy sent to FBI headquarters in Washington where a private screening was held.

Cooper played a longtime marshal of a small town in New Mexico who must face a criminal released from prison who is threatening to kill him. The American Left saw the film as an allegory of people, especially those in Hollywood, who were afraid to stand up to HUAC or to oppose Senator McCarthy. However, the movie did eventually gain the respect of people with conservative/anti-communist views.

J. Edgar and Clyde agreed with those who interpreted the film as an attack on their anti-communist movement, and were instrumental in getting its writer, Carl Foreman, called before HUAC to give testimony.

A screenwriter and producer, Chicago-born Foreman came from a working class Jewish family. One of the top screenwriters in Hollywood, he had scored great successes with such films as the 1949 *The Champion*, starring Kirk Douglas, and his 1950 *Cyrano de Bergerac,* which won an Oscar for José Ferrer, who was also suspected of having "communist leanings."

Foreman was not only writing *High Noon* but producing it with Stanley Kramer. Called before HUAC, Foreman testified that he had been a member of the Communist Party in 1941 but became disillusioned with Stalin's policies and had resigned. HUAC defined him as an "uncooperative witness," which automatically put him on the Hollywood blacklist. Unlike Kazan and Schulberg, Foreman had refused to name names.

Back in Hollywood, Kramer tried to get him kicked off *High Noon*, but he had contracts and demanded his legal rights. Kramer later claimed, "Foreman blackmailed me to keep him on. He threatened if I didn't, he would go before the committee and name me as a communist, which I definitely was not."

Even so, Foreman knew that *High Noon* would be his last assignment in Hollywood. After completion of the film, he moved to England, where he worked on scripts such as *The Bridge on the River Kwai*, using a pseudonym when his writing was channeled back to Hollywood.

The super American patriot, John Wayne, agreed with J. Edgar and Clyde that the film was an attack on McCarthy and his anti-communist drive. As the chief promoter of the Motion Picture Alliance for the Preservation of American Ideals, Wayne led the fight to "have Foreman run out of this country." The cowboy star denounced *High Noon* as "un-American."

Ironically, even though he was the major big-name attacker of *High Noon*, Wayne agreed to accept the Oscar for Gary Cooper when he won that year as Best Actor.

Although Cooper won the Oscar, the film, *High Noon*, in an upset defeat, did not. The Academy Award for Best Picture went to Cecil B. DeMille's *The Greatest Show on Earth*. This is still viewed as one of the biggest upsets in the history of the awards, ranking up there with Judy Garland's loss for *A Star Is Born*. Director Zinnemann later claimed, "The Academy chickened out. They were afraid of McCarthy. DeMille was one of that crazed senator's biggest supporters. *High Noon* deserved that Oscar but the nutty Right Wing won out that night."

Another fervent anti-communist, and a future U.S. president, Ronald Reagan, disagreed with Wayne about *High Noon*. "The main character of the sheriff has a strong dedication to duty, law, and the well-being of the towns-people, and I applaud that," Reagan said.

Eisenhower had the film screened at the White House and claimed, "I love it." But, as far as presidents go, the real champion of *High Noon* was Bill Clinton. "It is my favorite film," he said. He had it screened a record of seventeen times at the White House.

In 1959, Wayne wanted the last word when he teamed with director Howard Hawks to make *Rio Bravo*, which he considered the conservative response to the Cooper film. Hawks said, "I made *Rio Bravo* because I didn't like *High Noon*. Neither did Duke. I didn't think a good town marshal was going to run around town like a chicken with his head cut off asking everybody to help. And who saves him? His Quaker wife as played by Grace Kelly. That isn't my idea of a good Western."

David Niven, a close friend and former

John Wayne led an attack on Gary Cooper's **High Noon** *(poster above)* calling it "the most un-American thing I've ever seen in my life" in a *Playboy* interview in 1971. Yet on Oscar night, he agreed to accept the Academy Award on behalf of his friend, Cooper.

Wayne also claimed that he had no regret for getting the film's creator, Carl Foreman, blacklisted from Hollywood. Cooper himself had conservative views, but agreed to make the film anyway because he recognized its power and potential as a box office hit.

Grace Kelly and Gary Cooper (lower photo) were lovers both on screen and off during the making of *High Noon*.

lover of Grace Kelly, spent one afternoon drinking with her at the Monte Carlo Country Club. He asked her what she felt about the political controversy that had raged around *High Noon*. "To hell with all that," the future Princess Grace said. "I just wanted Gary Cooper to fuck me before he became too old to get it up."

***

J. Edgar was never afraid to tackle a high-profile target. "If I can investigate the private lives of U.S. presidents, I can most definitely take on lesser mortals," he told Clyde and his most trusted agents. "And that includes Einstein himself."

Albert Einstein, the German-born theoretical physicist, discovered the Theory for General Relativity and is today hailed as the Father of Modern Physics. In 1921, he won the Nobel Prize for Physics.

Arriving in New York in 1933, eighteen days before Hitler rose to power in Germany, Einstein was almost not allowed into the country. The State Department, the War Department, the Immigration and Naturalization Service, and most definitely J. Edgar's FBI had been told by pro-Nazi, anti-Semitic "sources" that the scientist was a secret spy for the Kremlin.

The Women's Patriot Corporation had sent J. Edgar an urgent letter, asking him to use his influence to deny entry to Einstein. The group stated, "Not even Josef Stalin himself is affiliated with so many anarchic communist front groups."

Fearing international ridicule for refusing entry to the world's most famous scientist and a Nobel prize winner, the State Department relented and allowed him into the United States.

The immigration trouble alerted J. Edgar that the United States may have allowed a dangerous "subversive" into the country. When Einstein heard that Hitler had seized power in Berlin, he decided not to return to his native Germany. After several months in Belgium, he moved temporarily to England before immigrating to the United States. He accepted a position of teaching physics at the Institute for Advanced Study at Princeton, an affiliation that lasted until his death.

After he settled into New Jersey, Einstein's file at the FBI began to grow. Amazingly, some of the most damaging accusations presented to J. Edgar came from Heinrich Himmler, head of the newly formed Nazi Gestapo. From Berlin, Himmler wrote J. Edgar a number of derogatory letters about Einstein, considering him "a dangerous communist and enemy to world peace. As a Jew, he wants to sow dissent between the peace-loving American people and the peace-loving German people."

Himmler charged that in the early 1930s, Einstein's apartment in Berlin "was a center for all extreme radical cabals" and that his summer house at Caputh was "a hiding place for Moscow envoys."

The Nazi also claimed that Einstein's office in Berlin had "been a cable drop for Russian spies." The Gestapo leader reported that Einstein's secretaries had extracted coded messages from telegrams and letters passed to the scientist and had sent data to Soviet couriers who in turn delivered the secrets directly to the Kremlin.

In reality, Einstein did not have an office in Berlin, but worked out of his home. He also had only one secretary, Helen Dukas.

The FBI did turn up evidence that Einstein had an affair with Margarita Konenkov, a Russian immigrant married to the sculptor Sergei Konenkov. She was later outed as a Soviet agent by a former Russian spy master, Pavel Sudoplatov, in his 1995 memoir, *Special Tasks*.

J. Edgar and Himmler became so cozy that he invited the Gestapo leader to the 1937 World Police Conference in Montreal. Himmler and J. Edgar were still corresponding just months before the Nazi attack on Poland, igniting World War II.

The FBI director also maintained links with KRIPO, the Nazi criminal police agency, which was conducting murderous attacks on Jews, homosexuals, and Gypsies. J. Edgar continued to correspond with this Nazi police group up until three days before the Japanese attack of Pearl Harbor on December 7, 1941. Of course, after Germany declared war on the United States, J. Edgar went on a campaign to round up Nazi spies in America.

During the Spanish Civil War, the FBI discovered that Einstein supported the Abraham Lincoln Brigade, composed of volunteer soldiers from the American Communist Party battling the dictator Franco.

As journalist Phil Shannon wrote: "Einstein was attacked by a ludicrous parade of sources, including informants suffering from schizophrenia and dementia, deranged crackpots, con artists, blackmailers, pro-Nazis, far-right nutters, anti-Semitic bigots, and apostate Stalinists, with self-serving allegations. Even so, the FBI case against Einstein being a subversive was running on empty."

Einstein's mail was opened, his phone bugged, and he was tailed by an agent. The FBI even rummaged through Einstein's garbage at Princeton, a technique known as "trash watch." In nearly a quarter of a century, Einstein's FBI file grew to some 1,800 pages, perhaps a lot more because J. Edgar ordered much of the really personal data destroyed upon Einstein's death.

As J. Edgar told his most trusted agents, "I want first to demonize Einstein and then neuter him." J. Edgar would continue his campaign to get the

Immigration and Naturalization Service to deport Einstein, an FBI lobbying that lasted as long as Einstein did.

J. Edgar was not alone. In those pre-war years, open anti-Semitism and pro-Fascist points of view were popular expressions. A conservative columnist, Jimmy Tarantino, ran an editorial advocating RED-FRONTING EINSTEIN SHOULD BE DEPORTED. "So who needs Einstein?" Tarantino asked. "Not the American people."

In 1940, Einstein became a naturalized U.S. citizen. He had a number of friendly chats with President Roosevelt, warning him that German scientists were working to develop an atomic bomb. He urged FDR to launch such research in America, assuming he would be asked to work on the project. "It will be a race to see which country destroys which country first," Einstein told the President.

Einstein's friendly talks with Roosevelt did not extend to J. Edgar, who was instrumental in preventing him from working on the Manhattan Project. J. Edgar convinced military intelligence that Einstein "was far too Red and would supply all our atomic secrets to the Kremlin."

Ironically, the Manhattan Project was riddled with Soviet spies who went undetected by J. Edgar until it was too late.

Einstein was deeply disappointed he was not appointed to work on the Manhattan Project, because he wanted "to wipe Nazism off the face of the earth." He saw many of his colleagues from Germany working on the bomb. One newspaper claimed that "without these European scientists, often Jews, the Manhattan Project would not have produced a firecracker."

J. Edgar's ear listened to every accusation presented against Einstein, regardless of how far-fetched. Charges included that the scientist was part of a communist conspiracy to take over Hollywood. He was also accused of working to invent a death ray or a "mental control" robot. Most of the accusations concerned unproven charges that he was a Soviet agent.

During the war, Einstein did contact J. Edgar to report several death threats, as Josef Goebbels had placed a bounty on his head. Einstein feared a Nazi spy assassination attempt on his life. One German magazine listed him under the category of "not yet hanged."

In the 1930s Goebbels had proclaimed that "Jewish intellectualism is dead," and he'd ordered the burning of Einstein's books and papers. On hearing of Einstein's fears, J. Edgar told Clyde and other agents, "We will not protect Einstein. The ugly fart is on his own."

After the war, on J. Edgar's instruction, Einstein's file grew every time he joined another civil rights group. "These are un-American organizations," J. Edgar claimed. "They are in essence Red fronts."

In 1947, Einstein said, "I came to America because of the great, great freedom which I heard existed in this country. I made a mistake of selecting America as a land of freedom, a mistake I cannot repair in my lifetime."

Although Einstein today is a beloved figure, that was not the case in the 1940s and 1950s. In 1945, a senior Democratic congressman from Mississippi, John Rankin, attacked Einstein. "It's about time the American people got wise to Einstein. He ought to be prosecuted." Rankin was a friend of the Franco regime in Spain. Rankin claimed Einstein was a "foreign-born agitator trying to spread communism around the world."

J. Edgar had his agents turn up the heat on Einstein when he appeared on the once-a-week NBC television show, *Today With Mrs. Roosevelt*, on February 12, 1950. Two weeks before that, Truman had announced that the United States was surging ahead of Russia in the development of a hydrogen bomb, which he claimed would be 100 to 1,000 times more powerful than those he'd ordered dropped on Japan.

On the former First Lady's show, Einstein had warned that the development of a hydrogen bomb might annihilate mankind. His appearance was greeted with a headline that proclaimed—DISARM OR DIE, SAYS EINSTEIN.

After hearing the broadcast, J. Edgar ordered agents to intensify their probe of Einstein. To his aides, he said that the Eleanor and Einstein show on NBC represented "Eve and the Snake combined. All they can offer America is a poison apple."

Up until near the time of his death, Einstein was urging witnesses not to testify before Senator McCarthy's subcommittee.

On April 18, 1955, Einstein died at the age of 76. Only then did J. Edgar close the FBI file on him.

By the end of the 20th century, Einstein's fame arguably topped his contemporaries. In 1999, *Time* magazine named him "Person of the Century," beating out even Franklin D. Roosevelt. His name has become synonymous with genius. A Gallup poll ranked him the fourth most admired person of the 20th century.

Today his estate still takes in ten million dollars a year from the sales of Einstein memorabilia, everything from coffee mugs to T-shirts.

***

J. Edgar also targeted celebrity Paul Robeson for intensive surveillance. It was an eerie prelude for his greater battle with Martin Luther King, Jr.

Somewhat forgotten today, the African-American Robeson was an athlete, an actor, a bass-baritone concert singer, and a major recording artist of his day. Eventually, he became tabloid fodder because of his political radicalism and activism in the burgeoning civil rights movement.

A nationally renowned football player from 1917 to 1920, he was the first major concert star to popularize Negro spirituals, and he was also the first black actor of the 20th century to star as William Shakespeare's *Othello* in a production with an all-white cast. In 1930, he appeared opposite Dame Peggy Ashcroft's Desdemona. His affair with the distinguished Ashcroft lasted on and off until the late 1950s. Two years before that, he'd appeared in the role of Joe in the London production of *Show Boat*, immortalizing himself by singing the definitive version of "Ol' Man River."

Robeson's links with the Soviet Union began in 1934 when he journeyed to Moscow, finding the country free of racism. However, when he stopped over in Berlin, he was nearly attacked by the Nazi *Sturmabteilung* (storm troopers).

After World War II, Robeson's fame as a civil rights activist grew steadily, which brought him into conflict with J. Edgar, who had him spied on every day of his life.

In July of 1946, horrified at the lynching of blacks in the South, Robeson appealed to President Truman. Joining him as co-chairman in the American Crusade Against Lynching was Albert Einstein, who became one of his closest friends. Robeson threatened Truman that if he did not do something about these lynchings, "the Negroes will." The President did not capitulate to Robeson's intimidation, and quickly showed him to the door of the Oval Office.

J. Edgar spread the word that Robeson was a card-carrying communist, but on October 7, 1946, Robeson issued a statement denying it. At one point he called J. Edgar "a cocksucking liar," but that was not printed, given the self-imposed censorship of that era.

Over dinner at Harvey's, J. Edgar and Clyde plotted to discredit Robeson by turning the second most popular African American, Jackie Robinson, against him. Robinson was the first black major league baseball player

Near the end of her life, the former First Lady, **Eleanor Roosevelt**, had become "A Lioness in Winter." After her death in 1962, the press hailed her as "the most famous woman on Earth."

On her NBC talk show, in direct contrast to Harry Truman's policies, Albert Einstein warned about the dangers of increasingly powerful atomic bombs.

After Einstein's appearance on her show, J. Edgar sent an urgent memo to FBI offices around the country: SEARCH OUT ALL DEROGATORY INFORMATION ON EINSTEIN.

of the modern era.

J. Edgar was particularly angered at a speech Robeson had made on April 20, 1949, at the International Student Peace Conference in Paris. He claimed that in the event of a war between the United States and the Soviet Union, blacks would not support their country because of their second-class citizenship status within America.

Even though he did not have to, Jackie Robinson agreed to testify before the HUAC. "Hoover convinced me there would be repercussions if I did not appear," Jackie said. "I was afraid my career in baseball would be seriously damaged, and I would harm future integration of black professional athletes."

Before HUAC, Jackie said, "If Robeson wants to sound silly when he expresses his personal views in public, that is his business and not mine." Jackie's carefully worded statement could hardly be construed as an attack on Robeson. "Racial discrimination is not a creation of communist imagination," Jackie said.

Even so, Robeson considered Jackie's testimony "a disservice to the black community."

After the hearing, Jackie left Washington immediately, a black newspaper, *New Age*, suggesting that he ran out of town before "being Jim Crowed by Washington's infamous lily-white hotels."

J. Edgar told his aides that he found Jackie's testimony "too nelly. I wanted more he-man attacks on Robeson."

Paul Robeson, the African-American singer born in Princeton, New Jersey, occupied a prominent place on J. Edgar's hit lists of communists to pursue.

An outstanding athlete, singer, and actor, he appeared in the Broadway revival of *Show Boat* in 1932, and that same year, in the film version of *The Emperor Jones*—a rare example at the time of a black starring in a major Hollywood production. He is forever remembered for his recording of "Ol' Man River" from the 1936 film version of *Show Boat*.

The singer earned the ire of J. Edgar because of his outspoken criticism of racism in America, claiming his people received fairer treatment in the Soviet Union.

For his stand, he became one of the tragic figures of blacklisting in the 1950s.

The FBI director pressured NBC in March of 1950 to cancel Robeson's appearance on Eleanor Roosevelt's television program, *Today With Mrs. Roosevelt*.

"I can just imagine what that man who loves white pussy and Horse Face, who, on occasion, went for nigger dick have to talk about," J. Edgar told his aides.

Largely because of J. Edgar's interference, Robeson had his passport revoked in 1950 under the McCarran Act, the State Department citing the star's frequent criticism while abroad of the U.S. treatment of blacks. Robeson was blacklisted from performing on stage, screen, radio, and television, although his right to have a passport was given back to him in 1958.

In 1952 Robeson was awarded the International Stalin Peace Prize by the Soviet Union, although he was banned from going there to accept it. When Stalin died, Robeson issued a statement to world press. Forgetting that Stalin, like Hitler, was responsible for the death of millions, Robeson claimed, "Throughout his deep humanity, by his wise understanding, Stalin leaves a rich and monumental heritage."

"Yeah, right," J. Edgar said, "that is, to those who survived the death camps."

During Robeson's blacklist, it became difficult in America to hear him sing on radio or even to buy his music. J. Edgar even wanted to have MGM cut the segment from its popular musical *Show Boat,* in which Robeson had sung the memorable "Ol' Man River."

When a would-be film producer, Martin Richards, wanted to make a documentary on Robeson, he went to the Library of Congress only to learn that most of the newsreel footage on the star had been destroyed or else the sound erased. When pressed for its whereabouts, a librarian informed him it was sent to the FBI, which did not respond to the Richards' request to turn over the lost footage. It is believed that J. Edgar destroyed the newsreels.

In his own appearance before the HUAC in May of 1956, Robeson refused to sign an affidavit affirming that he was not a communist. He reminded the HUAC that the Communist Party was a legal party before he invoked the Fifth Amendment against self-incrimination. He claimed that White America wasted the lives of sixty to a hundred million "of my people," who died on slave ships or on plantations in the South.

In the spring of 1961, Robeson journeyed to the Soviet Union for the last time. Disguised as a tourist, an FBI agent followed him there. He reported that Robeson attended "a wild party" in his hotel room in Moscow before locking himself in his bedroom and attempting suicide by cutting his wrists. He was brought to recovery in a local Russian hospital, later claiming that, "I had this powerful sense of emptiness and depression."

Plagued by years of ill health, Robeson at the age of 77 died on January 23, 1976 in Philadelphia, having suffered a stroke. The black press eulogized him, calling him "Gulliver among the Lilliputians."

***

J. Edgar and Clyde never liked the movies of Charlie Chaplin and always viewed him suspiciously, beginning a file on him. The first entry on him was in 1921 when William Z. Foster paid a social visit at the Chaplin Studio in Hollywood upon his return from the Red International Conference of Labor Unions in Moscow.

By the time of J. Edgar's death, the Chaplin file had mushroomed beyond 2,000 pages. Much of the data had been destroyed, however. Throughout three presidential elections when Foster ran for President of the United States on the Communist Party ticket, in 1924, 1928, and 1932, Chaplin supported his candidacy and helped finance his campaign.

Throughout Chaplin's heyday as the king of silent films in the 1920s, and on throughout the Depression era of the 1930s, and into the early years of WWII, J. Edgar and Clyde continued to add to their Chaplin dossier. At times they seemed more intrigued by Chaplin's sexual life than they did his left-wing political views.

The FBI established very early into their surveillance of Chaplin that he liked to seduce underage teenage girls. When he visited brothels, he always requested "the youngest whore." He virtually outed himself as a child molester when he said, "The most beautiful form of life is the very young girl just starting to bloom."

One of the most damaging reports to reach the FBI was that on occasion Chaplin liked to have sex with underage teenage boys who were "imported" from Mexico, seduced, and then sent back across the border.

Mildred Harris, Chaplin's first wife and a teenager herself, spread that gossip around Hollywood. So did 1920s heartthrob Ramon Novarro, who also preferred sex with young boys or at least very young men.

The FBI files showed that Chaplin seduced some of the leading actresses of his day, including Louise Brooks, Hedy Lamarr, Carole Landis (who committed suicide), Pola Negri (who was mostly lesbian), Edna Purviance (his co-star in silent films), Claire Windsor, and the nymphomaniac Lupe Velez when she was not otherwise occupied with Gary Cooper.

Chaplin also slipped in seductions with Aimee Semple McPherson, American most famous and controversial evangelist, as well as with Marion Davies, the mistress of press baron William Randolph Hearst.

He'd impregnated first wife Harris, an actress, before she turned "sweet sixteen." Lita Grey, his second wife and co-star of his 1925 *The Gold Rush*, bragged about his sexual prowess. "He told me that he was a stallion, and I had better get used to it. There were nights when he was good for as many as six 'bouts,' as he called them, in succession—with scarcely five minutes of rest in between."

Edgar often speculated on the size of Chaplin's penis, which the actor called "The Eighth Wonder of the World," claiming it was a thick twelve inches. Mae West, an expert on male genital size, seemed to agree. "Chaplin was short and his nose average, but his pecker was really big-time." J. Edgar always wanted to get a nude frontal of Chaplin, but never succeeded.

Orson Welles cast a dissenting vote about the size of Chaplin's penis. "I once showered with him. It was a little peanut."

Welles was referring to a shower they'd had together after a swim in his pool when he'd taken a script to him called *The Ladykiller*, in July of 1941. It was about the wife murderer Landru. Chaplin bought the script but changed the title to *Monsieur Verdoux*, which he didn't release until 1947.

Of course, J. Edgar and Clyde continued to monitor data about Chaplin and his political views, or what other people, both pro-Chaplin and anti-Chaplin, had to say on the star. J. Edgar's favorite remark came from Vladimir Lenin, the leader of the Russian Revolution, who claimed "Chaplin is the one man in the world I want to meet." Lenin's replacement, Josef Stalin, was also a great admirer of Chaplin, not just for his films, but also for his political views.

J. Edgar and Clyde had always plotted how "to get Chaplin," and a great opportunity occurred during the war years. One would think they had more important activities to pursue with the nation at war, but J. Edgar made a decision to divert a lot of the Bureau's resources to pursuing Chaplin's sex life.

The starlet, Joan Barry, became the one young woman Chaplin wished he'd never seduced. She brought a paternity suit against the actor in 1943, which led to an array of investigations and other charges.

As Gary Cooper said when he heard the news, "That gal dated high on the hog." She briefly had been the mistress of oil tycoon J. Paul Getty, arguably the richest man in the world at the time. Tiring of her, he passed her on to his friend A.C Blumenthal, the financier behind many movies. He, too, tired of her and passed her on to Chaplin.

In 1941, Chaplin seduced Barry with the promise he'd give her a starring role in a picture he was going to make called *Shadow and Substance*. The movie was never made. Apparently, Barry was a young woman of whom her older male lovers tired of quickly, and Chaplin gave her some money and wanted to get rid of her. After being promised stardom, she didn't want to let go of her prize catch.

She showed signs of severe mental illness, which was confirmed when she began stalking him. One night she broke into his home with a gun and threatened him. He wrestled the gun from her and threw her on the floor where he proceeded to rape her until he'd climaxed three times, or so she claimed. His second wife, Lita Grey, had suggested that he was capable of doing that.

In his autobiography, Chaplin recalled that once he'd had dinner with J. Edgar "many years ago. After one overcomes a rather brutal face and a broken nose, one finds him quite agreeable."

Such was not the case in 1942 when Chaplin dined at Chasen's in Los Angeles. He spotted J. Edgar and Clyde eating steaks at a nearby table. The men did not converse, although Chaplin nodded to J. Edgar on his way out of the restaurant. Unknown to the actor at the time, J. Edgar was in Los Angeles to investigate charges that Chaplin violated the Mann Act which made it against the law to transport a woman across the state line for purposes of seduction.

It was learned that Chaplin had transported Barry to New York when he appeared at Carnegie Hall, rallying supporters advocating the opening of a Second Front in Europe as a means of aiding the Russians in the East. Not only had Chaplin seduced Barry himself, but he had passed her around to his friends at an orgy staged at his hotel suite. Allegedly Chaplin had called Barry "the party favor."

On hearing this, J. Edgar told his agents, "If this is a White Slave violation, we ought to go after him vigorously."

At some point Clyde had interviewed the Hollywood financier, Blumenthal, who agreed to speak off the record if he'd be granted immunity. He confessed that since 1925, he'd attended orgies with Chaplin. "At the first one, Chaplin showed up with Louise Brooks, and they went at it from nightfall until the next day." He also testified that Chaplin often hired young girls to service men at these orgies. Reportedly, Blumenthal told Clyde, "Chaplin liked fourteen-year-olds. His favorite pastime was penetrating virginal hymens." Blumenthal also claimed that Chaplin told him that he practically kept an abortion clinic in Mexico in business.

J. Edgar voyeuristically read Clyde's reports on Chaplin. "It looks like we can get the fucker on the Mann Act."

Beefed up by J. Edgar's FBI reports, Charles Carr, the U.S. attorney in Los Angeles, presented his accusations to a Federal grand jury in January of 1944. He walked away with four indictments against the actor, the first an alleged violation of the Mann Act, the other three involving charges that Chaplin had violated Barry's civil rights by conspiring to have her flee Los Angeles after she was arrested for shoplifting.

Chaplin had been impressed with criminal defense attorney Jerry Giesler when he'd defended Errol Flynn on charges of statutory rape. The lawyer took on Chaplin's case, defending him against a largely hostile press. *Variety* called for Chaplin to "be drummed out of the industry."

In retaliation, and against the advice of Giesler, Chaplin shot back, charging Barry with being "an agent for a pro-Nazi cult." Even though a war was raging, Chaplin claimed that many pro-Fascists in Hollywood "are attacking me because I ridiculed Hitler in my film, *The Great Dictator*." After that outburst, which no one believed, Giesler advised Chaplin not to speak to the press about the case.

Time magazine reported "Auburn-haired Joan Barry, 24, who wandered from her native Detroit to New York to Hollywood in pursuit of a theatrical career, became a Chaplin protégée in the summer of 1941. She fitted into a familiar pattern. Chaplin signed her to a $75-a-week contract and began training her for a part in a projected picture. Two weeks after the contract was signed she became his mistress. Throughout the summer and autumn, Miss Barry testified, she visited the ardent actor five or six times a week. By midwinter her visits were down to maybe three times a week. By the summer of 1942 Chaplin had decided that she was unsuited for his movie. Her contract ended."

Conviction on all four counts would have subjected Chaplin to a sentence of twenty-three years in prison, with fines of up to $26,000. The jury acquitted Chaplin during his first trial on a charge of violation of the Mann Act.

Attorney General Tom Clark called Charles Carr in Los Angeles and told him to drop the other three cases of conspiracy. "We don't really have a case here." Clark overrode J. Edgar, who wanted Carr to continue to press the case against Chaplin.

But Barry was not going to go gently into that good night. On October 2, 1943 she'd given birth to a baby girl named Carol Ann. She claimed that Chaplin was the father and filed a paternity suit against him.

The Little Tramp was back in the headlines again in a most unattractive way. Long before Richard Nixon played dirty tricks, J. Edgar was a master of the art. He fed unfounded rumors about Chaplin to Hollywood's two most viperish columnists, Louella Parsons and Hedda Hopper. When they reported his accusations, he then issued FBI reports, claiming that "the press alleges. . . ."

In one column, published on December 27, 1943, Hopper wrote that Chaplin contributed $25,000 to the Communist Party but only $100 to the Red Cross. Parsons dredged up the old charge that the Queen of the Silent Screen, Mary Pickford, had once called Chaplin "a dirty old man."

Chaplin, along with Barry and Carol Ann, her infant daughter, were ordered to take blood tests. The tests revealed that Chaplin's blood type was O, Barry's blood type A, and Carol Ann's blood type B, making it highly unlikely that Chaplin was the biological father. Giesler moved for a dismissal of the charges against Chaplin. The judge denied the request. At that time blood tests could not be admitted as evidence in California state courts.

In a memo sent to J. Edgar on August 25, 1943, Robert Hood of the FBI in Los Angeles claimed that Chaplin's attorneys were "buying up male witnesses to testify that they were intimate with Berry (sic) at the time Carol Ann was conceived." He alleged that unlimited funds were being expended.

As bizarre as it sounds, Attorney General Clark and J. Edgar feared that Chaplin would skip bail and flee to the Soviet Union. He'd been invited by Stalin himself to pay a goodwill visit to Moscow. Barry testified that Chaplin had told her that he was considering a defection because Stalin had promised to make him a commissar over the lackluster Soviet film industry. Hood also told J. Edgar that Chaplin was taking lessons in Russian.

For her lawyer, Barry signed with Joseph Scott, whom a reporter compared to an Old Testament prophet. The trial opened on December 19, 1944, at which time jurors heard Scott denounce Chaplin as "a cheap Cockney cad, a pestiferous, lecherous hound, and a little runt of a Svengali." He even suggested that Chaplin had taken shots to change his blood type, although that was impossible.

Lita Grey, Chaplin's divorced second wife, claimed that her former husband had paid corrupt government officials to tamper with the blood test results.

The jury deadlocked on January 4, 1945, with seven voting for acquittal, five for conviction. The judge ordered a second trial which opened on April 12, 1945. This time nine jurors voted for convictions, the rest for acquittal. Instead of facing yet another trial, Judge Clarence L. Kincaid ruled that Chaplin should pay Barry $5,000 plus $75 a month in child support until Carol Ann turned twenty-one.

In the early 1950s, doctors diagnosed Barry as a schizophrenic and consigned her to a state mental hospital in California.

Although she faded from his life, J. Edgar did not. More troubles for Chaplin were on the way.

***

On March 7, 1947, Senator William Langer of North Dakota visited the offices of J. Edgar where he was shown excerpts from the file on Chaplin. Angered, the next day he addressed the Senate, asking why "a man like Charlie Chaplin, with his communistic leanings, with his unsavory record of law-breaking, or rape, or the debauchery of American girls 16 and 17 years of age, should remain in this country."

That same year HUAC subpoenaed Chaplin to come before their committee to testify. The actual hearing was postponed three times before it was finally cancelled. Working behind the scenes, J. Edgar had determined it was better to keep him off the witness stand and not allow him to present his side of the story. "Let the rumors and innuendos stand," J. Edgar advised. Richard Nixon also warned that if called "Chaplin is likely to ridicule and lampoon us in a movie."

Chaplin was invited to attend the premiere of his film, *Limelight*, in 1952. He accepted the invitation and flew to London, not knowing that J. Edgar would work to prevent his return to California.

J. Edgar met with James P. McGranery, President Truman's final appointee as Attorney General. After reading the FBI file on Chaplin, McGranery determined that the re-entry of Chaplin into the United States should be opposed on the grounds of "moral turpitude." The Attorney General was particularly incensed at the number of abortions Chaplin was said to have arranged. He agreed with J. Edgar that Chaplin could be barred under the law banning "political or moral undesirables."

On hearing of the legal troubles that awaited him back in the U.S., Chaplin decided not to return. He told the press, "Since the end of the last world war, I have been the object of lies and propaganda by powerful reactionary groups who, by their influence and the aid of America's yellow press, have created an unhealthy atmosphere in which liberal-minded individuals can be singled out and persecuted. Under the conditions, I find it virtually impossible to continue my motion picture work, and I have therefore given up my residence in the United States."

Eventually, Chaplin left England, settling in Vevey, Switzerland, with his fourth and final wife, Oona O'Neill, whom he'd married when she was eighteen years old. Her father, playwright Eugene O'Neill, had objected to the marriage.

Chaplin would not return to the United States until April of 1972, when he was invited by the Motion Picture Academy of Arts and Sciences to receive an honorary Oscar.

With only weeks to live, J. Edgar spent his fading energy trying unsuccessfully to prevent Chaplin's re-entry into the country. He failed, and the ailing eighty-two-year-old actor flew to Hollywood, where the Academy gave him the longest standing ovation in its history when Jack Lemmon presented him with his overdue Oscar.

***

J. Edgar had failed to pin the Red label on Chaplin, but, with the aid of Senator Joseph McCarthy, he would succeed in wrecking other lives be-

By blackmailing **Richard Nixon** *(left)*, J. Edgar managed to continue as FBI director during Nixon's first term as president.

On the surface, at least, J. Edgar maintained a friendly relationship with **Ronald Reagan** *(right)*. Guy Hotell later said, "If told that Reagan would one day become president of the United States, Eddie would never have believed it. For one thing, he would think that by the 1980s, Reagan would be far too old to hold another political office. Besides, Eddie thought a divorced actor without a lot of brain power could never become president."

Had Reagan ascended to the presidency during J. Edgar's lifetime, J. Edgar had already prepared his blackmail on him. The FBI director told Guy, "As head of the Screen Actors Guild, Reagan once raped a young woman, and I covered it up."

cause of some affiliation with communism, regardless of how tenuous.

As J. Edgar moved into the 1950s, his obsession with chasing after followers of "commonism" (he never could pronounce the word) remained at fever pitch. Riding piggy-back on McCarthy, the FBI director and the senator defined the final Truman years and the launch of the Eisenhower era. They continued on a headline-making streak that divided a nation.

After leaving office, Truman blasted McCarthy on TV. "McCarthyism is the corruption of truth, the abandonment of our historical devotion to fair play. It is the spread of fear and the destruction of faith in every level of our society. This horrible cancer is eating at the vitals of America, and it can destroy the great edifice of freedom."

J. Edgar was called upon to defend the senator. "I view him as a friend and believe he so views me. Certainly he is a controversial man. He is earnest and he is honest. He has enemies. Whenever you attack Communists, Fascists, even the Ku Klux Klan, you are going to be the victim of extremely vicious criticism."

None of Truman's criticism was quite as vicious as what one future president, Richard Nixon, told another future president, Ronald Reagan, one night in California when the two met together to see if they might join forces to help each other's future careers.

"Isn't it ironic?" Nixon asked Reagan, "that Hoover and McCarthy are chasing after Reds and faggots in the State Department, and both of them, the senator and director, have sucked more cocks than your secret girlfriend, this Marilyn Monroe thing."

CHAPTER TEN

Twelve days after the launch of the Korean War, J. Edgar sent a daring plan to the White House that would suspend *habeas corpus* and imprison some 12,000 Asian Americans suspected of disloyalty. The plan was shown to Harry S Truman on July 7, 1950, calling for mass arrests "to protect the country against treason, espionage, and sabotage." From a list provided by J. Edgar's office, the FBI could apprehend any person viewed as potentially dangerous to national security. Since 1946, J. Edgar and Clyde had been compiling this list of possible traitors.

Since the arrests in New York and California would cause the prisons in those states to overflow, J. Edgar proposed that the prisoners be jailed at military facilities across the country. This provocative plan evoked J. Edgar's participation in the notorious Palmer raids of 1920, which swept up thousands of people suspected of being communists or radicals.

In September of 1950, Truman vetoed as unconstitutional a law authorizing the detention of persons suspected of being a "dangerous radical." Opposing him, Congress passed the Internal Security Act of 1950, also known as the McCarran Act. Congress voted to override the President's veto. Truman never signed the bill.

***

Senator Joseph McCarthy had promised the Tydings Committee that he would name "the top Russian espionage agent in the United States," an employee of the State Department. At that point in their relationship, McCarthy was still on friendly terms with J. Edgar and Clyde, and was seen frequently with the two FBI honchos at Harvey's Restaurant, where they continued to dine for free, or at the race track, as all three men were avid fans and secret gamblers. J. Edgar always placed "safe bets," having been tipped off before as to which races were fixed by the Mafia.

Working around the clock, the best name that J. Edgar and Clyde could provide for McCarthy to throw under the bus was Owen Lattimore. Born in the U.S., Lattimore had been reared in China, where his parents taught English at a Chinese university. He became an author/educator and influ-

One of the major victims of Senator Joseph McCarthy's witch hunt for communists was **Owen Lattimore**, an expert on Far Eastern affairs. He is seen above *(left)* talking with **Chiang-Kai Sheck** in 1941.

William C. Sullivan, J. Edgar's number 3 man at the FBI, said, "We investigated the hell out of Lattimore, read every letter and memo, everything he ever wrote, but we never found anything substantial to use against him. McCarthy's accusations were ridiculous."

ential scholar of Central Asia.

After the Germans invaded the Soviet Union in June of 1941, President Franklin D. Roosevelt appointed Lattimore U.S. adviser to Chinese Nationalist leader Chiang Kai-shek. In 1944, Lattimore was given the post of helming the Pacific area for the Office of War Information. At this point he came under J. Edgar's surveillance.

When Lattimore accompanied Vice President Henry Wallace on a mission to Siberia and Mongolia in 1944, the scholar aroused J. Edgar's suspicions once again. He told his aides, "We don't have proof yet, but I think Lattimore is marching to the drum beat of the Kremlin. Both he and that Wallace."

At one point, Lattimore visited the Soviet Union's concentration camp at Kolyma and later wrote favorably about it, claiming the inmates looked strong and well fed. That was the nail in Lattimore's coffin as far as J. Edgar was concerned. McCarthy wanted a victim, and J. Edgar fingered Lattimore.

On December 14, 1948 Alexander Barmine, the former *chargé d'affaires* at the Soviet Embassy in Athens, wrote a letter to J. Edgar, claiming that Lattimore was a Soviet agent, based on what he'd been told by Soviet GRU Director Janis Berzin. Later, J. Edgar would arrange for Barmine to get in touch with McCarthy and have him repeat these accusations before the Senate Committee in 1951.

In a preliminary private meeting with the Tydings Committee before the actual public hearings, McCarthy lied and said he had not spoken to J. Edgar about the case. He also told Tydings and the senators, "If you crack this case, it will be the biggest espionage case in the history of the United States." Finally, he vowed, "I am willing to stand or fall on the Lattimore case."

Appearing before Tydings and other senators in March of 1950, McCarthy outed Lattimore as the top Soviet agent in the United States. Privately he'd told Tydings, "When Soviet spies land in the United States, they first report to Lattimore for their marching orders."

McCarthy cited Lattimore's "tremendous power" at the State Department, and called him the architect of the Far East policy of the United

States.

On that day, Lattimore was in Kabul, Afghanistan on a cultural mission for the United Nations. Denouncing the charges as "moonshine," he rushed back to America to testify before the Tydings Committee.

McCarthy summoned Louis F. Budenz, former editor of the Communist Party *Daily Worker*, who testified that Lattimore was a secret communist, but not a Soviet spy. "He often assists the Soviets in their foreign policy," Budenz lied.

After hearing the witnesses and McCarthy's reckless charges, the majority report cleared Lattimore, although some senators still felt he was a spy.

As it turned out, Lattimore did not work for the State Department at all. "We're still looking for his desk," said Tydings. It seemed that he had once given a speech to State Department employees on Far East matters five years ago. In response, the Tydings Committee published a report denouncing McCarthy and his claims against Lattimore as a hoax.

McCarthy got his revenge when Tydings ran for re-election in 1950 and was defeated by John Marshall Butler.

Roy Cohn, McCarthy's chief aide, distributed a *faux* composite picture of Tydings with Earl Browder, the former leader of the American Communist Party. The doctored photo merged a 1938 picture of Tydings listening to the radio and a 1940 photo of Browder delivering a speech. The suggestion was that Tydings was an eager listener to Browder's communist propaganda. The voting public in Tydings' state of Maryland fell for the libel.

Lattimore was not let off the hook so easily. In February of 1952, he was called to testify before the Senate Internal Security Subcommittee (SISS) headed by a dedicated anti-communist, Senator Pat McCarran, McCarthy's ally. Except for the McCarthy/Army hearings to come, this twelve-day session was the most acrimonious of all the investigative hearings, marked by shouting matches, even threats of physical violence between the opposing sides.

Budenz was brought in again to testify that Lattimore was both a communist and a spy for the Soviets, contradicting his previous testimony.

Finally, after seventeen months of controversial hearings, and after having summoned sixty-six witnesses and thousands of documents, the McCarran Committee issued a 226-page unanimous report. Lattimore was named as "a conscious and articulate instrument of the Soviet conspiracy," with the understanding that he had functioned in that role since the 1930s. He was indicted for perjury on seven counts. But within three years a Federal judge, Luther Youngdahl, would dismiss the charges, calling the so-called evidence "insubstantial and not judicable."

Thanks to insider tips, McCarthy and J. Edgar usually won at the race tracks, but they lost the ball game for the McCarran Committee. The controversy, however, destroyed Lattimore's academic career. He became one of the more prominent victims of McCarthyism.

Both J. Edgar and McCarthy wasted little time fretting over the Lattimore case, moving on to their next victims.

***

The man with the perpetually bloodshot eyes, Roy Cohn, was one of the most brilliant, ruthless, and controversial lawyers in America. He met and gained the attention of J. Edgar and Clyde when he served on the Justice Department's prosecution team at the espionage trials of Soviet spies Julius and Ethel Rosenberg. In gay bars, he proclaimed that it was he who influenced Judge Irving Kaufman to impose the death penalty on his fellow Jews, the Rosenbergs.

J. Edgar and Clyde bonded with Cohn, and soon he was seen dining with them at Harvey's Restaurant. "We share a lot in common," J. Edgar told him. The sharp wit of Cohn didn't need but a second to figure out what that meant, but he knew he had to take the first step in outing himself to gain greater intimacy with Clyde and his boss-lover.

Cohn would later confide to his best friend, literary agent Jay Garon, that "Eddie and I lived deep in the closet in those days, but I knew how to win him over and show him I was one of them. When Clyde excused himself to go to the men's room one night, I looked wistfully at him as he moved away, and whispered to Eddie, 'I wish I had a man like that in my life.' At first he looked astonished, but then his face relaxed. I had sent the signal. He'd received it. From then on, it was clear in our relationship that anything goes. And it did, year after year after year. Eddie and I were not only gay, both of us were two of the most despised people in America."

When McCarthy asked J. Edgar to recommend a legal aide for his staff, the FBI Director named Cohn. "He can spot Red a mile away, and he sees a commie around every corner," J. Edgar claimed. "Wait until you see him put a commie on the hot seat. Roy's grilling beats any police detective with a suspect under a blazing light."

"I'm considering this other aggressive young guy, Robert Kennedy, the ambassador's son," McCarthy said.

He was referring, of course, to Joseph P. Kennedy, who had been ambassador to England and was a close friend of J. Edgar's.

"Don't do it," J. Edgar cautioned. "There are already rumblings that

At a Senate hearing, **Joseph McCarthy** *(left)* places his hand over the microphone as his chief counsel, a young **Roy Cohn** *(right)* feeds him confidential information.

your boys are anti-Semitic. Let's face it: you and I are. And all the Kennedys, including the founding *padre*, are anti-Semitic. If you appoint Cohn over Kennedy, it will show Congress that all your boys don't say Jew followed by the word bastard."

Talented, but with a character compared to both a porcupine and a serpent, Cohn told McCarthy, "I am a living rebuttal to the libel that all Jews are communist sympathizers." Smart and savvy, the twenty-six-year-old stood five foot eight. His hooded eyes gave him the perpetual look of someone denied sleep. Under slicked back black hair, he had a mysterious scar that ran down his nose.

During the day, Cohn castigated and sought out "commie sex perverts" in the Department of State, whereas at night he trolled the gay bars, preferring butch and clean-cut military types, preferably "blond and uncut," a rather kinky requirement for a Jewish boy descended from ancestors who practiced the age-old rite of circumcision on their infants.

In spite of McCarthy's own private life, he publicly claimed that homosexuals should not be allowed to work in government because they might be subject to blackmail. Without ever proving it, he stated that he knew the Soviet Embassy employed a series of good-looking men to entrap government workers into sexual situations where they could subsequently be blackmailed to turn over confidential information.

Within just a few weeks, Cohn was seen sitting at Table 50 in Manhattan, where columnist Walter Winchell held court at the Stork Club, with J. Edgar on one side of him and Clyde on the other. Cohn fed Winchell confidential information about "American traitors."

One night at the club, when Winchell had gone to meet Clark Gable at the bar, J. Edgar asked him how "things" were going with McCarthy.

"We're getting along great," Cohn said. "One weekend he took me to his lakeside retreat in Wisconsin owned by a friend of his. He drank a lot of bourbon which loosened him up a bit. He gave it to me up the ass."

If J. Edgar and Clyde didn't show surprise at this revelation, it was because they already knew that McCarthy was a closeted homosexual. J. Edgar lived in dread that news of McCarthy's homosexuality would reach someone in the press and discredit all of their anti-communist maneuvers, as it invariably did.

In covering up his own homosexuality, J. Edgar was sometimes placed in the awkward position of concealing McCarthy's true sexual preference. In 1952, Attorney General J. Howard McGrath received a letter from a young Army lieutenant, David Sayer. He accused McCarthy of "brutally sodomizing me" at the Wardman Park Hotel in Washington after getting him drunk.

J. Edgar had Clyde conduct a perfunctory investigation, and it was indeed determined that Sayer and McCarthy, both of them drunk, had checked into the hotel at two o'clock one early morning without luggage. Occupants in nearby rooms reported a disturbance which had died down by dawn when an unshaven McCarthy departed the hotel. J. Edgar wrote Mc-Grath that the FBI had looked into the accusation and found it without merit.

At one point, Cohn was allowed to read the file the FBI kept on Mc-Carthy. Although his sexual affairs in Wisconsin were not known, as a young senator he was watched closely in Washington. Apparently at one time he had hired a University of Wisconsin graduate, John Steadman, with whom he had been intimate in their home state, to work with Veterans Affairs. Because of the housing shortage in post-war Washington, the young man had a rented room. McCarthy was seen leaving the man's room sometimes as late as three o'clock in the morning.

One night, McCarthy's friend was arrested for soliciting a soldier in the men's room of the Washington bus terminal. McCarthy placed an emergency call to J. Edgar, who arranged for Steadman to be immediately transported back to Wisconsin with no charges filed.

This incident did not entirely escape press notice. The *New York Post*, then a liberal newspaper, ran a seventeen-part series called "Smear, Inc., The One-Man Mob of Joe McCarthy." In 1947, the researchers, William V. Shannon and Oliver Pilat, wrote: "The man [meaning McCarthy] who flamboyantly crusades against homosexuals, as if they were the menace to the nation, employed one in his office staff for many months."

In a private meeting, J. Edgar remained late at the office, talking with Clyde and Guy Hotell, who had just prepared a memo for McCarthy attacking homosexuals in the State Department.

"Roy Cohn and Joe McCarthy are our friends right now," J. Edgar warned them. "I'm a good judge of character. I find that both of these firecrackers have it in them to blow themselves up. I visited their office. They're sloppy and inefficient. They don't prepare their cases well. They hurl accusations and then turn to us for evidence, even if there is no evidence—a very risky business."

"What we've got to do is give them love and kisses but remember they are both rattlesnakes. They could bite us at any minute with their poison, even turn on us if things don't go well. We'll sleep in the same bed with them, but remember it's sleeping with the enemy. When they go down, we've got to see to it they don't take us with them. But for the moment, at least, we'll play around with these two lover boys."

***

Francis ("Flip") Flanagan was a veteran Capitol Hill operative who accepted the position of general counsel to the McCarthy staff. Roy Cohn was chief counsel, a position coveted by the young and aggressive Robert Kennedy, who was appointed assistant counsel.

Flanagan and Cohn lunched together at the Mayflower Hotel in Washington. "You have a real enemy in Bobby Kennedy," Flanagan warned Cohn. "First off, he's not all that crazy about Jews. Second, you're not exactly a member of the Palm Beach Polo Club. Finally, you've got the job he covets."

Robert Kennedy's first position, working for Joseph McCarthy and having to deal with Cohn, came about through the father of the Kennedy clan, Ambassador Joseph P. Kennedy, Sr., a long-time friend of McCarthy.

On his first visit to Hyannis Port, McCarthy told Joseph and Rose, "I'm shanty Irish. You guys are lace curtain Irish."

"We are just two Irish Catholics trying to make our way in a Protestant and Anglo-Saxon nation," the Kennedy patriarch told him.

Before he left Cape Cod that weekend, McCarthy hit up Kennedy for a loan of several thousand dollars. The Kennedy patriarch obliged and didn't ask what kind of jam the young senator was in.

He left Hyannis Port not only with some of the Kennedy bootleg money, but with a broken rib. When McCarthy broke his rib playing touch football, Jack Kennedy "benched him forever," according to Bobby.

Years later, Bobby confided in Lem Billings a story he'd never told his brothers and certainly not Joe. Lem was Jack Kennedy's best friend, a relationship that had begun at Choate in 1933 and continued for a lifetime.

A homosexual, Lem was in love with Jack, and the whole Kennedy clan knew it, but strangely tolerated Lem and his life-long obsession with Jack, whom he'd met while showering at prep school.

Lem also became Bobby's confidant. Bobby claimed that when he was seventeen years old, he took McCarthy sailing on a small boat off the coast of Hyannis Port. "Of course, there were no toilet facilities," Bobby said. "When you had to go, you pulled down your trunks and urinated over the side of the boat. All my brothers did that when sailing on a small craft. Mc-

Carthy came and stood beside me. At first I thought he had to take a leak. He looked down at my penis and said, 'I could take care of that for you.' I quickly pulled up my trunks and told him I didn't go that route."

This blatant proposition might have ended the relationship between Bobby and McCarthy but, surprisingly, it didn't. In fact, in the years to come, Bobby would make McCarthy the godfather of his first child. And although privately McCarthy came on to Bobby, for public consumption, he dated two of the Kennedy sisters.

First, McCarthy dated Patricia Kennedy or "Pat" as she was called. She found that he had a "certain raw wit and charm when he wasn't drunk." But she eventually dumped him to marry the bisexual movie star, Peter Lawford. McCarthy then dated Eunice and told his colleagues in Washington, "This is the gal for me. The only gal I've ever loved."

When Eunice dumped him to marry R. Sargent Shriver, he sent her a wedding present inscribed: "To one who lost, Joe McCarthy."

Pat read it and said, "Oh, that Joe, pretending to be straight."

Before McCarthy eventually proposed marriage to one of his office aides, he told Cohn, "Years ago, I figured if worse came to worst, I might have to marry one of the Kennedy gals."

"It was Papa Joe who arranged for Bobby to work in Washington for the McCarthy committee," Jacqueline Kennedy once recalled to author Gore Vidal. "Jack didn't think it was a good idea, but he was overruled."

Seeking his approval, Joe called J. Edgar. "A great way for Bobby to break into politics," the FBI director told Joe. "McCarthy's a great guy when he's sober."

"I made millions off of booze, so I can't complain if a man has a drink or two," Joe told J. Edgar.

Lawrence J. Quirk, RFK's biographer, wrote: "Bobby was an ambitious 27-year-old with a black-and-white, good-guys versus bad-guys, rather narrow thinking that time and circumstances were later to force him to outgrow, and McCarthy's howling and raucous anti-communist 'crusade' seemed like a right and good thing, something he could get his teeth into, something he could believe in."

Latter day fans of the very liberal Bobby Kennedy have a hard time reconciling his early role as a "Red Witch Hunter" for McCarthy.

"At the end of his life, Bobby was completely different from the young man I met when I was dating Jack," claimed Jacqueline in discussing her brother-in-law and the man who became her lover after her husband was assassinated in Dallas in November of 1963.

In Washington, McCarthy introduced Bobby to the tyrannical Cohn, who made his dislike of the Kennedy son very obvious. Bobby, as he admitted later, "despised the brash little Jew on sight." Bobby also intensely disliked Cohn's aide, G. David Schine, a hotel tycoon's son who pursued anti-communism with a dilettantish interest, perhaps needing something to do.

After a week of working with Cohn and Schine, Bobby flew back to Hyannis Port for a meeting with Joe. "Schine and Cohn are a couple of queers," Bobby told Joe. "Cohn is definitely the bottom, as that Schine seems to manufacture testosterone by the cupful. They go about investigating an alleged communist like a bull in a china shop."

Behind their backs, Bobby mocked Cohn and Schine as "the lavender duo, too pushy and egotistical for me. Schine walks around the office like he's packing a footlong dick." Some of Bobby's experiences with them would be recalled in his book, *The Enemy Within*.

He told Jack and Teddy that, "Hoover and Clyde Tolson often dine with Schine and Cohn. Birds of a feather if you ask me. All four of

Eventually, **Robert Kennedy** *(top photo, left)* became one of the most liberal members of the U.S. Senate. But when he worked for the ultra-conservative Senator **Joseph McCarthy** *(right)*, the duo were known as the odd couple. Bobby told his family that McCarthy had fallen in love with him and that was why he refused to go out drinking with him at night. "I didn't want one thing to lead to another," Bobby claimed.

In the bottom photo (left to right) are **David Schine, McCarthy,** and **Roy Cohn** testifying at a Senate hearing on communism. Schine and Cohn were lovers, as the hearings would soon reveal.

them are hit-below-the-belt-kind of fags. They decide who is a communist and then set out to gather evidence, even when the person is innocent."

One afternoon at a Senate hearing, tension between Cohn and Bobby exploded. Bobby had objected to Cohn's briefs for McCarthy, claiming, "You're leading the senator into a trap."

Cohn told Bobby, "Listen, rich man's son, mind your own fucking business. You're an idiot."

At recess, an encounter in the men's room led to Cohn slugging Bobby. He struck back, bloodying Cohn's scarred nose. At that point Schine, the most athletic and muscular of the trio, entered the men's room and pushed Bobby away from Cohn. Bobby hastily headed toward the exit, as Cohn called out to him: "You don't belong on the committee. Get lost!"

It was advice that Bobby took, although McCarthy claimed he regretted his leaving and called Joe Kennedy, telling him, "Your boy did a fine job. He's the kind of man who will one day be president, providing he switches to the Republican Party."

Even though he came to recognize McCarthy as a tyrant, Bobby still had a bond with him and personally liked him. "He was sensitive and yet insensitive," Bobby later said. "He was very thoughtful of his friends, but he could be so cruel to others. He was always kind to me. I cared for him, although I realized what a heavy-handed character he was."

Over the years, Bobby tried to explain to his very liberal anti-McCarthy aides why he felt compassion for McCarthy, who had ruined so many lives. Kennedy aide Kenneth O'Donnell recalled Bobby's remembrance.

He said, "I guess there are two sides to me, a loving man to my wife and brothers. That's the gentler side of me. McCarthy brought out the Hun in me. I stuck with him, even though he fell in love with me. I assure you, it was an unrequited love on his part. Deep down in my darkest soul, I must have admired his aggression, although he used it for all the wrong reasons. Both of the two Joes in my life, my dad and the senator, were father figures to me. Both of them wanted to climb the highest mountain but fell off."

In time, Bobby would move left of center in liberal politics, but he never completely disowned his former boss. "The saddest thing about the country's 'Grand Inquisitor' was that he so desperately wanted to be liked, but ended up the most despised man in America," Bobby told his aides.

Censored by the Senate, attacked and vilified after 1954, McCarthy walked through the corridors of power in his final months like a burned-out wraith. He died in May of 1957. Bobby flew to his funeral in Appleton, Wisconsin.

A reporter for the *Milwaukee Journal* was surprised to encounter Bobby at the funeral. "He stood away from the other mourners, almost hiding behind a nearby tree. It was obvious he didn't want his presence known. After McCarthy was put into the ground, Bobby was seen hurrying to the Green Bay Airport. With his departure that day, I think the McCarthy era, which started with such a bang, ended with a whimper."

***

For thirty-seven years, Drew Pearson wrote the nation's most popular column, "Washington Merry-Go-Round" for the *Washington Post*. He was later assisted by Jack Anderson, who eventually took over the column for him. Most mornings, over coffee, the first editorial J. Edgar and Clyde read was Pearson's column.

Although the newspaperman and the FBI director maintained a surface politeness with each other, they privately loathed each other. During WWII, Vice President Henry Wallace claimed that the FBI had Pearson under constant surveillance. J. Edgar called him "the slut of columnists who writes pathological lies."

Privately, Pearson referred to J. Edgar and McCarthy as "the butterfly boys." Sometimes, if he had enough to drink, he referred to them as "those two anti-commie pansies."

Among political columnists, Pearson was the number one muckraker in America. He never had any qualms about publishing a story whether it was true or not. Based on leaks from within the government, his truth was often heavily embroidered, as he liked to emphasize the sensation in a news item. He combined facts with invented stories of his own.

FDR claimed Pearson was "a chronic liar." On his payroll was a staff of chauffeurs, waiters, politicians spilling the secrets on their enemies, bribed military personnel, and even a thief or two skilled at office break-ins.

The most widely read columnist in America, **Drew Pearson** *(above)*, was a bitter enemy of Senator Joseph McCarthy. "One time, he threatened to mutilate me so I couldn't go on television," Pearson claimed.

When it came to exposing McCarthy, the gadfly columnist was the man for the job. He leaked information about McCarthy's homosexuality, his bogus war record, and even that he used campaign money to speculate in the gyrating soybean market.

Pearson once revealed that McCarthy, between bouts of Senate testimony, retreated to the men's room to chug-a-lug a fifth of Irish whiskey while gulping down a handful of baking soda to quiet his diaphragmatic hernia.

The newspaperman liked to reveal the salacious details of a subject's sexual proclivities. In time, he would open the closet door of McCarthy himself. J. Edgar and Clyde both feared Pearson, knowing he could do to them what he was doing to McCarthy.

Sometimes J. Edgar felt Pearson had gone too far, and the two of them had epic battles. On December 12, 1941, Clyde through an informant told J. Edgar that Pearson was going to reveal "what really happened at Pearl Harbor and who was responsible." In anger, J. Edgar called Pearson and threatened to have him thrown in jail—and "you know I have the power to do that and to toss the key." Pearson didn't run the column, which had placed the blame for the Japanese attack on Pearl Harbor clearly on J. Edgar's failure to coordinate intelligence.

Pearson angered both General Dwight D. Eisenhower and J. Edgar when he was the first to report the 1943 wartime incident when General George S. Patton slapped a soldier, Charles Kuhl. J. Edgar, working with Army intelligence, never figured out who leaked that story.

The columnist also angered another general, Douglas MacArthur, when he wrote that he was actively campaigning for a promotion. MacArthur sued Pearson, but dropped his case when the columnist threatened to publish love letters from the general to Isabel Rosario Cooper, his Eurasian mistress.

J. Edgar wanted to move carefully around Pearson, who constantly threatened he'd write a series of articles about his private life with Clyde. In an impulsive decision to prevent that, J. Edgar made a deal to throw his friend McCarthy to this newspaper "wolf hound." Secretly he had Clyde leak Pearson incriminating details about McCarthy.

Since 1950, Pearson had written columns attacking America's "Red Hunter." McCarthy charged that David Karr, Pearson's aide, was "the KGB handler" for the columnist. An investigation by J. Edgar and Clyde turned up evidence that Karr had worked as a reporter in 1943 for the *Daily Worker*, the communist newspaper.

The battle heated up. In Las Vegas in 1952, McCarthy called Hank Greenspun, the editor of the *Las Vegas Sun*, a former communist.

Using secrets supplied by Pearson, who in turn had gotten them from J. Edgar, the hard-boiled publisher, Greenspun, exposed McCarthy as a homosexual within his newspaper.

Additionally, the *Las Vegas Sun* revealed that McCarthy had been sexually involved with Charles Davis, who was a confessed homosexual and onetime communist. The publisher also cited the arrest of one of McCarthy's "Intimates," Edward Babcock, an administrative assistant, who had been picked up for soliciting a sailor "for lewd and lascivious purposes."

An informant in Madison, Wisconsin revealed that McCarthy had spent the night in a Wausau hotel room with William McMahon, formerly an official of the Milwaukee Young Republicans during the Wisconsin Republican Convention. "From the sounds coming through the thin walls, these two perverts engaged in illicit sex with each other," the manager charged. The staff at the White Horse Inn in Milwaukee also claimed that over the years the senator had checked into a various rooms with various young men.

McCarthy immediately threatened to sue Greenspun for libel. He suspected that Pearson—not J. Edgar—was the source of the rumors. J. Edgar advised McCarthy not to do that. "So far the story's stayed in Vegas. Let's keep it there."

Enraged, McCarthy reluctantly agreed to do that after he calmed down and realized that a libel trial would virtually destroy his career, because the rumors were true and because he suspected that the defense would produce dozens of witnesses to testify about his various liaisons with young men.

However, back in Washington one evening, Pearson and McCarthy each selected the Sulgrave Club for dinner, eating at tables on opposite sides of the dining room and not aware of each other's presence. However, McCarthy encountered Pearson in the cloakroom. The senator attacked the columnist.

At that moment Richard Nixon entered the cloakroom to separate the two warriors. "Let a peaceful Quaker put an end to this."

The next day Pearson filed a lawsuit against McCarthy, charging him with "grabbing me by the neck and kicking me in the groin." McCarthy counter-charged that Pearson was "a communist tool."

***

On September 29, 1953, McCarthy married his office aide, Jean Kerr, a dedicated anti-communist. In the years leading up to their marriage, they had often fought and broken up. On three different occasions he had fired her.

J. Edgar, Guy Hotell, and Clyde speculated that he got married to quash rumors that he was a homosexual. The marriage did not succeed in doing that. If anything, after the McCarthy/Army hearings the rumors were red hot.

At parties and on other occasions, McCarthy came on strong with women, almost to the point of harassment. Some of the more naïve observers of the 1950s called him a womanizer; however, he never seemed to follow through on a conquest even when a woman indicated she might be willing to give him a tumble.

McCarthy's wedding attracted A-list guests, including J. Edgar and Clyde, John and Robert Kennedy, Patricia and Richard Nixon, Secretary of the Army Robert Stevens, and even Allen Dulles, director of the CIA. From the Vatican, the Pope sent his blessings.

Willard Edwards of *The Chicago Tribune* wrote, "At the age of forty-five, McCarthy got married only to quash stories that he was a homosexual." In writing that, he echoed an opinion already shared by J. Edgar and Clyde.

After the marriage, Clyde and J. Edgar behaved like a married couple visiting another married couple. As Cohn claimed, "Hoover used to come over with Tolson, and he loved Mrs. McCarthy's cooking. All of us would sit around, let our hair down, and exchange confidences, a very relaxed evening, although we were some of the most controversial people in America."

***

Drew Pearson's main investigative reporter, Jack Anderson, won the 1972 Pulitzer Prize for National Reporting the same year J. Edgar died. Clyde Tolson called Anderson "the lowest form of human being to walk on the face of the earth."

After Anderson began attacking J. Edgar and how he ran the FBI, the director told his aides. "We must silence his sources and spread scurrilous rumors about the fucker."

At one point, Anderson hired a detective to sort through J. Edgar's household garbage, although he turned up nothing incriminating. The FBI director, who had ordered many a garbage can associated with other suspects searched, was too clever to toss out anything revelatory about himself. As the detective reported to Anderson, "J. Edgar and Tolson must bare-back—not even a used rubber."

From J. Edgar's garbage, Anderson did learn that he drank Jack Daniels Black Label and brushed his teeth with Ultra-Brite. For a sore throat, he took Cepacol and for stomach acid, Gelusil.

After Pearson died, Anderson took over the "Washington Merry-go-Round" column and became the king of all muckrakers. He reached an audience of forty million readers and was published in a thousand newspapers.

Anderson's feud with J. Edgar began in the 1950s when he accused the FBI director of allowing the Mafia to go unchecked. J. Edgar called Anderson "lower than the regurgitated filth of vultures."

The columnist hastened the destruction of McCarthy and, in the years to come, wrote ex-

Jean Kerr *(left)* took time out on September 29, 1953, at St. Matthew's Cathedral in Washington to marry Senator *Joseph McCarthy,* who was called the most hated man in America.

As columnist Drew Pearson cattily remaked to his colleagues at *The Washington Post,* "That just proves there's somebody in the world for every person. Even Eva Braun loved Hitler."

Before her marriage, Kerr told reporters that she had firmly laid down "conditions" for their marriage.

Had he made a promise to her to give up young men? She declined to disclose what her conditions were. Robert Kennedy said, "I didn't think Joe was the marrying kind."

posés of J. Edgar himself.

Almost no major columnist had ever done that, but in the wake of Anderson's attacks, other newspapermen followed suit. Whatever the scandal, Anderson was on the scene with his interpretation—the Kennedy assassinations, Chappaquiddick, Watergate, fugitive Nazis, white supremacists, the Iran-Contra scandal.

Of all the newspaper men who ever lived, J. Edgar detested columnist **Jack Anderson** the most. "I wish him dead," J. Edgar often told Clyde and his aides.

With very few exceptions, Clyde always loathed the press, but in the beginning, he viewed Anderson as a friend of the FBI and fed him "special information."

But when Anderson started publishing a series of articles attacking J. Edgar and the Bureau, Clyde turned, referring to him as a "turncoat," ordering agents to "dig up the dirt."

At the FBI, Clyde's main job involved protecting "The Boss" from attacks.

Over the years, Anderson was called "part circus huckster, part guerrilla fighter, and part righteous rogue."

As he neared the age of eighty, nothing infuriated J. Edgar more than when the columnist wrote, "Hoover should have retired ten years ago. He would better serve his country as an elder statesman who could offer advice to his successor."

The year J. Edgar died, Anderson was the target of an assassination plot brewing within the White House. For years, Nixon had blamed Anderson's publication of a story he had revealed on the eve of the elections of 1960, about a secret loan from Howard Hughes to Nixon's brother, Don, for his loss of the presidential race to John F. Kennedy. Nixon's resentments had simmered ever since 1960.

Nixon himself never authorized any attempt on Anderson's life. But reports that later came out about those "White House plumbers," G. Gordon Liddy and E. Howard Hunt, claimed that this nefarious pair wanted to curry favor with Nixon by "righting a wrong of long ago." Doing away with Anderson would be "revenge at last" for Nixon, at least in their alleged view. If reports are to be believed, from within the White House, Liddy and Hunt plotted how to remove Anderson. Options they discussed included poisoning his aspirin bottle, staging a fatal mugging, or giving him a lethal dose of LSD. What saved Anderson's life was the diversion of the Watergate break-in.

Ironically, in this lifelong "Battle of the Titans," neither party ever fully succeeded in getting what he really wanted from the other. J. Edgar wanted to obtain Anderson's file on him, and the columnist wanted to obtain the FBI's file on him.

Anderson once admitted, "I used J. Edgar as a role model by bugging phones, savaging my victims, and ignoring fairness in the pursuit of an exposé."

***

J. Edgar never really destroyed either Drew Pearson or Jack Anderson, but he took delight in the disgrace of Joseph Alsop, a Harvard-educated "blue blood" of Connecticut whose ancestors had included Presidents Theodore Roosevelt and James Monroe. Entering journalism, he became a best-selling author when he published *The 168 Days* (1938) about FDR's unsuccessful campaign to enlarge the Supreme Court.

In WWII, he trained in Burma and joined the famous "Flying Tigers," until he was captured and interned in Hong Kong by the Japanese.

After the war, he became known for his newspaper column, "Matter of Fact." Unlike Pearson and Anderson, Alsop insisted on the accuracy of his information even if it meant exposing the illegal investigative methods of the FBI. Although a Republican, he supported JFK's bid for the presidency.

J. Edgar and Clyde were not fooled by Alsop's marriage to Susan Mary Jay Patten in 1961. They knew that this noted art connoisseur and collector was a closeted homosexual like themselves. When McCarthy objected to an article Alsop had written about him in the *Saturday Evening Post*, J. Edgar called McCarthy, informing him that Alsop was a homosexual.

In a speech the following day, McCarthy did not overtly accuse Alsop of being a homosexual, but did refer to him as "not being healthy and normal" during one of his attacks on "perverts and pederasts."

Confirmation of Alsop's secret gay life came in 1957 when Clyde opened a package delivered to the FBI from the Soviet Embassy. In it, there were a dozen photographs of a drunken Alsop in a Moscow hotel room with a Soviet agent, a tall, incredibly handsome blond giant of a man. The American reporter was photographed performing fellatio on the Soviet hunk as well as being sodomized by him.

When John F. Kennedy ran for president in 1960, Alsop lent him a vigorous support, even though he was descended from a long line of Republicans. When JFK took over the Oval Office, one of J. Edgar's first "official" duties was to visit him and show him the KGB photographs of Alsop and the Soviet agent. JFK dismissed J. Edgar and ordered him to destroy the photographs, a presidential command he did not obey.

In a confession, Alsop wrote a "detailed account of the incident and a narrative history of his homosexual sex life." It brimmed with revelations about his involvement with men on several continents, and even detailed his love affair with Arthur H. Vandenberg Jr., who had been the appointment secretary to Dwight Eisenhower.

For reasons of his own, Alsop delivered this highly personal document to the CIA, who in turn sent the dossier to J. Edgar and Clyde, each of whom read the papers with a certain glee.

In 1957, when Alsop wrote several articles critical of the Soviet Union, the KGB sent the incriminating sex photographs of him to some fifty journalists across America, although not one reporter chose to publish the information in the uptight Eisenhower era. At one point Alsop considered going public with details of his gay life to end the harassment, but ultimately did not.

In Gore Vidal's 1967 novel, *Washington, D.C.*, the character of a gay journalist was based on Alsop. Alsop's own memoir, lacking the spicy details, was called *I've Seen the Best of It* and published three years after his death in 1989.

***

General Eisenhower, in June of 1944, had successfully directed the greatest armada of all time, Allied troops landing on the coast of Normandy facing a blood bath. "It is not the end," he said, "but it is the beginning of the end. After the liberation of Paris, it's on to Berlin to destroy the Third Reich that Hitler had boasted would last a thousand years."

From a dirt-poor family in Kansas, Ike had risen to become one of the towering figures in world history even before he ran for President of the United States. Having commanded Allied forces in Europe during WWII, he'd become a popular hero.

He'd been offended by McCarthy's foam-at-the-mouth, anti-communist rabble-rousing, but didn't really understand J. Edgar's role behind the scenes. Ike was hardly soft on communism himself. As president he bullied North Korea into an armistice and presided over a bitter Cold War with the Soviet Union. He helped organize America's stockpiling of nuclear weapons, especially after Russia launched its Sputnik satellite into space in 1957.

J. Edgar, noting how thin Ike's "blackmail file" was, ordered Clyde and his agents "to dig up more dirt." He'd had plenty of blackmail on FDR, less so on Truman.

As Guy Hotell later recalled, "both Eddie and Clyde set out to look under every rock to see what they could find on Eisenhower and on Stevenson. With Stevenson, at least their investigation paid off. Ike had less scandal."

FBI agents looked into Ike's past, discovering he'd lost his virginity to a redhead known as Ruby Norman. "Ruby or Sadie always sounds to me like a hooker," the FBI director said.

Apparently, Ike was rather shy around girls until he met a teenager, Mamie Geneva Doud, the daughter of a Denver meat packer, whom he married on St. Valentine's Day, 1916, after a whirlwind romance.

During the war he was posted in London as the Supreme Commander. In England, he met a former model and movie actress, Kay Summersby, a member of the transport section of the women's Royal Army Corps. He was immediately attracted to this Irish lass, calling her "a double-breasted GI with a built-in foxhole."

Twenty years his junior, Kay virtually became his slave, pouring his coffee, laying out his clothes, and seeing that an aide kept his shoes shined.

Winston Churchill soon learned that Kay and Ike were a couple, as did King George VI. Ike and Kay showed up in Algeria, in Egypt, and in Palestine. She fell in love with her middle-aged general.

Apparently, Ike waited a long time before he put the moves on Kay, although eventually, J. Edgar and Clyde confirmed that they'd had an affair and were lovers, although the FBI did not know the true story of that relationship.

Long after J. Edgar and Eisenhower had died, a cancer-stricken Kay on her death bed worked on her memoirs called *Past Forgetting: My Love Affair with Dwight D. Eisenhower*. "It was like an explosion. We were suddenly in each other's arms. His kisses absolutely unraveled me. Hungry, strong, demanding, and I responded every bit as passionately. We were breathing as if we had run up a dozen flights of stairs."

But their passion evolved into disappointment for both of them. As she bluntly put it in her memoirs: "Eisenhower could not get an erection." Later at a secluded, guarded retreat, Telegraph Cottage, they tried on several occasions to make love. Finally, she concluded the obvious: Ike was impotent. At war's end, he decided that there was no more need for Kay in his life. He returned home to Mamie.

As author Nigel Cawthorne speculated, "One would wonder what damage the German propaganda machine could have caused if they had found out that Ike was impotent."

J. Edgar put it more colorfully, "World War II was fought between an impotent general and a Nazi leader with one ball."

***

In 1952, homosexuality was the love that dare not speak its name. For years J. Edgar and Clyde had been told that Ike's opponent, Adlai Stevenson, was a homosexual, although he tried to have affairs with certain movie stars to prove that he was straight. On his arm candy list were Ava Gardner, Shelley Winters, and Joan Fontaine.

The FBI interviewed Ellen Borden, the wealthy socialite whom Stevenson had married in 1928, divorcing her in 1949 after having three sons with her. Since 1935 they'd lived on a 70-acre plot of land near Libertyville, outside Chicago.

After her divorce and throughout the 1952 campaign, the ex-Mrs. Stevenson told such reporters as James ("Scotty") Reston that her husband was a homosexual. She also claimed that he had had numerous affairs and "is mentally and morally unfit for the presidency."

Suffering from what was diagnosed as "persecution paranoia," Ellen made an astonishing claim to journalist Arthur Krock. The bombshell she delivered was that one night in Chicago, Stevenson murdered a man and used his political influence to have the investigation squashed.

J. Edgar and Clyde seized on that accusation; if proven, the presidential race was all but over. The murder was said to have occurred in 1948. But after FBI agents combed through the records in Chicago, not a shred of evidence could be found to back up this charge.

Murder might be out of the question, but the homosexual label seemed to stick on Stevenson, or so J. Edgar and his agents determined. In Baltimore, Stevenson was said to have picked up a handsome young sailor, Bart Bennett Jr., and had taken him back to his hotel room "where he performed unnatural acts on me."

In another incident in Chicago, Stevenson was said to have asked a well-built room service waiter, Bruce Harwood, to revisit his bedroom after he finished work for the night. The young man placed the incident in April of 1950. Before an FBI agent, Harwood claimed that "Stevenson sucked my cock and gave me fifty dollars. He was fully dressed during our time in bed together."

Mamie Eisenhower *(top photo)* spent most of her life apart from her husband, General Eisenhower. After all, he had a war to win. When she moved into the White House, she said, "As an Army bride, I've spent most of my life in government housing, some places without electricity. For most of my life, money was as scarce as Ike was."

Below is **Kay Summersby,** Ike's wartime mistress. The beautiful English fashion model became his driver in wartime London. Away from Mamie, Kay was the woman he loved.

Since these homosexual acts were allegedly committed in a private bedroom, it is not known what led to Stevenson's arrest. Perhaps the two young men, when learning who Stevenson was, tried to shake him down for more money under threat of blackmail. When Stevenson refused to pay, the two young men may have carried through on their threat and gone to the police. At least that's what J. Edgar suspected. He also believed that Stevenson not only paid off the two hustlers, but used his influence to get the arrests removed from his record.

What really put Stevenson on J. Edgar's "Sex Deviate Index" at the FBI was a report that he had been arrested in a raid on a gay bar (the very existence of which was illegal at the time). He got out of jail by posting bond. Taking flight to Illinois, he forfeited that bail, although he was charged in a "morals arrest." J. Edgar ordered Clyde to assign two of his agents to track down this record, which was discovered and put in the growing file on Stevenson. News of this New York morals arrest first appeared in award-winning Curt Gentry's defining book, *J. Edgar, The Man and the Secrets* (1991).

"Hoover was the source of the whispers," he wrote. "The FBI supposedly obtained from local police, statements that Adlai Stevenson had been arrested on two separate occasions, in Illinois and Maryland, for homosexual offenses. In both cases, it was claimed that as soon as the police had learned his identity, Stevenson had been released and the arrests expunged from the records, though not from the recollections of the arresting officers. Hoover used the law enforcement grapevine to spread the story, who in turn shared it with favored reporters. Although most newspaper editors had the story, none used it. But it was widely circulated, as anyone who worked in the campaign could attest."

Among the politicos, McCarthy, as befitted his character, threatened to broadcast the arrest in a speech in Chicago he was delivering called "Pinks, Punks & Pansies." The senator wanted to make the whispers about Stevenson public knowledge. Referring to his speech, he said Stevenson fitted at least two of the Ps—"pink" and "pansy."

When the actual address came, in front of 1,700 supporters on October 27, 1952, in Chicago, it was carried on fifty television stations and more than 550 radio stations. McCarthy did not air charges of homosexuality, as threatened, but attacked Stevenson for being "the arch traitor of our time" for his defense in court of Alger Hiss. However, later in front of reporters for the *New York Daily News*, he constantly referred to Adlai as "Adeline."

Although McCarthy did not carry through with his threat to out Stevenson as a homosexual, J. Edgar's friend, Walter Winchell, was not so discreet in 1956 when Stevenson once again ran unsuccessfully against Ike. On his television program, Winchell claimed, "A vote for Adlai Stevenson is a vote for Christine Jorgensen," a reference to the former GI, George Jorgensen, who went to Denmark in 1952 and had a sex change operation. George emerged as "Christine," much to the delight of a bevy of handsome beaux wanting to try out this revolutionary new plumbing.

Winchell was forced off television after this broadcast, which shocked the easily shockable audiences of the Eisenhower era.

Confidential magazine reported that the rumors of Stevenson's homosexuality "burned the breasts of a nation and was the nastiest, most widely circulated hearsay in the annals of rumor mongering."

***

Ike had far more respect for J. Edgar than he did for McCarthy. Soon after taking office, Ike told his aides, "I don't want to get into a pissing contest with that Wisconsin skunk," meaning the senator. After the 1952 election Eisenhower assured J. Edgar that in spite of what he'd heard, "I still want you running the FBI."

To show his gratitude, J. Edgar revealed to Ike that one of his chief aides, the son of an influential GOP senator, was a homosexual. Ike fired the hapless victim the next day without an explanation.

J. Edgar still viewed Eleanor Roosevelt as an enemy. She'd been a U.S. delegate to the United Nations' General Assembly between 1946 and 1952, but out of respect for the incoming President-elect, she resigned her post, hoping to be reappointed. When J. Edgar heard of this, he made another visit to the Oval Office, with a dossier on the former First Lady, revealing her affairs with both women and men. Homophobic Ike passed on her, opting not to reappoint her.

After his ascension to the Oval Office, in 1953, Ike signed an executive order that stated that sexual perversion was sufficient grounds for firing somebody from any Federal job.

"There go J. Edgar Hoover and Clyde Tolson," a defeated Stevenson mockingly told his aides.

After countless firings, the *Washington Post* claimed, "The ancient Aztecs of Mayans used to sacrifice virgins annually to propitiate the gods. The State Department sacrifices homosexuals to gain money from the House Appropriations Committee." During the Cold War, more homosexuals were dismissed from Federal jobs than communists.

Wanting to stay in the loop, J. Edgar kept more FBI informants in the White House during Ike's two administrations, and spied on him more than he had on any other president, even FDR. He uncovered little scandal, other than the fact that his wife, Mamie, was an alcoholic and often staggered drunk around the White House, blaming it on some inner-ear problem.

Unlike FDR, Ike appeared to be conducting no affairs within the White House. All J. Edgar could learn from his spies was that Ike had some odd personal quirks. The President would get up in the morning and emerge from the bathroom totally nude. His valet, John Moaney, would bend down on his knees and personally put on the President's white boxer shorts.

As a young man, in winter, Ike had developed the odd habit of sometimes wearing tall socks, heavy boots, and a dress overcoat—nothing else. His fellow soldiers in the barracks called him "the flasher."

***

In 1960, J. Edgar made one final attempt to sabotage the political career of Stevenson. When JFK wanted him appointed Ambassador to the United Nations, J. Edgar arrived at the White House with his homosexual file on Stevenson. Both RFK and JFK ignored the file, and the President appointed Stevenson anyway. They had already been aware of these allegations for a long time.

Even when Stevenson was threatening to run again for President in 1960, with the support of Eleanor Roosevelt, both JFK and RFK told their aides not to air these gay rumors. As Bobby so graphically put it, "From what we've learned, it's been years since Adlai sucked a dick."

***

It was said that the downfall of Senator McCarthy began on the day he allowed G. David Schine to work as an unpaid "chief consultant" to the Senate Subcommittee on Investigations. The strapping, tall, blond-haired Schine, a Harvard dropout, was the heir to a hotel fortune. His chief qualification for the job was that he had written an anti-communist pamphlet which his father distributed within his hotels.

Had Schine not wanted to be a "Red Hunter," he might have fitted into the Tab Hunter 1950s movie star ideal. He was described as a pretty boy "in the style that one associates with male orchestra singers."

Born to New York hotel magnate Junius Myer Schine, David was a Harvard drum major for the university band. *The Harvard Crimson* wrote, "Schine lives in a style which went out with the era of the Gold Coast."

Roy Cohn told his best friend, the literary agent Jay Garon, that he'd picked up Schine in a bar and had begun an affair with him in a hotel room at the "Q Club" in Washington, Downstairs was the Quorum Club where

Senators, lobbyists, hookers, and businessmen seeking government contracts came for food, drink and pick-ups. A young John F. Kennedy was a frequent visitor. Lyndon B. Johnson often showed up with his protégé, Bobby Baker.

A wheeler-dealer and LBJ's right-hand man, Baker once revealed to J. Edgar and Clyde that, "Lyndon is much more closed mouth about his extramarital affairs than Jack Kennedy." He told the FBI men that Jack once introduced him to this beautiful French woman. "Bobby, look at this fine chick. She gives the best head in the United States," Kennedy claimed.

Incidentally, the small town, good ol' southern boy, the ambitious Baker, was viewed by J. Edgar as the leading pimp in Washington, hooking up politicos with what were referred to as "ladies of the evening" back in the 1950s.

From all reports, David Schine was basically straight, but for the sake of his unbounded ambition he was "willing to drop trou," as Guy Hotell claimed, "for the right party ready to advance his career. Obviously the unattractive Roy Cohn fitted his bill for career advancement. Bobby Baker referred to the unlikely duo as 'The Beauty and the Beast.'"

Schine proved his heterosexual credentials when he went to Hollywood and was reported dating two screen beauties, Rhonda Fleming and Piper Laurie. Or, as Schine put it, "I always try to seduce women Ronald Reagan's already had, as I admire his taste."

David's reported romancing with the beautiful Rhonda Fleming, with her flaming red hair, was superficial if they dated at all. There was gossip that they did. The actress often rode across the plains looking luscious in Technicolor opposite such stars as Glenn Ford. She made three pictures with Reagan, *The Last Outpost*, *Hong Kong*, and *Tropic Zone*. But he decided to marry starlet Nancy Davis instead.

***

Hailing from Detroit, the red-haired Piper Laurie toiled in programmers or out-and-out garbage, including Arabian Nights-type adventures such as *The Prince Who Was a Thief* with Tony Curtis, until Hollywood finally discovered what a skilled actress she was.

According to Piper's memoirs, *Learning to Live Out Loud,* published in 2011, her romance with Schine almost led to marriage. When she first dated him, she was unaware of his background and his relationships with Cohn and McCarthy. In fact, on their first date, he took her on the bus to the Cocoanut Grove night club at the Ambassador Hotel in Los Angeles, not knowing that his father owned it. They became lovers.

She claimed that Cohn often joined them for dinner at the Cocoanut Grove. At that time, she suspected that the young lawyer "might have a yen for me," not knowing that he was a homosexual. Once, he put McCarthy on the phone, and she spoke to him, not really knowing who he was.

Of course, during the McCarthy/Army hearings, Piper, along with the entire nation, became aware of Cohn's relationship with Schine. She later wrote: "Perhaps Cohn had a "crush" on David, as some of the papers implied, and just wanted him around. I thought it was entirely possible Roy had romantic or sexual yearnings for David, who was a handsome six-foot-four Adonis, but the speculation that they were a homosexual couple was silly to me. David was an ardent lover of women's bodies and loved making love. Perhaps I was naïve."

In the 1950s, the nature of a bisexual was hardly as well known as it is today.

David eventually proposed to her, in spite of the national scandal he was involved in. She accepted and even wore the engagement ring he presented, but she finally decided to break it off.

"The truth was, the relationship with David never felt right," she wrote. "He had fulfilled all of the superficial requirements for a husband, but I felt a darkness around him. He had never really opened himself up to me about McCarthy and Cohn, and I couldn't understand or accept that. This was not the guy for me."

***

Still a confidant of J. Edgar and Clyde, Joan Crawford told them she'd also seduced Schine on his Hollywood get-acquainted visit. He met her on a movie set one day, and she extended an invitation to dinner. Appealing to the voyeurism in J. Edgar and Clyde, she confided, "Dave has two and a half times more than Clark Gable; he's as long as Gary Cooper, but not as thick as my former husband, Franchot Tone."

Cohn was alleged to have been jealous of Schine's extracurricular adventures, and a terrible row ensued upon his return to Washington.

***

J. Edgar and Clyde liked Schine far better than McCarthy did, because Schine's father let them stay free at his Miami hotel during one of their "working vacations." Even so, J. Edgar ordered that Schine and Cohn be put under surveillance.

Schine and Cohn once joined J. Edgar, Clyde, and Guy Hotell on one of their Florida trips. They shared rooftop suites across from one another with a swimming pool between them. "Dave paraded around a lot before us in the buff," Guy said. "A low-hanging sausage and cut. After all, he was Jewish. Other than that, he looked like Hitler's ideal of the Aryan male."

J. Edgar snapped a frontal nude of Schine, which he added to his secret scrapbook.

***

Long before the Army hearings brought them down, Cohn and Schine set out on a whirlwind tour of Europe in the spring of 1953. Their job: to ferret out subversive literature from the libraries operated by the U.S. Information Agency. A London tabloid was blunt in a headline: COHN AND SCHINE, THE TWO LONDON LOVERS.

Theodore Kaghan, Deputy Director of the Public Affairs Division in the Office of the U.S. High Commissioner for Germany, called Schine and Cohn "junketeering gumshoes."

The downfall of Schine and Cohn began when "pretty boy" was drafted into the Army in November of 1953. He certainly met all the physical requirements. When he stripped down for his physical before an Army doctor, two young men whistled at the male beauty, which earned them a 4-F on the grounds of homosexuality.

The beautiful **Piper Laurie**, a budding starlet, and **David Schine** were snapped by a nightclub photographer on their first date at the Cocoanut Grove night club at the Ambassador Hotel in Los Angeles in 1952.

Cohn was unable to get his lover exempted from military service in spite of repeated phone calls. He then changed his tactics and tried to get him commissioned as an officer. The Army denied that pitch on the grounds that Schine had dropped out of Harvard.

At the time, Piper seemed unaware that David was the boy friend of Roy Cohn, who was serving as chief counsel on McCarthy's staff trying to ferret out communists in government offices. Since he took her there by bus, she feared he had little money.

Frustrated, Cohn made repeated calls to the Secretary of the Army, Robert Stevens, seeking to give Schine, who would be a private, privi-

Later, she found out that his father owned the hotel. Soon, David's lover, Roy Cohn, started joining them for dinner.

leges during basic training, something almost unheard of.

"David should be allowed a pair of mittens I gave him," Cohn said, "instead of the usual Army regulation gloves. Also I wish to buy him a pair of special boots, those with buckles and straps. I insist he be given a fur-lined hood with his overcoat. When on maneuvers, he should use a sleeping bag, which I have purchased for him, and an air mattress—not the cold, cold ground. It is imperative that he be given a pass every weekend to work with me on committee business."

Schine had to wear regulation Army clothing, but he did get more weekend passes than his fellow soldiers, reportedly to help with Mc-Carthy's investigation of rounding up communists. Waiting across from the barracks every weekend was Cohn in a chauffeured limousine to take his boyfriend to the Stork Club in Manhattan.

After an evening there, they would retreat to a free suite at the Wal-dorf-Astoria, arranged by Clyde himself, to "make up for lost time."

The chauffeur who used to drive them into Manhattan later claimed that once Schine got in the back seat of that limousine, Cohn couldn't wait to get at him. "He'd unzip his pants and give him a blow-job on our way into Manhattan," the driver claimed.

In his hunt for communists, McCarthy had the support of millions until he almost came unglued and began to attack the Army as being riddled with communists. Most Americans didn't believe that was true and seemed to turn against McCarthy when he attacked Secretary of Defense George Marshall, one of the country's most revered military men. McCarthy even accused Eisenhower of being lax in internal security in the Federal government.

American political circuses entered a new age when the McCarthy-Army hearings opened on April 24, 1954. By the millions, viewers were glued to their relatively new television sets. This was the first time TV expedited the downfall of a tyrant. More politicians would fall victim to the medium in the future. Television with its omnipotent eye could destroy a political career faster than all the newspaper columns in the country.

Instead of exposing communists in the Army, the military lawyers turned the focus on McCarthy's aides, especially the relationship of Schine and Cohn. The question was, what was the exact bonding of these two men, although the word homosexual was not uttered, following the decorum of the day. But it was clearly suggested. Cohn was left squirming in his seat when it was revealed that he had sought special privileges for his companion.

Secretary of the Army, Robert T. Stevens, claimed, "There is perversion here." He paused for effect before adding "a perversion of power." He reported a private remark that McCarthy had made to one of his aides. "Roy thinks that Dave ought to be a general and operate from a penthouse at the Waldorf-Astoria."

The Army called on Ray Howard Jenkins, a politically ambitious criminal lawyer from Knoxville, Tennessee, to press its case. "You and this boy, David Schine," Jenkins said on TV. He paused long enough to allow the word "boy" to sink into his audience. "You and this boy, David Schine, are almost constant companions, good, warm personal friends, are you not?"

Cohn admitted only that "we are friends pursuing the same goal on the committee." But Jenkins had scored his point, with the clear suggestion that they were two lovebirds.

After that hearing, "the hazel-eyed dynamo," as *Time* magazine called Cohn, became the subject of off-color jokes throughout Washington, even figuring into show business acts. Joe E. Lewis, the nightclub comic, sang, "I'm gonna love you like nobody's loved you, come Cohn or come Schine."

The hearings and the attack on the Army infuriated Ike, who in a surprise move enlisted the help of J. Edgar. At this point, the cunning FBI director decided that McCarthy and Cohn were going down, primarily because of the Schine affair.

Secretly, without McCarthy finding out, J. Edgar supplied the President's staff and the legal brass of the Army with "forty-four counts of improper behavior and pressure Cohn had brought on the Army." The FBI report included a threat that McCarthy and Cohn had made that they were going "to wreck the Army" if it did not give in to their demands regarding Schine. After reading his version of the report the FBI had prepared for him, Ike wrote across the top, "it's a pip!"

He ordered the Army to release the FBI report, although it was not identified as having been compiled by J. Edgar and the FBI. McCarthy shot back, claiming that the military was holding Schine "hostage" to keep his committee from pursuing "the Red Army." He didn't mean the Army of the Soviet Union, but communists in the American Army.

Fighting back, McCarthy demanded that Eisenhower's aides be hauled in to testify if the President himself had ordered this smear of Cohn and Schine. The White House evoked executive privilege, which would forbid his advisers to testify before Congress. Executive privilege would be invoked for years to come by future presidents as well, including Nixon.

The Army reached out for a "top gun," Joseph Nye Welch, to represent it and to oppose McCarthy. A Boston attorney and a Republican, Welch was a senior partner in the prestigious firm of Hale and Dorr. For his backup team, he drafted two young lawyers in his firm, one of whom was James St. Clair, who would later represent Nixon in the Watergate affair. He also drafted Fred Fisher, Jr., who had once joined the National Lawyers Guild, a left-wing organization which defended so-called radicals against criminal prosecution, including the Hollywood Ten and some communists who had violated the Smith Act, a 1940 law that made membership in the Communist Party illegal. That law would ultimately be overturned by the Supreme Court.

A man of great decency that seemed to have moral outrage on his side, Welch was the proper antidote for McCarthy's bombastic style. One of their most famous exchanges occurred when McCarthy aides produced a photograph of Schine and Army Secretary Stevens standing next to each other smiling. The next day Welch revealed that the original picture had been cropped and a third man removed from the photo. Welch asked, "Did you think this doctored photo came from a pixie?"

McCarthy interrupted. "Will counsel for my benefit define—I think he might be an expert on that—what a pixie is?"

Welch shot back, "I should say, Mr. Senator, that a pixie is a close relative of a fairy."

The audience broke into hysterical laughter, and even the naïve TV viewers of the 1950s knew that fairy was commonly used to describe a homosexual. This was a very back-door way of outing the gay relationship between Cohn and Schine.

One newspaperman, daring for the time, wrote that Welch's fairy reference "really fixed McCarthy and his pansy friends." That remark seemed to open the floodgates. Drew Pearson weighed in, claiming that "the supposedly fearless McCarthy is deathly afraid of pint-sized Cohn because the aggressive lawyer knows all the Senator's secrets, including extraordinary allegations about his personal life which can't be repeated here."

One reader wrote Pearson, "What is the big secret, the big mystery? It is obvious that Cohn is in love with Schine. Perhaps the hunk also has to service McCarthy too."

"Why have McCarthy and Cohn shown such passion in keeping Schine out of the Army?" one editorial asked. "This sordid relationship should be exposed for what it actually is, but which good taste prevents us from doing so here. J. Edgar Hoover should investigate." Of course, the FBI director knew all about Cohn's relationship with Schine and McCarthy's most closeted secrets.

McCarthy's final break with J. Edgar came when the Senator claimed he had a "carbon copy of a personal and confidential letter that J. Edgar had sent Army brass at Fort Monmouth, citing thirty-four security risks.

J. Edgar shot back, charging that McCarthy did not have access to FBI files, only "memos based on those files."

Richard Nixon was made aware of a very private meeting that J. Edgar had with Eisenhower in the Oval Office in 1954. "Hoover told Ike that Mc-Carthy had reached the point where he was actually impeding the investigation of communists. He also told him a hell of a lot more."

Because of his unreliable heart, Eisenhower at least considered the possibility of not seeking re-election in 1956. J. Edgar was not in the loop about his actual plans.

But through his intimate connections with Cardinal Spellman and Joseph Kennedy, the FBI director had learned that these two ringleaders had had had several secret meetings with McCarthy, wherein they'd promised to back him if he sought the Republican nomination for president in 1956.

Spellman promised he would deliver "an armada" of Catholic votes, and Kennedy claimed he'd be the chief source of money to get the campaign rolling until other millions started to flow into McCarthy's coffers. The Vatican, however, didn't plan to offer any support to Spellman, because, as the Cardinal told J. Edgar, "The Pope right now is pissed off at me. The Vatican has had to cover up just one too many of my little indiscretions."

It was at this time that J. Edgar turned over very confidential FBI reports that McCarthy, his aide Roy Cohn, and even Cardinal Spellman were homosexuals.

Eisenhower, according to what J. Edgar told Clyde and his other top aides, "looked shocked." Perhaps owing to his homophobic Army background, Ike had zero tolerance for gay people and didn't want them in any part of the Federal government, even as a mail carrier or a garbage collector.

It appears that J. Edgar's revelations were too hot for Ike to handle. At that point, both Spellman and McCarthy had millions of loyal followers, and Ike obviously didn't want to alienate them, and he especially didn't want to offend millions of American Catholics.

There is evidence that the President met with Herbert Brownell Jr., his attorney general. As Curt Gentry wrote in *J. Edgar Hoover, The Man and the Secrets*, "Just how seriously Eisenhower and Brownell took this sensational charge is not known, but Hoover himself, from the tone of his memorandum, seemed to give it more than passing credence. The timing of Hoover's decision to sever relations with McCarthy was fatal to the senator."

Back at the Army hearings, McCarthy confronted Attorney Welch on another issue. Cohn had dug up the fact that Fred Fisher Jr. worked for Welch's law firm. Before signing Fisher to help with the case for the Army,

Welch had asked him, "Are there any skeletons in your closet?" That is when Fisher had admitted his membership in the left-wing National Lawyers Guild. Consequently, he was not appointed to aid Welch in the Army hearings. Therefore, Fisher was not an issue until McCarthy tried to make him one.

When McCarthy accused Welch of having a member of the Communist Party on his staff, Welch cut him off, "Let us not assassinate this lad further, Senator," he said to McCarthy. "You have done enough. Have you no sense of decency, sir, at long last? Have you no sense of decency?"

The impact of Welch's rebuke virtually drove a dagger into McCarthy, as TV viewers across the country watched a political assassination, the beginning of the end of McCarthy's reign of fear. Welch with his old-fashioned sense of American fairness won the day and ultimately scored a triumph for the Army.

On December 12, 1954, McCarthy was censored by the U.S. Senate. After that day, J. Edgar told his aides, "The Senator from Wisconsin is dead meat. Let's wash the pig's blood off our hands."

Looking back over the old film clips of the era, one TV critic wrote, "The McCarthy-Army hearings were the birth of reality TV."

Cohn, who resigned after the hearing, later wrote of McCarthy, his mentor: "He came into American homes as humorless, demanding, dictatorial, and obstructive. With his easily erupting temper, his menacing monotone, his unsmiling mien, and his perpetual five o'clock shadow, he did seem the perfect stock villain."

After departing from McCarthy, Cohn moved to New York where he became a "killer lawyer," specializing in winner-take-all divorce cases. In New York he led a promiscuous homosexual lifestyle, involving literally dozens of male hustlers.

Writing his deathbed autobiography, Cohn was dictating to his co-author Sidney Zion. "Are you familiar with the term killer fruit?" Cohn asked. "Truman Capote, who knows about such things, says it's a certain kind of queer who has Freon refrigerating in his bloodstream. Diaghilev, for example. J. Edgar Hoover. Hadrian."

AIDS claimed Cohn in 1986.

Schine would go on to marry Hillevi Rombin of Sweden, Miss Universe of 1955.

Schine had a successful media career. His credits included the role of executive producer of the 1971 hit film, *The French Connection*, which won an Oscar as Best Picture. His music company provided songs for such singers as Lou Rawls, and he was a musician himself, once conducting the Boston Pops Orchestra. Of course, some left-wing musicians refused to appear on stage with him.

Schine died on June 19, 1996 at the age of 68. His son, Berndt, was piloting a private plane that went down, killing himself but also his father and mother, David and Hillevi.

Upon Schine's death, Tony Kushner wrote a one-act comedy, *G. David Schine in Hell*. In hell, he is reunited with Roy Cohn, Richard Nixon, Whittaker Chambers, and J. Edgar Hoover himself.

***

Lucille Ball and Desi Arnaz "double dated" with J. Edgar and Clyde on their visits to California and often shared a table with them at the Stork Club in Manhattan. J. Edgar was the instigator of these soirées because Clyde was still jealous of J. Edgar's attraction to Desi, which had led to physical violence at one point. Nonetheless, Clyde put up a brave front when he was forced into social situations with Lucille and Desi.

But something went wrong in J. Edgar's relationship with Desi in the early 1950s. Without warning and without explaining it to anyone, including Clyde, J. Edgar turned on the couple. He really had little on Desi, but he'd found a scandal in Lucille's

The McCarthy/Army hearings virtually ended the communist witch hunt orchestrated by the senator from Wisconsin.

The Army wisely hired "a country lawyer," **Joseph Welch**, who subtly exposed the homosexuality of David Schine, Roy Cohn, and even McCarthy himself without actually using the word "homosexual."

Welch appeared on the cover of *Life* magazine on July 25, 1954.

life that could be used to destroy her career. He called his long-time friend, the columnist Walter Winchell, and had him broadcast a "blind item" on his weekly television show. Winchell went on the air on Sunday night, September 6, 1953. At her ranch in Chatsworth, California, Lucille sat in her living room, listening to the broadcast as she did every week.

In his staccato style, Winchell, fed with information from J. Edgar, blurted out, "The top television comedienne has been confronted with her membership in the Communist Party."

As Lucille recalled in her memoirs, she thought, "I didn't know Imogene Coca was a communist."

No sooner had the accusation been broadcast than Desi called. "Did you know Imogene was a communist?" Lucille asked him.

"Lucy, it's *you!*" Desi shouted at her. "He's claiming *you* are the communist."

From that moment on, all Lucille could remember was that, "The shit

hit the fan."

Even though he was on the outs, Desi called J. Edgar, not knowing that he was the guilty party who had planted the item with Winchell. Still angry at him, J. Edgar refused his call.

Desi then called George Murphy and asked the song-and-dance man to call J. Edgar. Murphy, a famous movie star of that time, got J. Edgar on the phone. He later reported, "He was noncommital, very formal, but said he'd look into it, before quickly putting down the phone."

It wasn't until years later that it was learned how J. Edgar was tipped off by about Lucille's membership in the Communist Party. It had come from "America's leading expert on communism," Lela Rogers, long rumored to have been J. Edgar's so-called girlfriend.

In 1936, the year Lucille had registered as a communist voter, she had worked at RKO Studios during the day and at Lela's Little Theatre Group every Monday to Saturday night. Apparently, back then Lucille must have said something to Lela. As Lucille recalled, "During the Depression, it was less suspicious to be a communist than a Republican."

On March 19, 1936, Lucille gave in to her socialist grandfather, Fred Hunt, and went to downtown Los Angeles, where she registered as a communist. Her eccentric grandfather evoked the Lionel Barrymore character in the popular 1938 film, *You Can't Take It with You.*

Lela's daughter, Ginger Rogers, completely disagreed with J. Edgar and her mother. "Lucille was no communist, any more than I am, and I'm practically a member of the John Birch Society."

Even though she was the most famous actress in Hollywood, as American as mom and apple pie, Lucille knew that the merest link to communism would spell doom for her *I Love Lucy* series, and threaten the solvency of Desilu Productions. She lived in a state of constant fear until the matter was settled, hopefully in her favor.

Having decided not to go after Desi to seek his revenge (for what?), J. Edgar had supplied data about Lucille and her "communist affiliations" to the House Un-American Activities Committee.

William A. Wheeler, head of West Coast Investigations for the House Un-American Activities Committee, interviewed her. He was probing into the alleged communist activities of Hollywood stars.

Before that Winchell broadcast, Lucille had gone through two closed-door hearings about her alleged communist affiliation, once before the FBI and later before the House Un-American Activities Committee.

She and Desi had formed Desilu Studios, and their *I Love Lucy* series dominated weekly TV ratings for most of its ten-year run beginning on October 15, 1951. They were, in fact, the biggest stars in America.

Before a studio audience, Desi and Lucille prepared to film a segment of *I Love Lucy*, their first appearance since the communist charges broke.

Facing three hundred people, Desi said, "I want to talk to you about something serious. Lucy has never been a communist, not now, and never will be."

The applause of the audience lasted an entire minute.

"I was kicked out of Cuba because of communism," Desi continued. "We despise everything about it. Lucy is as American as Bernie Baruch and Ike Eisenhower. By the way, we both voted for Eisenhower—so ladies and gentlemen, don't judge too soon—read for yourselves. Read her story to be released tomorrow. Don't believe every piece of bunk you read in some papers." He then introduced Lucille, who came out in tears. "My favorite redhead, and that's the only thing red about Lucy and even that isn't legitimate."

Like a real trouper, she performed in her brilliant comedic way and went off the air saying, "God bless you for being so kind."

I Love Lucy stayed on the air, and it is still being broadcast on television sets around the world today.

Not all TV viewers were pleased with Desi's explanation. "My son didn't vote Red to please his grandpa—but he did die in Korea for his Uncle Sam," claimed M.S. Maloney of the Gold Star Mothers.

A major attack came from Westbrook Pegler, a popular columnist appealing to the zealots of the Far Right. He claimed that Lucille was cleared only because she was rich and famous. "She knew what she was doing when she registered with the communists, and I can tell you that the poor devils out there in Hollywood who fought the traitors in the movie business took terrible persecution. Socialist grandfather is a new variant on the whine of the crooked White Sox player who did it for the wife and kiddies!"

Trouble kept mounting, even though *I Love Lucy* remained number one on TV. The American Legion threatened to boycott Philip Morris cigarettes, her sponsor, and war veterans vowed never to watch her on television.

The Huntington *Herald-Dispatch* claimed, "Despite the almost frenzied efforts of the very best press agents and public advisers those capitalist dollars can buy, most thoughtful Americans are going to find it difficult to 'love' Lucy with the same old abandon."

Owned by William Randolph Hearst, the *Los Angeles Herald-Express* stubbornly ran a banner headline—LUCILLE BALL A RED.

Most protests had faded away when Dwight Eisenhower and his wife Mamie invited Desi and Lucille to a White House celebration dinner in honor of the President's birthday.

***

Between 1956 and 1971, the year before J. Edgar died, the FBI launched COINTELPRO (an acronym for Counter Intelligence Program). This was a series of often illegal and covert operations aimed at "surveilling, infiltrating, discrediting, and disrupting domestic political organizations."

The FBI authorized "whatever is necessary to destroy the enemy"— psychological warfare, smearing through *faux* letters, harassment, wrongful imprisonment, extra-legal violence and assassination. All this was done in the name of protecting national security.

Over a period of years, COINTELPRO operated against the Black Panthers and various perceived communist and socialist organizations. Persons associated with the civil rights movement, such as Dr. Martin Luther King Jr., became special targets, as did the Southern Christian Leadership Conference, the NAACP, the Congress of Racial Equality, and various civil rights advocates such as Marlon Brando, whom J. Edgar viewed as the "New Left."

The American Indian Movement came under suspicion, as did the Students for a Democratic Society and the Weathermen. Any group protesting the Vietnam War was targeted. As society moved forward, leaders in the women's rights movements were designated as lesbians. Both the Nation of Islam and the Ku Klux Klan were also targeted.

While it flourished, COINTELPRO caused considerable damage to thousands of American lives until it was brought down. Senator Frank Church of Idaho headed a special Senate investigating committee which castigated COINTELPRO, calling its techniques intolerable in a democratic society. The FBI was accused of violating the First Amendment right of free speech. Church cited "ridiculous" secret dossiers such as President Eisenhower being sent reports on the political and social contacts indulged in by Eleanor Roosevelt.

When J. Edgar learned that COINTELPRO had been officially terminated as of April of 1971, he told his aides, "We will go on as before, only now we'll be unofficial. We must continue our battle against the enemies of this nation with a lethal ferocity, using whatever means we may deem necessary."

***

Two presidents had each expressed hostile reactions to Joe Kennedy, FDR calling him "one of the most evil and disgusting men I have ever

393

known. Harry S Truman claimed he was "a god damn thief, a former bootlegger and drunk, and the most crooked man in the country. He makes our gangsters look like choir boys."

J. Edgar himself had a troubled relationship with Ambassador Kennedy, making the patriarch of a political dynasty wonder if the FBI director were friend or foe. On May 3, 1941 J. Edgar had reported to Franklin D. Roosevelt that Joe had met with Hermann Göring in Vichy, France, and had donated a "considerable sum" to Germany.

Whether this was true or not is not known. Apparently, FDR dismissed this shocking revelation as "one of Hoover's fantasies." But as ambassador to England, Joe had opposed America's getting involved in "England's war with Germany."

At times, J. Edgar worked to undermine the interests of Joe Kennedy; at other times he provided him with valuable information. Nixon said he felt that "Kennedy and Hoover worked on the barter system."

Ronald Kessler in his book, *Sins of the Father*, wrote: "The two men used each other: Joe constantly praised Hoover as the finest public servant in the land, while Hoover helped Joe by providing secrets about his enemies."

J. Edgar had long ago learned that Joe Kennedy and Spellman had plotted to run McCarthy for president on the Republican ticket in 1956. But after McCarthy's censure by the Senate, Joe came up with another radical idea—run J. Edgar for President instead. The patriarch of the Kennedy clan had a cunning mind, which involved not just running J. Edgar for president, but plotting the political futures of his sons, especially Jack.

Joe knew that J. Edgar's cherished dream had been to run for president in 1940, an ambition that was ruined when FDR decided to seek an unprecedented third term.

Instead of calling J. Edgar, Joe Kennedy wrote him a letter:

Dear Edgar,
I listened to Walter Winchell mention your name as a candidate for President. If that should come to pass, it would be the most wonderful thing for the United States. I would guarantee you the largest contribution that you would ever get from anybody.
Joe.

At three o'clock in the morning of the next day, J. Edgar turned on the light waking up Clyde. "Maybe old Joe has a good idea," J. Edgar said to his sleepy companion. "My running for president might be a brilliant move. Eisenhower is dying. I could make our neighbor Lyndon my Vice President. That Kennedy fucker will put up some of his bootleg millions. J. Edgar Hoover, President of the United States. I like the sound of that. Of course, my first official duty will be to appoint you director of the FBI. Between my job and your job we will become the two most powerful men on earth. Nothing can stop us!"

But as dawn broke across Capitol Hill, Clyde had returned J. Edgar to the earth.

"He's dangling the bait at me, but here's one shark who isn't biting," J. Edgar told Clyde, Guy Hotell, and Lou Nichols. "I have no intention of running for president. Did old Joe Kennedy think I was going to walk into that trap he's setting for me?"

Two weeks later, Joe followed up his letter with an hour-long phone call to J. Edgar at his home. He outlined why he thought he should seek the presidency. Actually Joe had a diabolical plan. He wanted J. Edgar to resign as FBI director and take on Eisenhower, knowing he would lose.

Privately Joe told his sons, Jack and Bobby, "Ike's unbeatable. He's brought peace and prosperity. Whoever gets the '56 nod will be a sacrificial lamb put up by the Democrats."

He said to Jack, "I want you to run for President in 1960. All of us know that Hoover has an extensive file on you which he could use to blackmail us. But if he's no longer heading the FBI, you can appoint whoever you want for the job, maybe one of our stooges, maybe even Bobby here."

Joe went so far as to have another job lined up for J. Edgar even if he didn't win the presidency. "I'll make you chief of my security." Joe knew that in that capacity he would go from gathering blackmail on "my boys to keeping their asses wiped and their names out of the scandal magazines."

J. Edgar assured Joe he'd get back to him. He waited a month before responding. "I feel I'm needed where I am," was his brief rejection.

A master of the two-face, J. Edgar also met privately with his ally at the time, Nixon, who confided in him. "When I'm president, and that's likely to happen sooner than later, I want you to know I plan to keep you on as director of the FBI."

"That's mighty kind of you, Dick," J. Edgar said.

"I've talked to Eisenhower's doctors about his heart," Nixon claimed. "They told me he'll not live to serve out his term and that he might die at the beginning of his second term, the way Roosevelt died at the beginning of his fourth time, allowing that bastard, Truman, to become president. As a sitting president, I'll be almost a shoe-in for the 1960 presidential race."

"Good thinking, Dick" J. Edgar told him.

At the Democratic convention of 1956, both Jack and Bobby showed a rare streak of independence from their father and sought to win a spot on the ticket for Jack, running as Adlai Stevenson's vice president. Joe had opposed that, knowing his son would lose. Joe feared "the Catholic issue" would make his son look like a loser on a ticket doomed for failure.

With Bobby's arm-twisting skill behind the scenes, Jack came within thirty-nine votes of winning the nomination, losing to coonskin-cap wearing Senator Estes Kefauver of Tennessee. As predicted by Joe, Ike went on to win the election, with Nixon retained on the ticket as his running mate, even though Ike was none too happy about that.

In discussing the Stevenson/Kefauver ticket, Joe had referred to them as "the queer and the muff-diver." Stevenson's closeted homosexual life was familiar to him, and "that moral crusader," Kefauver was known for patronizing whores in Washington and for his penchant for oral sex.

At the age of sixty-eight on September 13, 1956, Joe Kennedy entered a hospital to have his prostate gland removed. J. Edgar sent him a telegram, wishing him a speedy recovery. Joe responded by asking him to do whatever he could to prevent the showing of *Baby Doll*, a film based on a Tennessee Williams play. "It's about a child bride, it's indecent, and the worst thing that Hollywood has put out. I'll definitely get it banned in Boston."

Joe had a far more serious request in 1959 when Jack was plotting his run for the presidency on the Democratic ticket. "I know you have a file on my boy," Joe told J. Edgar. "I'm sure you have one on me, perhaps even Bobby and Teddy, surely not Rose. She's like Caesar's wife. Above reproach."

When Jack wins the presidency, better keep those files under lock and key," Joe said. "Get my drift, Edgar? You scratch our backs and we'll scratch yours."

"You've just made me an offer I can't refuse," J. Edgar said. "First, we'll see that Jack will run for president in 1960 and '64, then Bobby in '68 and '72. By the way, how old is Teddy?"

***

On looking back on those dark days of the great American witch hunt, author Matt Wilson wrote: "J. Edgar Hoover was the director, not of the FBI, but of the Great American Inquisition."

CHAPTER ELEVEN

In the 1950s, J. Edgar Hoover loudly proclaimed, "There is no organized crime in America," although he knew differently, having frequently been seen in the company of such gangsters as Frank Costello. "There are only minor criminals acting independently," the FBI director told reporters. He actually went so far as to have Clyde Tolson assign FBI agents to document the "nonexistence of organized crime in the U.S."

As the *New York Journal-American* asked in an editorial, "How paranoid can you get: Form a committee to investigate something that doesn't even exist? The trouble with that is that organized crime does exist throughout America, and it needs to be investigated, exposed, and arrests made."

J. Edgar's link with the Mafia is still a hotly debated subject, beginning with the allegation that gangster Meyer Lansky hired a "long-distance" photographer to snap a picture of J. Edgar performing fellatio on Clyde on the open terrace of their Miami Beach hotel suite.

Throughout most of his career, the FBI director was far more interested in rounding up suspected American communists than he was in routing mobsters. In his words, "I'd rather be dead than red!"

He found an ally in the mob in fighting communism, and understandably so. The Mafia thrived on exploiting capitalism, and it had also been a key factor in the FBI's success in preventing sabotage at American ports during WWII.

When queried, Clyde maintained that a ruthless gangster such as Carlos Marcello was no more than a "tomato salesman."

In 1959 in New York City, one of the hotbeds of organized crime, J. Edgar had assigned four hundred agents to weed out communists, but only four were assigned to investigating organized crime. All of that was about to change.

J. Edgar's relationship with the mob dates back to the 1930s, when he was seen on several occasions meeting with Frank Costello in Manhattan's Central Park. The FBI director was also spotted with this gangster at the Stork Club and at the Waldorf-Astoria. Costello was a source of illegal income for J. Edgar.

Along with Meyer Lansky, Costello and his "boys" dominated the il-

J. Edgar was seen on several occasions socializing with the Calabria-born **Frank Costello**, who was nicknamed "Prime Minister of the Underworld," when he became the most influential Mafia boss in American history, eventually the capo of the Luciano crime family.

Although there were many attempts on his life, Costello lived to be 82 years old, dying in 1973. But his longtime enemy, Carmine Galante, a year later, bombed his mausoleum.

Marlon Brando, who played Vito Corleone in the 1972 film *The Godfather,* used Costello as his role model.

legal off-track betting market. J. Edgar and Clyde made major use of Costello's services, according to Seymour Pollack, a former Lansky associate who later exposed J. Edgar's arrangement with the bookies.

"Hoover used to place bets in the hundreds or thousands with Sherman Billingsley, the owner of the Stork Club in Manhattan, or with Walter Winchell, who turned them over to his bookie. Hoover was seen placing two-dollar bets at the window, but these were just for show. The big bets were done in secret."

Lewis Rosenstiel, a multi-millionaire "philanthropist," who had links to both Costello and Lansky, handled J. Edgar's really big bets. One of his wives, Susan Rosenstiel, called it "a sweetheart deal. Hoover likes to gamble. My husband would call up his boys and place the bet. If Hoover won, he collected the money. If he didn't, Lou covered his losses."

The question remains, why did J. Edgar lose if he played only safe bets? Since horse racing dealt with jockeys and animals, mishaps occurred. One time, Fred Otash, Hollywood's most famous detective, was caught doping a horse and was arrested at the Santa Anita racetrack. J. Edgar and Clyde were at the track that day and had placed high bets on the mob's favorite horse.

The stricken horse didn't run that day.

Otash suffered a felony conviction, which was later downgraded to a misdemeanor and eventually expunged from his record. He was given a suspended sentence, but he lost his "gumshoe license," as he called it.

Rosenstiel had made his money by distilling and importing "booze" (as he called it) through his company, Schenley Industries. J. Edgar met him through another bootlegger, Joseph P. Kennedy.

As J. Edgar and Clyde soon discovered during the course of their friendship, Rosenstiel was a promiscuous homosexual who could "buy the best young men for sale," as he boasted to his like-minded FBI friends. He also was known for staging some of the best gay parties anywhere, enough to rival J. Edgar's other friend, the Woolworth heir Jimmy Donahue.

For years, Louis Nichols had been J. Edgar's press agent, creating exaggerated stories about the FBI director's accomplishments, real or imagined. But suddenly, even though Nichols was his mouthpiece, J. Edgar decreed to Clyde and others, "It's time for Lou to go."

There was a sinister motive for J. Edgar wanting to get rid of his faithful servant. On January 14, 1957, Drew Pearson in his column "Washington Merry-Go-Round," had written that, "Louis Nichols has been busy ingratiating himself with key senators, who have the impression that he is grooming himself to be Hoover's heir-apparent."

That was followed by another column on September 5, 1957, that claimed, "The FBI's amiable press agent, Louis Nichols, is cozying up to Vice President Nixon. Louis has his eye on J. Edgar Hoover's job and is keeping close to the powers-that-might-be."

After his enforced retirement from the FBI, Nichols approached Rosenstiel and asked him for a job. The former bootlegger immediately found a vacancy for him, giving him the title of vice president of liquor distributorship.

In his new job at Schenley Company, Nichols found himself working with J. Edgar's former enemy, Thomas Dewey, who Rosenstiel had hired as general counsel for his business.

Nichols went from representing J. Edgar to representing a gangster. He was called to testify before various Senate committees. At one he claimed, "Mr. Rosenstiel has never, directly or indirectly, had any dealings or associations with Meyer Lansky, Frank Costello, or any other underworld characters. Needless to say, I would never have become associated with him if there was the slightest taint on his record." Nichols must have wondered how J. Edgar and Clyde might ridicule his testimony.

Rosenstiel was still an intimate friend of Clyde and J. Edgar, so it was to their advantage that he tried to present a public image of his boss as squeaky clean. He did the same thing for years for J. Edgar. With such training, he was now putting up a good front for a man even more sinister.

***

The "Apalachin Meeting" near Binghamton, in New York State on November 14, 1957, has gone down in the annals of crime. The confab of mob leaders across America, with some imports from Italy, was held in the town of Apalachin at the home of mobster Joseph Barbara, known as "Joe the Barber."

Barbara was the Mafia boss of Northeastern Pennsylvania. The town of Apalachin lies about 200 miles northwest of New York City along the south shore of the Susquehanna River near the Pennsylvania border. The meeting was called to resolve *La Cosa Nostra* disputes over gambling, prostitution, and narcotics smuggling. The control of crime-riddled Havana was another hot topic to iron out, along with loan-sharking and the domination of New York's garment center trucking.

The meeting was the largest gathering of the mob in U.S. history. It is estimated that some one-hundred gangsters and their bodyguards showed up at Barbara's fifty-three acre estate. A local state trooper, Edgar D. Croswell, became suspicious of all these custom-made cars arriving in this small town, and he alerted local police to set up a roadblock.

One late-arriving member of the mob saw the roadblock being formed and called Barbara's estate to alert his fellow *Mafiosi*. The meeting hadn't even begun before its members dispersed in all directions. Some gangsters tried to escape in their cars but encountered the roadblock. Others abandoned their cars and fled into the woods, tossing their guns and cash so as not to be caught with it.

For weeks afterward, local residents reported finding one-hundred dollar bills scattered through the woods. Some fifty gangsters or bodyguards escaped, but fifty-eight mob members were apprehended.

When news reached J. Edgar in Washington, he at first dismissed the account, claiming that "this was not a gathering of a national crime syndicate, just a bunch of hoodlums getting together, probably for booze and babes."

To their surprise, J. Edgar and Clyde learned that Lucky Luciano, Frank Costello, and Meyer Lansky were not at the "summit." Clyde believed that this triad of gangsters tipped off local law enforcement officers because there was a civil war raging within *La Cosa Nostra*. The Neapolitan mobster, Vito Genovese, was trying to take control of areas formerly dominated by "The Unholy Three."

With news of the Apalachin meeting appearing on front pages across America, J. Edgar and Clyde were forced to respond to the menace. The FBI created its "Top Hoodlum program" to go after the syndicate's most powerful bosses. Even so, they worked behind the scenes, impeding the investigations of the Justice Department, providing little or no evidence to build up any prosecution against the arrested Mafioso.

It was during this major crisis for the FBI that J. Edgar had his first clash with Joseph Kennedy's son, Robert Kennedy. Having long ago abandoned "those queers," Joseph McCarthy and Roy Cohn, RFK was now working for Senator John McClellan's racket investigating committee.

Storming into J. Edgar's office, Bobby, the chief counsel for McClellan, demanded that J. Edgar turn over what dossiers he had on the arrested

Mafiosi.

Bobby later recalled, "After the meeting at Apalachin, which 70 people attended, I asked Hoover for files on each of them and they didn't have any information, I think, on 40. And what information they did have consisted mainly of newspaper clippings in contrast to the Federal Bureau of Narcotics, which had something on every one of them. The FBI didn't know anything, really, about these people who were the major gangsters in the United States."

That dire situation for the FBI, as described by Bobby, was about to change and drastically so.

Clyde sent out a bulletin from J. Edgar to all agents to investigate the top mobsters in their districts. In Chicago, a group of FBI agents, described as the "Young Turks," asked for authorization to bug Murray Humphreys, a Welshman turned Chicago mobster, who was the chief political and labor racketeer in his city. He bore two nicknames, "The Camel" and "The Hump."

Laurence Bergreen in his book, *Capone: The Man and the Era*, described Humphreys as "skinny and dapper and handsome in a sinister sort of way, a representative of the new breed of racketeer, part thug and part businessman."

Approval was granted for bugging and a fantastic amount of information began to pour in at FBI headquarters in Washington. From this illegal wiretapping, J. Edgar and Clyde learned more than they ever expected to. They also approved the bugging of the home phone lines of gangster Sam Giancana, a partner of Humphreys. Giancana would loom large in their investigations during the rapidly approaching Kennedy era.

So pleased was J. Edgar with the information coming over the line from Chicago that he extended permission to all FBI agents to bug homes. "My goal is to learn every dark secret of every public official in America," he told Clyde and his aides. The FBI dossiers grew on crooked judges, crooked congressmen, crooked senators, crooked mayors, and crooked police chiefs. They discovered everything from murders to voting frauds, or even what bank was going to be robbed the following night.

J. Edgar and Clyde especially liked "the personal stuff." They learned that tough guy, mobster Mickey Cohen, the so-called celebrity gangster, was banging everybody from the very tender and very young ass of actor Sal Mineo to an experienced "star fucker," Liz Renay, the nation's winner in the Marilyn Monroe look-alike contest.

The wiretaps of Humphreys became their favorite. The FBI learned that whenever a mob member anywhere in the country ran afoul of the law, a call was placed to Humphreys of the Chicago syndicate. "The Hump" often bragged, "I can fix anything. Cash is better than having our enemy killed."

Bugging also revealed that The Hump had both a wife, Mary Brendle Humphreys, and a mistress, Jeanne Stacy. In addition, he preferred kinky sex on the side, employing a leading Chicago madam to supply him "with fresh meat." He liked to be worked over by a beautiful young girl and a beautiful young boy, preferably black. If not that, then "dark Puerto Rico," would do, but, according to his requests, he definitely preferred chocolate.

J. Edgar was embarrassed when he learned that his former boss, Tom Clark, who had been appointed attorney general by Truman, was on the take. He had been bribed to grant parole to four Chicago members of Al Capone's gang in 1947. Humphreys' influence was so great that he even got Harry S Truman to designate Clark as a Supreme Court Justice. Some historians claim that appointment was brought about "by the mob's leverage over Truman himself."

Humphreys, with a criminal career which had included jail time, ended up dining with presidents and kings from Iran to the Philippines.

His mentally unstable daughter, Llewella, went to Italy where she had a torrid affair with Rossano Brazzi, a movie matinee idol of his day. Returning to America, she gave birth to a son, but in 1958, she was committed to a mental institution in Topeka, Kansas.

From Boston to New York, from Washington to California, the FBI-bugged phones supplied more and more damaging information on Jack and Bobby Kennedy and on Richard Nixon. "If the American public is dumb enough to elect one of these men for its president, I will certainly be able to extend my tenure as FBI director, even though I'll pass the age for mandatory retirement," J. Edgar claimed.

When Humphreys died of a heart attack on November 23, 1965, the *Chicago Tribune* presented his epitaph: NO GANGSTER WAS MORE BOLD. He was also immortalized in *The Godfather* books as the character of "Tom Hagen."

***

While he was learning the secrets of organized crime, J. Edgar took time out to read that his arch enemy of yesterday, master spy William J. Donovan, had died after resigning his post as ambassador to Thailand. He'd become afflicted with an arteriosclerotic atrophy of the brain.

From his apartment at 4 Sutton Place in Manhattan, "Wild Bill," as he was nicknamed, drifted off into la-la land, imagining Soviet tanks advancing over the Queensborough Bridge to conquer New York City.

Although publicly expressing his sympathy, J. Edgar spread the rumor that Donovan had died of syphilis which he'd contracted when he was head of the OSS during WWII. "It came about in one of the many sex orgies he'd staged with prostitutes," J. Edgar falsely claimed.

The death of his arch enemy had an emotional effect on J. Edgar. It was at this point in his life that he became increasingly paranoid. All FBI agents were ordered not to walk in his shadow. He ordered three of his agents to investigate any claim—"anywhere in the world"—believed to hold the secret of prolonging life. Within a period of one year, he visited fifteen different doctors in New York or Washington, imagining that he was suffering from various ailments. Apparently, most of these physicians assumed he suffered from hypochondria. By coincidence, his primary doctor was named Joseph Kennedy.

At night, J. Edgar convinced Clyde that both New York and Washington would suffer a nuclear attack in less than three years. That prediction was made in 1959. His crystal ball wasn't as far-fetched as it sounded, according to the memoirs of Nikita Khrushchev.

As the years went by J. Edgar's phobia about germs increased. He washed his hands at least three dozen times a day. He wouldn't touch a door knob leading into another room but insisted someone do it for him. This germ phobia almost paralleled that of the aviator mogul Howard Hughes. At the government's expense, an air filter system was installed in J. Edgar's private home. His claim was, "It can electrocute any germs."

A lot of this paranoia stemmed from an incident in 1958 in which J. Edgar had suffered a minor heart attack, reminding him of his own immortality. After that, he went on a strict diet, taking off thirty pounds in just three months, and ordering all FBI agents who were overweight to do likewise, even if it meant eating one celery stalk and one quarter of a small head of iceberg lettuce—no dressing—a day, perhaps three carrot sticks. One agent in Washington, following the diet too rigidly, collapsed and died at his desk.

The Eisenhower 1950s moved toward its inexorable end, as John F. Kennedy appeared as the possible nominee for President on the Democratic ticket, with Richard Nixon ready to grab the Republican nomination.

J. Edgar repeated to Clyde and his aides, "It doesn't matter which of these farts takes the prize. I've already got enough on both of them to end their presidency before it begins. If things keep going my way like this, I'll be director for life."

"What if it's Lyndon B. Johnson?" Guy Hotell asked.

"Dear old Lyndon and I have enough on each other to put both of us in jail."

***

It was only after Senator Joseph McCarthy died on May 2, 1957, that J. Edgar was informed about more tantalizing details of his private life. Clyde came to him with a report from two FBI agents that McCarthy had a fondness for "very young bellboys and elevator operators." In two cases that had come to the attention of the FBI, the boys involved were under sixteen years ago. "I knew ol' Joe was queer," J. Edgar told his aides. "I didn't know he was a pedophile."

To add more intrigue to the plot, J. Edgar also learned that in March of 1954 an attempt to assassinate the red-baiting senator had been planned but never carried out. On March 1, 1954, four Puerto Rican nationalists shot thirty rounds from semi-automatic pistols from the Ladies' Gallery (a balcony for visitors) onto the floor of the U.S. House of Representatives. Five congressmen were shot in the attack, including Alvin M. Bentley (R-Michigan) who took a bullet to the chest; Clifford Davis (D-Tennessee), Ben F. Jensen (R-Iowa), George Hyde Fallon (D-Maryland), and Kenneth A. Roberts (D-Alabama). Although wounded, in some cases gravely so, all of them survived.

The attackers—Lolita Lebrón, Rafael Cancel Miranda, Andres Figueroa Cordero, and Irving Flores Rodriguez were arrested, tried, and convicted, each given a minimum sentence of seventy years after their death sentences were commuted by President Eisenhower.

Under intense grilling by the police, one of the very young terrorists revealed the plot to kill McCarthy. Somehow the Puerto Ricans had learned of the senator's fondness for young boys during a secret pleasure trip to San Juan, with a stopover in Havana, where he was known to have patronized a bordello featuring male prostitution.

The scheme involved having a handsome and well-muscled Puerto Rican fifteen-year-old boy dress up as a Western Union messenger. According to the plot, he was to deliver a fake telegram to the senator's hotel room during one of his visits to Manhattan. A tight-fitting uniform was tailored for him.

Many of the terrorists' plans went wrong, including their shoot-out at Blair House in an attempt to assassinate Harry S Truman, whose family was staying there because of much-needed repairs going on at the White House.

The plot called for the fake messenger to knock on McCarthy's hotel room door and ingratiate himself inside using his seductive wiles.

When J. Edgar learned of this alleged scheme, details of which were later printed in Curt Gentry's exposé of the FBI, he ranted and raved.

"It is now 1962," he shouted at his aides. "This happened in 1954. Why wasn't I informed of this at the time? I'm going to get to the bottom of this incompetence."

*   *   *

From all reports, during his early days, J. Edgar "was wound up as tightly as a coiled spring" (Guy Hotell's words), but in later life he began to unwind a bit. He knew he had blackmail evidence on such future presidents as Kennedy and Nixon and that he could enjoy life more."

The debate continues to this day whether J. Edgar were gay and, if so, was he also a cross-dresser? That controversy raged anew after the November, 2011 release of the film, *J. Edgar*, directed by Clint Eastwood and starring Leonardo DiCaprio as J. Edgar with Armie Hammer as his faithful companion, Clyde Tolson.

Long before the release of that movie, the man (or woman) on the street had long ago heard that J. Edgar and Clyde were gay. J. Edgar dressed in drag has been depicted in comic strips, editorial cartoons, books, and is a favorite of stand-up comics.

Investigators Vasili Mitrokhin and Christopher Andrew made the somewhat outrageous claim that the rumor about J. Edgar's cross-dressing was hatched as a KGB plot to discredit the FBI.

At least three American presidents—Kennedy, Johnson, and Nixon—often mocked J. Edgar behind his back as a cross-dresser. His one-time boss, Robert Kennedy, then attorney general, once quipped to David Powers, "Do you think Hoover will show up today in one of Jackie's discarded Dior gowns?"

And J. Edgar's across-the-street neighbor, Lyndon Johnson, had first encountered the director tending his roses wearing what might have been his mother's housecoat.

In the Eastwood movie, *J. Edgar* (DiCaprio) gets beaten up by Clyde (Hammer) when he suggests that there might be a Mrs. Hoover, a reference to the Queen of the Sarong, the movie goddess Dorothy Lamour. Had she been alive and had sat through a screening of the film, she would have surely either cackled or else stood up and shook her fist at the screen, screaming, "That's bullshit!"

Whenever someone in his FBI office asked why he never married, J. Edgar pointed to a glossy studio portrait of Dorothy in a low-cut dress. He showed viewers her inscription which read, "With my sincere admiration and friendship—Dottie."

But that was the inscription from one of his best friends, hardly his lover. In Toluca Lake, California, one night, in the home of Gordon Howard, the California tycoon, Dorothy Lamour, in the presence of her husband (Bill Howard), author Darwin Porter, and TV director Stanley Mills Haggart, said, "Those romantic stories about Eddie and me are ridiculous, of course. I met Eddie when I was dating Sherman Billingsley at the Stork Club. A photographer was there from the *Daily News*. Sherman asked me if I would go over and pose with Eddie like I was his girlfriend. He didn't want him photographed cozying up with his real date for the evening, Clyde Tolson."

"At first I was reluctant to do so, but I found Eddie and Clyde to be great guys, and I started hanging out with them, especially in California when they came out to enjoy the race track season. They stayed with Bill and me. We always knew they were lovers, and Eddie liked to dress up on occasion. So what? He had a tough job and needed to relax from all the pressure of Washington and all that pretense of having to be a macho straight."

"In my opinion, Clyde was always deeply in love with Eddie. He loved Clyde back as far as he was capable of loving anyone. His mother did such a number on him I think he was afraid of loving a man. It was hard for him to give of himself. But Clyde was the only person he really opened up to, and that was very hard for him to do."

"In our home, he was very relaxed and let his hair down, or what hair he had to let down. Bill was always a little uptight, afraid one of the guys might make a pass at him. That was his Army background speaking. But he liked the boys, especially when Eddie prepared his lethal cocktails and manned the barbecue."

A much more learned response came from the widow of Dr. Marshall Ruffin, the psychiatrist who had attempted to help J. Edgar come to terms with his homosexuality. Mrs. Ruffin typed her husband's notes, claiming that the psychiatrist had written that the FBI director was "a bisexual with a failed heterosexuality."

According to her, J. Edgar at her husband's diagnostic clinic in Washington had confessed his homosexual link to Clyde Tolson and his penchant for cross-dressing.

"Hoover was definitely a homosexual, and my husband's notes would have proved that. Everybody then understood he was a homosexual—not just my husband." After seeking treatment, J. Edgar had ordered Dr. Ruffin to destroy all notes of their interviews.

Up until the day he died, J. Edgar continued to punish any person who publicly asserted that he was gay. In 1952, an officer in the CIA, Joseph

Bryan III, had told guests at a lavish dinner party (he was rich) that J. Edgar had a crush on a friend of his. "He's made several advances but my buddy turned him down. He's straight. Hoover is not."

Word reached J. Edgar about this "outrage." Somehow through methods not known, Bryan was intimidated "to back down and recant his charges," Guy claimed.

**

At the end of the Eisenhower era and at the beginning of the Kennedy presidency, Clyde was no longer the strapping Midwestern "Gary Cooper type" who had so enchanted J. Edgar in 1928. He had prematurely aged and was frequently in and out of hospitals. By 1957, he'd had three minor strokes and also suffered from duodenal ulcers and an abdominal aneurysm.

One of his eyes caused him such a problem he'd been hospitalized three times with it. After he'd gone through open-heart surgery, his speech had become hesitant. "I'm going to die, Eddie," he said. But he lived through that major operation and other ailments, even outliving J. Edgar, who was in far better health than his long-time companion.

Clyde wanted to retire, but J. Edgar insisted he keep his position, even though in time he could no longer fulfill his duties. On many days, he was too ill to report for work.

Of course, the physical passion of J. Edgar and Clyde had run its course, according to Guy Hotell. "I spent many a night at their place," he claimed. "They slept in separate bedrooms. I think Clyde no longer had sex with anybody. But Eddie was the lusty toad he always was. He went out on his own to have sex. He couldn't pick up a guy in a bar like an ordinary citizen. But he found Roy Cohn, Lewis Rosenstiel, and two or three connections on the West Coast that would supply him with young men for sale."

This was more or less confirmed by FBI agent John Dixson, who often met J. Edgar when he came by train to Manhattan, arriving at Penn Station as part of "a private visit." As Dixson or other agents remembered it, J. Edgar was often driven to the Rosenstiel's elegant townhouse.

One of the richest men in the world, Rosenstiel had known J. Edgar since the days of Prohibition, when he and Joseph P. Kennedy had made millions in bootleg liquor. By coincidence, Rosenstiel was also one of the best friends of Roy Cohn, with whom J. Edgar had worked so closely during the McCarthy hearings.

"He was just a little Jew lawyer when I met him," Rosenstiel said. "A cocky little bastard who loved cock even more than I did." Cohn and

Rosenstiel bonded almost immediately, and became in time two of the biggest connoisseurs of male hustlers in Manhattan.

It was well known to J. Edgar that Rosenstiel had a close "working relationship" with the gangster Frank Costello. Costello and Rosenstiel, in gangland parlance, were referred to, respectively, as "the Italian with the muscle and the Jew with the brains."

A Sicilian gangster, Costello was called "Prime Minister of the Underworld," and he became one of the most powerful of the Mafia bosses when J. Edgar knew him.

The FBI director also knew that Rosenstiel had business links with "the brains behind the Mafia," Meyer Lansky. They owned several enterprises, including casinos in Las Vegas. Both Rosenstiel and Lansky were said to have incriminating photographs of J. Edgar engaged in gay pursuits. Rosenstiel had secret cameras installed in his Manhattan townhouse and the bedrooms bugged.

The leading U.S. distiller, Rosenstiel also owned a 2,000-acre estate in Connecticut. He bugged the "playroom" in the basement where sex orgies were staged. The young men at these parties were personally selected by Cohn himself, who, incidentally, was Rosenstiel's chief counsel. At the time J. Edgar began visiting his Manhattan townhouse on East 80th Street and his country residence, Rosenstiel was taking in $50 million a year, an almost unheard of sum in 1950s dollars.

During one of their frequent Florida vacations, J. Edgar and Clyde (if he were well enough) flew on Rosenstiel's private DC-9 airplane and stayed at his mansion when not sailing on his super deluxe yacht.

Some of the public knew of J. Edgar's association with Rosenstiel, but the friendship was interpreted as the FBI director socializing with a famous philanthropist. Rosenstiel donated some $100 million to New York or Florida hospitals and to the University of Notre Dame or Brandeis University. In time he also became the principal benefactor of the J. Edgar Hoover Foundation.

J. Edgar also advised Rosenstiel about which politicians in Washington might be receptive to a gift, especially if he wanted to get legislation passed to benefit his distribution of liquor throughout the country. Reportedly, half a million dollars ended up in the coffers of Lyndon Johnson, the Senate Majority Leader.

According to reports, Rosenstiel was exceedingly generous to J. Edgar. When J. Edgar published the FBI ghost-written *Masters of Deceit*, Rosenstiel purchased 25,000 copies and mailed them to colleges and libraries across the country.

Susan Rosenstiel became his fourth wife. She'd been married for nine years to a husband she described as "99¼ percent homosexual." A month into her marriage to Rosenstiel, she discovered that he preferred sex with young men more than he did with her.

That discovery was made one day when she came back to their townhouse unexpectedly and caught her husband in bed with Cohn. Rosenstiel told her that they were relaxing, going over some legal matters.

Before slamming the door in their faces, she said, "Governor Thomas Dewey is also one of your attorneys. I've noticed you don't have legal sessions with him naked."

At one party at their Manhattan townhouse, Susan recalled J. Edgar, Cardinal Spellman, Cohn, and her husband wining and dining with Sam Giancana, the Chicago Mafia godfather, and Santos Trafficante, who ran the crime syndicate in Florida and Cuba.

When Castro came to power and seized all of Trafficante's Cuban enterprises, he vowed revenge when he was deported as an undesirable alien. J. Edgar was made aware of several unsuccessful attempts he made to assassinate Fidel Castro.

Ironically, during that summer of 1958 when J. Edgar was associating with gangsters, he finally was forced to admit that the Mafia did, in fact, exist after years of denying it. He issued a statement to the press: "The Mafia does exist in the United States as a special criminal clique or caste engaged in organized crime activity." He also claimed that gang members consisted mostly of Italian or Sicilian origin.

Eventually, after her bitter divorce from Rosenstiel, Susan became more "loose-lipped" about her multi-millionaire former husband, revealing shocking details about gay orgies to one of J. Edgar's biographers, Anthony Summers.

To Summers, she claimed that her husband took her on two different occasions to a male orgy taking place in the Blue Suite of Manhattan's Plaza Hotel, which had been rented to Cohn. She was invited because a few of the VIPs liked a woman to watch as they engaged in homosexual sex. She was told that J. Edgar would be there, but she was not to acknowledge that she knew who he was. "He might be dressed a little different," Rosenstiel warned her.

Ushered into the suite by Cohn, she was introduced to a man on the sofa as "Mary," an old-fashioned gay term to describe a fellow homosexual.

As she recalled, "He was wearing a fluffy black dress, very fluffy, with flounces, and lace stockings with high heels, and a black curly wig. He was sitting there in the living room of the suite with his legs crossed."

Later she claimed, the party retired to the master bedroom where she witnessed the arrival of two blond boys, presumably imported as the party favors of the evening. Indeed at this time Cohn had "imported" two young male hustlers from Denmark that he kept at the Plaza for two weeks, according to Cohn's best friend, the famous literary agent, Jay Garon. Although Garon did not attend the orgy described by Susan, he told the author that he went one night to the Blue Suite at Cohn's invitation where he got to spend two hours in the bedroom with the "oversexed Danes."

At the orgy, according to Susan, J. Edgar "took off his lace dress and panties. He was wearing a short garter belt. He lay down on the double bed, and the two boys worked on him with their hands. One of them wore rubber gloves."

She later claimed that both Cohn and her husband performed sodomy and fellatio on the two overworked hustlers from Scandinavia. Susan said that J. Edgar had the two men "only play with him. I didn't see him take part in any anal sex."

She also claimed that within a year she returned to Cohn's suite at the Plaza for another orgy where J. Edgar was also in drag. "His clothing this time was even more outlandish," she charged. "He had a red dress and a black feather boa around his neck. He was dressed like an old flapper like you see on old tintypes. After about half an hour some boys came, like before. This time they were dressed in leather. And Hoover had a Bible. He wanted one of the boys to read from the Bible. As he read—I forgot the passage—the other boy played with him wearing rubber gloves. And then Hoover grabbed the Bible, threw it down, and told the second boy to join in sex."

She recalled that she saw Edgar only once more, and that was in 1961 when he visited their estate. He arrived in a limousine at Connecticut accompanied by Cardinal Spellman.

At this particular dinner, Cohn, Spellman, and J. Edgar, the honored guests, dined on lobster and caviar, while enjoying the beautiful gold dinner service that had once belonged to Queen Marie of Romania. Everything was washed down by bottles of Mouton Rothschild served by a butler who looked like movie actor Basil Rathbone.

She did not attend "the entertainment" conducted in the den, but one of the hustlers, Derrick Stiller, said that Rosenstiel paid him and six other hustlers picked up at the Haymarket Bar in Manhattan to perform sex acts in alcoves with J. Edgar, Cohn, Rosenstiel, and Spellman.

This Blue Suite at the Plaza, the one referred to by Susan Rosenstiel, was rented to Cohn under an assumed name. Suite 233 was used by the lawyer in one of the shadiest and least explored episodes in his notorious career. Two New York tabloids learned of it but didn't risk publishing the details.

Cohn led an extravagant lifestyle, including having an expensive yacht, a lavish home, and a huge hustler bill. He was perpetually running short of cash when he would resort to blackmail, as he did so often in all of his high-profile divorce cases.

He employed boys, ages ten to fourteen, to service pedophiles in Suite 233, at which time they were secretly photographed. Of course, the child molesters were rich and always paid off rather than risk imprisonment.

J. Edgar virtually had to know about this, but never moved against Cohn, who was called "the man who knew too much."

"A blackmailer could always blackmail another blackmailer," Richard Nixon once said.

Susan continued with her revelations in 1970 when she was called to testify before the New York State Joint Legislative Committee on Crime, which was chaired by State Senator John H. Hughes. It was also learned during this investigation that Louis Nichols, once J. Edgar's trusted "mouthpiece," earned his salary of $100,000 a year by using his influence in Washington to get Congress to change the liquor tax laws, which saved Rosenstiel millions upon millions of dollars.

By so doing, Nichols increased the value of his own liquor stock by $7 million. When J. Edgar learned that, he went into a rage. "I made him. I picked him up off the street, and now he's pulling in millions based on the job I got for him. I'm working for a government salary, and he's hauling money to the bank in wheelbarrows."

Subsequently, J. Edgar assigned agents to follow Nichols. When Nixon lost the presidential election of 1960 to John F. Kennedy, and was considered finished politically, Nichols didn't think so. When Nixon flew into New York on business trips, Nichols would meet him at the airport in a chauffeured limousine.

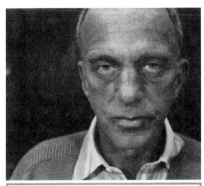

When this picture was taken, **Roy Cohn,** the most notorious attorney in New York, was facing death.

To the public, he continued to deny that he was a homosexual. He also refused to admit that he was dying of AIDS, insisting that it was cancer of the liver.

Columnist Liz Smith recalled encountering him at Le Cirque in Manhattan. "He looked awful. I'll never forget it. His face was very drawn, and he had sort of white chalky stuff at the edge of his mouth, like he was sick."

When he died, many of his enemies asserted, "So there is a God after all."

"This is brown-nosing," J. Edgar said. "I think Lou would lick the dingleberries off Nixon's asshole, if asked. He must think Nixon will be president one day. Take it from me, Nixon is finished in politics."

Although they remained friends until the end, Cohn's professional relationship with Rosenstiel ended in a disaster for him. In 1975, as Rosenstiel lay comatose and dying, Cohn came into his hospital room. He forced a fountain pen into Rosenstiel's feeble hand and lifted it to sign a Last Will and Testament, naming himself and Cathy Frank, Rosenstiel's granddaughter, beneficiaries.

Although he was accused in the 1970s and 80s of professional misconduct, including perjury and witness tampering, he was never convicted on any charge, in spite of overwhelming evidence.

However, in 1986 a five-judge panel of the Appellate Division of the New York State Supreme Court disbarred him for "unethical and unprofessional conduct, including misappropriation of client's funds, lying on a bar application, and pressuring a client to amend his will," the latter a reference to Rosenstiel. Cohn lost his license but it didn't really matter, as death within a month from AIDS came on August 2, 1986.

By that time, J. Edgar was long gone and never lived to see his former friend's disgrace.

After the McCarthy hearings and the senator's censure, J. Edgar abandoned him. But he still maintained some affiliation with Cohn, never really trusting the dangerous attorney, who might turn on him at any minute.

As author Burton Hersh put it, "Like scorpions investigating coitus, Roy Cohn and Hoover would continue to circle each other with wary fascination for decades."

***

A veteran cop turned private eye, the notorious Fred Otash lives today in the annals of Hollywood scandal, at least those scandals that were never exposed. He wrote a book called *Investigation Hollywood* in 1976, but it was a fairly vanilla account of some of his incredible adventures.

Before his death, he was said to be gathering notes for what he proclaimed "would be the most shocking book ever published on Hollywood." Apparently, he never completed the book; if he did, the manuscript seems to have disappeared.

One adventure that Otash could have written about would be his revelations about J. Edgar. The detective was a client of Lewis Rosenstiel. A close associate of Frank Costello, Rosenstiel flew Otash to Manhattan to bug his residence from the basement to the rooftop. Like President Richard

Nixon, Rosenstiel wanted everything documented. He trusted nobody, especially his friend, J. Edgar. "I want to entrap him," Rosenstiel told Otash.

In a call to his editor at Henry Regnery Company in Chicago, his previous publisher, Otash claimed he was going to send in a new manuscript "to blow the roof off the ceiling." Long after J. Edgar and even Clyde were in their graves, Otash was ready to tell what he knew not only about them but about a bevy of indiscreet movie people ranging from Howard Hughes to Lana Turner.

In his pitch for a big advance, Otash claimed that J. Edgar had been bugged and even secretly photographed having sex with a hustler at Rosenstiel's Manhattan address. Otash also said that he had "more than one" photograph secretly taken of J. Edgar in drag.

If his claims were true, his memoirs might have been the most scandalous book of the year. Otash also said he would crack the Marilyn Monroe Case—murder or suicide?—and "reveal stuff on Clark Gable, Judy Garland, Mickey Cohen, the Brothers Kennedy, and Frank Sinatra that would cause heart attacks."

As a detective, Otash specialized in extortion plots, sexual sadism, bugged bedrooms, cardinals and archbishops who swing, kidnappings, suicides, and presidential dalliances. In all, he was privy to more inside stories than any other detective in Hollywood history.

Most of his early duties involved the setup of abortions for the mistresses of movie stars. "I've had enough kids aborted to populate a small country," he said.

He was also the chief investigator for the tabloid scandal rag *Confidential.*

Although he was called in on the Lana Turner/Johnny Stompanato murder case, he was employed by the mob specifically to report on the affairs Kennedy was having on the West Coast. Today, he's best remembered for his private work investigating Marilyn Monroe and the Kennedy brothers. In the wake of Marilyn's death, J. Edgar ordered that Otash's files be confiscated and never returned. Perhaps they were destroyed, or else they exist today in some dark vault.

Otash told James Ellroy, the novelist, that he sometimes spied on JFK in action. Otash claimed that from what he'd seen spying on JFK, that he was "a two-minute man" and "hung like a cashew." In Ellroy's novel, *American Tabloid* (1995), the president was called "Badback Jack," because he used his bad back as an excuse for his lack of virility.

On October 8, 1992 an obituary writer, Myrna Oliver, wrote: "Otash prowled Hollywood by night in a chauffeured Cadillac full of women he called 'little sweeties,' and much like a fictional private eye conjured up by

Raymond Chandler, drank a quart of Scotch and smoked four packs of cigarettes a day."

Private detectives are supposed to keep silent about their revelations, except to their clients. But Otash often bragged of his inside knowledge.

Whenever he met a friend, he'd often begin his conversation by saying, "Did I tell you about the time. . . ." Then he'd relate a shocking incident from his vast repertoire. He once told columnist James Bacon one of his scandals. Of course, the journalist couldn't print it but privately gossiped about it.

One incident Otash related to Bacon allegedly occurred when he was a security guard at the Hollywood Ranch Market, which was experiencing a great deal of shoplifting. One afternoon, he caught James Dean stealing both a ham and a tinned caviar, "the expensive stuff, although he could afford to pay. It was my job to see that he was arrested. Charges were filed against him, but I learned later from someone in the police department that the case was mysteriously dropped. Someone important had intervened."

"Believe it or not, four months later I caught Dean stealing another ham at the market—no caviar this time," Otash claimed. "Instead of arresting him, I put the ham back on the rack and invited him for a freshly squeezed orange juice. I told him to cut out this shoplifting shit since he was making good money. What I really wanted to know was who got him off on the last charge."

"He looked at me with that smirky grin he had," Otash said. "'It was the most powerful man in America,'" he claimed. "'But I had to sing for my supper when I was driven in this big black limousine to La Jolla.'"

"As a detective, it didn't take me long to add two and two," Otash said. "I knew that Clyde Tolson and Hoover were staying in La Jolla at that time going to the race track. Suddenly, it made sense. Hoover could get anybody off from anything in those days, and Dean was his type. I'm also certain if you looked at that infamous book of Hoover's celebrity nudes, Dean posing with a big hard-on in that tree would be among his prized possessions. Some Dean biographers have written about the actor's claim to have been seduced by this 'bigwig in Washington.' It must have been Hoover. Eisenhower is definitely not a suspect."

***

In 1945, at the end of World War II, Scotty Bowers, a well-built, curly haired blond from southern Illinois, moved to Los Angeles. Shortly thereafter, he opened Scott's Gas Station at the corner of Fairfax and Hollywood Boulevard. Within eight months, it had become the most popular gas station among gays in Hollywood.

Getting a lube job at Scotty's came to mean something else. He hired as many as a dozen young men to pump gas and to escort certain gentlemen callers into the back rooms. There, the car owners could perform fellatio on these handsome, strapping former servicemen, or else become passive recipients of sodomy. Scotty hired only "tops."

Among the many patrons of the gas station were director George Cukor and the very closeted Spencer Tracy. Robert Taylor often stopped by to get "filled up," and Tyrone Power took some of the young men home with him to "perform the down and dirties," in the words of one gas jockey hustler.

"Most of Scotty's men were gorgeous," or so claimed Vivien Leigh, who visited the gas station accompanied by her friend Cukor. Most of Scotty's men were bisexuals and could accommodate either gender. Sometimes one of the gas jockeys was hired for private sessions at the homes of a married couple. Stars seeking lesbian encounters could also find Scotty's services fulfilling.

In his investigation, author Paul Young quotes a source who claimed that "Scotty was smarter than some of his competitors. He refused to accept money from his boys or his clients. He'd only accept gifts: gold watches, silver trinkets, stocks, bonds, you name it. Some of his regular clients, who greatly appreciated his services, even went so far as to give him pieces of property."

"You know, I've had my cock sucked by some of the biggest names in Hollywood, and this really big wig in Washington," **James Dean** once said.

Detective Fred Otash figured out that that bigwig was none other than J. Edgar himself, who ordered that Dean's arrest for theft in a supermarket be removed from police records.

J. Edgar's scrapbook contained a collection of obscene pictures secretly snapped of Dean, including one taken at a Hollywood party where he fellated a black man in front of other guests.

The subject of many newspaper and magazine articles, Scotty, in his late 80s as of this writing, is a Hollywood legend. When not running his gas station, he moonlighted as a bartender at star-studded Hollywood parties where he met many of his admirers.

Over the years, various stars had need for his services including Katharine Hepburn ("no women with skin blemishes"), Cary Grant, Rock Hudson, Tennessee Williams, even the Duke and Duchess of Windsor. (She was a closeted lesbian, the former king a closeted homosexual.)

Late in life, Scotty wrote his long-overdue memoirs, called *Full Serv-*

ice, a reference, of course, to the dual "services" provided by his filling station. The subtitle to his book is called "Secrets, Sex, and High Society in Hollywood's Golden Age."

Arguably, the most shocking revelation in *Full Service* is the weekend Scotty spent in the company of J. Edgar Hoover. He recalled meeting a rich young doctor from La Jolla at a lavish party off Doheny Drive in Beverly Hills. In the book, the physician is referred to only as "Ted" (with the last name withheld).

Scotty bonded with this doctor, who invited him to take care of food and beverage arrangements at a party at his home in La Jolla two weeks hence.

Right on schedule, Scotty arrived in just fourteen days at an elegant, modern beachfront home where Ted, clad in a bathing suit, welcomed him. Scotty found his kitchen fully stocked with everything from caviar to lobster, so he soon realized that he was the choice hunk of meat on the menu that weekend.

After Scotty had showered and "slipped into something more comfortable," he noticed from his bedroom window a large black sedan pulling into the driveway, its windows dark tinted. A young chauffeur, around twenty-eight years old, emerged from behind the wheel to open the door for his passenger. Out emerged a stocky man in his mid-60s with thinning black hair. He wore dark glasses.

A few minutes later Scotty was introduced to the distinguished guest as "John." At the time, the face of J. Edgar Hoover was one of the most recognizable in the world. The FBI director and the handsome young driver disappeared for two hours behind the closed door of an upstairs bedroom, which contained a king-sized bed.

When J. Edgar and the driver, who was called "Rick," emerged from upstairs, Scotty noticed that he wore a shoulder holster with a revolver strapped to his well-muscled body. Apparently "Rick" was J. Edgar's bodyguard, perhaps a young agent at the FBI.

In his memoirs, Scotty wrote, "So the rumors were true." According to his account, sex began after an elegant dinner, Ted pairing off with Scotty, and J. Edgar disappearing inside the Blue Room upstairs with the young bodyguard.

"The evening didn't end there," Scotty said. "We swapped around a bit—no group sex, no gangbanging, no foursomes, no orgies. Everyone was one-on-one, with two couples going their separate ways" and having their separate sexual encounters.

He claimed that he had sex with J. Edgar five times that weekend and just as often with Ted. Both Ted and J. Edgar tried out Rick, but Scotty was not asked to sample his charms. In bed, Scotty claimed, J. Edgar was "a very pleasant and gentle man," unlike his public image, but he gave no more tantalizing details. Did they kiss? Was J. Edgar a top or bottom? How was the penis? Cut or uncut? Large? Average? Small?

During the weekend, Ted opened the locked door to a spare bedroom filled with a large wardrobe of women's clothing. Scotty claimed he was asked to serve Saturday night dinner in drag. He also said that J. Edgar appeared that evening in costly gowns, changing his selection of wardrobe two or three times that night.

On Monday morning, Scotty said goodbye to Ted, J. Edgar, and his young driver, as he headed back to Los Angeles. He wrote that Ted remained a client for years "but I never saw Hoover ever again."

***

At a luncheon at Washington's Mayflower Hotel, Joseph P. Kennedy complained to J. Edgar, "I should have had my boy Jack gelded when he was fifteen years old. He can't meet a woman he doesn't fuck. Already he's gone through half the stars in Hollywood from Marlene Dietrich to Gene Tierney, even Jayne Mansfield—and that big-busted cow was pregnant at the time."

"At least he's not dating any more Nazi spies," J. Edgar said, noticing the frown that crossed the ambassador's brow.

The FBI director was referring to an affair JFK launched in November of 1941 with Inga Arvad, when he was an ensign in the Office of Naval Intelligence in Washington. She called him "Honeysuckle," and he nicknamed her "Inga-Binga."

At the age of fifteen, with her thirty-six-inch bust, she'd won the Miss Denmark contest. In 1936 she'd had an affair with Adolf Hitler during the 1936 Summer Olympics in Berlin. Der Führer found her "the perfect example of Nordic beauty."

This torrid affair came to the attention of Clyde and J. Edgar. The director told his aides, "The bitch is the Mata Hari of Washington, and that upstart Kennedy brat is fucking her and giving away naval secrets which she's reporting to Hitler himself."

JFK knew that J. Edgar's G-Men were following him and bugging his bedrooms. One night in bed with Inga, he addressed the hidden microphones. "Whoever is listening, the next sound you hear will be of me fucking her." He also said, "Hoover's on the take from the Mafia, which pays his heavy gambling debts. With the high costs of dresses and wigs these days, he needs financial assistance from the mob."

417

With the intervention of the ambassador, his son ended the affair and was shipped off to the Pacific.

J. Edgar and Clyde had met Arvad. The Nazi spy had been introduced to them at a party. Later she wrote that Clyde is "like a good boy expecting a promised candy bar." That comment angered J. Edgar.

The interference of J. Edgar into JFK's wartime affair caused a lasting bitterness between the two adversaries.

At their Mayflower Hotel luncheon, the ambassador leaned back after his third glass of Irish whiskey and informed J. Edgar, "The family has decided it's time to run Jack for President of the United States, in spite of the fact he's a Catholic. We know we can depend on you to keep the lid on any scandal."

"You can count on me, Joe," J. Edgar said. "We've been friends for years, and I've demonstrated to you that you can trust me."

"I'm counting on that," Kennedy said.

What J. Edgar didn't tell Joe Kennedy was that privately he was backing Lyndon B. Johnson for the Democratic nomination in the presidential race of 1960 which would pit JFK against Richard Nixon, another of J. Edgar's allies. Even though behind his back LBJ called J. Edgar "the queer bastard," they pretended to be warm friends—at least when they met up with each other.

Two weeks later at the same Mayflower Hotel luncheon table, J. Edgar informed Nixon that "you can count on me." He paused. "One-hundred percent."

Clyde was also at the luncheon, and he assured Nixon that, "We have a way of containing any embarrassing revelations that might rear their ugly heads. If an ugly head pops up, we'll chop it off with the sharpest axe the FBI has to offer."

J. Edgar and Clyde were well aware of the sexual misadventures of the candidate they mocked as "The Jack Rabbit," willing to hop between any open legs. Even more alarming was the in-

In the annals of political seductions, **Inga Arvad** *(right figure, above)* had a definite taste for powerful men, each of whom presided over huge portions of the world. She was seduced by both **Adolf Hitler** *(left)* and a young U.S. Navy officer, **John F. Kennedy.**

She often spoke of Hitler's "kind heart." J. Edgar became suspicious that hot-to-trot Jack Kennedy was revealing government secrets to his mistress.

This revelation led to JFK's being sent off to the Pacific to command PT 109—and the rest is history.

formation they were gathering that Joe Kennedy still had the mob connections he'd formed when he was a bootlegger during Prohibition.

Clyde had shown J. Edgar a photograph taken on a California golf course which revealed Joe playing golf with Johnny Roselli, who was the West Coast mob chief for Chicago Mafia boss Sam Giancana.

The FBI also had photographs secretly taken of Jack meeting with Meyer Lansky in 1957 in pre-Castro Havana. The Senator from Massachusetts had flown in with one of his best friends, Senator George Smathers of Florida, to patronize "only the most beautiful of the city's *putas*."

Through wiretaps, J. Edgar and Clyde learned that Joe was funneling money into a war chest presided over by Sam Giancana, whose instructions were "to buy the West Virginia primary" if necessary. As a Catholic, JFK was facing a difficult contest in a heavily Protestant state. But through buying off the unions and key officials, JFK emerged triumphant in the primary.

Joe also knew that the Chicago mob boss, Sam Giancana, his former ally from bootlegging days, knew that during the actual election in November, winning Illinois was crucial because it was a political swing state and would be essential for his son's election as president.

The FBI surveillance of Jack produced another dangerous link with Giancana. They shared the same mistress, Judith Campbell, a party girl who looked like Elizabeth Taylor. Introduced to JFK by his friend, Frank Sinatra, after the singer had tired of her, Judith had met Jack when he was a senator and hadn't yet announced his run for the presidency.

Born in New York City to a wealthy family who soon after moved to Los Angeles, Judith grew up in a 24-room Mediterranean villa where she met such celebrities as family friend Jack Warner and Cary Grant.

She later claimed that Bob Hope, one of her father's best friends, molested her in a beach house when she was a little girl. In later life, according to the FBI report, she "deep-throated" such Sinatra Rat Packers as Peter Lawford, Sammy Davis Jr. and Dean Martin.

In 1960, when Jack was running for president, she arranged a secret meeting at Miami Beach's Fontainebleau Hotel between JFK and Giancana. J. Edgar had ordered an FBI agent to spy on this rendezvous. To complicate matters even more, Judith was also a part-time mistress of Johnny Roselli, Giancana's "henchman" in Los Angeles.

Before he became president, Jack was revealed to prefer three-ways with two women at a time. Even though she denied it in her highly unreliable memoirs, Judith Campbell was often hired as "the second woman."

On the eve of the Democratic Convention in Los Angeles, Clyde had ordered agents to bug JFK's hotel suite. The bugging revealed that the man about to be nominated as the Democratic standard bearer had previously arranged a sexual tryst with both Marilyn Monroe and Judith Campbell in his bed.

When J. Edgar learned this, he told his aides, "I guess Kennedy couldn't get the real Elizabeth Taylor to join Monroe and himself, so he had to settle for Marilyn and a Taylor clone."

The FBI also learned that JFK had "enjoyed" two beautiful mulatto prostitutes when he'd been a guest of Frank Sinatra at his desert villa in Rancho Mirage, near Palm Springs, California.

Tapes of these sexual trysts with JFK, Marilyn, Judith, and the mulatto prostitutes were turned over to Lyndon Johnson's campaign, as the Texas senator was hoping to knock out Kennedy and carry the Democratic banner for himself that year. Although Johnson and his aides found the recordings voyeuristically amusing, they didn't seem to have a clue about how to release them, at least to the general public.

Just hours before the actual nomination on the floor, other disturbing information would be sent to the Johnson campaign from J. Edgar.

"The fag issue was also raised about twenty-four hours before the nomination," said Senator Smathers, who was a confidant of both JFK and LBJ.

Even though Bobby and Jack were notorious womanizers, the Johnson camp had been swamped with rumors that they were "queer on the side."

In David Talbot's book, *Brothers: The Hidden History of the Kennedy Years*, the author said:

"The Kennedy brothers' boyish good looks set off homophobic anxiety attacks among their enemies, including the sexually repressed Hoover. But this particular whispering campaign about the brothers, who were notoriously heterosexual, never went anywhere."

J. Edgar had already made Johnson aware that JFK's best friend, Lem Billings, was a homosexual and "probably gives him an occasional blowjob." The Kennedys had also been able to suppress charges against Billings when he was arrested for "lewd conduct" in a men's room in Washington.

At the last minute, J. Edgar and Clyde produced pictures of Bobby and Jack in drag taken at a drunken party on Martha's Vineyard.

Smathers was at that party. "It was Halloween. The whole thing was just a gag. For a laugh, Jack and Bobby put on some of Pat Lawford's clothes and paraded out to amuse the guests. Some jerk took a picture. It was bullshit! They are not cross-dressers. Come on. Hoover is the fucking cross dresser. I think Lyndon understood that and never released the pictures. After all, he had his own sexual scandals that might do him in."

On the road to the White House, both Jack and his brother Bobby had to deal with two dangerous adversaries, even though publicly they had to praise both Johnson and J. Edgar. As Talbot reported, "Jack and Bobby and their top aides were aware of Hoover's secret life and knew he wore funny clothes. The Kennedy brothers and Hoover had a stalemate. They knew enough about Hoover and Hoover knew enough about them." It appeared that each warring faction had enough ammunition to shoot down the other.

Even before he was nominated, Jack had sent J. Edgar a confidential memo, assuring him, "You will be one of the first appointments I make." Privately they had a very different opinion. In 1964, after Jack was assassinated, Bobby made a recording which he thought would be read only by future historians, but his comments through

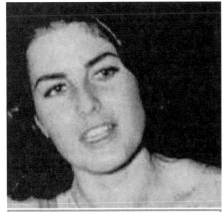

Judith Campbell (later **Exner**), an Elizabeth Taylor lookalike, had a reoster of potentially dangerous lovers, including Johnny Roselli, Sam Giancana, Frank Sinatra, and John F. Kennedy, whom she'd met while he was still a senator from Massachussetts.

Later in life, when she was criticized for her affair with a sitting president, she said, "I was 25 years old and in love. Was I supposed to have better sense and more judgment than the President of the United States?"

Before TV audiences in the 1970s, she told viewers that at the time, she didn't know who Senator Kennedy was. "I was not up on politics."

Not believing her, audiences booed her.

some informant reached J. Edgar. "Hoover is a dangerous man, a habitual blackmailer," Bobby charged. "He's rather like a psycho. Jack and I thought we could control him."

Facing the press, JFK had high praise for J. Edgar's accomplishments. Privately, he told aides David Powers and Charles ("Chuck") Spalding, "The two most overrated things in the world are the State of Texas and the drag queen running the FBI."

When it was clear to Johnson that he would not get the nomination, he still wanted to be on the ticket as Kennedy's vice presidential running mate. LBJ told Smathers, "One out of every four presidents dies in office. I'm a gambler, and I like to take a chance. Perhaps someone will shoot Kennedy, and I can take over."

During the campaign, Johnson also revealed to Smathers, "The queer bastard [a reference to J. Edgar] keeps sending me all this incriminating shit on Kennedy I can't use. Take that Nazi spy he used to bed. News that Kennedy had slept with Hitler's mistress who had also sucked off Herman Göring would cost him the Jewish vote. News that his best friend is a homosexual would cost him the Christian right—that and news he's a whoremonger. That he's fucking Marilyn Monroe might actually win him votes from redneck men, because that's what they'd like to be doing themselves."

When Johnson sent news that he wanted to be the "nominee for Veep," Jack told Bobby, "We're trapped. He's got us by the balls. I bet Hoover has turned over his complete FBI file on me to the Johnson camp."

Evelyn Lincoln, JFK's personal secretary, said, "I saw it happen. I was in and out of the room when Bobby and Jack made the decision they had to run with Johnson, even though they despised this tall Texan and didn't want him on the ticket. Johnson literally blackmailed himself onto the ticket."

In one of the closest elections in American history, the Kennedy/Johnson team narrowly defeated Richard Nixon.

It is still called "the stolen election." When Judith Campbell was leaving Chicago to go to Washington to have sex with the President-elect, Giancana told her, "Your boyfriend has become the leader of the Free World because of me."

Two weeks after the presidential election in November of 1960, Nixon called J. Edgar to thank him for his support. He was seemingly unaware of J. Edgar's behind-the-scenes support of Johnson. "The Kennedys taught me a thing or two about dirty tricks, and I thought I was the master. One day I'll get my revenge. I'll teach the fucking bastards what dirty tricks are all about. Watch me go!"

During his usual grapefruit and cottage cheese salad luncheon at the Mayflower Hotel, J. Edgar shared Nixon's promise of revenge with Clyde, Guy Hotell, and Louis Nichols.

***

The heir to the Camelot legacy, and the sexiest of all the Kennedys, John F. Kennedy, Jr. was born on November 25, 1960, a premature birth. His original due date was December 12. His father was President-elect John F. Kennedy, who had not yet moved Dwight D. Eisenhower out of the White House. His mother, Jacqueline Bouvier Kennedy, remained at the Kennedy compound in Palm Beach, not returning to Washington until the January inauguration of her husband.

John Jr. moved into the White House in February of 1961 and was given one of the largest rooms in the building, which Jackie had already transformed into his nursery. He'd inherited his sister Caroline's crib, on which Jackie had removed the pink bows and replaced them with blue ones. His bottle, prepared on a nearby gas stove, was given to him at six every morning. His morning nap was on the Truman Balcony, which a previous president had added to the White House and which was seeing its first infant in nearly seventy years.

Overnight, John Jr. had become most famous baby in the world, and he'd grow up to become America's Prince Charming, idolized by millions, especially when the cute little boy attended his father's funeral after the assassination. In 1999, millions more mourned JFK Jr.'s own untimely death in a private plane crash flying to New England to attend the wedding of a relative.

But before that happened, a glamorous life unfolded for him as the adorable son of the two most glamorous figures ever to inhabit the White House.

Almost from the date of John's birth, there were threats from kidnappers—some real, some from the deranged. He had been assigned a three-man Secret Service team to protect him.

The FBI director ordered that all these letters be sent to him, so that his agents could carry out an investigation.

J. Edgar knew that the kidnapping of the most celebrated baby in the world would provoke an international incident, dwarfing the infamy of the Lindbergh baby. "We don't want to be caught asleep when some kidnapper hoists a ladder to Junior's bedroom at the White House and hauls off this precious cargo. Jack Kennedy would have our heads."

From the very beginning, J. Edgar was fascinated by the infant. A spy he had planted in the White House fed him information. He learned that the nannies who changed John Jr.'s diapers nicknamed him "Big Boy." J. Edgar concluded that the boy had inherited his penis from the Bouvier side of his family, not from his father.

J. Edgar's informants picked up the most esoteric and trivial information on the young boy. He didn't like children's theater because he wanted to see dramas "where someone gets their head chopped off." Nikita Khrushchev in Moscow sent him a Russian puppy named "Pushinka." The boy also loved to visit a snake farm near Camp David where he would let a harmless cobra he named George crawl all over him.

John Jr.'s first attempt at a presidential "assassination" was when the communist dictator Marshall Tito of Yugoslavia was giving a speech at the White House. Playing upstairs on the Truman Balcony, Junior dropped a toy gun, its fall caught on camera, causing the Secret Service consternation.

J. Edgar was among the first to learn that John Jr. was a serious exhibitionist. When he learned to walk, he often appeared half-naked in the White House halls. When he grew older, he once visited a nude beach on Cape Cod, appearing completely naked.

J. Edgar was long dead when John Jr. appeared nude after his thirtieth birthday in 1990 on a beach in St. Barts in the French West Indies. A New York travel agent, Shelby Shusteroff, photographed him but has never made her coveted shots public, in spite of offers of huge amounts of money. Shusteroff claimed that the pictures were not taken for financial gain but for her own pleasure.

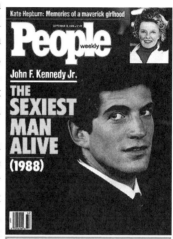

As a student at Brown University, John Jr. purchased a white-haired pig, which he kept in the basement of the Phi Phi fraternity house. He fed it well and planned to sell it for slaughter. To make the pig grow fatter, he personally castrated it with a Boy Scout pocket knife.

During his fraternity initiation, he was forced to swallow a live goldfish and then had to crawl around on a tile floor covered with the entrails of animals. He was then blindfolded and forced to search for a peeled banana in a toilet bowl filled with feces. He was later stripped down and tied, whereupon members proceeded to paddle his naked buttocks.

The kidnapping threats would continue throughout John Jr.'s life, and grew especially heavy during his second year at the New York University School of Law. He refused the FBI's offer of around-the-clock police protection.

A fellow classmate, Baird Jones, told biographer C. David Heymann, "Kidnapping threats were commonplace. I happened to know the people who ran the mailroom at NYU. One day they showed me some of the

J. Edgar died before **John F. Kennedy, Jr.** *(photo above)* became a promiscuous young man about town. But the FBI began compiling a dossier on his when he was a still a boy.

As "the most famous baby in the world," he was frequently subjected to kidnapping threats by extortionists who wanted to get their hands on some of the Kennedy millions.

J. Edgar was especially interested in what was said to JFK, Jr. by other people. At a party which he attended with his "guardian," Ted Sorensen, he was introduced to buxom Jayne Mansfield, with whom JFK Sr. had had an affair.

She told the young boy, "I preferred a man like your father as president. He was the kind of leader who will do it to a woman rather than to the nation."

threatening letters. It was incredible stuff, totally insane. One card stipulated that unless several million dollars changed hands, John would be kidnapped or killed. It surprised me that John was able to go about his business—ride his bike around town, get on the subway—without the slightest hesitation."

Under the Freedom of Information Act, the FBI files on John Jr. have been published, but they are among the most censored released by the Bureau. Almost none of them make any sense as the wording, for the most part, has been completely blacked out with a heavy pen. Many contain only the most innocuous words, as the juicy details have been censored.

Throughout JFK Jr.'s FBI file, the word "kidnapping" occurs the most frequently, although there are references to "abduction."

As documents, the files are virtually worthless, and many of the really scandalous have been removed. One document dated October 10, 1996, states,

> *"Supposedly, this was aborted because . . . scheme did not work. . . . was in charge of the plan and for making all the arrangements for the kidnapping. The plan also involved . . . who. . . . After kidnapping Kennedy, he would be taken to. . . . Kennedy would be held there until. . . ."*

The stuff that would make tabloid fodder was accumulated after J. Edgar's death in 1972 when JFK Jr. was only twelve years old. The FBI kept some sort of watch over JFK Jr. even beyond his death, investigating his mysterious plane crash, especially the charges that a bomb had been placed on board his private plane.

One of the most bizarre kidnapping schemes occurred after JFK Jr. was named *People* magazine's "Sexiest Man Alive." Three natives of Bogotá, Colombia, planned to abduct JFK Jr. when he was biking through Manhattan's Central Park.

Somehow he was going to be flown by private plane to Colombia. There, while held captive, he was going to be forced to make pornographic movies, both gay and straight, which his abductors felt—perhaps rightly so—would make millions of dollars—like a Paris Hilton sex tape, only so much more. Obviously that plan was never carried out.

In the spring of 1974, John Jr. was mugged in Central Park, with no Secret Service agent in sight, while riding his Italian-made ten-speed racer along a bike path to the tennis courts. His assailant turned out to be a twenty-year-old heroin addict who lived in Spanish Harlem. He stole John's bike and tennis racket but was later apprehended. Not wanting the publicity, Jackie urged that charges be dropped.

Considering some of the evidence the FBI collected on John Jr. as a grown-up young man, it is understandable why much of the data has never been made available. Perhaps many of his files were destroyed.

Like his promiscuous father, his son liked to seduce actresses, models, or just beautiful women.

Before his marriage to Carolyn Bessette, a six-foot-tall, blue-eyed beauty, JFK Jr. had a rather tender romance with Christina Haag, who lived with him in Washington during the summer of 1987. She recaptured their love affair in a memoir called *Come to the Edge*, published in 2011. Their romance blossomed when they were cast together in an off-Broadway play in New York City. The affair was a tale of the loss of young love.

He also had tumultuous affairs with actress Daryl Hannah and Madonna, neither relationship meeting the approval of his almost obsessively protective mother. He was said to have had a fling with Sarah Jessica Parker when she could escape from Robert Downey Jr. He claimed she once met him at JFK airport wearing a mink coat with nothing on underneath, a story denied by the actress.

By the late 80s and 90s, JFK Jr. had become tabloid fodder. In 1996, the *National Enquirer* headlined a story, JFK JR. & MODEL IN SEX TAPES SCANDAL, a reference to a rumored affair with supermodel Elle MacPherson.

He also dated other gorgeous models, including Julie Baker, a dead-ringer for his mother Jackie. One of his more bizarre relationships was with Paula Barbieri, the ex-girlfriend of O.J. Simpson and a model and actress.

His alleged affair with Princess Diana at the Hotel Carlyle on New York's Upper East Side made headlines around the world. One paper reported that Diana told Simone Simmons, her "natural healer" and clairvoyant, that John Jr. was "so much better than Charles."

Model Naomi Campbell struck out, but things heated up with singer Apollonia, who was "the main squeeze" of Prince, with whom she'd co-starred in the 1984 film *Purple Rain*. Jenny Christian, his girlfriend at Phillips Academy, claimed "he was extremely handsome, and it was a great romance."

There were so many more encounters watched by the FBI, including actresses such as Melanie Griffith and even Julia Roberts. He struck out with Irish singer Sinead O'Connor who once "shredded" the Pope. Maybe she hated Catholics. Also linked in the press to John Jr. were Sharon Stone and Princess Stephanie of Monaco. His so-called romance with Brooke Shields never seemed to get airborne.

John's tragic death in a plane he piloted occurred on July 16, 1999.

Also brought to a watery grave was his wife, Carolyn, and her sister, Lauren Bessette.

One tabloid carried a report that Bill Clinton had once told John, "We're going to run Hillary for President in 2008, and we want you to be on the ticket as her vice president. Your turn will come in 2016 and 2020."

***

Beginning in the spring of 1961, J. Edgar ordered that Marilyn Monroe should be put under surveillance. He wasn't all that concerned about her affairs with a parade of other men, plus an occasional woman such as a "weekend fling" with the "notoriously heterosexual" Elizabeth Taylor in a suite in Las Vegas. Instead, the FBI director focused mainly on her involvement with the Kennedy brothers and Peter Lawford, who was married to Patricia Kennedy at the time.

The diligent FBI agents came up with some tantalizing details: JFK had first seduced Marilyn when she was a budding starlet named Norma Jean Baker. When JFK returned from the Navy in 1946, he'd visited Hollywood, where he stayed with his close friend, actor Robert Stack. Stack's job was to introduce the future congressman from Massachusetts to a galaxy of stars and starlets, all of whom seemed eager to meet "the ambassador's son," as he was called. JFK was then at the height of his male beauty, charm, and flash, and it was easy for Stack to arrange liaisons for his horny young buddy.

JFK would have no recollection of the experience, but Marilyn did when she met him in 1954 during the course of her marriage to Joe DiMaggio. Now the international star, Marilyn Monroe, she remembered him and, when DiMaggio went to the bathroom, she gave JFK her phone number.

The next morning, Marilyn called her best friend, Jeanne Carmen. "Senator Kennedy couldn't take his eyes off me last night," she said.

During the final weeks of Marilyn's crumbling marriage to DiMaggio, she began an affair with JFK that was consummated during the times he was in California. Their venues ranged from the raunchy Malibu Cottage to the Chateau Marmont in Hollywood. She told columnist James Bacon, "Jack doesn't indulge in foreplay too much because he's on the run all the time."

Henry Rosenfeld, Marilyn's New York confidant, said Marilyn not only saw JFK at an apartment of a friend in Manhattan on 53rd Street near Third Avenue, but also visited him at his permanent suite at the Mayflower Hotel in Washington where, on occasion, he would also seduce Judy Garland.

Joe bragged to his son that he'd seduced Marilyn in 1950 when director John Huston had introduced them when she was making the film noir *The Asphalt Jungle*, a movie in which the budding starlet had a minor role.

When JFK became president, Marilyn in her delusion became more and more convinced that a divorce with Jackie was imminent. Her friend, Jeanne Carmen, warned her that the President would dump her when the novelty of seducing her had worn off."

"Not so!" Marilyn said. "We'll grow old together. I'll even learn to sit in a rocking chair like he does."

According to Lawford, he used to dress Marilyn up like an ugly secretary with a stringy black wig and slip her into the Carlyle. He even claimed that the blonde bombshell was slipped aboard Air Force One in dowdy disguise "for an airborne fuck."

The FBI learned that when Bobby was appointed Attorney General, JFK used the bedroom installed above Bobby's office at the Justice Department. During these sexual trysts, Bobby was conveniently absent.

When JFK flew to California, the meetings between Monroe and himself took place at the home of Patricia and Peter Lawford. Of all his sisters, Pat was the only one aware of his adulterous relationships.

Jeanne Carmen, in her tabloid tattle called *True Confessions of a Hollywood Party Girl*, claimed that she had a three-way with Marilyn and JFK at the Lawford home. She said the President told her that she should view Marilyn and herself as "pioneers of the New Frontier of the 1960s."

News of all these scandals were sent to J. Edgar and Clyde. Guy Hotell said "such stuff was their favorite bedtime reading. *Little Red Riding Hood* was too scary."

There was so much more to come. After the finalization of Marilyn's divorce from DiMaggio in 1955, she rented a small apartment in New York City. But she didn't invite JFK there since too many people might observe them. He would have her slipped into the swanky Hotel Carlyle to his penthouse suite. The hotel is famous as a venue for discreet liaisons among the most celebrated people in the world.

Her friend, Henry Rosenfeld, claimed Marilyn was as excited as a teenager to be having an affair with the handsome man who was going to become President of the United States. She confided to columnist Earl Wilson, "I think I make his back feel better—don't print that."

Before leaving a night club, she said, "Earl, you're a dear. Take a good look at me. You're looking at the future First Lady of the United States."

"But what about Jackie?" Wilson asked.

"He'll divorce the old bag. I heard it from Jack himself that she won't do all the things I'll do. She's too much of a lady, I guess."

Launched into an affair with Marilyn, the hottest thing on celluloid,

Jack placed a call to his father Joe Kennedy in Palm Beach. His father had been seducing movie stars since the 1920s, notably his long-running affair with silent screen vamp Gloria Swanson. But J. Edgar and Clyde were aware of many others—Constance Bennett, Evelyn Brent, Betty Compson, Viola Dane, Marion Davies (Hearst's mistress), Marlene Dietrich, Phyllis Haver, Sonja Henie, and, if Joe is to be believed, Greta Garbo.

In November of 1961, J. Edgar and Clyde at FBI headquarters had received an anonymous package. In it were sexually explicit photographs of Marilyn and the President. Who took these photographs is not known. The package carried a Los Angeles postmark. It is not known if the President knew of this delivery.

J. Edgar rather accurately concluded that in his private life JFK was "the most reckless man ever to occupy the Oval Office." As evidence, he cited his appearance in November of 1961 at a reception at the Beverly Hilton Hotel. "For all the world to see back then, Marilyn Monroe was his date," J. Edgar said.

J. Edgar learned that Joe was plotting Jack's re-election in 1964 and viewed Marilyn "as a walking time bomb." He called her and some sources claim he offered her a million dollars—"the price of silence."

The next day Marilyn told Carmen that she'd decided to drop JFK after all. "I've always thought that diamonds are a girl's best friend. Money can make a gal change her mind."

But as negotiations lingered into the Christmas season of 1961, and before her deal with Joe was consummated, he suffered a stroke. This once feared figure was left sitting in a wheelchair, helpless, mute, and drooling.

When J. Edgar with Clyde flew to see him, Rose Kennedy refused their admittance. She didn't want these two powerful power brokers to gaze in pity on a once-powerful man.

With Joe alive technically, but physically out of it, both J. Edgar and Clyde realized that they had to deal with JFK and RFK on their own. "The Jack Rabbit can be controlled, not that other rodent who sits in the Attorney General's office. We'll increase our surveillance of him. We've concentrated too much on Jack Kennedy. I hear Brother Robert is as much of a womanizer as his older brother, except he's more discreet. Round up your men. Let's keep our so-called boss under surveillance."

***

Using whatever means within his control, J. Edgar and Clyde pursued the nocturnal life of both Bobby and JFK with a certain ferocity. Instead of the Kennedy brothers, they called them "the Kennedy bastards."

With Joe Kennedy, their founding father, out of commission, Clyde predicted the brothers would grow wilder and wilder in their indiscretions.

The reports arriving at the FBI suggested that JFK was heavily sedated most of the time to avoid back pain.

J. Edgar's spies among the Secret Service in the White House were reporting on nude parties with prostitutes. Although J. Edgar at one point had no concrete evidence, he was informed that JFK, on occasion and as noted in numerous biographies, was fond of having himself photographed with beautiful women, sometimes pictured during fornication with him or else when one of the hired women was fellating him.

"I want to get hold of some of those pictures," he told Clyde and his aides. "No excuses."

It was rumored that Peter Lawford was called in to photograph a nude session with Marilyn and JFK at his home in Santa Monica. Marilyn confided to both Jeanne Carmen and Shelley Winters that the photos were taken in a large bathtub at Peter's home. Marilyn also claimed that Peter joined JFK and herself for a three-way.

The existence of these notorious photographs of Marilyn and JFK were first exposed in C. David Heymann's biography, *A Woman Named Jackie*. The whereabouts of the photographs, if they exist at all today, are not known, but J. Edgar was rumored to have obtained a copy of one of them.

Late in 1961, J. Edgar and Clyde began to pry into the private life of Bobby, watching him almost as closely as they did JFK because, as Attorney General, he was in a position to cause them the most damage, especially in his advocacy of civil rights and

Marilyn Monroe (*pictured in the top photo, above*) sings her most famous song, "Diamonds Are a Girl's Best Friend," in the hit movie, *Gentlemen Prefer Blondes*.

All three Kennedy brothers (*left to right*, **Bobby, Teddy, and Jack**) got to sample her charms, one at a time. Like some plaything, she was passed around from brother to brother. The brothers became duly alarmed when an out-of-control Marilyn threatened to destroy their carefully constructed political dynasty.

Marilyn entertained fantasies of marrying either Jack or Bobby, but not Teddy. "I call him my overgrown Teddy Bear—nothing more," she told her best friend, Jeanne Carmen.

his attack on organized crime. He'd once sent a memo to J. Edgar: "Hire more African-Americans in the FBI—and not just as a janitor or chauffeur."

In the FBI headquarters in Washington, J. Edgar shouted at Clyde and his aides, as he tossed the *Washington Post* on the floor. "Robert Kennedy is no saint. He must have paid someone to write this feature story on him. He's as big a whoremonger as his brother." Then he stormed into his office.

Within weeks, he was accumulating damaging evidence on his boss, the Attorney General. "He keeps his wife home barefoot and pregnant," Clyde said. "He travels all the time, and he always has a woman sent to his hotel bedroom."

RFK's latest affair was with the beautiful actress Lee Remick, who was ten years his junior. The report on him said he'd begun an affair with her after she visited Washington on the arm of her husband, Bill Colleran.

Another report claimed that Remick was overheard at a party saying, "I'm bored with my marriage and seducing married men is a big turn-on for me."

J. Edgar learned that her affair with Bobby had begun in 1962, the year when she won the Oscar as Best Actress for playing the alcoholic wife of Jack Lemmon in *Days of Wine and Roses*.

Through wiretaps, J. Edgar listened in on a conversation between Bobby and his brother-in-law, Peter Lawford. The Attorney General claimed he was flying to the West Coast and wanted to meet Remick. Lawford responded, "Sure, I'll introduce you. I'm also having an affair with her. But welcome aboard. The more the merrier."

Flying into Los Angeles, Bobby, according to the FBI report, spent the weekend with Remick at some friend's secluded home in Malibu.

Apparently, Remick fell for Bobby after their first two nights together. Before he left Los Angeles, she was urging him to divorce Ethel. She promised she'd divorce her husband.

Like Marilyn Monroe chasing after JFK, Remick pursued Bobby, even making unscheduled trips to Washington which she described to her husband as fundraising efforts for the Democratic Party. In 1962 Remick and Bobby were seen staying together in a villa on Palm Beach.

Bobby, according to reports, wanted to keep Remick on the string for occasional romps in the hay. He had no permanent plan for her in his life and he became alarmed to see her developing an obsession about him.

From both Bobby and Lawford, JFK heard what a "great gal" Remick was in bed. The President became intrigued and asked Lawford to schedule a meeting between them when he flew to the West Coast. He also advised Lawford that "Bobby's not to know."

431

Lawford, according to FBI surveillance, delivered Remick to JFK's hotel suite in Los Angeles, where she spent most of the night. She later told Lawford, "He wasn't the lover Bobby is. He just sort of lies down on his back and expects the woman to do all the work."

Bobby eventually heard about his brother's seduction of Remick. He told his office staff to, "Tell her to stop calling me. It's over. I've moved on."

***

From the beginning of Marilyn Monroe's affair with Bobby Kennedy, J. Edgar, Clyde, and their agents monitored the development of the sexual tryst. It began in early February during Bobby's trip to Los Angeles where he stayed at the home of his sister, Patricia Kennedy Lawford and her actor husband Peter. It would last on or off until the last day of her life and a confrontational meeting at her home in Brentwood only hours before she died.

When Peter asked RFK what star he most wanted to meet in Hollywood, his first choice had been MM.

In a letter to Arthur Miller's teenage son, MM praised Bobby's sense of humor and also claimed, "He's not a bad dancer either."

Peter later warned Bobby, "When Ethel's in the room, you shouldn't hold Marilyn so close when you dance with her. Her bosom was pressing into your chest, not to mention something else."

Joan Braden, a family friend of the Lawfords, recalled Marilyn's arrival at their home in Santa Monica. The blonde star was dressed in black lace, wearing no brassière. Throughout the night, Bobby devoted all his attention to her, finishing off a bottle of champagne with her. She even taught him how to do the twist. Right in front of Pat and Peter, Marilyn asked Bobby, "As Attorney General, have you ever arrested a woman in bed?"

"No, but I've done other things to them," he said.

Peter Lawford, brother-in-law to the Kennedy brothers, claimed "Bobby caught the adultery infection from Jack." Such was the case when he encountered a gorgeous 26-year-old movie star, **Lee Remick** (photo above). According to reports, "Bobby couldn't take his eyes off her."

Close friends claimed, "They were destined to hit the sack." Bobby wanted a casual affair, but Lee fell for him. She wanted each of them to divorce their respective spouses and marry each other, "but there was no way that Bobby was going to leave Ethel and all those children," according to Lawford.

After that night, Bobby made frequent trips to Los Angeles, promoting his book on organized crime. *The Enemy Within,* which he wanted developed as a film project.

Bobby's sister, Jean Kennedy Smith, wrote from Palm Beach, "Dear Bobby, I hear you and Marilyn Monroe are the new, hot item among Hollywood gossips."

After he finished a fourteen-country goodwill tour with Ethel, Bobby immediately called Marilyn for a rendezvous. Their affair was about to begin. At the time, Marilyn was also sending handwritten love poems to JFK at the White House.

One of Marilyn's closest friends, Jeanne Carmen, who lived nearby, remembered opening the door to Marilyn's house to discover Bobby Kennedy on the doorstep. When she heard who it was, Marilyn came rushing out of the bathroom. "She jumped into his arms," Carmen said, "and they started kissing madly. We had a glass of wine together before Marilyn reminded me that I had important business to take care of."

After that, Marilyn logged many calls to Bobby at the Justice Department. "She called him almost daily during the summer of 1962, her last on Earth," claimed Ed Guthman, a Kennedy press aide. Then he added a tantalizing note, one that hasn't yet been fully documented within the Kennedy scandals. "Judy Garland placed almost as many calls to Bobby as Marilyn. What was going on between Dorothy and Bobby? I never found out."

When Bobby wasn't on the West Coast, they talked for hours on the phone," claimed Hazel Washington, Marilyn's maid at the time. "I think they invented phone sex. Marilyn actually made love to Bobby on the phone. I heard everything."

"Jack was the first to sample the honeypot," Marilyn told Robert Slatzer, her friend. "Bobby had his turn. I wasn't in love with Jack, but I fell in love with Bobby."

Carmen also claimed that she went with Marilyn and Bobby to a nude beach near the present Pepperdine University north of Santa Monica. Marilyn, according to the report, wore a black wig, and Bobby had on sunglasses and a fake beard. Each of them went unrecognized. "Could you imagine what a sensation it would have been if a nude Marilyn Monroe and a nude Attorney General had been snapped on the beach by some photographer?" Carmen asked.

Bobby bragged about bedding Marilyn to Kennedy aide David Powers. Powers at first didn't believe him, calling him "the biggest bullshitter in the world." He later claimed, "Bobby wouldn't have the balls to play like that in the big league."

But Bobby claimed it was true. "Not only have I had Marilyn, but I think she's in love with me."

***

Nearly every person in America has heard about President Kennedy's affair with Marilyn. And at least a million have heard about her affair with Bobby. But only a few thousands know that she also had an affair with Teddy.

That revelation came to light in 2010, thanks to disclosures within formerly confidential files from the FBI. In June of 2010, after Teddy Kennedy's death from cancer in August of 2009, the Bureau released some 2,352 pages of formerly secret documents.

According to the files, there were several orgies staged at JFK's suite at the Carlyle. At least three included Marilyn Monroe as "guest of honor." Rat-packers Frank Sinatra, Sammy Davis Jr., Peter Lawford, and even Patricia Kennedy attended at least one of the orgies.

The FBI named Mrs. Jacqueline Hammond as a source of much of this information. Hammond was the divorced wife of a former U.S. ambassador to Spain.

Marilyn's eight-month affair with Teddy, which began at an orgy within the Carlyle attended by all three of the Kennedy brothers, extended until right before her murder.

Jack's younger brother, Teddy, had been very competitive about Judith Campbell Exner when she was the mistress of the president. He pursued her, and one night in Las Vegas, he openly propositioned her. But she turned him down, finding him "childishly temperamental."

After that orgy at the Carlyle, Teddy pursued Marilyn. One night in New York, she agreed to let him come to her apartment, where he found candlelight, roses, champagne, and Marilyn in a see-through nightgown.

"Teddy was all too eager," said Lawford when he learned about their coupling. "But the night Teddy met Marilyn at the Carlyle, he had to wait his turn, taking sloppy thirds after Jack and Bobby had finished with her. I was glad to hear that Teddy got to have Marilyn all by himself for a night and didn't have to wait in line."

Teddy's seduction of Marilyn, although known by many Kennedy aides, never surfaced in any public way during the star's lifetime.

The FBI documents were so explosive that Teddy's widow, Victoria, fought to have them squelched forever. She was ultimately defeated by a law court which upheld the Freedom of Information Act.

Teddy told Senator George Smathers, "I'm now screwing the woman whose poster Jack used to jack-off to when he was in the hospital. Marilyn Monroe herself. She told me I make better love than either of my two broth-

434

ers." Unknown to Teddy, she'd also told Bobby that he was a "far better lover than Jack."

Author Christopher Anderson claims, "Teddy, like the rest of his family, was engaged in an almost frantic pursuit of power, money, and sex."

In a particularly bizarre revelation, Carmen remembered drinking wine one late afternoon with Marilyn in her living room. The star was dressed in a stunning gown but wouldn't tell her friend where she was going. "I have a date tonight."

The doorbell rang and Marilyn hurried to the bathroom to check her make-up. "Be a doll, Jeanne, and get the door," she called out. Carmen was stunned to open the door to discover both John and Robert Kennedy, with two men standing behind them, presumably Secret Service agents. She ushered them into the living room. JFK claimed, "We don't have much time."

"Marilyn rushed out of the bathroom and gave each of them what looked like a prolonged tongue kiss," Carmen claimed. "Neither the President nor the Attorney General seemed embarrassed. Of course, Bobby and I had been intimate, so I didn't expect him to turn red-faced. I guess Jack Kennedy, considering his lifestyle, was beyond mere embarrassment at that point in his life."

She claimed that the brothers didn't stay long, and that both of them left very soon.

During her extensive grilling by the FBI, Carmen revealed these details but apparently Marilyn never confided any specifics about where she was taken that night by the Kennedy brothers.

Charles (Chuck) Spalding later revealed that JFK had told him that Marilyn was taken to the private villa of a friend of his in Bel Air. Teddy Kennedy arrived later. "Marilyn got to sample not

Beginning in 1961, when his brother, JFK, sat in the Oval Office, J. Edgar ordered the FBI to stay on the trail of young **Teddy Kennedy** *(photo above)*. "Who knows?" J. Edgar told his aides. "the little fucker might become president one day."

When Teddy went on a good will tour of Latin America, the FBI arranged for an undercover agent to be posted within his group. He reported back to the FBI that one night, Teddy rented an entire Chilean brothel for himself and his cronies.

Like his brothers, Bobby and Jack, Teddy also pursued Marilyn Monroe. But unlike Bobby and Jack, who spoke about divorcing their wives and marrying Marilyn, Teddy really meant it when he said he'd divorce his wife for the chance of becoming her next husband.

"I didn't really love Teddy like I did Jack and Bobby," MM told her friend Jeanne Carmen, "but he sure knows how to cuddle."

only Jack's charms but Teddy's and Bobby's that night. Of course, as president, JFK was first in line." At least that is what Spalding claimed that JFK had revealed to him.

If this testimony is true, it means that Marilyn and the Kennedy brothers were repeating the theme of their orgy at the Carlyle Hotel in New York, details of which were revealed in those FBI files.

Rumors still persist that Marilyn checked into Southern California's Cedars of Lebanon Hospital under an assumed name to have President Kennedy's child aborted. Others insist that is was Bobby's child. It has never been explained how Marilyn persuaded a doctor to perform an illegal abortion within a major U.S. hospital, when other movie stars were crossing the border into Mexico.

Never revealing the identity of the father, Marilyn claimed she had had a miscarriage. She told that to her publicist, Rupert Allen; her hairdresser Agnes Flanagan; and a Laguna Beach realtor, Arthur James. She was considering at the time buying a house in Laguna Beach.

Marilyn's gynecologist, Dr. Leon ("Red") Korhn, denied any abortion stories, although he did say that Marilyn had become pregnant three times, losing each fetus in a miscarriage because of the massive amounts of drugs and liquor she shared with the unborn.

Considering the timing, chances are that if any of the Kennedy brothers had been the father, it would be Bobby and not JFK. Marilyn made a crude joke to Slatzer about "Bobby baby-maker's big dick."

When Jackie learned the details of JFK's affair with Marilyn, she threatened to divorce him, which would have cost him the 1964 election, had he been alive to run for office.

According to Senator Smathers, the President told Jackie, "Look, it really is over. It was nothing anyway."

Jack told Smathers that his affair hadn't been worth it. "Jackie more or less gives me free rein around here, and I don't want to fuck this up. Let's face it: Marilyn's day has peaked in Hollywood. For these 36-year-old glamour gals, it's all downhill from there. I can live without Marilyn. In fact, she's become a god damn nuisance calling up all day. It's time for an *adios*."

There would be one more grand event incorporating the lives of Marilyn, Bobby, and JFK. It would eventually capture the imagination of the world and become part of the JFK/MM legend.

When Jackie learned that Marilyn had been invited to his birthday celebration, she said, "Screw Jack" and left the room. Then she packed to leave town, heading for Virginia.

On May 19, 1962, Marilyn ran away from the set of her film, *Some-*

thing's Got to Give, to sing for the President in New York City at a fund-raising birthday party at Madison Square Garden. Peter Lawford was the Master of Ceremonies.

After Marilyn missed her first cue, Peter introduced her as "the late Marilyn Monroe," a word usage that would soon after prove eerily prophetic.

She dazzled the world that night in her tight, glittering, almost transparent $12,000 Jean-Louis dress of "skin and beads." The flesh-colored dress had to be sewn on her. She didn't wear underwear, of course.

The President stared in fascination at Marilyn. "What an ass! Gene. What an ass!" that was JFK's comment to his writer Gene Schoor, who sat in the presidential box with him.

When JFK came onto the stage, he joked with the audience, "Now I can retire from politics after having 'Happy Birthday' sung to me in such a sweet, wholesome way."

After her appearance before the entire world, Marilyn retreated to her dressing room where she had to be cut out of her designer dress. After a bath, she headed for a party given by Arthur Krim, the theater magnate, president of United Artists.

Statesman/politico Adlai Stevenson was there. He later claimed, "I never got to dance with her. Bobby Kennedy put up strong defenses around her. He was dodging around her like a moth around the flame."

Dorothy Kilgallen reported in her column that Bobby danced with Marilyn five times. What she didn't report was that Ethel, in a far corner of the room, stood glaring at them with a bubbling fury about to spill over.

Before dawn the next day, Marilyn was slipped into the Carlyle where she later told Peter, "I had sex in one bedroom with Jack, then I came to the other bedroom and took care of Bobby." This was the last time the president, as far as it is known, ever saw Marilyn again. Bobby still lay in her future, his exact role the subject of ferocious debate today.

JFK was seen leaving the Carlyle at around 6am the following morning. Bobby left at ten o'clock that morning.

In a stern chastisement of her son, Rose Kennedy urged Bobby to drop Marilyn "and spare your family another disgrace."

Although the lid had been kept on them for years, by 1963, stories about JFK and Marilyn were about to break wide open in the press. JFK told Senator Smathers, "It's all become too public. I can't see her anymore."

JFK even sent William Haddad, a former *New York Post* reporter working at the time for the Peace Corps, to the top editors at *Time* and *Newsweek*, cautioning them not to print news about his alleged affair with Marilyn. "It simply isn't true," Haddad claimed.

Peter Lawford later said that "Marilyn couldn't get it through her head that the party was over. I kept telling her that she didn't know Bobby and Jack like I did. When they're through with a woman, they're toast. She really knew that, but somehow couldn't bring herself to admit it. She wrote constant letters to Jack at the White House begging him to take her back. At one point, she was so bitter she told me that Jack made love like a thirteen-year-old boy. When she wouldn't let up, Jack sent Bobby out here to cool her down."

Author Truman Capote was a close friend of **Marilyn Monroe** *(above photo, left)*. He'd wanted her to appear as Holly Golightly in *Breakfast at Tiffany's,* but the role went to Audrey Hepburn instead.

Capote often met Marilyn for lots of drinks. One night, she shared her dream with him. "**Jack Kennedy** *(right)* told me only last week that he plans to divorce Jackie and marry me. No later than 1964, I will be by his side when he seeks election. Imagine, me, First Lady of the land. I will preside over America from 1964 to 1968, but I'll be a very different First Lady from Jackie."

Like Jack, Bobby believed that his romance with Marilyn was becoming high profile, and he, too, retreated from her. He also claimed that she was consistently reckless because of her high consumption of alcohol and drugs. "Bobby is moving on from me the way Jack did," Marilyn told Peter. "The Kennedy brothers . . . they treat women like that. They use you, then they dispose of you like so much rubbish."

She also confided to Jeanne Carmen that she exempted Teddy from that charge. "He truly loves me, and wants to be with me anytime I'm willing. I let him do it because he loves it so much, but I'm not in love with Teddy. What I really want is for Jack and Bobby to make love to me at the same time. At the Carlyle one night, they both made love to me but not in the same bed at the same time."

In California, Bobby delivered the news to Marilyn in person. She was not to see Jack or him again. Nor was she to place any more calls to the White House or the Justice Department.

In hysterics, she began to scream after hearing this ultimatum from

Bobby himself. He tried to comfort her. When a man went to comfort Marilyn, that meant only one thing, sex. At least for a moment, he was overcome by her seductive charms.

But by the following morning, a clearer head would emerge on Bobby. Holding onto power, both for himself and his brother, was far more important to Bobby than bedding an aging sex symbol.

Marilyn refused to obey Bobby's ultimatum and continued to call both Jack and Bobby in Washington.

"Jack was the first to refuse my calls to the White House," Marilyn told Carmen. "And now Bobby won't speak to me at the Justice Department either. But Teddy is in touch with me. He still loves me and we're going to get together soon. I don't love Teddy, but I'm in love with the idea that one of the Kennedy brothers still worships me, unlike those older meanies."

"I've already sent word to both Jack and Bobby that I'm going to call a press conference and reveal everything about our relationships," Marilyn said. "But because of Teddy I will probably not do that. Peter Lawford is dead set against it too."

"Monroe could not accept that her affair with Bobby was over," said author Lucy Freeman, who interviewed Monroe's psychiatrist on several occasions. "Bobby's rejection reawakened her father's complete abandonment of her. Because of her father's early desertion, she created the sex goddess, the one that no man could possibly abandon."

RFK called Peter Lawford. The two men had never liked each other. The Attorney General ordered Peter to "cut Marilyn off from all contact with the First Family—see to that." Then he abruptly hung up the phone, offending Peter.

Not only had JFK and RFK abandoned her, but on June 2, 1962, her studio fired her. Fox press agents were instructed to launch a negative publicity blitz, defining their former star as mentally ill.

***

In March of 1962, JFK had gone an entire year without directly speaking to J. Edgar, and rumors circulated throughout FBI headquarters and Washington in general that he was going to be fired by JFK. His replacement, according to gossip, was to be William Boswell, the security director at the Department of State.

The President summoned J. Edgar to the White House for a luncheon that was to last a total of four hours.

His aide, Kenneth O'Donnell, was invited to attend, but for reasons not known Bobby was not at the meeting. Perhaps he'd been invited but couldn't stand dining with J. Edgar.

O'Donnell later recalled that JFK planned to take a risk and fire J. Edgar that day, but was restrained when the FBI delivered a bombshell that threatened Jack's presidency.

Marilyn Monroe remained a continuing problem. Not admitting any FBI surveillance, J. Edgar revealed that the mob, perhaps directed by Johnny Roselli and Sam Giancana, had secretly taped and in a few cases filmed sexual liaisons between the President and Marilyn. "All you need is some of their documentation to be released to the press, and you won't even need to seek re-election in '64. I view Miss Monroe as a possible time bomb that could explode at any minute and threaten your presidency. But you must decide that for yourself."

Jeanne Carmen, Marilyn's close friend, believed that she would have told all if she'd lived. She normally didn't like to carry on feuds, but she was deeply wounded by both JFK and RFK. "She wanted some kind of revenge, and she could have brought down the presidency," Carmen said. "She knew too much. She also attacked J. Edgar Hoover, claiming that the FBI had bugged her phone and her house. She took to calling me from pay phones."

At the White House, J. Edgar issued dire warnings against JFK's continuing involvement with Judith Campbell (Exner), Sam Giancana's girlfriend. It was all there in the FBI dossier. "Judith had unwittingly given J. Edgar the ammunition he needed to blackmail the President," wrote Scripps-Howard News Service reporter Dan Thomasson. Unaware that her phone was bugged, Judith had called JFK at the Oval Office from Giancana's tapped line.

The FBI director knew details about each incident of Judith acting as a go-between flying from Washington to see Giancana in Chicago. She'd even delivered top CIA intelligence on Fidel Castro that Giancana would use in a botched attempt to assassinate the Cuban dictator.

Bobby also issued a warning to his brother to cut off his affair with Judith, but for the next month JFK ignored both Bobby and J. Edgar. His affair with Judith continued into the summer.

O'Donnell once asked him why he was willing to take such a risk. JFK told his aide, "Because she's the best pussy I've ever sampled . . . the very best!"

Judith had already told the President that Giancana felt betrayed because Bobby was investigating him, despite the fact that he had been responsible for throwing the presidential election of 1960 to JFK.

She claimed that Giancana felt that the President could have restrained Bobby's investigation into his mob activities. "Jack Kennedy broke the code of the Mafia," Giancana said. "He did not live up to his bargain with me." One night he told her, "You know what we do with guys who do not live up to the code."

In 1974, eleven years after the death of JFK, Judith was summoned to testify before the Church Committee, a Senate investigation of U.S. government involvement in assassinations. She told only a fraction of what she knew, but was forced to admit that she'd had a sexual relationship with JFK.

She didn't want the notoriety, but she also feared for her life. She'd told an attorney, "They killed Sam," a reference to her lover, Sam Giancana. "They killed Johnny" (Roselli). "They killed Marilyn Monroe. They killed Jack . . . and Bobby too. I know they'll kill me."

She was obviously referring to Mafia hitmen. Labeled as a Mafia gun moll, Judith was hounded by the press and the FBI for years. Kennedy fans, steeped in the myth of Camelot, reviled her. Until the day aides such as David Powers died, the word from the Kennedy camp was that "there was no affair."

Near the time of her death, Judith told a friend, "I paid a high price for loving two powerful men." After a life of infamy, and suffering from breast cancer, Judith died at the age of 65 on September 24, 1999.

During his luncheon at the White House, J. Edgar had more to discuss than Marilyn Monroe or Judith Campbell. He issued a dire warning to the President: "We've been picking up rumblings that some forces—and we're not exactly sure who they are—are plotting an assassination of you. You must exercise more caution than ever at all public appearances."

JFK, according to O'Donnell, seemed to dismiss such concerns. "Since the day I became president, I always assumed that if anybody wants to trade my life for his, he can do so. It's the risk of being President. Just ask Abraham Lincoln."

O'Donnell later claimed that JFK lacked the courage to follow through on his original intent to fire J. Edgar. He obviously knew too much.

Finally, when J. Edgar excused himself to go to the toilet, JFK whispered to O'Donnell, "I bet he squats on the toilet to piss. Listen, I've been patient long enough. When Hoover comes back, get him out of here. Make up some excuse. The bastard is the biggest bore in Washington."

JFK also told O'Donnell, "If I can hold out a little longer with this faggot, I'll get rid of him anyway. There's a mandatory retirement age of seventy at the FBI. You do the math. It is now 1962, and Hoover was born in 1895."

***

441

After that confrontational luncheon whose dialogue involved a sex goddess, a gun moll, and the threat of a possible assassination of a sitting President, J. Edgar was assured that he'd get pretty much whatever he wanted from then on. That included permission from Bobby Kennedy to wiretap the phones of Martin Luther King, Jr., who was rapidly becoming J. Edgar's "most dangerous man in America." He believed that King was a communist whose intent was to overthrow the United States government.

After leaving the White House, J. Edgar was taken by black limousine back to FBI headquarters, where a nervous Clyde was waiting for him. "We're not getting fired, Junior," he proclaimed. "The Kennedys know I have enough blackmail on them to destroy them. I've got them by the balls and I'm squeezing."

J. Edgar had accurately assessed his own political power and the vulnerable spot the President was in. JFK remained immensely popular with the public, who did not know what was going on behind the scenes. J. Edgar's staff recalled that he looked jubilant when he returned from the White House.

He told Guy Hotell, Clyde, and two of his aides, "I did my duty. I warned Kennedy of the disturbing data that there is some plot afoot to assassinate him. Personally, even if I knew the exact time and place of the assassination, I would not intervene. Lyndon Johnson would become the President, and he has assured me that he would waive the mandatory requirement for me at the age of seventy. I plan to continue in this office until I'm at least eighty-two."

"But, Eddie," Clyde protested. "I'd like the two of us to retire. Won't you consider it?"

"Would you shut your fucking mouth?" J. Edgar snapped at him. "When I want your opinion, I'll ask for it. Power is very addictive. Once you've got it, it's hard to let go. Surely you of all people must understand that."

"I've always had a gut instinct for things, and there is one thing I know," J. Edgar continued. "During the 1964 race for the White House, Kennedy will be out of the picture. Johnson will sweep to victory on the Democratic ticket. Don't ask me how I know that, just accept it as the gospel truth. I'm never wrong about these things."

Someone in his office could have reminded him of Pearl Harbor, but no one dared do that.

442

CHAPTER TWELVE

Two men with huge egos, Attorney General Bobby Kennedy and FBI director J. Edgar Hoover, were on a collision course, with implications that affected the entire nation. As the 1960s dawned, J. Edgar was still on his "commie witch hunt," and wasn't all that keen for chasing mobsters the way he'd done during the John Dillinger era of the 1930s. He knew only too well how *Mafiosi* had infiltrated the worlds of politics and business, and he was well aware of Joseph Kennedy's links with the mob and President Kennedy's ties with Chicago mobster Sam Giancana.

J. Edgar was shocked when Bobby told him that one of his top priorities would involve going after organized crime. This worthy mission was launched in the midst of a world in crisis, with the Soviet Union threatening nuclear annihilation, a war festering in Vietnam, a potentially destructive arms race in full force, and millions of black Americans demanding their civil rights. Some of them, unlike Martin Luther King, Jr., advocated violence against the government.

When J. Edgar brought up the subject of home-grown communists, Bobby dismissed his fear. "Why go after American communists? Most of their fading membership rolls consist entirely of undercover FBI agents."

In a rebuttal to RFK's assessment that the U.S. Communist Party was "feeble," J. Edgar told a House committee that the party was "a Trojan horse of rigidly disciplined fanatics unalterably committed to bringing this free nation under the yoke of international communism."

When it came to investigating the criminal underworld or taking an initiative in civil rights, Bobby knew almost from the beginning of his administration that J. Edgar was what he called "a foot dragger." In frustration, Bobby set up his own investigation force within the Justice Department.

The FBI knew that the Freedom Riders in Alabama were going to be attacked by white bigots, but took no steps to prevent it. These activists were demanding the right of all Americans to use public transportation. "All the FBI men in the area did was take down notes," Bobby claimed. In his lack of compliance, J. Edgar was catering to his Southern conservative

Dr. Martin Luther King, Jr., is seen arriving at the office of J. Edgar on December 1, 1964 for a much-heralded meeting of two sworn enemies.

"I agreed to the meeting," J. Edgar recalled, "but I held this moral degenerate in utter contempt. He heard the tapes we'd recorded of him having sex with various women in hotel rooms. I told him then and there we'd release those tapes if he didn't stop calling for my resignation. At the end of the meeting, he asked me to pose with him in front of the press corps. I turned him down. 'Don't you ever attack me or the Bureau for as long as you live,' I told him, 'With the enemies you're making, that may not be a long time.'"

base in Congress who routinely supported him.

J. Edgar's main role in the civil rights movement involved investigating the private life of the Rev. Martin Luther King, Jr. "We will find a way to stop him," he told Clyde and his aides. "Put him under twenty-four hour surveillance, tap his phones, gather evidence to blackmail him. We know he's married and has a different woman sent to his suite every night. We also hear he has homosexual dalliances with studly black men, just like Franklin Roosevelt's pet, Sumner Welles. Go to work on it. I want to see a file on King that will reach the thickness of John Kennedy's, another womanizer with an occasional homosexual dalliance. It seems that all the big-time womanizers like to engage every third Thursday in perverted sex. Take Errol Flynn for example. Someone told me it is called 'the Don Juan complex.'"

From the beginning, King had a large mountain to climb, and authors such as Michael Hoffman in his *Holiday for a Cheater* weren't kind, calling King a "despicable hypocrite, an immoral degenerate, and a worthless charlatan."

Privately J. Edgar called King "a vicious liar, who supports himself by treachery and deceit. I know where he gets his marching orders. We got Dillinger, we'll get King."

In investigating King, the FBI went back to his past, even revealing that as a young man he attended the world premiere of the 1939 "racist" film, *Gone With the Wind*.

In 1957 he, along with Ralph Abernathy and other civil rights activists, founded the Southern Christian Leadership Conference, advocating a non-violent philosophy behind their protests. J. Edgar viewed the SCLC as a communist front.

On September 20, 1958, while King was signing copies of his book, *Stride Toward Freedom*, at a department store in New York's Harlem, he was stabbed in the chest with a letter opener. His attacker was Izola Curry, a deranged black woman. King narrowly escaped death.

"Thank God it was a Negro woman who tried to kill him," J. Edgar told his aides. "Not a white man. Otherwise, Harlem would be on fire tonight."

Eerily, J. Edgar was predicting the future violence that would emerge from King's assassination in the years to come.

J. Edgar had been incensed when King publicly called on the FBI to open its employment rolls to all races. In an attempt to derail both King's civil rights agenda and to re-establish his credentials as a hunter of American communists, J. Edgar fired off a memo to Bobby. "King's closest adviser is Stanley D. Levison, a white attorney and businessman who is his chief fundraiser and legal counsel. He is the actual brains behind King. Their aim is not to promote the agenda of civil rights. That is a mere cover for their true intent, which is a communist takeover of Washington. To achieve that end, they will use the civil rights movement."

Working behind the scenes, Levison had once funneled Soviet funds to the American Communist Party. He also edited King's book, *Stride Toward Freedom* and arranged to have it published. He even prepared King's income tax returns and controlled fundraising and agitation activities of the SCLC. Described as one of King's closest friends, he also wrote many of his speeches.

While investigating Levison, the FBI discovered that one of his chief aides, Jack O'Dell, had links to the Communist Party. Levison put him on the SCLC staff and payroll to assist with the organization's work in New York.

J. Edgar put through a personal call to the President, who chose not to pick up the phone.

As journalist Taylor Branch wrote in 1988, "The message was clear: that the troublesome Negro revolution was Moscow's skirmish line, and that only the omniscient Hoover knew the full details."

Although he was one of the great advocates of the civil rights movement, Bobby did grow alarmed that King didn't heed his warning and break from Levison. "Your goal is the right one, but associations with guys with communist backgrounds will only work against you," Bobby warned King, who paid him no attention.

King continued to irritate J. Edgar with his attacks on the FBI. One speech about conditions in Albany, Georgia, particularly enraged him. This southern town had mobilized thousands of its citizens for a frontal attack on segregation, attracting nationwide attention.

King said, "One of the great problems we face with the FBI in the South is that the agents are White southerners who have been influenced by the mores of the community. To maintain their status, they have to be friendly with local police and people who are promoting segregation. Every time I saw FBI men in Albany, they were with the local police force."

J. Edgar put through a call to King to tell him how misinformed he was. Clyde had called Albany and spoken to the agents there, finding that four of the five men were from the North. J. Edgar was deeply insulted when King refused to take his call. He would never forgive the minister for that.

***

As one investigative reporter claimed, "Marilyn Monroe was under lockstep surveillance, and she could not even fart without blowing air into J. Edgar Hoover's ear. Monroe's entire house was bugged—audio and video. The guy who bugged her house was later killed in prison to keep the rumor that her murder was actually videotaped out of the realm of absolute proof."

On August 5, 1962, an emergency call was placed to J. Edgar in Washington. His West Coast agent sounded hysterical. "Mr. Hoover, Marilyn Monroe is dead."

"I know," the FBI director said before slamming down the phone. That left the agent wondering how he knew that before authorities in Los Angeles were notified. In the wake of Marilyn's death, extra FBI agents were rushed to the West Coast.

The most elaborate cover-up in Hollywood history began even before Monroe's body was sent to its "eternal peace" in a cemetery.

J. Edgar and Clyde were kept busy as well, as the director didn't want one shred of evidence to remain showing that he had had Monroe under surveillance.

Whatever evidence he had gathered on the Kennedys would guarantee that he could keep his job in the event that a Kennedy dynasty ever really began—JFK, Bobby, Teddy, an ongoing line of presidents with more on the way. As he told Clyde and his aides, "America just might become an elected monarchy."

J. Edgar ordered his FBI agents in Los Angeles to seize Marilyn's phone records. There was a great potential for blackmail there. But he was furious when he learned that he was too late. The phone records had already been seized by the L.A. police.

Ironically, the death of Marilyn Monroe opened a door of opportunity for William H. Parker, the Los Angeles Police Chief. A close friend of Bobby Kennedy, he coveted J. Edgar's job. If JFK were re-elected in 1964, he wanted Bobby to use his influence to have the President fire J. Edgar and name him the new Attorney General.

In a daring move, Parker knew he could save Bobby from a lot of embarrassment. He authorized his policemen to remove Marilyn's phone records from the company's files. Once they had done that, Parker studied the calls and realized that most of them were to Bobby at the Attorney General's office.

If revealed, the public would know for the first time that Marilyn was having an affair with Bobby, or at least an observer might assume that.

Via special courier, these telephone records were delivered to Bobby at the office of the Attorney General in Washington.

The Kennedy brothers *(left to right)*—**JFK, Bobby,** and **Teddy**—often passed women around, including **Marilyn Monroe**. As President of the United States and as Attorney General, both JFK and RFK were vulnerable to scandal, and each of them became duly alarmed at an out-of-control Marilyn, who threatened to destroy their political dynasty. To remove her from the scene, both Jack and Bobby urged her to remarry Joe DiMaggio, thinking he might keep her under control.

Marilyn told them, "Joe is too possessive. He is capable of physical violence."

She entertained fantasies of marrying either Jack or Bobby, but not Teddy. "He's just a plaything for me," she told Jeanne Carmen. "I call him my overgrown Teddy bear."

It is believed that most of the hardcore facts about Marilyn's involvement with the Kennedy brothers remained locked in FBI files, if not destroyed.

Bobby had only recently denounced J. Edgar's continuing pursuit of American communists as "sententious poppycock." But after Marilyn's death and knowing the incriminating data J. Edgar had on the Kennedy link with her, he changed his tune. Suddenly, he praised J. Edgar's pursuit of communism. "I hope Mr. Hoover will continue to serve the FBI and America in general for many, many years to come."

On hearing this, J. Edgar told his aides, "We've silenced the Kennedys forever thanks to Miss Monroe."

After Monroe's death, Bobby and J. Edgar almost never talked again.

"The Big Chill" had set in, as both the FBI director and the Attorney General went their separate ways, giving each other wide berth.

J. Edgar avoided talk of Marilyn. He and Clyde told only a few trusted friends, including Ethel Merman, Guy Hotell, and Dorothy Lamour, "Monroe was murdered. It was not a suicide."

He chose not to reveal the identity of the person who murdered her, although it was obvious that he knew. Clyde also knew who killed Marilyn.

Langdon Marvin, a Kennedy aide, remembered being called to RFK's Hickory Hill estate in Virginia during January of 1964. There his boss handed him a dozen or so letters, ordering him to "get rid of them—burn them."

Marvin did as he was told, and shredded each of the letters. Later he learned from RFK they were "love missives" to both JFK and RFK from Marilyn herself. "I should have saved them. If genuine, they would be worth a fortune if sold today to collectors."

Director George Cukor later said, "Marilyn was not a lady who would have taken aging well. Her forties would have been a horror for her. She didn't have the integrity of a true actress—she would not have welcomed the richness of character interpretations, as a true actress would have. She was a star trading on certain gimmicks, and in her heart she knew that."

***

A sleek black limousine sped through the starless night, leaving Manhattan. It was three o'clock in the morning in March of 1963. In the back seat sat the world's most famous singer, Frank Sinatra, between two buxom blonde hookers whose names he did not care to know. "Tonight I'm going to find out if both of you are true blondes. Or, if like Marilyn Monroe, you peroxide your pussies."

"Where are you taking us?" asked one of the hookers.

"I've got to go to a graveyard to take a leak," he said.

"Why a graveyard?" she asked. "Won't a toilet bowl do?"

"Hell, no! This is one special piss I've been saving up after a night of drinking. I've been holding it in."

Sinatra was heading for the gravesite of the newspaper columnist Lee Mortimer, who had died of a heart attack in New York on March 1. In life he had been Sinatra's chief attacker, exposing his mob ties. Mortimer not only had tied Sinatra to the Mafia, but to the Communist Party.

At Mortimer's gravesite, Sinatra's driver had to guide the drunken entertainer to the grave. Once there, Sinatra unzipped his tuxedo pants and hauled out his penis, which he called "Big Frankie." He urinated on the gravesite before tucking it all back in and heading back to his limousine. In the rear with the two blondes, he ordered the driver to take them back to New York. "Revenge is sweet," he said. "Too bad I didn't need to take a crap."

Sinatra's hatred of Mortimer dated from 1947 when the Chicago-born columnist, radio commentator, crime reporter, lecturer, night club show producer, and author was at the peak of his career.

Among other achievements, Mortimer was one of the leading crime reporters in the nation. As a journalist, he had led the pack attacking Sinatra for his ties to the mob, with exposés dating back to 1947 when Sinatra arrived in Havana carrying two million dollars in illegal profits for mob boss Lucky Luciano.

From that day, Sinatra's hatred of Mortimer grew. Gangster Johnny Roselli suggested to Sinatra that Mortimer should be "wiped off the map." Although he would have been delighted, Sinatra turned down the idea because "too many fingers of suspicion would be pointed at me."

Mortimer not only attacked Sinatra because of his mob links but became the chief critic of his music and his movies. When *It Happened in Brooklyn* was released, Mortimer called it "a terrible, terrible picture. Stay away. Also stay clear of the cheap hoodlums he befriends. As for his fans, they are imbecilic, moronic, screemie-meemie autograph kids."

At FBI headquarters, J. Edgar and Clyde were more concerned that Sinatra was a communist and not by the intimate terms he maintained with the mob.

J. Edgar and Clyde always suspected Sinatra was a communist, ever since he'd published an open letter to Henry Wallace in 1947. In *The New Republic*, Sinatra urged him to run for President "to take up the fight we like to think of as ours—the fight for tolerance, which is the basis of any fight for peace."

Secretly, Clyde met frequently with Mortimer, feeding him information for his column, not just about Sinatra but about other celebrities as well. Their relationship at one point became intimate, and Clyde was seen leaving Mortimer's apartment on several nights.

Under the headline SINATRA FACES PROBE ON RED TIES, Mortimer wrote that "Sinatra is one of Hollywood's fellow leading travelers on the road to Red fascism."

Mortimer's attacks on Sinatra were picked up by other newspapers throughout the country, one editorial calling Sinatra "a pawn of the Kremlin."

The singer was never called to testify before the House Un-American Activities Committee, but he was frequently mentioned during the hear-

Columnist **Lee Mortimer** (top photo) detested **Frank Sinatra** *(inset photo)* and repeatedly attacked him in the press.

When Sinatra encountered Mortimer at a club, he beat him with fury, which led to Mortimer suing the singer, in spite of threats of physical harm from the mob.

Sinatra had Mortimer investigated, discovering that he and Clyde Tolson were having an affair. Sinatra's evidence was turned over to the FBI.

J. Edgar never saw it. It was intercepted and destroyed before it was delivered to the Bureau chief.

ings when it was claimed that he had links to communist front groups. In *The New York Times Index* for 1949 there is only one entry for Sinatra that year—"Sinatra, Frank: See U.S. Espionage."

In retaliation, Sinatra hired two detectives to investigate Mortimer. The detectives were able to obtain an affidavit from a young man who claimed that Mortimer had performed fellatio on him, for which the young man was paid. Sinatra wanted to go public with the accusation, but his press agent, George Evans, talked him out of it.

The detectives also discovered that Mortimer was having an affair with Clyde, and J. Edgar apparently didn't know about it. Behind Evans' back, Sinatra gathered up this evidence and had it mailed anonymously to J. Edgar. It is believed that the FBI director's faithful secretary, Helen Gandy, intercepted the dossier and destroyed it before J. Edgar could read it.

On the night of April 8, 1947 at Ciro's in Hollywood, Sinatra ran into Mortimer. He came right up to the columnist's table. "You're a fucking homosexual," he shouted. Then he struck Mortimer in the face. Arising from the table, the reporter was grabbed by two of Sinatra's burly bodyguards who held him while he was pounded by Sinatra's Hoboken-trained fists.

"I'll kill you, I'll kill you!" Sinatra shouted in front of some fifty witnesses.

Nat Dallinger, a photographer for King Features Syndicate, rushed to Mortimer's aid but could not stop Sinatra's assault. Dallinger called reporters to cover the incident, and he was also the one who delivered the badly beaten journalist to the West Hollywood Emergency Hospital.

The story of Sinatra's assault held the public spellbound. J. Edgar ordered the West Coast FBI office to send him all the details. It wasn't a case over which he had jurisdiction, but ever since the 1940s he'd had a voyeuristic interest in Sinatra. Perhaps not knowing of Mortimer's affair with his lover, Clyde, J. Edgar always viewed the journalist as a "friend of the family."

Upon reading of the attack, Sinatra's boss at MGM, Louis B. Mayer, said, "If President Eisenhower himself had been assassinated, it wouldn't have gotten this kind of newspaper coverage." He urged Sinatra to "settle this goddamn mess—and soon—or you'll never work another day at MGM."

To the police, Sinatra falsely claimed that Mortimer had called him "a dago bastard." Sinatra was charged with assault and battery, and his gun permit was revoked.

The columnist sued Sinatra for $25,000 but settled for $9,000 and an apology. In addition, Sinatra ran up legal bills totaling $25,000. All in all, in today's dollars that would be worth about $100,000 out of pocket.

When Mortimer sued Sinatra, he received at least eight death threats from the mob, which he turned over to Clyde at FBI headquarters.

Even after Sinatra's settlement with Mortimer, the reporter continued to snipe at him, calling him "Lucky" Sinatra, suggesting his link to Lucky Luciano.

Three years after his attack on Mortimer at Ciro's, the columnist was beaten unconscious at the Riviera Club in Fort Lee, New Jersey. The dive was owned by mobster Willie Moretti, Sinatra's mentor and close friend who helped launch his singing career in his New Jersey "casino barns."

After all this bad publicity, Sinatra's career took a "big nosedive," much to the delight of J. Edgar.

Even his own P.R. man, Evans, claimed, "Frankie is losing fans every day and may soon become a has-been."

At MGM, Mayer released Sinatra from his contract, Columbia Records asked him to give back an advance. He was also fired from his radio show. It appeared that Sinatra had become another one of the many victims of McCarthyism. But unlike so many others, he turned out to be the comeback kid, beginning with his Oscar-winning performance as Maggio in *From Here to Eternity* in 1953.

Following Sinatra's death in 1998, reporters pressed the FBI to release its file on him under the Freedom of Information Act. The dossier was six inches thick and 1,275 pages long. It is believed that this file was only one-fourth of the actual dossier that the FBI had compiled on Sinatra over the decades. The rest of the file may either have been destroyed by Helen Gandy, J. Edgar's secretary, or else hidden away somewhere in a vault.

Jeff Leen, of the *Washington Post*, in 1999 wrote: "Spanning five decades, the documents detail the curious and complex relationship between the nation's greatest entertainer and its most powerful law enforcement agency. Born in suspicion and contempt, this relationship proved to be protean and became unexpectedly intimate—a dance of interdependence. In a strange way, Sinatra and Hoover's FBI needed each other. Sinatra gave the FBI what every law enforcement agency needs to stay engaged and in business, a threat that must be tracked. The FBI gave Sinatra what every celebrity needs: protection from lunatics and extortionists. In Sinatra and Hoover, popular culture met the politics of fear."

In the words of the former boyfriend of Jackie Onassis, journalist Pete Hamill, "Frank Sinatra was the most investigated performer by the FBI since John Wilkes Booth."

It was said that the Sinatra files offer a secret history of the American Century.

***

Months before, J. Edgar had warned President Kennedy about the danger of affairs with Marilyn Monroe and Judith Campbell (Exner).

In the summer of 1963, J. Edgar claimed that it was imperative that he meet with both President Kennedy and Bobby, the Attorney General, in the Oval Office. The message he sent requesting the meeting was brief but emphatic: *YOU ARE INVOLVED WITH THREE SECURITY RISKS. YOUR PRESIDENCY MAY NOT SURVIVE.*

After reading that, JFK could hardly turn down J. Edgar's request. He called Bobby at once to set up the confrontation.

At the height of the Cold War, President Kennedy and, to a lesser extent, Bobby, had become victims of a self-styled "Honey Trap" plotted by the KGB from bases in London and Washington. The purpose of their plot was to use beautiful young women, actually Soviet spies, to seduce prominent politicians and extract secrets from them to send behind the Iron Curtain.

Soviet intelligence in America had provided the Kremlin with data that both JFK and RFK were womanizers, especially the President.

JFK had avidly followed news of the Profumo affair, perhaps fearing that the investigation in London might stretch all the way to Washington.

Even before meeting with J. Edgar in their tensest meeting ever, he suspected what the FBI director was going to reveal to him—and he was right.

Perhaps signaling the beginning of the end for Camelot, J. Edgar had done a thorough investigation of Ellen Rometsch, rumored to be an East Germany spy. Meeting her in Washington at Bobby Baker's Quorum Club,

JFK had begun an affair with her, finding her "another Elizabeth Taylor look-alike." A small-town Texas boy, Baker was Lyndon Johnson's major aide. LBJ told J. Edgar and Clyde, "Baker is a wheeler-dealer like I am. He's the first person I talk to in the morning, the last one at night."

The Quorum Club, sometimes known as "The Q Club," was a gathering place for senators, lobbyists, and businessmen seeking government contracts. JFK was immediately enchanted by Rometsch, who wore heavy makeup, including blood-red lipstick on her "Deep Throat" mouth and "glossy upswept ebony hair that looked more like a big pink Teutonic *houri* bred for the trade," in the words of author Burton Hersh, who also noted that she was known for her "sloe-eyed, come-hither manner."

Baker was the Capitol's leading practitioner of "get-a-contract-with-a-girl" form of doing business. At the Q Club, he employed several prostitutes from communist countries, most notably Ellen Rometsch but also Mariella Novotny. London-born Suzy Chang was also suspected of being a foreign agent. At the FBI, J. Edgar and Clyde had discovered that the President had become sexually involved with all three women. RFK himself was also implicated.

Pictures don't lie: At this complicated "summit meeting" in **JFK**'s Oval Office, **J. Edgar and Bobby Kennedy** clearly detested each other and chose not to look into each other's eyes during the tense confrontation.

J. Edgar is shown revealing that he knew that both the President and the Attorney General were cavorting with KGB spies, sometimes within the White House. Evoking a warning that would be made to a future president, Richard Nixon, less than a decade later, the chief G-Man told JFK: "There is a cancer growing on the presidency."

At long last, JFK's womanizing had caught up with him. A Senate investigation scheduled for after his return from Dallas would have exposed details about his many, often reckless, affairs to millions of American voters.

RFK later told Kennedy aide Kenneth O'Donnell, "Jack and I have been fucking the wrong broads. In the future, we'll fuck only Stars & Stripes women, not Hammer & Sickle whores."

When Baker introduced Rometsch to JFK, she was clad in a scanty black, skin-tight uniform, with black mesh hose. She stood against the background of a wall painting depicting a voluptuous nude woman.

After a night with the spy, JFK called Baker the following morning. "It was the best time I've ever had in my whole life. Send her over again on an as-needed basis."

Clyde at the FBI had wiretapped Baker's phone and heard this.

The FBI also heard Rometsch's opinion of JFK. "Jack was as good as it got with oral sex—made me happy."

As early as October of 1961, a top-level FBI memo had claimed that, "It was alleged that the President and the Attorney General had availed themselves of services of playgirls," a reference to the prostitutes working The Q Club.

An East German spy and a *femme fatale,* **Ellen Rometsch** could have evolved into a time bomb for JFK had he not been assassinated in Dallas.

Journalist Clark Mollenhoff of the *Des Moines Register* claimed, "Had John F. Kennedy lived to run for president in 1964, his House of Cards would have come tumbling down. Perhaps I would have seen to that. I had the goods on that fucker. Sex scandals crippled the government of Harold Macmillan in London. I would have done the same for Camelot."

Rometsch became one of the regulars at the naked pool parties at the White House, these events under FBI surveillance by J. Edgar's spies among the President's Secret Service.

On occasion JFK arranged for Rometsch to be sent to the Justice Department, where Bobby got to sample her charms in the secret bedroom above his office. He, too, praised her skill as a seductress. In Washington, she was referred to as "The Fellatio Queen of the Potomac."

She was not the Mata Hari of Washington. J. Edgar liked to reserve that appellation for himself. From the beginning, he had monitored the affair of the East German with the President. Under Clyde's direction, the FBI accumulated 478 pages within the file they devoted to her.

After his meeting with J. Edgar and the President, Bobby ordered Rometsch deported to West Germany. LaVern Duffy, one of RFK's aides, personally escorted her to Europe aboard an Air Force plane.

News of Rometsch's affair with the Kennedy brothers reached a Senate investigating committee.

During October of 1963, a month or so before JFK's assassination, the noose had already begun tightening around the throat of Bobby Baker. On October 7, 1963 he had been forced to resign as secretary to the Senate. Lyndon Johnson was also trying to limit his connection with Baker and had cut him off. There was a suspicion that LBJ was involved in political corruption, an example of which was the awarding of a $7 billion contract for a fighter plane to Texas-based General Dynamics.

Unlike Johnson, JFK was not connected with

454

Baker through any financial misdeeds, but through sexual liaisons.

"There's only one man in Washington who can suppress this investigation of Baker, or at least contain it," JFK told his brother Bobby in front of his aide, Kenneth O'Donnell. "That's J. Edgar, the old queen himself. Of course, in spite of past favors—financially in Lyndon's case, sexually in mine—both of us might have to toss Baker under the bus. I can just see the headlines: KGB PROSTITUTES SERVICE THE WHITE HOUSE."

The President deliberately made the word "prostitutes" plural. As the scenario unfolded, it seemed that Baker had also introduced JFK to two more prostitutes—Mariella Novotny and Suzy Chang—who may have been Soviet spies. Mariella was a bleached blonde Czech and Suzy was a Chinese beauty.

To make matters worse, and glaringly obvious to anyone searching for bait, these two beautiful hookers had been key players in the Profumo scandal that was already rocking the Macmillan government in London.

Had JFK lived, thanks to this particularly incendiary situation, his womanizing would probably have reached the press in spite of any attempted cover-up.

According to J. Edgar's FBI surveillance, JFK had done little to conceal his illicit involvements with the foreign prostitutes. As a senator in the late 1950s, he had invited Suzy to dinner at "21," one of the most highly visible dining spots on the celebrity circuit in New York City. Gossip columnist Walter Winchell, a frequent visitor to "21," spotted the handsome young senator and the prostitute, but chose not to write about it in his influential column.

In London, Mariella, an on-again, off-again striptease dancer, became a notorious prostitute. She traveled to the United States in 1960 in the company of Suzy. Both women were eventually hired by Bobby Baker at the Quorum Club.

Both RFK and JFK had affairs with the notorious **Mariella Novotny**, who maintained links to a Soviet spy ring. The FBI arrested Mariella on March 3, 1961 and charged her with solicitation involving men "in high elective office in the United States."

At the time of her mysterious death in February of 1983, she was writing a tell-all memoir. Her friends suggested she was murdered. One of her closest women friends said, "We always knew that Mariella would be killed by American or British agents, probably the CIA."

Her unfinished memoirs disappeared after she was found dead.

In time, Suzy and Mariella were introduced to the two Kennedy brothers, with whom they each had affairs. Baker arranged the introductions.

The daughter of two Chinese immigrants, Suzy had been born in New York City in 1934. During the late 1950s in London, she became involved with osteopath and pimp Stephen Ward, who rounded up prostitutes such as Christine Keeler and Mandy Rice-Davies for sex parties with key members of Her Majesty's government, including John Profumo. Ward turned out to be a prophet. He told party girl Keeler, "I believe Kennedy will be assassinated. He will not be allowed to stay in such an important position of power in the world. I can assure you of that." Ward never explained what led him to that conclusion.

One of Ward's friends was Prince Philip, Duke of Edinburgh, who sat for a portrait painted by Ward. "He's a snob," Ward later said, "not the man he used to be at my parties. I knew him before he married . . . what's her face, Elizabeth."

Although both of the Kennedy brothers had managed to keep news about their adulterous affairs out of the papers, there were various printed hints of what was going on. The *New York Journal-American*, in a blind item, wrote that "a man who holds a very high elective office in the Kennedy administration is linked to a Chinese prostitute."

Both Mariella and Suzy were not only named as members of the same spy ring that had trapped Profumo a few months earlier, but both women had "connections" to antagonistic communist adversaries of the U.S.

Mariella moved to New York, where she opened an international brothel. After her return to London, she was questioned by Scotland Yard and admitted that she had had sex with JFK in 1960 "at a New York hotel." She also claimed that her second encounter with the President was simultaneously with two other prostitutes on West 55th Street in Manhattan.

In New York, her partner was Harry Allen Towers, a Soviet agent, who had previously fled from England and was last seen in what was then known as Czechoslovakia.

Mariella's testimony could have been particularly damaging to JFK. Reportedly, she tied up the leader of the Free World for a "mild beating." S&M was her specialty.

Novotny was described by Christine Keller, the famous prostitute at the center of the Profumo scandal: "She had a tiny waist that exaggerated her ample figure. She was a siren, a sexual athlete of Olympian proportions—she could do it all. I know. I saw her in action. She knew all the strange pleasures that were wanted and could deliver them."

Later, Jack reportedly told his brother, "I couldn't keep up with her. I hope you could."

"Nobody ever said I had a bad back," Bobby answered.

In an unpublished memoir written right before her death in the 1970s,

Novotny maintained that she had been "recruited" by Peter Lawford to have group sex with JFK right before his inauguration.

In addition to Profumo, Keeler was also having sex with Eugene Ivanov, a naval *attaché* at the Soviet Embassy in London. There was a fear that she was transferring to him government secrets learned during pillow talk with Profumo.

Keeler was known to have visited New York, with Mandy Rice-Davies. Robert Kennedy asked Hoover to see if FBI agents could find out if the President had slept with either girl, especially Keeler. Of course, Bobby could have simply asked his brother, but since JFK slept with so many prostitutes, he simply could not remember.

This revelation appeared in a book called *An Affair of State: The Profumo Case and the Framing of Stephen Ward* by Phillip Knightley and Caroline Kennedy (no, not that one).

The book said that "Robert Kennedy had a right to be concerned. On July 23, 1963, according to an FBI internal memorandum, the tape recording which Christine Keeler had made with her new manager, Robin Drury, mentioned President Kennedy as one of Keeler's lovers. All that needs to be said about this allegation is that if Keeler had indeed slept with Kennedy, then it would have been completely out of character for her to have kept it quiet upon her return to London. She would have told everyone. The fact that she never mentioned it until she was recounting her memoirs for sale to Fleet Street strongly suggests that she invented it to make them a more valuable property."

Apparently, Keeler had wanted to have sex with JFK, but he died before she could orchestrate it. However, because of her notoriety, she received many offers for sex. She claimed that movie stars Warren Beatty, Maximilian Schell, and George Peppard "banged" her.

In February of 1983, Mariella Novotny was found dead in London. Police reported an overdose of drugs as the cause, but Keeler didn't believe that. "I think she was murdered. She knew too much."

As the investigation of Baker continued in Washington, more and more roads were leading directly to the Oval Office. The press became aware of the unfolding scandal.

Wesley Pruden, editor of *The Washington Times*, claimed, "A few brave Republicans were screwing up the courage to make something out of it, on the grounds that a President shouldn't be taking off his clothes with a *femme fatale* from the 'Evil Empire.'"

When word leaked out about this impending GOP assault, Bobby Kennedy, in his role as Attorney General, asked J. Edgar Hoover of the FBI to threaten and intimidate inquisitive Republicans in Congress.

Seeking to gain favor with Bobby, whom the FBI director despised, Hoover came through. He warned Republicans on Capitol Hill not to investigate the JFK/Ellen Rometsch affair. "If you do, I'm going to open all of your closets, and believe me, there are skeletons in there that will get you impeached."

J. Edgar reminded the senators—most of them "bitter opponents of civil rights"—that many of them had used "Negro prostitutes for sleepovers. Surely, you gentlemen wouldn't want this shocking fact exposed to your lily white voters back home, especially when many of you are coming up for re-election this year."

RFK then forced J. Edgar to meet with Mike Mansfield, the Democratic leader of the Senate, and Everett Dirksen, the Republican counterpart. Details about that meeting have been suppressed. J. Edgar obviously had "blackmail on everybody in Washington," as he privately proclaimed to the Senate leaders. In the aftermath of this meeting, the Senate Rules Committee decided not to investigate the Rometsch scandal.

In exchange for this favor, Bobby told J. Edgar that his job at the FBI was secure and allowed him to proceed with his wiretaps on Martin Luther King, Jr.

Betraying RFK, J. Edgar, behind his back, ostensibly worked to suppress the scandal, but also wanted it leaked. Information was supplied by him at various points to investigative reporters Courtney Evans and Clark Mollenhoff. Subsequently, Mollenhoff wrote an article incorporating a highly veiled version of the information in a story for the *Des Moines Register*.

In it, he claimed that the FBI had established "that a beautiful brunette had been attending parties with congressional leaders and some prominent new Frontiersmen from the executive branch of government. The possibility exists that her activity might be connected with espionage is of some concern, because of the high rank of her male companions."

Mollenhoff later claimed, "Had JFK lived to run for president in 1964, his House of Cards would have come tumbling down. Perhaps I would have seen to that. I had the goods on that fucker. Sex scandals crippled Macmillan's government. I would have done the same for Camelot."

During the closing months of JFK's presidency, the attorney general was kept busy "putting out brush fires," as he characterized it. Some of those fires were threatening to become major conflagrations.

Fearing that he would become the central figure in a U.S. version of the Profumo scandal, JFK as President ordered David Kirkpatrick Bruce, U.S. ambassador to the Court of St. James's, to provide him with a daily behind-the-scenes report on the Profumo scandal then cresting in London.

"To quote Ike, I want to be as clean as a hound's tooth when I run for president in 1964," JFK told Ben Bradlee of *The Washington Post*. "I plan to dump Lyndon. I considered a Democratic governor here and there, but I've come up with an unbeatable choice to offer the Democratic National Convention. A Kennedy/Kennedy ticket. I'll serve out my terms, then Bobby takes over for two terms, and by then we will have groomed Teddy to fill in for two terms. At some point, son John-John will be old enough to run. We could carry this a little further. Caroline might become the first woman president of the United States. Perhaps we could have her run for Senator from New York to get her launched into politics."

That was JFK's political fantasy. The more realistic Lyndon Johnson had a different take: "Not that I'm one to throw stones," LBJ told Bobby Baker, "but I think Jack's womanizing is about to be exposed as a national security risk. You're looking at the next President of the United States. After Jack steps down, I'm the obvious choice to get the nomination. And even win the election. Who are the Republican shitheads to run against me? Barry Goldwater? Ronald Reagan? Get serious."

In 1967, almost four years after JFK's assassination and before the 1968 assassination of Bobby Kennedy, Bobby Baker was convicted on seven of the nine counts of fraud on which he was charged. "I vomited breakfast in the men's room," he later recalled. He had to serve eighteen months in a federal penitentiary. His case has been called "The most bizarre Washington scandal of the 1960s."

Back in Washington during that fateful November of 1963, the case against the president was about to explode. Scheduled for a few days after what would have been his return from Dallas, JFK would have been questioned by a Senate committee about his "relationship with KGB prostitutes."

Journalist John Simkin wrote, "I think it possible that John Kennedy's relationship with Ellen Rometsch played a role in the cover-up of his assassination. LBJ and Hoover both knew that JFK had a sexual relationship with a KGB spy. Did this influence Bobby Kennedy's decision not to publicize his own doubts about the assassination of his brother?"

Some of the most tantalizing "what if's" associated with this case raise some questions:

1. WHAT IF J. EDGAR HOOVER HAD NOT GOTTEN INVOLVED AND DIDN'T THREATEN ALL THOSE SENATORS WITH THE INFORMATION HE WAS HOARING?

2. WOULD THE INVESTIGATION OF THE PRESIDENT HAVE GONE FORWARD?

3. AND WOULD KENNEDY, IN THAT CASE, HAVE BEEN IN DALLAS ON NO-VEMBER 22, 1963?

***

J. Edgar was "seriously pissed off" that he and Clyde had to cut short their annual vacation at La Jolla in California where they enjoyed placing "safe bets" on the horses, having been tipped off by the mob before game time.

Predictably, J. Edgar had opposed Martin Luther King's march on Washington, as had President Kennedy, who feared it would evolve into a public relations backlash, thereby damaging his civil rights agenda. Working behind the scenes, J. Edgar ordered the FBI to investigate celebrities participating in the march, including Joan Baez, Bob Dylan, and Peter, Paul & Mary.

He personally called Charlton Heston, who refused to give in to his demand to stay out of Washington. At that point J. Edgar threatened Heston. "We have nude pictures of you."

Heston had been an artist's model, often clad only in a velour posing pouch. But one day while changing his underwear for the pouch, one young man had snapped a picture of the star's genitals.

J. Edgar also warned Heston, "Do you want word to get out that you fucked a very young Sal Mineo?"

Despite these threats, which could have spelled disaster for his movie career, Heston still flew to Washington.

Before the march, J. Edgar and Clyde filed an FBI dossier on its organizer, a Pennsylvania-born black, Bayard Rustin. They discovered that Rustin

A triumphant moment in the career of **Dr. Martin Luther King, Jr.**, involved his speech, "I have a Dream" in front of the Lincoln Memorial in Washington, DC.

What was not known at the time was that he delivered the speech even as J. Edgar was threatening to reveal his womanizing, his alleged link to communists, even some rumored homosexual dalliances.

But King moved bravely ahead, even though he'd heard recordings of the wiretapped conversations that he'd had in bugged hotel suites during his sexual dalliances on the road.

had been arrested on a morals charge in a men's toilet where he committed an act of fellatio on a vice cop. When arrested, he protested to the policeman, "But you came in my mouth." He was booked and charged anyway.

Many civil rights leaders attacked Rustin's sexuality, but King stood by him. Rustin's sexuality came in for severe attacks from both white segregationists in the South and "Black Power" militants.

In the 1970s, long after the march, he would become a public advocate on behalf of gay and lesbian rights. Giving testimony on behalf of the New York State Gay Rights Bill in 1986, he gave his famous "The New Niggers Are Gays" speech.

Before the march, FBI secret tapes revealed King talking about Rustin. "I hope Bayard doesn't take a drink before the march," the minister said. "He might grab one little brother, 'cause he will grab one when he has a drink."

On that same tape, King was trying to explain his adultery to his close allies. "I'm away from home 25 to 27 days a month. Fucking's a form of anxiety reduction." King often talked about being the "Dr. Jekyll and Mr. Hyde in all of us." After listening to the tapes, J. Edgar claimed King was "a tomcat with obsessive degenerate sexual urges."

King's wife, Coretta, once said that her husband was a "guilt-ridden man."

The same could be said of J. Edgar himself.

On August 28, 1963, King led a triumphant march of 250,000 African Americans and their supporters to the foot of the Lincoln Memorial in Washington. It was to be the apogee of his political career. For J. Edgar watching the march on television, "It is my darkest day," perhaps not realizing that the word "darkest" could be interpreted two ways.

Many African Americans claimed that under pressure from the White House, the march had become too sanitized. Malcolm X called it "the Farce of Washington," and the Nation of Islam warned its members not to attend.

For most people, the march was a success, the largest protest march in the history of Washington. King's "I Have a Dream" speech electrified the crowd. His most ardent fans ranked it up there with Lincoln's Gettysburg Address or Franklin D. Roosevelt's "a date that will live in infamy" speech after the Japanese attack on Pearl Harbor.

J. Edgar took a more skeptical view. Noting the numerous charges of plagiarism that had plagued King for some of his writings, J. Edgar skeptically said, "Good speech. Who did he steal it from?"

***

As the autumn winds of 1963 blew through the cherry trees of Washington, J. Edgar feared his days in office were numbered. Lyndon Johnson had called and told him that if JFK were re-elected, he was considering him for an ambassadorship to Switzerland, where he had ancestral links. Perhaps jokingly, Johnson also told him that Robert Kennedy had recommended him for Boxing Commissioner.

J. Edgar called the White House and requested an urgent meeting with President Kennedy. Without the presence of Bobby, the *tête-à-tête* took place in the Oval Office, and was viewed as an off-the-record meeting with no notes taken.

It can be assumed that J. Edgar promised the President that he would rescue him from the brewing Ellen Rometsch scandal. Perhaps he promised that he would do what he could to prevent the Senate from holding public hearings. In return for pulling off this coup, J. Edgar demanded that JFK raise the mandatory retirement age for FBI officials when they reached the age of seventy.

The President's response was not recorded. This would be only the sixth meeting between J. Edgar and JFK since he assumed office. It would also be their last.

After that meeting and little more than three weeks hence, Jack and Jackie would be riding in their motorcade through the streets of Dallas, where they were greeted with waving crowds, not knowing that an assassin's bullet lay at the end of the trail.

At that moment when his brother was getting his head blown off in Dallas on November 22, 1963, Robert Kennedy was sitting by his pool at Hickory House in McLean, Virginia

President Kennedy had only moments to live when a bystander snapped this shot of him with First Lady **Jacqueline Kennedy** in the seat beside him. The pink pillbox hat she wore was about to become the most famous fashion accessory in the world.

The whereabouts of that hat is unknown today, although there's a rumor it was acquired by a drag queen in Connecticut.

The skies over Dallas were blue and bright, but it was twilight time for a president as he rode into history on November 22, 1963. Before flying to Texas, JFK tore a groin muscle while swimming. He was forced to wear a stiff shoulder-to-groin brace that locked his body in a rigid and upright position.

When struck by the first bullet, he remained erect for the fatal shot. He didn't slump over, and thereby remained in a stiff position to receive the final shot.

with U.S. Attorney for the Southern District of New York, Robert Morgenthau. The men were having a bowl of New England clam chowder and talking over ways to "de-ball" Roy Cohn, RFK's nemesis.

Ethel brought out an extension phone to her husband. "Hoover wants to speak to you."

From FBI headquarters in Washington, J. Edgar's message was brief. "The President has been shot." He put down the phone.

No sooner than that, a call came in from the hospital in Dallas where the slain President had been taken.

Within ten minutes, J. Edgar called again. "It appears your brother's wounds are critical."

"You may be interested to know," RFK said, "that my brother is dead."

As the Attorney General later recalled, J. Edgar did not appear upset in any way—"not quite as excited as if he were reporting the fact that he had found a communist on the faculty of Harvard University."

One aspect of the assassination that intrigued J. Edgar was that John Connally, the Governor of Texas, was riding in the same open-top limousine with JFK and his wife Jackie. A close friend of Johnson, Connally was at the top of the list of men who were viewed as a replacement of J. Edgar as FBI director.

J. Edgar had learned this upsetting rumor when lying in a New York hospital on New Year's in 1963, recovering from prostate surgery. He told Clyde and his aides, "Nothing like a prostate surgery to remind you of your own mortality. But I'll rise from this bed and carry on. You can count on me."

With three television sets blaring in his office, J. Edgar could hardly fail to notice that the entire nation seemed to be "treating Kennedy's assassination like news of the Second Coming," in his disgruntled words. "He was a whoremonger who nearly got New York and Washington blown off the face of the earth, yet he's being hailed as a fallen hero."

The next day, urgent calls from all over the world were coming in to J. Edgar's office, with personalities as diverse as Richard Nixon or Prince Philip phoning from Buckingham Palace in London. But J. Edgar told his secretary, Helen Gandy, to hold all calls. He and Clyde were going to the Pimlico Racetrack in Baltimore.

The day of celebrating the death of JFK was not one of total jubilation. At the track during the sixth race, Clyde complained of a sudden numbness in his right shoulder. His right eye seemed to be experiencing some sort of a spasm. He sat down. An aide nearby noticed Clyde's distress. J. Edgar had a lot of money riding on the race, and he hardly seemed to notice. Only when the aide nudged J. Edgar to look at his distressed friend did he focus on Clyde. "Oh, you're such a hypochondriac."

Nonetheless, the aide and J. Edgar walked Clyde from the stands to a waiting limousine, where he was taken to the hospital in Baltimore. There he was diagnosed as having had a transient ischemic attack, called a TIA or mini stroke.

Clyde was released that afternoon and driven back to Washington where he was put to bed. J. Edgar spent most of the time at his office at FBI headquarters. The President had died, and Lee Harvey Oswald had been arrested as the suspected assassin.

To his everlasting regret, J. Edgar lost his chance to interview Oswald before a night club sleazeball named Jack Ruby fatally shot him as he was being transferred to a more permanent lockup in Dallas.

At FBI headquarters, J. Edgar put Clyde and the FBI on full alert to get all information they had on Jack Ruby and Oswald. He was particularly terrified if the FBI had had any links with them in the past. "We may have to do a little housekeeping," he told his aides. "The blame game is on in the Kennedy assassination. We don't want any fingers pointing at us. I was falsely blamed for being unaware of the oncoming attack on Pearl Harbor. I don't want the American public to blame me for Kennedy's assassination, although I know of no man who deserved it more the way he was jeopardizing national security with his reckless life."

***

For the next nine months, during most of which Bobby Kennedy remained in a sort of daze, JFK's brother would still be J. Edgar's boss before stepping down as Attorney General. At a time when both men might have been communicating daily to see who murdered JFK, they would rarely speak and then only in the briefest of terms.

The new President, Johnson, called J. Edgar at the rate of four or five times daily. He warned J. Edgar to spend less time investigating who killed Kennedy—"and more time looking into who might kill my favorite Texan. I fear I'm targeted for assassination too. Don't be caught asleep at the wheel."

In response, J. Edgar offered him his bulletproof limousine and extra security guards not associated with the Secret Service when he made public appearances. "Lyndon trusts me completely," J. Edgar told his aides, "and I won't let him down."

When not on the phone, J. Edgar took on one of the most major tasks of his administration. "There's a shitty mess to be cleaned up in Texas over this Oswald thing," he told his aides. "Both Lyndon and I know that slimy little pervert wasn't the only assassin. But too thorough an investigation might extend to very dangerous levels and even lead to an overthrow of this government. We can't allow this to happen."

Normally the Attorney General's Office would have conducted an inquiry into a presidential assassination, but Bobby remained at home traumatized. In his absence, J. Edgar took over the investigation and opposed any other commission being formed to look into it.

When Johnson told him he was appointing a commission, J. Edgar asked him if he could head it. This was one of the few times when LBJ turned him down, appointing Earl Warren, Chief Justice of the Supreme Court, instead.

When J. Edgar heard that Michigan Congressman Gerald Ford had been nominated, he was delighted. "He's our man. We've got blackmail on him."

It was revealed that the future American president had been secretly taped by the FBI when he took various women to the suite registered in the name of lobbyist Fred Black at the Sheraton-Carlton Hotel in Washington. Bobby Baker, LBJ's disgraced former aide, also had a key to the suite. He'd later claim that, "Sometimes Jerry would call me and tell me not to use my key to the suite. It was going to be occupied for two hours that afternoon."

Women viewed Ford in those days as a good-looking football player who had been a male model in New York, often posing with his lover, the beautiful Phyllis Brown, modeling ski clothes for such magazines as *Look*. In his autobiography, Ford claimed they had "a torrid four-year love affair."

J. Edgar ordered Clyde to gather up all pictures of Ford snapped when he was a male model, the only U.S. President to have worked as a male model. He once posed for the cover of *Cosmopolitan* magazine, but apparently refused to do frontal nudes, in spite of repeated offers, especially from gay photographers in New York.

"I picked Ford because he can become your eyes and ears on the Warren Commission," Johnson told J. Edgar. "He played football too long without a helmet. He's also too dumb to walk and fart at the same time."

Actually Johnson was wrong in his latter assessment. Throughout his 1974-1977 presidency, and during his failed 1976 election battle with his Democratic rival, Jimmy Carter, Ford farted frequently. On every occasion, he blamed it on a nearby member of his Secret Service, lecturing a hapless agent to "Show a little class."

The new President's most famous utterance was "I am a Ford, not a Lincoln."

"The Beefcake Chief Executive," President **Gerald Ford**, was the most athletic president in American history. He was offered contracts to play pro football by both the Detroit Lions and the Green Bay Packers, but turned them down to go to Yale and study law while coaching football (*top photo*). He also showed off his splendid physique in the boxing ring, where he caused bobbysoxers to swoon.

In 1939, Ford posed for the cover of *Look* Magazine. After that, and for three years into the future, he was a male model appearing on the April, 1942 cover of *Cosmopolitan* (*lower photo, above*) with his beautiful mistress, **Phyllis Brown**.

His reputation as a clod came only when he was president, and never before that, when he was referred to as "a stud."

Johnson may have been wrong about Ford's farting, but he was right in believing that Ford would be an acquiescent cheerleader for the FBI during his term on the Warren Commission. William C. Sullivan, J. Edgar's number three man at the FBI, later said, "Ford looked after FBI interests. He came through for us, keeping us advised on what was going on behind closed doors. He was our man, our informant."

Sometimes Ford brought J. Edgar news he didn't want to hear. He wanted to dominate all investigations and clashed with key figures on the commission who opposed that. J. Edgar developed a particular distaste for J. Lee Rankin, the chief counsel for the Commission who wanted to investigate why Oswald was heading toward Jack Ruby's apartment in Dallas immediately after the assassination. On hearing that, J. Edgar said, "We'll put a stop to that little probe."

In the weeks following JFK's assassination, J. Edgar became obsessed with covering up the FBI's former dealings with Oswald and Ruby.

***

Since 1959, the FBI had been aware of Lee Harvey Oswald. Police authorities in Dallas even went so far as to suggest to the Warren Commission that Oswald had performed "various tasks for FBI agents." That accusation caused J. Edgar to explode.

In Fort Worth, Texas, on June 26, 1962, FBI agents had interviewed Oswald upon his return from Russia. Two months later, in August of 1962, when the local

Bureau was alerted that Oswald was receiving communist literature such as *The Worker*, Oswald was interviewed at his apartment.

When Oswald, along with his wife Marina, moved to Dallas in March of 1963, Special Agent James Hosty was given the job of "checking up periodically on Oswald." After his first encounter with him, Hosty scribbled on his file: "This guy is a nutcase and should be watched."

J. Edgar was horrified that his FBI had been in contact with Oswald, as he and Clyde worked to conceal any FBI role in his life. "We'll cover our tracks or else I'll become an old man on a pension hobbling around my house on a cane," he told aides.

To protect himself, he censured, transferred, or suspended without pay seventeen of his once-trusted agents in Texas. In time, that toll would rise to more than thirty agents. "Such gross incompetency can hardly be overlooked," he chastised them.

In a remark that virtually caused J. Edgar to have a mini-stroke, the FBI's Hosty spoke a day after the President's assassination. "We knew that Lee Harvey Oswald was capable of assassinating the President of the United States, but we didn't dream he would do it."

J. Edgar worked behind the scenes to get the Warren Commission to define Oswald as the lone assassin.

The suspected assassin of President Kennedy, **Lee Harvey Oswald,** a former U.S. marine who had briefly defected to the Soviet Union, holds up his manacled hands at police headquarters in Dallas, where he had been arrested for questioning about the death of both a Dallas police officer and JFK.

At this very hour, Oswald is depicted as he is about to become one of the most famous names in America, with one of the most recognizable faces. Earlier, he'd told the police, "I'm being framed. I didn't shoot Kennedy, although millions of his enemies will make a hero out of the man who did it. But it wasn't me."

New testimony about the type of ammunition used in the assassination has raised questions about whether Oswald acted alone, according to a study by researchers at Texas A&M University.

William C. Sullivan, his number three man, said he was told to, "Get this thing over with—and quick! We don't want to be chasing a hundred conspiracy theories. Let's face it: historians are still debating the assassination of Lincoln."

In front of his most trusted aides investigating the case, J. Edgar told them, "There are no co-conspirators. There is no international conspiracy."

"These instructions were uttered before the investigation had really begun," Sullivan claimed.

Kenneth O'Donnell and David Powers, two of JFK's most trusted aides, believed the fatal shots were fired from behind a fence in front of the motorcade rather than from the book depository. But J. Edgar told them, "There is no way. Testify that the bullets came from the building."

In spite of J. Edgar's efforts to contain them, accusations continued to emerge. Marina Oswald claimed she was led to believe that her husband "worked for the American government." Witnesses in New Orleans, where Oswald lived for a time, reported seeing him in the company of FBI agents.

In Dallas, Allen Sweatt, a deputy sheriff, came forward with the charge that the FBI was paying Oswald $200 a month as an informant. The Warren Commission, under pressure from J. Edgar, chose not to investigate these claims.

J. Edgar also suppressed evidence, as when the FBI turned over Oswald's address book. One page containing the name, address, and car license plate number of Hosty, his FBI contact in Dallas, had been removed. J. Edgar also suppressed a note that Oswald had left at the FBI office in Dallas, in the wake of Hosty's visit to his home. When Oswald learned that Hosty had interviewed his wife, Marina, he went by the local Bureau. In his note he threatened to blow up the office if the FBI didn't stop "bothering my wife." The FBI took no notice of that. When J. Edgar heard of this threat, he instructed the FBI in Dallas to destroy Oswald's threat.

After J. Edgar ordered Hosty to flush Oswald's threatening note down the toilet, his career with the FBI became a nightmare of transfers to different locales, probations, and suspensions without pay.

Under heavy pressure from the FBI, Marina Oswald testified before the commission, claiming that her husband shot the President. She later recalled meeting J. Edgar. "I was chilled from top to bottom. It was as if you met a dead person. He had a coldness like someone from the grave."

In Sullivan's words, "Every day, Hoover tried to put out a brush fire, sometimes a forest fire. Allegations were coming out of the woodwork like termites."

Waggoner Carr, the Attorney General of Texas, told the press that Oswald was an undercover agent for the FBI. This charge was denied by J. Edgar.

Later, the charge emerged that Jack Ruby was also an FBI informant, and this, too, was denied by J. Edgar, although it emerged that FBI agents did have contacts with the nightclub owner. His FBI file listed Ruby as a

P.C.I. meaning "potential criminal informant."

Records revealed that Ruby had been contacted nine times by the FBI between March 11 and October 2 in 1959, regarding criminal matters in Dallas. J. Edgar demanded that this disclosure be removed from the commission's report to the public, and its members agreed. "Such a disclosure might be too suggestive to the public at large," J. Edgar warned the commission.

The only member of the Warren Commission that J. Edgar continued to trust was future President Gerald Ford. In a touch of irony, he learned that one of the women that Ford seduced "on numerous occasions" was none other than Ellen Rometsch herself, the East German spy whose involvement with JFK in 1963 was threatening his presidency as he flew to Dallas. These assignations between Ford and Rometsch took place in a suite rented by lobbyist Fred Black at the Sheraton-Carlton Hotel in Washington.

"Pills and booze had laid Betty Ford low, and I guess Jerry had to take his fun where he could find it," J. Edgar told his aides.

He prevailed on Ford to alter the commission's report to claim that the President was shot from behind the neck. JFK was actually shot through the back. By claiming he was shot through the neck and not the back established the downward angle required by the "magic bullet" theory where a single bullet was said to have entered Governor Connally's body after exiting from the slain President's body.

During his occupancy of the Oval Office in 1975, Ford became very candid and admitted that he had suppressed "certain FBI and CIA surveillance reports that indicated that JFK had been caught in a crossfire in Dallas."

It wasn't until 1979 that the Assassinations Committee in Washington reported that "the FBI probe of the murder of the President had been seriously flawed," and that the Warren Commission was more or less chastised for relying too heavily on the advice of J. Edgar.

The chief counsel for the Warren Commission, J. Lee Rankin, later said, "He may not have believed it himself, but Hoover wanted the lone assassin theory to prevail. Perhaps he knew too much, meaning that an extended investigation would expose a lot of people in government. He knew a hell of a lot more than he told the commission, and he also suppressed vital evidence."

Perhaps the most revealing comment J. Edgar ever made on the assassination was said to Billy Byars, Jr., the son of Humble Oil millionaire Billy Byars, Sr., who was a close friend of Clyde and J. Edgar and sometimes dined with them.

It was later revealed that on J. Edgar's phone log on the day of the assassination, he placed only three calls—one to Bobby Kennedy, another to the chief of the Secret Service, and a third to Byars Sr. in Texas.

As revealed to author Anthony Summers, Byars Jr. claimed he once asked J. Edgar, "Do you think Lee Harvey Oswald did it?"

According to the account Byars Jr. gave to Summers, the director said, "If I told you what I really know, it would be very dangerous to this country. Our whole political system would be disrupted."

LBJ's mistress, Madeleine Brown, later claimed that her very angry suitor told her, "It had something to do with American intelligence and oil" before storming out the door.

Until the day he died, J. Edgar was hounded by inquiries and pressure to reopen the investigation of "The Crime of the Century." In all cases he had a pat response: "OSWALD DID IT, ALONE. CASE CLOSED."

In summation, as author Burton Hersh wrote: "Wriggling inside Hoover's hammerlock, the Warren Commission coughed up the monolithic single-shooter version of events that the Director demanded. Anything less could mean the FBI was guilty of dereliction of duty. Privately, Hoover knew better."

The ill-conceived conclusion of the Warren Commission, much of it orchestrated by J. Edgar and his staff, claimed that the assassination of John F. Kennedy was the work of one "quixotic misfit with grandiose pretensions, Lee Harvey Oswald, who acted alone in shooting the President from the sixth floor of the Texas School Book Depository overlooking Dealey Plaza in Dallas."

Although he'd been the chief advocate of such a theory, J. Edgar told

President Nixon *(left)* listens intently to the political opinions of **Gerald Ford** *(right)*. Nixon once told Nelson Rockefeller (Ford's future vice president) that, "I find Jerry a bit klutzy."

When Spiro Agnew was forced to resign as Nixon's vice president, Ford stepped up to fill his shoes. When Nixon was forced to resign from office over the Watergate scandal, Ford was automatically elevated to the Oval Office. On August 9, 1994, he became the only man in American history to have been foisted upon the nation by circumstances—twice—and not by an election.

When in 1976 he at last ran for office as part of an election, he lost to a peanut farmer from Georgia, Jimmy Carter.

Clyde and his trusted aides, that he didn't actually believe that Oswald had acted alone "but that's what we're going to run with."

By May of 1964, J. Edgar in seven months would turn seventy, but Lyndon finally waived the mandatory retirement age and praised him as "an anathema to evil men."

The Senate passed a resolution honoring his fortieth year with the Bureau, citing his unrelenting crusade against the underground world of America.

Life magazine claimed that "The Roman Senate conferred god status on a few emperors while they were still in office. That more or less has happened to J. Edgar Hoover with the passage of Senate Resolution #706. Of course, Hoover has been at least a demi-god for a very long time."

What was J. Edgar doing during this time of glory? Working frantically behind the scenes, he was trying to suppress new evidence about himself as a young man. Once again his arrest record on a morals charge with a young fisherman in New Orleans had surfaced, and he had to eradicate this blight on his record for all time.

***

With Bobby Kennedy at long last out of the Attorney General's office, J. Edgar felt he could relax a bit. When he congratulated Lyndon Johnson over his upset victory in the 1964 elections, in which LBJ had triumphed over ultra-conservative Barry Goldwater, Johnson too seemed relieved to have Bobby off his staff. The President told J. Edgar, "From now on, I want to be surrounded by men loyal enough to kiss my ass in Macy's window and say it smelled like a rose."

When Bobby left his role as Attorney General in September of 1964 to pursue a role as elected Senator from New York, LBJ referred to him as "the little runt." RFK had called Johnson "a venomous Texas rattlesnake." Even so, J. Edgar had learned that Bobby had sent out a feeler to run as Johnson's Vice President in the '64 election, feeling LBJ needed his name recognition to help him win the November election. But LBJ bitterly rejected him. "Tell him to go back to fucking Jackie Kennedy and leave the politics to me."

J. Edgar had told LBJ, who loved gossip, that Jackie, in her loneliness and desperation, had transferred her love for JFK onto his brother, Bobby, and that his wife, Ethel, knew about it.

Both Johnson and J. Edgar lived in fear of exposure. At one point magazines such as *Life* were constantly threatening to expose them, especially the origins of the President's wealth, made through shady dealings in Texas, and J. Edgar's link to oil millionaires and some leading figures within the Mafia.

So far, J. Edgar had been able to put out brush fires about his private life. But every now and then there was a flare-up, such as when there was a robbery at Roy Cohn's "harem-scarem" townhouse on Manhattan's East Sixty-Eighth Street "where J. Edgar was often invited to enjoy the best entertainment money can buy," a reference to a string of muscled, well-endowed male hustlers.

Cohn called J. Edgar and told him that burglars had made off with his collection of sex tapes. The FBI director had never trusted Cohn, and he feared that he might have secretly taped him indulging in sex with young men.

Immediately J. Edgar swung into action, not considering that the crime was technically the province of the New York Police Department. It is not known how his agents tracked down the robbers and confiscated the stolen merchandise. J. Edgar returned the cash and jewelry to Cohn, but told him, "I'm keeping the sex tapes for my viewing pleasure." They were never returned.

Later in a 1980 interview, Cohn described the stolen films as "kinky— even to me."

The Cohn tapes were added to J. Edgar's obscene file, cabinets of which he kept at FBI headquarters, although certain tapes were taken home for private viewing with Clyde. Eastman-Kodak had presented him in 1936 with a 16mm Kodascope projector, and it was still in use for his private screenings.

The banjo-eyed Roy Cohn, as he moved into middle age, was still a fixture in J. Edgar's life. In Manhattan, he was a big spender, living far beyond his means and still hanging out with the A-list, including Barbara Walters, Cardinal Spellman, and even Aristotle Onassis. Cohn was the first to tell J. Edgar that he felt the Greek shipping magnate was going to marry Jackie, even though he was carrying on an affair with Maria Callas.

J. Edgar also learned through Cohn that Onassis was a fellow cross-dresser and kept a young man stashed in an apartment in Paris and another in Athens, where he subjected them to beatings for his sadistic pleasure.

As author Burton Hersh put it, "Barely thirty, Roy Cohn soon laid his spoor across Manhattan, reconfirming his reputation as the Western World's second most sinister mama's boy. He had a gift for outrageous business practices and high-wire finagling in the courts." Presumably, the number one mama's boy was J. Edgar himself.

Behind the scenes, Cohn was known for his manipulation and once bragged to literary agent Jay Garon, "I never step out the door without a trio of judges in my breast pocket."

As late as July of 1964, Cohn had called J. Edgar, "Anything new from that shit Robert Kennedy?"

"Let me put it this way," J. Edgar told him. "Jimmy Hoffa is enemy number one. You are enemy number two."

Like Johnson and J. Edgar, Cohn was relieved to hear that Bobby had moved on to another venue within a few months of his brother's assassination. But he was still plagued by the "Get Cohn Squad," and was under investigation at the Internal Revenue Service. The probe was led by Robert Morgenthau, the U.S. Attorney for the Southern District of New York, who had discovered illegal wiretaps, mail fraud, and the abuse of surveillance. J. Edgar refused Morgenthau's request to turn over his FBI file on Cohn.

Cohn had also entertained J. Edgar on *Defiance*, a steel-hulled, 100-foot yacht. He'd often ordered his skipper to leave the various ports where it had docked at three o'clock in the morning to avoid marina fees. The *Defiance* was often the scene of orgies.

J. Edgar may have sailed with Roy and a bevy of hustlers four or five times, although he complained that the only food Cohn ever kept onboard were cans of Bumble Bee tuna and peanut and jelly sandwiches.

Cohn always received his paid companions lying nude on top of a large fur piece that covered the bedroom in his stateroom.

Nicholas von Hoffman in his book, *Citizen Cohn*, wrote: "The boat saw every kind of service. There were floating bacchanals when, late at night, hull down in the water of a cargo of drunken revelers, Roy sent one of the hands, who had a knack for such talent scouting, to the marina bars to come back with young men and women for sex." Why the women? Cohn was also a voyeur who liked to watch men have sex with women.

When Cohn ran short of money, he turned the yacht into a fiery furnace to collect the insurance money. Regrettably, his first mate was trapped in the flames and burned to death.

Agent William C. Sullivan, who had achieved the post of assistant director of the Domestic Intelligence Division in 1961, left the Bureau with bitter memories in 1971. He was well aware of J. Edgar's "Obscene File."

"He didn't just like porno, he wanted only the vilest kind. He especially liked to see young men—boys, really—getting sodomized by brutes of men. Some of the stuff came from Mexico—women with horses, shit like that, even snuff films. Of course, anything about Marilyn Monroe or Martin Luther King was his favorite pre-nap viewing material."

Cohn's sex tapes remained some of J. Edgar's favorite viewing material, but around Christmas of 1965 a mysterious package arrived at FBI headquarters.

The FBI later discovered that it had been sent by a former aide to Jimmy Hoffa, the boss of the Teamsters Union who had once targeted RFK for blackmail.

Sullivan claimed that J. Edgar's favorite sex tape was of Marilyn Monroe performing fellatio on Bobby Kennedy, or at least a man J. Edgar claimed was the former Attorney General. He showed the tape to Sullivan and several of his most trusted agents. The nude man's face did not appear but Marilyn was clearly visible. Sullivan had seen Bobby in a bathing suit, and the chest in the film definitely looked like that of Bobby's.

Sullivan said that it was a silent three-minute, black-and-white loop. A nude Marilyn appears on her knees giving a blow-job to a man.

J. Edgar said that the loop was secretly taken with a hidden camera that had been planted in Monroe's bedroom in Brentwood.

It was later reported that J. Edgar, in January of 1966, showed the film to Clark Clifford, who had been one of JFK's aides and was serving as an adviser to LBJ.

Clifford said that he later met Jackie Kennedy at a dinner party hosted by Diana Vreeland, the editor of *Vogue*. "Jackie cornered me and asked me if I knew about the sex tape of Bobby and Marilyn. I denied knowing anything about it. She didn't really believe me, but didn't press me either."

***

With permission reluctantly obtained from then Attorney General Bobby Kennedy, J. Edgar and his agents bugged the hotel rooms of Martin Luther King, Jr., wherever he went from Atlanta to Los Angeles, from Honolulu to New York. President Kennedy was already dead when on February 22, 1964, FBI agents rented an adjoining suite next to King's at the Hyatt House in Los Angeles. For two days they monitored King.

The information on these tapes has never been made available under the Freedom of Information Act. However, Sullivan privately told one of the editors at W.W. Norton, the publisher of his memoirs, *The Bureau: My Thirty Years in Hoover's FBI*, that an orgy was staged. From the tapes, according to Sullivan, King was heard having sex with various women. He was also heard mockingly discussing the late President Kennedy's sex life. "I think he got more poontang than me," King is alleged to have said. He also made reference to the widowed Jackie Kennedy. "Now that's one white woman I'd like to plow myself. She probably didn't get much from Kennedy's little weenie."

Sullivan was one of the few who heard the tapes, but there is no way of verifying if what he claimed is accurate.

The FBI's Sullivan was one of the men responsible for creating the myth of J. Edgar. He sent his boss a memo, calling King "the most dangerous Negro of the future in this Nation from the standpoint of Communism, the Negro, and national security." To stop King, Sullivan suggested that the FBI might have "to resort to tactics that some might not consider legal." After the march, and with great hesitation, Bobby had agreed to move ahead with the wiretaps. "Hoover had so much blackmail at the time on the Kennedy brothers, I didn't think Bobby had a lot of choice in the matter," Sullivan said.

King was also recorded at an orgy at the Willard Hotel in Washington. The FBI wiretap revealed a wild party going on in the living room of the suite, followed by sexual encounters with King in the bedroom with what sounded like three different women. The FBI also recorded the sounds of an orgy at the Los Angeles Hyatt House when the civil rights leader returned for another visit.

In 1997, Bernard Lee, one of King's associates, won a victory in court. The FBI transcripts of the illegal King wiretaps will be sealed until 2027.

Almost every story in the newspapers about King infuriated J. Edgar, including the news that he'd been designated as recipient of the St. Francis Peace Medal from the Catholic Church. After King met with the Pope, J. Edgar wrote, "I am amazed that the Pope gave an audience to such a degenerate."

When the director learned that King was going to win the Nobel Peace Prize, J. Edgar wrote, "He could well qualify for the top alley cat prize!"

What doubly infuriated J. Edgar was that for years he had long coveted the Nobel Peace Prize for himself. In spite of letters of endorsement from prominent Americans, year after year J. Edgar failed to get the votes from the Nobel Committee, who did not necessarily view him as a man of peace.

A historic meeting between King and J. Edgar was arranged at FBI headquarters in Washington. King was accompanied by Ralph Abernathy, who recalled that J. Edgar never smiled, was "colder than an igloo, and referred to Martin and me as 'boys.' Martin got nervous in front of Hoover and started biting his nails. He knew all the shit Hoover had on him."

After the meeting, King told his aides, "Old Man Hoover talks too much. He gave me two minutes, then lectured me for fifty minutes on the glories of the FBI and all it was doing for the American Negro."

Before King flew to Oslo to accept the Nobel Peace Prize, J. Edgar ordered the FBI to step up its harassment of King. He was put under even heavier surveillance. At one point, the FBI sent in a false fire alarm to a secret hideaway where King was having sex with two unidentified white women. "He was literally smoked out of his bed," Sullivan later reported to J. Edgar.

J. Edgar had succeeded in pinning the homosexual label on presidential candidate Adlai Stevenson, and he set about to do the same slander to King.

Noting a general attitude of homophobia within the religious black community, J. Edgar hired three agents to gather evidence that King, like many known womanizers, occasionally engaged in homosexual activities.

According to Sullivan, Clyde Tolson emerged with three young men from Atlanta, each signing an affidavit and agreeing to testify in court that King had performed fellatio on them.

The case against King was still pressing forward at the time of King's death. Sullivan never knew if these young mulatto men—no dark-skinned ones—were actually bribed to render testimony, or if Clyde and his agents had actually discovered King indulging in some homosexual acts, which could be used to widely discredit him.

When King died, the file was destroyed, and "those boys just faded into the background never to be heard from again," according to Sullivan.

Under orders from J. Edgar, FBI agents continued to smear King. Nearly all the incriminating data, including photographs supplied to newspapers, were never printed. James Eastland, the Democratic senator from Mississippi, was given a surveillance film loop of King entering his hotel suite with a blonde-haired white woman. Berl Bernhardt, staff director of the Civil Rights Commission, was furnished with rather perfunctory data that King had homosexual dalliances.

J. Edgar sent an FBI tape to President Johnson in which King is heard inviting Ralph Abernathy to have a sexual encounter. Others who listened to the tape claimed it was "mere locker room joshing," such as when a football player will grab his genitals to mock a fellow player who lost the game. "Come over here, girlie man, and get some of this."

Using an infrared camera, the FBI obtained pictures of King lying naked on his bed with his gay assistant, a fully dressed Bayard Rustin. Like Johnson himself, King often pulled off all his clothes and talked to key staff members while completely nude. There is no evidence that these were sexual encounters, just idiosyncratic behavior. When Rustin learned of these pictures, he denied that he and King ever had sexual relations.

Eventually, J. Edgar's case that King was a closeted homosexual petered out. In spite of circumstantial evidence, the director managed to convince no one except Clyde, Roy Cohn, Cardinal Spellman, Richard Nixon, and one of his chief aides, William C. Sullivan.

King's frequent attacks on the FBI intensified into an all-out war. J. Edgar was given a bulletin that King had sent out to his affiliated groups, claiming that "Hoover is old and getting senile. Let's hit him from all sides in order to force President Johnson to censure him publicly."

Under Sullivan's direction, the FBI compiled a composite tape of the surveillance of King, including only the most embarrassing episodes. These recordings, along with an anonymous letter, were mailed to King's head-quarters in Atlanta. The letter stated:

KING,

In view of your low grade . . . I will not dignify your name with either a Mr. or a Reverend or a Dr. And, your last name calls to mind only the type of King such as King Henry the VIII. . . .

King, look into your heart. You know you are a complete fraud and a great liability to all of us Negroes. White people in this country have enough frauds of their own but I am sure they don't have one at this time that is anywhere near your equal. You are no clergyman and you know it. I repeat you are a colossal fraud and an evil, vicious one at that. You could not believe in God. . . . Clearly you don't believe in any personal moral principles.

King, like all frauds your end is approaching. You could have been our greatest leader. You, even at an early age have turned out to be not a leader but a dissolute, abnormal moral imbecile. We will now have to depend on our older leaders like Roy Wilkins a man of character and thank God we have others like him. But you are done. Your "honorary" degrees, your Nobel Prize (what a grim farce) and other awards will not save you. King, I repeat you are done.

No person can overcome facts, not even a fraud like yourself. . . . I re-peat—no person can argue successfully against facts. You are finished. . . . And some of them to pretend to be ministers of the Gospel. Satan could not do more. What incredible evilness. . . . King you are done.

King, there is only one thing left for you to do. You know what it is. You have just 34 days in which to do (this exact number has been selected for a specific reason, it has definite practical significant [sic]. You are done. There is but one way out for you. You better take it before your filthy, abnormal fraudulent self is bared to the nation.

Three days after the tapes were sent, J. Edgar branded King "the most notorious liar in the country."

Some historians have claimed that the intent of Sullivan's letter was to drive King to commit suicide to avoid personal embarrassment.

King did not bow to pressure but in a very depressed state flew with Coretta to Oslo to accept his prize.

Back from Oslo, King increased his opposition to America's war in Vietnam, earning him "the eternal loathing" of Johnson and J. Edgar. King claimed that the U.S. interest was solely to turn Vietnam into an American colony. As far-fetched as this accusation was, millions of his followers believed him. He didn't stop there, claiming that the U.S. was "the greatest purveyor of violence in the world today," citing the outrageous claim that America had murdered one million Vietnamese—"mostly poor, helpless children."

Life magazine called his provocative statements "demagogic slander that sounded like a script for Radio Hanoi."

King's main attack was that the United States was diverting its money and resources that could have been spent on welfare within the country. He charged that all the money being spent on the war was leading "America toward a spiritual death."

"Only an assassin's bullet can stop the tongue of this liar," an infuriated J. Edgar told his aides, including Sullivan. "We must discredit, neutralize, and expose this man. Send agents to Zurich to ferret out secret Swiss bank accounts. I bet he's stashing away millions overseas."

***

Many of the secrets about J. Edgar or Clyde Tolson emerged after their deaths. Perhaps journalists during their life spans were too intimidated by the pair to probe too deeply into the secrets these FBI men kept in the closet.

A startling article appeared in the *New York Post* on February 11, 1993, written by Murray Weiss. He exposed an extortion ring in 1966 that was broken up by the Manhattan district attorney, Frank Hogan, and his "Racket Squads."

Two blackmailers, Edward Murphy and Sherman Kamingsky, operated a racket called "The Chicken and the Bulls." They hired well-built, heavily endowed hustlers to prey on older, prosperous-looking men who they would meet at airports and in hotel lobbies, soliciting them for sex to later blackmail them, often with photographs from cameras installed in shabby hotel rooms to which they took their johns for sex.

Sometimes one of the ringleaders of the group would burst into a hotel room with a photographer and catch a victim in bed having sex with one of the young hustlers.

Many prominent people were entrapped in this scam, including movie star Rock Hudson and William Church, a Navy admiral stationed at Key West, Florida, who committed suicide when outed. A prominent congressman, Peter Frelinghuysen, Jr., a Republican who represented New Jersey in the House of Representatives from 1953 to 1975 was also outed. News of the congressman's arrest first appeared in a book, *Bobby and J. Edgar*, by Burton Hersh.

The raid turned up a candid photograph of J. Edgar posing with Kamingsky. The files of the pair revealed that J. Edgar was one of the outfit's best customers. Apparently young men were sent to Clyde and J. Edgar gratis. Obviously, Murphy and Kamingsky didn't dare make trouble for J. Edgar, and rewarded him with young men of his choosing.

When J. Edgar learned of Hogan's raid, he sent Clyde to New York. All evidence, including that candid photograph of J. Edgar, was removed from the files.

After his imprisonment, Kamingsky mysteriously disappeared, though he was reported to have fled to Colorado, selling wigs and raising rabbits.

Murphy was known as a "chicken hawk," meaning an adult male who has sex with young boys. After serving time in prison, he became somewhat of a gay icon. When J. Edgar died, he admitted that he supplied young men to both J. Edgar and Clyde.

"They wanted mature men, not boys," Murphy claimed. He also supplied much younger hustlers to Roy Cohn, which the lawyer used to entrap rich pedophiles in his suite at the Plaza Hotel. "Mother Murphy," as he was called, said, "I never pretended to be a saint."

Four months after Murphy's death in 1989, he was named Honorary Grand Marshall of the Lesbian and Gay Pride Parade in New York.

In 2006, a journalist wrote, "The story of Edward Murphy is fascinating, the way scandalous secrets are, the way evil fascinates. It is also the story of the pre-Stonewall era. Murphy combined prostitution, blackmail, and strong-arm tactics into a lucrative enterprise that ran for ten years until he was brought down by the Manhattan attorney general and a battery of Irish Catholic New York City detectives. It is a story with all the best ingredients—greed, lust, pride, honor, and most of all, irony."

***

J. Edgar came very close to being outed as a homosexual on the floor of Congress by Cornelius E. (Neil) Gallagher, a Democrat from New Jersey's 13th Congressional District and a major member of the House Government Operations Committee and a key figure on the House Committee on Foreign Affairs. He was almost picked as Lyndon Johnson's running mate in 1964, but the President abandoned that idea after J. Edgar visited the Oval Office and presented FBI files on Gallagher. Subsequent to that meeting, Hubert Humphrey was chosen as Johnson's vice presidential running mate.

Sharp-witted and good-looking in a rugged way, Gallagher was as charming as Frank Sinatra on one of his good hair days. One of the most popular congressmen in Washington, he was also a WWII hero based on his command of a rifle company in Europe. Later he saw action in Korea and was wounded three times, receiving eight decorations.

His troubles began on August 9, 1968 when *Life* magazine exposed his links with the Mafia.

In its ground-breaking series on the Mob and its enterprises, *Life* exposed Gallagher as "a tool and collaborator of a Cosa Nostra gang lord, Joe Zicarelli, a New Jersey *capo*. His fellow *Mafiosi* called him "Joe Bayonne," a reference to his hometown, a New Jersey industrial waterfront city opposite Manhattan's financial district. The magazine claimed that the Zicarelli/Gallagher business enterprises extended from Montréal in Canada to Santo Domingo in the Dominican Republic.

The FBI, under J. Edgar's orders, had put Gallagher under surveillance in 1960. In one bugged and wiretapped conversation, Zicarelli was overheard telling another mob member, "Gallagher is a thing of beauty, like a two-star sapphire pinky ring."

One scheme the mobster and the congressman concocted was to have laetrile imported and hawked as a cure for cancer. The ingredients were extracted from the pits of apricots and peaches. In defending this enterprise, Gallagher said, "Look, if Bonnie and Clyde had a cure for cancer, you'd listen." The U.S. Pure Food and Drug Administration rejected the claim.

After the *Life* exposé, Gallagher's attorney, Larry Weisman, called him, informing him that, "Mr. Hoover is demanding that you resign from Congress and give up your campaign for re-election." Gallagher adamantly refused.

In a devious move by J. Edgar, he had the FBI spread rumors about Gallagher's wife, claiming that a minor mob figure had died in her bedroom while making love to her. As the story went, Gallagher came home, found the body, beat up his wife, and placed the corpse in his basement until two burly Mafia members showed up to remove the body from his house and secretly bury it. "Even Goebbels didn't have the terrible capacity to spread such a lie about a good and decent woman," Gallagher said.

To get revenge on J. Edgar, Gallagher visited the offices of attorney Roy Cohn. The crooked lawyer and the crooked congressman had been allies since Cohn got Gallagher off on a porno charge in his home state of New Jersey. A company Gallagher owned had been distributing obscene pictures of women in a magazine that was a rip-off of Hugh Hefner's *Playboy*.

In Cohn's office, Gallagher presented him the draft of a speech he planned to deliver on the floor of the House of Representatives. At first Cohn thought it was a draft of his resignation speech.

With astonishment, Cohn read:

"Mr. Speaker, it has been called to my attention that the director of the FBI and the deputy director of the FBI, Clyde Tolson, have been living as man and wife for some twenty-eight years at the public expense. As members of Congress, we have an oversight duty and that oversight is to make sure that the funds which go to the FBI are properly spent and don't end up providing armored cars to this couple to take them to the racetrack and pay for their gambling debts, their hotels, their expensive dinners, or their breakfast the next morning after one of their cuddly nights together."

Cohn issued his sternest warning that he should not make that speech to the House.

"I may go down, but I'm taking the old fag with me," Gallagher threatened.

The next day, Cohn in near panic called Gallagher. "I just talked to Mr. Hoover. He is issuing a statement repudiating the transcript of the FBI wiretaps. You are exonerated."

Gallagher didn't deliver that speech alleging J. Edgar's homosexuality. Actually, all the congressmen were well aware of J. Edgar's reputation. Instead, Gallagher delivered another devastating speech.

"Mr. Speaker, the FBI is corruption at its worst, and its central figure is J. Edgar Hoover. It is he whose unchecked reign of absolute power has intimidated this Congress to the extent that a serious question has not been asked about his management of the FBI for ten years—maybe longer. He has become the American Beria, destroying those who threaten his empire, frightening those who should question his authority, and terrorizing those who dissent from his ancient and anachronistic view of the world."

Gallagher didn't completely escape the hook. During the Nixon administration, he was tried and convicted of income tax evasion and perjury and sentenced to serve two years at Allenwood (Pennsylvania) Federal Prison.

As one of his last acts of duty as FBI director, J. Edgar in 1972 reviewed the Gallagher file for a final time. He wrote across it, "He is like an octopus spewing forth its black fluid to hide his true character."

Virtually on his deathbed, Cohn wrote Gallagher, telling him that J. Edgar had wrongly defamed his wife as part of his campaign to blackmail Gallagher into resigning from Congress. By then, of course, J. Edgar was conveniently dead.

***

Toward the end of his life, J. Edgar not only struggled to suppress stories of his homosexuality, but he tried on several occasions to muffle rumors of his black ancestry.

The author Gore Vidal, who grew up in Washington, D.C. in the 1930s, told biographer Anthony Summers: "Hoover was becoming famous, and it was always said of him—in my family and around the city—that he was a mulatto. People said he came from a family that had 'passed.' It was the word they used for people of black origin, who, after generations of inbreeding, have enough white blood to pass themselves off as white. That's what was always said about Hoover."

Hollywood in a major way dealt with this theme of passing in the 1934 film *Imitation of Life*, starring Claudette Colbert and based on the Fannie Hurst soaper.

The first major exposé of J. Edgar's alleged ancestry was published in a book, issued in 2000, called *Secrets Uncovered: J. Edgar Hoover—Passing for White?* by Millie L. McGhee, an influential California educator. In her memoir, she merges a 200-year-old oral family history with modern genealogical data.

As a little girl growing up in McComb, Mississippi, McGhee heard of her family's links to J. Edgar. She traced the lineage to Clarence Allen, called "Big Daddy," by his family. Standing seven feet tall and very light skinned, he was her grandfather on her mother's side. The relation, as she described it, was "J. Edgar Hoover was my Big Daddy's father's brother's child."

Research has shown that J. Edgar's grandfather and great-grandfather lived in a segregated black area of Washington, DC, where the census classified them as "colored." McGhee claimed that her relatives were warned of "dire consequences" if they spoke about their genetic link to J. Edgar.

As rumors grew stronger in the 1960s, J. Edgar dispatched FBI agents to track down the source of this gossip. Blacks interviewed claimed J. Edgar was "a soul brother," others referring to him as "some kind of spook."

In his 1995 book, *FBI Secrets: An Agent's Exposé*, Wesley Swearingen, a former special agent, claimed that privately within the Bureau, agents speculated about J. Edgar's origins, noting "his tight wiry hair and his unusual facial characteristics." They also speculated that maybe there was a little hanky-panky in his family tree, which they talked about as having been painted by a "tarbrush."

A copy of J. Edgar's birth certificate revealed that it was not filed until 1938, when the FBI director was forty-three years old. He never applied for a birth certificate until the death of his mother, Annie Hoover.

Although dismissed by many historians, McGhee's account would not be surprising in view of the evidence compiled by such scholars as sociologist Robert Stuckert of Ohio State University, whose research revealed that about twenty-one percent of whites in America have black ancestry within four generations.

J. Edgar was certainly no champion of either gay rights or black civil rights, and did much to hamper the movement led by Martin Luther King, Jr. The specter of racial intermarriage horrified him, and he didn't want blacks to become FBI agents. Richard Gid Powers in his book, *Secrecy and Power: The Life of J. Edgar Hoover* (1987), claimed that Bureau personnel used the word "Nigger" instead of Negroes in 90 percent of their reports.

If J. Edgar had been exposed to have had black ancestry, he would have been excluded from a high government position, according to the rules of segregation which had been reinstituted throughout the Federal Civil Service during the administration of President Woodrow Wilson.

As McGhee writes in her memoir: "While researching my roots, I was surprised to find that J. Edgar Hoover's name was listed in my family's pedigree chart. After much study and findings of other records in libraries and National Archives, it was clear to me that he was indeed part of us. Big Daddy told me that Hoover was his second cousin, and I believe him."

Gore Vidal once said, "There are two things that were taken for granted in the Washington of my youth—that Hoover was a faggot and that he was black."

***

On March 29, 1968 the Rev. Martin Luther King, Jr. and his colleague, Ralph Abernathy, flew into Memphis to support black sanitation public works employees who were striking for higher wages. They were booked into their familiar suite (#306) at the Lorraine Motel.

On April 3, King appeared at the Mason Temple where he delivered his last speech, uttering the words, "I've Been to the Mountaintop."

David J. Garrow, author of *The FBI and Martin Luther King Jr.*, wrote about how prophetic this speech was. "King's emotional remarks about death, and his fatalistic attitude toward it, combined with the sound of the heavy rain and thunder, created an atmosphere that was exceptionally eerie. Rarely before had any of his assistants heard him speak publicly about such subjects."

The next day at 6:01pm, King walked out on the second-floor balcony of the Lorraine Motel for some fresh air. Suddenly, a bullet penetrated through his right cheek, smashing into his jaw. The little missile traveled down his spinal cord before coming to rest lodged in his shoulder.

Abernathy heard the shot and rushed out of the suite to come to King's aid. An ambulance was summoned, and King underwent emergency surgery but was pronounced dead at St. Joseph's Hospital at 7:05pm. A biographer, Taylor Branch, claimed that an autopsy revealed that although King was only thirty-nine years old "he had the heart of a sixty-year-old man."

Within thirty minutes of King's shooting, J. Edgar heard the news at FBI headquarters in Washington. He summoned Clyde, William Sullivan, and his most trusted aides. "We must hunt down King's killer," he said. "If we don't, black America will burn the inner cities."

In that, J. Edgar was a bit of a prophet. When television and radio spread the news of the assassination, a wave of black riots broke out in dozens of cities, including Washington itself, Chicago, Baltimore, Kansas City, and Louisville, Kentucky. Bobby Kennedy urged supporters to follow King's policy of nonviolence, to no avail.

After the tense meeting in his office, J. Edgar turned to Clyde. "Tomorrow, Big Guy, you and I are going to the races." He'd extended the same invitation to Clyde when JFK was assassinated.

Even though King was dead, J. Edgar could not bring himself to abandon his smear campaign. He ordered two agents in Tennessee to track down the rumor that King and Abernathy had entertained three white women in their suite the night before the assassination.

J. Edgar even spread the word to Jack Anderson, a columnist he detested on most occasions, that King had been involved with the wife of a doctor in Los Angeles and that the enraged husband may have flown to Memphis to kill him in a jealous rage. Anderson later interviewed the woman who did admit to an affair with King. But her husband was firmly anchored in California at the time of the assassination. Anderson did note that she was an "incredibly beautiful woman. At least King had good taste."

Watching the rapidly changing events unfold on his office TV, J. Edgar was aware that conspiracy theories would abound in the aftermath of the assassination of King. Conspiracy theories were still raging over the death of JFK. What J. Edgar may not have suspected was that many African Americans would blame him for King's death.

Abernathy put the blame solidly on the FBI. "Martin was killed by someone trained or hired by the FBI, acting on orders of Hoover himself."J. Edgar fired back at this accusation. "Coretta King and Abernathy are deliberately plotting to keep King's assassination in the news by pulling the ruse of maintaining that King's murder was definitely a conspiracy and not committed by one man. This, of course, is obviously a rank trick to keep the money coming in to them."

The FBI trail led to James Earl Ray, a dirt-poor high school dropout from Illinois, who had served in the Army during WWII in Germany. He had been convicted of several robberies, beginning as early as 1949, and had served time in Leavenworth Federal Penitentiary. After his last robbery in 1959, he had been sentenced to twenty years in the Missouri State Penitentiary. In 1967, a year before King's assassination, Ray had escaped in a truck transporting bread from the prison bakery.

Agents picked up his trail which took him to St. Louis and Chicago before he settled in Toronto, Montréal, and finally Birmingham.

In 1967, he drove from Alabama to Puerto Vallarta in Mexico. Under the alias of Eric Starvo Galt, he became a porn director, using mail order equipment to film young prostitutes of both sexes.

The FBI learned but never revealed, according to William Sullivan, that he soon switched to child porn, using underage Mexican girls and boys, some as young as ten. Apparently, he never exported this child porn into the United States, but dealt exclusively with pedophiles in Switzerland and Germany through mail order.

From Mexico City, agents sent J. Edgar and Clyde copies of these

The alleged assassin of Martin Luther King, Jr., **James Earl Ray** *(above)*, remains a man of mystery. Speculation continues to this day as to who killed the Rev. King in Memphis. Even J. Edgar has been accused of masterminding the plot.

Ray had a long police record of robberies. In Mexico, he filmed and distributed child porn, featuring underage teenage girls and boys. Sometimes he starred in these porn movies himself, taking on numerous partners. After King's assassination, Ray lived for a time in Portugal, where various prostitutes supported him.

Abandoning Lisbon, he landed in London, where he tried to rob a bank, but bungled the job.

porn films. In one, Ray is seen sodomizing a beautiful young Mexican boy who looks no more than thirteen years old. In another, he seduces three teenage Mexican girls in the same bed. There were many close-up shots of Ray's penis, of which he seemed to be proud.

Leaving Mexico on November 16, 1967, Ray drove to Los Angeles where he was a bartender and studied ballet, because he liked the way he looked in tights. In 1968, he aided segregationist George Wallace in his run for the presidency.

As part of a cross-country drive during March of 1968, he arrived in Atlanta, where he avidly followed King's appearances, reading in the *Atlanta Constitution* about his upcoming scheduled arrival in Memphis. From his seedy rooming house, Ray packed his single piece of luggage and drove to Memphis after buying a rifle with accessories.

On June 8, 1968, a little more than two months after King's death, Ray was captured as he tried to leave London's Heathrow Airport to fly to Ian Smith's white supremacist Rhodesia.

J. Edgar deliberately held back news of Ray's arrest in London for two days before releasing it to the press. He waited for the appropriate moment so that he would interfere with another headline—the funeral of his nemesis, the assassinated Bobby Kennedy.

The UK quickly agreed to extradite Ray to Tennessee, where he was charged with King's murder. He confessed to the shooting on March 10, 1969, but recanted this confession three days later, claiming the FBI threatened him with the death penalty if he didn't confess. His recantation was ignored, and his guilty plea earned him a sentence of ninety-nine years in prison. The method of execution at the time in Tennessee would have been electrocution. Ray's lawyers claimed he was a scapegoat similar to the way many conspiracy theorists viewed Lee Harvey Oswald in the assassination of John F. Kennedy.

In June of 1977, Ray escaped prison but was later recaptured and returned to jail. In an interview in 1988, he claimed, "I was framed to cover up an FBI plot to kill King." In 1997, Dexter Scott King, the son of the slain leader, meet with Ray in prison and publicly supported his efforts to obtain a new trial.

William C. Sullivan at the FBI said, "I was convinced that Ray killed King, but I doubt if he acted alone. He was so stupid that I don't think he could have robbed a five-and-ten-cent store. He was also sloppy, leaving the rifle he used to shoot King in an alley and beer cans covered with fingerprints in the trunk of his abandoned car. Someone taught Ray how to get a false Canadian passport, how to get out of the country, and how to travel to Europe."

In 1978, the Congressional Assassinations Committee concluded that there had indeed been a conspiracy in the murder of King, but found no evidence that the FBI was involved.

Conspiracy theories abound to this day and perhaps forever more. In 2000, the Justice Department completed its investigation without finding enough evidence to support allegations about a conspiracy.

The Rev. Jesse Jackson was present in Memphis at the time. He said, "I will never believe that Ray had the motive, the money, and the mobility to have done it himself. Our government is very involved in setting the stage for and I think the escape route for Ray."

King's friend and colleague, James Bevel, also weighed in with the theory that Ray did not act alone. "There is no way a ten-cent white boy could develop a plan to kill a million-dollar black man."

***

J. Edgar and Clyde had long maintained a file on Marlon Brando, but he came under renewed surveillance when he attended the funeral of Martin Luther King, Jr. in Atlanta. Brando made the claim to actor Anthony Franciosa, with whom he shared a room in a hotel, that King had been "eliminated" by J. Edgar because of the minister's opposition to the Vietnam War. He would later repeat some of these same accusations in a 1979 *Playboy* interview.

"J. Edgar Hoover hates black people, hated Martin Luther King," Brando told such guests as Peter Lawford, singer Eartha Kitt, Sammy Davis Jr., and author James Baldwin. "If King had stayed in the civil rights area, he might be alive today. But when he got on the issue of the war in Vietnam, his fate was sealed."

By early 1968, Brando had become more radicalized than ever, and he enjoyed a brief romance with the Black Panthers, an African American revolutionary leftist group active from 1966 to 1982. It had been founded by Bobby Seale and Huey Newton.

From the beginning, J. Edgar Hoover had denounced the Black Panthers as "the greatest threat to the internal security of the country." He was horrified to learn that such celebrities as Brando, Jane Fonda, and Jean Seberg were supporting a cabal that the FBI stated wanted to overthrow the U.S. government.

Through his secret internal organization, COINTELPRO, J. Edgar and Clyde directed a campaign of infiltration of the Black Panthers, using surveillance, police harassment, and in some cases actual assassination. By 1969, party membership peaked at 10,000 members before it began to decay because of legal woes, jail terms, internal conflicts, expulsions, or just defections, as was the case with Brando.

Bobby Seale bonded with Brando even though he was a "white boy from Nebraska." When King died, Seale called Brando and asked him to pay his airfare to Atlanta. According to an FBI report, the actor came through and also paid the fares of Earl Niel, the Panthers' minister of religion, and a third Panther member, a woman with the title of "Captain of the Sisters."

Wherever Seale and Brando went, an FBI agent was on their trail. One night they followed the pair to the home of Eldridge Cleaver, the dogmatic author who was one of the leaders of the Panthers. Cleaver's wife, Kathleen, later recalled, "Brando couldn't take his eyes off my husband, and he and Eldridge talked until dawn."

After King's funeral, Brando also attended the funeral of Bobby Hutton, the seventeen-year-old treasurer of the Panthers, who had been gunned down by the police in Oakland. Two FBI agents were at the funeral where Brando gave a brief eulogy on April 12, 1968.

A campaigner for civil rights, actor **Marlon Brando** *(right figure in photo above)* was photographed at the funeral of Bobby Hutton in 1968. Hutton was the slain seventeen-year-old treasurer of the Black Panthers.

The bisexual Brando was rumored to have had brief flings with certain members of the Panthers, including Bobby. J. Edgar leveled the same charges against actresses Jean Seberg and Jane Fonda.

In time, Brando seemed to lose interest in the advancement of African Americans, and turned his attention to the plight of the American Indians, accusing the government of committing genocide on these Native Americans and robbing them of their lands.

When he later appeared on a television talk show hosted by Joey Bishop, Brando accused the Oakland police of "murdering little Bobby." His statement was greeted with a six-million-dollar libel suit from the Oakland police. Brando's attorneys had to fight the case all the way to the Supreme Court before the actor was absolved of any damages.

It was during this time that the bisexual Brando had a brief affair with the black author James Baldwin, who also had an FBI file. Shelley Winters, another one of Brando's lovers, referred to the Brando/Baldwin mating as "The Beauty and the Beast." Baldwin was known for his writing, not his looks.

In Paris, Baldwin told the author of this book, "After King's death, Brando fantasized that he should take up the sword of Martin Luther King. He saw himself, a white man, leading black America to a second emancipation."

Brando even told *Newsweek* that he was giving up his film career to devote his full attention to the cause of "advancing civil rights for the American Negro. I might dye my skin black and live like an African American to better understand the plight of these downtrodden people," Brando claimed, although quickly forgetting that offer.

Every statement he made, regardless of how outrageous, was recorded in his personal FBI dossier, much of which had been destroyed by the time J. Edgar died.

Actress Jean Seberg, who would later become an FBI target of surveillance, remembered attending a gathering of Black Panther supporters at a private home in Los Angeles. The FBI had two undercover agents at the party. Seberg arrived with Abby Mann, the screenwriter and producer. They listened to Brando give a long, mumbling, and rambling speech, pleading for funds for the Poor People's Campaign to feed impoverished African Americans.

Seberg whispered in Mann's ear, "What is this? A take-a-nigger-to-lunch gathering? Brando's the biggest shit I've ever heard."

In the spring of 1968, Brando, as well as Seberg and Jane Fonda, were accused of sleeping with members of the Black Panthers. Brando, a self-admitted bisexual, had a months-long affair with Ellsworth Jackson, a mulatto piano player he met in San Francisco. He supported Jackson for several months before the entertainer disappeared somewhere in France.

Brando, according to FBI reports, also had affairs with other "Hollywood Bad Boys," such as Montgomery Clift and James Dean.

J. Edgar and Clyde became voyeuristically intrigued by Brando's sex life, finding that he'd seduced both Vivien Leigh and Laurence Olivier when he'd briefly lived with them during the making of Tennessee Williams' *A Streetcar Named Desire*. He'd also seduced such gay authors as Williams himself and Truman Capote, who was always mocking J. Edgar's gayness at his A-list *soirées*. Some of Brando's other A-list conquests, the FBI learned, included Cary Grant and Doris Duke, the tobacco heiress.

On a tantalizing note, one FBI report claimed that Brando referred to his penis as "my noble tool," claiming that it had performed its duties "through thick and thin and without fail."

It was also learned that Brando had had a long-running affair with Marilyn Monroe, beginning in 1946 when he picked her up in a 10th Avenue hooker bar in Manhattan, back when she was known as Norma Jean Baker.

One of J. Edgar's favorite pictures for his obscene scrapbook was taken of Brando in 1952 when he was photographed performing fellatio on his roommate, TV actor Wally Cox.

By May of 1968, Brando, who had a short attention span, had become disenchanted with the Black Panthers, as he told Bobby Seale. He was driven away by the extremists, many of whom advocated "driving the white man out of America," leaving it for the Indians and the blacks. He particularly objected to some who said that if the Black Panthers asked a member, he or she should kill both their father and mother. "That's too Gestapo for me," Brando told Shelley Winters. "I'm out of here."

After breaking with the Panthers, Brando never publicly criticized them. When he split with Seale, he refused to take any more of his phone calls. In 1978, in an interview with *Playboy*, he said, "Bobby is a vicious, pernicious symbol of something that is destructive in our society. To other people, he's a poet, an aristocratic spirit."

J. Edgar scribbled across Brando's file, "He's the ultimate *Ugly American*," a reference to Brando's 1963 film, in which he played an American ambassador to an Asian country whose arrival stirs up pro-communist elements.

***

From the White House, an urgent call came in to J. Edgar from President Lyndon Johnson, who had been awakened from his sleep by a member of the Secret Service.

A sleepy Clyde answered the phone to hear, "It's Lyndon. Roll over and tell lover boy I want to speak to him . . . and now."

Awakened by the call, J. Edgar picked up the phone.

"Kennedy's been shot in Los Angeles. There's no hope for the fucker. I'll send Air Force One to retrieve the body when he does croak. Get onto this case! I'm not going to be blamed for his murder like I was that day in Dallas."

When Johnson had announced that he would not be a candidate for President in the 1968 elections, he had picked his Vice President, Hubert Humphrey, as his choice for the Democratic nomination. It seemed inevitable that Richard Nixon would win the nomination on the Republican ticket.

Senator Eugene McCarthy entered the fray but was later challenged by Robert Kennedy, who held a "carpetbagger" Senate seat from New York, not his native Massachusetts.

If given a choice, J. Edgar would be forced to go with his old enemy,

490

Bobby, because McCarthy had publicly claimed that if elected president his first official duty would be to fire J. Edgar.

Bobby refused to take such a position, knowing the blackmail J. Edgar had on him, including explicit details of his affair with his brother's widow, Jackie, which was a sure-fire way to turn off voters.

Since January of 1966, RFK had taken an adamant stand against the war in Vietnam, although it still had wide support among Americans at that time. "If we regard bombing as the answer in Vietnam, we are headed straight for disaster."

After losing a primary in Oregon to McCarthy, (RFK's 38.8% vs. McCarthy's 44.47%), Bobby swept to victory on the night of the California primary, 46% vs. 42% against McCarthy. At the Ambassador Hotel in Los Angeles, Bobby emerged downstairs, entering to face a wildly enthusiastic crowd assembled in the Empire Ballroom.

Rising early from bed, J. Edgar and Clyde even skipped breakfast at the Mayflower Hotel, a ritual with them, to read reports coming across the wire from the FBI in Los Angeles. A portrait was emerging of what happened.

He told Clyde and his aides, "The Messiah of the Generation Gap is dead. Americans are such fools they probably would have elected him the 37th President of the United States—and then where would we be at the FBI?"

A few months earlier, Clyde had told FBI agents, "I hope somebody shoots and kills the son of a bitch."

At 12:15am on June 5, 1968 in Los Angeles, RFK had left the podium after thanking his supporters, including singer Rosemary Clooney, who had gathered at the Ambassador Hotel. Originally, he was to have taken a different route, but the *maître d'*, Karl Uecker, took his hand and guided him toward the back of the hotel and the kitchen for a rear exit.

His last handshake was with a Mexican busboy, Juan Romero.

Suddenly, Sirhan Bishara Sirhan emerged from behind an ice machine, rushing past Uecker and firing into RFK with a .22 caliber Iver-Johnson Cadet revolver.

As Sirhan fired the shots, he shouted, "Kennedy, you son of a bitch!" as witness Richard G. Lubic later reported.

RFK had been shot three times, one bullet, fired at a range of about an inch, entering behind his right ear and scattering brain fragments. Two other bullets entered at the rear of his right armpit, one exiting from his chest and the other coming to rest in the back of his neck. A fourth bullet passed through his jacket.

In addition to RFK, five bystanders were wounded.

Romero cradled the senator's head and placed a rosary in his hand.

RFK asked Romero, "Is everybody safe, OK?"

"Yes, yes," Romero said, "everything is going to be OK." Captured by *Life* photographer, Bill Eppridge, this moment became the iconic image of RFK's assassination.

A group of men forced Sirhan against a steam table and disarmed him. But at one point he wrestled free and grabbed the revolver again, only to be subdued again.

George Plimpton, one of the men who helped subdue Sirhan, later claimed, "He was Satan himself. I'll never forget those cold, utterly expressionless eyes of this terrorist."

As Sirhan was being hauled off by the police, one witness reported that his last words before forced out of the kitchen were, "Will I be on television?"

Journalist Pete Hamill, a future boyfriend of Jackie Onassis, was one of the men who helped subdue Sirhan.

Of the seventy-seven people in the pantry that night, eighteen of them were later singled out as key witnesses.

FBI agents were quick to deliver information about the identity of the assassin. A Palestinian refugee with a passport from Jordan, Sirhan was a Christian Arab born in Jerusalem and harboring violent anti-Zionist beliefs. A diary found at his home contained the words, "RFK must die! RFK must be killed!" He violently opposed the senator's support of Israel.

Sirhan was a stable boy at the Santa Anita racetrack in Arcadia, California. On two different occasions, he had encountered J. Edgar and Clyde at the races.

Doctors at the Good Samaritan Hospital in Los Angeles worked frantically to save Bobby's life, although they must have known from the beginning how hopeless that was.

When doctors advised the family that he could not survive, Ethel refused to "pull the plug." She ran screaming down the hospital corridor, "I can't kill Bobby!"

It took the strong will of the widowed Jackie Kennedy, survivor of an even bigger assassination, to put an end to RFK's life.

Only weeks before, he'd told her broken heart that he had to end their love affair now that he was seeking the presidency. All of this information was funneled into the office of J. Edgar. He even had a "plant" within the Kennedy family circle, though perhaps not a blood relative.

Bobby died at 1:44am PDT on June 6. For twenty-six hours after the shooting, his heart had continued to beat.

In the immediate aftermath of the assassination, both Johnson and J. Edgar concluded they might be next on someone's hit list. J. Edgar immediately ordered another layer of armoring for his FBI limousine.

Once again, as in the assassinations of JFK and King, J. Edgar invited Clyde to the races at Pimlico, near Baltimore, the following day. "I just can't stand the idea of missing the opening race," J. Edgar said. Before going to the tracks, he wired the widowed Ethel Kennedy. "If my associates or I can be of help in this trying time, please let us know. Bobby's passing leaves a deep void in the hearts of the entire nation, and we pray that God's comforting hand will sustain you in your bereavement."

It wasn't until after J. Edgar's death that the final report was released on RFK's death. Initially the FBI claimed that thirteen bullets were fired, yet Sirhan's gun could fire only a round of eight.

Many Kennedy historians today conclude that two gunmen were involved, although J. Edgar, for reasons of his own, insisted to his final day that Sirhan was the sole assassin.

On one report, J. Edgar wrote, "Another nutbag psycho taking out another Kennedy—that's all there is to it. No conspiracy."

There was only one time J. Edgar wavered from his theory that Sirhan was the sole assassin. As revealed by William C. Sullivan, "For one afternoon, he came to suspect Aristotle Onassis. Hoover was among the first to know that Onassis wanted to marry Jackie—not for love, but for the prestige. Since she was in love with Bobby Kennedy, he stood in Onassis' way, and he was a man who usually got what he wanted. For the first time, Onassis had come up with a younger man as tough and iron-fisted as he was. But now both of Jackie's men, Jack and Bobby, were dead meat."

At the time of RFK's assassination, the shipping tycoon was beguiling the former First Lady with expensive gifts, including a diamond-and-ruby necklace originally intended for opera diva Maria Callas, his other girlfriend.

Ever since WWII, J. Edgar had disliked Onassis with great intensity calling

In April of 1968, the accused assassin of Robert F. Kennedy, **Sirhan Sirhan**, is seen being escorted out of the courtroom by two police officials, following his conviction for the brutal murder.

To many investigative reporters, including Shane O'Sullivan, author of *Who Killed Bobby?*, the killing of the presidential candidate is still "an unsolved murder." The mystery also remains about who was that girl in the polka-dot dress?

She was with Sirhan in the kitchen pantry of the Ambassador Hotel in Los Angeles. Right after the shooting, she was seen fleeing down a fire escape screaming, "We shot him! We shot him!"

him both a criminal and a spy. As the biographer of Onassis, Peter Evans, wrote: "Hoover, was a great believer in the no-smoke-without-a-fire theory, and he was always convinced that the Greek was getting away with something."

Although Sirhan testified that he "killed Kennedy with twenty years of malice aforethought," in 2011 he made the preposterous statement that, "I have no memory of the shooting."

Convicted on April 17, 1969, he was sentenced to death. But in 1972, the sentence was commuted to life in prison.

Writing in his journal, John Bartlow Martin claimed that RFK evoked the spirit of Manolete, Spain's greatest matador. "His fans kept demanding more and more of Manolete in the bullring. He kept giving it until there was nothing left to give but his life—and so he gave them that. So did Bobby."

When J. Edgar read that, he scrawled, "sentimental claptrap!"

On a bizarre note, the only autopsy pictures J. Edgar ever locked up in his personal filing system, away from the main FBI network, were the gruesome color photos of Robert Kennedy's nude body being dissected. In the months ahead, he would on occasion remove these photos and study them carefully.

One of Sirhan's lawyers, Lawrence Teeter, in an attempt to win a new trial, claimed as late as 2003 that Sirhan had been "hypnotized and framed," a sort of Manchurian Candidate as depicted in two movies, the first with Frank Sinatra.

A government conspiracy was suggested. Privately but not in court, Teeter, who died in 2005, told his associates, "I can name who murdered Bobby Kennedy. It was none other than J. Edgar Hoover, who hated him. He knew that if he didn't eliminate him, Kennedy would become President of the United States and fire him."

Teeter also made the claim that Sirhan's revolver contained blanks and that he meant "only to frighten Kennedy."

William C. Sullivan, after he split from J. Edgar and left the FBI in 1971, added a bizarre footnote. "It had nothing to do with solving who murdered Bobby Kennedy, but Hoover some way, somehow—he moved in mysterious ways—obtained a secret film loop depicting Sirhan masturbating in his lone cell while looking at a campaign publicity photo of Bobby he'd removed from the prison library."

***

Henry Fonda, a rather conservative actor, was always deeply disturbed about his daughter, Jane Fonda, and her involvement with revolutionaries,

494

including the Black Panthers, to which she contributed money. He once received a threat in the mail—ARRANGE DELIVERY AT THE APPOINTED TIME OF $50,000 IN SMALL BILLS—OR YOUR DAUGHTER WILL BE KILLED.

Other death threats poured into Jane's world daily, but some supporters in the press called her "the next Susan B. Anthony."

Jane's political activities made her more and more distant from her father. When asked about her by a reporter, the veteran actor said, "Daughter? What daughter? I don't have a daughter."

Fonda turned the threatening letters over to FBI, and they were personally read by J. Edgar. At that time, he had targeted Jane with his Counter Intelligence Program.

He'd also launched a smear campaign against her, sending a fake letter to *Daily Variety* that Jane was heard at a fund-raiser, shouting, "We will kill Nixon and other mother-fuckers who get in our way."

J. Edgar's nemesis, columnist Jack Anderson, said, "Because of Jane's political activism, she headed the Enemies List of both Nixon and Hoover. Both men considered the actress very dangerous, even more frightening than a terrorist."

During the early 1970s, J. Edgar ordered that Jane be put under almost constant surveillance, perhaps spending some $1.8 million of government money trailing her. She was followed at a large Labor Day rally in Pennsylvania where she supported a band of ragtag veterans; she was trailed to the banks of the Delaware River, where she gave a speech attacking the Vietnam War. Jane claimed that the Nixon administration was "a beehive of cold-blooded killers."

Jane's biographer, Patricia Bosworth, in *The Private Life of A Public Woman*, wrote: "Jane Fonda's files at the FBI reveal the Bureau's obsessive, illegal, and ultimately fruitless surveillance of Jane as she opposed the Vietnam War. It went on for years. The files

During her tour of North Vietnam in July of 1972, **Jane Fonda** earned, indelibly, the name "Hanoi Jane," a moniker that will probably haunt her forever.

She is seen here singing to North Vietnamese soldiers while seated on an anti-aircraft gun designed to shoot down American pilots. She's wearing a Vietnamese pantaloon and blouse, and a Vietnamese soldier's helmet.

Years later, during her more mature years, she referred to the incident as a betrayal of U.S. soldiers.

495

chart the intensive interest in the actress on the part of Nixon and the dirty tricks that were employed against her, including pressuring the Justice Department to charge her with treason. FBI agents opened her mail, tapped her phone, combed through her past, and even planted a false story in the press she wanted to kill the president."

In 1970, on a six-week anti-war tour through some sixty colleges, signs went up—COME HEAR BARBARELLA SPEAK! Unknown to Jane, a bodyguard assigned to her was a secret FBI agent.

At the Cleveland International Airport, she was arrested. The next morning headlines read: JANE FONDA CAUGHT SMUGGLING DRUGS. JANE FONDA ARRESTED FOR ASSAULTING A POLICE OFFICER. After spending a night locked in a cell with a woman who had dismembered her lover, Jane was freed on bail and the drug charge eventually dropped. It was discovered that she was actually carrying prescription medicine, not drugs, in her handbag.

J. Edgar also wanted spicy details of her first marriage to Roger Vadim, the French director who had helmed her in *Barbarella* in 1968. Vadim was also known as "the man who discovered Brigitte Bardot."

The FBI learned from informants that Jane may have engaged in lesbian activities during her marriage to Vadim, who insisted on bringing other women home to their bed.

Vadim later said, "Jane seemed to understand and, as always, went all out—all the way." This was duly noted by J. Edgar.

Unlike most gorgeous movie stars, Jane did not seem to have that many involvements with other A-list stars, with such exceptions as Warren Beatty or else Donald Sutherland, her co-star in the 1971 *Klute*.

Near the end of her marriage to Vadim, the FBI learned he'd told Rock Hudson, "Married to Jane is like babysitting for Lenin."

The FBI also learned of her involvement with the long-haired activist Tom Hayden, one of the "Chicago Seven," whom she eventually married. Friends said she was captivated by "Hayden's brilliance and his knowledge of Vietnamese culture." As Jane bragged to her friends, "And the sex was terrific too."

Jane followed her own beliefs, even after a stern warning from her father. He'd told her that if he ever discovered her to be a communist, he would "turn you in to Hoover himself."

She often used her elegant New York apartment for meetings of the Black Panthers. For a while she was rumored to be having an affair with the handsome, charismatic Huey Newton, one of the co-founders of the Panthers. She called him "as beautiful as Harry Belafonte."

The FBI file on the actress was marked—JANE FONDA, ANAR-

CHIST.

It was later learned that Jane was also spied upon by the Secret Service, the State Department, and the CIA. Nixon had ordered a "punitive" IRS audit of her financial records.

J. Edgar and Clyde learned of Jane's alleged sexual involvements, not only with members of the Black Panthers but of U.S. Army men she met while performing with the F.T.A. troupe.

This traveling group, whose full name was "Fuck the Army," was founded on February 16, 1971, and was closely monitored by the FBI. Jane saw the entertainers as providing an alternative for right wing Bob Hope's USO tours. "We will amuse soldiers with acts they really want to see," she said. "We will carry a message of civil disobedience."

Of course, the Army would not allow them to perform on military bases, but they found nearby coffeehouses, even high school gyms, in which to entertain the soldiers with their anti-war skits. Most of their acts were secretly recorded by undercover FBI agents sent by J. Edgar.

In 1972, Jane made the most controversial trip of her life, flying to North Vietnam in the midst of its war with the United States. The FBI had informants in Hanoi during her controversial visit and tracked her every move, even recording her propaganda broadcasts. After that trip, which caused outrage among millions of Americans, she was forever labeled "Hanoi Jane."

The image of her perched on an anti-aircraft gun, poised to shoot down American pilots, became the most iconic image of her life. In later years, she claimed that "my two-minute lapse of sanity has haunted me for the rest of my life."

When this picture was later spread across the frontpages of American newspapers, a massive cry went up, charging her with treason. J. Edgar at FBI headquarters was bombarded with letters that he should personally arrest her upon her return to the United States.

"Pinko slut" was one of the kinder descriptions of Jane that arrived at FBI headquarters.

When Jane's plane touched down at Kennedy Airport in New York on July 27, 1972, she wore black Vietnamese silk pajamas and a coolie hat. Her arrival was secretly photographed by an undercover FBI agent.

Jane, of course, outlived her two major enemies, with J. Edgar dying in 1972 and Nixon's political career beginning to unravel that same year over the Watergate scandal. She told a reporter, "The people who wanted to put me in jail are going to jail themselves."

***

George Wallace, running on an anti-integration platform in 1968, actually called J. Edgar and asked him to appear on the ticket as his vice presidential running mate. Knowing Wallace didn't have a chance to occupy the White House, J. Edgar politely turned him down.

When Nixon triumphed over Hubert Humphrey in that '68 presidential election, J. Edgar was already seventy-three years old, three years past the mandatory retirement age of seventy. But he felt no immediate threat from Nixon. That would come later.

In appointing John Mitchell as Attorney General, Nixon warned J. Edgar a second time not to investigate his background. Privately, J. Edgar told his aides, "Mitchell is the biggest liar ever to set foot in Washington. He even fabricated a story that he served on that god damn PT-boat crew commanded by that whore-mongering fart, John F. Kennedy."

It was perjury that got Mitchell sentenced to prison over the Watergate break-in in 1977, but by then J. Edgar was in the cold, cold ground.

In his continuing disputes with J. Edgar, William C. Sullivan finally walked out of the Bureau in October of 1971, telling colleagues that he found "Hoover a disgusting man, not sane, a child-molesting pervert, and a corrupt official who should have been forced out of office long ago."

At one point, Sullivan, right before his death, was dictating his memoirs, but as some observers at the FBI noted after reading the book, "He left out a lot of the real juicy stuff that would have damaged Hoover's reputation forever."

Retiring Attorney General Ramsey Clark received a private memo from FBI agents in Los Angeles, citing J. Edgar's increasing "senility and megalomania." No longer was the press afraid of him. Editorials across the country demanded to know if Nixon planned to appoint a new FBI director.

Once, J. Edgar had been a revered hero to Americans, but public opinion was going against him, against the Vietnam War, and against his opposition to civil rights movements, which he continued to label as "communist inspired."

But as Nixon swept into office, he told Clyde, "Dick will save us." During Nixon's time in exile after losing to JFK, J. Edgar and Clyde had been a frequent visitor at the home of Richard and Patricia Nixon. "He's my buddy and always will be," J. Edgar told his aides. "Of course, everybody in public life makes a mistake here and there."

Before Johnson left office, J. Edgar received an urgent call from him. "I want extra protection from the FBI, not just the Secret Service. I've looked after you. Now you've got to look after me. I'm the most hated man in America because of the Vietnam War, and I need your help."

J. Edgar assured his old friend that "protection from crackpots out to shoot you will be provided—rest assured of that."

Actually J. Edgar had little concern for his longtime friend now that he was losing his power. All his attention was focusing on the newly elected president from California, Richard Milhous Nixon.

***

J. Edgar went so far as to plant an underground FBI agent on October 20, 1968 among the observers at Jackie Kennedy's marriage to Aristotle Onassis on his private Greek island of Skorpios.

When J. Edgar read that Onassis gave his age as sixty-two, he ordered Clyde to look into his file. Passport documents at the Department of State revealed that Onassis was actually born in 1900.

J. Edgar planted an FBI spy at the October, 1968 wedding of **Jacqueline Kennedy** to shipping magnate **Aristotle Onassis**.

Rose Kennedy said, "Jackie is one of the world's most expensive women to maintain, and Onassis has one of the world's greatest fortunes."

In Rome, *L'Espresso* Magazine noted that the 39-year-old former First Lady of The United States was marrying "this grizzled satrap, with his liver-colored skin, thick hair, fleshy nose, and wide horsey grin, who buys an island, then has it removed from all the maps to prevent the landing of castaways."

J. Edgar pounced on that report with a certain glee, claiming, "That proves my point. Onassis is a liar and a total fraud. He even lies about his age, like that old Nazi spy, Marlene Dietrich."

By 1968, Jack and Bobby Kennedy had been assassinated, but there remained one Kennedy brother that J. Edgar considered a possible threat— their younger brother Teddy.

Nixon had telephoned J. Edgar, telling him that a "spy" within the Kennedy camp had informed him that Teddy was positioning himself to challenge Nixon during his bid for re-election in 1972. "He must be stopped, and there's plenty of shit you can get on this little whoremonger."

"I'm already on the job," J. Edgar assured Nixon. "We here at the FBI have been keeping a file on him since 1961 when Jack Kennedy became president, defeating you—the man who should have won the office, and actually did, had it not been for voter fraud."

In addition to details about a string of sexual affairs with women, a great deal of Teddy's FBI files—in fact, hundreds of pages, deal with death threats against him. Most of them were in the vein of . . . "two down and one to go!"

One of the most intriguing threats against Teddy came from Sirhan Sirhan, in prison for fatally shooting RFK in 1968. He was said to have offered a guarantee of one million dollars to a fellow prisoner about to be released if he would assassinate the third Kennedy brother. The prisoner declined and reported Sirhan's offer to the warden. The question remains, how did Sirhan, a former stable boy, have access to one million dollars—that is, if the offer were serious?

Throughout most of the 1960s, J. Edgar and Clyde had sustained a "Deep Throat" as a plant within Teddy's camp. That was a reference to the label Carl Bernstein and Bob Woodward had given the "mole" inside the Nixon White House during the Watergate scandal. The FBI's mole supplied the Bureau with details on Teddy's secrets that never saw newsprint during his lifetime.

At this jaded point in his life, when he knew so much about so many prominent Americans, J. Edgar was hardly surprised at any revelation. But Helen Gandy, his secretary, told friends that, "Mr. Hoover was shocked to learn that Teddy Kennedy was having an affair with Jackie even after her marriage to Onassis. The younger brother seemed to be following in the footsteps of his older brother, the Attorney General."

A member of "Kennedy's Irish Mafia," JFK legal aid David Powers, saw the affair unfold. J. Edgar learned that Powers had told his cronies, "Let's face it. Teddy has had the hots for Jackie ever since he laid eyes on her when he was just a kid. If Jackie went for two of the brothers, why not a third?"

When J. Edgar, Clyde, and their aides read these FBI reports from inside Teddy's camp, the FBI director proclaimed, "I find this some of the most titillating exposés I've ever read. Teddy goes in for sloppy seconds. He was the last brother to fuck Marilyn Monroe after Bobby and Jack were done with her, and the last to fuck Jackie after John Kennedy was assassinated and that awful Bobby Kennedy dumped her when he announced he was going to run for President."

Journalist Leon Wagener was the first to break the story. He quoted a source close to Teddy who claimed, "When Ted finally made love to Jackie, he fulfilled the dream he'd had to possess his brother's beautiful wife. Obviously he knew it was a grievous sin and an insult to his late brother, but he couldn't control himself."

Wagener quoted another family insider who asserted, "Ted in his diaries wrote about his romance with Jackie in great detail and didn't want his family, especially his wife, Vicki, and his son, Congressman Patrick J.

Kennedy, to read it now when it could cause great hurt."

Before he died, Teddy confessed his "sin" to a priest and asked for forgiveness.

Powers revealed to Kennedy insiders, who included Ted Sorensen, that "the Kennedy family has long known that Teddy was more than a brother-in-law to Jackie. But it's a subject that dare not speak its name. No one wants to talk about it. The revelations about Bobby and Jackie were already too much for this overburdened family. The thing between Jackie and Teddy was just too much to handle."

One night in Boston, Teddy told Powers, "I've always been in love with Jackie, right from the beginning, although I was barely 21 when I met her. She's always been special to me. When Jack died, I knew she was seeing Bobby, too, but that didn't stop me. Bobby couldn't always be with her."

"She was trapped in a miserable marriage with Onassis," Teddy said. "After Bobby died, she turned more and more to me as her confidant. We once took a romantic trip to Greece together. It was the happiest moment of my life."

Jackie's friendship with Teddy began when he was still an undergraduate at Harvard, and she agreed to help him with his term paper on art history, a subject he didn't know much about and she did.

Neither Teddy nor Bobby wanted Jackie to marry Onassis. But when Teddy saw that she was determined to go through with it, he agreed to fly with her to Greece and handle financial matters with her new groom. He didn't welcome the task "but for you, Jackie, I'll do it. Someone has to see that your interests are protected."

Of the many powerful men she knew, Jackie wanted Teddy to negotiate the details of a pre-nuptial agreement with Onassis. During the most intense of the negotiations, Jackie flew to Athens on a shopping expedition, leaving her husband-to-be with her brother-in-law and lover.

Onassis was known as a hard bargainer, but Teddy found him willing

Coveting his brother's former wife, **Teddy Kennedy** shares an intimate moment with **Jacqueline Onassis**. According to author Gore Vidal, when Teddy and Jackie came together, they made "the Devil's pact."

According to insiders, the pact involved the promotion of the legend of Camelot, with the goal of transforming Teddy into the living symbol of a Kennedy-style liberalism. While this was going on, they fell in love.

As Jackie told author Truman Capote, "I'm in love with two men at the same time, both Bobby and Teddy. What to do?"

to relent to his demands. The senator revealed that Jackie's income from the Kennedy Trust was only $175,000 a year, which shocked Onassis. "So little money for such a rich family," he told Teddy, who quickly explained that Bobby had been supplementing that with a check for $50,000 a year. Teddy also pointed out that by marrying again, Jackie would lose her $10,000 annual widow's pension from the government as well as the protection of the Secret Service.

Onassis assured him that he would replace the pension and also ensure that she was protected. He invited Teddy to inspect his kennel of well-trained German shepherd police dogs which would patrol Skorpios.

When Jackie returned from Athens, Teddy reported that the negotiations had gone splendidly, and that Onassis had agreed to everything—and more. To celebrate, Onassis invited both of them for a party aboard the *Christina*. Knowing Teddy's fondness for beautiful young women, he arranged for eight of them to be flown in from Athens.

Partly as a means of concealing his affair with Jackie, Teddy deliberately made a play for one of the blonde bimbos. For whatever reason, Onassis had invited Nico Mastorakis, a professional journalist and photographer, aboard as well.

When Mastorakis snapped a photo of Teddy, soaked in ouzo and holding a blonde in his arms, the senator became furious. He grabbed the camera from Mastorakis and tossed it overboard. "If you report any of this," Teddy shouted at him, "I'll have your ass."

The next day, Jackie and Teddy told Onassis they had to discuss private Kennedy business, and he turned over the *Christina* and its crew to them to sail to an uninhabited nearby island. He assigned two of his security guards to accompany them. Suspicious of their motivations, Onassis ordered one of his guards to discreetly spy on Jackie and Teddy.

Once they arrived at the island, Teddy asked one of the guards to direct them to its most secluded cove. The guard found a beauty spot for them with warm water and white sands. Teddy instructed the guard to stand at a lookout point and signal if anyone was coming, and he also asked the guard to turn his eyes away to allow them some privacy.

Of course, the guard didn't do as instructed and spied relentlessly on his two charges. He later reported to Onassis that he'd seen them nude and lying together on a blanket, kissing each other passionately. And whereas the Greek tycoon had long ago learned about Jackie's affair with Bobby, it was the first time that Onassis learned that Teddy was also sexually involved with his sister-in-law.

Although Onassis decided not to confront Jackie with this indiscretion, he vowed to get "revenge" on Teddy. He did not specify what that revenge would be.

Somehow, Teddy learned that Onassis had uncovered details of his affair with Jackie. "Onassis is powerful and he's ruthless," Teddy told Powers. "He could easily put out a contract on me. He's killed others, maybe Bobby himself."

The Massachusetts senator had long been suspicious that Onassis had been behind the assassination of his beloved brother, Bobby. Reportedly, his diaries revealed that Teddy lived in "constant terror" that Onassis might have him murdered. "I'd wake up in a cold sweat, fearing a killer was in the house."

***

On July 1969, as astronauts were setting foot on the surface of the moon, a car on the island of Chappaquiddick, off Martha's Vineyard, going twenty miles an hour, was headed for Dike Bridge, a wood-timbered span angled obliquely to the road. It was unlit, with no guardrail.

The driver of the vehicle was an inebriated Teddy Kennedy. In the passenger seat sat a pert blonde beauty, Mary Jo Kopechne, one of the so-called "Boiler Room Girls," who worked in the secretarial pool for the Kennedy brothers. Ostensibly, Teddy had volunteered to drive Mary Jo to the departure point of the ferry headed back to Edgartown on Martha's Vineyard, but it seemed he had other plans for her that evening.

The car veered off the bridge and crashed into a pond. Teddy managed to free himself through the driver's door and swam to safety. But Mary Jo, trapped in the car, was left to drown.

As it turned out, Teddy would not report the accident to the police until the following morning. Newsmen around the country learned of the accident and flocked to Martha's Vineyard.

One of the greatest of all the scandals associated with the Kennedy brothers was about to unfold. At FBI headquarters in Washington, J. Edgar and Clyde already knew the details before they became frontpage news around the world.

One of the many amazing stories that never surfaced for public consumption that night was that an FBI agent telephoned J. Edgar at his home in Washington.

Around 1:45am, he was informed that Teddy's car had sunk into the pond and that the senator had escaped with his life but "a female passenger had drowned." Obviously J. Edgar was having Teddy trailed that night, and perhaps on many other nights, hoping to accumulate blackmail evidence on him in the way he had on his brothers. That was, in case Teddy ever became president. Above all else, J. Edgar wanted to have enough ev-

idence on Teddy to blackmail him into not firing him should he ever be in a position to do so.

It was never explained why this mysterious FBI agent didn't attempt to rescue Mary Jo after Teddy fled from the scene. He'd been spying on Teddy and had obviously seen him leaving the party with the young blonde, and had then proceeded to tail them. He could have saved her, but perhaps he was more concerned with protecting his anonymity, no doubt on orders from the FBI chief himself, and as such, he never came to the rescue. The FBI agent was apparently instructed not to report the accident and not to let anyone know that Teddy had been the driver. J. Edgar seemingly wanted Teddy to hang himself with the consequences of this tragedy.

One of Teddy Kennedy's most trusted advisers privately told Kennedy staffers that on the night of **Mary Jo Kopechne**'s last car ride, which ended in a watery grave on Chappaquiddick, Teddy was going to ask her to abort their child. He saw it as the only way to save his political career and maintain his image as a devout Catholic.

If Teddy had immediately reported the fact that his car had plunged off a bridge and into a pond, it might have saved her life, in the event that she had been trapped in an air pocket.

But he did not, and instead tried to create a false alibi for himself after he swam across the channel to the neighboring island of Martha's Vineyard.

After abandoning his car, with Mary Jo trapped inside, Teddy walked to the departure point for the Edgartown ferry, which had long ago shut down for the night. Amazingly, in his weakened condition, he swam the 500-foot channel, although he later claimed he almost drowned.

Back in his room, he took off his clothes and collapsed, but still made no calls. He later said, "I had not given up hope all night long that, by some miracle, Mary Jo would have escaped from the car."

Although he could have, the FBI agent chose not to alert the police, letting the hours go by as Teddy mulled over what to do.

Nixon's former counsel, John Dean, testified that, "Politically until Chappaquiddick, Nixon was convinced that he was going to be running against Teddy Kennedy. After Chappaquiddick, he wasn't sure, but I think he certainly wanted to make sure, if it did happen, that he could hang Chappaquiddick around Kennedy's neck."

With that resolve, Nixon called J. Edgar once again, demanding more details that the police might have overlooked.

On Nixon's instructions, J. Edgar and his agents investigated the background of the doomed girl. An FBI agent obtained a statement from her fellow co-worker. "Mary Jo was nothing but a whore. She'd go to bed with any man who had Kennedy written on his zipper."

As the FBI probed deeper, J. Edgar and his men discovered that early in 1968 Mary Jo had had an affair with Bobby.

When she joined his secretarial pool, Bobby and Mary Jo launched a torrid sexual tryst still going on at the time of his assassination.

According to an FBI report, after mourning Bobby's death, she switched her affections to Teddy. From a secret source in a hospital on Martha's Vineyard, J. Edgar learned that Mary Jo was pregnant with Teddy's child at the time of her death.

All of this information was presented to Nixon, who filed it away for safekeeping, although he came to believe that after Chappaquiddick, Teddy would not have the political clout or support to seek the presidency on the Democratic ticket.

"Good work, Edgar," Nixon wrote in a memo. "You've given me enough to clip off Kennedy's balls if it comes to that."

Wherever Teddy went, an FBI "mole" was sure to be there. Such was the case when Teddy was on a plane with Senator Walter Mondale in April of 1971. Operating on little sleep, Teddy jumped up from his seat, shouting, "They killed Jack and they killed Bobby. Now they're trying to kill me. They're trying to kill me!" Mondale and two other men had to subdue him.

J. Edgar learned that when Teddy traveled, he had a doctor with him. In most places, an ambulance was alerted of his arrival in case there was an assassination attempt at an airport.

On a bizarre note, J. Edgar ordered the FBI in Denver to investigate a report that Teddy was about to be slain with a crossbow.

Upon Teddy's death, a 2,352-page document was released under the Freedom of Information Act. By that time the personal file that J. Edgar maintained on Teddy had presumably been destroyed.

***

Ever since Elvis Presley burst onto the music scene in the 1950s, J. Edgar expressed his loathing of "this girlie" boy, although he seemed to have some bizarre fixation on him.

J. Edgar spent much of his declining years trying to gather proof that Elvis was a bisexual. After investigating the lives of such "lady killers" as Howard Hughes and Errol Flynn, J. Edgar suspected all men who drifted night after night from woman to woman to be closeted homosexuals suffering "the Don Juan complex," as he called it.

When Elvis went into the Army and was stationed in West Germany, the FBI was monitoring his activities from their agents in Europe.

Among those figures appearing in the file was Dr. Laurenz Landau, a South African dermatologist Elvis visited in November of 1959. He falsely claimed he was ninety-eight years old but didn't look a day over forty. Elvis wanted his skin to remain "forever young" and sought treatment from Landau.

Finally, the singer submitted to Landau's Aroma Therapy treatment, in which an "elixir" of roses, carnations, orange blossoms, and resins were rubbed over Elvis's entire body. He required a totally nude Elvis to submit to ten treatments a week, although he much preferred him to have twenty.

As Elvis's biographer, Alanna Nash, wrote: "Elvis was a sucker for shit like that because he was terrified of getting old and because his skin was pretty rough in places. He had pores big enough to hide a tank."

The "doctor" also controlled Elvis' diet, feeding him honey and yogurt.

At twenty-four years of age, Elvis was "in a tizzy" about growing old. Reports are sketchy, but J. Edgar and the FBI learned that at some point Landau tried to masturbate Elvis when he developed an erection during skin treatments.

When Elvis kicked Landau out of his house, the doctor threatened to blackmail him, claiming that he'd had a different preteen or young fourteen-year-old German girl in his bedroom every night. If Elvis didn't pay blackmail money, he would go to the police and make a charge that Elvis was a pedophile.

This fascinated J. Edgar, who even obtained a copy of the report that Elvis made to MPs who came to grill him when Landau showed up at Army headquarters in Germany making charges against Elvis.

J. Edgar was convinced that Elvis was both bisexual and a pedophile, and once considered having him arrested when he brought Priscilla Beaulieu into the United States.

The FBI even rounded up statements that members of Elvis' Memphis Mafia made after parting company with Elvis. Lamar Fike, once a close friend, said: "When it came to sex, you've got to remember that Elvis was more interested in titillation than anything else. He didn't like penetration that much because he was uncircumcised, and sometimes in intercourse tore his foreskin and he'd bleed."

All these reports made tantalizing bedtime reading for J. Edgar and Clyde.

An FBI agent even trailed Elvis and his boys to Paris when he went on leave from the Army in West Germany.

In a memo from an unknown agent in Paris, it was reported that Elvis visited transvestite bars around Place Pigalle and became "involved" with a beautiful British drag queen. The note said: "He has an obsessive interest in transvestitism and may, in fact, be a transvestite himself. Mr. Presley is alleged to have taken to his hotel an astonishing beautiful female looking performer from the Moulin Rouge in Paris. Reportedly, he told his cronies that back in his hotel suite, he discovered 'she had a dick bigger than mine.'"

One night Elvis and his Mafia encountered the columnist Dorothy Kilgallen, who was in Paris pursuing a story that Elvis was hanging out with "all those girls, or guys, as the case may be." When Elvis spotted her, he fled from the club. Some of the girls were so beautiful at the drag clubs, that Elvis was constantly asking his pals, "Is it a he or she?"

Lamar Fike, one of Elvis' "Memphis Mafia," traveled to Paris and Frankfurt with his boss. Fike reported that Elvis dated a female contortionist one night at a club in Frankfurt and spent six hours in her dressing room. "He came out of there wringing wet."

The FBI also kept a running list of all the women Elvis seduced. The singer bragged that he'd seduced 1,000 women before his marriage to Priscilla. Apparently, he never claimed how many women he seduced after his marriage.

At one point he seemed partial to blondes, seducing not only Marilyn Monroe, who wanted him to co-star with her in *Bus Stop*, but her clones such as Mamie Van Doren and Jayne Mansfield. He considered all blondes to be prostitutes. He even seduced Diana Dors, called "the English Marilyn Monroe."

The most startling information J. Edgar picked up about Elvis came from Dee Presley, Elvis' stepmother. Dee had married Vernon after the

Although Richard Nixon agreed to meet with **Elvis Presley** in the Oval Office, J. Edgar ducked out on greeting him personally during Elvis' visit to FBI headquarters in Washington. J. Edgar's secretary, Helen Gandy, falsely claimed that J. Edgar was out of town.

Even though he didn't meet Elvis personally, and even though Elvis wasn't viewed as a threat to national security, J. Edgar spent a lot of time going over files on his personal life.

J. Edgar wanted to accumulate information that Elvis was a bisexual, especially revelations that he'd had an affair with actor Nick Adams.

J. Edgar also wanted the FBI to investigate if Elvis had had an incestuous affair with his mother, Gladys.

death of Elvis' beloved mother Gladys. *The National Enquirer* revealed excerpts from a book she was writing. In her manuscript she claimed that Elvis and Gladys had a sexual relationship and that Elvis had a "secret gay life." She said that Vernon had revealed that to her during their marriage.

J. Edgar wanted the incest theme explored more thoroughly and received a report from a woman named Kim Tracy, who alleged that she had had a five-month affair with Elvis while he was stationed with the Army in West Germany. She also claimed that she became pregnant with Elvis' baby but had a miscarriage. "During lovemaking he would scream out "mama, mama" at the moment of climax. She also said that during intercourse, he would call her Gladys.

The only concrete evidence J. Edgar and the FBI turned up to indicate that Elvis was bisexual was his extended involvement with actor Nick Adams, who had been the best friend and lover of James Dean. Elvis was fascinated with the late actor and would endlessly watch *Rebel Without a Cause* in which Adams also had a brief role.

Adams was known in Hollywood as a "star-fucker," according to FBI reports. In the words of biographer Albert Goldman, Nick was "forever selling himself"—and Elvis had plenty of money.

A close bond between Elvis and Adams was formed the first night they met when Elvis accepted an offer to be Nick's "date" for a preview of the film *The Last Wagon* (1956). Elvis wanted to "hang" with Adams and asked him to show him Hollywood, especially the places Dean had patronized. Within a week, Adams told another one of his lovers, Sal Mineo, that he and Elvis were sleeping together. According to Adams, Elvis preferred oral sex and mutual masturbation. Penetration, apparently, was never an option between them.

In Washington, J. Edgar and Clyde seem to savor this relationship.

Back in the 1950s Elvis was seen driving his white Cadillac all over Los Angeles with Nick in the seat beside him. They patronized the old Villa Capri when it was on McCadden Place, and were seen dining at Googie's Restaurant on Sunset Boulevard.

When Elvis returned to Graceland, he left Nick an airplane ticket. Nick flew to Tennessee two days later. Sometimes at Graceland, Elvis, according to reports, would have a lover's quarrel with Nick, and Nick would be forced to sleep with Vester Presley, Elvis' uncle.

A tabloid ran a story that Nick and Elvis shared the same bed at Graceland. Late at night, Elvis and Nick could be seen riding their twin Harley Davidson motorcycles around Memphis.

To legitimize their relationship, Elvis hired Nick to accompany him on cross-country tours.

Eventually, Elvis tired of Nick, and they separated. Nick announced to the press that he was writing a tell-all book. Nick's dead body was discovered on February 6, 1968 at his house in Coldwater Canyon in Los Angeles. There was no suicide note. Rumors still persist to this day that Col. Tom Parker, Elvis' manager, had him murdered. Nick's memoirs were not found in the house after his death.

One of Adams' closest friends, Broderick Crawford, said "Nick made a lot of mistakes, but his biggest mistake was to threaten Elvis with blackmail and let Col. Parker hear about that."

At the time of his death, J. Edgar still maintained an "open file" on Elvis as he sunk deeper into drugs and degradation.

While having a massage from a buxom blonde at Graceland, Elvis on an impulse decided he wanted to fly to Washington to meet both Richard Nixon and J. Edgar.

On December 21, 1970 Nixon agreed to meet with a cape-wearing Elvis in the Oval Office. Aides reported that the President seemed uncomfortable around Elvis, but was willing to be photographed shaking his hand. Elvis expressed his patriotism for America and denounced the "hippie drug culture," although he was alleged to have been on drugs himself during the meeting. He asked Nixon for a Bureau of Narcotics and Dangerous Drugs Badge, which was granted.

With a "mole" planted in the White House, J. Edgar wanted to know all the details of the Nixon/Presley meeting, including Elvis' wardrobe of amber-tinted sunglasses, a cardinal purple velvet cape, a cane, a white shirt with a high collar, and a black suede suit. The President noted that Elvis was wearing eye shadow and mascara. Nixon later told Bob Haldeman, his chief aide, that Elvis was "a gay blade."

As in all such meetings, there is often one very awkward moment. That came when Nixon opened his desk drawer and removed clasps with presidential seals to give to Elvis and his cohorts. "Remember, they have wives, too," Elvis said.

When Nixon didn't immediately offer equivalent souvenirs for the wives of his friends, Elvis said, "Now I know why they call you 'Tricky Dicky.'"

Nixon quickly responded, "Now I know why they call you 'Elvis the Pelvis.'"

Before leaving, Elvis did the unthinkable. Evoking Sammy Davis Jr., he actually hugged Nixon in a tight embrace. When he broke away, the President patted Elvis on the shoulder. As they were being photographed, Nixon said, "You dress kind of strange, don't you?"

Elvis responded, "Well, Mr. President, you got your show, and I got mine."

After the meeting, Nixon told the press that Elvis "could send a positive message to young people."

In his initial letter to Nixon, Elvis told him that he was about to be named one of the "Ten Outstanding Young Men of America," and noted "we share something in common," since Nixon himself had once obtained that honor.

When Elvis called the FBI and asked to meet J. Edgar during his tour of the Bureau's headquarters in Washington, FBI agent, M.A. Jones, wrote: "Mr. Presley's sincerity and good intentions notwithstanding, he is certainly not the type of individual whom the Director would wish to meet. It is noted at the present time he is wearing his hair down to his shoulders and indulges in the wearing of all sorts of exotic dress."

On December 31, 1970 at FBI headquarters, Elvis and six members of the Memphis Mafia had been flown in by private jet. An FBI agent told Elvis that J. Edgar was out of town but that a tour could be arranged "for you and your boys."

No member of the public was allowed into the building with weapons, but Elvis brought in a derringer and a .25 automatic. Amazingly, the FBI agents did not confiscate his guns.

There is evidence that J. Edgar wished he had come out to greet Elvis. During his tour Elvis had told FBI agents that "J. Edgar Hoover is the greatest living American." He claimed he'd read three of his books, including *Masters of Deceit*.

In an FBI memo sent to J. Edgar the next day, an agent wrote: "Mr. Presley claimed that he is of the opinion that the Beatles laid the groundwork for many of the problems we are having with young people by their filthy unkempt appearances and suggestive music while entertaining in this country during the early and middle-1960s. He also advised that the Smothers Brothers, Jane Fonda, and other persons in the entertainment business industry of their ilk have a lot to answer for me in the hereafter for the way they have poisoned young minds by disparaging the United States in their public statements and unsavory activities."

"Mr. Presley advised that he wished you, Mr. Hoover, to be aware that he, from time to time, is approached by individuals and groups in and outside the entertainment business, whose motive and goals he is convinced are not in the best interests of this country, and who seek to have him lend his name to their questionable activities. In this regard, he volunteered to make such information available to the Bureau on a confidential basis whenever it came to his attention."

Elvis' Memphis Mafia concluded that their boss was volunteering to be

"Hoover's stoolie."

Four days later, J. Edgar responded to Elvis' praise, sending him a letter in which he said, "Your generous comments concerning the Bureau and me are appreciated, and you may be sure that we will keep in mind your offer to be of assistance."

Fike said that Elvis later learned that J. Edgar was at FBI headquarters at the time of their visit, but chose not to receive the singer and his Memphis Mafia. "Hoover was probably in his office giving head to Clyde Tolson," Fike later claimed.

With all the sexual accusations removed from Elvis' FBI file, the sections that remained for publication dealt mainly with death threats made against him, complaints about his public performances; an extortion attempt; mention of a paternity suit; theft by larceny of an executive jet he owned, and how J. Edgar Hoover responded to citizen complaints.

Originally, the FBI file was thick with anecdotes about Elvis until J. Edgar's longtime secretary, Helen Gandy, shredded "the really personal stuff."

***

Far removed from Nixon's one known affair with a possible Chinese spy, Marianna Liu, J. Edgar and Clyde became far more intrigued with Nixon's bizarre relationship with Charles Rebozo, nicknamed "Bebe," meaning "Baby" in Spanish. Before J. Edgar himself became a guest at Bebe's home at Key Biscayne Florida, in December of 1971, he had his agents complete a security check on Bebe, turning up some "disturbing" information.

Born of Cuban immigrants to Tampa, Bebe was voted the "most beautiful boy in high school."

He became the lover in the late 1920s of Donald Gunn, a rather wealthy young man who paid the bills. In 1931, Bebe married Donald's sister, Claire Gunn, but after four years she claimed the marriage was never consummated. He later remarried her for another two years, perhaps under some sort of arrangement.

He took yet a final wife, Jane Lucke, his lawyer's secretary, but the marriage didn't take. She later said Bebe's favorite things were Richard Nixon, his car, and me a very distant third." His third and final marriage was called "antiseptic."

As Nixon biographer Fawn Brodie, noted: "Nixon seemed to have been willing to risk the kind of gossip that frequently accompanies close friendships with a perennial bachelor like Rebozo. This despite Nixon's known public aversion to homosexuals, and his acute sensitivity to the damage

During his presidency, **Richard Nixon** *(left)* spent far more time with his best friend, **Bebe Rebozo** *(right)* than he did with his wife, Patricia.

Because Bebe ("Baby" in Spanish) was well known in Miami's homosexual circles, rumors arose about the two men spending so much time together. Bebe was even assigned his own bedroom and office within the White House.

Nixon and Bebe swam nude together at his home on Key Biscayne. The president also shared several "shady dealings" with Bebe, who maintained notorious links to the mob.

"I don't know how anyone could make love to Nixon, but if there's one person on earth who can stomach the fucker, it's that Cuban faggot, Rebozo, down there in Miami," said Lyndon B. Johnson.

that the label of homosexual on a friend could bring to a public man."

Senator George Smathers of Florida took a more cynical view. He often dined with Nixon when he came to see Bebe at Key Biscayne. "I think Bebe's love of Nixon just grew and grew, starting when he became Vice President but bursting into full bloom when he became the actual President. Being President of the United States can make one power-hungry guy fall madly in love with you."

Bebe was well-known in Miami's homosexual community. When Nixon was not in residence, he threw Saturday night male-only barbeques at his Key Biscayne home, where he had a longtime affair with a handsome flight attendant on Pan American, Patrick LeLand. Bebe was bisexual, conducting a three-year affair with big-busted Margaret Foresman, the blonde-haired editor of *The Key West Citizen*.

Foresman claimed that with Bebe, Nixon could be quite playful, wrestling together in the pool at Key Biscayne. "When I visited and Nixon was there, we slept in different rooms. But one night around three in the morning when I was heading for the bar in the living room, I secretly spied Nixon emerging from Bebe's bedroom wearing just the top to his pajamas."

"I knew when we sailed over to Eleuthera in The Bahamas one week, Nixon and Bebe shared a bedroom and put me in my own quarters somewhere else on the property. One time I returned to Bebe's home three hours earlier than I said and spotted them sunbathing in the nude around the pool. I slipped out of the house again and came back at the appointed time I told them. By then they were fully dressed and sitting around Bebe's living room enjoying their first of many cocktails that night."

Bobby Baker, LBJ's top aide, claimed that his boss knew that Bebe and Nixon were "close like lovers. Bebe loved Nixon more than he loved anybody. He worshipped Nixon. Nixon was his God. His Little Jesus."

Columnist Jack Anderson later revealed that both Nixon and Bebe had stashed away hidden bank accounts in Switzerland. During Nixon's presidency, Bebe's net worth went from $750,000 to $4.5 million.

As for his wife Patricia, Nixon communicated with her mainly through memos signed "The President," or so J. Edgar was informed.

General Alexander Haig, Nixon's last chief of staff, was overheard mocking Nixon's limp-wristed friend and joking about his gay relationship with Nixon, according to author Anthony Summers.

Henry Kissinger, Nixon's Secretary of State, claimed he always resented the presence of Bebe, who was frequently sneaked in and out of Nixon's suite when the President traveled outside the United States. "His presence was always there as I was trying to talk foreign policy with Nixon. Sometimes a drunken Nixon would call me at three o'clock in the morning, with Bebe's foreign policy crackpot ideas. Nixon always warned me, 'Better take his advice, or it'll be your ass, Henry.'"

During Nixon's time in the White House, it is estimated that he spent one out of every ten days with Bebe, and the President made fifty trips to Key Biscayne to see his friend.

Bebe, as J. Edgar discovered, was a close friend of Santos Trafficante, the Tampa Godfather, and also a close friend of Alfred ("Big Al") Polizzi of Cleveland, who was a drug trafficker with syndicated links to gangster Meyer Lansky. Bebe was partners with Polizzi in developing a Cuban shopping center in Miami. The FBI labeled Polizzi as "one of the most influential members of the underground in America."

An FBI agent in Miami reported that in addition to Trafficante, Polizzi, and Lansky, Bebe frequently entertained Vincent ("Jimmy Blue Eyes") Alo, a close cohort of Lansky.

During Nixon's presidency, Bebe had access to 1600 Pennsylvania Avenue, where he was given a private office and a designated bedroom. J. Edgar had long suspected that Bebe was Nixon's "bag man" to the Mafia and to the eccentric mogul Howard Hughes, the loopy billionaire Nixon referred to as "Daddy Warbucks."

After J. Edgar's death, Bebe would come under investigation during the Watergate scandal for transferring a $100,000 bribe from Hughes to Nixon.

Eventually, Nixon established a residence next to Bebe's in Key Biscayne. The press nicknamed it the Florida White House.

J. Edgar did not live to see the disgrace of both Bebe and Nixon. Columnist Jack Anderson speculated that Archibald Cox, the Watergate Special Prosecutor, had been fired because he had started to investigate Bebe's role in accepting covert payments for Nixon.

Through Nixon's resignation and the President's subsequent fall, Bebe remained his loyal friend to the end.

Bebe frequently joined Nixon during his years of "exile" in California and was at his bedside nursing him through his final illness in 1994.

The "first friend" would live four more years, dying on May 8, 1998.

In Bebe's last interview with *The Miami Herald*, he said, "Richard Nixon was everything they say he's not. He's a very sensitive man, very thoughtful and, of course, very brilliant. "For forty-four years, he enriched my life."

***

Billy Byars, Jr. was the son of a rich Texas oilman, Billy Byars, Sr., who often entertained J. Edgar and Clyde. Byars Jr. remembered how outspoken J. Edgar was in private company with his wealthy friends, calling Bobby Kennedy "a despicable little shit" or Richard Nixon "a dirty little son of a bitch. Right from the beginning, Nixon never met up with a bribe he didn't want to pocket."

J. Edgar's association with Byars Jr. and some of his friends almost led to his own involvement in a homosexual scandal that even the FBI might not have been able to cover up. J. Edgar soon discovered that he and Byars Jr. shared certain mutual interests.

Byars Sr. and his wife, Emily had adopted the boy. Junior liked to claim that his biological parents were of Russian royalty. Actually, he may have been the offspring of a waitress and a Texas trucker. At one time his father kicked him out of his home in Texas allegedly because of his homosexuality, but they later reconciled.

Apparently, Byars Jr. never offered an explanation as to why his father was one of only three men J. Edgar called on the day of the assassination of John F. Kennedy. Because that mysterious call was made, Byars Sr. often figures in conspiracy books written after JFK's murder.

In his book on J. Edgar, author Anthony Summers claimed that Byars' house in Los Angeles, at the summit of the Laurel Canyon, was for a while "a haven for adult homosexuals and male teenagers." One of J. Edgar's chauffeurs, who refused to give his name, later maintained that he delivered J. Edgar (without Clyde) one night to this haven.

Byars Jr. was the founder of Lyric International, which produced physique photographs of boys and young men from the late 1960s until

1973. Lyric's major film was *The Genesis Children*, featuring extensive full nudity of preteen and teenage boys. The boys were both American and European, some of whom came from Germany.

The boys are seen frolicking entirely in the nude in the surf and engaging in other activities such as climbing cliffs. There is no boy-on-boy sex, as Byars did not endorse pornography. However, one of his associates, Guy Strait, did specialize in boy pornography.

In *The Genesis Children*, there are many close-ups of the boys' pelvic areas.

Deland Anderson, who went under various pseudonyms, was a child pornographer who recruited some of the teenagers for Lyric films. He also pimped those boys who were willing to various pedophiles. During its short existence, Lyric distributed ninety magazines featuring teenagers, and made films with extensive nudity of young men and boys.

Anderson maintained that a few of the boys who appeared in these films were supplied to Clyde and J. Edgar during their vacations in La Jolla. Byars Jr. lived in a bungalow next to J. Edgar's at the Del Charro Hotel in La Jolla. There is no evidence that he participated in any of this peddling of young flesh.

Many liaisons with young boys and J. Edgar and Clyde were arranged by Anderson. The kids called the FBI director "Mother John," and for some reason called Tolson "Mother Mike."

In addition to J. Edgar and Clyde, these teenage boys were also supplied "to some of the biggest names in Hollywood," according to Deland Anderson, who disappeared from the radar screen late in 1973 when newspapers began writing exposés about him.

When the police seized Anderson's address book, one tantalizing address was the home address and phone number of Fred Astaire.

Anderson said that he had been told that J. Edgar and Clyde had been lovers when they were young men, but in their dotage they preferred three-way sex with young boys to stimulate their sagging libidos. "My boys just regarded them as two old queens and were willing to go with them because they paid well. One Saturday night I personally drove four boys to Hoover's cottage. The boys were in there for four hours before they were released. Each was given a hundred-dollar bill, but I took half of it for my fee."

Anderson recalled that J. Edgar had been particularly impressed with a nude photograph of a muscled, heavily endowed fifteen-year-old boy. "But before I could arrange a rendezvous between Hoover and the kid, the director insisted I take him to the barber. He always preferred a young man with a crewcut and detested what he called 'long-haired hippies.'"

After J. Edgar's death, Byars Jr. was indicted, along with thirteen other men, for child molestation and making movies depicting sex acts with boys. By that time, Byars had left the United States to live the life of an expatriate.

The Lyric Studio came to a notorious end in 1973. The Meese Commission, appointed by Ronald Reagan, announced its demise as the destruction of "the first known child pornography ring brought to public view."

The Los Angeles Times headlined the story as "14 Men Indicted in Sex Movies Featuring Boys Ages 6 to 17."

Criminal justice proceedings against the defendants more or less wound down with light sentences or $500 fines. One teenager provocatively claimed he was "dangled over a cliff by two L.A. policemen until I confessed to having sex with Hoover."

Robin Lloyd in his book, *For Money or Love: Boy Prostitution in America*, claims that Lyric films still command a high price "in the chicken market," especially one film featuring a blond-haired thirteen-year-old boy.

***

Nixon's top aides, H.R. ("Bob") Haldeman and John Ehrlichman, intensely disliked J. Edgar, and on six different occasions convinced the President to fire him. At the last minute in each case Nixon backed down, fearing the FBI director would take his revenge and expose Nixon's most guarded secrets.

Behind J. Edgar's back, Haldeman arranged a meeting between Nixon and Peter Pitchess, the sheriff of Los Angeles County, who was regarded as a suitable replacement for J. Edgar. John Connally was also a candidate for the position. As governor of Texas, he had ridden in that limousine in Dallas in which JFK was assassinated.

Through his spies within the White House, J. Edgar learned of the manipulations of Ehrlichman and Haldeman. The director ordered an investigation into their private lives. "I've been hearing scandalous stories," he told Clyde and his top aides, "but I need proof to present to the President about the two men in whom he's put his trust."

Instead of firing J. Edgar, Nixon invited him for a weekend at Camp David. "And bring your boy, Mr. Tolson," Nixon added. At seventy, Clyde was hardly "a boy" any more. At Camp David, Nixon told J. Edgar that his new boss and Attorney General was to be John Mitchell. The name was familiar to J. Edgar. Mitchell was a noted New York municipal bond lawyer, the director of Nixon's 1968 race for the White House, and one of Nixon's closest personal friends.

Nixon had already warned J. Edgar not to make his usual investigation of the Mitchells' background. The only warning J. Edgar gave Nixon was about Mitchell's wife, Martha. An alcoholic, she was known for her erratic behavior and her utter lack of discretion. Tanked up on enough booze, she would virtually spill secrets best confined to the closet. Mitchell also was not the model of discretion.

When reporter Carl Bernstein was about to expose his involvement in the Watergate affair, Mitchell issued a warning to Bernstein's publisher: "Katie's gonna get her tit caught in a big fat wringer if that's published." The reference, of course, was to Katharine Graham. She was not intimidated by Mitchell. If anything, his threat caused her to order her reporters to probe deeper.

Months into the Nixon presidency, Haldeman and Ehrlichman began to resent J. Edgar's easy access to Nixon, and behind the scenes they worked to limit it.

Nixon's two top aides, **Bob Haldeman** *(left)* and **John Ehrlichman**, wanted their boss, Richard Nixon, to fire J. Edgar. But when the FBI director heard about this through his "mole" within the White House, he ordered that the two men be investigated. What FBI agents learned shocked even J. Edgar.

Haldeman and Ehrlichman, sometimes with young members of Nixon's Secret Service, often staged homosexual orgies at the Watergate Complex. When Nixon was staying with Bebe Rebozo in Key Biscayne, Haldeman and Ehrlichman also staged nude swimming parties in the White House pool with well-built young men.

During their careers in the Nixon administration, Ehrlichman and Haldeman became known as "The Berlin Wall," which was a play on their German family names and their shared penchant for keeping visitors away from Nixon. They were, in essence, his "gatekeepers."

Bob Haldeman proudly referred to himself as Nixon's "son of a bitch," and he never shied away from firing staffers in person. The only man he wanted to fire, but couldn't, was J. Edgar himself.

Ehrlichman also held J. Edgar "in total disgust." Together "The Berlin Wall" set out to undermine the FBI director and get him fired.

In striking back, J. Edgar delivered what he told Clyde and his aides was a "bombshell." As first revealed in Anthony Summers' biography of J. Edgar, the FBI was told that Haldeman, Ehrlichman, and yet a third Nixon aide, Dwight Chapin, were indulging in homosexual sex within the White House, along with five members of Nixon's Secret Service.   Chapin was innocently smeared in these allegations, but the FBI had a strong case against Nixon's two top aides. As it happened, one of J. Edgar's under-cover agents was one of the youngest and best-looking members of the Secret Service.

The agent told J. Edgar that although he was straight, he had been propositioned by Ehrlichman, no doubt because of his good looks, to join the homosexual cabal. The agent went on to testify that after he'd refused, Ehrlichman had threatened to dismiss him from the Secret Service.

Through their informants, the FBI had accumulated names, dates, and places of homosexual orgies, some of which, ironically, had transpired within the Watergate complex, the venue for Nixon's ultimate downfall. Attorney General Mitchell had already been alerted to the bombshell J. Edgar had delivered to Nixon.

One night after a cruise aboard the president yacht *Sequoia*, Mitchell met privately with Haldeman and Ehrlichman. "I know boys will be boys sometimes when they get together," he said, referring to the homosexual reports. "But Hoover is sending a warning to us. Stop all this pressure in trying to get Nixon to fire J. Edgar. If you persist, you will be exposed. A scandal like this could bring down the presidency. Welcome to Washington, boys. It's a dirty game, and you'd better know it now."

Ehrlichman and Haldeman waited to see how Nixon was going to handle the exposure of their secret sex lives.

Hoping to smooth things over, Nixon accepted J. Edgar's invitation to dinner at his private home where Clyde was the co-host. The President invited Ehrlichman and Haldeman to go with him. J. Edgar graciously received them, feeding them tender, thick steaks flown in as a gift from Texas oilman Clint Murchison, "Elizabeth Taylor's favorite chili" from Chasen's Restaurant in Beverly Hills, and tree-ripened fresh fruit from a Florida ranch that specialized in exotic flavors.

Ehrlichman found J. Edgar's house "gone to seed." Haldeman later told Mitchell, "I felt I was in the house of some old auntie with lace doilies on the chair and male nude statues placed around, with erotic homosexual friezes from Roman days in the bathroom. In case Hoover had a peep-hole, I fluffed it a bit when I went to take a piss."

Mitchell told this story to his blabbermouth wife, Martha, who spread the gossip at Washington cocktail parties.

Nixon learned that an aide had heard Clyde Tolson tell Sullivan, "Whoever is elected in 1972, Eddie knows he's finished at the FBI—and that means even if Nixon is re-elected. I understand that as each week goes by, Nixon plots another scheme to fire us."

Nixon's reactions to these revelations are not known. There is speculation that he already was well aware of the behind-the-scenes trysts within the White House. When he was away, Haldeman and Ehrlichman sometimes staged nude all-male swimming parties in the White House pool, where John F. Kennedy had cavorted with naked prostitutes.

J. Edgar didn't seem to feel the noose tightening. He told colleagues, "I'm flying down to Key Biscayne around Christmas. I don't want Nixon to see how bad off Clyde is, so I'll leave him at our hotel when I call on Nixon and his lover boy, Bebe Rebozo."

On J. Edgar's birthday on New Year's Day, Nixon always made a show of wishing him the happy returns of the day. Once again J. Edgar was assured he could remain as FBI director "as long as you choose, or as long as I'm President."

Because of strokes and open-heart surgery, Clyde wanted to retire and live on his government pension, but J. Edgar refused to give him permission. He kept him on the payroll, even though on many a day Clyde was too weak or sickly to show up for work. Because of his failing eyesight, he had to have a secretary read his mail to him.

As time went by, and passion's fire between the two G-Men had long ago died down, they became like a bickering straight couple, constantly nagging at each other.

Instead of being sympathetic to Clyde's rapidly declining health, J. Edgar seemed to hold him in contempt. One day at a luncheon at the Mayflower Hotel, Clyde stumbled and fell. Two waiters rushed to his side, but J. Edgar ordered them away. "Let the asshole get up by himself," he told the waiters.

Even though he faced repeated temptations to fire J. Edgar, Nixon called out for him in the midst of the Watergate crisis. He shouted to his aides, "Where in the fuck is J. Edgar Hoover now that I need him?"

***

On May 1, 1972 a feeble old man of seventy-seven walked into the Mayflower Hotel for his last luncheon, ordering a fresh grapefruit salad with cottage cheese, followed by coffee. His gray-brown hair, at least what remained of it, was straight and thin, no longer the spiky, curly hair of his youth. Still holding himself erect, his dark brown eyes looked slightly dazed, as if he were daydreaming.

Clyde, his beloved companion for all these years, was too weak and feeble to lunch with him that day, as he had so faithfully every day for years.

J. Edgar, the legendary G-Man of yesterday, had entered twilight time, the sun setting on one of the most notorious careers in U.S. government service.

Three hours earlier, his new chauffeur, Tom Moton, had driven him to FBI headquarters where he took a private elevator to his office. Before his arrival, word spread that, "He's on the way up."

The deputy associate director, Mark Felt, reported that, "Hoover was alert, forceful, typically aggressive."

He called his secretary, Helen Gandy, who had been with him for forty-four years, into his office. "If something ever happens to me, you know what to do." She had long ago been instructed to shred his personal files when he died.

She later claimed that she felt, as never before, "Edgar had a sense of his own mortality. That was made clear when he heard that Clyde had been taken to the hospital that morning for some medical tests."

The first dossier Helen put on J. Edgar's desk was the beginning of a series of the *Washington Post's* exposés on the FBI, written by his dreaded enemy, Jack Anderson. Anderson's column, according to Helen, "devastated J. Edgar, raising his blood pressure to dangerous levels."

Jack Anderson had written:

"FBI chief J. Edgar Hoover, the curmudgeon of law enforcement, fiercely resisted a White House suggestion that he spare a few hundred agents to crack down on drug abuses. But he can spare agents to snoop into the sex habits, business affairs, and political pursuits of individuals who aren't even remotely involved in illegal activity.

"Hoover's gumshoes have loaded FBI files with titillating tidbits about such diverse figures as movie actors Marlon Brando and Harry Belafonte, football heroes Joe Namath and Lance Rentzel, ex-boxing champs Joe Louis and Muhammad Ali, black leaders, Ralph Abernathy and Roy Innis.

"It's no secret that the FBI hounded the late Martin Luther King, Jr., the apostle of racial brotherhood and nonviolent protest. We have seen FBI reports on his political activities and sex life. The FBI is now watching the widow, Coretta King."

Anderson also claimed that "Hoover's gumshoes go out of their way to find out who's sleeping with whom in Washington and Hollywood. A famous movie star has been the subject of investigation, even though he has no criminal record or fingerprint data. His FBI contains nothing but rumors about his sex life, showing that he is definitely a homosexual." Anderson did not name the actor.

Over the intercom, J. Edgar ordered Helen to bring him the files on Rock Hudson. At his desk, he went over it carefully. It was all there, including his *faux* marriage to a secretary Phyllis Gates, a well-known lesbian. Hudson's list of seductions was long: porn star Paul Baresi, studio publicist Tom Clark, Errol Flynn, actor Jon Hall, Liberace, Sal Mineo, George Nader, Tyrone Power, Merv Griffin, Jim Nabors, and talent agent Henry Willson.

A surprising number of women were also on the list—Elizabeth Taylor, Joan Crawford, Mamie Van Doren, and Frank Sinatra's longtime girlfriend, Marilyn Maxwell.

The FBI even had a report that at a Hollywood party, Hudson had propositioned pint-sized Mickey Rooney who turned him down. "Rock, you know I like girls."

Many members of the Bureau felt that reading Anderson's column that day hastened J. Edgar's death.

When Helen came in to see J. Edgar after he returned from his lunch, she found him staring out the window. "I want to live to see the new building completed sometime in 1974." He was referring to the new $102 million FBI building going up on Pennsylvania Avenue.

In the office he reached for her hand. In her fifty-four years of service to him, he had never touched her before. "I must remind you," he said, "my personal files must never fall in the hands of our enemies. You have never failed me before. Of all the people at this Bureau, you are the only one who is indispensable."

He looked deeply into her eyes, imbedded in a face that biographers have claimed "evoked Cerberus at the gate."

Before he left that day, he told her, "Our greatest enemy is time. I hear the sound of time's winged chariot very loud in my ears."

Helen officially retired on the day J. Edgar died, but she spent the next few weeks destroying his personal papers, blackmail evidence he'd accumulated on everybody from the Kennedys to Nixon, from Joseph McCarthy to Eleanor Roosevelt and Marilyn Monroe.

She was left $5,000 in his will, and continued to live in Washington until 1986 when she moved to Deland, Florida to live with a niece. An avid trout fisherman, she died of a heart attack on July 7, 1988.

***

After his last day on the job, J. Edgar's chauffeur drove him to Clyde's

apartment. His associate director had long ago given up sleeping over at the home of his boss. Back from the hospital, he looked weak and feeble after suffering a series of debilitating strokes.

He was hardly coherent, fussing over an early dinner prepared by his housekeeper. She'd cooked Omaha steaks, baby peas, baked potatoes, and prepared for each of them three scoops of banana nut ice cream, their favorite.

After dinner, J. Edgar embraced Clyde, the recipient of thousands of embraces over the decades. His chauffeur delivered him to his home at 10:15pm. He said goodnight to his housekeeper, Annie Fields, and spent an hour out in his backyard with his two Cairn terriers, "G-Boy" and "Cindy." He retired to bed, perhaps around 11:30om.

An hour later, he was rudely awakened by the urgent ringing of a telephone on his nightstand.

J. Edgar picked up the phone to hear the drunken voice of President Nixon. "It's Dick," he said. "Edgar, it pains me to inform you of this, but I must. In the morning, I'm holding a press conference to announce the new director of the FBI. I hope you will understand my decision. A scandal is about to break in California, a real nasty one. About young boys and stuff. If you step down without protest, I think we can cover it up and protect your stellar reputation."

Perhaps J. Edgar did not need to be told what that scandal was. He already knew.

Helen Gandy was J. Edgar's long-time secretary. She was so loyal to him that she destroyed his personal files after his death so as not to embarrass him.

Clint Eastwood's movie, *J. Edgar*, depicts Leonardo DiCaprio, cast as the FBI's director, proposing marriage to Gandy.

But before her death in 1988, the usually tight-lipped Gandy said J. Edgar never showed any interest in her other than as a loyal secretary.

However, at the end of WWI, perhaps for the sake of appearances, J. Edgar did conduct a *faux* romance with his former secretary, a woman named "Alice." She soon abandoned him, running off with a young Army officer returning from the war in Europe.

"I wouldn't exactly call it love between Eddie and Alice," Gandy said, refusing to reveal the woman's last name.

According to John Ehrlichman and Bob Haldeman, J. Edgar did not ask who his successor was.

"Good night, Mr. President," he said in a weak voice. "I have served my country well, given distinguished service. I have fought all enemies, both foreign and domestic." He put down the receiver.

In the middle of the night he suffered a fatal heart attack.

***

Nixon was alerted in the early morning hours when J. Edgar's body, clad in his pajama bottoms, was discovered by the side of his bed by his housekeeper, Annie.

"Jesus Christ," Nixon said. "That old cocksucker."

He immediately ordered eighteen of his Secret Service men to go to J. Edgar's home and remove his private records, which he kept in the basement. "Get them before Clyde Tolson shreds them."

Later that morning, Nixon told the press that J. Edgar "was a legend in his own lifetime, serving forty-eight years under eight American presidents with total loyalty, unparalleled ability, and supreme dedication."

He immediately ordered a state funeral. It attracted 25,000 mourners. His body lay in state on the same bier that once had borne the body of the assassinated Abraham Lincoln. The funeral did not come off without incident. The coffin weighed more than half a ton and two of the eight pall-bearers were injured trying to lift the massive weight.

An Army guard presented Clyde with a U.S. flag that had draped J. Edgar's coffin. It was a public recognition of their special friendship.

That day, Nixon also announced that the new FBI headquarters would bear the name of J. Edgar Hoover in gold letters.

***

For one day, Clyde was the director of the FBI, but he submitted his resignation to Nixon that afternoon. "Without Eddie around, there is no more need for me to carry on," he told Helen Gandy. "Nixon would have fired me by tomorrow anyway."

Clyde inherited J. Edgar's estate of $551,000 and moved into J. Edgar's house, where he remained until he died, venturing out only twice.

On May 2, 1974, the second anniversary of J. Edgar's death, a weak, feeble Clyde went out of his house for only the second time since the death of his long-time companion. He walked with a cane to where a chauffeur waited to take him to the Congressional Cemetery.

At the cemetery, Clyde walked slowly to the grave of J. Edgar and placed a red rose on the burial site. Perhaps he also looked at the plot of land adjoining, where he would be buried himself.

After private words uttered over the grave, he returned to the limousine, where he was driven back to his lonely home where he had received nobody in the wake of J. Edgar's death.

He had spent the previous two years destroying more and more of J. Edgar's files which had been stored in his apartment. He wanted no papers left behind that would damage the reputation of the longtime director of the FBI.

On the third anniversary of J. Edgar's death, Clyde was preparing once again to be driven to the cemetery with his red rose.

But he feared he'd never make it. His final call was to Helen Gandy, J. Edgar's long-time secretary. He inquired about her health and complained of his own. He melodramatically told her, "I'll soon be joining Eddie for eternity."

Death came to him on April 14, 1975. His secrets were buried with him beside J. Edgar.

J. Edgar *(left)* and **Clyde Tolson** *(right)* spent many happy moments together at various racetracks.

Here, they're seen in 1947 at La Jolla in California, playing safe bets with insider information obtained from the mob, who often fixed the race.

The racetrack was also a venue for various "celebrations," including the assassinations of John F. Kennedy, Martin Luther King, Jr., and Robert F. Kennedy.

ABOUT THE AUTHOR

Darwin Porter has been fascinated by the FBI ever since his widowed mother began dating a G-Man who presented him with a Junior G-Man badge in the mid 1940s.

Porter never became an FBI agent himself, but turned his investigative skills into reporting.

Over the years, he gathered stories from dozens of Hollywood celebrities and FBI men, many in retirement in Florida. Sometimes, they spoke freely about their experiences in the FBI. Many others, however, preferred to keep their secrets, and those of J. Edgar Hoover and Clyde Tolson, to themselves.

Today, Porter is one of the world's leading celebrity biographers, having written books on such diverse figures as Katharine Hepburn, Paul Newman, Howard Hughes, Marlon Brando, Humphrey Bogart, Michael Jackson, Steve McQueen, the Kennedys, and Frank Sinatra.

He is also the co-author of the popular *Hollywood Babylon* series, and is also the co-author of *Damn You, Scarlett O'Hara,* which exposed the complicated and deeply anguished private lives of Laurence Olivier and Vivien Leigh.

Currently, Porter is working on *Marilyn at Rainbow's End,* destined for a publication during the Spring of 2012 and devoted to exploring the mysterious final years in the life of blonde sex goddess Marilyn Monroe.

When not traveling, Porter lives in New York City.

INDEX

537

Marvin, Langdon 448
Mary of Scotland 282
Massing, Hede 268
Master Race, The 290
Masterman, J.C. 171
Masters of Deceit 408, 510
Mastorakis, Nico 502
Mattachine Society, The 273, 290
"Matter of Fact" 375
Matthews, James B. 120
Mature, Victor 334
Maxwell, Elsa 327
Maxwell, Marilyn 521
May, Gary 269
Mayer, Louis B. 67, 102, 145, 153, 229, 280,
    303, 305, 451
Mayflower Hotel (Washington, DC) 27, 78, 130,
    139, 155, 274, 427, 519
Mazzini, Ricky 95
McCarey, Leo 306
McCarran Act, the (aka The Internal Security Act
    of 1950) 360
McCarthy, Eugene 490, 491
McCarthy, Frank 198
McCarthy, Joseph 10, 212, 241, 262, 266, 270,
    316, 317, 318, 349, 358, 359, 360, 361,
    362, 363, 364, 366, 367, 369, 371, 372,
    379, 381, 383, 385, 388, 389, 394, 404, 521
McClure Hotel (Wheeling, West Virginia) 316
McCoy, George 269
McEvoy, Freddie 191, 192
McFarlin, M.W. 142
McGhee, Millie L. 482, 483
McGranery, James P. 358
McGrath, J. Howard 365
McKellar, Kenneth D. 72
McKinley, William 13
McLaghlen, Victor 153
McLeod, Dr. Donald Campbell 3
McMahon, William 371
McMurty, Larry 59
McNeil Island Penitentiary (Washington State)
    76
McPherson, Aimee Semple 353
McQueen, Steve 292
Meese Commission, The 516
Meet Nero Wolfe 290
Meet the Press (NBC) 269
Melvin Purvis Junior G-Men Clubs 65
Men in Battle 289
Mencken, H. L. 34
Menjou, Adolphe 278, 298, 303
Mercer, Lucy (see Rutherford, Lucy Mercer) 137
Merchants National Bank (South Bend, IN) 61
Merman, Ethel 87, 88, 89, 90, 107, 212, 213,
    231, 236, 327, 328, 448
Message for Garcia, A 172

Meyer, Johnny 193
MGM (Metro-Goldwyn-Mayer) 101, 103, 451
MI-5 124
MI-6 170, 171, 173, 174, 176
Miami Herald, The 514
"Mickey Mouse" 157, 278
Midkiff, Myra 315
Midnight Cowboy 92
Miller, Arthur 281, 284, 342, 432
Miller, Earl 41, 42, 132
Miller, Merle 229
Miller, Paula 342
Milligan, Maurice 222
Million Dollar Studs, The 260
Milwaukee Journal, The 369
Mineo, Sal 460, 521
Miranda, Rafael Cancel 404
Mitchell, John 498, 516, 518
Mitchell, Martha 517, 518
Mitchell, William D. 31
Mitchum, Robert 291
Mitrokhin, Vasili 405
Moaney, John 381
Moats, Alice Leone 260
Mollenhoff, Clark 454, 458
Mondale, Walter 505
Monroe, Marilyn 31, 45, 280, 323, 335, 413,
    420, 422, 427, 428, 429, 432, 434, 437,
    439, 446, 447, 448, 452, 473, 474, 489,
    500, 507, 521
Monsieur Verdoux (aka *The Ladykiller*) 354
Monte Carlo Country Club (Monaco) 346
Montgomery, Robert 277, 278, 280
"Moon of Manakoora, The" 87
Moon Over Burma 87
Morales, Angel 100
Moretti, Willie 254, 451
Morgan, J.P. 10
Morgan, Ted 185
Morgenthau, Henry 222, 309
Morgenthau, Robert 463, 473
Morris, Chester 37
Mortimer, Lee 448, 449, 450, 451
Motion Picture Alliance for the Preservation of
    American Ideals 109, 305, 344
Motion Picture Association of America (MPAA)
    289
Motion Picture Country Home (Los Angeles)
    294
Moton, Tom 520
Mr. Lincoln's Whiskers 295
Muehlebach Hotel (Kansas City) 30
Mulligan, Gerry 321
Mundt, Karl Earl 311
Muni, Paul 279, 284
Murchison, Clint 236, 518
"Murder, Inc." 115, 116

542

544

If you liked this book, check out these other titles from
BLOOD MOON PRODUCTIONS
Entertainment About How America Interprets Its Celebrities

Blood Moon Productions is a New York-based publishing enterprise dedicated to re-searching, salvaging, and indexing the oral histories of America's entertainment industry.

Reorganized with its present name in 2004, Blood Moon originated in 1997 as The Georgia Literary Association, a vehicle for the promotion of obscure writers from America's Deep South.

Blood Moon's authors, administration, and staff are associated with some of the writing, research, and editorial functions of THE FROMMER GUIDES, a subdivision of John Wiley & Sons, a respected name in travel publishing. Blood Moon also maintains a back list of at least 20 critically acclaimed biographies and film guides. Its titles are distributed within North America and Australia by the National Book Network (www.NBN-Books.com), within the U.K. by Turnaround (www.Turnaround-uk.com), and through secondary wholesalers and online retailers everywhere.

Since 2004, Blood Moon has been awarded almost 20 nationally recognized literary prizes. They've included both silver and bronze medals from the IPPY (Independent Publishers Assn.) Awards; four nominations and two Honorable Mentions for BOOK OF THE YEAR from Foreword Reviews; nominations from The Ben Franklin Awards; and Awards and Honorable Mentions from the New England, the Los Angeles, the Paris, the New York, the San Francisco, and the Hollywood Book Festivals.

For more about us, including a free monthly subscription to our scandalous celebrity dish, **BLOOD MOON'S DIRTY LAUNDRY,** and access to a growing number of videotaped book trailers, click on **WWW.BLOODMOONPRODUCTIONS.COM** or refer to the pages which immediately follow.

Thanks for your interest, best wishes, and happy reading.

Danforth Prince, President
Blood Moon Productions Ltd.

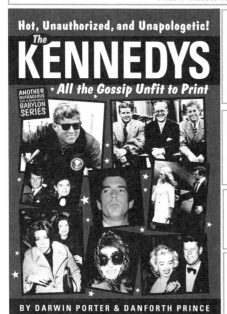

FRANK SINATRA, The Boudoir Singer

All the Gossip Unfit to Print
from the Glory Days of Ol' Blue Eyes

"Every time I sing a song, I'm actually making love on stage. Call me 'The Boudoir Singer.'" —Frank Sinatra

"When Sinatra dies, they'll donate his zipper to the Smithsonian." —Dean Martin

"F-R-A-N-K-I-E-E-E-EE! Take my virginity!" screamed a bobby-soxer in midtown Manhattan in 1943

"Our problems were never in bed," said Ava Gardner, his greatest love. "We were always great in bed. Ten pounds of Frank, 110 pounds of cock."

Even If You Thought You'd Heard It All Already,
You'll Be Amazed At How Much This Book Contains
That Never Got Published Before.

Vendettas and high-octane indiscretions, fast and furious women,
deep sensitivities and sporadic psychoses, Presidential pimping, FBI coverups,
Mobster mambos, and a pantload of hushed-up scandals about

FABULOUS FRANKIE AND HIS MIND-BLOWING COHORTS
Winner of a literary award from the 2011 New England Book Festival.
Hardcover, 465 pages with LOTS of photos

ISBN 978-1-936003-19-8 $26.95

"Womanizer Sinatra's Shocking Secret Sins are revealed in a blockbuster new book, in-cluding his raunchy romps with Liz Taylor, Marilyn Monroe, Jackie-O, and Nancy Reagan. Every time the leader of the Free World would join him in Palm Springs, the place was a sun-kissed brothel, with Kennedy as the main customer." **THE GLOBE**

The Most Amazing "True Crime" Story Ever Published, Available in the June, 2012 from Blood Moon Productions.

Less than an hour after the discovery of Marilyn Monroe's corpse in Brentwood, a flood of theories, tainted evidence, and conflicting testimonies began pouring out into the public landscape.

In honor of Marilyn, and as an insight into the American experience of celebrity death on the 50th anniversary of the murder of the Love Goddess, biographer Darwin Porter has compiled, with commentary, an intriguing roundup of the conspiracies, and dark secrets behind Hollywood's most notorious mystery: Who Killed Marilyn?

This relentless page-turner, a lip-smacking and juicy read, examines the mass hysteria that followed in the wake of Marilyn's assassination. No death in the 20th century, other than that of JFK himself, ever sparked more cover-ups, lies, criminal thefts of vital data (including body parts), bribes, perjury, myths, incompetent investigating, distorted medical records, unauthorized leaks, outrageous rumors, and a blitzkrieg of bizarre books that obscured more than they revealed.

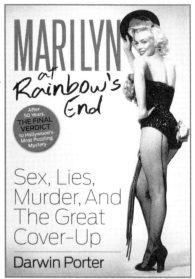

Like the sirens of Greek mythology, Marilyn was an irresistible temptress who captivated powerful men. On her road to ruin, the once-vulnerable waif had mutated into a temperamental vixen, seducing and then provoking dangerous men who presided over the economic and military mechanisms of the Free World and the innermost sanctums of organized crime.

Filled with rage, hysteria, and depression, "and fed up with Jack's lies, Bobby's lies," she sought revenge and mass vindication. Her revelations at an imminent press conference could have toppled political dynasties and destroyed criminal empires. Marilyn had to be stopped.....

This investigative book treats the reader like a member of the jury, laying out evidence, stripping it of its links to the self-interest of whoever gave it, and separating what really happened from thousands of distorted and misleading testimonies. Ultimately, all juries must render a verdict. The rendering of history's final verdict was, until now, crippled because of eyewitnesses who radically changed their testimonies as many as three times as the years drifted by.

Into this steamy cauldron of deceit, Marilyn herself emerges as a most unreliable witness during the weeks leading up to her murder. Her own deceptions, vanities, and self-delusion poured toxic accelerants on an already raging fire.

In the aftermath of the shattering events of August 5, 1962, as Marilyn's nude body—the object of the desire of literally thousands of men—was wheeled in for voyeuristic doctors to examine and dissect, a legend was already being born.

MARILYN AT RAINBOW'S END

SEX, LIES, MURDER, AND THE GREAT COVER-UP, BY DARWIN PORTER

Softcover, 480 pages, ISBN 978-1-936003-29-7 $22.95

WHAT does a man really have to do to make it in Show Biz?

Finally—A COOL biography that was too HOT to be published during the lifetime of its subject. TALES OF A LURID LIFE!

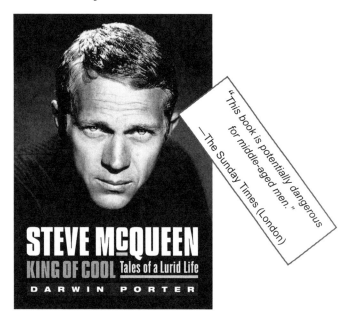

"This book is potentially dangerous for middle-aged men."
—The Sunday Times (London)

The drama of Steve McQueen's personal life far exceeded any role he ever played on screen. Born to a prostitute, he was brutally molested by some of his mother's "johns," and endured gang rape in reform school. His drift into prostitution began when he was hired as a towel boy in the most notorious bordello in the Dominican Republic, where he starred in a string of cheap porno films. Returning to New York before migrating to Hollywood, he hustled men on Times Square and, as a "gentleman escort" in a borrowed tux, rich older women.

And then, sudden stardom as he became the world's top box office attraction. The abused became the abuser. "I live for myself, and I answer to nobody," he proclaimed. "The last thing I want to do is fall in love with a broad."

Thus began a string of seductions that included hundreds of overnight pickups--both male and female. Topping his A-list conquests were James Dean, Paul Newman, Marilyn Monroe, and Barbra Streisand. Finally, this pioneering biography explores the mysterious death of Steve McQueen. Were those salacious rumors really true?

Steve McQueen   King of Cool   Tales of a Lurid Life
Darwin Porter

A carefully researched, 466-page hardcover with dozens of photos

ISBN 978-1-936003-05-1 $26.95
Also Available for E-Readers

PAUL NEWMAN

THE MAN BEHIND THE BABY BLUES,
HIS SECRET LIFE EXPOSED

Darwin Porter

THE MOST ACCURATE AND COMPELLING BIOGRAPHY OF THE ICONIC ACTOR EVER PUBLISHED

Drawn from firsthand interviews with insiders who knew Paul Newman intimately, and compiled over a period of nearly a half-century, this is the world's most honest and most revelatory biography about Hollywood's pre-eminent male sex symbol, with dozens of potentially shocking revelations.

Whereas the situations it exposes were widely known within Hollywood's inner circles, they've never before been revealed to the general public.

If you're a fan of Newman (and who do you know who isn't) you really should look at this book. It's a respectful but candid cornucopia of information about the sexual and emotional adventures of a young man on Broadway and in Hollywood.

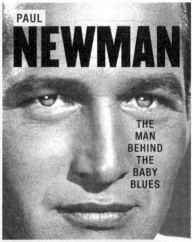

Hardcover, 520 pages, with dozens of photos. Also available for E-readers "One wonders how he ever managed to avoid public scrutiny for so long."

ISBN 978-0-9786465-1-6 $26.95

PAUL NEWMAN WAS A FAMOUS, FULL-TIME RESIDENT OF CONNECTICUT. SHORTLY AFTER HIS DEATH IN 2009, THIS TITLE WON AN HONORABLE MENTION FROM HIS NEIGHBORS AT THE NEW ENGLAND BOOK FESTIVAL

This is a pioneering and posthumous biography of a charismatic American icon. His rule over the hearts of American moviegoers lasted for more than half a century. Paul Newman was a potent, desirable, and ambiguous sex symbol, a former sailor from Shaker Heights, Ohio, who parlayed his ambisexual charm and extraordinary good looks into one of the most successful careers in Hollywood.

It's all here, as recorded by celebrity chronicler Darwin Porter--the giddy heights and agonizing lows of a great American star, with revelations never before published in any other biography.

KATHARINE THE GREAT

HEPBURN, A LIFETIME OF SECRETS REVEALED

BY DARWIN PORTER

Katharine Hepburn was the world's greatest screen diva--the most famous actress in American history. But until the appearance of this biography, no one had ever published the intimate details of her complicated and ferociously secretive private life.

Thanks to the "deferential and obsequious whitewashes" which followed in the wake of her death, readers probably know WHAT KATE REMEMBERED. Here, however, is an unvarnished account of what Katharine Hepburn desperately wanted to forget.

Katharine
The Great

HEPBURN
A Lifetime of Secrets
Revealed

Darwin Porter

The First Book of Its Kind, A Fiercely Unapologetic Exposé of the Most Obsessively Secretive Actress in Hollywood

Softcover, 569 pages, with photos $16.95

ISBN   978-0-9748118-0-2

Also Available for E-Readers

This is What Happens When A Demented Billionaire Hits Hollywood

HOWARD HUGHES
HELL'S ANGEL
BY DARWIN PORTER

From his reckless pursuit of love as a rich teenager to his final days as a demented fossil, Howard Hughes tasted the best and worst of the century he occupied. Along the way, he changed the worlds of aviation and entertainment forever.

This biography reveals inside details about his destructive and usually scandalous associations with other Hollywood players.

"The Aviator flew both ways. Porter's biography presents new allegations about Hughes' shady dealings with some of the biggest names of the 20th century"
—New York Daily News

"Darwin Porter's access to film industry insiders and other Hughes confidants supplied him with the resources he needed to create a portrait of Hughes that both corroborates what other Hughes biographies have divulged, and go them one better."
—Foreword Magazine

"Thanks to this bio of Howard Hughes, we'll never be able to look at the old pinups in quite the same way again."
—The Times (London)

Winner of a respected literary award from the 2011 Los Angeles Book Festival, this book gives an insider's perspective about what money can buy—and what it can't

814 pages, with photos $32.95; Also available for E-Readers

ISBN 978-1-936003-13-6

BRANDO UNZIPPED

An Uncensored *Exposé* of America's Most Visible Method Actor
and Sexual Outlaw

by Darwin Porter

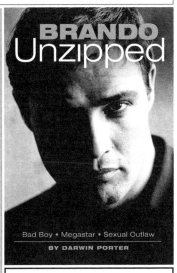

MERV GRIFFIN
A LIFE IN THE CLOSET

Darwin Porter

"Darwin Porter told me why he tore the door off Merv's closet.......*Heeeere's Merv!* is 560 pages, 100 photos, a truckload of gossip, and a bedful of unauthorized dish."

Cindy Adams, The NY Post

"Darwin Porter tears the door off Merv Griffin's closet with gusto in this sizzling, superlatively researched biography...It brims with insider gossip that's about Hollywood legends, writ large, smart, and with great style."

Richard LaBonté, BOOKMARKS

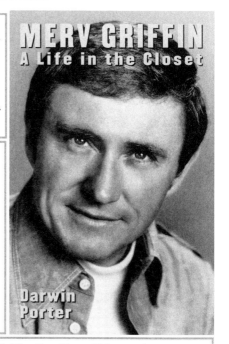

Merv Griffin, A Life in the Closet

Merv Griffin began his career as a Big Band singer, moved on to a failed career as a romantic hero in the movies, and eventually rewrote the rules of everything associated with the broadcasting industry. Along the way, he met and befriended virtually everyone who mattered, made billions operating casinos and developing jingles, contests, and word games. All of this while maintaining a male harem and a secret life as America's most famously closeted homosexual.

In this comprehensive biography—the first published since Merv's death in 2007—celebrity biographer Darwin Porter reveals the amazing details behind the richest, most successful, and in some ways, the most notorious mogul in the history of America's entertainment industry.

HOT, CONTROVERSIAL, & RIGOROUSLY RESEARCHED

HERE'S MERV!

Hardcover, with photos. Also available for E-Readers.
ISBN 978-0-9786465-0-9 $26.95

Jacko
HIS RISE AND FALL
The Social and Sexual History of Michael Jackson

Darwin Porter

He rewrote the rules of America's entertainment industry, and he led a life of notoriety. Even his death was the occasion for scandals which continue to this day.

This is the world's most comprehensive historical overview of a pop star's rise, fall, and to some extent, rebirth as an American Icon. Read it for the real story of the circumstances and players who created the icon which the world will forever remember as "the gloved one," Michael Jackson.

"This is the story of Peter Pan gone rotten. Don't stop till you get enough. Darwin Porter's biography of Michael Jackson is dangerously addictive."
The Sunday Observer (London)

"In this compelling glimpse of Jackson's life, Porter provides what many journalists have failed to produce in their writings about the pop star: A real person behind the headlines."
Foreword Magazine

"I'd have thought that there wasn't one single gossippy rock yet to be overturned in the microscopically scrutinized life of Michael Jackson, but Darwin Porter has proven me wrong. Definitely a page-turner. But don't turn the pages too quickly. Almost every one holds a fascinating revelation."
Books to Watch Out For

This book, a winner of literary awards from both *Foreword Magazine* and the Hollywood Book Festival, was originally published during the lifetime of Michael Jackson. This, the revised, post-mortem edition, with extra analysis and commentary, was released after his death.

Hardcover 600 indexed pages with about a hundred photos

ISBN 978-0-936003-10-5. $27.95 Also available for E-readers

HOLLYWOOD BABYLON
STRIKES AGAIN!

THE PROFOUNDLY OUTRAGEOUS VOLUME TWO OF
BLOOD MOON'S BABYLON SERIES

Winner of the Los Angeles Book Festival's Best Nonfiction Title of 2010, and the New England Book Festival's Best Anthology for 2010.

"Monumentally exhaustive... The Ultimate Guilty Pleasure" Shelf Awareness

Volume Two of Blood Moon's overview of exhibitionism, sexuality, and sin as filtered through 85 years of Hollywood indiscretion.

Hot, Unauthorized, and Unapologetic!

HOLLYWOOD BABYLON
Strikes Again!

Volume #2
of the Babylon Series

ities!

All That Nudity!

All Those Scandals!

...and All That Sin!

BY DARWIN PORTER & DANFORTH PRINCE

"If you love smutty celebrity dirt as much as I do, *then have I got a book for you!*"
The Hollywood Offender

"*These books will set the graves of Hollywood's cemeteries spinning*" **Daily Express**

Hollywood Babylon Strikes Again!
Darwin Porter and Danforth Prince
Hardcover, 380 outrageous pages, with hundreds of photos

ISBN 978-1-936003-12-9 $25.95

OUT OF THE CELLULOID CLOSET, A HALF-CENTURY REVIEW OF
HOMOSEXUALITY IN THE MOVIES
A Book of Record, Reference Source, and Gossip Guide to 50 Years of Queer Cinema

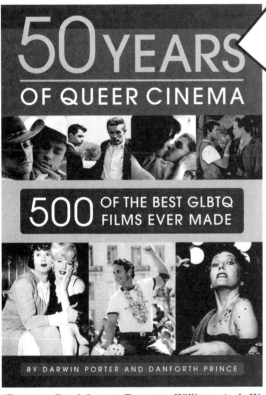

Winner of the
New England Book Festival's
Best GLB T Title of 2010

"In the Internet age, where every movie, queer or otherwise, is blogged about somewhere, a hefty print compendium of film facts and pointed opinion might seem anachronistic. But flipping through well-reasoned pages of commentary is so satisfying. Add to that physical thrill the charm of analysis that is sometimes sassy and always smart, and this filtered survey of short reviews is a must for queer-film fans.

"Essays on Derek Jarman, Tennessee Williams, Andy Warhol, Jack Wrangler, Joe Gage and others—and on how *The Front Runner* never got made—round out this indispensable survey of gay-interest cinema."

RICHARD LABONTÉ
BOOK MARKS/QSYNDICATE